PAGE 317

Of the Making of Nationalities There is No End

Volume One

Paul Robert Magocsi

Of the Making of Nationalities
There is No End

Volume One

Carpatho-Rusyns in Europe and North America

With an Introduction by
Christopher M. Hann

EAST EUROPEAN MONOGRAPHS
Distributed by Columbia University Press, New York

1999

EAST EUROPEAN MONOGRAPHS, No. DXL

Composition and layout by Gabriele Scardellato.

ISBN 0-88033-438-X
Library of Congress Catalog Card Number 99-72628

Contents

Part II
Carpatho-Rusyns in North America

VOLUME TWO

Part III
Speeches and Debates

Part IV
Bibliographical Works

Maps

Tables

Preface

To complete the paraphrase inspired by a passage on learning from the Book of Ecclesiastes, the full title of this two-volume work should read: Of the Making of Nationalities There is No End, And Much Diversity is a Richness of the Human Spirit. Put another way, the various peoples, or nationalities inhabiting our planet all deserve to have their cultures preserved and fostered, because it is their manifold diversity that makes life worth living.

One of those peoples are the Carpatho-Rusyns. For the past quarter of a century this people has been an important part of my scholarly research. These two volumes contain 41 chapters of studies, most of which have been published before in a wide variety of serial publications or collected works. Because of the on-going interest in Carpatho-Rusyns, especially since the Revolutions of 1989, and because these studies are not easily available, several colleagues sugggested that I publish them in book form. I am particularly grateful to Christopher Hann of the Institute for Advanced Study (Wissenschaftskolleg) in Berlin and to Tom Trier of the Danish Refugee Council in Copenhagen for their introductory essays that help to place each volume in a wider perspective.

With the exception of Chapters 21, 39, and in part 29, I have decided not to revise or to update the texts in any substantive manner. I have, however, tried to impose upon them some grammatical and stylistic consistency. Also, since these studies were originally published in different journals, it was almost always necessary to begin by defining "who, what, and where" are the Carpatho-Rusyns. The first, otherwise popular introductory essay was included here as Chapter 1 in order to answer such questions, and this kind of information has been removed wherever it may have appeared at the beginning of the original version in many of the subsequent essays. Despite such editorial deletions, it is inevitable that some degree of repetition still remains. For this I beg the reader's indulgence.

On a technical note, the question of transliteration into the Roman alphabet from several Cyrillic alphabets has been resolved in favor of retaining whichever standard transliteration system (Library of Congress and International) was used in the original publication. The transliteration of Rusyn texts follows that used for Ukrainian with the following emendations: ô=ô; ѣ=î; ы=ŷ; and specifically for Vojvodinian Rusyn: и=i. Rusyn texts using the Roman alphabet (usually from the United States) appear in their original form. Placenames are rendered according to the official language used in the country where the places are currently located; therefore, in the Slovak form for Prešov in Slovakia; the Ukrainian form for Užhorod/Uzhhorod in Ukraine; the Polish form for Nowy Sącz in Poland, etc.

Finally, I wish to express my deepest appreciation to three colleagues—Dr. L'ubica Babotová (Prešov University), Professor Emeritus Catherine Chvany (Massachussetts Institute of Technology), and Professor Patricia A. Krafcik (The Evergreen State College)—who kindly proofread the entire two-volume text. Their concern for accuracy greatly improved the work. Any errors that may remain are, of course, my responsibility.

PRM

Introduction:
On Nation(alitie)s in General, and One
Potential Nation(ality) in Particular

I t is a pleasure and a privilege to be asked by Professor Magocsi to contribute an introduction to this volume, the first of two in which he has assembled the most important of the shorter contributions that he has made to Carpatho-Rusyn studies over the last quarter of a century. The two volumes complement each other. Together they also complement the numerous longer works that he has produced in the same period, both scholarly monographs and more popular publications. It is tempting to see these two volumes as the completion of an *oeuvre*, but this would almost certainly be premature. The accelerating number of studies in recent years is an indication that Professor Magocsi's contributions to Carpatho-Rusyn studies are by no means exhausted.

This volume is made up principally of studies dealing with the history, culture, language, and political orientation of Rusyns in their homeland in central Europe. These articles are grouped together in Part I. Part II contains six studies which deal with the past and present development of Carpatho-Rusyns in North America. I do not see it as my role to provide detailed comments on any of these materials. Professor Magocsi's prose is admirably clear and his arguments do not need further elaboration by me. Instead, what I should like to do is to try to situate his work in the context of wider debates in the social sciences about collective identities in the modern world.

I personally find the Rusyn case of enormous interest in its own right. This is a consequence of having spent some time as an anthropologist working with these people, or at any rate with closely related people in an adjacent section of the Carpathians.[1] Recognizing that not all readers will share such a background, I shall try here to highlight what I see as the important general issues raised by the Rusyn case. The goal is to stimulate the reader to explore Magocsi's detailed arguments in order to make his or her own evaluation.

A word of warning at the outset: my own opinions and scholarly orientations do not always coincide with those of Professor Magocsi.[2] I shall make my disagreements plain, knowing that this is what he expects of me, and hoping that this, too, will encourage readers to tackle the substantive chapters and make up their own minds on contentious matters.

In my view the key issues are implicitly raised in the very title that he has given to these volumes. I disagree with his claim that "of the making of nationalities there is no end." Understood literally, this implies that each and every human being might constitute a sovereign nationality. Professor Magocsi is not, in fact, a radical individualist, but we do differ in the importance we attach to *scale* in determining the outcome of nation-building processes. Furthermore, I think that nationality is unlikely to remain as important a source of identity in the twenty-first century as it has become for so many people in the twentieth. For me, the making of nationalities is a constrained process that scholars must try to understand in specific historical contexts. I shall return to these points below.

First, however, we need to clarify what is meant by the concept of nationality. I therefore begin by examining this term in the context of the recent social-science and historical literature on ethnicity, nationalism, and collective identities generally. I then turn to examine Magocsi's arguments with respect to the Carpatho-Rusyns, first in North America and then in Europe. Finally, I return to more theoretical issues and suggest that it might be fruitful to compare the work of Paul Robert

[1]C.M. Hann, *A Village Without Solidarity: Polish Peasants in Years of Crises* (New Haven, Conn., 1995). The village in question is now known as Wisłok Wielki. It falls within the eastern district of the so-called Lemko zone, although a few indigenous families still remain in the village today.

[2]For an earlier comparative critique, see my "Intellectuals, Ethnic Groups and Nations: Two Late-Twentieth-Century Cases," in Sukumar Periwal ed., *Notions of Nationalism* (Budapest, 1995), pp. 106-128.

Magocsi with that of a scholar who followed a very different approach, the late Ernest Gellner.

Nations, nationalities, identities

What is a nationality? The question is not as simple as it looks. For many people, nationality is the identity that is recorded in their passport, and this name will be closely related to the name of an internationally recognized culture as well as the name of a state. This is the case, for example, for the great majority of the inhabitants of contemporary Germany and France. In fact, there is a major difference in the citizenship legislation of these two European countries, as a consequence of which it has been much easier for immigrants to France to obtain citizenship (French nationality) than it has been for the corresponding immigrant population in Germany. This is not, however, the sense in which Professor Magocsi is using the term nationality.

His aim can be better illustrated using the example of my own country, Great Britain. I hold British nationality in the sense that I am, and have been from birth, a subject of Queen Elizabeth II. In another sense, however, my identity is something other than British. It is not English, although that is my mother tongue, and I have worked in English universities for most of my life. My nationality, in Professor Magocsi's sense, is Welsh, because that is where I was born and brought up, as were my parents before me. It is an identity that means more to me, in some subjective ways that are rather hard to define, than any other identity, even though I do not speak the language and have not lived in Wales for the last thirty years.

The term nationality is closely related to nation. I am not quite sure why Professor Magocsi prefers to use the former term, but I do not think that it matters particularly. He might equally well have used "ethnic group" in his title, or even "people." All of these overlapping terms direct attention to a basic form of collective belonging in the modern world. Nation is probably the term that has generated the largest explanatory literature, but it has the drawback that it is often closely tied to the state, both in academic analyses and in popular perception. Nationality feels more appropriate to describe a group such as the Carpatho-Rusyns, classified by Professor Magocsi as a "stateless people" (see Chapter 2). Thus Rusyns can be said to constitute a *nationality* within the Slovak *nation*, or the Ukrainian *nation*, or indeed within the American *nation*.

As for "ethnic group," this term has come to replace tribe in many anthropological accounts of non-Western societies. It has also been widely applied to minority immigrant groups within the Western world, and Professor Magocsi himself often uses this term in the North American context. It is less securely established, however, in accounts of the indigenous populations of European regions. There is also a sense sometimes that an ethnic group may denote a lower order of collectivity, that several *ethnic groups* might coexist within the same *nationality*. Some of these nuances could be useful in addressing the arguments of Professor Magocsi. For example, some of his critics might suggest that the Rusyns are a regionally based ethnic group within the Ukrainian nation(ality). It is important to be clear that Magocsi rejects such viewpoints. He argues instead that the Rusyns constitute a people, a nation(ality), on the same ontological level as Ukrainians and the other nation(alitie)s that surround their homeland—Poles, Slovaks, Hungarians, and Romanians. In the diaspora context one might speak of Rusyn-American culture, but it would make little sense, in his view, to speak of Rusyn-Ukrainian culture.

What are these entities we call nationalities? Are they groups that were always there? If not, how did they emerge? The scholarly literature in this field has reached enormous dimensions, but there is a wide measure of consensus that nation(alitie)s have developed under specific conditions in a relatively recent phase of world history.[3] In a recent wide-ranging analysis, the historical sociologist Liah Greenfield has argued that the idea of a nation is "the constitutive element of modernity."[4] For her, national identity, nationality in Magocsi's sense, is the most generalized identity that people hold in the modern world. It was

[3]Anthony Smith, *The Ethnic Origins of Nations* (Oxford, 1986), draws distinctions between "primordialists" and "modernists" and between modern nations and pre-modern *ethnies*. Smith himself settles on an intermediate position which emphasizes that, even when nations have seemingly recent origins, they are nonetheless based on much older ethnic (cultural) traditions. Wide-ranging samples of the literature now available in this field can be found in two anthologies compiled by John Hutchison and Anthony Smith: *Nationalism* (Oxford, 1994) and *Ethnicity* (Oxford, 1996).

[4]Liah Greenfield, *Nationalism: Five Roads to Modernity* (Cambridge, Mass., 1992), p. 18.

not always thus, and Greenfield's work is an attempt to explore the main historical processes, semantic as well as institutional, by which a national "style of thought" has spread to most parts of the world over the last four centuries. Her approach, inspired by the German sociologist Max Weber, emphasizes subjective meanings: in other words, we can speak of national identity only when this forms part of the actor's own consciousness. Characteristics that we typically call "ethnic" may provide a sort of objective "raw material" for the formation of nation or nationality, but they do not in themselves guarantee that it will be formed. Actual outcomes will be determined by a great many political contingencies, and above all by the role played by intellectuals.[5]

Of the five substantive chapters that constitute Greenfield's study, each describing a distinct path to modernity, several are relevant to the work of Paul Robert Magocsi. The closest is the one that deals with Russia, where *ressentiment* against the early advantages enjoyed by the West led to a strong assertion of indigenous values and the eventual spread of "particularistic pride," that is, national identity, even among people who previously did not acknowledge any collective secular label. In this respect, Russian peasants of the nineteenth century were little different from those elsewhere in eastern Europe.

Poland is an interesting case because it demonstrates how a national idea could gain ground despite the absence of any political entity called Poland in this period. It was relatively easy to develop an argument that the peasant speakers of Polish dialects, virtually all of them united also by their Roman Catholic faith, should be incorporated into the Polish nation, a concept previously restricted to aristocratic and gentry elites. It was more tricky to argue (though many Polish intellectuals nonetheless did so) that their state should also incorporate millions of other peasants in the east who did not meet either the linguistic or the religious criterion but who had no self-evident alternative to Polishness at the level of national identity. In the painful course of twentieth-century history, most of this *masa ethnograficzna* has come to acquire a national identity as Ukrainian or Belorusan. The mythologies of these

---

[5]For the most influential model of the role of the intellectuals in the successive phases of national movements in eastern Europe, see Miroslav Hroch, *Social Preconditions of National Revival in Europe: A Comparative Analysis of Patriotic Groups among the Smaller European Nations* (Cambridge, 1985).

states insinuate, as does the Polish, that the national cultures of today can be projected back into the distant past; but this is to impose a retrospective and misleading tidiness on complex historical processes of settlement, migration, and identity formation onto which the concept of nation(ality) has only recently bestowed some measure of order.

The people who form the subject of this volume can also be considered as a part of this *masa ethnograficzna*. Understood broadly, they were East Slavs living since at least the later Middle Ages both north and south of the Carpathian Mountains in states known as Poland and Hungary respectively (see Chapter 1 for Professor Magocsi's historical overview).

Greenfield's treatment of the English case is interesting. She sees this, quite plausibly, as the birthplace of the idea of the modern nation, and therefore of nationalism. It is, however, problematic to assume that anything resembling a modern patriotism was widely disseminated in English society in the sixteenth century. Nationality in Magocsi's sense did not develop until much later. It is also, at least from my perspective, a little problematic to overlook the case of Wales, politically united with England from 1531 yet retaining distinctive customs and traditions. The symbols of modern Welsh national identity were shaped later, largely by Romantics in the nineteenth century.[6] If we accept Ernest Gellner's definition of nationalism as the principle that the political unit should coincide with the national unit,[7] then far from being the paradigmatic case, the political entity of England and Wales, later joined by Scotland and Ireland, seems to present a direct and continuing challenge.

If Wales cannot be adequately squeezed into Greenfield's narrative of the English case, neither can the Carpatho-Rusyns be squeezed into her analysis of Russia. These two stateless nations seem to confirm the truth of Professor Magocsi's title for this volume, but they are by no means identical. Whereas most inhabitants of Wales, whether they can speak Welsh or not, do seem to have a sense of belonging to a Welsh nation(ality), this remains to be established in the case of the Rusyns,

---

[6]Philip Morgan, "From Death to a View: The Hunt for the Welsh Past in the Romantic Period," in Eric Hobsbawn and Terence Ranger, eds., *The Invention of Tradition* (Cambridge, 1983), pp. 43-100.

[7]Ernest Gellner, *Nations and Nationalism* (Oxford, 1983), p. 1.

for whom we have no adequate studies of contemporary identifications.

The bulk of the present volume is written on the assumption that the group under analysis exists as such. The objective grounds on which a self-conscious identity could be based are extensively presented. But Professor Magocsi is well aware that this is insufficient. He is in agreement with Greenfield, and with most anthropologists, in attaching greater importance to subjective factors: a nation(ality) is a nation(ality) if its members believe it to be one and act as if it is one. Given favorable political circumstances, the classification will be confirmed by neighboring groups and come to seem "natural" to all parties.[8]

The argument in North America

It may be useful to reverse the order in which the topics are presented in this volume and review the position of Rusyns in North America before addressing the nationality issue in the homeland. I want to emphasize the intimate links between the two, and to point out that Paul Robert Magocsi's scholarly formation and personal engagement began not in the homeland but in North America. He is proud to identify himself as a third-generation Carpatho-Rusyn American.[9] Through publications such as *Our People*, Professor Magocsi has done more than any other individual to earn recognition for this group in contemporary North America. It is worth recalling that he began his work in the 1970s, when scholarly interest in ethnic and national identity issues was strongly affected by popular currents in the United States, and in particular the "roots" phenomenon. He has discussed this climate himself in interviews (see Volume Two, Chapter 2).

From a historical point of view, the key question is to what extent the experiences of North American migrants had an impact on identity

---

[8]Subjective factors are stressed in the Soviet tradition of *ethnos* theory; see, for example, Viktor Kozlov, "On the Concept of the Ethnic Community," in Yulian Bromley, ed., *Soviet Ethnology and Anthropology Today* (The Hague, 1974), pp. 73-81. They are central to as well modern Western approaches, such as the highly influential work of Frederick Barth, *Ethnic Groups and Boundaries: The Social Organization of Cultural Difference* (Oslo, 1969).

[9]It may be worth noting that Professor Magocsi prefers to avoid a second hyphen in this group designation, thereby avoiding some of the issues to which Greenfield draws attention in her discussion of "hyphenated Americans."

debates in the homeland. The latter were in full swing at precisely the period when migration rates to the New World were at their highest, that is, in the decades preceding World War I. It seems clear that the appreciation of nationality gained in the United States and Canada did feed back to central Europe, both in correspondence and through return migration. American influences played a role in the revival of Ortho-doxy and of pro-Russian political orientations in these years, since in the absence of a well-developed Ukrainian movement this was the cate-gory into which immigrants from the Carpathian region could most easily be slotted (see Chapter 3). As anthropologists have shown in many other parts of the world,[10] the new forms of mobility and contact with persons of many different nation(alitie)s prompted migrants to simplify and standardize the various local and regional identifications they took with them to North America. They began to assert that they, too, belonged to a nation(ality).

Professor Magocsi treads a careful balance in Chapter 22, "Made or Remade in America." He recognizes the consequences of the immigra-tion for identity formation but denies that this amounts to the cons-truction or invention of identity, since there is, in his view, a solid basis in the objective circumstances of the homeland for asserting a different nationality status. This seems to me an eminently reasonable strategy, avoiding the pitfalls of both the primordial vision—"our nation(ality) has always existed in essentially its present form"—and the postmoder-nist "presentism" which would have us believe that identities can be manipulated at will, regardless of the weight of the past and objective cultural differences.

The other essays in Part II of this volume document the later development of the diaspora communities. Professor Magocsi reviews a range of activities, including the press, literature, and political activity. The general picture that emerges is one of a minority people which has been slow to organize and take advantage of the opportunities of North American society, a slowness that is readily understandable in terms of its relatively late arrival, fragmentation and

---

[10]The studies of the "Manchester School" in the Copperbelt region of Zambia are a classical source; see, in particular, J. Clyde Mitchell, *The Kalela Dance*, Rhodes-Livingstone Papers, No. 27 (Manchester, 1954); and A.L. Epstein, *Scenes from African Urban Life: Collected Copperbelt Essays* (Edinburgh, 1992).

low level of cultural development. The picture is overall a positive one, however, for there is no doubt that Rusyns have become well integrated into American society. They have made valuable contributions in virtually all fields, from the Marines' capture of Iwo Jima in World War II to Andy Warhol's pop art. At the same time they have formed associations to nourish their traditions and shown increasing interest in their history. In all this they have followed the same basic pattern as numerous other groups. The Carpatho-Rusyn case would seem to exemplify the attractive elements of a contemporary multicultural society.

The penultimate chapter of this section deals with Canada, which has been Paul Robert Magocsi's home and academic base for almost two decades. Although the present volume contains no reference to this work, during the period 1990-1997 he was director of the Multicultural History Society of Ontario, responsible for the project which led to the *Encyclopedia of Canada's Peoples*. This monumental work describes the evolution of 130 groups in all, including the aboriginal peoples (classified as a single group, with multiple subdivisions), the so-called Founding Nations (British and French), and the numerous groups formed by more recent immigrants.

I mention these points because they strike me as germane to understanding Professor Magocsi's larger concerns. One of his goals, of course, has been to document and explain the history and culture of the nation(ality) he calls the Carpatho-Rusyns, both in North America and in Europe. In the United States it seems clear that, generations after the main waves of migration, the group sustains a separate collective identity from the Slovak and the Ukrainian. I do not think anyone would dispute that Professor Magocsi has played the leading role in shaping and clarifying a Carpatho-Rusyn identity since the 1970s. In short, in North America the cause of the Carpatho-Rusyns has clearly succeeded and Professor Magocsi's contribution is an achievement that few social scientists can hope to emulate. He has shown himself in this work to have a humane commitment to enabling ordinary people to answer questions that matter to them very dearly, by helping them to understand to which group they belong in some ultimate sense. While many academic theorists have argued that the future of democracies throughout the world lies in collective mutual recognition of identity differences, Professor Magocsi's work with and for Rusyns goes farther by putting these ideals into practice. I am reminded also of William H.

McNeill, the great Chicago historian, who returned in 1985 to his native Canada to lecture in Toronto about the importance of engaging with cultural diversity. For McNeill, such "polyethnicity" is the normal condition of humanity and the age of allegedly monoethnic "nation-states" a short-lived aberration in modern history.[11]

But how does this approach, with its underlying polyethnic values that look so unambiguously positive on the North American scene, translate into the past and present of the homeland? The paradoxical fact is that, whereas the status of the Carpatho-Rusyns in North America seems assured, the jury is still out on the issue as to how far a separate Rusyn nation(ality) exists in the homeland.

The argument in the homeland

Members of the Carpatho-Rusyn ethnic group in North America presumably ground their affiliation ultimately in a belief in the existence of a clearly defined group with a clearly defined territory in the heart of Europe. In this they have been strongly supported by Professor Magocsi, though it is worth pointing out that possession of a currently identifiable homeland may not necessarily be a precondition for the viability of a collective identity in North America (see Chapter 22).

If one accepts that nation(ality) is historically shaped and the product of both objective cultural differences and subjective awareness, then how one sets about defining the precise object of study is fraught with difficulty. If one defines the subject to be "the Carpatho-Rusyns," one is open to the accusation of presupposing the existence of what needs first to be demonstrated through research. This problem has dogged a great deal of anthropological research. Early fieldworkers, some of them doubtless influenced by the development of nationalism in their countries of origin, all too often presented reports on "the X," with the implication that this tribe formed a bounded group with a unique culture, analogous to an ideal type of modern nation(ality) in modern Europe. Closer inspection usually showed that this alleged uniqueness was far from the reality.

In Paul Robert Magocsi's case, the problem is compounded by the

---

[11]William H. McNeill, *Polyethnicity and National Unity in World History* (Toronto, 1986). For the parallels in Magocsi's work, see especially Chapter 38 in Volume Two of this work.

terminology available. What are we to call the nation(ality) that forms the subject of this book? The obvious answer would be to use the name they use for themselves. While the term *Rusyn* is indeed the most widely used, the self-designation *Rusnak* is also widespread. Imposing the anglicized Latinization "Ruthenian" is not a solution: this term has been applied in the remoter past to a much larger East Slav population, including the people we now recognize as Ukrainians, Belarusans, and Russians. Ethnographers in the last two centuries have used the terms Lemko, Boiko, and Hutsul, but each has been a source of controversy. In the case of Lemkos, there are some in Poland today for whom this term has some elemental force: they consider Lemko to be their nationality, in Professor Magocsi's sense of the term.[12] The logic of his position requires him to respect this orientation (see Chapter 14, and Volume Two, Chapter 28). Nevertheless, Professor Magocsi himself invokes objective criteria in maintaining that these terms have been "superseded." In any case, he argues, overall these categories "never had any meaning for the inhabitants themselves" (Volume Two, p. 133) The term he has preferred in North America has been the hyphenated Carpatho-Rusyn, yet this has never been widely adopted in the homeland.

I do, however, find the introduction of a territorial element through the geographical adjective to be a helpful move. It parallels the move made by some anthropologists half a century ago, when they defined their object of study as "any convenient locality" rather than "the X," with implications of a bounded cultural unity.[13] The convenient locality selected by Professor Magocsi when he began his work in the 1970s was the Subcarpathian region that had belonged historically to Hungary before being transferred after World War I to Czechoslovakia and then after World War II to the Soviet Union. It was always obvious that this politically defined unit was significantly smaller than the corresponding cultural unit, since villages with similar linguistic and religious characteristics were to be found in neighboring districts of

---

[12]I have discussed the position of Lemkos in C.M. Hann, "Ethnicity in the New Civil Society: Who are the Lemko-Ukrainians?" in Laszlo Kurti and Juliet Langman, eds., *Beyond Borders: Remaking Cultural Identities in the New East and Central Europe* (Boulder, Colo., 1997), pp. 17-38.

[13]Edmund Leach, *Political Systems of Highland Burma* (London, 1954), p. 5.

Slovakia, Hungary, Romania, Ukraine, and Poland (as well as non-contiguous communities in former Yugoslavia). I think that it is more helpful to look at the larger territory and to consider Rusyn interaction with their neighbors. Professor Magocsi was always interested in this broader picture and has published extensively on the Galician region, north of the Carpathian watershed.[14] Yet in much of his early work, Rusyn and Carpatho-Rusyn referred exclusively to the Subcarpathian region from which the material side of his own family and that of most of the American Rusyns originated.

While Communism lasted it was hardly worth worrying about whether the Rusyns of eastern Slovakia and the Rusnaks of Poland (including both Lemkos and Boikos) really belonged to the same group as the Rusyns of Ukraine's Transcarpathia. With the subsequent changes in the political climate, however, it has become practical, even "convenient," for Professor Magocsi to expand the geographical framework and to explore the position of the Rusyns as a definable and potentially unifiable group across all present political boundaries. Certainly he wants to include in the new nation(ality) those labeled Lemkos by Polish ethnographers, most of whom were forcibly removed from their homeland by the Polish authorities in 1947. He is right to point to strong north-south links in this part of the mountains in earlier years.

On the other hand, he argues that north-south links were weaker in the more eastern districts and, therefore, does not lay claim to the Boikos and Hutsuls, who currently seem overwhelmingly to accept that their nationality is Ukrainian (see especially Chapter 2). It is precisely at this point, however, that the "objective" dimension of Professor Magocsi's argument faces its most serious difficulties, for it is by no means easy to draw a sharp ethnographic boundary between the Rusyns and their Ukrainian neighbors. Just as Polish ethnographers documenting the Lemko case in the 1930s struggled to find the precise eastern boundary between Lemkos and Boikos, so Magocsi today has a difficult (critics would say impossible) task in distinguishing Carpatho-Rusyns from the much larger nationality of Ukrainians.

---

[14]See his *Galicia: A Historical Survey and Bibliographic Guide* (Toronto, 1983) and *The Roots of Ukrainian Nationalism: Galicia as Ukraine's Piedmont* (Toronto, forthcoming).

This brings us to the heart of the matter. Rusyns can be clearly distinguished from most of their neighbors by the basic cultural elements of language and/or religion (although in some cases, notably in interaction with Hungarians, the pattern became complicated by high rates of assimilation). But, in the case of Ukrainians, their religion is the same as that of Rusyns, and the linguistic differences show a pattern of continuous variation, making it hard to impose any sharp boundary. Such factors need not create an insuperable barrier to the formation of a separate nationality. For instance, comparable continuities in religion and dialectal speech once prevailed between Germany and Holland, and to some extent they still persist between Ukraine and Russia. Nevertheless, we have no trouble today in recognizing Germans and Dutch, Ukrainians and Russians, as separate nationalities. Is there any essential difference between these cases and that of the Rusyns? Clearly for Paul Robert Magocsi there is none.

The question now is whether, following half a century in which the debates about a new identity were almost entirely suppressed, the post-Communist climate has provided an opportunity for new elite groups to succeed where their forerunners had failed. A remarkable case of nation(ality) building has been unfolding in late-twentieth-century central Europe. We can note the parallels with nineteenth-century efforts, above all in the production of language materials and the standardization of a fourth East Slavic language, which was successfully achieved for Rusyns in Slovakia in 1995 (see Chapters 4, 15, and 16).

The picture at present, however, is somewhat confused. Although there is certainly more contact across state borders than had been possible in the Communist period, there is not as yet a well defined Rusyn movement that transcends these boundaries. In Poland, work has been continuing on the standardization of a Lemko language, different both from literary Ukrainian and from the newly standardized Slovak Rusyn. Both Lemko Rusyn and Slovak Rusyn are gradually becoming institutionalised, that is, they are beginning to be taught in schools and to be used in newspapers and in radio and televsion broadcasting. Yet it remains to be seen whether a *demand* for building up the culture of this new nationality will develop. In other words, the reception, the subjective *internalization* of this new national identity, is proceeding slowly. Outside small circles of intellectuals, I see no evidence that it is making headway at all.

Scholarship and politics in the 1990s

The work of Paul Robert Magocsi, so in tune with the *Zeitgeist* in North America, has proved contentious and controversial in the homeland. Of course, within academic circles he has always courted controversy. The academic reception of *The Shaping of a National Identity* made this clear in the late 1970s. No matter how hard the author tried to justify his arguments on scholarly grounds, opponents accused him of a blatant anti-Ukrainian bias. For some critics, it was disingenuous of Professor Magocsi to claim that his work was neutral, "value free" scholarship: merely to raise the possibility that the people of this region could have developed an identity other than the Ukrainian was, from the standpoint of his critics, tantamount to staking out a political claim. Yet, so long as the Soviet bloc remained intact, these animated academic debates, samples of which are included in Volume Two (Chapter 26), had no impact on conditions in the homeland.

The collapse of Communist rule, beginning in 1989 in east-central Europe and extending within two years to the Soviet Union itself, created a quite new situation, one that came as a surprise to Professor Magocsi as it did to virtually everyone else. To put it very simply, the new circumstances gave him an opportunity to become, for the first time, practically involved in the affairs of the homeland. Perhaps he felt that he had no choice in the matter. His work over many years had been designed to show that there had existed in the United States, and that there might exist in central Europe a Rusyn nation(ality) separate from the Ukrainian, which had been ultimately suppressed under Communist political conditions. With the removal of those constraints between 1989 and 1991, Professor Magocsi was now able to make regular visits to the Transcarpathian oblast of Ukraine where the great bulk of Rusyns live, and to observe the putative nation(ality) close up. He has played an active role in the work of linguistic standardization and has been a member of the executive board of the World Congress of Rusyns since 1991 (representing the United States). There have been frequent tensions with post-Communist governments, notably with officials of the new government in Kiev who have rejected notions of a separate Rusyn nation(ality) with much the same dogmatism as their predecessors.

Elsewhere in eastern Europe, such sources of tension have boiled over into open hostilities and violence. The Carpathian region has been mercifully free of such excesses, and perhaps Professor Magocsi should be given some of the credit for this. On the other hand, critics can argue that, given the experience of Bosnia and Kosovo, any attempt to create a new nation(ality) against the wishes of present governments is a recipe for destabilization and potentially worse. Critics have included not only new public officials (many of them, of course, ex-Communists looking to play the nationalist card) but also—and this may be more disturbing to Professor Magocsi—local scholars with whom he has had longstanding ties and who themselves had suffered under Communist rule. For instance, Mykola Mušynka in Prešov has argued that Rusyn identity should not be considered as more than a "temporary fashionable trend." In a clear rebuke, he states: "I consider contemporary efforts to create a distinct Rusyn people a question of politics rather than nationality, and all the more so not a scholar's responsibility" (see Volume Two, p. 172).

It is important to note that, in these years of feverish practical activity, Paul Robert Magocsi has insisted on the priority of cultural work and emphasized that his own role is entirely scholarly. In essence, he wants to play the same facilitating role that he has played for roots-seekers in North America. He disavows political leadership and argues for recognition of cultural rights, not changes in political boundaries. When he has become involved, it has been at the request of local activists, whom he has supported with scholarly arguments but never sought to upstage. He can point to the undoubted fact that some local people are genuinely committed to the Rusyn identity. Why should they and their children have an unwelcome Ukrainian national identity foisted upon them, or assimilate into Polish or Slovak society, just because their traditional culture is bracketed by the authorities with the remote high culture of Kiev rather than their own Carpathian homeland?

Even if the Ukrainian state were less intransigent, both within Transcarpathia and in the neighboring districts of bordering states, the cultural mechanisms working to promote a Ukrainian identification among Rusyns are formidable. Given this climate, many readers, especially those imbued with the values of modern multicultural societies in western Europe and North America, will conclude that, in his support of initiatives within the realm of culture to extend the identification choices open to the people of this region, Professor Magocsi's involvement here is no less positive than it has been in North America. Others would draw the line differently and refrain from active participation in any cultural organizations in countries other than one's own that have agendas which inevitably carry political implications. That would be my own position—but I concede that I might feel differently if I had ties of descent to this group and had played the sort of public role that Professor Magocsi has undertaken for decades on behalf of communities in North America.

In any case, it is important to recognize that, as in the nineteenth century, in the post-Communist late twentieth century the stance of an authoritative academic can still have political consequences. Professor Magocsi recognizes this, and a careful analysis of his writings shows that he accepts the implied responsibility. At the end of the day the future status of the *Rusyn* nationality will be the outcome of a complex political process. It is too early to comment on whether new elites can succeed in persuading their wider communities that their *objective* differentiating cultural features are sufficiently strong to bring about a *subjective* ethnogenesis, a sense of belonging to the *Rusyn* nationality. It seems to me that, if a breakthrough does come about, it is likely to be as the result of external activities and the application of international conventions and the provisions of the European Union, rather than as the result of pressure from the Rusyns themselves in their new organizations. But whether the all-important internal convictions can be engineered through this sort of external pressure must be doubtful.

Culture and groupist social ontology

It is not premature, however, to attempt further analysis of the scholarly issues raised by the Rusyn case. In some respects, Paul Robert Magocsi's program exemplifies the modern social-science approach to questions of collective identity. Only the terminology is a little different: whereas Professor Magocsi speaks usually of a nationality, which he equates with a "people," the dominant terms in anthropology are ethnicity and ethnic group. The word "culture" is used freely by everybody. The etymologies and semantic complexities are richly complex but not vital for the points I wish to make here.

The most important insight, which has been more and more persuasively elaborated over the last few decades, is that, whatever the labels we use to describe them, none of these collectivities can be considered primordial. They emerge in specific historical circumstances, as the outcome of action by creative human beings interacting with each other. As Professor Magocsi himself puts it, "Nationalities are, after all, not absolute social categories . . . " (Volume Two, p. 185). The entire framework of his 1978 monograph, *The Shaping of a National Identity,* is built around this plasticity: namely, the dominant national orientation of the people of this region *could* in other circumstances have evolved differently. Alternatives were available which at various times were hotly debated by the intellectuals who constructed those national identities, until eventually political circumstances dictated the triumph of one version over the others. That, in a nutshell, is Magocsi's argument. And this is the position that allows him to become engaged alongside those wishing to advance an alternative conception under the changed political circumstances of the post-1989 era.

I call this a moderate constructivist approach and I think it has much to commend it. It is moderate because Professor Magocsi is fully aware that outcomes are contingent and open to intellectual guidance only within broad limits. Their location and history created several possibilities for the Rusyns, but these did not include kinship with, say, Germans, even though German influence in this region was not negligible in certain periods. The successful creators of a nationality need to invest it with a distinctive history, and this may often draw freely on elements of imagination and myth. Nevertheless, analysts need always to recognize that the actual movement of peoples and cultural traits in the past imposes certain constraints on the formation of identities.

From this point, which though very obvious is often overlooked in the contemporary literature, we can see how the weight of the past complicates the task of those wishing to promote the cause of the Rusyns. The paradigm of primordial group identities survived for a long time in anthropology, partly because many early studies were based on isolated groups. Sometimes the people were physically isolated, for example, on an island; in other cases they were less remote but still showed unambiguous cultural boundaries, as in the languages they spoke. The resulting paradigm of a world made up of relatively integrated and homogenous cultural blocks has dominated much anthropological work this century and remains a widely influential way of social classification both inside and outside the academy. Gradually, however, scholars have become aware of two major problems: first, such a paradigm is increasingly unrealistic in the context of accelerating globalization; second, the paradigm bears an uncomfortable affinity to the assumptions that underpin the nationalist world-view. As a consequence, the old concept of culture has come under heavy attack in recent years.

Paul Robert Magocsi is, of course, much too astute an analyst of the Carpatho-Rusyn case to argue that their claims to form a nation(ality) rest on a culture that can be neatly differentiated from that of neighboring nationalities. It is precisely because the boundaries are fuzzy that there has been scope to contest and negotiate collective identities over the last two centuries. Ultimately, as we have seen, it is the subjective elements of consciousness, loyalty, and commitment that will play the decisive role in determining whether or not a Rusyn nationality emerges and is sustained. In these respects, I think that Professor Magocsi's stance conforms to the views currently held by most social scientists.

Yet it seems to me that there is a further step that Professor Magocsi does not take. This is the more radical step of questioning what Rogers Brubaker has recently called a "groupist social ontology."[15] If the "objective" cultural grounds are not sufficient, what justification do we have for continuing to carve up the world into bounded groups with the presumption that they have some fundamental significance for all of their members? Might the subjectivities be more complex and resist the attempts of intellectuals to channel them into this mould?

One reply, of course, is that, for many people in the world, the bounded collectivities that Professor Magocsi calls nationalities are extremely important and likely to remain so. There is ample evidence in his own publications that his work on behalf of a Rusyn identity has brought satisfaction and a dignity they would not otherwise feel to the descendants of migrants from the Carpathian region, people who have felt a need to supplement their American identity with some knowledge of their roots. But what proportion of migrants and their descendants have actually felt this need? Does this provide sufficient grounds for working to validate such a group loyalty in the academy? What wider social benefits follow from this model of multicultural citizenship, compared with a bland hegemony based on the obliteration of cultural differences?

It seems to me that both the multiculturalism that Professor Magocsi espouses in North America and its justification, the nationality principle

---

[15]Rogers Brubaker, "Myths and Misconceptions in the Study of Nationalism," in John A. Hall, ed., *The State of the Nation: Ernest Gellner and the Theory of Nationalism* (Cambridge, 1998), p. 296.

that he supports in the homeland, are based ultimately on the "billiard ball" model of the world. Billiard balls have hard edges, they may bump into and bounce off each other, but there are no contaminating interactions. Does the billiards table (or, for that matter, the "salad bowl" that seems to have replaced the "melting pot" as most favored image in the ethnicity literature) provide a helpful metaphor for the kind of cultural interaction taking place today and the identities generated by these processes? Both in the homeland and in North America, Professor Magocsi's approach to the Rusyns has a bias towards hardness and boundedness.

This ontology undoubtedly has deep resonance today. It is true that some current trends can in the short term strengthen the need to be sure of one's nationality—recent events in the Balkans have shown this all too vividly. But others, notably the globalization of consumption, are undermining older ideas of cultural distinctiveness. Local differences will continue to be asserted and reasserted, often on the basis of something considered traditional; but whether having a nation(ality) identity can retain the centrality that it has had for most people for most of this century, as a fundamental building block for the self, seems to me highly doubtful.

The problem of scale

Let me reiterate that the model of a world neatly divisible into nation(alitie)s does remain important to millions of human beings, and no amount of academic deconstruction should allow us to forget this. Nevertheless, this is a model that scholarly analysis must question, and the best academic analyses of nationalism have indeed called it into question. The outstanding example is the work of Ernest Gellner, who has produced what is probably the most influential body of work in this field.[16] Gellner argued, as a committed "modernist," that nations were not primordial units but the outcomes of successful nationalist movements. Those who see things the other way around had already fallen into the nationalists' ontological trap.

I think that in principle Paul Robert Magocsi agrees with Gellner's position. His general aims and methods, however, could hardly be more

[16]For the impact of Gellner's work, see John Hall's introduction in *ibid.*, pp. 1-20.

different. Gellner was above all concerned to advance a general theory of nationalism and to understand how it fitted into the course of history. His theory emphasized the impact of industrialization, a proposition that at first sight looks quite inappropriate to cases like the Ukrainian or the Rusyn, even though his elaborate imaginative construction of "Ruritania" was intended to encompass such cases.[17] This model is deliberately abstracted from geographical specifics and historical events. It is, in short, a most unusual approach for an anthropologist.

Paul Robert Magocsi, though ostensibly working as a historian and political scientist, comes curiously closer to the usual specifications of anthropology. He is no primordialist, and his historical-constructivist approach distances him from the social ontology of the dogmatic nationalist, who believes that his group has maintained its unique national qualities over the long term. Professor Magocsi shares with Gellner a conviction about the importance in modern conditions of one most basic form of identity, that of belonging to a nation(ality). Their reasoning, however, is different. For Gellner, a national identity is the *sine qua non* of life in a developed industrial society; he pays little attention either to the historical roots of the new high culture or to the subjective satisfaction that such an identity brings to group members. Professor Magocsi, in contrast, has devoted enormous energy to documenting the precise details of the culture, both in his scholarly work and in other publications aimed more at non-academic "roots-seekers." The nationality is not there to serve macrosociological functions, it is there to meet psychological needs. It can achieve this, however, only if duly recognized as a concrete and bounded social reality.

What criteria determine which of the many thousands of potential groups or cultures acquire this status, this capacity to convey to their members the experience of belonging to a concrete social reality? I have already suggested, on the basis of my personal experience, that Wales has managed to do so. Professor Magocsi would clearly like to see the Rusyns do so as well. He is quite clear that size is not an important consideration, as he demonstrated through his analysis of the successful establishment of an autonomous cultural entity by a few

---

[17]See, in particular, Gellner, *Nations and Nationalism*, pp. 59-62.

thousand people living in the tiny principality of Monaco.[18]

Gellner takes a different view on this issue of scale. True, he first implies that each and every one of the world's 8000 linguistic communities might plausibly come forward and organize a successful national movement.[19] But he qualifies this with an argument about the scale minimally necessary for a viable nation, if it is not to be "parasitic." For Gellner, "the relevant shared culture is that of the modern-type primary school, not of the old folk culture."[20] Such a view follows from his general theories about the division of labor in a modern industrial state, which depends on a "high culture," and in particular on a standardized language, to ensure efficient communication and the necessary levels of mobility. Brendan O'Leary takes the case of Iceland, with a population of 250,000, as defining the minimum for a viable high culture.[21]

Professor Magocsi claims that there are at present potentially up to one million Rusyns in the Carpathian homeland, the great bulk of them citizens of Ukraine. It remains to be seen, however, if this number will prove enough to establish a new nationality today. Geographically and culturally it would be hard to think of a sharper contrast to Iceland than the case of the Rusyns, whose homeland lies in the heart of a continent. Perhaps the minimum needs to be set somewhat higher in the case of "Ruritanian" people without such clear linguistic or other cultural boundaries separating them from their neighbors?

To return to the question I posed above, I agree with Professor Magocsi that there is no essential difference between the case of Carpatho-Rusyns and the emergence of other nation(alitie)s in areas of cultural complexity, including the emergence of the Ukrainian and Belorusan identities as distinct from each other and from Russian. There is no *a priori* reason why the Rusyns who experienced Hungarian rule before 1918 could not have formed a nationality distinct from those

[18]Paul Robert Magocsi, "Monégasque Nationalism: A Terminological Contradiction or Practical Reality?" *Canadian Review of Studies in Nationalism,* XVIII, 1-2 (Charlottetown, Prince Edward Is., 1991), pp. 83-94.

[19]Gellner, *Nations and Nationalism,* pp. 44-45.

[20]Ernest Gellner, "Scale and Nation," *Philosophy of the Social Sciences,* III (London, 1973), p. 13.

[21]Brendan O. Leary, "Ernest Gellner's Diagnoses of Nationalism," in Hall, *State of the Nation,* p. 59.

across the mountains who had rather different experiences under Austrian rule. There is no *a priori* reason why now, at the end of the century, Rusyns both north and south of the mountains should not come together to form a nationality separate from the Ukrainian nationality, the major cultural centers of which are still remote. If this, Professor Magocsi's scenario, were to come about, Ernest Gellner's model would need modification, and not only with regard to arguments of scale.

The Gellner model predicts that national awareness is likely to develop in peripheral regions, where elites see a greater pay-off in promoting a new high culture than in participating in that of an economically more advanced region some distance away. Such a model might possibly be applied to the recent history of Slovakia. But can it now be applied on a smaller scale to Rusyns? Is it really possible that the same logic which led Slovak intellectuals to develop a national movement and a capital city in Bratislava could lead Rusyns to establish their own metropolis in, say, Prešov, or perhaps Uzhhorod? Since the great majority of Rusyns live in Ukraine, the latter would seem a more plausible location. Can it be argued that Rusyn elites in Ukraine might have good reason to cultivate their own nationality, not as an alternative to competing in a more advanced labor market to the west but in order to escape from the chaos of their post-socialist economy? Certainly Ukraine in the 1990s has hardly approached Gellner's ideal type of a modern industrial state.

To my mind, however, there is no realistic basis in the Carpathian region for the development of a viable state. Professor Magocsi confines himself to cultural issues and is fully aware that any calls for a separate state would be provocative and dangerous (see Volume Two, Chapters 32, 38). It is entirely consistent that he should formulate arguments about the impending end of the nation-state (see Chapter 38). But for Gellner this is highly premature and a *real* nation(ality), that is, one that is not to be parasitic vis-á-vis its neighbors, is subject to a kind of "objective" material testing. If this test is undertaken in the Carpatho-Rusyn case, the answer has to be that this territory is geographically unsuited to the development of an integrated industrial infrastructure. It lacks large cities, and those that it has are populated mainly by non-Rusyns. Moreover, because they are small they are often unattractive to the most able Rusyns, who prefer to realize their ambitions in Kiev, in Cracow, in Bratislava, or in Budapest. The inhabitants of "1000 villages" were simply never strong enough or numerous enough to establish their own nation(ality), and I think this remains true today. They can aspire to standardize their "folk culture," but, because the material bases for the "modern-type primary school culture" are still missing, I believe that Gellner's model is not in serious danger.

Conclusion

Paul Robert Magocsi, like Liah Greenfield in historical sociology and Ernest Gellner in anthropology, believes that human beings in the modern world have some fundamental, basic level of collective identity. Professor Magocsi calls this type of identity nationality. He has devoted most of his scholarly career to showing that one of the nationality options available in central Europe was and remains that of *Rusyn*. He has been extraordinarily successful in these endeavors, which in the changed political circumstances of the post-1989 era have spilled over from the closed world of journals and newsletters in North America to have a significant impact on identity debates within the European homeland. His work has served to foster a positive group identity in the North American diaspora. It has also attracted criticism, above all from Ukrainians, who see the Rusyns as a part of a single Ukrainian nationality.

I have suggested that the case of the Carpatho-Rusyns is of more general interest, both for the study of how nationalities emerge within homelands and for the study of how new types of groups, most commonly labeled ethnic groups, emerge following migrations. Both types of collectivity are modern. My main criticism of Professor Magocsi is that, while recognizing the constructed character of these new collectivities, he attributes to this form of group a force that I do not think it is capable of sustaining. For some people, certainly, the need to have one most basic level or type of identity is strong, and this must command our attention and our respect. But we must recognize this as itself the product of modern historical circumstances, which are continually changing.

Despite the clear evidence of increased loyalty to the categories of nation and nationality in the early post-Communist years, I think that the force of these categories is waning, faster in some regions than in others. It is probably too late for a new nationality to emerge in this region. Comparisons with cases such as Macedonia or Chechnya miss the point that these were estabished nationality categories throughout decades of Communist rule, which was not the case for the Carpatho-Rusyns. It seems that the most likely future is one that will see the emergence of "hyphenated Ukrainians," in the sense that most Rusyns will seek to reconcile Ukrainian nationality with the more specific ties that they feel to their Carpathian homeland. Whatever the precise pattern to emerge in the homeland, it will be interesting to see what consequences this has for the descendants of these people who live in the United States.

Despite reaching such conclusions, which certainly differ from those of Paul Robert Magocsi, it must be quite obvious to the reader that my criticisms and disagreements imply a compliment. The work of Professor Magocsi on the Rusyns demands the attention and engagement not only of anthropologists but of anyone with serious interests in the issues of collective identity in the modern world. His combination of emancipatory humanitarian motivation and high-level scholarship can be an inspiration, even to those who wish to proceed in somewhat different directions. It is no mean feat to be able to reconcile the academic demonstration of the *contingency* of the Carpatho-Rusyn nationality with the program of multicultural advocacy which asserts the *authenticity* of this identity for all those who wish to embrace it.

Let me conclude with a more explicit compliment. I have touched already on the contrast between the approaches of Paul Robert Magocsi and Ernest Gellner. I have been privileged to know both these scholars, each of whom has family origins in the heart of Europe but whose motivations, styles, and levels of analysis are so very different. Gellner's *oeuvre* is complete—he died suddenly in 1995, having just completed a further statement on nationalism that has since appeared posthumously.[22] Magocsi, happily, as the recent pieces in these two volumes show, is still at the height of his powers. Long may he remain there.

Even if my pessimistic prognoses for the Carpatho-Rusyn case, based on Gellnerian assumptions, turn out to be correct, that would not diminish the lasting scholarly value of the evidence and arguments marshaled in the volumes before us. Let us suppose that my scenario is accurate, and that it becomes clear in the next few years that the

---

[22]Ernest Gellner, *Nationalism* (London, 1997).

great majority of East Slavs in their Carpathian homeland do not embrace a Rusyn nationality. Let us suppose that this nationality weakens noticeably in North America as well. I would confidently expect Magocsi to rise to the new challenge and to work out in future publications a more comprehensive theory of social identity in an age of accelerating globalization. I would expect the Magocsi theory to complement the Gellnerian prototype by providing a full and historically sensitive account of why, contrary to the title of this collection, there are, after all, limits to the making of nationalities, and limits to the importance of nationality per se. If it called into question that groupist social ontology which nationalists and academic analysts have shared for much too long, the fame of this new theory would surpass even that of Gellner's.

Chris Hann
Berlin, Germany

Part I

Carpatho-Rusyns in Europe

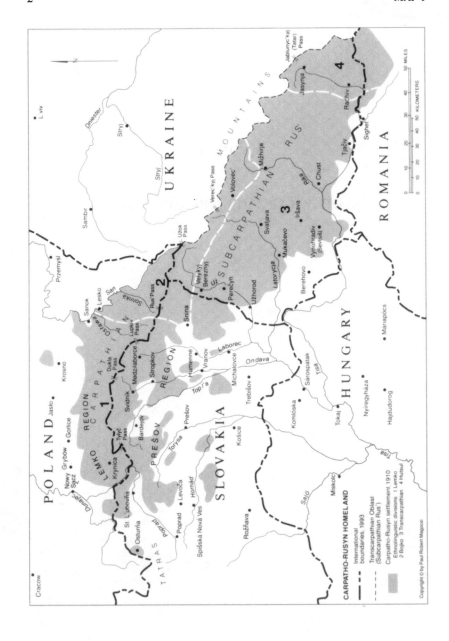

CARPATHO-RUSYN HOMELAND

International
boundaries, 1993

Transcarpathian Oblast
(Subcarpathian Rus')

Carpatho-Rusyn settlement 1910
Ethnolinguistic divisions 1 Lemko
2 Bojko 3 Transcarpathian 4 Hutsul

Copyright © by Paul Robert Magocsi

CHAPTER 1

The Carpatho-Rusyns[*]

C arpatho-Rusyns live in the very heart of Europe, along the northern and southern slopes of the Carpathian mountains. Their homeland, known as Carpathian Rus', is situated at the crossroads where the borders of Ukraine, Slovakia, and Poland meet. Aside from those countries, there are smaller numbers of Carpatho-Rusyns in Romania, Hungary, Yugoslavia, and the Czech Republic. In no country do Carpatho-Rusyns have an administratively distinct territory.

Geography and economy

Three-quarters of the Carpatho-Rusyns in Europe are found within the borders of Ukraine, specifically in the Transcarpathian region (historic Subcarpathian Rus'). In Slovakia, Carpatho-Rusyns live in the northeastern part of the country, in an area popularly known as the Prešov Region. On the northern slopes of the Carpathians, they had trad-

---

[*] The first three sections of this chapter initially appeared as part of the brochure, *Carpatho-Rusyns* (Orwell, Vt: Carpatho-Rusyn Research Center, 1995; 2nd revised ed., 1997), which appeared as well in Slovak, *Karpatskí Rusíni* (Prešov: Karpatorusínske výskumné centrum, 1995); in Ukrainian, *Karpats'ki rusyny* (Prešov: Karpats'ko-rusyns'kyi doslidnyi tsentr, 1995); in a joint Vojvodinian Rusyn/Serbian/ English edition, *Karpato-Rusini/Karpato-Rusini/Carpatho-Rusyns* (Novi Sad: Ruske slovo, 1995); in Hungarian, *A Ruszinok* (Budapest: Magyarországi Ruszinok Szervezete, 1996); and in Polish, *Rusini Karpaccy* (Orwell, Vt: Carpatho-Rusyn Research Center, 1996). The last section, "History," first appeared in the *Carpatho-Rusyn American*, XVIII, 4 (Fairfax, Va., 1995), pp. 6-7; XIX, 1 and 2 (1996), pp. 4-5 and 4-6.

itionally lived in southeastern Poland, in an area known as the Lemko Region. After World War II, the Lemko Rusyns were deported to Ukraine and other parts of Poland. Among those who remained in Poland, a few thousand eventually managed to return to their Carpathian homeland, although most continue to reside in scattered settlements in the southwestern part of the country (Silesia). Finally, there are several Carpatho-Rusyn villages just south of the Tisza River in the Maramureş region of northcentral Romania, and a few scattered settlements in northeastern Hungary.

Beyond the Carpathian homeland, Rusyns live as immigrants in neighboring countries. The oldest immigrant community, dating back to the mid-eighteenth century, is in the Vojvodina (historic Bačka) and Srem regions of former Yugoslavia, that is, present-day northern Serbia and far eastern Croatia. In the Czech Republic, Carpatho-Rusyns reside primarily in northern Moravia and the capital of Prague, where most immigrated just after World War II. The largest community outside the homeland is in the United States, where between the 1880s and 1914 about 225,000 Carpatho-Rusyns immigrated. They settled primarily in the industrial regions of the northeastern and north-central states where most of their descendants still live to this day. Smaller numbers of Carpatho-Rusyns immigrated to Canada and Argentina in the 1920s and to Australia in the 1970s and 1980s.

Carpatho-Rusyns do not have their own state. At best they function as a legally recognized national minority in some—but not all—of the European countries where they live. As has historically been the case with stateless minority groups, Carpatho-Rusyns have been reluctant to identify themselves as such or have simply not been recorded by the governments in the countries where they have lived. Therefore, it is impossible to know precisely the number of Carpatho-Rusyns in any country. A reasonable estimate would place their number at 1.6 million persons worldwide.

Until 1945, the vast majority of Rusyns in the Carpathian homeland inhabited over 1,100 small villages that averaged in size between 600 and 800 residents. Aside from Carpatho-Rusyns, most villages also had a small number (usually 5 to 15 percent) of inhabitants belonging to other national groups. These generally included a few Jewish families (small shopowners and tavern keepers as well as farmers), Romany/ Gypsies who often lived on the outskirts of the village, and a Magyar, Polish, Slovak, or Czech official (gendarme, notary, schoolteacher).

NUMBER OF CARPATHO-RUSYNS WORLDWIDE		
Country	Official Data	Estimate
UKRAINE Transcarpathia (650,000) Lemko Rusyns (90,000)	—	740,000
SLOVAKIA	49,000	30,000
POLAND	—	60,000
YUGOSLAVIA	19,900	25,000
ROMANIA	1,000	20,000
CZECH REPUBLIC	1,700	12,000
CROATIA	3,500	5,000
HUNGARY	—	3,000
UNITED STATES	12,500	620,000
CANADA	—	20,000
AUSTRALIA	—	2,500
Total		1,637,500

The Carpatho-Rusyns were mostly employed as farmers, livestock herders (especially sheep), and in forest-related occupations. The mountainous landscape that characterized Carpathian Rus' never allowed for extensive agricultural production. Thus, Carpatho-Rusyns were usually poor and often forced to survive by working in neighboring countries or by emigrating permanently abroad, especially to the United States.

After World War II, industrial enterprises were established in or near the Carpathian homeland, and many Rusyn villagers moved to nearby cities. Those cities (Užhorod, Mukačevo, Prešov, Humenné, Košice, Michalovce, Sanok, Nowy Sącz, Gorlice, Novi Sad) were most often located outside Carpatho-Rusyn ethnolinguistic territory. As a result, many Rusyns who migrated to cities intermarried, attended schools using the state language, and gave up their identity as Carpatho-Rusyns.

Language, identity, and culture

Carpatho-Rusyns belong to the Slavic branch of Indo-European peoples. Their dialects are classified as East Slavic, but because they live in a borderland region, Carpatho-Rusyn dialects are heavily influenced by Polish, Slovak, and Hungarian vocabulary. These influences from both the east and west, together with numerous terms from the Church Slavonic liturgical language and vocabulary unique to Carpatho-Rusyns, are what distinguish their spoken language from other East Slavic languages like Ukrainian.

In contrast to their West Slavic (Polish and Slovak), Magyar, and Romanian neighbors, Carpatho-Rusyns use the Cyrillic alphabet. Their national name, *Rusyn* (also spelled *Rusin*), connects them to the east, since *Rus'* was the name of the inhabitants and territory of a large medieval state centered in Kiev. The many names by which Carpatho-Rusyns have called themselves or were called by others—*Carpatho-Russian, Carpatho-Ukrainian, Rusnak, Ruthene, Ruthenian, Uhro-Rusyn*—all relate to their traditional association with the East Slavic world of the Rus'.

Despite the seeming confusion about names, the most appropriate designation is *Carpatho-Rusyn*, or simply *Rusyn*. This is the name the nineteenth-century national awakener Aleksander Duchnovyč used in poetic lines in what became the national credo—"I was, am, and will remain a Rusyn"—and it is the name he used in the first line of the national anthem—"Subcarpathian Rusyns, Arise from Your Deep Slumber." *Carpatho-Rusyn* and *Rusyn* are also the names used by most of the new cultural organizations and publications established in the European homeland since the Revolution of 1989. In Poland, Carpatho-Rusyns call themselves Lemkos. This is a new name. Before the twentieth century Lemkos, too, called themselves Rusyns or Rusnaks. Aware of their origins, recent publications and organizations in Poland often use the term *Lemko Rusyn* to describe their people.

When, in the seventeenth century, Carpatho-Rusyns began to publish books, they were written either in the vernacular Rusyn speech or in Church Slavonic, a liturgical language (functionally similar to Latin) used by East Slavs and South Slavs who were of an Eastern Christian religious orientation. In the nineteenth and twentieth centuries, Carpatho-Rusyn writers continued to use the Rusyn vernacular, and also began to use Russian and Ukrainian for their literary language. The so-called "language question" was always closely related to the problem of national identity.

Ever since the nineteenth century, Carpatho-Rusyn leaders have argued about their national identity. Some have felt that Rusyns are a branch of the Russians, others that they are a branch of the Ukrainians, still others that they form a distinct central European Carpatho-Rusyn nationality. Each orientation has used language, whether Russian, Ukrainian, or Carpatho-Rusyn, as a means to identify themselves. Today there are only two national orientations—the Rusyn and Ukrainian. The Ukrainian orientation argues that Rusyns are a branch of Ukrainians and that a distinct Carpatho-Rusyn nationality cannot and should not exist.

Since the Revolution of 1989, there has been a Carpatho-Rusyn national revival in all countries where they live, and efforts have been undertaken, especially in Slovakia and Poland, to create a standard Carpatho-Rusyn literary language for use in schools and publications. Rusyns in Yugoslavia's Vojvodina have had a literary language that has been used uninterruptedly in publications and schools ever since the first decades of the twentieth century.

Carpatho-Rusyns have a distinct literary tradition that dates back to the seventeenth century. Regardless of what language writers may have used—Rusyn, Church Slavonic, Russian, Ukrainian—their literary works have embodied the essence of Rusyn life and the mentality of its people. Among the most dominant themes have been a love for what is considered the pristine beauty of the Carpathian mountains and a characterization of Carpatho-Rusyns as a God-fearing and stoical people, who are seemingly destined to be controlled by natural forces and by foreign governments over which the individual has little power or influence. Each Carpatho-Rusyn region has its own literary founding father: Aleksander Duchnovyč (1803-1865) and Aleksander Pavlovyč (1819-1900) for the Prešov Region and Subcarpathian Rus'; Volodymyr Chyljak (1843-1893) for the Lemko Region; and Gabor Kostel'nik (1886-1948) for the Vojvodina.

Today there are Rusyn-language newspapers, journals, and books in virtually every European country where Carpatho-Rusyns live. The works of playwrights are performed by the professional Aleksander Duchnovyč Theater in Prešov, Slovakia; the semi-professional Djadja Theater in Ruski Kerestur and Novi Sad, Yugoslavia; and the amateur theater of the Lemko Association in Legnica, Poland. The best known current Rusyn-language writers are: in Ukraine—Volodymyr Fedynyšynec', Dmytro Kešelja, Ivan Petrovcij, and Vasyl' Sočka-Boržavyn; in Slovakia—Anna Halgašova, Mykolaj Ksenjak, Marija Mal'covska, and Štefan Suchŷj; in Poland—Olena Duc'-Fajfer, Volodymyr Graban, Stefanija Trochanovska, and Petro Murianka-Trochanovskij; in Yugoslavia—Natalija Dudaš, Irina Hardi-Kovačevič, and Djura Papharhaji; and in Hungary—Gabriel Hattinger-Klebaško.

Aside from various forms of folk culture, such as embroidery, painted Easter eggs, and folk music and dance performed by professional ensembles in Prešov and Užhorod and by numerous amateur ensembles elsewhere, Carpatho-Rusyns are most noted for an outstanding form of native architecture in the form of wooden churches. Perched on the top of hills, the majority of churches were built in the eighteenth and early nineteenth centuries.

During the first half of the twentieth century, Carpatho-Rusyns also created a unique school of painters, the so-called "Subcarpathian Barbizon," of whom the leading figures were Josyf Bokšaj, Adal'bert Erdeli, Fedir Manajlo, and Ernest Kondratovyč. About the same time, Rusyn life in the Lemko Region was captured on canvas by the world-renowned naive artist, Nykyfor Drovnjak. In more recent times, painters like Anton Kaššaj, Andrij Kocka, Volodymyr Mykyta, and the sculptors Mychajlo Belen' and Ivan Brovdij in Transcarpathia, as well as the painters Orest Dubaj, Štefan Hapak, Deziderij Millyj, and the political satirist Fedir Vico in Slovakia have produced a body of creative work that is replete with themes depicting Carpatho-Rusyn life and its environment.

Several museums exist with permanent exhibits of Carpatho-Rusyn folk art, icons, and painting. The most important and wide-ranging collections are in Svidník and Užhorod, with more specialized museums in Bardejov (icons), Medzilaborce (modern art), Nowy Sącz (icons), Sanok (icons), and Zyndranowa (on Lemkos). Open-air ethnographic museums (*skanzens*) with traditional Carpatho-Rusyn domestic architecture are found in Svidník and Užhorod. Similar museums in Bardejovské Kúpele, Humenné, and Sanok also include examples of Carpatho-Rusyn material culture.

Numerous scholars are engaged in studying the history, language, literature, ethnography, art, and music of Carpatho-Rusyns. Many are connected with scholarly institutions, such as the Institute of Carpathian Studies at Užhorod State University (Ukraine), the Institute of Rusyn

Language and Culture (Slovakia), the Department of Ukrainian and Rusyn Philology at the Bessenyei Pedagogical Institute (Hungary), the Department of Rusyn Language and Literature at the University of Novi Sad (Yugoslavia), the Society for Rusyn Language and Literature (Yugoslavia), and the Carpatho-Rusyn Research Center (United States). There are as well several scholars outside of the homeland countries who specialize in Carpatho-Rusyn themes, including Aleksander Duličenko (Estonia), Sven Gustavsson (Sweden), Paul Robert Magocsi (Canada), and Ivan Pop (Czech Republic).

Religion

Like their language and culture, Carpatho-Rusyn churches share elements from both the eastern (Slavia Orthodoxa) and western (Slavia Romana) Christian worlds. Religion has remained for Carpatho-Rusyns wherever they live the most important aspect of their lives. This is so much the case that in the popular mind Carpatho-Rusyn culture and identity have often been perceived as synonymous with one of the traditional Carpatho-Rusyn Eastern Christian churches.

The earliest ancestors of the Carpatho-Rusyns believed, like other Slavs, in several gods related to the forces of nature. The most powerful of these pagan gods was Perun, whose name is still preserved in the Carpatho-Rusyn language as a curse. Christianity first was brought to the Carpathians during the second half of the ninth century. Popular legends supported by scholarly writings suggest that Carpatho-Rusyns received Christianity in the early 860s from the "Apostles to the Slavs," Cyril and Methodius, two monks from the Byzantine Empire. As would be the case throughout the Slavic world, several pagan customs practised by Rusyns were easily adapted to the Christian holy days. Thus, the mid-winter festival of *koljada* was merged with Christmas and Epiphany; the festival of spring with Easter; and the harvest and summer solstice festival of Kupalo with the feast of John the Baptist.

Cyril and Methodius as well as their disciples were from the Byzantine Empire. Therefore, when the Christian church was divided after 1054, the Carpatho-Rusyns remained within the Eastern Orthodox sphere nominally under the authority of the Ecumenical Patriarch of Constantinople. Religious affiliation helped to distinguish Carpatho-Rusyns from their Slovak, Hungarian, and Polish neighbors who were Roman Catholic or Protestant. As Eastern Christians, the Carpatho-

Rusyns used Church Slavonic instead of Latin as the language in religious services; followed the liturgy of St. John Chrysostom; received both species (leavened bread and wine) at Communion; had married priests; and followed the old Julian calendar so that fixed feasts like Christmas eventually fell two weeks later than the western Gregorian calendar, on January 7. The Carpatho-Rusyns were distinguished as well from fellow East Slavic Christians (Ukrainians, Belorusans, Russians) by certain practices and rituals borrowed from their Latin-rite neighbors, but in particular by their liturgical music. That music, still in use today, consists primarily of congregational and cantorial singing (no organ or other instrument is permitted). Based on traditional East Slavonic chants and influenced by local folk melodies, it is known as Carpathian plain chant (*prostopinje*).

In the wake of the Protestant Reformation (which affected neighboring Magyars and Slovaks) and the Catholic Counter-Reformation, the government and local aristocracy began in the late sixteenth century to try to bring the Orthodox Carpatho-Rusyns closer to the official Roman Catholic state religion of the two states in which they lived at the time—the Hungarian Kingdom and Polish-Lithuanian Commonwealth. The result was the creation between 1596 and 1646 of a Uniate Church, that is an Eastern Christian Church in union with Rome. The Uniates were allowed to retain their Eastern rite and traditions, but they had to recognize the Pope in Rome, not the Ecumenical Patriarch of Constantinople as the ultimate head of their church. Hence from the seventeenth century, Carpatho-Rusyns were either Orthodox or Uniates. In 1772, the Uniates were renamed Greek Catholics. Eventually, in the United States they became known as Byzantine Catholics.

Although in practice there is not much difference between the Orthodox and Greek Catholic religious service (Divine Liturgy), there has nonetheless been constant friction between adherents of the two churches from the seventeenth century to the present in both the European homeland and the United States. The situation was made worse by the intervention of European secular authorities who at certain times persecuted and even banned entirely either the Orthodox or Greek Catholic Church.

Today, many Carpatho-Rusyn villages and cities have both a Greek Catholic and an Orthodox church. Also, in each country where Rusyns live there is at least one Greek Catholic and one Orthodox bishop. In general, among Carpatho-Rusyns worldwide, there are today an equal number of Greek Catholic and Orthodox adherents. In Ukraine's Transcarpathia, the region with the largest number of Carpatho-Rusyns, the situation is more complex. Of the 1,210 parishes registered in 1993, 38 percent were Orthodox and 17 percent Greek Catholic. The rest were Roman Catholic (5 percent) and Reformed Calvinist (7.5 percent)—both primarily among Magyars, as well as a growing number of Jehovah's Witnesses (17 percent), evangelical sects (6.6 percent), and Baptists (4 percent), all of whom have become widespread among Carpatho-Rusyns, most especially during the last decade.

With regard to church jurisdiction, the Greek Catholic eparchies of Mukačevo (Ukraine), Prešov (Slovakia), Hajdúdorog (Hungary), and Križevci (former Yugoslavia), as well as the Archdiocesan/Metropolitan Province of Pittsburgh (United States) are each self-governing and under the direct authority of the Vatican. The Orthodox eparchy of Mukačevo-Užhorod is part of the autonomous Ukrainian Orthodox Church within the Patriarchate of Moscow; the eparchy of Prešov is within the Orthodox Church of Slovakia; and the eparchies of Przemyśl-Nowy Sącz and Wrocław-Szczecin are in the Autocephalous Orthodox Church of Poland. In the United States, the Orthodox are either within the self-governing (autocephalous) Orthodox Church in America, or the American Carpatho-Russian Orthodox Greek Catholic Church under the Ecumenical Patriarch of Constantinople.

History

The ancestors of the Carpatho-Rusyns can be traced to Slavic peoples who began to appear in the valleys of the Carpathian Mountains in small numbers during the fifth and sixth centuries. Their presence is related to the question of the original homeland of the Slavs and the invasion into east-central Europe by nomadic peoples from central Asia.

Today most scholars agree that the center of the original homeland for all Slavic peoples was the region just north of the Carpathian Mountains in what is today eastern Poland, southwestern Belarus, and northwestern Ukraine. During the 440s, an Asiatic people known as the Huns crossed through the Slavic homeland and burst into east-central Europe, bringing with them Slavic peoples, some of whom settled in Carpathian Rus'. A century later, one of the tribes living in the original Slavic homeland known as White Croats had begun to settle in the valleys of the northern as well as southern slopes of Carpathian Rus'.

In the course of the sixth and early seventh centuries, the White Croats built fortified towns to protect their own people as well as the surrounding countryside which still included some Slavic settlers who had settled there earlier during the Hunnic invasions. During the seventh century, many of the Slavic tribes began to move out in various directions from their original homeland. Whereas some White Croats remained behind in Carpathian Rus', most moved southward into the Balkan peninsula. Their descendants are the modern Croats.

The first important event in the history of Carpathian Rus' occurred during the second half of the ninth century. In the early 860s, two missionaries from the Byzantine Empire, the brothers Cyril and Methodius, set out to bring the Christian faith to the Moravian Empire, which at the time was centered in what is today the eastern Czech Republic (Moravia) and western Slovakia. To this day, Carpatho-Rusyns believe that before their mission to Moravia Cyril and Methodius themselves brought the Christian religion to Carpathian Rus'—even establishing a bishopric at the fortified center of Mukačevo—or that this was accomplished during the 880s by the disciples of the Byzantine missionaries. Regardless of who actually did the conversion, it does seem certain that there was some kind of Christian presence in the Carpathians well before the end of the ninth century.

The very end of that same century brought another event that eventually was to have a profound effect on Rusyn historical development. Sometime between 896 and 898, a new Asiatic warrior people, the Magyars (ancestors of the modern-day Hungarians), crossed the crests of the Carpathians and settled in the region known as Pannonia, that is, the flat plain between the middle Danube and lower Tisza Rivers. From their new home, the Magyars eventually built a state called Hungary.

When the Magyars first crossed the Carpathians, they captured the White Croat hill fortress of Hungvar (modern-day Užhorod). There they defeated the semi-legendary Prince Laborec', who was later to become one of the first heroes of Rusyn history. Despite their military victory, the Magyars were initially unable to take control of Carpathian Rus', which during the tenth and for most of the eleventh century remained a sparsely-settled borderland between the kingdom of Hungary to south and the Kievan Rus' principality of Galicia to the north. In the absence of any outside political control. Slavs from the north (Galicia) and east (who actually arrived from Podolia via the mountain passes of

Transylvania) continued to settle in small numbers in various parts of the Carpathian borderland, which the Hungarians and other medieval writers referred to as the *Marchia Ruthenorum*—the Rus' March. These new immigrants, from the north and east, like the Slavs already living in Carpathian Rus', had by the eleventh century come to be known as the people of Rus', or Rusyns. The term *Rusyn* also meant someone who was a Christian of the Eastern (Byzantine) rite.

Rusyn migration from the north and east, in particular from Galicia, continued until the sixteenth century and even later. This was possible because the mountains, especially in western Carpathian Rus' (the Lemko Region), were not very high and were crossable through several passes. The sixteenth century also witnessed another migration into Carpathian Rus', this one by Vlach shepherds from the south. The Vlachs were originally of Romanian origin, although they were quickly assimilated by the Rusyns. The Vlachs moved throughout the entire range of the Carpathians as far west as Moravia. Their name *Vlach* soon came to mean a profession (shepherd) and legal status (tax-free person) rather than a nationality (Romanian).

The preceding discussion of early history suggests the complex origins of the Carpatho-Rusyns. They were not, as is often asserted, exclusively associated with Kievan Rus', from which it is said their name *Rusyn* drives. Rather, the ancestors of the present-day Carpatho-Rusyns are descendants of: (1) early Slavic peoples who came to the Danubian Basin with the Huns; (2) the White Croats; (3) the Rusyns of Galicia and Podolia; and (4) the Vlachs of Transylvania. Moreover, because Carpatho-Rusyns received Christianity over a century earlier than Kievan Rus', it is likely that they used the name *Rusyn* and were called by others *Rusyn* (Latin: *Rutheni*) even before the arrival of subsequent Rusyn migration from the north and east. On the other hand, because their Eastern-rite Christian religion derived from Orthodox Byzantium, Carpatho-Rusyns maintained cultural and religious ties with the Kievan Rus' principality of Galicia to the north, with Moldavia/Transylvania to the south, and with other Orthodox lands (central Ukraine and later Russia) farther east. Carpathian Rus' was not, however, under the political hegemony of Kievan Rus' or of any other East Slavic political entity during the Middle Ages nor at any time until the second half of the twentieth century! Instead, Carpathian Rus' has historically been within political and cultural spheres that are firmly part of east-central Europe.

By the second half of the eleventh century, Rusyn lands south of the

Carpathians came under the control of the kingdom of Hungary. Hungarian rule remained firmly entrenched until 1526, after which most of the kingdom was conquered by the Ottoman Turks. The small amount of land that still constituted Hungary, including Rusyn-inhabited territory, was divided between the Austrian Habsburg Empire and the semi-independent Hungarian principality of Transylvania. The Ottoman presence lasted until the outset of the eighteenth century, when the Habsburgs finally gained control of all of Hungary, including Transylvania. Consequently, Habsburg Hungary was to rule Rusyn lands south of the Carpathians until 1918.

North of the mountains, the Rusyn-inhabited Lemko Region that had been within the nominal sphere of the medieval Rus' principality of Galicia was, in the mid-fourteenth century, incorporated into the kingdom of Poland. Polish rule lasted until 1772, when Galicia was annexed by the Habsburg Empire and made into one of the provinces of Austria. Thus, from the late eighteenth century until 1918, all Carpatho-Rusyns found themselves under Habsburg rule, whether in the Hungarian kingdom or in the Austrian province of Galicia.

Although since the early Middle Ages Carpatho-Rusyns never had any political independence, they were recognized as a distinct group within the multinational Hungarian and Polish kingdoms and later the Austro-Hungarian Empire. In earlier times, when Carpathian Rus' was sparsely settled, Rusyn and Vlach mountain dwellers were treated for many decades as a privileged group that did not have to pay taxes. By the sixteenth century, however, most Carpatho-Rusyns were reduced to the status of peasant serfs dependent on either Hungarian, Polish, or later Austro-German landlords. Finally, during the last few decades of the Habsburg Empire's existence, between the 1870s and 1918, there was an attempt, especially in the Hungarian kingdom, to eliminate the Carpatho-Rusyns as a group through a policy of state-supported national assimilation.

Carpatho-Rusyns were able to survive as a distinct people largely because of their association with Orthodox Eastern Christian churches in the otherwise Roman Catholic social and political environment of Hungary, Poland, and later Habsburg Austria-Hungary. Among the most important symbols for Carpatho-Rusyns of their Orthodox eastern-rite identity was the Monastery of St. Nicholas on Monk's Hill (Černeča hora) near Mukačevo. This religious center, which in the fifteenth century became the residence for bishops, was founded in the 1390s by

Prince Fedir Koriatovyč. Koriatovyč was a prince of Podolia invited by the king of Hungary to administer the fortress of Mukačevo and the surrounding lands that included several Rusyn villages. As lord of Mukačevo, he is considered by Carpatho-Rusyns to be among their important national leaders.

The sixteenth century began a period of transformation in the socioeconomic and religious life of Carpatho-Rusyns. North of the mountains, Polish landlords expanded their estates into the Lemko Region where the local Rusyn peasant population became enserfed. This meant that landlords steadily acquired control over all aspects of a peasant's life, including the amount of work a peasant family had to perform on the landlord's estate, the amount of taxes a peasant household had to pay, even when and to whom peasants could marry. In order to ensure that these duties were fulfilled, Rusyn peasants were forbidden to leave their property, even temporarily, without the permission of the landlord. In practice, the serf became legally tied to the land.

South of the mountains the Hungarian government also passed laws (1514) that established serfdom in the countryside. Those laws were for some time not enforceable, however. This is because Hungary was invaded by the Ottoman Turks, who annihilated the Hungarian army in 1526, and who within a few decades came to control nearly three-quarters of the country. For nearly the next two centuries all that remained of Hungary was a small strip of territory under Habsburg Austria (primarily what is today Slovakia and part of Croatia) and the semi-independent principality of Transylvania (present-day central Romania) in the east. The Catholic Habsburgs spent as much time fighting their rivals for control of Hungary—the Protestant princes of Transylvania—as they did the Ottoman Turks.

Tucked in between Transylvania and Habsburg-controlled Hungary was Carpathian Rus', which for most of the late sixteenth and seventeenth centuries was ravaged by the conflicts between the military forces of Catholic Austria and Protestant Transylvania. Villages were frequently destroyed by marauding troops and the size of the Rusyn population declined because of flight or death by disease brought by soldiers in the wake of foreign invasions. Frustrated with their fate, many Rusyns joined Hungary's independent Transylvanian princes in their struggle against the Habsburgs. For instance, during the last great anti-Habsburg rebellion, the troops serving the Transylvanian Hungarian

Prince Ferenc II Rákóczi (who was raised in the family castle of Mukačevo) were made up largely of Rusyn peasants. Even though Rákóczi was finally defeated in 1711, a Hungarian legend arose about how the Rusyns proved themselves to be a people most faithful (*gens fidelissima*) to "their" prince and country. Another result of the defeat of Rákóczi was the full implementation of Austrian Habsburg rule throughout all of Hungary. For Carpathian Rus' this meant the influx of new Austro-Germanic landlords, like the Schönborn family, which during the eighteenth century came to control large tracts of land and numerous Rusyn villages.

The Carpatho-Rusyn Orthodox church in Hungary was also caught up in the political rivalry between Catholic Austria and Protestant Transylvania. The fate of Orthodoxy was closely tied to developments in Poland, where that country's Catholic rulers were becoming increasingly alarmed at the rapid spread of Protestantism within their realm. Faced with such political and religious rivalries, several Orthodox priests and a few bishops, first in Poland and then in Hungary, decided to join the Catholic Church and to recognize the authority of the Pope. This was confirmed by agreements reached at the Union of Brest (1596) and the Union of Užhorod (1646), after which the Uniate church came into being. In the course of the next century, the Orthodox church was banned and all Carpatho-Rusyns became officially Uniate or, as they came to be known after the 1770s, Greek Catholic. Unlike the Orthodox, the Uniate/Greek Catholics were recognized as a Habsburg state church, and in 1771, they received their own independent Greek Catholic eparchy (diocese) of Mukačevo. Financially supported by the Austrian Habsburg authorities, the Greek Catholic Church by the late eighteenth century operated elementary schools and academies for seminarians in which the Rusyn and Church Slavonic languages were taught. From these institutions came Greek Catholic clerics (Ioanniky Bazylovyč, Mychajlo Lučkaj), who during the second half of the eighteenth and first half of the nineteenth centuries wrote the first histories of the Carpatho-Rusyns.

The rise of nationalism throughout Europe during the nineteenth century also reached the Carpatho-Rusyns. They became particularly active as a group following the revolution of 1848 and what turned out to be Hungary's failed war of independence against Habsburg Austria. The short revolutionary period of 1848-1849 did, however, produce three important results: the abolition of serfdom; the arrival on the throne of a new Habsburg emperor, Franz Joseph (who was to rule until 1916); and the beginnings of a Rusyn national revival. The Rusyn national revival was largely the work of two individuals. One was the Greek Catholic priest Aleksander Duchnovyč (1803-1865), who in the 1850s founded the first Rusyn cultural society (in Prešov), published the first literary almanacs and elementary schoolbooks, and wrote the lines to what became the Rusyn national credo: *Ja Rusyn byl', jesm i budu* (I was, am, and will remain a Rusyn). His name is also associated (perhaps incorrectly) with the Rusyn national anthem: *Podkarpatskî rusynŷ, ostavte hlubokyj son* (Subcarpathian Rusyns, Arise from Your Deep Slumber). The other was Adol'f Dobrjans'kyj (1817-1902), a member of the Hungarian parliament and Austrian government official who between 1849 and 1865 attempted to create a distinct Rusyn territorial entity within the Habsburg Empire.

Following political changes in the Habsburg Empire during the 1860s, the last decades of the nineteenth century turned out to be a difficult time for Carpatho-Rusyns. The empire was transformed into the Austro-Hungarian Dual Monarchy, which in practice meant that the Hungarian authorities could rule their "half" of the state without any intervention by the imperial government in Vienna. By the 1870s, the Hungarian government set out on a course to enhance the status of the Magyars and their language and culture. As a result, the Carpatho-Rusyn national revival was stopped by the rise of Hungarian chauvinism. At the same time, widespread poverty caused in part by an increase in population and land shortages forced thousands of young men and entire families to emigrate. A few thousand Carpatho-Rusyns moved to the Bačka region (Vojvodina) in the southern part of the Hungarian Kingdom, where the first Rusyn colonists had arrived as early as 1745. A much larger number, estimated at about 225,000, left between the 1880s and 1914 for the industrial regions of the northeast United States.

The mid-nineteenth century cultural revival led by Duchnovyč and Dobrjans'kyj was able to preserve a sense of Carpatho-Rusyn national identity. It was not successful, however, in the effort to obtain autonomy or other political status specifically for Carpatho-Rusyns. All that was to change with the outbreak of World War I in 1914. For the next four years, thousands of Carpatho-Rusyns served loyally in the imperial Austro-Hungarian army where many died or were wounded on the eastern front against Russia or in the killing fields of northeastern

Italy. The war years also brought another kind of tragedy, especially for Rusyns in the Lemko Region. In 1914-1915, as tsarist Russia occupied most of Galicia, Austrian officials suspected Lemko Rusyns of treason and deported nearly 6,000 to concentration camps, especially at Talerhof near the city of Graz in Austria.

When the war ended in late 1918, the Austro-Hungarian Empire ceased to exist. Carpatho-Rusyn immigrants in the United States had already begun to meet in the summer of 1918, and under their leader Gregory Žatkovyč (1886-1967) they eventually supported the idea of a fully autonomous "Rusyn state" within the new country of Czechoslovakia. The idea of Carpatho-Rusyn autonomy or statehood was also accepted in the European homeland. At the same time, the postwar republic of Hungary responded be creating an autonomous Rusyn Land (Rus'ka Krajina) in December 1918, while Carpatho-Rusyn leaders were meeting between November 1918 and January 1919 in various national councils that called for union with either Hungary, Russia, Ukraine, or Czechoslovakia. Finally, in May 1919, Carpatho-Rusyns living south of the mountains met in Užhorod, where they decided that their homeland, Carpathian Rus', should be united as a "third state" with the new republic of Czechoslovakia.

The Lemko Rusyns north of the mountains expected to be part of Carpathian Rus' as well, but were rejected by Czechoslovakia. Instead, they created an independent Lemko Rusyn Republic based in the town of Gorlice. The Lemko Republic lasted for nearly sixteen months until March 1920, when its government headed by Jaroslav Kačmarčyk was arrested and its territory incorporated into Poland. Finally, the 10,000 or so Rusyns living in the Vojvodina (Bačka) region of southern Hungary joined a Serbian-dominated national congress and voted in November 1918 to be part of the new kingdom of Serbs, Croats, and Slovenes (later Yugoslavia).

During the interwar years, Carpatho-Rusyns in Czechoslovakia lived for the most part in the province of Subcarpathian Rus' (Podkarpats'ka Rus'). They had their own governor, elected representatives in both houses of the national parliament in Prague, and Rusyn-language schools. This was also a period when Rusyn cultural life flourished and when nearly one-third of the population left the Greek Catholic Church and "returned" to the Orthodox faith of their forefathers. Although Rusyns were considered one of the three "state peoples" of Czechoslovakia, they did not receive the political autonomy they were promised in 1918-1919. Moreover, about 100,000 Carpatho-Rusyns in the Prešov Region were administratively separated from Subcarpathian Rus' and given only the status of a national minority within Slovakia. Despite such political problems, compounded by existing difficult economic conditions made worse during the Great Depression of the 1930s, the Carpatho-Rusyns did enjoy an extensive national revival and marked improvement in their educational and cultural status during Czechoslovak rule. In particular, they learned how to live in a democratic society governed by the rule of law.

One result of the newly-found freedom was an increase in religious and national tensions. Left basically to themselves within a democratic Czechoslovakia, the Greek Catholic and Orthodox churches clashed with each other in competition for new adherents and for control of church property, while supporters of the Carpatho-Rusyn, Russian, and Ukrainian national orientations—each with its own organizations, schools, and publications—tried to convince the masses that they were either Rusyns, Russians, or Ukrainians.

In Poland, the Lemko Rusyns had no specific political status and no hopes for any kind of autonomy. Nevertheless, the Polish government during the 1930s did allow instruction in Lemko Rusyn in elementary schools and the establishment of Lemko civic and cultural organizations. Also, in response to the growing Orthodox movement, in 1934 the Vatican created a special Greek Catholic administration for the Lemko Region so that it was no longer under the direct control of the Ukrainian Greek Catholic hierarchy.

On the eve of World War II, the status of Carpatho-Rusyns changed substantially. As a result of the Munich Pact of September 30, 1938, Czechoslovakia became a federal state. In early October, Subcarpathian Rus' finally received its own long-awaited autonomous government headed by Andrej Brodij (1895-1945). By November 1938, a second autonomous government headed by the local pro-Ukrainian leaders, Avhustyn Vološyn (1874-1945) and Julijan Revaj (1899-1978), changed the province's name to Carpatho-Ukraine. That same month, Hungary annexed a southern strip of Carpatho-Ukraine that included its main cities Užhorod and Mukačevo. Then, on March 15, 1939, when Hitler destroyed what remained of Czechoslovakia, Carpatho-Ukraine declared its independence, but was immediately annexed by Hungary. For the rest of the war, Subcarpathian Rus' (Carpatho-Ukraine) remained under Hungarian rule, while Carpatho-Rusyns in the Prešov Region remained in what became an independent Slovak state closely allied to Nazi Germany.

Meanwhile, north of the mountains, the Lemko Rusyns found themselves under German rule after Poland was destroyed in September 1939 and the Lemko Region was annexed to Hitler's Third Reich. Finally, in the wake of the German-led invasion of Yugoslavia in the spring of 1941, the Vojvodina with its Carpatho-Rusyn inhabitants was annexed to Hungary. Thus, during World War II, Carpatho-Rusyn lands were ruled by either Nazi Germany, or by its allies, Hungary and Slovakia.

For most of the war years, the Carpatho-Rusyn homeland did not suffer any military damage and the economic situation was relatively stable. This did not mean, however, that certain segments of the population were exempt from the suffering caused by the new political conditions. In 1939-1940, nearly 40,000 Carpatho-Rusyns, mostly young males opposed to Hungary's annexation of Subcarpathian Rus', fled across the mountains into eastern Galicia, the former Polish region that after September 1939 was annexed to the Soviet Union. The young refugees, who expected to be welcomed to join in the fight against fascism, were instead arrested, accused of crossing into Soviet territory illegally, and sent to concentration camps. Three years later, those who survived were allowed to join the new Czechoslovak Army Corps set up to fight alongside the Soviet Army against Hitler.

At home in Subcarpathian Rus', which was renamed Subcarpathia (*Kárpátalja*) by the Hungarians, Carpatho-Rusyns had a modicum of cultural freedom. The "Uhro-Rusyn" language was taught in schools, and Rusyn publications and cultural societies were permitted as long as they were pro-Hungarian in political orientation. Expressions of pro-Ukrainian sentiment were forbidden, however. The war years were particularly harsh toward the over 100,000 Jews, who alone made up nearly one-quarter of the population in Subcarpathian Rus'. In the spring of 1944, the Hungarian and Slovak authorities under pressure from Germany deported virtually all of the region's Jewish inhabitants to the Nazi death camps where they perished. As a result, the Jewish presence, which for several centuries had been an integral part of the Carpatho-Rusyn environment, ceased to exist.

In the fall of 1944, the German army, together with its Hungarian and Slovak allies, was driven from all parts of Carpathian Rus' by the Soviet Army. Among the victorious Soviet forces was the Czechoslovak

Corps with its large contingent of Rusyn soldiers. During the course of the war, the Allied Powers (United States, Great Britain, France, the Soviet Union) had agreed that Subcarpathian Rus' should again be part of a restored Czechoslovak state. In October 1944, however, the Soviet Generalissimo, Josif Stalin, suddenly changed his mind. With the help of local Communists, the Soviets prepared the ground for the annexation of Subcarpathian Rus' to what was described as the "Soviet Ukrainian motherland." No general plebiscite was ever held, and in June 1945 a provisional Czechoslovak parliament (in the absence of Carpatho-Rusyn representation) ceded Subcarpathian Rus' to the Soviet Union. As for other Carpatho-Rusyn territory, the Prešov Region remained within Czechoslovakia; the Lemko Region became part of a restored Poland; and the Vojvodina became part of the republic of Serbia within a federated Yugoslavia.

Within a few years after the end of World War II, all Carpatho-Rusyns found themselves under Communist rule, either in the Soviet Union or in countries under Soviet domination. The last of these countries to become Communist was Czechoslovakia. That took place in 1948, the same year Yugoslavia freed itself from the Soviet bloc, although it still remained Communist.

Communist rule had a particularly negative impact on traditional Carpatho-Rusyn life. During the first few years after World War II, the Greek Catholic Church was outlawed; land was taken from the individual farmers who were obliged, often against their will, to work in collective or cooperative farms; and the Rusyn nationality was forbidden. Anyone who might claim his or her identity as Rusyn was forcibly listed in official documents as a Ukrainian. The Rusyn language was banned in schools and in all publications.

An even worse fate befell the nearly 180,000 Lemko Rusyns living in Poland. About two-thirds were encouraged to emigrate voluntarily to the Soviet Ukraine in 1945 and 1946. Then, in the spring of 1947, those Lemkos who had remained in the Carpathians were driven from their homes by Polish security forces. The Lemkos were forced to live in the former German lands of western and northern postwar Poland (in particular Silesia). As for the Lemko Region itself, many age-old Rusyn villages were destroyed, while others were taken over by Polish settlers.

The only exception to the sad fate of Carpatho-Rusyns during the post-World War II Communist era was Yugoslavia. In the Vojvodina and the neighboring Srem region, Rusyns were recognized as a distinct nationality with their own government-supported schools, publications, cultural organizations, radio, and television programs. The Greek Catholic Church was also allowed to function in Yugoslavia. Finally, in 1974, when the Vojvodina became an autonomous province within the republic of Serbia, the Rusyns became one of the five official nationalities in the region.

Despite the harshness of Communist rule, the Carpatho-Rusyns did from time to time protest their fate. In Poland during the late 1950s, Lemkos began to return illegally to their native mountain villages, and by the 1980s about 10,000 did succeed in reestablishing new homesteads or in buying back their old houses. Some Lemkos also tried to set up their own cultural organizations and publications distinct from Ukrainians, but they were blocked in those efforts by the Polish government.

In neighboring Slovakia, Carpatho-Rusyns protested their reclassification as Ukrainians by identifying themselves as Slovaks and sending their children to Slovak schools. The result was large-scale assimilation among Carpatho-Rusyns in the Prešov Region whose numbers declined by two-thirds, most especially after the policy of forced Ukrainianization was implemented in 1952. During the Prague Spring of 1968, when Czechoslovakia's leaders tried to "humanize" Communism, Carpatho-Rusyns in Slovakia's Prešov Region demanded the return of their nationality as well as the re-establishment of Rusyn schools and publications. Those efforts were cut short, however, by the invasion of the country by the Soviet Union and its allies on August 21, 1968. Within a year of the invasion, the hard-line pro-Soviet Czechoslovak Communist authorities once again banned all activity that might in any way be connected with a distinct Carpatho-Rusyn identity. Only the Greek Catholic Church, which was restored in Czechoslovakia in June 1968, was allowed to survive, although it rapidly dropped its former Carpatho-Rusyn orientation and became an instrument of slovakization. Thus, the four decades of Communist rule following World War II brought to an end many aspects of traditional Carpatho-Rusyn life and led to the virtual disappearance of the group as a distinct nationality.

Carpatho-Rusyns, like every other people in central and eastern Europe, were profoundly influenced by the reforms that began in the Soviet Union after the accession to power in 1985 of Mikhail Gorbachev as head of the Soviet Communist party. The first changes actually took place among the Lemko Rusyns in Poland, who as early as 1983 organized an annual folk and cultural festival (Vatra). The goal of the Vatra was to restore among Lemkos the idea that they belonged to a distinct nationality that was neither Ukrainian or Polish, but Carpatho-Rusyn.

The Carpatho-Rusyn national revival really got underway only after the fall of Communism in 1989. During the next two years, a new organization to promote the idea of a distinct Carpatho-Rusyn nationality was established in each of the countries where Rusyns live: the Society of Carpatho-Rusyns (Obščestvo podkarpatskych Rusynov) in Ukraine, the Rusyn Renaissance Society (Rusyn'ska Obroda) in Slovakia, and the Lemko Association (Stovaryšŷnja Lemkiv) in Poland. This same period saw as well the establishment of new organizations among Rusyns outside the Carpathian homeland, such as the Society of Friends of Subcarpathian Rus' (Společnost přátel Podkarpatské Rusi) in the Czech Republic, the Ruska Matka in Yugoslava, and even the Organization of Rusyns in Hungary where it was thought Rusyns had long ago disappeared through assimilation already by the end of the nineteenth century. Also, for the first time since World War II, Rusyn-language newspapers and magazines began to appear, including *Rusyn* and *Narodnŷ novynkŷ* in Slovakia, *Podkarpats'ka Rus'* and *Rusyns'ka bysida* in Ukraine, *Besida* in Poland, and *Rusyns'kyj žyvot* in Hungary.

The greater ease of travel following the fall of Communism allowed Carpatho-Rusyns new opportunities for cross-country cooperation. As a result, in March 1991, the first World Congress of Rusyns and, in November 1992, the first Congress of the Rusyn Language were held, both in Slovakia. The cultural and organizational activities that have taken place since the Revolution of 1989 have in varying degrees been assisted by the governments of all the countries where Rusyns live, except Ukraine. In March 1991, Rusyns were even recognized and recorded as a distinct nationality in the census of the former Czech and Slovak Federated Republic.

In the wake of the Revolution of 1989, the vast majority of Carpatho-Rusyns in Europe found themselves living in new countries. In the summer of 1991, the Rusyns of Yugoslavia became divided by a new state boundary between a smaller Yugoslavia (that still included the Vojvodina) and a newly independent Croatia. Unfortunately, the Carpatho-Rusyns of Croatia (about 2,500 in the area near Vukovar) were in the war zone between Croatia and Serbia and suffered much material losses and forced deportation as part of Serbia's policy of ethnic cleansing. At the end of 1991, when the Soviet Union collapsed, the Carpatho-Rusyns in Transcarpathia voted overwhelmingly in favor of an independent Ukraine. Finally, in January 1993, the Czechoslovak state broke up, so that the Prešov Region Rusyns now live in an independent Slovakia.

Today, the governments of Slovakia, Poland, the Czech Republic, Hungary, and Yugoslavia recognize Carpatho-Rusyns as a national minority. Rusyn organizations in each country are concerned primarily with preserving the group's existence as a distinct nationality through cultural activity, such as publications and the work of scholarly institutions, schools, and theaters. In Ukraine's Transcarpathia, however, the emphasis has been on political activity, in particular efforts to obtain autonomy.

In December 1991, at the same time that the citizens of Ukraine voted in a referendum for their independence, 78 percent of the inhabitants of Transcarpathia voted in favor of autonomy (self-rule) for their province. To date, neither the Ukrainian government nor its parliament has implemented the promised autonomy voted on by over three-fourths of Transcarpathia's population in a legal vote. In an attempt to put pressure on Ukraine to fulfill the results of the December 1991 referendum, a "Provisional government of the Republic of Subcarpathian Rus'" was formed in Užhorod in May 1993, headed by Professor Ivan Turjanycja. In June 1994, Turjanycja was also elected a deputy to the regional parliament (Oblasna Rada), and since that time the struggle to achieve autonomy for Subcarpathian Rus' (Transcarpathia) in Ukraine has been carried out within the framework of the regional parliament.

The Carpatho-Rusyn revival that began in the 1980s has not been greeted with universal favor. Those individuals in each country who accept a Ukrainian self-identity and who head pro-Ukrainian organizations reject all efforts by Carpatho-Rusyns to assert their national identity. Local Ukrainian leaders state categorically that "there cannot and should not be" a distinct Carpatho-Rusyn nationality. This is because the pro-Ukrainians believe that all Rusyns are simply a regional variant or "branch" of the Ukrainian nationality. Such views are particularly widespread in Ukraine, the only country that refuses to recognize Carpatho-Rusyns as a distinct people.

Despite such denials as expressed by the Ukrainian government and by nationalistic elements within the Ukrainian population, the idea of a distinct Carpatho-Rusyn nationality and culture continues to be greeted favorably, both in neighboring countries where the group lives as a minority (Slovakia, Poland, Hungary, Yugoslavia) as well as by several non-governmental organizations based in other countries who are concerned with fate of minority cultures and languages in Europe.

CHAPTER 2

Mapping Stateless Peoples:
The East Slavs of the Carpathians[*]

I n 1996, I published a large-scale map (1: 355 000) entitled
Carpatho-Rusyn Settlement at the Outset of the 20th Century
(henceforth: C-R Settlement Map). The map depicted over 1,300 villages inhabited by Carpatho-Rusyns between the years 1900 and 1921,
with comparative reference to the years 1881 and 1806.[1]

Carpatho-Rusyns have never had their own state nor even an administrative entity that encompassed all the territory where they have lived.
Consequently, some criteria other than officially recognized borders had
to be found in order to decide what should be depicted visually as
Carpatho-Rusyn territory. This essay is an attempt to explain the conceptual basis of the C-R Settlement Map which, with several smaller
maps has begun to function as a didactic tool for those who in recent

[*] This study was prepared for the XIIth International Congress of Slavists held in
Cracow, August 27–September 2, 1998. It was first published in *Canadian Slavonic
Papers*, XXXIX, 3–4 (Edmonton, 1997), pp. 301-334.

[1] Paul Robert Magocsi, *Carpatho-Rusyn Settlement at the Outset of the 20th Century with Additional Data from 1881 and 1806/Rosselenia karpat'skŷkh rusyniv
na zachatku XX stolitia z dalshŷma dannŷma z 1881-ho i 1806-ho roku* [Or-
well, Vermont], 1996. A second revised edition appeared in 1998.

MAP 2

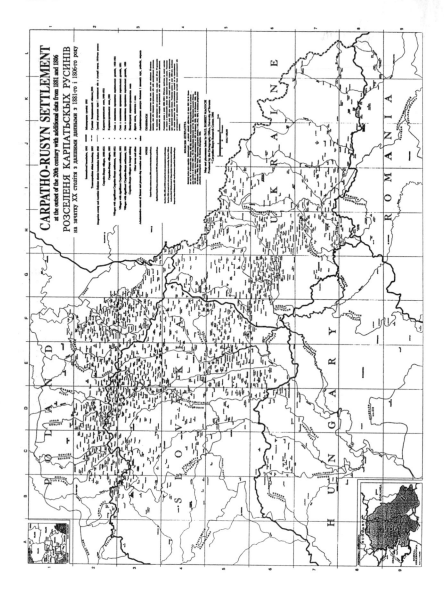

years support the idea of a distinct Carpatho-Rusyn nationality.[2]

My first encounter with the problem of depicting on a map the territory inhabited by a people that has no state dates back to the mid-1970s. At that time, I was commissioned to prepare 89 maps for the *Harvard Encyclopedia of American Ethnic Groups*. These maps were intended to show the homelands of each of the peoples represented in the encyclopedia, some of whom had their own state, some of whom did not. Authors of the entries were asked to submit along with their text a sketch map with some of the elements they would like to have depicted. I remember vividly the map that accompanied the entry on the Basques, whose homeland straddles the present-day borders of Spain and France.

The Basque sketch map included no state borders or even a reference to either Spain or France. The Basque homeland could therefore have been anywhere, and this caused the encyclopedia editors—imbued with Harvard's characteristic intellectual condescension—to dismiss the map outright as an example of myopic nationalism. Not unexpectedly, the final map that I drew for the encyclopedia made clear that the Basque Land (Euzkadi) was firmly a "part" of Spain and France.[3]

It took several years to extricate myself from the tyranny of contemporary state boundaries and to realize that the "borderless" map by the Basque author was in one sense as legitimate as my published corrected version in which the Basque homeland was rendered subordinate to Spain and France. Why was the Basque author's version of spatial reality also legitimate? Because when asked about their homeland, at least some Basques respond in categories that disregard con-

---

[2]Smaller versions of the map have appeared from 1987 through 1997 in each issue of the quarterly *Carpatho-Rusyn American* (Pittsburgh, Pa. and Fairfax, Va.); in a brochure entitled *Carpatho-Rusyns* that has appeared in various editions: English, Ukrainian, and Slovak (Orwell, Vt., 1995), Vojvodinian Rusyn and Serbo-Croatian (Novi Sad, 1995), Hungarian (Budapest, 1996), Polish (Orwell, Vt., 1996); and at least once in the print media of all countries where Rusyns live: *Rusyn*, I, 1 (Medzilaborce, Slovakia, 1991), inside cover; *Besida*, IV, 2 (Krynica, Poland, 1992), insert; *Podkarpats'ka Rus'* (Uzhhorod, Ukraine), September 9, 1993, p. 3; and *Rusynskŷi zhyvot*, I, 1 (Budapest, 1994), p. 2. Both the small and large versions of the map are featured since 1995 on the Carpatho-Rusyn World Wide Web Internet site—http://www.carpatho-rusyn.org/carpatho.

[3]Stephen Thernstrom, ed., *Harvard Encyclopedia of American Ethnic Groups* (Cambridge, Mass., 1980), p. 173.

temporary and historic state boundaries. And why is this so? Because they know that as Basques they have lived in their own homeland before Spain or France had ever come into existence. Hence, Basque "boundaries" have as much justification to be depicted on maps as any latter-day and often changing state boundaries.

Such an approach implies that there may be different kinds of boundaries. Some are "real" because they have been agreed to by governments, confirmed by surveyors, and depicted with lines on a map. Others are "real" because a group of people with a common historical memory are aware of and believe in their existence. Does this mean that boundaries in the second category are merely imagined and are, therefore, unreliable because imaginations can vary from individual to individual? Or do there exist quantitatively objective criteria which can be used to determine the boundaries of stateless peoples?

The stateless people under consideration here are the Carpatho-Rusyns. They are depicted on the C-R Settlement Map as living on contiguous territory within the present-day state boundaries of Ukraine, Slovakia, Poland, and Romania. All these territories were before World War I part of Austria-Hungary. The Carpatho-Rusyn inhabited lands within each present-day country are also known by regional names: (1) Subcarpathian Rus' (*Podkarpats'ka Rus'*) or Transcarpathia (*Zakarpattia*) in Ukraine; (2) the Prešov Region (*Priashev'ska Rus'/Priashevshchyna*) in Slovakia; (3) the Lemko Region (*Lemkovyna/Lemkivshchyna*) in Poland; and (4) the Maramureş Region (*Maramorosh*) in Romania. Aside from these four regions which form a compact territory, there are as well isolated Carpatho-Rusyn villages or groups of villages (islets) in nearby southeastern Slovakia, northeastern Hungary, and farther south in the Vojvodina (historic Bačka and Srem) of Yugoslavia's republic of Serbia.

Carpatho-Rusyns are linguistically and culturally an East Slavic people who live along a linguistic-cultural boundary, the other side of which is inhabited by West Slavic (Poles and Slovaks), Finno-Ugric (Magyars), and Romance (Romanian) peoples. Problems have arisen whenever scholars have attempted to determine with any degree of exactitude the extent of the Carpatho-Rusyn areal. Particularly problematic is the southwestern boundary with the Slovaks. There is also difficulty in delineating an eastern boundary, assuming there should be an eastern boundary at all. Put another way, to what degree are

Carpatho-Rusyns distinguishable from fellow East Slavs, specifically the Ukrainians of neighboring historic Galicia?

Previous studies

There is a sizeable literature dealing with the extent of Carpatho-Rusyn territory.[4] The earliest studies began to appear in the mid-nineteenth century, a time when the first population censuses were being conducted in a systematic fashion in Austria-Hungary and the empire's inhabitants were being asked by governmental functionaries to define themselves in terms of the language they spoke, their religion, and eventually their national identity. Such questions caused confusion, and the inhabitants of certain villages often identified themselves differently from one census to the next. This prompted scholars to analyze the relationship between the official statistics and ethnolinguisitc "reality." The most comprehensive works, which dealt with settlement on the southern slopes of the Carpathians were by the Russian historian Aleksei L. Petrov and the Ukrainian historian Stepan Tomashivs'kyi.[5]

---

[4]The literature is surveyed in Stepan Tomashivs'kyi, "Etnografichna karta Uhors'koï Rusy," in Vladimir I. Lamanskii, ed., *Stat'i po slavianoviedieniiu*, Vol. III (St. Petersburg, 1910), pp. 181-189; Jan Húsek, *Národopisná hranice mezi Slováky a Karpatorusy* (Bratislava, 1925), pp. 5-12; and Bohdan Strumins'kyi, "Terytoriia: istorychnyi narys pohliadiv," in idem, ed., *Lemkivshchyna: zemlia—liudy—istoriia—kul'tura*, Zapysky Naukovoho tovarystva im. Shevchenka, Vol. CCVI (New York, Paris, Sydney, Toronto, 1988), pp. 11-86.

[5]Of Petrov's numerous studies on the subject, of particular relevance here are: "Zamietki po ètnografii i statistikie Ugorskoi Rusi," *Zhurnal Ministerstva narodnago prosvieshcheniia*, CLXXIX, 2 (St. Petersburg, 1892), pp. 439-458—reprinted in his *Stat'i ob Ugorskoi Rusi* (St. Petersburg, 1906), pp. 1-18; *Prediely ugrorusskoi riechi v 1773g. po offitsial'nym dannym: karty*, Sbornik Otdieleniia russkago iazyka i slovesnosti Imperatorskago akademii nauk, Vol. LXXXVI (St. Petersburg, 1909); *Prediely ugrorusskoi riechi v 1773g. po offitsial'nym dannym: izsliedovanie i karty*, Zapiski Istorichesko-filologicheskago fakul'teta Imperatorskago S.-Peterburgskago universiteta, Vol. CV (St. Petersburg), 1911; and *Národopisná mapa Uher podle úředního lexikonu osad z roku 1773* (Prague, 1924), with map 1:468 000.

Tomashivs'kyi's major contribution is an ethnographic map based on the Hungarian census of 1900, with commentary, statistics, and index: Stepan Tomashivs'kyi, "Etnografichna karta Uhors'koï Rusy," in Vladimir I. Lamanskii, ed., *Stat'i po slavianoviedieniiu*, Vol. III (St. Petersburg, 1910), pp. 178-269 and map 1:300 000 (St. Petersburg, 1906). Tomashivs'kyi's map was reviewed at length with supplemental information by Oleksander Nazariïv, "Etnohrafichna terytoriia uhors'-kykh ukraïntsiv-rusyniv," *Zapysky Naukovoho tovarystva im. Shevchenka*, CII

The controversial boundary between Rusyns and Slovaks prompted the most literature, as some of the leading Slavists from the pre-World War I era attempted to delineate a "correct" boundary. Among the more important contributions to the debate were by the Norwegian Slavist Olaf Broch,[6] the Galician-Ukrainian ethnographer Volodymyr Hnatiuk,[7] the Czech philologist František Pastrnek,[8] the Russian linguist Aleksei Sobolevskii,[9] the Czech archaeologist and anthropologist Lubor Niederle,[10] and the Slovak linguist Samuel Czambel.[11] Although they did not participate in the polemics among the aforementioned Slavists, the maps and statistical compilations of the Austrian official, Karl von Czoernig,[12] and the Magyar scholars Elek Fényes, Pál Balogh, and most recently Edit Tamás,[13] contributed to the

(L'viv, 1911), pp. 164-191. Aside from the ethnographic map, Tomashivs'kyi also undertook a detailed critique of Hungary's censuses in "Uhors'ki rusyny v s'vitli madiars'koï uriadovoï statystyky," *ibid.*, LXI (L'viv, 1903), pp. 1-46, and in "Prychynky do piznannia etnohrafichnoï terytoriï Uhors'koï Rusy teper i davnishe," *ibid.*, LXVII (L'viv, 1905).

[6]Olaf Broch, *Studien von der slowakisch-kleinrussischen Sprachgrenze im ostl. Ungarn* (Kristiania, 1897) and *Weitere Studien von der slowakisch-kleinrussischen Sprachgrenze* (Kristiania, 1899).

[7]Volodymyr Hnatiuk, "Hungarian-Ruthenica," *Zapysky Naukovoho tovarystva im. Shevchenka*, XXVIII, 2 (L'viv, 1899), pp. 29-38; "Rusyny Priashivs'koï eparkhiï i ïkh hovory," *ibid.*, XXXV (L'viv, 1900), pp. 1-70; and "Slovaky chy Rusyny?: prychynok do vyiasnennia sporu pro natsional'nist' zakhidnykh rusyniv," *ibid.*, XLII, 4 (L'viv, 1901), pp. 1-81.

[8]F. Pastrnek, "Rusíni jazyka slovenského: odpověd' panu Vlad. Hnat'jukovi," in Vladimir I. Lamanskii, ed., *Stat'i po slavianoviedieniiu*, Vol. II (St. Petersburg, 1906), pp. 60-78.

[9]A. Sobolevskii, "Kak davno russkie zhivut v Karpatakh i za Karpatami," *Zhivaia starina*, IV, 3-4 (St. Petersburg, 1894), pp. 524-526.

[10]Lubor Niederle, "K sporu o ruskoslovenské rozhraní hranici v Uhrách," *Slovanský přehled*, V (Prague, 1903), pp. 345-349; "Ještě k sporu o rusko-slovenskou hranici v Uhrách," *ibid.*, VI (1904), pp. 258-261; and "Nová data k východní slovenské hranici v Uhrách," *Národopisný věstník českoslovanský*, II (Prague, 1907), pp. 1-3.

[11]Samo Czambel, *Slovenská reč a jej miesto v rodine slovanských jazykov*, Vol. I (Turčiansky Sv. Martin, 1906).

[12]Karl Freiherr von Czoernig, *Ethnographie der oesterreichischen Monarchie*, 3 vols. (Vienna, 1855-57).

[13]Elek Fényes, *Magyarországnak és a hozzá kapcsolt tartományoknak mostani állapotja statisztikai és geographiai tekintetben*, 6 vols. (Pest, 1833-40), esp. vols. III and IV; Pál Balogh, *A népfajok Magyarországon* (Budapest, 1902); Edit Tamás,

debate about the southern extent of the Carpatho-Rusyn area.

The attempts by scholars to determine the boundaries of the Lemko Region on the northern slopes of the Carpathians have also produced an extensive literature. The most comprehensive map of the region together with statistical data on individual villages and towns was prepared by the Galician-Ukrainian geographer, Volodymyr Kubiiovych, who reconstructed data based on various censuses conducted between 1900 and 1931.[14] With regard to the specific extent of the Lemko Region, the western and northern boundary with Poles has been less difficult to define than the eastern boundary.[15]

Ever since the early nineteenth century scholars have debated whether Lemko-Rusyn territory extends as far east as the San River, or whether it ends somewhere to the west along the Solinka, Osława, or Wisłok River valleys.[16] Since the 1930s, the number of works on the Lemko Region has increased substantially, and the question of the

"A szlovák-magyar-ruszin nyelvhatár a történelmi Zemplén és Ung megyében," in Judit Katona and Gyula Viga, eds., *Az interetnikus kapcsolatok kutatásának újabb eredményei* (Miskolc, 1996), pp. 267-284.

[14]Volodymyr Kubiiovych (Kubijovič), *Etnichni hrupy pivdennozakhidn'oï Ukraïny (Halychyny) na 1.1.1939/Ethnic Groups of the South-Western Ukraine (Halyčyna—Galicia) 1.1.1939* (Wiesbaden, 1983). This work contains statistical data for Ukrainian-inhabited Galicia; the accompanying map (1:250 000) has an insert covering "Zakhidnia Lemkivshchyna/Westernmost Part of Halyčyna."

[15]On the northern and western boundary of the Lemko region, see the early work by Dionizy Zubrzycki, *Granice między ruskim i polskim narodem w Galicji* (L'viv, 1849)—German edition: *Die Grenzen zwischen der russinischen und polnischen Nation in Galizien* (L'viv, 1849); and Tit Myshkovskii, "Iugozapadnaia ètnograficheskaia granitsa Galitskoi Rusi," *Nauchno-literaturnyi sbornik Galitsko-russkoi matitsy*, LXIX [VIII] (L'viv, 1934), pp. 3-9.

In contrast to the southern slopes of the Carpathians, in the Lemko Region there was only one islet of East Slavic settlement separated by some distance from the compact territory along the mountain crests. This consisted of eight villages north of the town of Krosno near the bend of the Wisłok River inadvertently left off the first edition of the C-R Settlement Map but added in the second edition.

[16]Those scholars who favored the San River as the eastern Lemko boundary include Wincenty Pol, Ivan Vahylevych, Aleksei Torons'kyi, and Iakiv Holovats'kyi. Those who consider the boundary to be along a line farther west include Denys Zubryts'kyi, Izydor Kopernicki, and Ivan Zilyns'kyi. See the discussion in Roman Reinfuss, "Łemkowie jako grupa etnograficzna," *Prace i materiały etnograficzne*, Vol. VII (Lublin, 1948-49), esp. pp. 89-94; and Strumins'kyi, "Terytoriia," pp. 25-35.

eastern boundary continues to be debated by Polish and Ukrainian linguists,[17] ethnographers,[18] and geographers.[19] Despite the results of multidisciplinary research there is still no consensus on the eastern boundary.

Characteristics of the C-R Settlement Map

How, then, does the 1996 C-R Settlement Map differ from the preceding literature and what does it add to our understanding of where precisely the Carpatho-Rusyn homeland is located? First, a few words about the content of the map. It shows 1,300 villages (1,447 in the revised 1998 edition) where 20 percent or more of the inhabitants were Carpatho-Rusyn in the period 1881 to 1921, together with other villages which had more than 20 percent Carpatho-Rusyn habitation in the year 1806. The vast majority of villages are on contiguous territory along the southern and, in part, northern slopes of the northcentral ranges (Beskydy, Bieszczady, Gorgany) of the Carpathian Mountains. There is also an inset map of the Vojvodina (historic Bačka and Srem) where Rusyn immigrants from what is today northeastern Hungary and Ukraine's Transcarpathia settled beginning in the mid-eighteenth century.

Superimposed on this pattern of villages are three levels of boundaries: present-day state boundaries, the boundary of the Transcarpathian oblast in Ukraine, and the boundaries of counties (*megye/Comitat/župa*) in the former Hungarian Kingdom and the districts (*Bezirk/*

[17]Józef Szemlej, "Z badań nad gwarą łemkowską," *Lud Słowiański*, III, 2 (Cracow, 1934), pp. 162-177; Zdzisław Stieber, "Wschodnia granica Łemków," *Sprawozdania z Czynności i Posiedzeń PAU*, XL, 8 (Warsaw, 1935), pp. 246-249—French edition: "La frontière orientale des Lemki," *Bulletin internationale de l'Académie polonaise des sciences et des lettres*, no. 7-10 (Cracow, 1936), pp. 232-236; Ivan Zilyns'kyi, "Pytannia pro lemkivs'ko-boikivs'ku hranytsiu," *Lud Slowiański*, IV, 1 (Cracow, 1938), pp. 75-101.

[18]Jan Falkowski and Bazyli Pasznycki, *Na pograniczu łemkowsko-bojkowskiem* (L'viv, 1935; reprinted Warsaw, 1991); Roman Reinfuss, "Problem wschodniego zasięgu etnograficznego Łemkowszczyzny," *II. zjazd sprawozdawczo-naukowy poświęcony Karpatom wschodnim i środkowym* (Warsaw, 1938), pp. 1-11; idem, "Etnograficzne granice Łemkowszczyzny, *Ziemia*, XXVI, 10-11 (Warsaw, 1936), pp. 248-253; and idem, *Lemkowie jako grupa*, esp. pp. 84-102.

[19]Stanisław Leszczycki, "Zarys antropogeograficzny Łemkowszczyzny," *Wierchy*, XIII (Cracow, 1935)—reprinted in Walery Goetl, ed., *O Łemkowszczyźnie* (Cracow, 1935), pp. 14-40; Ihor Stebel's'kyi, "Heohrafiia liudyny," in Strumiņs'kyi, *Lemkivshchyna*, pp. 113-146.

okruh) of the former Austrian Habsburg province of Galicia that existed as administrative units at least until 1918.

On the reverse side of the map is an index that lists over 3,600 names of villages (4,300 names in the revised 1998 edition) according to the following criteria: present-day name; historic name(s); and several linguistic variants (Carpatho-Rusyn, Hungarian, Polish, Romanian, Serbo-Croatian, Slovak, Ukrainian).[20] Determining an appropriate name for a given place was not straightforward. Among other things, a Carpatho-Rusyn standard does not exist for all areas covered on the map,[21] while each Rusyn village south of the Carpathians has two, often significantly different names in Hungarian, as well as variants (not provided) in the Czech and Russian languages that were in official use in Subcarpathian Rus'/Transcarpathia at various times in the twentieth century.[22] All the names in the index

[20]Slovak place-names follow the main forms used in the invaluable *Retrospektívny lexikon obcí Československej socialistickej republiky 1850-1970*, Vol. II: *Abecedný prehl'ad obcí a častí obcí v rokoch 1850-1970*, Pt. 2: *Slovenská socialistická republika* (Prague, 1978), which provides for each village the former Hungarian and in some cases German names, as well as Slovak names in various historic orthographies. Romanian place-names are from Coriolan Suciu, comp., *Dicţionar istoric al localităţilor din Transylvania*, 2 vols. (Bucharest, 1968).

[21]There is a standard only for the territory of Subcarpathian Rus' (present-day Transcarpathia in Ukraine); in 1927, the Czechoslovak government approved a Rusyn name for each settlement (using the Cyrillic alphabet in its etymological script). See the explanation and index in *Statistický lexikon obcí v republice československé . . . na základě výsledků sčítání lidu z 15. února 1921*, Vol. IV: *Podkarpatská Rus* (Prague, 1928), pp. x-xii and 63-68. Rusyn names for the Prešov Region in Slovakia were taken from Iurii Pan'ko, ed., *Orfografichnyi slovnyk rusyn'skoho iazŷka* (Prešov, 1995). Rusyn names in the Lemko Region were taken from the dictionary (*słowniczek*) of place-names in Janusz Rieger, "Toponomastyka Beskidu Niskiego i Bieszczadów Zachodnich," in *Łemkowie: kultura—sztuka—język* (Warsaw and Cracow, 1987), pp. 133-168, although I have added ы/ŷ to distinguish that characteristic Carpatho-Rusyn vowel from и/y. Rusyn names for villages in present-day Hungary, Romania, and southeastern Slovakia which were not indicated in the above sources were taken for the most part from Tomashivs'kyi, "Etnografichna karta."

[22]During the height of the magyarization efforts before World War I, the Hungarian names for most Carpatho-Rusyn villages south of the Carpathians were changed between 1900 and 1910. The government's goal was to make the names sound less Slavic. For instance, Kolbasov (Slovak)/Kovbasuv (Rusyn), which had been Kolbaszó in Hungarian until 1900, became Végaszó. Analogously, Negrovo (Rusyn)/ Nehrovo (Ukrainian), which had been Negrova in Hungarian became Maszárfalva. With regard to orthography on the C-R Settlement Map, the older Hungarian phoneme *cz* has been replaced by modern spellings (i.e., Rakaca, instead

are cross-referenced to a main entry that is in the dominant/official langauge of the country in which the village is located today: Polish in Poland, Ukrainian in Ukraine, etc. It is the present-day official forms that appear on the map itself.[23]

The sources used to compile the C-R Settlement Map were governmental and church censuses on which individuals were asked to identify their language ("mother tongue") or their nationality. Before turning to the reliability of such sources and the reasons for choosing one census over another, first a word about the criteria used for determining the group identity of what is called here Carpatho-Rusyns. This requires a brief definition of a people or nationality.

of Rakacza), and contemporary forms are used for compound names (i.e., Alsóremete, instead of Alsó-Remete).

Czech names, which had official status between 1919 and 1938, are found in *Statistický lexikon obcí*, Vol. IV, pp. 49-63; Russian names, which had official status from 1945 to 1991, are found in N.N. Semeniuk et al., eds, *Istoriia gorodov i sel Ukrainskoi SSR: Zakarpatskaia oblast'* (Kiev, 1982); and Georg Heller, *Comitatus Bereghiensis, Comitatus Unghensis,* and *Comitatus Marmarosiensis/Comitatus Ugocsiensis*, Veröffentlichungen des Finnisch-Ugrischen Seminars an der Universität München, Serie A, Vols. 15, 17, 18 (Munich, 1983-85).

[23]Ukrainian forms posed a special problem. Aside from the numerous name changes after 1945, which were basically intended to slavicize what were perceived to be Hungarian-sounding forms (i.e., Niagovo became Dobrians'ke; Trebushany—Dilove; Voloskoe—Pidhirne), Soviet Ukrainian orthography differed from Ukrainian orthography in the West. This was particularly evident in place-names with the traditional ending *o* that were changed to *e* (i.e. Poroshkovo became Poroshkove; Mukachevo—Mukacheve, although Mukachiv in Ukrainian publications in the West), or that were simply shortened (Iablonovo—Iabluniv; Tiachovo—Tiachiv). After 1991, the local authorities in independent Ukraine have sought to return in part to orthographic forms that are not associated with the Soviet era.

Nevertheless, there is still inconsistency, so that while Poroshkove has again become Poroshkovo, Pidhirne has not become Pidhirno. Finally, in an attempt to respond to the sensitivities of Magyar-inhabited districts in southern Transcarpathia, the oblast government has approved the older Hungarian names in both their Ukrainian and Hungarian forms. Thus, Vuzlove has become Bat'ovo (Hungarian: Bátyú), Ivanivka has become Ianoshi (Hungarian: Jánosi). For further details, see Anikó Beregszászi, "Language Planning Issues of Hungarian Place-Names in Subcarpathia," *Acta Linguistica Hungarica*, XLIII, 3-4 (Budapest, 1995-96), pp. 373-380. The Ukrainian names used on the C-R Settlement Map, including the recent changes implemented since 1991, are found in *Zakarpats'ka oblast: dovidnyk administratyvno-terytorial'noho podilu na 1. VI. 1996 roku*, 3rd. edition (Uzhhorod, 1996).

Conceptual issues

Scholars have wrestled with the problem of defining a nationality ever since the nineteenth century, when an interest in different peoples and in the ideology of nationalism became a dominant concern in Europe and then gradually in other parts of the world. Some commentators have argued that a nationality is defined by the presence of certain observable "objective" characteristics, such as territory, historical tradition, ethnographic characteristics, and most especially language. Others have argued that regardless of the presence of all or some of such observable common characteristics, a population cannot be considered a distinct people or nationality unless its individual members are aware of such a common identity. In other words, there needs to be present a national will.

In the case of the Carpatho-Rusyns, they have traditionally used terms derived from the noun Rus' to describe themselves: *rusynŷ* (Rusyns), *rusnatsi* (Rusnaks), *podkarpats'ki rusynŷ* (Subcarpathian Rusyns), *karpatorossŷ* (Carpatho-Rusyns), as well as to describe their attributes: *rus'kŷi iazŷk* (Rusyn language), *po-rus'kŷ, po-rusnats'kŷ* (in the Rusyn or Rusnak language), *rus'ka vira* (adherent of the Rus' or Eastern Christian faith).[24] Such ethnonyms, which were built around the noun Rus' and which encompassed both a religious and linguistic identity, helped to distinguish Carpatho-Rusyns from their Polish, Slovak, Magyar, and Romanian neighbors to the north and south, as well as from Jews, Germans, and Roma (Gypsies) who lived in towns and villages within and immediately adjacent to the Carpatho-Rusyn areal.[25]

Nomenclature, however, does not by itself help to distinguish Carpatho-Rusyns from other East Slavs. This is because at least until the 1920s, the Ukrainians of Galicia and Bukovina also called

[24]The noun Rus' and its derivatives also figure in the names given by outsiders and by Carpatho-Rusyns themselves to their homeland: *Karpats'ka Rus'* (Carpathian Rus'), *Marchia Ruthenorum* (The Rus' March), *Podkarpatská Rus* (Subcarpathian Rus'), *Priashevs'ka Rus'* (Prešov Rus'/Region), *Ruténföld* (Ruthene Land), *Rusinsko* (Rusinia), *Rus'ka Kraïna* (Rus' Land), Ruthenia, *Zakarpats'ka Rus'* (Transcarpathia Rus').

[25]The noun Rus' also formed the basis of the names given to Carpatho-Rusyns by neighboring peoples: *magyarorosz/orosz* (Hungarian), *Rusin* (Polish), *Rusín/Rusnak* (Slovak), *rutén* (Hungarian), *Ruthener* (German).

themselves Rusyns. Consequently, Ukrainian authors considered the ethnonym Rusyn to be an older name for Ukrainian, while Russian authors considered it to be a regional name for Russian. From such a perspective, there is no need to define a Carpatho-Rusyn areal distinct from the rest of the East Slavic world. Instead, the East Slavs on both sides of the Carpathians are subdivided into three ethnographic groups—Lemkos, Boikos, and Hutsuls. These groups may have distinct ethnographic characteristics, but they are viewed as part of an East Slavic ethnolinguistic continuum, whether as a branch of the Ukrainian nationality or a branch of an even more encompassing Russian nationality.[26]

The major shortcoming of this approach is that the three-fold ethnographic classification scheme does not respond, so to speak, to the reality on the ground. For instance, none of the so-called Lemkos and very few of the so-called Boikos living on the southern slopes of the Carpathians have ever called themselves Lemkos or Boikos, but instead use the terms Rusyn or Rusnak to describe themselves. Linguists, moreover, do not speak of Boiko dialects on the southern slopes of the Carpathians. In other words, the people that ethnographers consider to be Boikos living south of the mountains in a territory that coincides with virtually all of Subcarpathian Rus'/Transcarpathia do not describe themselves as Boikos and are classified by linguists as speaking dialects that are different from Boiko dialects north of the mountains.[27]

---

[26]Russophile authors put less of an emphasis on ethnographic differentiation than on seeing the Carpatho-Rusyn areal as part of the Little Russian branch of a larger Russian or "common Russian" (*obshcherusskii*) nationality. Cf. Grigorii Kupchanko, *Nasha rodina* (Vienna, 1896; reprinted New York and Berlin, 1924); and Timofei D. Florinskii, *Zarubezhnaia Rus' i eia gor'kaia dolia* (Kiev, 1900). Ukrainophile authors have developed an extensive literature on the three ethnographic regions which comprise lands on both sides of the Carpathians and that, in turn, are considered part of the Ukrainian nationality. Cf. Iurii H. Hoshko, ed., *Hutsul'shchyna: istoryko-etnohrafichne doslidzhennia* (Kiev, 1987); Iurii H. Hoshko, ed., *Boikivshchyna: istoryko-etnohrafichne doslidzhennia* (Kiev, 1983); and Bohdan O. Strumins'kyi, *Lemkivshchyna: zemlia—liudy—kul'tura*, 2 vols. (New York, Paris, Sydney and Toronto, 1988).

[27]See Georgij Gerovskij, "Jazyk Podkarpatské Rusi," in *Československá vlastivěda*, Vol. III: *jazyk* (Prague, 1934), pp. 460-480 with map, who speaks of a group of closely related "Subcarpathian dialects" throughout what most others call the "southern Boiko" region; and Iosyf O. Dzendzelivs'kyi, "Stan doslidzhennia henezy ukraïns'kykh diialektiv," *Movoznavstvo*, XV, 1 [85] (Kiev, 1981), esp. pp. 49-50,

If the ethnographic scheme, with its arguments about similarities between people on the northern and southern slopes of the mountains, is
rejected as a valid conceptual framework, how does one justify including within the Carpatho-Rusyn areal (1) the Lemko Region in historic
Galicia, which is north of the Carpathians; and (2) the southeastern
corner of Transcarpathia where the inhabitants have traditionally used
the name Hutsul just as do the inhabitants immediately on the northern
slopes of the mountains? Even more important, how can one justify
speaking at all of a Carpatho-Rusyn areal distinct from the rest of the
East Slavic world?

Put quite simply, the C-R Settlement Map reflects the views of
political activists and writers who at least since the second half of the
nineteenth century have, like the Basques mentioned at the outset of
this essay, come to believe in the existence of a definable homeland
called Carpathian Rus'. They have based their belief on the presence
among the area's inhabitants of a national will expressed in the form of
a common historic tradition. Admittedly, there has also been a Russian
national will and a Ukrainian national will expressed at various times
among the region's East Slavic inhabitants, and those are subjects
worthy of attention in their own right. The object of this essay, however, is to explain the evolution of the Rusyn national will and therefore
the justification for the areal depicted on the C-R Settlement Map.

Since the establishment of the first states in east-central Europe, the
crests of the Carpathian Mountains formed an administrative boundary
that separated the inhabitants on the southern slopes from those on the
northern slopes. Those same Carpathian crests also coincided with a
dividing line that determined different geographic spheres. The southern
slopes are part of the Danubian Basin. All rivers, transportational patterns, and centers of trade and commerce point in a southward direction.
For nearly a millennium the dominant state structure in the Danubian
Basin was the multinational Kingdom of Hungary, of which the Carpa-

---

who speaks of four basic dialectal groups throughout all of Transcarpathia. The
recently published authoritative *Atlas ukraïns'koï movy*, Vol. II (Kiev, 1988), plate
IV, indicates that Boiko dialects exist only in Galicia, while most East Slavs south
of the Carpathians speak what are classified as "Transcarpathian" dialects with only
a small area of Hutsul dialects in the far east. On the C-R Settlement Map, the
Hutsul area comprises the town of Rakhiv and 27 villages east of, but not including,
Velykyi Bychkiv, which represents less than one percent of all Rusyn villages.

tho-Rusyn area was an integral part. Thus, while it is true that there may be some similarities in the language and religion of the East Slavic inhabitants on both sides of the Carpathian Mountains, those living on the southern slopes were until as recently as 1945 part of an entirely different geo-political sphere.[28]

The question of the relationship with other East Slavs became an issue of concern in the course of the nineteenth century, when, under the impact of nationalism, local leaders began to seek a group identity based on cultural instead of political criteria. Initially, mid-nineteenth century reformers like Adol'f Dobrians'kyi, argued that all the East Slavic Rusyns living within the Austrian provinces of Galicia and Bukovina formed, together with Hungary's Uhro-Rusyns, one people.[29] This people, moreover, deserved to have its own administrative unit based on nationality criteria within what reformers hoped would become a reconfigured Austria-Hungary.

The political realization of such a broader definition of Rusyns turned out to be impractical for two reasons: (1) Austria-Hungary was unable and unwilling to transform itself into a federal state based on nationality units; and (2) as Rusyn leaders north and south of the Carpathians increased their personal and organizational contacts, they began to realize that whatever linguistic and religious similarities they may have had were not strong enough to overcome their differences brought about by having lived for centuries in divergent political and geographic

[28]For recent attempts that argue for Subcarpathian Rus'/Transcarpathia as a distinct central European geo-politcal unit whose present-day inhabitants of various nationalities represent an amalgam called the "Transcarpathian people," see Ivan Pop and Volodymyr Halas, "Stanú sa Zakarpatci štátotvorným národom?," *Medzinarodné otázky*, III, 2 (Bratislava, 1994), pp. 33-42; Ivan Pop, "Podkarpatská Rus a Zakarpatská Ukrajina—historický úděl a perspektivy malé země a malého národa mezi střední a východní Evropou," in *Euroregio Egrensis* (Prague, 1994), pp. 27-36; Ivan Pop, "Homo totalitaricus?: istoriia Zakarpattia, krytychni rozdumy," *Karpats'kyi krai*, VI, 5-7 (Uzhhorod, 1996), pp. 4-22; and Alexander Duleba, "Základné geopolitické charakteristiky Zakarpatska," in *Zakarpatsko* (Bratislava, 1995), pp. 187-233.

[29]On the broader definition of Carpatho-Rusyns, see Iakov Golovatskii [Holovats'kyi], "Karpatskaia Rus': geografichesko-statisticheskie i istorichesko-etnograficheskie ocherki—Galichiny, sievero-vostochnoi Ugrii i Bukoviny," *Slavianskii sbornik*, I (St. Petersburg, 1875), pp. 1-30 and II (1877), pp. 55-84; and A. Petrov, *Ob ètnograficheskoi granitsie russkago naroda v Avstro-Ugrii: o somnitel'noi 'vengerskoi' natsii i o nedielimosti Ugrii* (Petrograd, 1915).

spheres. One contemporary from the Russian Empire, who otherwise was convinced that on both sides of the Carpathians "live the very same Rusyn people speaking the very same language," nonetheless admitted: "Characteristically, Hungarian Rus' is completely separated not only from Ukrainian territory [in the Russian Empire] but from its nearest neighbor, Galicia, as well. There has been and there still is no spiritual unity between Hungarian Rus' and Galician Rus'. The political and historical conditions in Hungarian Rus' have proven to be an even more divisive factor than the mountains that separate Galicia from Hungary."[30] The growing strength of the Ukrainian national movement in Galicia during the last decades of the nineteenth century only further alienated the articulate elements among Rusyns living south of the mountains, who consistently rejected the efforts of pro-Ukrainian activists like Mykhailo Drahomanov and Volodymyr Hnatiuk to establish contacts and cultural cooperation.[31]

On the other hand, the sense of a distinct Carpatho-Rusyn identity based on historical tradition was enhanced by developments connected with the drive for political autonomy. Ever since the mid-nineteenth century, Rusyns living south of the Carpathians had been concerned with attaining political autonomy for a territory which they argued was inhabited by a distinct people. As early as 1849, the Austrian government created the Uzhhorod military district, which in practice became a Rusyn-led administrative entity. Although short-lived, the Uzhhorod district set a precedent which Carpatho-Rusyn spokespersons hoped to restore even during the new wave of magyarization in the 1860s and 1870s, when religious and secular leaders continued to submit to the Hungarian government petitions for the creation of a Carpatho-Rusyn autonomous region.[32]

By the twentieth century, the principle that Carpatho-Rusyns were

---

[30]L. Vasilevskii (Plokhotskii), "Vengerskie 'rusnaki' i ikh sud'ba (pis'mo iz Avstrii)," *Russkoe bogatstvo*, No. 3 (St. Petersburg, 1914), p. 368.

[31]For the texts of Rusyn reactions to Drahomanov and Hnatiuk, see Paul Robert Magocsi, *The Shaping of a National Identity: Subcarpathian Rus', 1848-1948* (Cambridge, Mass., 1978), pp. 60-63.

[32]On these little-known efforts, see the petitions submitted to the Hungarian government cited in Mária Mayer, *Kárpátukrán (ruszin) politikai és társadalmi törekvések, 1860-1910* (Budapest, 1977), pp. 27-35; English edition: *The Rusyns of Hungary: Political and Social Developments, 1860-1910* (New York, 1997), pp. 28-37.

deserving of political autonomy because they formed a distinct national group was accepted by every state that ruled the region. Hence, the autonomous Rus'ka Kraïna (1918-1919) was created in post-World War I Hungary, Subcarpathian Rus' (1919-1938) in the new state of Czechoslovakia, Carpatho-Ukraine (1938-1939) in post-Munich federated Czecho-Slovakia, and Transcarpathian Ukraine (1944-1945) in an international political vacuum—although in the presence of the Soviet military—during the closing months of World War II.[33] There was, moreover, a remarkable consistency in the territorial extent of these autonomous units. Each one, beginning with the very first one back in 1849, comprised the four historic Hungarian counties of Ung/Uzh, Bereg, Ugocsa/Ugocha, and Máramaros/Maramorosh.

There was as well a degree of consistency in the geopolitical goals of Carpatho-Rusyn leaders. They continued to demand that Rusyn-inhabited regions in at least three other counties—Szepes/Spish, Sáros/Sharysh, and Zemplén/Zemplyn in present-day northeastern Slovakia—be included within any Rusyn autonomous province. Their demands were even formally recognized by the international community, when two treaties at the Paris Peace Conference (Saint Germain, 1919 and Trianon, 1920) accepted the principle that "the Ruthenes south of the Carpathians" be endowed with "the fullest degree of self-government compatible with the unity of the Czecho-Slovak state."[34]

It is certainly true that in practice no government ever delivered fully on its promises of autonomy for Carpatho-Rusyns. What is important in this discussion, however, is that the very recognition of some degree of autonomy for a Rus' land south of the Carpathians instilled in the inhabitants a sense of a distinct Carpatho-Rusyn political as well as cultural/national identity. Such an awareness was codified and promoted by numerous publications, including textbooks used in schools between 1919 and 1944, that provided a new generation of young people with a conceptual framework that considered the history of Subcarpathian Rus' (including all Rusyn lands south of the Carpathians) as well as Rusyn literature and art as phenomena with their own internal evolution

---

[33]For documents on the Subcarpathian Rusyn autonomous tradition in the twentieth century, see P. Hod'mash, comp., *Od avtonomnoï Podkarpats'koï Rusy do suverennoï Zakarpats'koï Ukraïnŷ* (Uzhhorod, 1996).

[34]*Traité entre les Principales Puissances Alliées et Associées et la Tchécoslovaquie* (Paris, 1919), pp. 26-27.

distinct from that of their neighbors.[35]
Such theoretical constructs were reflected in practice. Throughout the interwar years, Carpatho-Rusyn political and civic activists living in the Prešov Region argued they were only "temporarily" under a Slovak administration, and they repeatedly demanded to be united with their brethren in neighboring autonomous Subcarpathian Rus'. Those demands were reiterated as late as 1945, a time when Subcarpathia was about to be annexed to the Soviet Union.[36] At the far southeastern corner of the Carpatho-Rusyn areal, recent documents have come to light to show that there, too, in early 1945, representatives of the dozen or so villages in the Maramureş Region of Romania requested that they be united with their brethren in Transcarpathia.[37] And as for settlements to the south that were separated from compact Carpatho-Rusyn territory, older residents in several villages of present-day northeastern Hungary retain an active historical memory that their ancestors are Rusyns (*ruténok*) from the Carpathians, while farther south the Rusyns of the Vojvodina in Yugoslavia have a well developed literature that makes it clear that their ancestral home is in the Carpathian Highland (*Hornïtsa*).[38]

[35]Among works in this genre were: Yrynei M. Kondratovych, *Ystoriia Podkarpatskoî Rusy dlia naroda* (Uzhhorod, 1924; reprinted 1991); Evgenii Nedziel'skii, *Ocherk karpatorusskoi literatury* (Uzhhorod, 1932); *Ystoriia podkarpatorus'koi lyteraturŷ* (Uzhhorod, 1942); and A. Yzvoryn [Evgenii Nedziel'skii], "Suchasnî rus'kî khudozhnyky," *Zoria/Hajnal*, II, 3-4 (Uzhhorod, 1942), pp. 387-418 and III, 1-4 (1943), pp. 258-287.

[36]Ivan Vanat, *Narysy novitn'oï istoriï ukraïntsiv Skhidnoï Slovachchyny*, Vol. II: *1938-1948* (Bratislava and Prešov, 1985), pp. 29-63 and 218-223; Paul Robert Magocsi, *The Rusyns in Slovakia: An Historical Survey* (New York, 1993), pp. 71-95.

[37]On February 4, 1945, 426 delegates from seventeen villages gathered at Sighet, the regional administrative center on the left bank of the Tysa/Tisza River in Romania, to form the First Congress of National Committees that issued a manifesto calling for unification of Maramureş with Transcarpathia. Omelian Dovhanych, "Maramaros'kyi z"ïzd," *Karpats'kyi krai*, IV, 1-2 (Uzhhorod, 1994), pp. 36-37.

[38]Miron Žiroš, *Živa Hornïtsa I: demohrafiino-etnohrafiini drahopis* (Budapest, 1996); István Udvari, "Rusyns in Hungary and the Hungarian Kingdom/Rusiny v Vengerskom Korolevstve" and Ljubomir Medjesi, "The Problem of Cultural Borders in the History of Ethnic Groups: The Yugoslav Rusyns/Problem kulturnikh hranïtsokh u istoriï etnïchnikh zaiednïtsokh: iuhoslavianski Rusnatsi," in Paul Robert Magocsi, ed., *The Persistence of Regional Cultures/Tryvalist' rehional'nykh*

If an argument can be made that Rusyns south of the Carpathians have a common political culture and a sense of historic tradition that is distinct from other East Slavs, how does one justify the inclusion of the so-called Lemko Region north of the mountains within the framework of a Carpatho-Rusyn areal? At first glance it might seem that the ethnographic principle is being invoked after it has been rejected in the case of Carpatho-Rusyn lands father east. In fact, it is historical tradition as well as in part geography that has helped to create a sense of communality across the crests of the mountains.

With regard to geography, it has always been relatively easy for the inhabitants of the Lemko Region to maintain commercial, cultural, and familial relations with East Slavs immediately to the south, because the Beskyd ranges—roughly between the Poprad River in the west and the Osława River in the east (the present-day boundary between Poland and Slovakia)—have the lowest elevations throughout the Carpathians and are penetrated by several routes that cut through accessible passes (Tylyč/Tylycz, Dukl'a/Dukla, Lupkiv/Łupkow).[39]

Not surprisingly, then, when at the close of World War I the East Slavs of the Lemko Region organized for the first time to decide their political future, the strongest orientation among them called for unity with their Rusyn brethren living south of the mountains.[40] It was, in fact, the political demands of the Lemko Rusyns that resulted in the first maps which conceptualized in visual terms the idea of an entity called Carpathian Rus', whose territory basically coincided with the villages from the 1900-1921 period shown on the C-R Settlement Map. The Lemko-inspired concept of a Carpatho-Rusyn homeland was submitted to the Paris Peace Conference in 1919,[41] and it was only

---

kul'tur (New York, 1993), pp. 105-162 and 103-165.

[39]On the wide range of contacts across the Beskyd ranges, see Roman Reinfuss, "Związki kulturowe po obu stronach Karpat w rajonie Łemkowszczyzny," in Jerzy Czajkowski, ed., *Łemkowie w historii i kulturze Karpat*, Vol. II (Rzeszów, 1992), pp. 167-181.

[40]On the various political orientations among the Lemkos after World War I, see Paul Robert Magocsi, "The Ukrainian Question Between Poland and Czechoslovakia: The Lemko Rusyn Republic (1918-1920) and Poltical Thought in Western Rus'-Ukraine," *Nationalities Papers*, XXI, 2 (New York, 1993), pp. 95-105—reprinted below, Chapter 13.

[41]Anthony Beskid and Dimitry Sobin, *The Origin of the Lems, Slavs of Danubian Provenance: Memorandum to the Peace Conference Regarding Their National*

after the Czechoslovak government refused to accept their request for unification that the Lemkos formed on the northern slopes of the Carpathian Mountains an independent Lemko Rusyn Republic that was to last sixteen months (December 1919 to March 1920). Despite the failure to unite politically after World War I, Lemko writers and historians have kept alive a tradition that the Lemko Region and its East Slavic inhabitants are culturally part of a Carpathian Rus' homeland on both sides of the Carpathian Mountains.[42]

As for the territorial extent of the Lemko Region north of the Carpathians, the boundary with Polish-inhabited villages remained stable until 1945, after which Lemko Rusyns were deported en masse from their homeland.[43] And whereas Polish and Ukrainian ethnographers and linguists continue to disagree on the region's eastern boundary (see above, notes 16-19), Lemko historical tradition is governed by the precept that "the border of the Lemko Region extends . . . in the east to the San River."[44]

There is still the question of whether the historic inhabitants of the Lemko Region should be distinguished at all from other East Slavs (i.e.,

---

Claims (Prešov, 1919). The idea of Carpathian Rus' political unity was kept alive by Lemko and other Rusyn immigrants in the United States and was revived during World War II. See the June 1942 resolution with map in "Amerykanskyi Karpatorusskyi Kongress," in *Karpatorusskyi kalendar 1943* (Yonkers, N.Y., 1942), pp. 17-34. In early 1945, the Lemko Workers' and Peasants' Committee in Gorlice informed Carpatho-Rusyns meeting in Prešov that they wished to unite with them. Cf. Vanat, *Narysy*, pp. 219-220.

[42]Lemko historical ideology is outlined in Ivan Teodorovich, "Lemkovskaia Rus'," *Nauchno-literaturnyi sbornik Galitsko-russkoi matitsy*, LXIX [VIII] (L'viv, 1934), pp. 10-21; in the popular history by Yvan F. Lemkyn [Ioann Polans'kyi], *Ystoryia Lemkovynŷ* (Yonkers, N.Y., 1969); and Olena Duc'-Fajfer, "The Lemkos in Poland/Lemkŷ v Pol'shchŷ," in Magocsi, *Persistence of Regional Cultures*, pp. 83-103 and 80-102.

[43]Between 1945 and 1947, the postwar Communist government of Poland, as part of its agreement with the Soviet Union on population exchanges, encouraged all East Slavs within its new borders to emigrate voluntarily to the Soviet Ukraine. Those who refused were forcibly resettled in former German territories that had just become part of western and northern Poland (Silesia, Pomerania, East Prussia). Villages in the Lemko Region were either abandoned (marked by an x on the C-R Settlement Map) or resettled by Poles. In the 1960s, some Lemko Rusyns began to return to their native villages, and today there are about 15,000 to 20,000 living again in the Lemko Region.

[44]Teodorovich, "Lemkovskaia Rus'," p. 10.

Ukrainians) north of the Carpathians. In this regard, it is instructive to note why East Slavs living west of the San River began to call themselves by the regional name *Lemko*. During the first decade of the twentieth century, local leaders became displeased with the Ukrainian national movement that was radiating from L'viv throughout eastern Galicia. Since in Polish (the functional language throughout Galicia before World War I) the term *Rusini* was used to describe all East Slavs north of the Carpathians, articulate spokespersons living west of the San River wanted to distinguish themselves from what they considered the pro-Ukrainian *Rusini* in eastern Galicia. Hence, they replaced their own historic name *Rusyn* with a new ethnonym, *Lemko*.[45] Such a name change, as we have discussed above, did not affect negatively the Lemko sense of commonality with fellow Rusyns on the southern slopes of the Carpathians.

Statistical data

Now to return to the question of sources used in the C-R Settlement Map. Based on the assumption that the definition of a people is best gauged by how individual group members identify themselves, census data seems the most readily available source to determine self-identity. Like any data, census reports are problematic. For instance, at the data-gathering stage, it is possible that the individual being interviewed does not understand the question being asked, or that he or she may be intimidated and therefore provide an answer assumed to be acceptable to the census enumerator and the "authorities" posing the question. Then there is the problem of classifying the answers once the raw data is collected. As an example, it is quite possible that on a single census conducted in the Carpatho-Rusyn area the following answers might be

---

[45]The term *Lemko* actually appeared as early as 1831, and it was used in publications throughout the nineteenth century. It did not, however, begin to be used as an ethnonym by the populace at large until the first decades of the twentieth century. As for its etymological origin, Lemko derives from the adverb *lem* (only), which is actually used in most Carpatho-Rusyn dialects north and south of the mountains as far as the Borzhava River valley in central Transcarpathia. On the evolution of the name and its adoption as an ethnonym, see Duc'-Fajfer, "Lemkos in Poland," pp. 84/81-82; and Bohdan Struminsky, "The Name of the Lemkos and of Their Territory," in Jacob P. Hursky ed., *Studies in Honor of George Y. Shevelov, Annals of the Ukrainian Academy of Arts and Sciences*, Vol. XV (New York, 1981-83), pp. 301-308.

given in response to the question of native language or nationality: *rusyn, rus'kyi, uhro-rus', karpatoros, lemko.* How should census enumerators classify these responses in the final report? Should there be listed five separate nationalities/language; should one of the terms be used to represent all five variant answers; or should some other "known" classification such as Russian or Ukrainian be used?

Despite the potential shortcoming of censuses, they are still the only sources we have for determining the identity of the inhabitants over a large territory and with the possibility of comparison over different periods of time. The data for the C-R Settlement Map was based largely on pre-World War I data, in particular the Hungarian census of 1910.[46] This data is relatively more reliable than later censuses because it asked persons to identify their mother tongue, not nationality.[47] If, for instance, the question "nationality" had been asked, it is likely that an inhabitant of Rusyn, or Slovak, or Jewish background would have replied Hungarian, or Austrian, or Habsburg, because the respondant would have associated nationality with citizenship in the Hungarian Kingdom, Austrian Galicia, or the Habsburg Monarchy.

To underscore this point, we need only look at the census conducted a little over a decade later by the ostensibly more democratic Czechoslovak government. In Czechoslovakia's 1921 and 1930 censuses, the question of nationality instead of mother tongue was asked. Among the answers a respondant was urged to give—and that were later tabulated and eventually published in the census reports for the country's two eastern provinces, Slovakia and Subcarpathian Rus'—were: Czechoslovak, German, Magyar, Rusyn,[48] or Jewish. The political tenden-

---

[46]*A magyar szent korona országainak 1910. évi népszámlálása,* Magyar statisztikai közlemények, új sorozat, Vol. XLII (Budapest, 1912).

[47]Mother tongue (Hungarian: *anyanyelv*) meant the language usually spoken at home.

[48]The rubric for Rusyns in the village-by-village census data (*Statistický lexikon*) was designated simply as *ruská*, which in Czech means Russian. In the summary report for the 1921 statistics, the word *ruská* was followed by a parenthesis that read (Great Russian, Ukrainian, Carpatho-Rusyn). Cf. *Sčítání lidu v republice československé ze dne 15. února 1921,* Vol. I (Prague, 1924), pp. 84-85. The introduction to the village-by-village census report for 1930 explained: "Because of lack of space, the second rubric under nationality is marked only as 'ruská'; this, of course, also indicates those persons who stated their nationality as Ukrainian, Carpatho-Rusyn, Rusyn, or Rusnak." *Statistický lexikon obcí v republice*

tiousness of such an approach is obvious. One result was that according to official census data there were no Slovaks in Slovakia, only "Czechoslovaks." Moreover, since the inhabitants in question, regardless of nationality, were by 1921 citizens of Czechoslovakia, they could rightly describe themselves as Czechoslovak. This is, in fact, what happened in many villages in northeastern Slovakia. Hence, among the same people who throughout the nineteenth century had described themselves as Rusyn (in answer to the mother tongue question), in 1921 and in 1930 there were some who described themselves as Czechoslovak and others as Rusyn.

To distort matters even further, Slovak publicists and scholars, reacting to what they perceived as manipulation of census data by Czechs in the central government in Prague, simply "translated" the term *Czechoslovak* into Slovak, thereby transforming all "Czechoslovak nationals," whether of Rusyn, Jewish, German, and even Magyar background, into Slovaks.[49] Thus, the pre-World War I Hungarian census reports, which ask the question of mother tongue, provide a better insight than any later censuses into the national identity of the inhabitants on the southern slopes of the Carpathian Mountains.

With regard to the Lemko Region north of the Carpathians in the historic province of Galicia, I did not have access to the Austrian statistics for either 1900 or 1910. Hence, I used data from Poland's 1921 census, which provided the following nationality rubrics: Polish, Rusyn, German, Jewish, other.[50] While it is generally true that mother tongue is a more reliable indicator than national identity, the question regarding nationality in the 1921 Polish census does have validity. This is because on the same census there is data on religious affiliation. It

---

československé . . . na základě výsledků sčítání lidu z 1. prosince 1930, Vol. IV: *Země podkarpatoruská* (Prague, 1937), p. x.

[49]An excellent illustration of the distortion resulting from "statistical slovakization," accompanied by a map indicating the Slovak-Rusyn ethnographic boundary according to the 1930 statistics, is found in: Ladislav A. Potemra, "Ruthenians in Slovakia and the Greek Catholic Diocese of Prešov," *Slovak Studies*, I (Rome, 1961), pp. 199-220. Cf. the earlier polemic commissioned by the patriotic Slovak League: Ján Ruman, *Otázka slovensko-rusínskeho pomeru na východnom Slovensku* (Košice, 1935).

[50]Główny urząd statystyczny Rzeczypospolitej Polskiej, *Skorowidz miejscowości Rzeczypospolitej Polskiej*, Vol. XII: *Województwo Krakowskie*, and Vol. XIII: *Województwo Lwowskie* (Warsaw, 1924-25).

is interesting to note that the figures for Rusyn nationality and Greek Catholic religion are virtually identical. Since north of the Carpathians there has generally been a correlation between Poles as Roman Catholics and Rusyns as Greek Catholics, this lends weight to the validity of the nationality response in the 1921 Polish census data.

The next question was how to define in statistical terms a Carpatho-Rusyn settlement (village or town)? Is the presence of any number of Rusyns, even one, sufficient? Or, do all the inhabitants have to be Rusyn? Most maps that show nationality or religious affiliation employ the principle of a simple majority; that is, 50 percent or more of a settlement's inhabitants must be of a given identity to be included. Considering the complexity of ethnocultural borderlands, the C-R Settlement Map includes solid green symbols (dots, squares, triangles) for places with 50 percent or more Rusyn inhabitants, and open symbols for places with 20 to 49 percent Rusyn inhabitants. The vast majority of settlements in the 20 to 49 percent category are on the southern slopes of the Carpathians and generally beyond the contiguous Carpatho-Rusyn area. There are also a few villages within the area that were not included because less than 20 percent of their inhabitants were Rusyn.[51]

Mapping the data

With regard to its visual impact, the C-R Settlement Map adopts what might be called the maximalist approach. Since it is meant to show chronological evolution, the map does not depict the status of the Carpatho-Rusyn population at a particular point in time, but rather all villages and towns that *at any time* were inhabited by 20-49 and 50 percent or more Carpatho-Rusyns. To achieve this result, the Hungarian census of 1910 and the Polish census of 1921 were used as the base, to which were added other villages that had 20 to 49 percent and 50 percent or more Rusyn inhabitants according to the 1921 Czechoslovak census and the 1900 and 1881 Hungarian censuses.[52]

---

[51]Among such villages are Slovak-inhabited Lenartov and Stebnícka Huta in the Prešov Region, and German-inhabited Nimets'ka Kuchava and Nimets'ka Mokra in Transcarpathia.

[52]*Statistický lexikon obcí v republice československé . . . na základě výsledků sčítání lidu z 15. února 1921*, Vol. III: *Slovensko* and Vol. IV: *Podkarpatská Rus*

Finally, to such governmental data was added a new source not available to scholars who had previously described or mapped the Carpatho-Rusyn area. This is the census conducted in 1806 by the Greek Catholic Eparchy of Mukachevo, which at the time covered the entire Rusyn area south of the Carpathians in the historic Hungarian Kingdom.[53] Of the twelve questions on the church census, one indicated which language—Rusyn, Magyar, Slovak, or Romanian—was used by the parish priest during the homily. In contrast to the liturgical part of the service, which was in Church Slavonic, the homily was a personalized message given in a language which parishioners could readily understand. Although the church census was not intended as an inquiry about mother tongue or nationality, it is perhaps because of the indirect nature of the question that we are able to obtain an impartial insight into the linguistic and nationality composition of settlements south of the Carpathians as early as 1806.

Not every village where the Greek Catholic priest delivered his homily in Rusyn was included on the C-R Settlement Map, however, only those where 50 percent or more of the inhabitants understood (and likely spoke) Rusyn. In order to determine whether a village's inhabitants were at the time at least 50 percent Rusyn, the number of Greek Catholics listed in the 1806 census was compared to the total population of each village. Since the 1806 census did not include information on the total number of inhabitants in a given village, that data was derived from the next chronologically closest source, the comprehensive geographical dictionary for the entire Hungarian

---

(Prague, 1927-28); *A magyar korona országainak 1900. évi népszámlálása*, Magyar statisztikai közlemények, új sorozat, Vol. I (Budapest, 1902); *A magyar korona országaiban az 1881. év elején végrehajtott népszámlálás*, Vol. II (Budapest, 1882).

[53]The eparchy covered twelve Hungarian counties: Abaúj-Torna, Bereg, Borsod, Gömör, Máramaros, Sáros, Szepes, Szabolcs, Szatmár, Ugocsa, Ung, and Zemplén, which today are within the boundaries of Slovakia, Ukraine, Hungary, and Romania. The complete census with explanatory data was published by István Udvari, comp., *A munkácsi görögkatolikus püspökség lelkészségeinek 1806. évi összeírása*, Vasvári Pál Társaság füzetei, Vol. III (Nyíregyháza, 1990). For a summary of the data, see István Udvari, "Perepis' prikhodov Mukachevskoi greko-katolicheskoi eparkhii 1806 goda," in Ryszard Łużny, Franciszek Ziejka, and Andrzej Kępiński, eds., *Unia brzeska: geneza, dzieje i konsekwencje w kulturze narodów słowiańskich* (Cracow, 1994), pp. 163-173.

Kingdom published in 1851 by Elek Fényes.[54]
There are 223 Carpatho-Rusyn villages from the 1806 census data (distinguished by a separate triangular symbol), most of which are in present-day southeastern Slovakia and northeastern Hungary. These regions were not shown on most previous maps depicting Carpatho-Rusyn settlement, and their appearance here supports the earlier views of Slavists like Pavel Šafárik and Lubor Niederle that "all of eastern Slovakia is, in fact, slovakized Rus' territory (*vlastně poslovenštěná Rus*)."[55]

There is, of course, another way to depict the Carpatho-Rusyn area; that is, to plot those villages and towns inhabited by Carpatho-Rusyns at a particular point in time. This is what Aleksei Petrov did for the year 1773 and Stepan Tomashivs'kyi for 1900 on large-scale maps with village by village statistics on the southern slopes of the Carpathians.[56] As an example of what such an approach would yield over a longer period of time, it might be useful to depict sequentially that part of the Carpatho-Rusyn area which has changed most dramatically; namely, the area of present-day northeastern Hungary and eastern Slovakia where Carpatho-Rusyn, Slovak, and Magyar settlement patterns interact.

---

[54]For instance, the 1806 church census indicated that the village of Szőled (Abaúj-Torna county) a total of 303 Greek Catholic inhabitants. Fényes describes Szőled as a Rusyn-Magyar-Slovak village with Greek Catholic, Roman Catholic, and Lutheran (Evangelical) adherents. The 302 Greek Catholics represented 60.5 percent of the population and, therefore, the village is indicated on the C-R Settlement Map for 1806.

Fényes also indicated several villages not listed as Rusyn-speaking parishes in the 1806 census but that were either exclusively Rusyn (Vernárd/Vernár, Telgard/Švermovo, Sumjác/Šumiac in Gömör county and Sislóc/Šyšlivci in Ung county) or mixed Rusyn-Magyar/Magyar-Rusyn, i.e., primarily Greek Catholic inhabitants with some Roman Catholics and/or Protestants. These villages were added to the second (1998) edition of the map. On the other hand, a few villages in Sáros, Abaúj-Torna, and Zemplén counties described by Fényes as Slovak were deleted on the second edition. Elek Fényes, *Magyarország geographiai szótára*, 4 vols. (Pest, 1851; reprinted Budapest, 1984).

[55]Lubor Niederle, *Slovanský svět* (Prague, 1909), p. 93. According to Pavel Josef Šafařík, *Slovanský národopis* (1842), 4th ed. (Prague, 1955), pp. 32-33, the Slovak-Rusyn boundary was formed by the Topl'a River from Bardejov in the north to its mouth near where it joins the Latorica River in the south, with the exception of the Sotak triangle on its east bank bounded by Stropkov, Snina, and Humenné. Šafařík's boundary is reconstructed on a map in Strumins'kyi, "Terytoriia," p. 49.

[56]See above, note 5.

A quick glance at the attached seven maps (pages 53-59) depicting Rusyn settlement south of the Carpathians in 1806, 1881, 1900, 1910, 1921, 1930, and 1991 reveals in graphic fashion a reduction in the number of villages where at least 50 percent of the inhabitants identified as Carpatho-Rusyn.[57] With their backs to the mountains, the Rusyn "retreat northward" has nevertheless not always been consistent, and it was quite common for the inhabitants of a single village to claim they were Rusyn in one census, Slovak in the next, and yet again Rusyn. The change in identity or language from census to census was most evident in villages south of Stará L'ubovňa, around Svidník and Stropkov, and to the north and southeast of Uzhhorod. It becomes quite obvious, however, that because of frequent changes in identity, a trend toward assimilation with the state nationality, and more recently out-migration, that the geographic area inhabited by Carpatho-Rusyns in eastern Slovakia has been reduced dramatically during the nearly two centuries from 1806 to 1991.

The first major reduction occurred during the five decades between 1841 and 1890, at a time when, according to one Czech statistician, 176 Rusyn villages in eastern Slovakia were slovakized, 37 were magyarized, while only one Slovak village was rusynized.[58] This was also a period when most of the Rusyn villages in present-day northeastern Hungary were magyarized. The second major reduction occurred about a century later, between 1945 and 1990, with the result that today there are only a handful of villages in eastern Slovakia (and none in the Lemko Region of southeastern Poland) where 50 percent or even 20 to 49 percent of the inhabitants describe themselves with an East Slavic ethnonym (Rusyn, Lemko, Ukrainian, Russian).

The recent decline since World War II has been the result of a number of factors: the manipulation of statistical data, demographic

---

[57]The shaded areas on the maps represent villages with 50 percent or more Rusyn inhabitants based on published census reports indicated above in notes 46, 48, 50, 52, and 53 as well as in the unpublished data from the Krajský štatistický úrad, Košice, "Národnost' obyvatel'stva podl'a obcí v okresoch východného Slovenska, r. 1991," supplied to the author by the Institute for Social Sciences of the Slovak Academy of Sciences (Spoločenskovedný ustav SAV), Košice, Slovakia. With regard to the latter source, the responses for Rusyn and Ukrainian were combined.

[58]Jaromír Korčák, "Etnický vývoj československého Potisí," Národnostní obzor, III (Prague, 1933), p. 270. For further details, see Húsek, Národopisná hranice, pp. 461-484.

change (caused by voluntary out-migration, involuntary resettlement, a decline in birth rates), and national assimilation.[59] It would certainly be useful to explore further the reasons for the precipitous decline of Carpatho-Rusyns in the twentieth century and to determine whether it is correct to assume—as many writers do—that national assimilation is a uni-directional process. The latter assumption would seem to be challenged by the unexpected revival of a Rusyn-language instruction in elementary schools in a few villages in Hungary (Múscony and Komlóska) and in Slovakia that had either been magyarized or slovakized but that since the political changes of 1989 are returning to their ancestral Rusyn heritage. These are questions, however, for another essay.

Conclusions

The concern here has been to reveal some of the problems connected with mapping a stateless people. At the very least, the C-R Settlement Map has succeeded in plotting the exact location in relation to historic and contemporary administrative borders of all villages whose inhabitants at some time between 1806 and 1921 identified themselves as Rusyn. With regard to the question of the Carpatho-Rusyn area as representing the homeland of a distinct people, this is only one way that the East Slavic inhabitants and their leaders perceived themselves during the past two centuries. The area has been perceived in other ways: as smaller in size yet still representing the homeland of a distinct people, or as part of a larger Ukrainian or Russian national territory to the north and east. In the end, one thing seems clear. As the homeland of a distinct people, the Carpatho-Rusyn area has changed in the past and is likely to continue to change in the future despite the best efforts of scholars to fix it permanently in time and space through lines and symbols on a map.

---

[59]For details on post-World War II developments on both sides of the Carpathians, see Pavel Mačų, "National Assimilation: The Case of the Rusyn-Ukrainians of Czechoslovakia," *East-Central Europe*, II, 2 (Pittsburgh, 1975), pp. 101-131—reprinted below, Chapter 11; and Kazimierz Pudło, *Łemkowie: proces wrastania w środowisko dolnego Śląska, 1947-1985* (Wrocław, 1987).

MAP 3   53

RUSYN SETTLEMENT SOUTH OF THE CARPATHIANS   1806

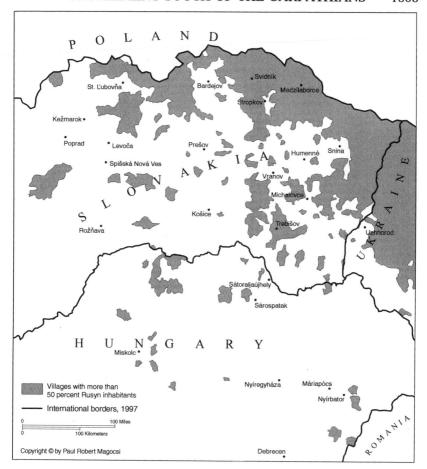

Villages with more than 50 percent Rusyn inhabitants

International borders, 1997

0   100 Miles
0   100 Kilometers

Copyright © by Paul Robert Magocsi

MAP 4

RUSYN SETTLEMENT SOUTH OF THE CARPATHIANS 1881

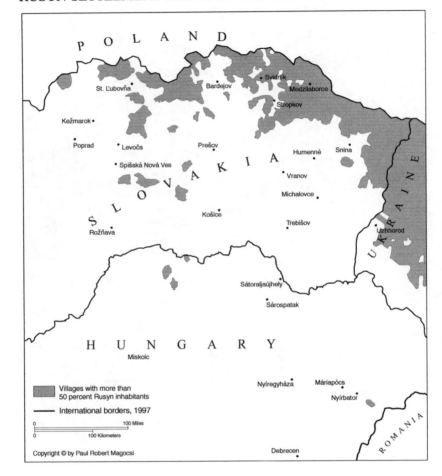

POLAND

St. Ľubovňa
Bardejov
Svidník
Medzilaborce
Stropkov

Kežmarok

Poprad
Levoča
Spišská Nová Ves
Prešov
Humenné
Snina
Vranov
Michalovce

SLOVAKIA

Košice
Trebišov
Rožňava
Uzhhorod

UKRAINE

Sátoraljaújhely
Sárospatak

H U N G A R Y
Miskolc

Villages with more than
50 percent Rusyn inhabitants

International borders, 1997

0   100 Miles
0   100 Kilometers

Copyright © by Paul Robert Magocsi

Nyíregyháza
Máriapócs
Nyírbator

Debrecen

ROMANIA

MAP 5   55

RUSYN SETTLEMENT SOUTH OF THE CARPATHIANS   1900

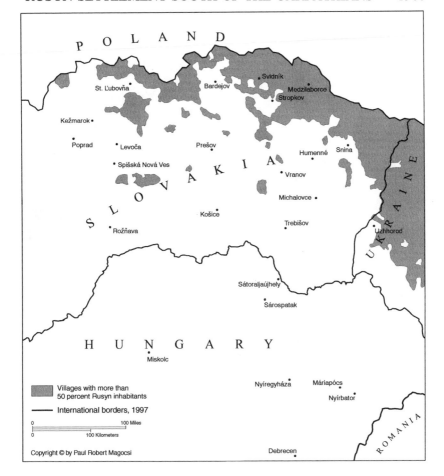

P O L A N D

St. Ľubovňa Bardejov Svidník Medzilaborce Stropkov

Kežmarok

Poprad Levoča Prešov Humenné Snina

Spišská Nová Ves K I A Vranov

S L O V A Michalovce

Košice Trebišov Uzhhorod

Rožňava

UKRAINE

Sátoraljaújhely

Sárospatak

H U N G A R Y
Miskolc

Villages with more than
50 percent Rusyn inhabitants

International borders, 1997

0   100 Miles
0   100 Kilometers

Copyright © by Paul Robert Magocsi

Nyíregyháza Máriapócs

Nyírbator

Debrecen

ROMANIA

RUSYN SETTLEMENT SOUTH OF THE CARPATHIANS 1910

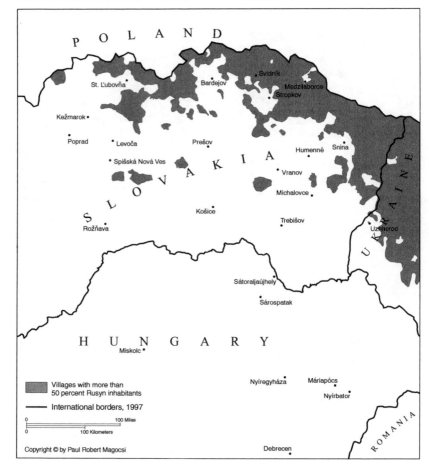

MAP 7   57

RUSYN SETTLEMENT SOUTH OF THE CARPATHIANS   1921

POLAND

St. Ľubovňa   Bardejov   Svidník   Medzilaborce

Stropkov

Kežmarok

Poprad   Levoča   Prešov   Humenné   Snina

Spišská Nová Ves   SLOVAKIA   Vranov

Michalovce

Košice

Rožňava   Trebišov   Uzhhorod

UKRAINE

Sátoraljaújhely

Sárospatak

H U N G A R Y

Miskolc

Villages with more than
50 percent Rusyn inhabitants

Nyíregyháza   Máriapócs

Nyírbator

International borders, 1997

0   100 Miles

0   100 Kilometers

ROMANIA

Copyright © by Paul Robert Magocsi   Debrecen

RUSYN SETTLEMENT SOUTH OF THE CARPATHIANS 1931

Villages with more than
50 percent Rusyn inhabitants

International borders, 1997

0   100 Miles
0   100 Kilometers

Copyright © by Paul Robert Magocsi

MAP 9   59

RUSYN SETTLEMENT SOUTH OF THE CARPATHIANS   1991

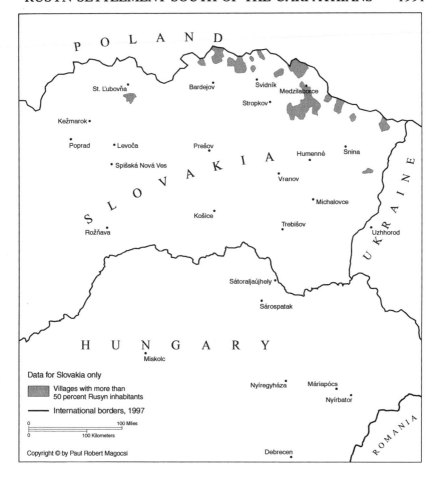

P O L A N D

St. Ľubovňa   Bardejov   Svidník
                                                Medzilaborce
                              Stropkov

Kežmarok

Poprad   • Levoča   Prešov   Humenné   Snina
            • Spišská Nová Ves   A K I A
                                                Vranov
                                   O V

                                                        • Michalovce
                          Košice
                                          Trebišov
Rožňava   Uzhhorod

U K R A I N E

Sátoraljaújhely •

Sárospatak

H U N G A R Y
        • Miskolc

Data for Slovakia only

[shaded] Villages with more than   Nyíregyháza   Máriapócs
         50 percent Rusyn inhabitants   Nyírbator

───── International borders, 1997

0   100 Miles
0   100 Kilometers   R O M A N I A

Copyright © by Paul Robert Magocsi   Debrecen

Religion and Identity in the Carpathians: Eastern Christians in Poland and Czechoslovakia*

> The worst thing that has happened in the world during the past few years is the appointment of the Pole, Wojtyła, as Pope. His aggressive brand of Catholicism has had a particularly negative impact on our people.
>
> —Comments of an Orthodox priest in Czechoslovakia, 1986

The above uncompromising statement by a popular young priest in a small mountain village in far northeastern Czechoslovakia captures in essence the centuries-old religious animosities that continue to persist in the Carpathian region. The message is undeniable and reflects a

---

*This essay was orginally commissioned for an international conference, "Contemporary Central European Religious Movements," held at the University of Michigan, October 4-6, 1987. The presentation at Michigan was published as "Carpatho-Rusyns: A Tortuous Quest for Identity," in Ladislav Matějka, ed., *Cross Currents*, Vol. XII (New Haven, Conn.: Yale Unniversity Press, 1993), pp. 147-159. A revised version of the essay was presented at an international conference, "The Millennium of Christianity in Rus': The Impact of Christianity on the History of the Eastern Slavs," held at the Kennan Institute for Advanced Russian Studies of the Wilson Center in Washington, D.C., May 26-28, 1988. The revised Washington text, reproduced here, was first published in Boris Gasparov and Olga Raevsky-Hughes, eds., *Christianity and the Eastern Slavs*, Vol. I: *Slavic Cultures in the Middle Ages/California Slavic Studies*, Vol. XVI (Berkeley, Los Angeles, and Oxford: University of California Press, 1993), pp. 116-138.

reality known to many—that the dichotomy between the Orthodox and Catholic cultural and religious spheres remains great, and that any successes garnered by one side are inevitably viewed by the other as a direct threat to the national as well as religious concerns of Eastern Christians living in Poland and Czechoslovakia's Carpathian region.

The Carpathian region refers to the mountains and valleys of the north-central Carpathian ranges inhabited by East Slavs who historically have been known as Rusnaks or Rusyns, and who in modern parlance are referred to as Ukrainians.[1] With the initial entry of the Slavs into the Christian world during the ninth and tenth centuries, the Carpathian region became firmly part of the sphere of Eastern Christianity. The strong sense of religious and ethnic conceptual bonding as expressed through the terms Rusnak/Rusyn remained undisturbed until the last decades of the nineteenth and the outset of the twentieth century, when local leaders influenced by the idea of nationalism and by the statistical and other demands of modern state bureaucracies began to argue that the traditional religious mode of self-identity was too vague and that the populace must think instead in terms of ethnolinguistic or national categories.

Thus, there began attempts at terminological precision together with the formulation of a national alongside a religious identity. The practical result, however, has not been clarity, but on the contrary, profound confusion that to a large degree still exists. This confusion is reflected by the fact that the East Slavs in the Carpathians have been described by others and by themselves as either Rusyns, Rusnaks, Lemkos, Ruthenians, Russians, or Ukrainians, terms which are at certain times and for some members of the group mutually-exclusive national identities and at other times complementary identities that form and reflect a kind of hierarchy of multiple loyalties. Looked at in another way, the terminological question can be seen as a struggle between the religious-based universalism of the faithful Eastern Christian masses as expressed in their association with the concept Rus', and the attempts of an often secular intelligentsia which prefers to emphasize the ethnonational particularities of the group. Nonetheless, the people

---

[1]On the question of nomenclature, see Paul Robert Magocsi, *The Shaping of a National Identity: Subcarpathian Rus', 1848-1948* (Cambridge, Mass., 1978), pp. 277-281.

themselves have seemed historically to prefer Christian universalism to ethnic particularism. Here we will use the historic terms Rus' or Carpatho-Rusyn to describe the population of the Carpathian region. Today basically two Eastern Christian churches, the Orthodox and Greek Catholic, serve the East Slavic Rusyns in the Carpathian region. Although both derive from the same theological base, they are divided along jurisdictional lines that bring to the fore the whole question of the western Catholic and eastern Orthodox spheres of religious and cultural influence in Europe. Indeed, the presence of Christianity in the Carpathians, whether the result of the ninth-century mission of Cyril and Methodius and their disciples, or the post-tenth century arrival of Christian migrants from Kievan Rus', predates the division between the eastern Orthodox and western Catholic worlds that began in 1054.[2] While the Carpathian region remained Eastern Christian, it was politically part of Roman Catholic Poland and Hungary, located along the Orthodox borderlands of those states in an area that witnessed periodic attempts at church union between the thirteenth and fifteenth centuries: Galicia in 1247; Constance, 1414-1417; Florence, 1439.

Finally, a qualified success in these unionistic efforts took place in 1596, when at Brest-Litovsk in the Polish-Lithuanian Commonwealth, several Orthodox bishops agreed to enter into union with Rome. The resultant Uniate Church, as it was known, switched its jurisdictional allegiance from the Orthodox ecumenical patriarch in Constantinople to

---

[2]The question of the beginnings of Christianity in the Carpathians is a controversial one. Local historians have accepted as a given the introduction of Christianity by Cyril and Methodius or by their disciples in the late ninth century, with both the eparchies of Mukačevo south of the mountains and Przemyśl to the north supposedly having come into existence already in the ninth century. The earliest written records derive from a much later period—eleventh century for Przemyśl and late fourteenth century for Mukačevo.

For the popular version of the Cyril and Methodian mission, see the interwar history textbook by Yrynej Kondratovyč, *Ystorija Podkarpatskoji Rusy dlja naroda* (Užhorod, 1924), pp. 10-14. The most systematic scholarly critique of this popular view is found in Aleksej L. Petrov, *Drevnjejšija gramoty po istorii karpato-russkoj cerkvi i ierarchii, 1391-1498 g.* (Prague, 1930), esp. pp. 1-5. Most recently, a Greek Catholic historian in Czechoslovakia has argued not only that the Byzantine missionaries were in the Carpathian region, but that they went there *before* going to Moravia (863) and that it was *from* Carpathian Rus' that Kiev received Christianity one century later: Stepan Pap, *Počatky Chrystyjanstva na Zakarpatti* (Philadelphia, 1983).

the Catholic Pope in Rome, but it was allowed to retain its Eastern Christian practices, including the liturgy of St. John Chrysostom said in Church Slavonic not Latin, a married priesthood, and the Julian calendar. The 1596 Union of Brest that affected lands in the Polish-Lithuanian Commonwealth was followed half a century later by the Union of Užhorod in 1646, which affected the lands in the Hungarian Kingdom.[3]

It should be stressed that the introduction of the union between 1596 and 1646 took on from the outset the negative characteristics of an all-or-nothing situation. Backed by the Polish and later Hungarian Roman Catholic hierarchies and secular governments, the Uniates were initially recognized as the only legal form of Eastern Christianity in the region. For the most part, the adherents of the "old faith" (*stara vira*)—Orthodoxy—were forced either to accept the union or to emigrate eastward to Slavic lands under the control of Muscovy. In the Carpathian region, however, Orthodox adherents with their own hierarchs were able to survive until the late eighteenth century.[4] By then all Carpatho-Rusyn villages became Uniate or Greek Catholic, as the church came to be officially called in the Austrian Empire which by 1772 had come to control the whole area.

It should also be remembered that from the very beginning, local Orthodox prelates considered the Union of Brest and Union of Užhorod to be uncanonical and therefore illegal. And when there were no longer any local Orthodox hierarchs left in the region, the anathematic views toward the Uniates/Greek Catholics were maintained by the hierarchy of the Russian Orthodox Church in Muscovy and later the Russian Empire. It is not surprising, therefore, that after the partitions of Poland (1772-1795), when the Russian Empire gained large territories inhabited by Greek Catholics, the tsarist government gradually banned the church.

---

[3]For details on these unions, see Oscar Halecki, *From Florence to Brest* (Rome, 1958) and Michael Lacko, *The Union of Užhorod* (Cleveland and Rome, 1968); and a discussion of the basic problems and literature in Paul Robert Magocsi, *Galicia: A Historical Survey and Bibliographic Guide* (Toronto, 1983), pp. 81-86.

[4]An Orthodox eparchy with its own bishop survived in the eastern part of the Subcarpathian Rus' (Transcarpathia) under the protection of Protestant Transylvania until 1711, while north of the mountains the Orthodox Eparchy of Przemyśl had throughout the seventeenth century an Orthodox as well as Greek Catholic bishop until 1691, when it became definitively Greek Catholic.

This was accomplished at first unilaterally through governmental decrees (before 1796), then with the assistance of the Greek Catholic and Russian Orthodox hierarchies (1830s). The last Greek Catholic diocese on Russian territory (Chełm/Kholm) was abolished in 1875.[5]

Despite persecution in the Russian Empire, the nineteenth century proved to be the best era in the history of Greek Catholicism. This was connected with the policy of the Austrian government, in particular the Josephine reforms and enlightened ideas that dominated state policy at the precise moment when, in 1772, the Habsburgs acquired Galicia and the vast majority of Greek Catholics. Already one year before, the Habsburg rulers had raised Mukačevo to the status of an independent Greek Catholic diocese (previously it had been subordinated to the Roman Catholic archbishopric of Eger), while in Galicia, the Greek rite was made equal to the Roman rite and by 1808 the metropolitan status of L'viv-Halych was restored in Galicia.[6]

Initially, however, such positive government intervention only helped to continue a trend that had existed in Greek Catholic circles since the church had come into being in 1596; namely, the tendency for the hierarchy and priesthood to assimilate culturally and linguistically to the dominant culture. In the case of Galicia, this meant Polish culture, while south of the mountains in the Hungarian Kingdom it meant Hungarian culture. Part of the assimilatory trend included changes in Eastern Christian liturgical practices, such as the adoption of the western Gregorian calendar, replacement of Church Slavonic with Polish, Hungarian, or Slovak, and by the twentieth century the imposition of celibacy for the priesthood. These trends developed at different speeds and, in some cases, were reversed or never even implemented. For instance, the trend toward polonization of the Greek Catholic hierarchy ended with the onset of Austrian rule in Galicia in 1772, then began again at the outset of the nineteenth century until it was definitively reversed after 1848, so that under the leadership of certain metropolitans (Hryhorij Jachymovyč, Andrej Šeptyc'kyj) the church became a catalyst of national consciousness and stood in the

---

[5]For details, see W. Lencyk, *The Eastern Catholic Church and Czar Nicholas I* (Rome and New York, 1966).

[6]The metropolitanate of L'viv-Halych, established in 1303, ceased to exist in 1401.

forefront of the Rus'-Ukrainian national movement in Galicia.[7] Thus, at least in Galicia, the Greek Catholic Church, which during the first half of the nineteenth century was an instrument of cultural assimilation, had by the outset of the twentieth century become the popular symbol of Ukrainian nationhood.

On the other hand, south of the mountains in Hungary, this same period saw the Greek Catholic Church become an instrument of national assimilation, with some of the hierarchs and many priests of the Diocese of Mukačevo becoming leading magyarones who helped promote state efforts to magyarize the local Rusyn population. Part of this trend witnessed the creation of a new Greek Catholic vicariate (1873) and then diocese (1912) at Hajdúdorog. Hungarian gradually replaced Church Slavonic as the liturgical language and the local Rusyn population became completely magyarized.[8]

The point is that in the eyes of many Rusyn patriots, whether among the intelligentsia or masses, the Greek Catholic Church had become or was becoming the symbol of compromise and subservience to the Roman Catholic world of Poland and Hungary. Changes in religious practices seemed sure to be followed by linguistic and national assimilation and the eventual disappearance of the Rusyns as an East Slavic people. Attitudes such as these led some individuals on a search for eastern spiritual renewal, which in part took the form—depending on one's view—of a "descent into the schism of Orthodoxy" or a "return to the Orthodox faith of our fathers."

Throughout all the Greek Catholic territories in the Austro-Hungarian Empire, it was precisely in the Carpathian region where the Orthodox revival had its greatest following. This was due to several factors: (1) the return of immigrants from America (who had converted to Orthodoxy in the New World); (2) the interest of Pan-Slavic circles in the Russian Empire; and (3) the innate conservatism of the Carpathian mountain inhabitants who instinctively felt themselves different

---

[7]See John-Paul Himka, "The Greek Catholic Church and Nation-Building, 1772-1918," *Harvard Ukrainian Studies*, VIII, 3-4 (Cambridge, Mass., 1984), pp. 426-452.

[8]Magocsi, *Shaping of a National Identity*, pp. 55-58; Atanasij V. Pekar, *Narysy istoriji cerkvy Zakarpattja*, Vol. I (Rome, 1967), pp. 95-112; Imre Timko, ed., *A Hajdúdorogi Bizánci Katholikus Egyházmegye jubileumi emlékkönyve 1912-1987* (Nyíregyháza, 1987), esp. pp. 17-29 and 158-181.

from—and therefore suspicious of—non-mountain dwellers, whether or not they happened to be of the same faith or nationality.[9] Moreover, from the very outset, the "return to Orthodoxy" was often a conscious religious and national act, since Orthodoxy was depicted by its apologists and came to be viewed by its new adherents as the "true faith" of the East Slavic Rus' *qua* Russian people. Such views not only coincided with the late nineteenth-century brand of Russian Pan-Slavism and Neo-Slavism, they also responded to the Christian universalist preferences of the Rusyn masses, since the Russian Orthodox Church integrated within its fold many ethnic elements, the dominant Slavic component of which was considered part of a so-called common Russian people (*obščerusskij narod*).[10]

Therefore, by the twentieth century several symbolic dichotomies prevailed throughout Carpathian society. From the perspective of Greek Catholics, their church represented the perfect compromise for Eastern Christianity, since it allowed for the survival of the Eastern rite and of the East Slavs, whether as Rusyns or Ukrainians, in a western Christian political and cultural environment. Based on such premises, Orthodoxy was considered not only the misguided faith of schismatics from the fold of "universal" Catholicism, but also a potential if not actual threat to Austria-Hungary because it preached the ethnonational unity of Rusyns and Russians and looked forward to the day when tsarist Russia would expand its despotic grasp up to and beyond the Carpathians.

The Orthodox felt their church represented a return to the "original" faith of Rusyns and all East Slavs, so that its existence served as a guarantee against foreign or Western (that is, Polish or Hungarian) national assimilation. In that context, argued the Orthodox, the Greek Catholics not only were preparing the ground for assimilation to Polish

[9]The impact of returning Carpatho-Rusyn immigrants on the Orthodox revival in the homeland deserves scholarly attention which it has heretofore not received. The role of Orthodox sympathizers in the Russian Empire (in particular Count Vladimir Bobrinskoj) also should be analyzed. For some interesting insights, see the statement of a contemporary Russian Orthodox activist: Michail Saryč, *Bratskij privjet bratjam i sestram-karpatorussam, živuščim v predjelach karpatskich gor i v Amerikje* (St. Petersburg, 1893); and the annual reports: *Otčet o djejatel'nosti Galicko-russkago blagotvoritel'nago obščestva v S.-Peterburgje*, 2 vols.: *za 1912/1913-1914 god* (St. Petersburg, 1913-14).

[10]For the best elaboration of the Orthodox East Slavic ideology as it pertains to the Carpathian region, see O. Mončalovskij, *Svjataja Rus'* (L'viv, 1903).

or Hungarian culture (Ukrainian was, by the way, viewed as an artificial bastardized form of the Polish language and its acceptance a sure step on the road to eventual complete polonization), they also slowly but surely were dropping all the tenets and practices of Eastern Christianity until it would not be long before Greek Catholics would be no different from Roman Catholics.

As long as the Austro-Hungarian Empire existed, the Orthodox revival in the Carpathians was kept to a minimum, even if it required trials from time to time against its adherents whose religious conversion was equated with state treason.[11] However, with the collapse of Austria-Hungary in 1918 and the creation of relatively religiously tolerant new political authorities in the Carpathian region—Poland north of the mountains and Czechoslovakia to the south—the Greek Catholic-Orthodox rivalry took on a new dynamism. The Rusyn masses began to express their national as well as religious preferences by large-scale "conversions" to Orthodoxy. Thus, among Rusyns south of the mountains in Czechoslovakia, nearly one-quarter (112,000) of the 460,000 Greek Catholics became Orthodox during the 1920s, while during the same period north of the mountains in Poland, about the same percentage, one-quarter (50,000) of Rusyns, known locally as Lemkos, did the same.[12]

Moreover, the religious change was often marked by violence, as parishioners locked Greek Catholic priests out of their churches, drove them from their parish houses, and installed Orthodox priests (*popy*), who were often newly-arrived refugees from lands farther east that had

---

[11]The first of these trials occurred in 1882 in L'viv (against Olga Grabar and others) followed by Marmaroš Sighet in 1913-1914 (against Archimandrite Aleksej Kabaljuk and others) and L'viv in 1914 (against Simeon Bendasjuk and others). Cf. René Martel, "La politique slave de la Russie d'avant-guerre: le procès ukrainien de Marmarosz-Sziget," *Affaires étrangères*, VI, 10 (Paris, 1936), pp. 623-634 and VII, 1 (1937), pp. 58-64; Bohdan Svitlynskij, "Avstro-Uhorščyna i Talerhof," in *Voennye prestuplenija habsburgskoj monarchii, 1914-1917 gg.* (Trumbull, Conn., 1964), annex, pp. 1-40; Konstantin M. Beskid, *Marmarošský proces* (Chust, 1926).

[12]For the situation in the Carpathian region in Czechoslovakia, see Magocsi, *Shaping of a National Identity*, pp. 178-185; and Ivan Vanat, *Narysy novitn'oji istoriji ukrajinciv Schidnoji Slovaččyny, 1918-1938*, Vol. I (Bratislava and Prešov, 1979), pp. 175-189. For the situation in Poland, see Ivan Teodorič, "Lemkovskaja Rus'," *Naučno-literaturnyj sbornik Galicko-russkoj maticy*, VIII [LXIX] (L'viv, 1934), pp. 16-23.

come under Soviet control.[13] South of the mountains in Czechoslovakia, the pro-Orthodox movement was in large part a reaction against the pro-Hungarian tendencies of the Greek Catholic hierarchy and village priesthood—a reaction, moreover, that was welcomed and at times directly supported by the Czechoslovak authorities for their own political reasons. North of the mountains in Poland, the pro-Orthodox movement was motivated by a reaction against the westernizing liturgical orientation and Ukrainian national preferences of certain circles in the Greek Catholic Church, in particular within the Eparchy of Przemyśl-Sambir-Sanok which had jurisdiction over the Lemko Rusyns.[14] Because they considered Ukrainianism as a separatist and anti-Russian (therefore in peasant eyes anti-Rusyn as well) phenomenon, the local Lemko Rusyns saw in Orthodoxy their national as well as spiritual salvation.

Not surprisingly, the Vatican was alarmed by the seemingly wholesale flight to Orthodoxy. To stem the tide, in Czechoslovakia it replaced the former pro-Hungarian (magyarone) bishops of the two Greek Catholic eparchies (Mukačevo and Prešov) with nationally pro-Rusyn and politically pro-Czechoslovak candidates.[15] In Poland, Rome felt obliged to take a more radical step by detaching the Lemko-

---

[13]The center of the Orthodox movement south of the Carpathians was in the village of Ladomirová, just outside of Svidník in northeastern Czechoslovakia, where in the early 1920s Archimandrite Vitalij Maksimenko established the Holy Trinity Monastery and printshop to propagate the faith. Cf. Paul R. Magocsi, *The Rusyn-Ukrainians of Czechoslovakia* (Vienna, 1983), pp. 40-41; and Vanat, *Narysy*, Vol. I, pp. 178-179.

[14]The bishop of the Greek Catholic Eparchy of Przemyśl-Sambir-Sanok was actually a Lemko, Josafat Kocylovs'kyj (1876-1947, consecrated 1917), who was one of the leading "westernizers" in the Greek Catholic Metropolia of L'viv-Halych. Kocylovs'kyj favored celibacy and other Latin-rite influences in opposition to the "easternizing" predilections of Metropolitan Šeptyc'kyj. As for the eparchial priesthood, it was for the most part deeply embued with a Ukrainian national sentiment. Tadeusz Duda, "Stosunki wyznaniowe wśród Łemków greckokatolickich zamieszkalych na terenie obecnej diecezji tarnowskiej w XIX i XX wieku," *Tarnowskie Studia Teologiczne*, X, I (Tarnów, 1986), pp. 240-243.

[15]The pro-Hungarian Greek Catholic bishops of Prešov, István Novak (1879-1932, consecrated 1913) and of Mukačevo, Antal Papp (1867-1945, consecrated 1912), each of whom refused to swear an oath of allegiance to the new Czechoslovak state, were replaced eventually by Petro Gebej (1864-1931, consecrated 1924) in Mukačevo and by Pavel Gojdič (1888-1960, consecrated 1927) in Prešov.

inhabited Carpathian region from the jurisdiction of the Ukrainian-dominated Greek Catholic Eparchy of Przemyśl. The result was the creation in 1934 of a Lemko Apostolic Administration, placed directly under the Vatican and headed by a pro-Lemko Rusyn (that is, not a sympathizer of the Ukrainian national orientation), whose presence was intended to suggest to the remaining Greek Catholics that their church and their children would not be turned into instruments of Ukrainianization.[16]

Considering its own traditional anti-Ukrainian orientation, the Polish government welcomed the Lemko Apostolic Administration as a limited but positive step in controlling Ukrainian influence in the southeastern part of the country. On the other hand, Ukrainian spokespersons branded the apostolic administration as a Polish-inspired Vatican plot to tribalize, divide, and eventually assimilate the Ukrainian nationality, of whom Lemko Rusyns were considered a part.[17] As for the Lemko Rusyn population, it generally welcomed the creation of what was now considered its "own" Greek Catholic church.[18] This move by the Vatican, based on precedent among immigrants from the Carpathian region in the United States, did in fact contribute to stabilizing membership and in cutting further losses to Orthodoxy.[19]

---

[16]The first apostolic administrator was the Reverend Vasylij Mascjuk (1899-1936), who was followed in 1936 by another Lemko, the Reverend Jakiv Medvec'kyj (1880-1941). The new Greek Catholic administration included 111 parishes and 127,305 faithful. See the statistics and historical survey (stressing the distinctiveness of Lemkos and their Christian descent from the SS Cyril and Methodian mission) in *Šematyzm Greko-Katolyckoho duchovenstva Apostol'skoji administraciji Lemkovščyny 1936* (L'viv, 1936).

[17]For a summary of the Ukrainian understanding, see the introduction by Vasyl' Lenčyk to the reprinted edition of the 1936 *Šematyzm* (Stamford, Conn., 1970); and the earlier Mykola Andrusjak, "Der westukrainische Stamm der Lemken," *Südost-Forschungen*, VI, 3-4 (Leipzig, 1941), pp. 536-575.

[18]For the contemporary Lemko view strongly critical of "Ukrainian infiltration," see "Što musyme o sobi znaty y pamiataty!," *Kalendar 'Lemka' na zvyčajnŷj rok 1935* (Przemyśl, 1934), pp. 133-134; and the discussion by one of the clerical supporters of the Apostolic Administration, I.F. Lemkyn [Ioann Poljans'kyj], *Ystoryja Lemkovynŷ* (Yonkers, N.Y., 1960), pp. 168-170. For a non-partisan review of those events, see Duda, "Stosunki," pp. 243-246.

[19]It was part the realization that Rusyn Greek Catholic immigrants from south of the Carpathians who were living in the United States could not get along with their increasingly Ukrainian-oriented religious brethren from Galicia that prompted the Vatican to establish separate administrations (1916) and then dioceses (1924) for

Hence, by the 1930s, a tenuous balance was reached between the two variants of Eastern Christianity in the Carpathian region. Some villages became all Orthodox or all Greek Catholic; others were split between the two orientations, each of which had its own church. However, this balance and relative stability was brutally upset after World War II with the arrival of a new political force in the area—the Soviet Union.

By late 1944, all the Greek Catholic territory that formerly had been part of the Austro-Hungarian Empire came firmly under the control of the Red Army. And within one year, most of that territory was incorporated into the Ukrainian S.S.R., leaving at most about 300,000 Rusyns beyond direct Soviet control within the new boundaries of Poland (circa 180,000 in the Lemko Region) and Czechoslovakia (circa 120,000 in northeastern Slovakia).

While the officially atheistic Soviet Union at best tolerated Russian Orthodoxy, especially since the *modus vivendi* reached between Stalin and the church during World War II, it was certainly not going to allow on its territory what was now hailed as the historic instrument of Polish and Hungarian feudal domination over the Rus' people and at present the agent of Vatican and western imperialism—namely, the Greek Catholic Church. Thus, the Soviet government was simply following the precedent tsarist Russia, and aided by Russian Orthodox Church hierarchy—which in any case never recognized the legality of the Union of Brest and Greek Catholicism—organized in 1946 a church sobor in L'viv, which abrogated the 1956 union.[20]

As a result of the 1946 L'viv *Sobor* (church council), the Greek Catholic priests in former eastern Galicia (L'viv, Przemyśl, Stanyslaviv eparchies) were given the choice to become Orthodox, and 1,111 (37.6 percent) of the 2,950 accepted the offer. As for the remainder who refused, a few hundred went underground, while an estimated 1,600

---

immigrants from Austrian Galicia and the Hungarian Kingdom—the present-day distinct Ukrainian Catholic Church and Byzantine Ruthenian Catholic Church. Accepting pre-World War I political boundaries, Lemko immigrants were separated from their Rusyn brethren and placed within Galician-Ukrainian dioceses.

[20]The proceedings of the L'viv Sobor were published first in *Dijanija Soboru hreko-katolyc'koji cerkvy u L'vovi, 8-10 bereznja 1946* (L'viv, 1946) and more recently in a revised version: *L'vivs'kyj cerkovnyj sobor: dokumenty i materialy, 1946-1981* (L'viv, 1984), with a slightly abridged English version: *The Lvov Church Council: Documents and Materials, 1946-1981* (Moscow, 1983).

were put in prison, where they lingered with few exceptions until their deaths in Soviet camps.[21] Three years later, in Soviet-controlled Transcarpathia (formerly Subcarpathian Rus' in Czechoslovakia), the Greek Catholic Eparchy of Mukačevo was liquidated and the church and its faithful officially transformed into Orthodox. Unlike in Galicia, there was no sobor held in Transcarpathia as had been the case in L'viv. Instead, the "act of reunion" was simply declared to be in effect following the reading of a proclamation during a service on August 28, 1949 in the cathedral church in Užhorod.[22]

With Greek Catholicism officially eliminated on Soviet territory, it survived for the moment only in the Carpathian region of southeastern Poland and northeastern Czechoslovakia. However, since that time the situation in both these countries has been particularly complicated.

After the new Soviet-Polish and Soviet-Czechoslovak borders were formed in 1945, efforts were made on both sides to follow the trend at the time in international relations, which favored the transfer of populations in an effort to make political and ethnic boundaries coincide, that is, to eliminate the problem of national minorities which—so it was felt—had contributed to if not caused World War II. In this regard, Rusyns from the Carpathian region (in return for Poles and Czechs from Soviet territory) were given the option to emigrate eastward to the Soviet Ukraine. In Poland's Lemko region, about 120,000 opted or were administratively encouraged to go east; in northeastern Czechoslovakia, only 12,000 Rusyns accepted the invitation. This eastward trek to the Soviet Union from Poland took

---

[21]*Martyrolohija ukrajins'kych cerkov*, Vol. II: *Ukrajins'ka katolyc'ka cerkva: dokumenty, materialy, chrystyjans'kyj samvydav Ukrajiny*, ed. Osyp Zinkevyč and Taras R. Lončyna (Toronto and Baltimore, 1985), p. 74. For greater details, see *First Victims of Communism: White Book on the Religious Persecution in Ukraine* (Rome, 1953).

[22]For the Greek Catholic view of these events, see Pekar, *Narysy*, pp. 159-170; Vasyl' Markus, "Nyščennja hreko-katolyc'koji cerkvy v Mukačivs'kij Jeparchiji v 1945-50 rr.," *Zapysky Naukovoho tovarystva im. Ševčenka*, CLXIX (Paris and New York, 1962), pp. 386-405; and Michael Lacko, "The Forced Liquidation of the Union of Užhorod," *Slovak Studies*, I: *Historica*, No. 1 (Rome, 1961), pp. 145-157. For the Russian Orthodox view in praise of the historically justified return to the true faith, see Bishop Savva (of Mukačevo and Užhorod), "30th Anniversary of the Reunion of the Zakarpatskaya Region Greek Catholics (Uniates) with the Russian Orthodox Church," *Journal of the Moscow Patriarchate*, No. 1 (Moscow, 1980), pp. 21-24.

place in 1945-1946 and from Czechoslovakia in 1947. Nonetheless, about 40,000 Lemko Rusyns still remained in southeastern Poland and another 110,000 in northeastern Czechoslovakia.[23]

As for Poland, the new pro-Soviet government resolved the problem in a simple way. Claiming that the local Lemko Rusyns were aiding anti-Soviet Ukrainian partisans who were holed up in the Carpathian Mountains, during the spring and summer of 1947 the Lemkos were forcibly removed from their homes and resettled in the so-called "Recovered Lands" (*Ziemie odzyskane*), the formerly-German territories of Silesia (especially near Wrocław) and along the Baltic Sea that had become part of Poland in 1945.[24] Therefore, with regard to the historic Eastern Christian churches in Poland's Carpathian region, the problem was resolved. There simply ceased to be any problem because there were no more Eastern Christians.

In legal terms, Poland's Communist authorities accepted the Soviet view that after the L'viv *Sobor* of 1946 the Greek Catholic Church ceased to exist in historic Galicia, which included lands in post-1945 Poland that had been under the jurisdiction of the Eparchy of Przemyśl and then the Lemko Apostolic Administration. Based on such a premise, Polish government decrees were issued in 1947 and 1949 which respectively nationalized Greek Catholic church property and

[23]For a discussion of the Lemko Rusyn eastward migration in the context of other European population movements at the time, see Joseph B. Schechtman, *Postwar Population Transfers in Europe, 1945-1955* (Philadelphia, 1962), pp. 151-179. On the lesser known emigration from northeastern Czechoslovakia, see Vanat, *Narysy*, Vol. II: *1938-1948* (1985), pp. 264-266.

[24]Although it seems that plans for the deportation of Lemkos (and Ukrainians from neighboring lands in postwar southeast Poland) were already prepared, it was the death of General Karol Świerczewski in a battle with the Ukrainian Insurgent Army (the Banderite UPA) in March 1947 that provided the official justification for removal. The forced deportation was carried out between April and July 1947 (often with only a few hours notice), despite the fact that the remaining Lemkos in Poland lived primarily in the western Lemko region (west of the Dukla Pass) where the UPA carried on only limited activity and where the local population was traditionally anti-Ukrainian.

On the deportation and the new life of Lemkos in the "Recovered Lands," see Andrzej Kwilecki, "Fragmenty najnowszej historii Łemkow," *Rocznik Sądecki*, VIII (Nowy Sącz, 1967), esp. pp. 274-287; his *Łemkowie: zagadnienie migracji i asymilacji* (Warsaw, 1974); and Kazimierz Pudło, *Łemkowie: proces wrastania w środowisko Dolnego Śląska, 1947-1985* (Wrocław, 1987).

then legalized the seizure on the grounds that it belonged to "juridical persons" whose "existence and activities lost their purpose as a result of resettlement of their members to the Soviet Union."[25] As a result of these decrees, the Greek Catholic Church in Poland was "delegalized," allowing for the official "non-recognition" of the Greek Catholic rite in Poland from that time until the present.

In practice, after 1947, the Lemko Greek Catholic Apostolic Administration (with its 129 parishes and 127,580 faithful as of 1943) ceased to exist. Church property in the depopulated Lemko Rusyn villages was left to decay and eventually disappear. In those Lemko villages resettled by Poles, former Greek Catholic churches were often appropriated by the Roman Catholic Church, in a few instances given to the Orthodox Church, or in the case of wooden ones, left to decay or to be torn down, using what remained of the structures for firewood.[26]

South of the border in Czechoslovakia, the vast majority of the population remained in place. There were two reasons for this. In contrast to the historic tradition of antagonism between Poles and East Slavic Rusyns and Ukrainians north of the Carpathians, on the southern slopes of the mountains the past was basically marked by friendly relations between Slovaks and Rusyns. Moreover, the isolated extremist views directed at Rusyns living on "Slovak land"[27] were neutralized

---

[25]Cited with further details in Bohdan R. Bociurkiw, "The Suppression of the Greek Catholic Church in Postwar Soviet Union and Poland," in Dennis J. Dunn, ed., *Religion and Nationalism in Eastern Europe and the Soviet Union* (Boulder, Colo. and London, 1987), p. 106.

[26]In the palatinate of Rzeszów, which included most of the Carpathian Lemko region as well as former Ukrainian-inhabited villages beyond the San, the vast majority of the 220 churches that disappeared between 1939 and 1972 were not destroyed as a result of World War II, but because of neglect during the post-1947 decades of peace. Ryszard Brykowski, "Zabytkowe cerkwie," *Architektura*, XXXVII, 5 (Warsaw, 1983), pp. 53-58.

For a useful introduction to what occurred in Lemko villages after the deportations and resettlement by Poles, see C.M. Hann, *A Village Without Solidarity* (New Haven, Conn., 1985), pp. 17-39.

[27]Ostensibly, the leader of the Slovak nationalists during the interwar years, the Reverend Andrej Hlinka, had once quipped that it might be preferable to ship the Rusyns eastward. This attitude was to resurface at times of political instability as during the deportation of Lemkos and the Banderite problem in neighboring Poland (1945-1947) and the Prague Spring (1968-1969).

in the new postwar political situation in Czechoslovakia in which the powerful Communist party had a relatively high number of functionaries of Rusyn background.[28] Therefore, aside from the truly voluntary nature of the eastward emigration of 12,000 Rusyns in 1947, there was to be no attempt at forced deportation to the Soviet Union or westward to other parts of the Czechoslovak republic.

However, after Czechoslovakia came to be ruled exclusively by a Communist regime in February 1948, the Soviet model in religious affairs was soon adopted. This sealed the fate of the Greek Catholic Church. In April 1950, Czechoslovakia's Communist officials invited 80 Greek Catholic priests to a "peace rally" in Prešov. By previous agreement with local Orthodox leaders, the "peace rally" was transformed into a church council (sobor) and, following the Soviet model, the union with Rome was abolished, making all former Greek Catholics become Orthodox. Like the rest of the Orthodox Church in Czechoslovakia, the new Orthodox parishes initially became part of the Russian Orthodox Moscow Patriarchate.[29] Of the 301 Greek Catholic priests at the time, one-third became Orthodox. The remainder who refused to convert were arrested and, when finally released, forbidden to serve as priests. Bishop Pavel Gojdič and his suffragan Vasyl' Hopko were also arrested, the former dying in prison in 1960.[30]

---

[28]On Slovak attitudes and the high number of Rusyn Communist activists after World War II, see Pavel Mačů, "National Assimilation: The Case of the Rusyn-Ukrainians of Czechoslovakia," East-Central Europe, II, 2 (Pittsburgh, Pa., 1975), pp. 126-127.

[29]The Orthodox jurisdictional question south of the Carpathians was complicated. With the expansion of Orthodoxy during the interwar years in both eastern Slovakia and Subcarpathian Rus', the new church with its Eparchy of Mukačevo-Prešov was placed in 1931 under the Serbian patriarch in Belgrade. In 1945-1946, the Orthodox in Soviet Transcarpathia (Subcarpathian Rus') and in Eastern Slovakia were released from the jurisdiction of the Serbian Orthodox Church to become respectively the Eparchy of Mukačevo and the Czechoslovak Exarchate of the Russian Orthodox Moscow Patriarchate. Finally, in 1951, the Orthodox in Eastern Slovakia, organized into the Eparchies of Prešov and of Michalovce, became part of a distinct Czechoslovak Autocephalous Orthodox Church, retaining since then close ties with the mother church in Moscow. Pavel Aleš, "Cesty k autokefalite," in Pravoslávny cirkevný kalendár 1981 (Bratislava, 1980), pp. 79-86; and Andrew Sorokowski, "Ukrainian Catholics and Orthodox in Czechoslovakia," Religion in Communist Lands, XV, 1 (Kent, England, 1987), pp. 59-60.

[30]For the Greek Catholic view of these events, see Pekar, Narysy, pp. 170-176; Lacko, "The Forced Liquidation," pt. 2: "Liquidation of the Diocese of Prešov," pp.

Thus, by 1950, it seemed that the Greek Catholic problem had been resolved in east-central Europe. The homeland where the church had flourished was now firmly in Orthodox or, in part, Roman Catholic hands. Ironically, within the Soviet bloc, it was only in ostensibly anti-Slavic Hungary (where the Eparchy of Hajdúdorog had long ago taken on a purely Hungarian character) and otherwise staunchly pro-Soviet Bulgaria (whose adherents in union with Rome numbered less than 5,000) that Greek Catholicism survived as a legal church.[31] However, despite their Communist governments and even strongly pro-Stalinist orientation, neither Poland nor Czechoslovakia was the Soviet Union. As a result, the relatively less rigid approach of Warsaw and Prague to religious matters allowed for new movement on the Eastern Christian front.

In Poland, following the political changes in October 1956, a church-state *modus vivendi* provided a "tolerated but not recognized" status to the Greek Catholic rite within the Roman Catholic Church. This meant that Lemko Rusyns and fellow Greek Catholic Ukrainians scattered throughout the western and northern parts of the country were permitted to have services conducted at some fifty "pastoral points" by the approximately fifty surviving Greek Catholic priests who were now designated bi-ritual assistants in Roman Catholic parishes. In practice, Greek Catholic services were held in Roman Catholic chapels provided the resident priest agreed.[32] In effect, the hierarchy of the Polish Roman Catholic Church was mildly tolerant of these activities, while the response among the lower echelons of the Polish priesthood ranged

158-185; and Julius Kubinyi, *The History of the Prjašiv Eparchy* (Rome, 1970), pp. 169-178. For the local Orthodox view, see Aleš, "Cesty," p.84 and Ilija Kačur, *Stručný prehl'ad histórie pravoslávnej cirkvi v bývalom Uhorsku a v Československu* (Prešov, no date), pp. 166-171. For the Czechoslovak Marxist view, see Ivan Bajcura, *Ukrajinská otázka v ČSSR* (Košice, 1967), pp. 128-132.

[31]In neighboring Romania, the union was abolished and the Greek Catholic faithful absorbed into the Romanian Orthodox Church in October 1948, while in Yugoslavia, which had broken with the Soviet bloc in 1948, the Greek Catholic Diocese of Križevci (which included Rusyn communities originally from south of the Carpathians as well as local Croats and Ukrainian immigrants and their descendants from Galicia) continued to function.

[32]By 1977, large concentrations of Greek Catholics were identified in 156 Roman Catholic parishes, including 16 located in the Tarnów and Przemyśl Roman Catholic dioceses, which cover the Lemko Region. Bociurkiw, "The Suppression," pp. 107 and 118, n. 57.

from Christian solidarity with to fierce opposition against their Greek Catholic brethren.

Also, beginning in 1956, some Lemkos were allowed to return to their ancestral villages—provided they could arrange to convince Polish families to sell them back their confiscated homesteads. By the mid-1960s, about 3,000 had returned, and this process of resettlement in the Carpathian homeland has continued so that today there are about 10,000 Lemko Rusyns living once again on the northern slopes of the Carpathians.[33] This has meant that the Eastern Christian presence, which had been physically removed by 1947, has now returned in the form of both a semi-legal Greek Catholic and fully legal Orthodox community.

The numbers are albeit small, with the estimated 10,000 Lemko Rusyns living in the Carpathians being divided more or less evenly between Orthodox, Greek Catholics, and non-believers. In response to this mini-revival, the Polish Autocephalous Orthodox Church established (or reestablished) in 1983 a new Eparchy of Przemyśl and Nowy Sącz, specifically for the Lemko Carpathian region. It is based in Sanok, has 33 parishes served by 14 priests, and is headed by a bishop of Lemko Rusyn background, Adam Dubec.[34] In 1985, a symbolically major event took place in the small Lemko Rusyn village of Zyndranowa, where the first Orthodox church newly constructed in the region since before World War II was opened. Two other Orthodox churches are under construction in Krynica and in the town of Gorlice.

This activity among the Orthodox has caused concern within Polish Roman Catholic circles and has forced a slight change in their traditionally intolerant attitude toward Greek Catholics. When the first Greek Catholics began returning to the Carpathian region, it was not uncommon to find Roman Catholic Polish priests—often under the influence of their own parishioners—refusing access to chapels in their churches for Greek Catholic services. With the recent increase in Orthodox activity, however, the Roman Catholics feel such "schismatic" activity needs to be stopped and that allowing Greek Catholics to

---

[33]Kwilecki, "Fragment najnowszej historii," pp. 287-288; and Kwilecki, *Łemkowie*, pp. 198-200.

[34]The Orthodox understanding is that the eparchy in 1983 is a restoration of what ceased to exist in 1691. Mykola Syvic'kyj, "Vidrodžennja peremys'koji," *Cerkovnyj kalendar na 1985 rik* (Sanok, 1984), pp. 165-169.

function easily might be the best way to achieve that goal. Moreover, the favorable pronouncements of Pope John Paul II toward Ukrainian (Greek) Catholics in the West, and the four recent visitations by the secretary of the Vatican's Congregation for the Oriental Churches (Archbishop Myroslav Marusyn) to Poland's Greek Catholics has raised the latter's status. These developments culminated in 1989 with the pope's appointment of Msgr. Ivan Martynjak as bishop to Poland's primate, Cardinal Glemp, with responsibility for Greek Catholics throughout the country.[35]

Despite such improvements in their status, the Greek Catholics in Poland remain under the jurisdiction of the Polish Roman Catholic Church. In the Carpathian region, there are today 13 parishes served by 3 priests. Of those parishes, 2 (Komańcza and Krempna) managed somehow to survive throughout the postwar events, 5 (Kulaszne, Łosie, Nowica, Pętna, Uście Gorlickie) were established in the 1960s following the initial return of Lemkos, and 6 (Gładyszów, Gorlice, Krynica, Olchowiec, Rozdziele, Rzepedź) have come into being since 1979.[36] All but one of the Greek Catholic parishes carry on their services in Roman Catholic churches, that is, at the discretion of the local Roman Catholic priest. It was therefore of great symbolic importance when a large new Greek Catholic church, the first of its kind to be constructed since World War II, was opened in 1987 in the village of Komańcza.

On the southern slopes of the Carpathian Mountains in Czechoslovakia, the fate of Eastern Christianity in the past four decades has been significantly different. The efforts at political liberalization in the 1960s that culminated in the Prague Spring of 1968 also prompted Czechoslovakia's former Greek Catholics to demand the restoration of their church. In June 1968, their efforts were met with success as the Dubček government legalized the existence of the Greek Catholic

---

[35]Archbishop Marusyn's visitations took place in 1984, 1985, 1986, and 1987, and some included the Lemko Region. An important indication of support for Poland's Greek Catholics occurred during the last visit of Pope John Paul II to Poland (June 1987), when he attended mass at the Basilian Greek Catholic Church in Warsaw.

[36]See the statistics in the first Greek Catholic church almanac published in Poland since before World War II: *Hreko-katolyc'kyj cerkovnyj kalendar 1987* (Warsaw, 1987), pp. 74-78.

Church.[37]

One immediate question that arose concerned church property. Who now had the legal right to it—the Orthodox who held it since 1950 or the Greek Catholics who wanted it back? This thorny issue was to be resolved by the mechanism of a plebiscite. Among the first symbolic steps of the plebiscite was the return of the Prešov Eparchy's cathedral church to the Greek Catholics in July 1968. In the course of the next year, plebiscites were held in about 210 parishes, only five of which opted to remain Orthodox. In the end, the government recognized the existence of 205 Greek Catholic and 87 Orthodox parishes.[38]

In many ways, the political and cultural turmoil that marked Czechoslovakia's Prague Spring played itself out in Rusyn villages through the mode of religion and a return to the Orthodox-Greek Catholic conflicts that had characterized the interwar years. Immediately after the legalization decree was issued, a delegation of 100 Orthodox priests delivered a protest to the president of Czechoslovakia against the reestablishment of the Greek Catholic Church.[39]

At the village level, while there were peaceful transfers of property from the Orthodox to Greek Catholics, there were also several cases marked by assaults and the physical removal of Orthodox priests, breaking down of church doors, stoning of services, and in at least one instance the death of a Greek Catholic curate at the hands of an

---

[37]The texts of the resolution of the Greek Catholic clergy requesting the legal reconstitution of their church, dated April 10, 1968, and of the Czechoslovak governmental decree, signed by then vice-prime minister (and later president) Gustav Husák, approving the restoration and dated June 13, 1968, appeared in *Kalendár gréckokatolíkov 1969* (Trnava, 1968), pp. 46-50. An English translation of the governmental decree is found in Michael Lacko, "The Re-establishment of the Greek Catholic Church in Czechoslovakia," *Slovak Studies*, XI: *Historica*, No. 8 (Cleveland and Rome, 1971), pp. 164-165.

[38]*Ibid.*, pp. 166-171.

[39]For the Orthodox view of the Prague Spring, including opposition to restoration of the Greek Catholic Church, aided by the arrival of Czechoslovakia during early 1968 of "107 church figures—Vatican agents who were wolves in sheep's clothing," see the articles by the Orthodox Rusyn lay activist in Prague, Ivan S. Šlepec'kyj, sent by him in 1968 to the Prešov Ukrainian newspaper, *Nove žyttja*, but only published in the West: "Komu potrebna unyja s Rymom na Prjaševščyni?," *Karpatorusskyj kalendar Lemko-Sojuza na hod 1970* (Yonkers, N.Y., 1970), pp. 77-80 and "V spravach demokratyzacyy Prjaševščynŷ," *Karpatorusskyj kalendar' Lemko-Sojuza na hod 1969* (Yonkers, N.Y., 1969), pp. 35-39.

Orthodox priest. The situation was made even more ominous in that most of the plebiscites were carried out after August 21, that is in the presence of Soviet armed forces throughout the country. While it is known that some Orthodox priests garbed in sacred vestments greeted the Soviet troops as "liberators and defenders of Orthodoxy," vicious rumors began to circulate according to which the Orthodox supposedly had invited the Soviets and that it was the Orthodox who were identifying the Greek Catholics as "counterrevolutionaries" to the interventionist forces.[40]

Nonetheless, despite the return beginning in early 1970 to a Soviet-style regime in Czechoslovakia which repealed many of the achievements of 1968, the restoration of the Greek Catholic Church has not been rescinded. It continues to function openly and with its own ecclesiastical structures, although like many Czech and Slovak Roman Catholic dioceses it did not have its own bishop until the revolutionary events of 1989. Moreover, the existence of a legal Greek Catholic Church in eastern Slovakia in the decades since 1968 proved to be a source of embarrassment to Soviet authorities in neighboring Transcarpathia, where an underground Greek Catholic Church was, since the 1970s, increasing its activity. The movement in Soviet Transcarpathia was, in part, encouraged by the improved status of its co-religionists and co-nationals on the other side of the border in Czechoslovakia.[41]

---

[40]For details, see Lacko, "The Re-establishment," pp. 164-165; and Athanasius B. Pekar, "Restoration of the Greek Catholic Church in Czechoslovakia," *Ukrainian Quarterly*, XXIX, 3 (New York, 1973), pp. 284-288; and the rejection of such accusations by the Orthodox in their official organ, *Zapovit sv. Kyryla i Mefodija*, XI, 5, 6, 7 (Prešov, 1968).

[41]By the second half of the 1970s, Greek Catholic laymen in the western regions of the Ukrainian S.S.R. led by Josyf Terelja of the Transcarpathian oblast were, at great personal risk (often resulting in imprisonment and exile), openly sending official requests to the Soviet government, the United Nations, and the governments of western countries, requesting the restitution of the Greek Catholic Church in the Soviet Union. Then, during Gorbachev's *glasnost*, the underground Greek Catholic hierarchy has revealed itself publicly, holding ever more liturgies and ordaining new priests, including several from the Ukrainian emigration in the West. Discussions now are underway between the Vatican, the Soviet authorities, and the Russian Orthodox Church on legalization of the Greek Catholic Church in the Soviet Union, although the jurisdictional format of a renewed church is still to be decided. See *Martyrolohija*, pp. 531-589 and 651-665; and the monthly newsletter, *Church of the Catacombs/Ukrainian Press Service* (St. Catharine's Ont., 1986-present).

But why did Czechoslovakia's Communist authorities or, more precisely in the new post-1968 federalist situation, the Slovak authorities, allow the survival of the Greek Catholic Church in their country? The answer, in part, is to be found in the nationality problem and this, in turn, leads to the further question. How has the restoration of Greek Catholicism and therefore the renewal of the Orthodox-Greek Catholic dichotomy in the Eastern Christian world of the Carpathians affected the way in which the local population views itself and is viewed by others with regard to the question of national identity? Whereas some aspects of the conflict over national ideology are evident in Poland's Lemko Region, the number of Rusyns living there is too small to make any conclusive judgements.[42] South of the mountains in Czechoslovakia, however, the critical mass is large enough to see some trends.

First of all, it should be remembered that as part of the post-World War II Soviet influence in Poland and Czechoslovakia, the nationality question, like the religious question, was ostensibly resolved as a result of the so-called "iron laws" of Marxist historical evolution, albeit helped along administrative decrees and their legal enforcement. This meant that the nearly century-old question of who the East Slavic Rus' population of the Carpathians was in national terms—Russian, Ukrainian, or a distinct Rusyn nationality—was decided. They were Ukrainian. But like the religious question, the nationality question turned out to be not so easily resolved.[43]

---

[42]In an atmosphere of political discussion that has prevailed since 1980 in Poland during and even after the rise and fall of the Solidarity movement, the question of the Lemkos has been revived once again. The issue concerns whether they should be considered Ukrainians (as they have been officially designated by the Polish government since 1945) or a distinct Lemko Rusyn nationality with the right to their own organizations. So far, it seems that this debate (carried on among Lemkos and among interested Poles and Ukrainians) has been the concern of the secular intelligentsia, without any particular role being played by either the Greek Catholic or Orthodox churches.

For details, see the series of articles in the *Carpatho-Rusyn American*, X, 1, 2, 3, 4, and XI, 1 (Fairview, N.J., 1987-88).

[43]The following discussion is based largely on Maču, "National Assimilation." See also Magocsi, *Rusyn-Ukrainians*, pp. 49-55; Bajcura, *Ukrajinská otázka*, pp. 132-134 and 149-160; and Pavol Uram, "K niektorým otázkam vývoja ukrajinského školstva v ČSR v rokoch 1945-1960," *Zborník prác učitel'ov ÚML UPJŠ*, No. 5 (Košice, 1978), pp. 243-252.

When in 1952 the Rusyn population of northeastern Czechoslovakia was administratively declared to be Ukrainian—a decision that meant among other things having Ukrainian instead of Russian taught in the early 322 elementary and secondary schools—large numbers of people reacted by voluntarily declaring themselves to be Slovak. They demanded and received Slovak schools in their villages. By 1966, there were only 72 elementary and secondary schools left in Rusyn communities that were not in Slovak, i.e., that provided instruction in Ukrainian. Then, with the heady days of the Prague Spring when demands of all kinds were being made to correct the injustices of the neo-Stalinist past, alongside the demand for a return of the Greek Catholic faith there was a call for the return of Rusyn schools and for recognition of Rusyns as a distinct nationality. Indeed, planning was begun to restore instruction in the local Rusyn dialect in the schools, which would have meant a rejection of Ukrainian instruction and the return of Slovak schools. But the Warsaw Pact intervention put an end to those and all other "counterrevolutionary" ideas. As we have seen, Czechoslovakia's Rusyns did get back their Greek Catholic Church, but at what cost?

The price, in fact, has been to see that the church becomes an instrument of slovakization. Indeed, the general trend toward assimilation was already well underway. For instance, if in the 1930 census, 91,079 persons in northeastern Czechoslovakia claimed Rusyn as their nationality, in 1959-60, when Ukrainian was the only possible choice, a mere 35,435 opted to do so.[44] It is uncertain whether the several proposals for changes away from the Ukrainian cultural and educational policy made in 1968-1969 would have made any difference in an individual's decision to emphasize a sense of Rusyn identity. The brutal destruction of the Czechoslovak experiment from the East only convinced many traditionally pro-Czechoslovak Rusyns that they had better throw in their lot fully with their West Slavic brethren by identifying with them nationally as well as linguistically and politically.

In this context, the Greek Catholic Church has been an unwitting partner in the assimilation process. At the moment of its restoration in June 1968, the question of who was to serve as bishop in the restored diocese of Prešov became acute. The last bishop, Pavel Gojdič, had

---

[44]Mačul, "National Assimilation," pp. 104 and 129-130.

diocese of Prešov became acute. The last bishop, Pavel Gojdič, had died in prison in 1960, but his auxiliary and successor Vasyl' Hopko survived, was released in 1964 for confinement in an old-age home, and finally in 1968 was rehabilitated and allowed to return to Prešov to lead the restoration process of the Greek Catholic Church. However, from the very outset, pro-Slovak forces within the church vowed that no Rusyn should ever again head the diocese.

To justify their views, the Slovak Greek Catholic faction pointed to official Czechoslovak nationality statistics, which allowed since Communist rule only for Ukrainian identity, not a Rusyn one. Accordingly, there were only 35,000 (1960) Ukrainians in northeastern Czechoslovakia, which represented a mere 11 percent of the total Greek Catholic population estimated at 315,000.[45] Slovak Greek Catholic activists, who otherwise were generally suspicious of most data and statements issued in the past by the Czechoslovak Communist authorities, accepted at face value the official statistics. As for the "Rusyn revival" of 1968, whose spokesmen challenged Slovak views on statistics and other matters, it was dismissed as the machinations of anti-Slovak extremists or perhaps even pro-Soviet agitators.

Such attitudes were held not only by Slovak Greek Catholics in eastern Slovakia, they were also promoted by powerful Slovak financial circles in the West, which put pressure on the Vatican to appoint a Slovak to head the restored Greek Catholic Eparchy of Prešov.[46] In the end, the recently-released and rehabilitated Bishop Hopko, who was allowed to return to Prešov in 1968 to lead the movement to restore the Greek Catholic Church and who was to be recognized as bishop by the Dubček government, was finally allowed to travel to Rome in December 1968 for an audience with the Pope. However, when the bishop returned a few weeks later, he discovered (according to a letter of the Sacred Congregation for Oriental Churches, dated December 22,

---

[45]Based on relatively reliable statistics of 1930, and taking into consideration natural increases and post-World War II emigration, there should have been approximately 130,000 Rusyns in Slovakia in 1968. Magocsi, *Rusyn-Ukrainians*, p. 64, n. 91.

[46]See the interview with the leading activists, the Canadian industrialist, Stephan B. Roman, and then auxiliary Greek Catholic Bishop of Toronto, Michael Rusnak in Benedykt Heydenkorn, "Rozmowy z bpem Rusnakiem i St. Romanem," *Kultura*, No. 1/2 [256/257] (Paris, 1969), pp. 148-153.

1968) that he was removed as head of the Prešov Eparchy and made subordinate to a Slovak administrator, the Reverend Ján Hirka.[47] Thus, the chance to have the appointment of a Greek Catholic bishop to the Eparchy of Prešov recognized by the Czechoslovak government was missed in 1968-1969 because of internal nationality controversies. Bishop Hopko was effectively removed from any real influence and died in 1976.

In the absence of a bishop, the eparchial authorities under administrator Hirka gradually engaged in the slovakization of church practices throughout all parishes, including the estimated 75 in Rusyn villages. While the liturgy remained in Church Slavonic in both Rusyn and Slovak parishes, the homilies and other non-liturgical parts of the service became Slovak.[48] Church publications were also increasingly slovakized, with the largest printings of the monthly journals (the Slovak edition *Slovo* and Ukrainian *Blahovistnyk*) and the annual almanacs being today in Slovak instead of in Ukrainian or in Rusyn dialect as had been the case in the early years of the church's restoration after 1968.[49]

Finally, in the wake of Czechoslovakia's Velvet Revolution of November 1989 and the end of Communist rule, the Vatican was able

---

[47]For the opposing interpretations of Hopko's fate in 1968-1969, see the Slovak view by Lacko, "Re-establishment," p. 174; and the Rusyn/Ukrainian views by: A. Pekar, *Bishop Basil Hopko, S.T.D., Confessor of the Faith* (Pittsburgh, Pa., 1979), pp. 15-30, idem, "Restoration," pp. 288-296; and the anonymous *Tragedy of the Greek Catholic Church in Czechoslovakia* (New York, 1971), pp. 25-66.

[48]The figure for the number of Rusyn Greek Catholic parishes was provided to the author during an interview in Prešov (June 1988) with the administrator Hirka, who based his calculations on data from the *Schematizmus slovenských katolíckych diecéz* (Trnava and Bratislava, 1978), pp. 417-456. According to the administrator, the reason for increasing slovakization is that he is unable to find priests who are able or willing to speak Rusyn.

[49]In an interview with the author (August 1989), then administrator Hirka blamed the decline in the printing of *Blahovistnyk* on its editor, the Reverend Stepan Pap, who dropped the sections written in Rusyn dialect and transformed the monthly into a Ukrainian publication which, according to Hirka, readers did not want. Also according to Hirka, Pap's Ukrainian-language *Biblijnyj katychyzm dlja hrekokatolykiv* (Trnava and Bratislava, 1984) simply sat in storage gathering dust because of a lack of reader demand. The Reverand Pap (who has died since) told me in August 1989 that as former editor he was not allowed to publish in Rusyn because government-owned printing shops refused to print works in an "unofficial" language.

to raise Hirka to the rank of bishop. Not surprisingly, at his massive and well-publicized installation in February 1990, the Slovak aspect of the Greek Catholic Eparchy of Prešov was clearly emphasized. The newly-won freedoms in Czechoslovak society have also encouraged some Greek Catholic priests and laypersons to prepare Rusyn-language translations of liturgical and prayer books, and to demand their use in Rusyn parishes. While Bishop Hirka has promised to respond to the needs of all his flock, including Rusyns, it is still too early to know whether the Greek Catholic officials who surround him are able or willing to reverse the pro-Slovak orientation within their church.[50]

In response, the Orthodox Church, with its approximately 20,000 faithful, its own cathedral churches in Prešov and Michalovce, and its 74 parishes spread throughout the countryside, prides itself once again as the defender of the East Slavic Rus' world in the face of Vatican and Slovak religious and national assimilationist encroachments as carried out through the medium of the Greek Catholic Church.[51] After all, for the Orthodox world, Greek Catholicism remains the bastard child of Roman Catholic Jesuit machinations in Eastern Europe, and for many Orthodox it seems particularly ironic that Greek Catholicism has been allowed to survive and do its "destructive work" among Eastern Slavs in Poland and Czechoslovakia right on the doorstep of the "Orthodox" Soviet Union. Furthermore, the traditional Rus'/Russian orientation of many Rusyns in Czechoslovakia makes such views quite palatable, and it seems no coincidence that those villages which were most reluctant

---

[50]Bishop Hirka stated in 1988 that he had commissioned several Rusyn-language religious books (in the Latin alphabet) that were slated for publication in early 1989. They have still not appeared. The priests and laypersons who have prepared their own Rusyn texts (in Cyrillic alphabet) say that the bishop refuses to grant them the required episcopal imprimatur in order that they be printed and used in services. See the discussion of these matters in "The Revolution of 1989," *Carpatho-Rusyn American*, XII, 4 (Fairview, N.J., 1989), pp. 7-8; "Revolution of 1989 Update," *ibid.*, XIII, 2 (1990), pp. 4-7; and the interview with Bishop Hirka on the eve of his installation and entitled: "Ja ljublju rusyniv," *Nove žyttja* (Prešov), February 16, 1990, p. 5.

[51]The statistical data is drawn from the *Pravoslávny cirkevný kalendár 1981* (Bratislava, 1980), pp. 57-61. While it is true that most Orthodox parishes use only Church Slavonic in the liturgy and Rusyn dialect (often heavily mixed with Church Slavonicisms) for homilies, Orthodox publications (including the montly *Zapovit Kyril i Mefodija*, annual almanacs, and its first catechism, *Cesta k Bohu* [Bratislava, 1984]) are now primarily or exclusively in Slovak.

to accept Slovak schools and a Slovak identity are precisely those which remained Orthodox.

Thus, when all is said and done, the nationality question and problems of national identity that were ostensibly resolved in the Carpathian region just after World War II continue to be expressed consciously or unconsciously through the medium of religion. As in the past, so too in the present, Christianity and its temporal structures remain a shield for nationalist passions and, alas, national hatreds.

CHAPTER 4

The Rusyn Language Revisited[*]

I n 1929, a Rusyn satirist named Marko Barabolja wrote "a one-act dramatical work" that poked fun at the idea of an autonomous territory called Subcarpathian Rus'. This political entity was supposed to exist in the far eastern region of the former Czechoslovakia. One of the play's characters recalled that only recently writers in Subcarpathian Rus' had begun to create a literature. That, in turn, led to the question of what language should be used for this new literature.

"Those were the days," quipped Barabolja's character," when the language question [*jazykovyj vopros*] was the dominant issue, a time

---

[*] An early version of this essay, with greater emphasis on the period before 1945, was commissioned by a Yale University project on Slavic languages and published under the title, "The Language Question Among the Subcarpathian Rusyns" (see below, note 3). The Yale study also appeared under the same title in a booklet with illustrations (Fairview, N.J.: Carpatho-Rusyn Research Center, 1979; reprinted 1987) and in a translation into Vojvodinian Rusyn, "Pitanje jazika medzi podkarpatskima rusinami," *Tvorčosc*, X (Novi Sad, 1984), pp. 6-22.

The version that appears here was originally prepared for an international conference held in Bratislava, January 1995, in conjunction with the announcement of the codification of the Rusyn language in Slovakia. It was first published in the *International Journal of the Sociology of Language*, No. 120 (Berlin and New York, 1996), pp. 63-84; then in both English and in Slovak ("Rusínska jazyková otázka znova nastolená") in a volume of proceedings connected with the codification announcement: Paul Robert Magocsi, ed., *A New Slavic Language is Born: The Rusyn Literary Language of Slovakia/Zrodil sa nový slovanský jazyk: Rusínsky spisovný jazyk na Slovensku* (New York: Columbia University Press/East European Monographs, 1996, pp. 19-47 and 15-40.

86

moreover that was the most romantic in the history of Subcarpathia. Just imagine, everywhere in cities and villages, in reading rooms, theaters, government offices, and cafés, no matter where people were, everywhere they talked continually about the language question."[1] Six decades later, when the Revolution of 1989 unfolded throughout east-central Europe and the Soviet Union, it seemed as though nothing had changed. Once again, wherever Rusyns lived, they were talking about the language question. And they are still doing so today! This is because the Rusyn language question, like language questions past and present among all peoples, is intimately related to the issue of national identity. As Rusyns continue to wrestle with the problem of who they are, so too has the language question become a problem that once again has to be addressed and hopefully resolved.

Ever since the second half of the nineteenth century, Rusyn intellectual and political life has addressed and tried to resolve the following dilemma: are Rusyns part of the Russian nationality, or the Ukrainian nationality, or do they comprise a distinct Slavic nationality known as Rusyn or Carpatho-Rusyn?[2] Not surprisingly, the supporters of these orientations have argued that the appropriate literary language should be either Russian, or Ukrainian, or a distinct Rusyn language. This on-going and still unresolved debate is what constitutes the Rusyn language question.

There is a substantial literature dealing with the language question, or more precisely the development of a literary language among Rusyns before 1945, including monographic studies by Georgij Gerovskij, František Tichý, Mykola Štec', and Paul Robert Magocsi.[3] Considering

---

[1]Marko Barabolja, "Oj, stelysja ty, barvinku, na joho mohyli!," *Pčôlka*, no. 6 (Užhorod, 1929), p. 158—recently reprinted in Marko Barabolja, *Proekt avtonomiji: tvory* (Užhorod, 1991), pp. 27-31.

[2]For details, see Paul Robert Magocsi, *The Shaping of a National Identity: Subcarpathian Rus', 1848-1948* (Cambridge, Mass. and London, 1978).

[3]Georgij Gerovskij, "Jazyk Podkarpatské Rusi," in *Československá vlastivěda*, Vol. III (Prague, 1934), pp. 460-517; František Tichý, *Vývoj současného spisovného jazyka na Podkarpatské Rusi* (Prague, 1938); Mykola Štec', *Literaturna mova ukrajinciv Zakarpattja i Schidnoji Slovaččyny* (Bratislava, 1969); Paul R. Magocsi, "The Language Question Among the Subcarpathian Rusyns," in Riccardo Picchio and Harvey Goldblatt, eds., *Aspects of the Slavic Language Question*, Vol II: *East Slavic* (New Haven, Conn., 1984), pp. 49-64.

the existence of such studies and the space limitations allotted to this essay, only the main developments before 1945 will be touched on here. The era before 1945 may be subdivided into four stages or periods, each of which differed in terms of the kind of language or languages that were favored. Those periods are: (1) the seventeenth and early eighteenth centuries; (2) the late eighteenth century to 1848; (3) 1848 to 1918; and (4) 1919 to 1944.

One theme has prevailed throughout all the above periods as well as the era from 1945 to the present. That theme concerns *dignitas* or prestige. All linguists agree that Rusyns living on both sides of the Carpathian Mountains speak a series of dialects which, based on their phonetic, morphological, and lexical characteristics, belong to the family of East Slavic languages. There is also agreement that Rusyn dialects are distinguishable from other East Slavic dialects by the high number of loanwords and other borrowings from neighboring Polish, Slovak, Hungarian, and to a lesser degree Romanian.[4]

There is disagreement, however, as to the relationship of Rusyn dialects to other East Slavic languages. Most linguists classify them with Ukrainian; while a few consider them part of a common-Russian (*obščerusskij*) linguistic area that comprises together modern Russian, Belarusan, and Ukrainian. Regardless what classification scheme is adopted, there still remains what might be called a basic psycholinguistic problem. In essence, do or can Rusyn dialects have a sufficient degree of *dignitas* to serve as the basis of a distinct literary language? Or do they intrinsically lack prestige, leading to a situation where the linguistic medium for Rusyns has to be taken from an already existing norm, whether Russian, Ukrainian or some other language? The

---

[4]The literature on Rusyn dialects is very well developed. The standard work is by Ivan Pan'kevyč, *Ukrajins'ki hovory Pidkarpats'koji Rusy i sumežnych oblastej* (Prague, 1938). There are also multivolume linguistic atlases by Josyf Dzendzelivs'kyj, Zuzanna Hanudel', Vasyl' Latta, Petro Lyzanec', Zdzisław Stieber and unpublished dialectal dictionaries by Ivan Pan'kevyč and Mykola Hrycak. See Josyf Dzendzelivs'kyj, "Stan i problemy doslidžennja ukrajins'kych hovoriv Zakarpats'koji oblasti URSR ta Schidnoji Slovaččyny," in Mychajlo Ryčalka, ed., *Žovten' i ukrajins'ka kul'tura* (Prešov, 1968), pp. 255-291; and the bibliographies by Olena Pažur, *Bibliohrafija pro doslidžennja ukrajins'kych hovoriv Schidnoji Slovaččyny* (Prešov, 1972), and Vida Zeremski et al., *Bibliografija Rusnacoch u Jugoslaviji, 1918-1980*, Vol. II (Novi Sad, 1990), esp. pp. 178-198.

question of *dignitas*, then, has historically pervaded and is still present in any debate regarding the language question among the Rusyns.

The Rusyn language question before 1945

The earliest Rusyn-language texts that came into relatively widespread use date from the seventeenth century. This was a time when the Protestant Reformation was making its strongest impact in northeastern Hungary and neighboring Transylvania. Although conversion to Lutheranism or Calvinism did not have any serious impact among Rusyns, their own clerical leaders were influenced by the Reformation's emphasis on living languages as the best way to communicate with the masses. Thus, the first printed books for Rusyns, a *Cathechism* (1698) and *Primer* (1699) prepared under the auspices of the Greek Catholic Bishop Joseph de Camillis (1641-1706), were written in "a simple dialect in order to be understood by the people."[5] Despite criticism in certain quarters for not using the traditional liturgical language, Church Slavonic, most of the religious polemics and other writings from this earliest period were in Rusyn vernacular.

The next period, which begins in the second half of the eighteenth century, witnessed a reaction against the "vulgarization of the church language" that supposedly characterized the earliest writings in Rusyn.[6] This meant that Church Slavonic, which because of its association with the Divine Liturgy of the Eastern rite had the appropriate *dignitas*, became the preferred language in publications destined for Rusyns. Although it was a literary language used in sacred books and in other communication among clerics throughout the Eastern Christian (Orthodox and Greek Catholic) world, Church Slavonic never had a single standard. Its form depended on the skill of individual authors who, when they lacked knowledge of a given word, would often borrow from the ʼimmediate linguistic environment in which they lived. The resultant variants of Church Slavonic were known as recensions, and the recension of Church Slavonic that developed among the Rusyns

---

[5]From the introduction to Josif de Camillis, *Katechysys dlja naouky Ouhrorouskym ljudem* (Trnava, 1698), p. ii.

[6]The descriptive phrase quoted here is by Ivan Paňkevyč, "Zakarpats'kyj dialektnyj variant ukrajins'koji literaturnoji movy XVII - XVIII vv.," *Slavia*, XXVII, 2 (Prague, 1958), p. 181.

came to be known as Slaveno-Rusyn (*slaveno-ruskyj*).

When, under the impact of the Theresan and Josephine enlightenment, church-run elementary and secondary schools began in the 1770s to be established throughout the Austrian Empire, several teachers prepared grammars and other textbooks for instructional use. The first of these was a grammar by Arsenij Kocak (1737-1800) completed in the 1770s,[7] followed in the first half of the nineteenth century with grammars by Mychajlo Lučkaj (1789-1843) and Ivan Fogorašij (1786-1834) and by the widely-used primer of Ioan Kutka (1750-1812).[8] Both authors reflected well the era in which they lived, one in which the ideas of Pan-Slavism emphasized the cultural unity among all the Slavic peoples as the most desirable goal.[9] Lučkaj, in particular, regretted the trend among many Slavic peoples to create "their own languages." He feared this proliferation of languages would lead to their being "swallowed up by other [larger] languages."[10] Church Slavonic, therefore, should be promoted, because it was already understood by the educated elite among all the East Slavs and South Slavs. In this regard, Rusyns had a special role to play, since they were the living preservers of the "one language . . . Rusyn or Carpatho-Rusyn" [*unica Dialectus . . . Ruthenica, aut Karpato-ruskaja*], which had not yet been "corrupted" and was closest to Church Slavonic.[11] Lučkaj's grammar, then, which recorded Rusyn vernacular and pointed

---

[7]The manuscripts of Kocak's "Hrammatyka russkaja" (1772-1778) and "Škola ili učylyšče hramatyky ruskoj" were published for the first time with an extensive analytical introduction by the compiler, Josyf Dzendzelivs'kyj, in *Naukovyj zbirnyk Muzeju ukrajins'koji kul'tury u Svydnyku*, Vol. XV, tom 2 (Bratislava and Prešov, 1990), pp. 73-284.

[8]Michael Lutskay, *Grammatica Slavo-Ruthena* (Buda, 1830); Ivan Fogorossi, *Rus'ko ouhorska ili madjarska hrammatyka* (Vienna, 1833); [Ioan Kutka], *Bukvar' jazyka ruskaho* (Vienna, 1797), 4th ed. (1846). Lučkaj's grammar was reprinted in facsimile version and translated into Ukrainian by P. M. Lyzanec' and Ju. M. Sak: Mychajlo Lučkaj, *Hramatyka slov"jano-rus'ka* (Kiev, 1989). Kutka's primer was also printed in facsimile and with an afterword by István Udvari (Nyíregyháza, 1998).

[9]Lučkaj was well known throughout the Slavic world and was one of five figures singled out in a pantheon listed in Jan Kollár's renowned spic poem, *Slávy dcera* (1832), 4th ed. (Prague 1868), p. 249.

[10]Lutskay, *Grammatica*, p. vii.

[11]*Ibid.*, p. viii.

out how it differed only slightly from Church Slavonic, was to be the model for the Slavic world.

There were other Pan-Slavic sympathizers, however, such as L'udovít Štúr (1815-1856), who did not shirk from codifying distinct languages, in his case Slovak. When some of his countrymen urged Rusyns to use Slovak as their literary language, Štúr responded to them with a rhetorical formulation: "Who asks here that Rusyns should accept the Slovak language as their own? Why they have their own beautiful Rusyn [rusínsky] language."[12]

It was the call of Štúr and a few other Slovak activists that prompted a change of attitude toward language among Rusyn cultural activists, in particular Aleksander Duchnovyč (1803-1865), the most influential figure during the third period that began in 1848. Duchnovyč came to be known as the "national awakener of the Carpatho-Rusyns" (narodnyj buditel' karpatorossov), and he is still revered today as the most important of all Rusyn cultural figures past and present. Already on the eve of the revolution of 1848, Duchnovyč published a primer based entirely on the Rusyn dialects of his native Prešov Region in northeastern Slovakia.[13] He also wrote a wide body of poetry and edited the first literary almanacs, all in Rusyn vernacular.

But even Duchnovyč was unable to sustain full confidence in the Rusyn vernacular as an instrument of literary endeavour. As early as 1852, he asked: "Which German, Frenchman, or Englishman writes as the average person speaks? None! . . . We must liberate ourselves from the mistakes of peasant vulgarisms and not fall into the mire of peasant phraseology. . . ."[14] To escape from the Rusyn "mire," Duchnovyč like his predecessors turned to Church Slavonic, and then more often to Russian.[15] The pro-Russian or Russophile trend was even more

---

[12]Slovenskje národňje novini (Bratislava), March 6, 1846.

[13]A.D., Knyžycja čytalnaja dlja načynajuščych (Buda, 1847), 2nd ed. (1850), 3rd ed. (1852). Reprinted in Oleksandr Duchnovyč, Tvory, Vol. II (Bratislava and Prešov, 1967), pp. 97-271.

[14]Zorja halycka, V, 50 (L'viv, 1852), p. 498.

[15]In 1853, Duchnovyč published a grammar Sokraščennaja grammatika ruskago jazyka (Buda, 1853), reprinted in Duchnovyč, Tvory, Vol. II, pp. 321-371, whose language was russianized (according to some without his consent) by his countrymen Ivan Rakovs'kyj and a Russian Orthodox priest in Budapest, Vasilij Vojtkovskij.

pronounced in the writings of Duchnovyč's contemporaries and successors: whether in polemical tracts by the dynamic political activist, Adol'f Dobrjans'kyj (1817-1901), or in several grammars of the Russian language by Kyrylo Sabov (1838-1914), Ivan Rakovs'kyj (1815-1885), Evmenij Sabov (1859-1934), and in dictionaries by Aleksander Mytrak (1837-1913) and Emiljan Kubek (1859-1940).[16] These works set the Russian-language standard used in Rusyn schools, newspapers, and cultural life in general until nearly the end of the nineteenth century.

Rusyn cultural and language developments were not, of course, taking place in a vacuum. Late nineteenth-century Austria-Hungary, in particular its Hungarian authorities, were uneasy about the foreign policy goals of their neighbor to the east, the Russian Empire. Among Russia's goals was to support what tsarist officials and propagandists argued were the best interests of the Slavic peoples in Austria-Hungary. Promoting the Russian language (and the Orthodox religion) among the Rusyns was, therefore, favored by tsarist Russia but not by Hungary.

In response, the Hungarian government sponsored translations into the Rusyn vernacular of several textbooks for use in its state-run elementary schools.[17] The new Rusyn standard was formulated by Vasyl' Čopej (1856-1934), who in 1883 published the first dictionary using the Rusyn vernacular, specifically the lowland dialects of today's Transcarpathian region. Čopej stressed that the "Rusyn language is

---

[16]A. Iv . . . tsch [Adol'f Dobrjans'kyj], "Nomenclation der österreichisch-ungarischen Russen," *Parlamentär*, no. 7 (Vienna, 1885), and his "Ugro-russkoe narječie v nastojaščem i prošlom," in A. L. Petrov, *Materialy dlja istorii Ugorskoj Rusi* (Petrograd, 1905), pp. 186-188; Kirill Sabov, *Grammatika pis'mennago russkago jazyka* (Užhorod, 1865); János Rakovszky/Ioann Rakovskij, *Orosz nyelvtan/Russkaja grammatika* (Buda, 1867); Eumén Szabó/Evmenij Sabov, *Orosz nyelvtan és olvasókönyv/Russkaja grammatika i čitanka* (Užhorod, 1890); Aleksandr Mitrak/Sándor Mitrák, *Russko-mad'jarskij slovar'/Orosz magyar szótár* (Užhorod, 1881); Emil Kubek/Emilij Kubek, *Ó-szláv-, magyar-, ruthén, (orosz) német szótár/Staroslavjanskij-ougorskij-russkij-njemeckij slovar'* (Užhorod, 1906).

[17]These included a translation of the Hungarian-language primer and first-grade reader by Pál Göncze into Rusyn by Vasylij Čopej, *Rus'ka azbuka j pervonačal'na čytanka dlja pervoho kljasa narodnych škol* (Budapest, 1881); and another translation by Avhustyn Vološyn, *Azbuka j perva čytanka dlja pervoho klassa narodných škol na rus'kom jazŷcî* (Budapest, 1898), 2nd ed. (1913).

independent and in no way can be considered a dialect of Russian."[18] The trend toward use of the Rusyn vernacular for instruction in schools was continued during the first decade of the twentieth century in widely-used primers by Mychal Vrabel' (1866-1923) and Avhustyn Vološyn (1874-1945).[19]

The fourth stage in the evolution of the Rusyn language question began in 1919 under profoundly new political circumstances. The Austro-Hungarian Empire had fallen and Rusyns were living in several new countries. The vast majority (about 80 percent) that had lived in the far eastern portion northeastern Hungary found themselves in Czechoslovakia (three-quarters in the province of Subcarpathian Rus'/Transcarpathia and one-quarter in the Prešov Region of Slovakia). Rusyns living north of the mountains in the Lemko Region of former Austrian Galicia were incorporated into Poland. As for the small group (about 20,000) who lived in the Bačka and Srem regions of southern Hungary, they were joined to the province of Vojvodina in Yugoslavia. The language question among the Rusyns during this fourth period, 1919-1944, evolved differently in each of the three countries where they lived.

Within Czechoslovakia, the legal status of Rusyns and, therefore, the status of their language also varied. In Subcarpathian Rus', which was in theory a province with international guarantees for Rusyn autonomy, the "local language" was alongside Czech one of the two official "state" languages. In Slovakia, on the other hand, Rusyns were a national minority, whose language was guaranteed for use in schools only in those areas where they comprised more than twenty percent of the population.

In practice, the democratic nature of the new Czechoslovak republic provided an important incentive for instruction and publications in the

---

[18]Laslov Čopej/László Csopei, *Rus'ko madjarskyj slovar'/Rutén-magyar szótár* (Budapest, 1883), p. x. Čopej understood the "Rusyn or Little Rusyn language" (*rus'kyj abo maloruskyj jazŷk*) to comprise what in modern-day terms are Ukrainian, Belorusan, and the various East Slavic dialects south of the Carpathians. *Ibid.*, p. xxiii.

[19]M. V[rabel'], *Bukvar'* (Užhorod, 1898), 4th ed. (1910); Avhustyn Vološyn, *Azbuka uhro-rus'koho j cerkovno-slavjanskoho čtenija* (Užhorod, 1901), 4th ed. (1919); Ágoston Volosin, *Gyakorlati kisorosz (ruszin) nyelvtan* (Užhorod, 1907), 2nd ed. (1920).

"local language." The government did not for the most part interfere in the language debates.[20] As a result, the 1920s and 1930s were, as the satirist Barabolja pointed out, the decades when people everywhere "talked continually about the language question." While everyone agreed that the "local language" should be adopted for official and educational purposes, no one was certain what specifically was meant by the term. As in the past, the·issue of *dignitas* played a large part in determining which language should be used. Some felt that the local dialects should form the basis of a distinct Rusyn literary language that would evolve from the late nineteenth-century dictionary of Čopej and the primers and grammar of Vološyn, which went through several new editions and were widely used in Subcarpathian schools.[21]

Others, including newly-arrived émigrés from Polish-ruled eastern Galicia, felt that Rusyn was simply a dialect of Ukrainian, which should serve as the literary language. To introduce Ukrainian to the region in a gradual manner, the Galician-Ukrainian writer Volodymyr Birčak (1881-1952) compiled a series of readers for secondary schools,[22] and

---

[20]The Czechoslovak authorities consulted with academicians in Prague who: (1) advised against creating a new literary language for the Rusyns; (2) recognized Rusyn dialects as part of the Ukrainian language; yet (3) also argued that since Ukrainians "were part of the Great Russian people," Russian should be taught as well. See Magocsi, *Shaping of a National Identity*, pp. 136-138.

[21]Avgustyn Vološyn, *Azbuka karpato-rus'koho j cerkovno-slavjanskoho čtenija*, 7th ed. (Užhorod, 1924). His still heavily Russian-influenced *Metodičeskaja grammatika ugro-russkogo literaturnogo jazyka dlja narodných škol* (Užhorod, 1901) became the vernacular *Metodyčeska hrammatyka karpato-russkoho jazŷka* (1919) and, in its sixth edition, the *Metodyčna hramatyka rus'koho jazŷka dlja nyzšych klas narodných škol* (Užhorod, 1930). For upper levels he wrote the *Praktyčna hramatyka rus'koho jazyka*, 2nd ed. (Užhorod, 1928).

Among Vološyn's more popular readers in use during the interwar years were: *Čytanka dlja II. klassŷ narodných škol* (Užhorod, 1921); *Mala čytanka dlja II. y III. klasŷ narodných škol* (Užhorod, 1921), 4th rev. ed. (Prague and Prešov, 1937); *Čytanka dlja IV. y V. škôl'ných rokôv narodných škol* (Užhorod, 1932); *Čytanka dlja rus'koî molodeži dlja IV., V. y VI. klas narodných škol*, 3rd ed. (Užhorod, 1925); *Čytanka dlja rus'koî molody dlja VI-VIII. škôl'ných rokôv narodných škol*, 5th ed. (Užhorod, 1932).

[22] Volodymyr Byrčak, *Rus'ka čytanka dlja I. klasŷ gymnazijnoî y horožanskych škol* (Prague, 1922), 2nd ed. with title added *Vesna: rus'ka čytanka . . .* (Prague, 1925); *dlja II. klasŷ* (Prague, 1922); *dlja III. klasŷ* (Prague, 1923); *dlja IV. klasŷ*

linguist from Galicia, Ivan Pan'kevyč (1887-1958), prepared a grammar of the Rusyn language. Although written in the traditional etymological alphabet and using special symbols to depict vowel sounds unique to the Subcarpathian region, Pan'kevyč's grammar was based on the dialects of the high mountainous area (the Verchovyna), which were closest to the Ukrainian speech in Galicia.[23] By the late 1930s, other émigrés from Galicia in cooperation with local pro-Ukrainian Subcarpathian activists produced school texts that were in standard Ukrainian using the modern phonetic alphabet.[24]

The third trend was represented by the Russophiles. These included local activists who carried on the tradition of the nineteenth-century national awakener Duchnovyč, together with Russophile émigrés from Galicia who helped the "locals" write in correct Russian. The standard text for this orientation was a grammar published in 1924 under the editorship of a local priest, Evmenij Sabov (1859-1934), although it was written in large part by a Russian émigré from pre-war tsarist ruled Warsaw, Aleksandr Grigorjev (1874-1945). The "Sabov grammar" did not even pretend to reflect local Rusyn speech, since it contained "the Russian literary language in its written and not its spoken form."[25] The goal of this grammar was to help its users read local "Carpatho-Russian" authors (who until then wrote in a Russian language corrupted by local dialectisms) and, in particular, to enjoy "Puškin, Gogol', Lermontov, and other classics of Russian literature."[26] Like the Ukrainian

---

(Prague, 1924; 2nd ed., 1928).

[23]Yvan Pan'kevyč, *Hramatyka rus'koho jazŷka dlja molodšych klas škôl serednych j horožanskych* (Mukačevo, 1922), 3rd rev. ed. (Prague, 1936).

Several local authors using the language of Pan'kevyč prepared introductory texts for elementary schools: E. Egreckyj, M. Huljanyč, and A. Markuš, *Podkarpatorus'kyj bukvar'* (Užhorod, 1923); A. Markuš, S. Boček, and N. Šutka, *Rôdne slovo: učebnyk rus'koho jazŷka dlja narodnŷch škol* (Užhorod, 1923); Aleksander Markuš and Julijan Revaj, *Bukvar': čytajte y pyšît'* (Prague, 1931; 2nd ed., 1937).

[24]A. Štefan and I. Vasko, *Hramatyka ukrajins'koji movy* (Mukačevo, 1931); Jaroslav Nevrli, *Hramatyka j pravopys ukrajins'koji movy* (Užhorod, 1937); Franc Ahij, *Žyva mova* (Užhorod, 1938).

[25]Evm. Iv. Sabov, ed., *Grammatika russkago jazyka dlja serednich učebnych zavedenij Podkarpatskoj Rusi* (Užhorod, 1924), p. 1.

[26]*Ibid*, p. 5.

orientation, the Russian orientation also had other primers and grammars.[27] Each of the three orientations had its own cultural organizations, newspapers, journals, writers of poetry, prose, and drama, and of course polemicists to defend the various language orientations. The school system in Subcarpathian Rus' used all three languages—Rusyn, Ukrainian, Russian—as symbolized by the grammars of Vološyn, Pan'kevyč, and Sabov.

In neighboring Slovakia during the interwar years, the situation was somewhat simpler. For all intents and purposes, a Ukrainian orientation did not exist. Most secular and religious activists spoke of the desirability of maintaining their local "Carpatho-Rusyn traditions." These traditions included use of a language that, in practice, was not Rusyn vernacular but rather Russian with a varying number of local dialectisms. Already in 1920-1921, the Greek Catholic school system published a primer and a heavily-dialectal reader by Ivan Kyzak (1856-1929) and a grammar of Russian by Aleksander Sedlak (1862-1927).[28]

In Poland as in Czechoslovakia, the language question among the Lemkos (the local name for Rusyns) was closely linked to the policy adopted by the central goverment in Warsaw for minority schools. For most of the 1920s, the textbooks used in the Lemko Region were either in Ukrainian or in Russian, which reflected the language dichotomy that prevailed in Galicia while it had been part of the Austro-Hungarian Empire. [29]In the early 1930s, however, the Polish government and the

[27]M. Iv. Vasilenkov, *Naša rječ: metodičeskaja grammatika dlja russkich narodnych škol Podk. Rusi* (Mukačevo, 1925); I. Doboš and P. Fedor, *Karpatorusskij bukvar'* (Užhorod, 1925), 3rd rev. ed. (1930); P. Fedor and M. Vasilenko, *Svět: kniga dlja čtenija dlja 2-3. škol'nych godov*, 2nd rev. ed. (Mukačevo, 1931); Michail Mikita, *Kniga dlja čtenija dlja 4-5. škol'nych godov*, 4th ed. (Mukačevo, 1932); Michail Mikita and Vasilij Popovič, *Rodina: kniga dlja čtenija VI-VIII. škol'nych godov* (Mukačevo, 1931).

[28]Ioann F. Kizak, *Bukvar' dlja narodnych škol eparchiji Prjaševskoj* (Prague and Prešov, 1921); Ioann Kyzak, *Čytanka dlja narodných škol* (Prešov, 1920); Aleksandr Iv. Sedlak, *Grammatika russkago jazyka dlja narodnych škol eparchii Prjaševskoi* (Prešov, 1920).

[29]For details, see Paul R. Magocsi, "The Language Question in Nineteenth-Century Galicia," in Riccardo Picchio and Harvey Goldblatt, eds. *Aspects of the Slavic Language Question*, Vol. II: *East Slavic* (New Haven, Conn., 1984), pp. 49-

local Greek Catholic Church administration (the Lemko Apostolic Administration) favored instruction in Lemko-Rusyn vernacular. A primer and reader attributed to a local teacher Meletij Trochanovs'kyj were published, and by the end of the 1930s these texts were used in most Rusyn schools in the Lemko Region, which eventually became Polish schools with some instruction in Lemko Rusyn.[30]

The situation among the small Rusyn minority in the Bačka that after World War I became part of Yugoslavia was yet again different. There the local intelligentsia adopted the vernacular principle and developed a literary standard based on the local speech of the inhabitants. That speech was substantially different from Rusyn as spoken in the Carpathian homeland and, instead, was a transitional dialect very close to eastern Slovak dialects, in particular those of the central and southern Zemplín region. While scholars argued about whether the Bačka-Rusyn speech should be classified with a West Slavic (Slovak) or East Slavic (Rusyn/Ukrainian) language, the speakers themselves called their language Rusyn (*ruskij jazik*) and identified themselves as Rusnaks (*rusnaci*).[31]

The formation of a Bačka-Rusyn standard is intimately tied to the work of one person, Gabor Kostel'nik (1886-1948), who published his first book of poetry in 1904 and then a grammar in 1923. Kostel'nik was of the pro-Ukrainian orientation, and he actually wrote his grammar in the local vernacular as only the first step that would eventually "open the road to a Rusyn-Ukrainian literary language."[32] Despite his hopes, there were to be no publications or school instruction in Ukrainian for the Rusyns of the Vojvodina (Bačka).

There was also a language question among Rusyns in the United

---

64.

[30]*Bukvar: perša knyžečka dlja narodných škol* (L'viv, 1935). A reader was included in the above book. Ukrainophile Lemkos also produced a reader that was used in a few schools during the interwar period: *Perša lemkivs'ka čytanka* (L'viv, 1934).

[31]The debate about classifying the speech of the Bačka/Vojvodinian Rusyns was carried out before World War I between the Galician-Ukrainian ethnographer, Volodymyr Hnatjuk, and the Slovak philologist, František Pastrnek.

[32]Gabor Kostel'nik, *Hramatika bačvan'sko-ruskej bešedi* (Sremski Karlovci, 1923), p. 2. This grammar was reprinted in Havrijil Kostel'nik, *Proza* (Novi Sad, 1975), pp. 207-312.

States, where before World War I an estimated 225,000 had immigrated. In the New World, the immigrants published several newspapers, books, and other works, and they established a school system connected with their Greek Catholic and Orthodox churches in order to pass on to children knowledge of their Rusyn heritage. Aside from importing school texts from the European homeland (the primers and readers of Vološyn were especially popular), Rusyn Americans published a series of their own language books for use in schools and as a normative guide for their publications.

These books can be classified into three linguistic orientations. Those approved for use by the Greek Catholic Church basically used the "traditional Carpatho-Rusyn language" of the late nineteenth century, in which authors tried to write in Russian while including a large number of Rusyn and Church Slavonic words. This "American Rusyn" language was best represented in a grammar and reader by Joseph P. Hanulya (1874-1962) and in a few other elementary primers.[33] The second orientation, used almost exclusively in Orthodox publications and schools, was standard Russian.[34] During this period, only the Lemko-Rusyn immigrant Dmitrij Vislockyj (1888-1968) produced a textbook written exclusively in the Rusyn vernacular.[35]

The fourth stage came to a close during World War II, when the Rusyn language question took a new turn, most especially in Subcarpathian Rus'. In March 1939, Hungary drove out the short-lived autonomous Carpatho-Ukrainian government (which had ruled since November 1938) and annexed the former Czechoslovak province which

---

[33]Iosif Hanulja, *Grammatika dlja amerikanskich rusinov* (McKeesport, Pa., 1918); Iosif P. Hanulja, *Čitanka dlja amerikanskoj rus'koj molodeži* (McKeesport, Pa., 1919; 2nd ed., 1935); Petr Iv. Mackov, *Novyj bukvar' dlja greko-kaftoličeskich russkich dětej* (Homestead, Pa., 1921).

[34]Ivan G. Boruch, *Rodnaja rěč': vtoraja kniga dlja čtenija i besěd ustnych i pis'mennych upraženij v školě i v sem'ě* (New York, 1916); Stepan F. Telep, *Russkij bukvar' dlja cerkovno-prichodskich škol v Sěvernoj Amerikě* (Mayfield, Pa., 1937; 2nd ed., 1938); V. Ternavcev, *Naša škola: bukvar' i pervoe čtenie* (New York, 1938); Stepan F. Telep, *Praktičeskij područnik grammatiki dlja cerkovno-prichodskich škol v Sěvernoj Amerikě* (Mayfield, Pa., 1940); Ioann Gr. Dzvončik, *Pervaja russko-angliiskaja kniga dlja čtenija* (Philadelphia, Pa. 1943).

[35] Van'o Hunjanka [Dmitrij Vislockyj], *Karpatorusskij bukvar'* (Cleveland, Ohio, 1931).

it renamed simply Subcarpathia (Kárpátalja). Although Hungarian authorities allowed the Russian orientation to function, they forbade the use of Ukrainian. Officially, it returned to the so-called Uhro-Rusyn orientation, which a short-lived Hungarian democratic regime had introduced in Subcarpathian Rus' in early 1919. At that time, the Hungarian authorities acted quickly to publish a reader and an anthology of literature and to set up a Department (*Katedra*) of Rusyn Language and Literature at the University of Budapest which began to function in 1919-1920.[36] With the return of Hungarian rule in 1939, Uhro-Rusynism meant, as well, a return to local traditions that would be neither Russian nor Ukrainian.

The first step in that direction was the publication of five readers for elementary schools,[37] and a grammar for secondary schools by a local Greek Catholic priest and official in the Hungarian Ministry of Education, Julij Maryna (1901-1983). The language was quite similar to that used in the late nineteenth century, that is, Russian with a heavy influence of local Rusyn dialectisms.[38] More influential was the language adopted by the newly-founded Subcarpathian Academy of Sciences in its publications, including a Rusyn grammar by Ivan Harajda (1905-1945). Harajda hoped to find a "true compromise" that would reflect Rusyn vernacular speech as well as incorporate certain words that supposedly had become accepted—and expected—as part of the traditional "Carpatho-Rusyn language." Many, however, appeared to be borrowings from Russian (*dovol'no, tol'ko, prosviščatysja*, etc).[39]

---

[36]Jador [Stryps'kyj], *Čytanka dlja doroslych* (Mukačevo, 1919) and O. Rachivs'kyj [Aleksander Bonkalo], *Vyimky yz uhors'ko-rus'koho pys'menstva XVII-XVIII vv.* (Budapest, 1919). On the Department of Rusyn Language and Literature at the University of Budapest, see the brief biography of its holder in Alexander Bonkáló, *The Rusyns* (New York, 1990), p. xiii-xiv. Also at this time a dictionary of Rusyn verbs was prepared by Tonij Romanuv [Antal Hodinka], *Hlaholycja: sbyrka vsîch hlaholov pudkarpats'ko-rusyns'koho jazŷka* (1922), although it only recently appeared as: Antal Hodinka, *Ruszin-magyar igetár*, compiled by István Udvari (Nyíregyháza, 1991).

[37]*Pervyj/Drugij/Tretij/Četvertyj/Pjatyj cvět dětskoj mudrosti dlja I./II./III-IV./V-VI./VII-VIII. klassa narodnoj školy* (Užhorod, 1939).

[38]Julij Marina, *Grammatika ugrorusskogo jazyka dlja serednich učebnych zavedenij* (Užhorod, 1940).

[39]Yvan Harajda, *Hrammatyka rus'koho jazŷka* (Užhorod, 1941).

Thus, the era before 1945 ended without any solution to the language question. Wherever Rusyns lived, they used either Russian, Ukrainian, or the local Rusyn vernacular in their schools and publications. Moreover, polemics between defenders of the three orientations reached a new intensity in the first half of the twentieth century and no consensus seemed in sight.[40] All was to change, however, with the establishment after 1945 of a new political order throughout the Rusyn homeland.

Ukrainianization and the "end" to the language question

In late 1944, the Soviet Army 'liberated' Subcarpathian Rus' from Hungarian control. Although the Soviets initially agreed with the other Allied Powers to restore the province to postwar Czechoslovakia, Stalin changed his mind. Consequently, the political wing of the Soviet Army was ordered to give support to local Subcarpathian Communists, who in turn arranged in November 1944 for the populace to request unification with the "Ukrainian motherland." In June 1945, Czechoslovakia formally ceded to the Soviet Union the province of Subcarpathian Rus', which became the Transcarpathian oblast of the Soviet Ukraine.

As early as 1924, the Fifth Congress of the Comintern had addressed the identity question in western Ukrainian lands. Regardless which "foreign occupier" might still be ruling those lands and regardless what the people themselves may have thought, the Rusyns were declared to be a branch of the Ukrainian nationality. The Fifth Comintern's decision was reiterated one year later by the Communist party (Bolshevik) of Ukraine and accepted by the Subcarpathian Communist party in 1926 with a resolution that in part read: "It is obvious that we

---

[40]Among the numerous polemical works from this period are: Avhustyn Vološyn, *O pys'mennom jazŷcî podkarpatskych rusynov* (Užhorod, 1921); Igor Iv. Gus'naj, *Jazykovyj vopros v Podkarpatskoj Rusi* (Prešov, 1921); Evm. I. Sabov, *Russkij literaturnyj jazyk Podkarpatskoj Rusi i novaja grammatika russkago jazyka* (Mukačevo, 1925); N. Zorkij, *Spor o jazykě v Podkarpatskoj Rusi i češskaja Akademija Nauk/Kak osvědomljaet d-r Ivan Pan'kevič češskuju publiku o našich jazykovych djělach* (Užhorod, 1926); *Za ridne slovo!: polemika z rusofilamy* (Mukačevo and Užhorod, 1937); G. I. Gerovskij and V. Krajnjanica, eds., *Razbor grammatiki ugrorusskogo jazyka* (Užhorod, 1941); Aleksander Bonkalo, "Rus'kyj lyteraturnŷj jazŷk," *Zorja/Hajnal*, I, 1-2 (Užhorod, 1941), pp. 54-71.

are part of the Ukrainian people. . . . and finally we will end . . . all 'language questions' [and dispense] with the names 'Rusyn', *'rus'kyj'*, or *'russkij'*."[41]

It took nearly two more decades before the 1924-1926 decisions could be implemented by the new Soviet authorities in Transcarpathia. By late 1944, all schools for the indigenous East Slavic population taught in literary Ukrainian according to Soviet norms, and Ukrainian was in theory considered the titular language of the country to be used in the local administration. In actual practice, however, the Russian language was taught as a subject in all schools; it became the dominant language at the newly-founded Užhorod State University; and it served as the operative language in most official and public transactions. This meant that both the Ukrainian- and Russian-language orientations from the pre-1945 era were in large measure satisfied—or equally dissatisfied—with Soviet policy.

Only the Rusyn orientation was banned. The very name *Rusyn* was associated with the "unenlightened" pre-Soviet past and was linked in Soviet propaganda with the bourgeois Czechoslovak and fascist Hungarian regimes that had occupied the province, as well as with the "reactionary" Greek Catholic Church which in 1949 was abolished entirely. From 1945 until nearly the very end of Soviet rule in 1991, not a single publication in Rusyn vernacular appeared in Transcarpathia. Even the language of published local folk songs and tales was ukrainianized as were the few reprints of pre-Soviet Transcarpathian literature.

Soviet policy regarding the national and linguistic identity of the Rusyns was also implemented in neighboring countries that came under Communist rule, first Poland and then Czechoslovakia. The language situation among the Lemko Rusyns was in a sense simplified by the fact that they were all deported from their Carpathian homeland—first "voluntarily" in 1945, then the remainder forcibly in 1947. Two-thirds were resettled in the Soviet Ukraine, those who remained behind (40,000-50,000) were forcibly resettled in Poland's "recovered" western (formerly German) territories, most especially Silesia. The Lemkos who were resettled in Poland's "West" were considered by the government to be part of the country's Ukrainian minority.

---

[41]*Karpats'ka pravda* (Užhorod), December 5, 1926.

When, after 1956, Poland allowed the creation of organizations and publications for some of its national minorities, the Lemkos also hoped to have their own organizations. This was not permitted, however, although a Lemko branch of the government-funded Ukrainian cultural society existed for awhile and a Lemko dialect page (*"lemkivska storona"*) appeared in that organization's weekly newspaper. Since the Lemkos scattered throughout the country were living in a Polish environment, many enroled their children in Polish-language schools. When in certain communities Lemkos had the possibility to attend minority language schools or classes, they were given instruction in Ukrainian.

In Czechoslovakia, specifically the Prešov Region of northeastern Slovakia, the situation was even more complex. The Communists did not come to power until 1948, and it was to be another four years until the language question was "resolved." From 1945 until 1952, the situation was truly paradoxical. All of the group's cultural and political organizations were called *Ukrainian*, yet in actual fact the language of their publications, theatrical performances, and instruction in schools was Russian. This approach responded to the interwar tradition in eastern Slovakia that was continued during World War II, whereby instruction at the very elementary levels was in Rusyn vernacular but at the higher and *gymnasium* levels in Russian. New Russian-language textbooks were published and some teachers were imported from the Soviet Union for instruction throughout the 275 elementary and nearly 50 higher-level schools (1948/1949) throughout the Prešov Region.[42]

In 1950, the Czechoslovak Communist government, following the Soviet model, abolished the Greek Catholic Church throughout the country and took over control of the school system. Then, in June 1952, the nationality and language policy was abruptly changed. Russian-language instruction in all schools was replaced with Ukrainian, and a new "cultural organization of Ukrainian workers" was established to promote publications and other cultural activity that followed Soviet

---

[42]Among the textbooks in use were: Aleksandr Ljubimov, *Načal'naja grammatika dlja 6-8 goda obučenija narodnych škol* (Prešov, 1944); Ivan Vanca, *Novyj bukvar' dlja l-ogo goda russkich narodnych škol* (Prešov, 1945); and M.M. Lichvar, *Naša reč': kniga dlja čtenija dlja 2-go i 3-go godov obučenija načal'noj školy* (Prešov, 1947).

Ukrainian linguistic and ideological models.

Initially, language guidelines were provided by a brief guide to Ukrainian orthography for specific use in former Prešov Region Russian-language schools.[43] But this gradualist approach was almost immediately replaced by the importation of textbooks from the Soviet Ukraine, and the adoption of literary Ukrainian without any consideration for local Rusyn conditions. This policy was also adopted by the Department (Katedra) of Ukrainian Language and Literature which was established in September 1953 at Šafárik University in Prešov to train teachers for service in the new Ukrainian-language school system.

As a result of such short-sighted linguistic practices and the abrupt bureaucratic manner in which Ukrainian was introduced—all carried out during the height of Stalinist repression—the Rusyn populace reacted by sending their children to Slovak schools in neighboring towns or by demanding Slovak instead of Ukrainian schools in their villages. This process of voluntary slovakization spread rapidly during the 1960s. If in 1948, when the Communists, had come to power, there were 322 Rusyn (actually Russian-language) schools with over 23,000 pupils, when Communist rule disappeared in late 1989 there were only 15 schools left with just 900 pupils, in which a few subjects were taught in Ukrainian.[44] Thus, the Rusyn language question in Slovakia was "resolved" as in Soviet Transcarpathia by the adoption of Ukrainian. The cost, however, was a two-third's decline in the number of Rusyns who willingly assimilated and adopted a Slovak national identity.

The situation among the Rusyn minority in Yugoslavia's Vojvodina was entirely different. There the Rusyn nationality and the Rusyn language were officially recognized. In fact, by 1974, Rusyn became one of the five official languages of the autonomous province of the

[43]*Korotki pravyla ukrajins'koho pravopysu dlja vžytku Prjašivščyny* (Prešov, 1952). This work was actually written by the distinguished linguist and pedagogue, Ivan Pan'kevyč, who worked in interwar Subcarpathian Rus' and then moved to Prague during the war. Because the Communists suspected Pan'kevyč of being a Ukrainian bourgeois nationalist, the guidebook was simply signed by the "research staff" of the Cultural Union of Ukrainian Workers.

[44]Ivan Vanat, Mychajlo Ryčalka, and Andrij Čuma, *Do pytan' pisljavojennoho rozvytku, sučasnoho stanu ta perspektyv ukrajins'koho škil'nyctva v Slovaččyni* (Prešov, 1992).

Vojvodina. With liberal funding from the Communist (but non-Soviet dominated) Yugoslav government, a Rusyn-language publishing house, press, elementary and secondary school system, and radio and television programming came into being. A series of school grammars, a codification of grammatical norms, and a terminological dictionary were prepared by Mikola Kočiš (1928-1973).[45] In order to enhance further knowledge and use of the Bačka-Srem or Vojvodinian variant of Rusyn, in 1973 a professorship and by 1981 a Department (Katedra) of Rusyn a Language and Literature was established at the University of Novi Sad, and in the early 1970s a Society for Rusyn Language and Literature came into being. While some Rusyn cultural activists in Yugoslavia believed that their people were part of the Ukrainian nationality, they never switched to the Ukrainian language, but continued to publish, teach, and develop further what scholars in other parts of the world were, by the 1980s, describing as a sociologically complete distinct "Slavic micro-language."[46]

Like the Rusyns in Yugoslavia, Rusyns in the United States also began after World War II to prepare grammars, phrasebooks, and even dictionaries that used a vernacular-based Rusyn language instead of the variants of Russian that were popular in the 1920s and 1930s. Some of these new texts used the Latin alphabet, which made understanding easier for American-born students who otherwise spoke and were educated primarily in English.[47]

---

[45]Mikola M. Kočiš, *Macerinska bešeda: gramatika za V-VI, VII i VIII klasu osnovnej školi* [3 pts.] (Novi Sad, 1965-68), 2nd ed.: *Gramatika ruskoho jazika za V i VI klasu osnovnej školi* (Novi Sad, 1974-77); Mikola M. Kočiš, *Priručni terminološki rečnik srpskochrvatsko-rusinsko-ukrajinski* (Novi Sad, 1972); Mikola Kočiš, *Pravopis ruskoho jazika* (Novi Sad, 1971).

[46]The term was popularized by A. D. Duličenko, *Slavjanskie literaturnye mikrojazyki* (Tallin, 1981), who considers Vojvodinian Rusyn one of the twelve micro-languages within the Slavic world. By the late 1970s, the Vojvodinian-Rusyn language phenomenon had captured the attention of Slavic linguists worldwide, including Henrik Birnbaum (United States), Aleksander Duličenko (Estonia), Sven Gustavsson (Sweden), Horace Lunt (United States), and Jiří Marvan (Australia), among others.

[47]John Slivka, *English-Rusin Dictionary* (Brooklyn, N.Y., 1973—unpublished) and his *Rusin-English Dictionary* (Brooklyn, N.Y., 1973—unpublished); Atanasij Pekar', *Lekciî z rus'koho jazŷka/Lessons in Ruthenian* (Pittsburgh, Pa., 1975—unpublished); Paul R. Magocsi, *Let's Speak Rusyn/Bisidujme po-rus'kŷ:*

The return of the Rusyn language question

The political changes that began in the Soviet Union during the late 1980s and that culminated in the Revolution of 1989 had a profound impact on all countries where Rusyns lived. The Communist regimes that for four decades had determined nationality and language policies collapsed, as did most of the countries where Rusyns lived. In December 1991, those living in Soviet Transcarpathia found themselves in an independent Ukraine. By mid-1992, the Rusyn community in Yugoslavia was divided between two countries, with the Vojvodina remaining in a reduced Yugoslavia (Serbia-Montenegro) and the Srem becoming a war-torn zone that was theoretically part of an independent Croatia. Finally, in January 1993, Rusyns in the Prešov Region were living in an independent Slovakia.

The profound changes in state structures and political systems that took place between 1989 and 1992 underscored what many had for some time suspected. Despite its propandistic statements, the Communist regimes repressed but did not resolve certain social problems. Among those problems was the question of national identity and language among Rusyns. On the eve of 1989, several cultural activists began to express their dissatisfaction with the Ukrainian-language orientation and argued the case for publications in Rusyn vernacular. In Poland, a few collections of poetry were published in the Lemko variant of Rusyn, and at the outset of 1989 a Rusyn-language magazine (*Besida*) began to appear. Meanwhile, in the Prešov Region of what was still Communist Czechoslovakia, a small circle of Greek Catholic activists led by Father František Krajnjak (b. 1957), prepared for publication several church manuals in the local Rusyn dialect (the area around the town of Medzilaborce).[48] The goal was to propagate the faith, especially to young people, in a language that they could most easily understand.

Prešov Region Edition (Englewood, N.J., 1976; 3rd ed., 1989); and Paul R. Magocsi, *Let's Speak Rusyn/Hovorim po-rus'kŷ: Transcarpathian Edition* (Fairview, N.J., 1979).

[48]In the late 1980s, Krajnjak actually set up a small "language commission" to help with his work. Of the half a dozen religious texts he prepared, to date only one has been published in parallel Cyrillic- and Latin-alphabet Rusyn texts: František Krajnjak, *Malŷj grekokatolyc'kŷj katechizm pro rusyns'kŷ dity* (Prešov, 1992).

These tentative first steps to publish in the Rusyn vernacular were transformed by the political changes that took place in late 1989 and 1990. In all countries where Rusyns lived, new Rusyn cultural organizations were established, and each one was based on the principle that Rusyns comprise a distinct nationality and should have their own literary language. Several of the organizations also began to publish a newspaper or magazine in the˙Rusyn vernacular. These included in Ukraine: *Otčij chram* (Užhorod, 1990-91) and *Podkarpats'ka Rus'* (Užhorod, 1992-present) of the Society of Carpatho-Rusyns (Tovarystvo/Obščestvo Karpats'kych Rusynov); in Slovakia: *Rusyn* (Medzilaborce and Prešov, 1990-present) and *Narodnŷ novynkŷ* (Prešov, 1991-present) of the Rusyn Renaissance Society (Rusyns'ka Obroda); and in Poland: *Besida* (Krynica, 1989-present) of the Society of Lemkos (Stovaryšŷnja Lemkiv). Also, the professional Ukrainian National Theater in Prešov, Slovakia, which since the early 1950s performed in Ukrainian, changed its name in late 1990 to the Aleksander Duchnovyč Theater and since then has been presenting most of its plays in Rusyn.

The rebirth of a Rusyn national and language orientation came as a surprise to the Ukrainian cultural, educational, and publishing institutions. Their spokespersons—many of whom were before 1952 advocates of a Russian orientation—thought that the nationality and language question had been resolved, whether by Communist-inspired administrative decree or as a result of the 'natural' evolution of history. The first reaction of the Ukrainianists was to poke fun at the initial efforts of the pro-Rusyn activists and their amateur-like proclamations that large-scale dictionaries and a codified Rusyn literary standard were about to appear imminently.[49] When, however, the rhetoric was replaced by concrete publications and linguistic work, and it became evident the Rusyn orientation was not about to disappear, Ukrainians argued that Rusynism was little more than a politically-inspired 'anti-historical' and 'anti-scholarly' aberration provoked by elements who wished to undermine Ukraine and to assimilate further "Rusyn-Ukrainians" living abroad in Slovakia and Poland.

[49]For such claims, see the Rusyn enthusiast from Transcarpathia, Volodymyr Fedynyšynec', *Myrna naša rusyns'ka put'* (Prešov, 1992), esp. pp. 24-28; and the critical Ukrainian reaction by Mykola Myšynka, *Rusynizm na antyukrajins'kij osnovi: perša knyžka 'Rusyns'koji obrody'* (Prešov, 1992).

Thus, by the early 1990s there was a full-fledged return to the polemics about language and national identity that had characterized the interwar years.[50] There were attacks, for instance, about the very idea of a magazine called *Rusyn* before it even appeared. Ukrainian polemicists and scholars were convinced that "from the standpoint of philology, there is simply no reason to create a so-called Rusyn literary language."[51]

Aside from polemics, the Ukrainian orientation faced its own problems, especially in Poland and Slovakia where at best Ukrainian has the status of a minority language. In Slovakia, for instance, Ukrainian spokespersons agreed with their Rusyn critics that the manner in which the Ukrainian language was administratively implemented in the early 1950s had a negative impact on its reception. In an attempt to reverse the perception among many local Rusyns that Ukrainian was a foreign language, there were calls after 1989 to bring Ukrainian closer to its potential users by adding more local dialectal words. Also, to emphasize the Ukrainian argument that the name *Rusyn* is just an older form for *Ukrainian*, a new hybrid term, *Rusyn-Ukrainian*, was adopted to describe the East Slavs in the Carpathians.[52] As recently as 1994, the head of the Union of Rusyn-Ukrainians in Slovakia proclaimed that "our organization has used and will continue to use the contemporary Ukrainian literary language with a highly democratic [sic] infusion of regional dialects."[53] In actual fact, however, Ukrainian publications and radio broadcasts in Slovakia, Ukraine, and for the most part in Poland avoid any local dialectisms.

Meanwhile, the Rusyn orientation has argued that the Ukrainian

---

[50]Among the numerious polemical pamphlets by Ukrainians, all fiercely critical of the Rusyn movement are: Jurij Baleha and Josyf Sirka, *Chto my je i čyji my dity?* (Kiev, 1991); Mykola Mušynka, *Polityčnyj rusynizm na praktyci* (Prešov, 1991); Oleksa Myšanyč, '*Karpatorusynstvo': joho džerela j evoljucija u XX st.* (Kiev, 1992); Stepan Hostynjak, *Pro četvertyj schidnoslov"jans'kyj narod ta pro plačeni vyhadky j nisenitnyci kupky komediantiv* (Prešov, 1992); and Ivan Vanat, *Do pytannja pro tak zvanu ukrajinizaciju rusyniv Prjašivščyny* (Prešov, 1993).

[51]Mikuláš Štec, *K otázke 'rusínskeho' spisovného jazyka* (Prešov, 1991), p. 22.

[52]The justification for the hyphenated name is found in Mikuláš Štec, *Rusíni či Ukrajinci* (Prešov, 1992).

[53]Viktor Koval', "Zvit Rady Sojuzu rusyniv-ukrajinciv Slovac'koji respubliky," *Nove žyttja* (Prešov), January 3, 1994, p. 2.

language and nationality policy during the four decades of Communist rule has led to large-scale assimilation in Poland and Slovakia and to the degradation (some even speak of "genocide") of traditional Rusyn life and culture in Ukraine. In an attempt to reverse this process and to restore a sense of Rusyn identity, one of the movement's primary goals is the codification of a standard Rusyn literary language. Aside from the newspapers and magazines mentioned above and a few Rusyn books that have appeared in Slovakia, Poland, and even Hungary, there have been several attempts at creating a Rusyn literary standard. All have appeared since 1992 and include: in Ukraine—a grammar by Ihor Kerča and Vasyl' Sočka-Boržavyn, and a poetic guide to dialectal words by Ivan Petrovcij[54]; in Slovakia—an orthographic rule book and terminological dictionary by Vasyl' Jabur and Jurij Pan'ko, and a primer and reader by Jan Hryb[55]; and in Poland—two grammars by Myroslava Chomjak, and a 9,000-word Lemko-Polish dictionary by Jaroslav Horoščak.[56]

These burgeoning efforts on the part of a Rusyn literary language which have occurred in three different countries began as the relatively isolated creative acts of individual authors. The result was the development of almost as many different standards as there were authors, compilers, and editors. In an attempt to put some order and coordination into these efforts, a working seminar on the Rusyn language was convened in Bardejovské Kúpele, Slovakia on November 6-7, 1992. Rusyn writers and editors from Ukraine, Poland, Slovakia, Yugoslavia, and Hungary joined with scholars from those countries and from the United States, Sweden, Switzerland, and Monaco to discuss: (1) theoretical issues concerning language-building, especially among "small" peoples; (2) and practical ways in which the Rusyn codifiers can coordinate their efforts.

The results of the November 1992 seminar, which has come to be

---

[54]Y. Kerča and V. Sočka-Boržavyn, *Rusyn'skŷj jazŷk: očerk kompleksnoji praktyčnoji gramatykŷ* (unpublished typescript, 1992); Ivan Petrovcij, *Dialektarij, abož myla knyžočka rusyns'koji bysidŷ u viršach* (Užhorod, 1993).

[55]See below, notes 58 and 59.

[56]Myroslava Chomjak, *Gramatŷka lemkivskoho jazŷka* (Legnica, 1992) and *Lemkivska gramatŷka dlja dity* (Legnica, 1992); Jaroslav Horoščak, *Peršyj lemkivsko-pol'skij slovnyk/Pierwszy słownik łemkowsko-polski* (Legnica, 1993).

known as the First Congress of the Rusyn Language, were as follows. The participants accepted the "Romansch model," that is to allow the development of four standards based on dialects in the countries where Rusyn live: Ukraine, Poland, Slovakia, and Yugoslavia. One standard, Vojvodinian Rusyn in Yugoslavia, already exists; the three others for Transcarpathia, the Lemko Region, and the Prešov Region need to be codified. The participants also agreed to meet periodically to exchange views on their own codifying work as well as to agree on as many principles as possible that will form the basis of an eventual "fifth" Rusyn literary standard, or *koiné* that would be common to all regions. Regardless of which standard is formed, it was decided that Rusyn should appear in the Cyrillic alphabet and be based on the "living spoken language in each of the regions where Rusyns live (Subcarpathia, Lemko Region, Prešov Region, Vojvodina)."[57]

The First Congress of the Rusyn Language also proposed the creation of "a theoretical and applied language institute," which two months later actually came into being in Prešov, Slovakia. The newly-formed Institute of Rusyn Language and Culture has, since its establishment in January 1993, served as a coordinating center for the work of Rusyn language codifiers in all countries where they live. Its first director, Jurij Pan'ko, published a preliminary set of rules for orthography and morphology and completed with input from codifiers in other countries a dictionary (1,100 entries) of Rusyn linguistic terminology.[58] Under

---

[57]"Scholarly Seminar on the the Codification of the Rusyn Language," *Carpatho-Rusyn American*, XV, 4 (Pittsburgh, Pa., 1992), pp. 4-5—reported on favorably in several professional journals: *Österreichische Osthefte* (Vienna), *Scottish Slavonic Review* (Glasgow), *International Journal of the Sociology of Language* (Berlin and New York), *Europa Ethnica* (Vienna), *Revue d'études slaves* (Paris), *Canadian Review of Studies in Nationalism* (Charlottetown), *Slovanský přehled* (Prague), *Nova dumka* (Zagreb), *Slavia* (Prague), and *Zeitschrift für Slawistik* (Berlin). The only negative assessment, which talked of "deceit, lies, and faleshoods," was the polemic by the Ukrainian ethnographer Mykola Mušynka, *Seminar dlja 'izbranných'* (Prešov, 1992).

[58]Jurij Pan'ko, *Normý rusyns'koho pravopysu* (Prešov, 1992) and his *Rusyn'sko-rus'ko-ukrajin'sko-sloven'sko-pol'skýj slovnyk lingvistyčnych terminiv* (Prešov, 1994). Despite the declared intent of the author that the rules (*normý*) were only proposals for discussion and only about orthography, Ukrainian critics analyzed them as if they were a new standard, then rejected them on principle because they did not conform to Ukrainian grammatical patterns. Cf. Mykola Štec' and Jurij

its present director, Vasyl' Jabur, the institute has published a *Rulebook for the Rusyn Writing System*, a 42,000-word orthographic dictionary, a primer and reader for elementary schools, and is completing work on a grammar.[59] Finally, the institute is expecting to be transformed into a Department (*Katedra*) of Rusyn Language and Literature at the School of Education (Pedagogical Faculty) of Šafárik University in Prešov.[60]

Conclusion

Thus, the language question that has been part of Rusyn cultural and political life ever since the seventeenth century is still alive and well on the threshold of the twenty-first century. That there are and will continue to be polemics about the issue is not at all surprising, because as the distinguished sociolinguist Joshua Fishman commented after returning from the first Rusyn language congress in 1992:

> The replacement of one literary elite by another is never an easy or pleasant affair, and the old-guard self-defined Ukrainian elite can be expected to campaign vigorously against the 'Young Turks,' Rusyn self-defining elites who [themselves] are self-declared candidates for the 'perks' that have until now supported the Old Guard's Ukrainian ethnic and linguistic orientation.[61]

Nonetheless, the struggle between the Rusyn and Ukrainian elites is only one, and ultimately not the most important aspect of the problem. For a language to succeed it must have users and therefore be accepted by the people for whom the literary standard has ostensibly been created. And this brings us back to the issue of *dignitas*, which has

Mulyčak, *Analiz norm pravopysu t.zv. rusyns'koji movy* (Prešov, 1992)—reprinted in *Ukrajins'ka diaspora*, II, 4 (Kiev, 1993), pp. 66-79.

[59]Vasyl' Jabur et al., *Pravyla rusyns'koho pravopysu* (Prešov, 1994); Jurij Pan'ko et al., *Orfografičnŷj slovnyk rusyn'skoho jazŷka* (Prešov, 1994); Jan Hryb, *Bukvar' pro rusyn'skŷ dity* (Prešov, 1994) and *Čitanka pro rusyn'skŷ* (Prešov, 1994).

[60]Vasyl' Jabur, "Treba kadrovo posylnyty Inštytut," *Narodnŷ novynkŷ* (Prešov), March 30, 1994, p. 2.

[61]"A brief post-script by a non-Rusyn participant"—Joshua A. Fishman—in Paul Robert Magocsi, "Scholarly Seminar on the Codification of the Rusyn Language," *International Journal of the Sociology of Language*, No. 104 (Berlin and New York, 1993), p. 124.

been a constant theme from the very outset of the Rusyn language question over three centuries ago. In the past, several linguistic forms were at one time or another proposed as worthy of use as literary languages: the Rusyn vernacular, Church Slavonic, Russian, Ukrainian, and even Hungarian, Slovak, or Polish. Today, the field has been narrowed down to two alternatives—Rusyn and Ukrainian—and when the emotion-laden polemics and scholarly arguments are stripped away, the issue is once again *dignitas*. Are the local dialects—as pro-Rusyn activists argue—able to be codified, and will they be perceived as worthy to represent the needs of a people at all levels of their cultural, administrative, and educational life? Or, as the pro-Ukrainian activists argue, are such language-building efforts unnecessary, because "Rusyn-Ukrainians" already have a literary language in the form of Ukrainian which is capable of satisfying all their needs?

The Rusyn language question has, indeed, been revisited. It seems certain that in all countries where Rusyns live there will continue to be writers who will produce publications and school textbooks in both Rusyn and Ukrainian. Less certain is the degree to which one or both of these languages—and national orientations—will be accepted as their own by the indigenous East Slavic populace of Carpathian Rus'.

CHAPTER 5

Rusyn Organizations, Political Parties, and Interest Groups, 1848–1914[*]

The revolutionary year 1848 was a veritable "springtime" for the Rusyn people living in the northeastern corner of the Hungarian Kingdom.[1] In contrast to other nationalities in the Habsburg Empire, the Rusyns of Hungary did not experience in the first half of the nineteenth century any of the developments normally associated with the early stages of national movements, such as the compilation by intellectuals of the group's language and folklore, or the establishment of cultural organizations and schools to propagate the specific national heritage. The year 1848, however, did begin a process for Rusyns in which their leaders became active in the intellectual and organizational

---

[*] This essay was commissioned in 1989 by the Austrian Academy of Sciences for inclusion in the multi-volume German-language history of the last decades of the Habsburg Empire—*Habsburgermonarchie, 1848-1918*, Vol. VIII: *Vereine, Parteien und Interessenverbände*. The piece was completed in 1992 and revised in 1998, but not yet published in the above-mentioned volume. It appears here for the first time.

[1] In the nineteenth century the term *Rusyn* was used not only by the East Slavs in northeastern Hungary, but also by those living in the neighboring Austrian provinces of Galicia and Bukovina. To distinguish the Rusyns of Hungary, their leaders often used the terms *Uhro-Rusyn* or *Subcarpathian Rusyn*. Unless otherwise indicated in this essay, the term *Rusyn* will apply to those East Slavs residing south of the Carpathians in northeastern Hungary, that is in territories which after 1918 became part of the new state of Czechoslovakia—the Prešov Region of northeastern Slovakia and the semi-autonomous province of Subcarpathian Rus'.

MAP 10 113

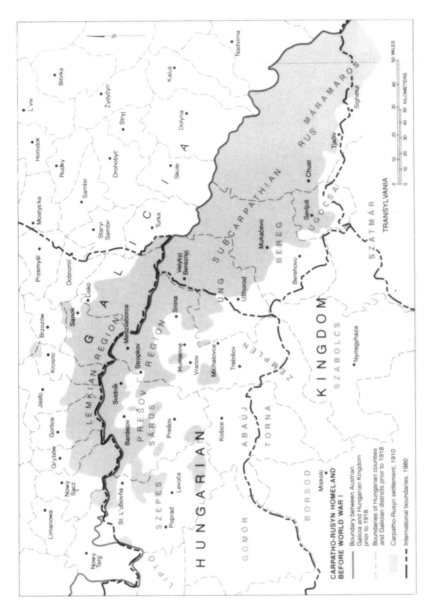

CARPATHO-RUSYN HOMELAND
BEFORE WORLD WAR I

——— Boundary between Austrian
Galicia and Hungarian Kingdom
prior to 1918.

———— Boundaries of Hungarian counties
and Galician districts prior to 1918

Carpatho-Rusyn settlement, 1910

—·—· International boundaries, 1980

stage as well as in the political stage of what indeed became a national revival.[2] As for organizational life, the period 1848 to 1918 did witness the creation of the first organizations devoted primarily to the propagation of Rusyn culture and education. While it is true that Rusyns never had their own political parties during this period, this does not mean that politics were absent from the minds of some of their leaders. In actual fact, Rusyn political aspirations during the second half of the nineteenth century were linked for the most part with one individual, Adol'f Dobrjans'kyj (1817-1901). Dobrjans'kyj was a native of the Prešov Region, the Rusyn-inhabited area that is in the northeastern corner of what is today Slovakia. Coming from the far western portion of Rusyn territory, Dobrjans'kyj interacted often with Slovak national activists and was even elected in 1848 to the Hungarian Parliament from the Banská Štiavnica district in central Slovakia.

Whereas Dobrjans'kyj favored cooperation with Slovaks, his main political program called for the unity of all Rusyns living in the Habsburg Empire, that is, his own group in northeastern Hungary together with those in the neighboring Austrian provinces of Galicia and Bukovina.[3] Not surprisingly, such goals were viewed by Hungarian leaders as a direct threat to the territorial integrity of the lands of the Crown of St. Stephan. Regardless of Hungarian concerns, the ambitious Dobrjans'kyj was given the opportunity to put his case before the emperor and the imperial government.

While unity with Rusyns in Galicia and Bukovina never came about, the Rusyns of Hungary did experience an initial stage of administrative unity in the form of the Užhorod district (the counties of Ung, Bereg, Ugocsa, and Máramoros). The Užhorod district was part of the Košice military region, which the Austrian government imposed on Hungary

[2] For a discussion of the three stages as applied to all Ukrainian lands, see Paul Robert Magocsi, "The Ukrainian National Revival: A New Analytical Framework," *Canadian Review of Studies in Nationalism*, XVI, 1-2 (Charlottetown, Prince Edward Island, 1989), pp. 45-62.

[3] For details on Dobrjans'kyj's political program, see Ivan Žeguc, *Die nationalpolitischen Bestrebungen der Karpato-Ruthenen 1848-1914* (Wiesbaden, 1965), pp. 43-71; and J. Pereni [József Perényi], *Iz istorii zakarpatskich ukraincev, 1849-1914* (Budapest, 1957), pp. 43-87; Ivan Kolomiec, *Social'no-èkonomičeskie otnošenija i obščestvennoe dviženie v Zakarpat'e vo vtoroj polovine XIX stoletija*, Vol. II (Tomsk, 1962), pp. 428-462.

during the era of martial law that followed the defeat in 1849 of the Hungarian revolution. Dobrjans'kyj was appointed advisor and deputy to the imperial administrator of the Užhorod district, which he in fact administered and which he considered the basis for a future "Rusyn district" in which his policies for national autonomy could be implemented.[4]

The experiment with the Rusyn district lasted only a few months (November 1849-March 1850), during which time Dobrjans'kyj used the Rusyn language alongside Magyar and German at public events and distributed appointments to his Rusyn colleagues. The result was the creation of what became known as "Dobrjans'kyj circle," an interest group that promoted the idea of territorial unity for all Rusyns in the Habsburg Empire. Dobrjans'kyj himself remained the most active spokesperson on behalf of Rusyns. When his call to unite the Rusyns of northeastern Hungary with the Rusyns in neighboring Galicia and Bukovina proved impossible to achieve, he instead concentrated his energies on creating an autonomous region for the Rusyn-inhabited counties in Hungary. The proposed region would have its own local administration headed by a Rusyn national congress.

The electoral campaigns of 1861, 1865, and 1869 marked the height of Rusyn political activity within the Hungarian Kingdom. Aside from Dobrjans'kyj, who was elected in 1861 and 1865, a few other candidates who were of Rusyn background and who represented their people's national interests won seats as deputies in the lower house of Hungary's parliament—Jurij Markoš, Aleksander Šeregij, Štefan Markoš, Štefan Silagij, Emanuel Hrabar (father of the famed Russian art historian Igor Grabar), Aleksander Nehrebec'kyj, and Ivan Pastelij. Their campaigns were often accompanied by the appearance of petitions and other public statements on behalf of Rusyn interests.[5]

It was Dobrjans'kyj, however, who was the central figure behind the political demands put forth in the name of the Rusyn people. In 1868, he decided to leave Hungarian political life, retiring to his estate in a

---

[4]Žeguc, *Die Nationalpolitischen Bestrebungen*, pp. 47-50; L'udovít Haraksim, *K sociálnym a kultúrnym dejinám Ukrajincov na Slovensku do roku 1867* (Bratislava, 1961), pp. 157-159.

[5]For further details, see Maria Mayer, *The Rusyns of Hungary: Political and Social Developments, 1860-1910* (New York, 1997), pp. 28-57.

small Rusyn village (Čertižné) in far northern Zemplén county (present-day Slovakia). From "retirement," he continued to remain active in Rusyn cultural and religious life and to publish several historical works. In 1881, he decided to leave Hungary for the relatively more tolerant atmosphere in Austrian-administered Galicia, but one year later he was implicated in a treason trial in L'viv, and although he was acquitted, he was barred from returning to Hungary. He eventually settled in the town of Innsbruck in Austria's Tyrol province where for three decades he lived until his death in 1901.[6] With the departure of Dobrjans'kyj from the Hungarian Parliament in 1868, Rusyn organized political life effectively ceased.

While Rusyns never had their own political parties, they did manage to create a few cultural organizations. Again, Adol'f Dobrjans'kyj was to play an important role. Even more active in organized cultural life, however, was Dobrjans'kyj's contemporary, the Greek Catholic priest, Aleksander Duchnovyč (1803-1865). Like his secular colleague, Duchnovyč came from the westernmost Rusyn territory (in present-day Slovakia) and was associated, in particular, with the city of Prešov, the seat of a Greek Catholic eparchy. Duchnovyč was to become the most popular Rusyn writer and the father of the Rusyn people or, as he is popularly known, the "national awakener" (*narodnyj budytel'*).

Aside from his own publications, which included the first Rusyn-language schoolbook and the texts for the national credo (*Ja rusyn byl, jesm' i budu*), Duchnovyč also founded in 1850 what could be considered the first cultural organization for Hungary's Rusyns, the Prešov Literary Institution (Literaturnoe Zavedenie Prjaševskoe). While this organization never had a legal charter and functioned out of Duchnovyč's home in Prešov, it nonetheless did have concrete achievements. These included twelve publications, among which were three volumes of the first Rusyn literary almanacs (*Pozdravlenie Rusynov*, 1850, 1851, 1852) and Duchnovyč's own very popular prayer book (*Chlîb dušy*, 1851).[7]

<hr/>

[6]On the later stages of Dobrjans'kyj's career, see Stepan Doboš, *Adol'f Ivanovič Dobrjanskij: očerk žizni i dejatel'nosti* (Bratislava, 1956), pp. 91-141.

[7]Olena Rudlovčak, "'Prjašivs'ka literaturna spilka' Duchnovyča i literaturne žyttja tohočassja," in idem, *Bilja džerel sučasnosti* (Bratislava and Prešov, 1981), pp. 51-106.

This first Rusyn cultural organization, dependent as it was on the financial and organizational support of basically one person, lasted only three years. Another decade was to pass before the next Rusyn organization came into existence. This was the Society of St. John the Baptist (Obščestvo sv. Joanna Krestitelja i Predteči), established in Prešov in 1862. Its founders, Duchnovyč and Dobrjans'kyj, managed to attract 400 members among whom were several Slovaks as well as Rusyns. The society had a definite purpose: to reverse the increasing tendency among young people to become magyarized and instead to educate them to be of "future service to the [Rusyn] national movement and renaissance."[8]

Directed as it was toward students, the St. John the Baptist Society's most notable achievement was the establishment in 1864 of a Greek Catholic student residence in Prešov known as the Alumneum. The society's founders were especially concerned with preserving a sense of Rusyn national consciousness among young people and, at least initially, it became a platform for Dobrjans'kyj's political ideas. By 1870s, however, the Hungarian government had embarked on a policy of magyarization that was intended to assimilate, in particular, the educated elements among the country's non-Magyar nationalities. Very helpful for achieving Hungarian state goals was the new Greek Catholic bishop of Prešov, Mykola Tovt (1838-1882), who in 1877, just one year after his consecration, succeeded in having the society's statute changed and its administration placed directly in the hands of the bishop. From then on, until the end of the fall of Austro-Hungary in 1918, the St. John the Baptist Society continued to exist, although its Rusyn cultural character was eliminated and its only real activity consisted of operating the Alumneum student residence according to the dictates of the ruling Greek Catholic bishop of Prešov.[9]

Not long after the St. John the Baptist Society began operating in

---

[8]Statement of Duchnovyč cited in Olena Rudlovčak, "Oleksandr Duchnovyč: žyttja i dijal'nist'," in Oleksandr Duchnovyč, *Tvory*, Vol. I (Bratislava and Prešov, 1968), p. 140.

[9]The Society of St. John the Baptist continued to exist formally until 1945, when its property was nationalized. The most comprehensive discussion of various aspects of the society is found in studies by Olena Rudlovčak, Josyf Šelepec', Andrij Čuma, Mychajlo Ryčalka, and Ljubycja Babota in an entire issue of *Karpats'kyj svit*, I (Prešov, 1993).

Prešov, farther east Rusyn activists within the Greek Catholic Eparchy of Mukačevo began to make plans for their own organization. Already in 1864, clerics at the Užhorod's Greek Catholic seminary formed the so-called Theological Society (Hittani Társulat). Before long members of this group requested governmental approval to establish a literary society which came into being in 1866 under the name, the Society of St. Basil the Great (Obščestvo sv. Vasiliia Velikago).[10] It was not long before the leadership of this new organization changed from a group of local priests to the political activist and parliamentary deputy, Adol'f Dobrjans'kyj.

The primary goal of the St. Basil Society was, in the opening words of its charter: "the promotion of the spiritual and moral education of Greek Uniate Catholics in the eparchies of Mukačevo and Prešov."[11] To achieve this goal the society intended "to collect, edit, publish, finance, and distribute textbooks for the needs of schools in the aforementioned eparchies, as well as other enlightening and useful books . . . and journals written in Rusyn and Hungarian."[12] The society did meet with some success. Its membership rose from 350 to 700 in its first four years, and it was able to publish several school texts, an annual almanac (*Misjacoslov*, 1868-89), and the first newspapers for Rusyns to appear in the homeland: *Svît* (Užhorod, 1867-71), *Novyj svît* (Užhorod, 1871-72), and *Karpat* (Užhorod, 1873-86).

The active publishing program of the St. Basil the Great Society, in particular its concern to reach students and a broad segment of the population, forced it to address a very practical issue. This was what later came to be known in the cultural and political history of Rusyns

---

[10]The most detailed history of the society is still: Julij Gadžega, *Istorija 'Obščestva sv. Vasilija Velikago'* (Užhorod, 1925); and the supplement by Iosif V. Kaminskij, *Dodatki k istorii O-va Vasilija Velikago v 1895-1902 godach* (Užhorod, 1937). See also Y.M. Kondratovyč, "Korotka ystorija Obščestva sv. Basylija Velykoho," in *Juvylejnŷj yljustrovanŷj kalendar' na rok 1928* (Užhorod, 1927), pp. 41-48, and the discussion in Mayer, *Rusyns in Hungary*, pp. 19-28 and 74-92; Žeguc, *Die nationalpolitischen Bestrebungen*, pp. 74-76; and Kolomiec, *Social'no-ékonomičeskie otnošenija*, pp. 244-265.

[11]"Charter of the Literary Society of Subcarpathian Greek Uniate Catholics, December 15, 1864," from a translation of the complete text in Mayer, *Rusyns in Hungary*, p. 268.

[12]*Ibid.*

as the "language question." That issue, in turn, was related to the nationality question. In short, were the East Slavic inhabitants living in the mountainous terrain of northeastern Hungary part of the Russian nationality or the "Little Russian" (Ukrainian) nationality?[13] And even if their dialects were "Little Russian" (Ukrainian), did the fact that they lived for a thousand years in Hungary transform them into a distinct Rusyn nationality? Or perhaps they were no more than Greek Catholic Magyars who spoke a variety of magyarized Slavic dialects in much the same way that the Slavic Macedonians were—in the opinion of Greek publicists—little more than Slavophone Greeks?

The struggle to answer the nationality question had an obvious impact on the language question and, in turn, on how organizations like the St. Basil the Great Society would decide what literary forms to use in its publications. Since initially the society was under the influence of Dobrjans'kyj and several Greek Catholic clerics like Ivan Rakovs'kyj (1815-1885), Aleksander Mitrak (1837-1913), Ivan Sil'vaj (1838-1904), Anatolij Kralyc'kyj (1835-1894), Jevhenij Fencyk (1844-1903), Viktor Kimak (1840-190?), and Kyril Sabov (1838-1914), its initial orientation was clearly Russophile. This meant that in its earliest years the St. Basil Society's publications appeared in Russian, or more likely in an approximation of Russian that was laden—depending on the ability of each author—with numerous borrowings from the Church Slavonic literary language and from local Rusyn dialects. This uncodified language was traditionally described in the East Slavic cultural sphere as Slaveno-Rusyn, by its defenders as "Carpatho-Russian," and by its critics as a macaronic jargon (*jazyčie*).

The choice of Russian, regardless of how correctly or incorrectly it was written, also had serious political implications. Ever since the 1848-1849 revolutionary era, Adol'f Dobrjans'kyj, who among his other activities had served as the Habsburg governmental liaison with the tsarist Russian armies that crushed the Hungarian revolutionaries in 1849, was under constant surveillance by the Hungarian government until he was permanently barred from the country after 1882. Even before that, however, Hungarian governmental pressure and the implementation of a policy of magyarization toward the kingdom's non-

---

[13]For further details, see Paul Robert Magocsi, *The Shaping of a National Identity: Subcarpathian Rus', 1848-1948* (Cambridge, Mass., 1978), pp. 42-75.

Magyar peoples was to have a negative impact on Rusyn cultural life. Particularly active in this regard was the new bishop of Mukačevo, Stepan Pan'kovyč/István Pankovics (1820-1874, consecrated 1867), who took the position that "if we now live under the rule of the Magyars, then we should become Magyars."[14] Bishop Pan'kovyč blocked the efforts of the St. Basil Society to construct its own Civic Center, or National Home (Narodnyj Dom), and he was instrumental in dispersing the region's Russophile-oriented cultural activists. Several priests were isolated in remote villages (Jevhenij Fencyk, Ivan Sil'vaj, Aleksander Mitrak), others were encouraged to take up posts outside the eparchy (Kyril Sabov), or still others emigrated of their own accord to Russia (Mychal Mol'čan, Vladimir Terleckij). Finally, in 1873, Dobrjans'kyj and Rakovs'kyj were removed as co-chairmen of the St. Basil Society which entered a period of stagnation marked by the occasional publication of a textbook and an annual almanac. It was also during the 1870s and 1880s that the St. Basil Society moved away from the Russophile position on language and began to favor the use of a language based on the local Rusyn vernacular. This trend was connected largely with the appearance on the scene of a group of younger clerical and secular writers led by Jevmenij Sabov (1859-1934), Jurij Žatkovyč (1855-1920), and Vasyl' Čopej (1856-1934), and in the 1890s by Vasyl' Hadžega (1864-1938), Avhustyn Vološyn (1874-1945), and Hijador Stryps'kyj (1875-1946).[15]

In 1895, there was a concerted effort to revive the St. Basil Society. This was in part connected to the establishment in Hungary of the Catholic People's party, which was opposed to the magyarization policies of the ruling govermental Liberal party. The new Catholic People's party was supported by Mukačevo's Greek Catholic bishop, Julij Fircak (1836-1912, consecrated 1891), who in turn promoted a revival of the St. Basil Society.

This time the younger pro-Rusyn activists were the dominant force in the organization, and the first concrete result was the appearance of

---

[14]This statement was attributed to the bishop by one of his Russophile-oriented priests, Ivan Sil'vaj, as quoted in the latter's "Avtobiografija," in I.A. Sil'vaj, *Izbrannye proizvedenija* (Bratislava, 1957), p. 144.

[15]Nykolaj Lelekač, "Podkarpatskoe pys'menstvo na počatku XX vîka," *Zorja-Hajnal*, III, 1-4 (Užhorod, 1943), pp. 229-257.

a newspaper called *Nauka* (1897-1914), written in the vernacular Rusyn language and in the Cyrillic alphabet. In 1895, the society took over responsibility once again for publishing the annual almanac, and it also published in 15,000 copies an elementary school Rusyn-language primer, *Azbuka* (1898), by Mychal Vrabel'. The main object of these publications was to stem the assimilation of Rusyn youth who were increasingly subjected to magyarization in the state school system, as well as to defend and preserve the Eastern-rite traditions and use of Church Slavonic as a bilingual language (not Hungarian as some were proposing) in the Greek Catholic Church. In practical terms, the St. Basil Society's program of publications and dissemination of information was enhanced by the acquisition in 1895 of its own printshop.

Cognizant of the new realities in Hungary, the St. Basil Society also published a Hungarian-language newspaper for the eparchy (*Görögkatolikus szemle*, 1899-1918). Not only did its revised charter completed in 1898 call for the expansion of activity to cover the entire Hungarian Kingdom, it also declared that the society's publication program would address the needs of "all Greek Catholic village schools, whether their language was Rusyn or Hungarian."[16]

The adoption of a new charter required the approval of the Hungarian government, which took two years to respond. When it finally responded in August 1900, the authorities demanded the charter be altered in order to give government authorities more direct control over the society's activity. The government's reaction reflected its increasing concern with what it called the rise of Pan-Slavism throughout the Habsburg Empire and, in particular, tsarist Russia's interest to protect—and eventually annex—lands inhabited by people it described as "Russians" living in "Rus' Abroad" (Zarubežnaja Rus').[17] The government in Budapest was well aware that among these "Russians abroad" were the Rusyns of northeastern Hungary, and despite the latter's protestations of loyalty to Hungary and their change from a

---

[16]The proposals for the revised charter are discussed in Mayer, *Rusyns in Hungary*, pp. 85-87.

[17]The most concrete form of Pan-Slavic infiltration from Russia came in the form of the Orthodox movement which began in 1900 with the conversion of a few Greek Catholic villages to Orthodoxy. See *ibid.*, pp. 124-152; and the contemporary pamphlet, T.D. Florinskij, *Zarubežnaja Rus' i eja gor'kaja dolja* (Kiev, 1900).

Russophile to Rusynophile national and linguistic orientation, they remained a constant source of suspicion. This was the context which led St. Basil Society members to reassess their options. In 1902, the executive board decided to dissolve the society and to transfer its property, in particular the printshop and book inventory, to a newly formed commercial and enterprise known formally as the Unio Book Publishing Shareholding Company. While the company continued to publish the newspapers (*Nauka*, *Görögkatolikus szemle*), annual almanacs, and other school textbooks and religious literature that had been the work of the St. Basil Society, Unio could hardly be considered a national organization. Hence, at the outset of the twentieth century, organized Rusyn political and cultural life was reduced to the activity of one institution—a printshop whose publications included a newspaper and some books written in the Rusyn language.

During the second half of the nineteenth century, the Rusyns of Hungary were culturally and politically active, although their organized corporate life was decidedly underdeveloped. In contrast to most other stateless peoples in the Habsburg Empire and other parts of east-central Europe, the Rusyns never had their own political parties, theaters, or libraries, even reading clubs, and by the outset of the twentieth century they no longer had cultural organizations. This was because most of the local intelligentsia, whether clerical or secular, had gradually and willingly embraced the Hungarian government's policy of assimilating the kingdom's non-Magyar peoples. This trend was most graphically evident in the very names of the newest organizations and student clubs comprised of Rusyn members that were formed at the time, such as the National Committee for Magyars of the Greek Catholic Rite (Görög Szertartású Katholikus Magyarok Országos Bizottsága, established in 1898) and the Union of Magyar Greek Catholics (Magyar Görögkatolikusok Egyesülete, established in 1902), both based far from the Rusyn-inhabited homeland in the country's capital of Budapest.[18]

---

[18] While it is true that there were also Greek Catholics of Slovak and Magyar ethnicity, the leadership and leading activists in the Budapest organizations were magyarized Rusyns (known derogatorily as magyarones), such as Jenő Szabó, Endre Rabár (Andrij Hrabar), Emil Demjanovics, and Ignác Roskovics. For details on the

In short, well before the outbreak of World War I in 1914, which four years later resulted in the collapse of the Austro-Hungarian Monarchy, Hungary's Rusyns had at best a printshop, but no cultural or civic organizations, no political parties, nor even informal interest groups whose goals were to defend and preserve the integrity of a Rusyn nationality. This led one observer to comment in 1916 that: "In ten years, Rusyn youth will be Magyar not only in spirit but in language also. Fruitless will be any attempt by other Slavic peoples ... to strive to free their [Rusyn] brethren: This is because in the Carpathians there will be no [Slavic] brethren, only Magyars everywhere!!"[19]

Budapest group of magyarone Rusyns, see Mayer, *Rusyns in Hungary*, pp. 153-189; and M. Mayer, "Beiträge zur Geschichte der Ruthenen (Karpatoukrainer) um die Jahrhundertwende," *Acta Historica Academiae Scientiarium Hungaricae*, XIX, 1-2 (Budapest, 1973), esp. pp. 139-147.

[19] Agoston Stefan, cited in Magocsi, *Shaping*, p. 74.

CHAPTER 6

The Rusyn Decision to Unite
with Czechoslovakia*

During the last months of 1918 profound political and social changes took place throughout the Austro-Hungarian Empire. After the dissolution of Habsburg administrative authority in late October, Poles, Ukrainians, Czechs, Slovaks, Serbs, Croats, and Romanians organized national councils that eventually were to determine the political future of these former subject peoples. Rusyns[1] living in the northeastern counties of Hungary also participated in this process, and from November 1918 to May 1919 they formed many councils which proposed various political alternatives: autonomy within Hungary, complete independence, or union with Russia, the Ukraine, or the new state of Czechoslovakia. Although these choices reflected the political and cultural allegiances that were traditionally attractive to Rusyn leaders, the particular international situation in 1919 proved favorable to only one—union with Czechoslovakia.

At a time when the national minorities demanded separation from the Habsburg Empire, Hungarian politicians under the leadership of Count

---

*First published in *Slavic Review*, XXXIV, 2 (Seattle, Wash., 1975), pp. 360-381. Reprinted in Harvard Ukrainian Research Institute Offprint Series, No. 3 (Cambridge, Mass., 1975).

[1]In the first published version of this study, the editor of the *Slavic Review* proposed using the term *Ruthenian* instead of *Rusyn*. In response to the author's original text and in keeping with the rest of this volume the term *Rusyn* will be used.

Mihály Károlyi also rejected the former regime and, on October 31, 1918, formed a "revolutionary" government in Budapest. This new, liberal-minded government included a Ministry for Nationalities, headed by Oszkár Jászi, whose task it was to develop a program of autonomy for the national minorities and thus preserve the territorial integrity of Hungary.[2] But the many centuries of Hungarian rule, which culminated in an extensive policy of magyarization and defeat in war, virtually doomed from the start any enlightened policy that the new Hungarian leaders might have proposed. National independence closely allied with desires for social liberation made the governments in Prague, Bucharest, and Belgrade seem more attractive than Budapest.

Rusyns also expressed desires for national and social liberation, especially after soldiers who returned home told of the revolutions taking place in the former Russian Empire. At secret meetings held in Uzhhorod in September 1918, two former Subcarpathian prisoners of war informed Rusyn leaders of the recent events in Russia and Ukraine, and then discussed the feasibility of greater autonomy within Hungary or perhaps union with their brethren beyond the Carpathians. To explore the latter possibility, it was decided to send the young *gymnasium* professor, Avhustyn Shtefan,[3] to Vienna in order to meet with parliamentary representatives from Galicia. The latter suggested that, in accord with Wilson's principle of self-determination, the best course of action would be to form national councils throughout the Subcarpathian region.[4]

Following this recommendation, the Rusyn intelligentsia (primarily priests, lawyers, and teachers) organized around four centers: Prešov, Uzhhorod, Khust (Hungarian: Huszt), and Iasynia (Hungarian: Kőrösmező). The geographical location of these towns interestingly coincided with their proposed political aims. Prešov, to the west, eventually became the center of the pro-Czechoslovak movement;

---

[2]Oszkár Jászi, *Revolution and Counter-revolution in Hungary* (London, 1924), p. 38.

[3]Avhustyn Shtefan, a Subcarpathian Ukrainophile, should not be confused with Dr. Agoston Stefan, the local Magyarone who served as governor of *Rus'ka Kraina* in 1919.

[4]Petro Stercho, *Karpato-ukraïns'ka derzhava* (Toronto, 1965), pp. 112-114; Avhustyn Shtefan, *Ukraïns'ke viis'ko v Zakarpatti* (Toronto and New York, 1969), p. 9.

Uzhhorod and later Mukachevo on the central lowlands represented the pro-Hungarian solution; Khust, farther east, declared for union with the Ukraine; and finally Iasynia, in a remote sector of the Carpathians, became the center of a short-lived, independent political entity.

The first national council (Russka Narodna Rada) met on November 8, 1918, in Stará L'ubovňa (Hungarian: Ólubló), a small town located in the western most portion of Rusyn ethnographic territory within present-day Czechoslovakia. Delegates from the surrounding counties of Sáros and Szepes gathered under the leadership of a local priest, Emiliian Nevyts'kyi, and drew up a manifesto which stated that those present were "imbued with the democratic spirit of the times" and "in protest against any force from foreign powers over our Rusyn (*rus'kii*) land."[5] Nevyts'kyi also wanted to gauge the attitude of the local population, and during the month of November he sent out two questionnaires. In both of these, there was clear evidence that the L'ubovňa Council was oriented toward union with the Rusyns living north of the Carpathians:

> We are Rusyns! Because we live in the Carpathians, we are called Carpathian Rusyns. But we know that Rusyns similar to us live beyond the Carpathians. Their speech, customs , and faith are the same as ours, as [they] are our brothers. With them we ethnographically form one great multi-million people.[6]

Other questions formulated the issue of Rusyn political fate as a choice between "remaining with Hungary" or "uniting with Rus' (Ukraine)." The available evidence reveals that Rusyns in the region around Stará L'ubovňa were generally opposed to Hungary, but not necessarily united behind any one political solution: some favored union with Rus' (Ukraine), some complete independence, others union with Czechoslovakia.[7]

---

[5]Cited in Ortoskop [Mykhailo Tvorydlo], *Derzhavni zmahannia Prykarpats'koi Ukrainy* (Vienna, 1924), pp. 9-10. For the text of another L'ubovna declaration, see Petro K. Smiian, *Zhovtneva revoliutsiia i Zakarpattia, 1917-1919 rr.* (L'viv, 1972), p. 31.

[6]Reprinted in Zdeněk Peška and Josef Markov, "Příspěvek k ústavnim dějinám Podkarpatské Rusi," *Bratislava*, V (Bratislava, 1931), pp. 526-527.

[7]M. Tvorydlo analyzed 55 completed questionnaires which he had in hand. As for remaining with Hungary, 51 were opposed, 2 for, 2 abstained. In response to

An attempt to secure autonony in Hungary was also initiated in early November by the Greek Catholic priests, Petr Gebei, Avhustyn Voloshyn, and Simeon Sabov. On November 9, more than one hundred persons gathered in Uzhhorod to form a national council. Referring to the "errors" of "Rusyns in many places who want to unite with the Ukraine," Reverend Sabov declared: "This movement, the Rada uhrorus'koho naroda [Council of Uhro-Rusyn people] is not separatist; on the contrary, it wants in fact to serve the territorial integrity of Hungary."[8] The resolution issued by the Uzhhorod Council began with professions of loyalty, and among the demands were included special autonomy for the Greek Catholic Church, agricultural, social, and industrial reforms, and other privileges for national minorities as proposed by the Károlyi government. The Council claimed itself the sole legal representative for the Rusyn people and began to negotiate with Hungarian officials in Budapest. Magyarone Rusyns in both Máramaros and Ugocsa counties met during the following weeks to proclaim loyalty to Hungary and to declare their support for the council in Uzhhorod.[9]

On December 10, 1918, thirty-six members of the Uzhhorod Council were invited to Budapest by Dr. Oreszt Szabó, a native of Subcarpathia and official in the Ministry of Interior who was appointed adviser to the government on Rusyn affairs. Among those present at the meeting were representatives of a Budapest-based Uhro-Rusyn political party (formed

---

whether union with Rus' (Ukraine) was desired, 28 were favorable, 20 wanted complete independence, 2 for Hungary, 5 for the Ukraine, but if not possible, for Czechoslovakia. These figures are only a sample, since it is not known how many questionnaires were completed and returned to Nevyts'kyi. Ortoskop, *Derzhavni zmahannia*, pp. 11-12.

[8]Speech quoted in I.V. Kaminskii, "Vospominaniia," published during 1933 in the Uzhhorod newspaper, *Karpatorusskii golos*, no. 26, and in Ortoskop, *Derzhavni zmahannia*, p. 22. On the Uzhhorod Council, see Avhustyn Voloshyn, *Spomynŷ* (Uzhhorod, 1923), pp. 89-90; Alois Raušer, "Připojení Podkarpatské Rusi k Československé republice," in J. Zatloukal, ed., *Podkarpatská Rus* (Bratislava, 1936), pp. 66-67; I.N. Mel'nikova, "Kak byla vkliuchena Zakarpatskaia Ukraina v sostav Chekhoslovakii v 1919 g.," *Uchenye zapysky Instituta slavianovedeniia*, III (Leningrad, 1931), pp. 111-112; Stercho, *Karpato-ukraïns'ka derzhava*, pp. 114-115; Smiian, *Zhovtneva revoliutsiia*, pp. 36-41.

[9]Gábor Darás, *A Ruténföld elszakításának előményei, 1890-1920* (Budapest, 1936), pp. 98-99.

on December 8) who promised "to stand or fall on the side of Hungary," and several more skeptical leaders like Stepan Klochurak and Dr. Mykhailo Brashchaiko who protested that no decisions should be made without first consulting the population at home. As a result of the meeting, a memorandum was addressed to Prime Minister Károlyi expressing "the hope and faith that in its decisions the Peace Conference would devote special attention" to the Rusyns of Hungary.[10] Until such time, demands were made for national and internal administrative autonony, and protests lodged "against the taking of territory by Czechs, Slovaks, Romanians and other nations."[11]

In an attempt to satisfy Rusyn demands, the Károlyi regime adopted an autonomy project, Law No. 10 of December 21, 1918, which called into existence the autonomous province of Rus'ka Kraina. However, this province comprised only those Rusyns living in the counties of Máramaros, Bereg, Ugocsa, and Ung; the inclusion of other Rusyn areas (parts of Zemplén, Sáros, Abaúj-Torna, and Szépes counties) would be postponed "until the time for the conclusion of a general peace."[12] The law further provided for full autonomy in internal matters (education, religion, national language) which were to be clarified after the establishment of a Rusyn National Assembly (Rus'kii Narodnii Sobor). The executive organs for Rus'ka Kraina were placed in a Ministry with headquarters in Budapest and a governor with a seat in Mukachevo.

The activity of the pro-Hungarian Uzhhorod Council and its initial success in negotiations with the Budapest government was met by opposition from various parts of Subcarpathian Rus'.[13] On November

---

[10]The memorandum is reprinted in Kaminskii, "Vospominaniia," no. 30. The program of the Uhro-Rusyn political party appears in Proklamatsiia do uhro-rus'koho naroda (Budapest, 1919), pp. 25-26. See also Karpato-rus'kii vîstnyk (Uzhhorod), December 23, 1918; Kaminskii, "Vospominaniia," nos. 27-28; Darás, A Ruthénföld, pp. 99-103.

[11]Kaminskii, "Vospominaniia," no. 30.

[12]"Narodnŷi zakon chysla 10 pro samoupravu rus'koho narodu zhyvushchoho na Uhorshchynî," reprinted in Ortoskop, Derzhavni zmahannia, pp. 32-33. An English translation is available in Peter G. Stercho, Diplomacy of Double Morality: Europe's Crossroads in Carpatho-Ukraine, 1919-1939 (New York, 1971), pp. 309-400.

[13]The occurrence of anti-Hungarian activity prompted Antonii Papp, the pro-government bishop of Uzhhorod, to send to all his priests a circular which requested

19, the L'ubovňa Council reconvened in Prešov. About 200 peasants and 40 priests gathered under the leadership of the Beskid family, in particular Dr. Antonii Beskid, who replaced E. Nevyts'kyi as chairman. Beskid was in close contact with Russophile leaders from Galicia (Andrei Gagatko, Dmitrii Vislotskii, and others) who originally wanted the Rusyn inhabited lands both north and south of the Carpathians to be united with Russia. The Prešov Council issued a manifesto which included general demands for "self-determination" and "national freedom," and called for a delegate to be present at the future "international peace conference"; however, it did not yet mention unification with any particular state.[14]

The following weeks witnessed a struggle between the Nevyts'kyi and Beskid factions in the Prešov Council. Nevyts'kyi still maintained the hope, expressed at smaller meetings in Bardejov (November 27), Svidník (November 29), Stropkov (November 30), Medzilaborce (December 2), and Humenné (December 3), that union with Rus' (Ukraine) should be brought about.[15] Beskid, on the other hand, pushed for a more practical solution—association with the new Czechoslovak state. To secure this goal he met in Turčiansky Svätý Martin with the Slovak National Council. On November 30, that body called upon "our brother Rusyns": "With the greatest love, we beg you as a free people to come closer to us, to unite with us."[16]

that they aid in controlling "the secret agitation for union with Ukraine or Czechoslovakia" as well as the "anti-Christian Social-Democratic radical agitation." The appeal was dated Uzhhorod, November 28, 1918, and is reprinted in Ortoskop, *Derzhavni zmahannia*, pp. 22-123, and in an edited version in *Taiemne staie iavnym: dokumenty pro antynarodnu diial'nist' tserkovnykiv na Zakarpatti v period okupatsiï* (Uzhhorod, 1965), doc. 51.

[14]Reprinted in Peška and Markov, "Příspěvek," pp. 524-526.

[15]Orotoskop, *Derzhavni zmahannia*, pp. 13-14; Mykola Andrusiak, "Istoriia Karpats'koï Ukraïny," in *Karpats'ka Ukraïna* (L'viv, 1939), p. 98. Unfortunately, the resolutions of these smaller councils have never been published or summarized in any of the existing literature.

[16]The Slovaks also promised "full autonomy" in ecclesiastical and educational affairs as well as the establishment of a university in the near future. "Proclamation of the Slovak National Council, Turčiansky Sv. Martin, November 30, 1918," reprinted in Peška and Markov, "Příspěvek," pp. 527-528. See also Karol A. Medvecký, *Slovenský prevrat*, Vol. I (Trnava, 1930), pp. 60-61. The failure to fulfill these promises was to be a source of constant friction between Rusyn leaders and

Beskid was supported in his efforts by the Galician Russophiles, who realized that Russia was a lost cause and thus hoped that Czechoslovakia would save Rusyn lands north of the Carpathians from future Polish control. On December 21, members of the so-called Russian (Galician) Council of Lemkos joined with the Beskid faction to form a Carpatho-Russian National Council (Karpato-Russkaia Narodnaia Rada). From the beginning, this group favored unification with Prague; moreover, the continuing political and military instability in both Galicia and Russian Ukraine made the Czechoslovak solution seem more feasible than ever. Nevyts'kyi's protests went unheeded, and by the end of December the arrival of Czech Legionnaires in eastern Slovakia further advanced the aims of Beskid so that in early January the Prešov Council could declare openly for union with Czechoslovakia.[17] Opposition to the pro-Hungarian Uzhhorod Council was also substantial in the eastern county of Máramaros, where sentiment for Ukraine was widespread. At a series of three meetings held at Khust on November 3, 7, and 10, the few Hungarian supporters present were overwhelmed by the rhetoric of a Rusyn lawyer, Dr. Iulii Brashchaiko, who called for union with Ukraine.[18] Similarly, on December 8, 1918, a Carpatho-Rusyn National Council (Karpats'ka-Rus'ka Narodna Rada) was formed at Svaliava (Szolyva). Those present rejected the Uzhhorod Council because "it is Magyar" and decided to address a memorandum to the Peace Conference which in turn should send an armed force "so that the Rusyn people could free themselves from the thousand-year-old [Hungarian] yoke and unite with Greater Ukraine where Rusyns live also."[19]

Continued anti-Hungarian sentiment was evident at a meeting in Marmaţiei Sighetul (Hungarian: Máramarossziget) arranged by the Budapest government on December 18, 1918. In an attempt to engender support for the Hungarian cause, the first speaker proclaimed that "the

the Czechoslovak government.

[17]Ortoskop, *Derzhavni zmahannia*, pp. 13-17.

[18]Raušer, "Přípojení Podkarpatské Rusi," p. 66; Smiian, *Zhovtneva revoliutsiia*, pp. 34-35; Darás, *A Ruthénföld*, p. 103.

[19]"Protokol Narodn'oho Zibrannia v Svaliavi, December 8, 1918," reprinted in Ortoskop, *Derzhavni zmahanniia*, pp. 18-19. See also Augustin Stefan, *From Carpatho-Ruthenia to Carpatho-Ukraine* (New York, 1954), p. 20 and Smiian, *Zhovtneva revoliutsiia*, pp. 35-36.

Rusyn ... people can find happiness only as a part of Hungary," but this speech was continually interrupted by cries of "we don't need anything from the Magyars, long live Ukraine, let us go to Ukraine."[20] Consequently, a Maramorosh Rusyn National Council (Maramoroshs'ka Rus'ka Narodnia Rada) was formed under the chairmanship of Dr. Mykhailo Brashchaiko and a manifesto adopted which called for union with Ukraine and the convocation of a new national council to be held at Khust on January 21.

Among the signatories to the Maramorosh manifesto, it is interesting to find the name of Dr. Agoston Stefan, a leading member of the Uzhhorod Council who had just returned from negotiations with Hungarian leaders in Budapest. Stefan, soon to become governor of the autonomous Rus'ka Kraina, was a well-known Magyarone, yet at the same time he signed a resolution calling for union with Ukraine. In fact, many Rusyn leaders were participants in councils which professed antithetical political ends. Such a phenomenon was indicative not only of a certain degree of opportunism on the part of these individuals, but also reflected to a large extent the unstable and rapidly changing conditions in Subcarpathian Rus' after the war.

It is perhaps necessary to emphasize what Subcarpathian leaders meant when they called for unification with Ukraine. Most held the traditional view that Ukraine was a Rus' land similar to their own. The relations they had with Galicia were usually with the Russophile intelligentsia, hence Subcarpathians were either unsympathetic toward or unaware of actual Ukrainian national and political goals. Many might favor unification of all Ukrainian lands, but not separation from Russia or the use of Ukrainian instead of Russian as a literary language. Hence, the head of the L'ubovňa Council, E. Nevyts'kyi, could formulate a manifesto calling for union with Rus' (Ukraine) as well as sign a Galician memorandum which claimed that all Rusyns are part of the Great Russian nation and that Ukrainianism was a dangerous separatist movement created by Austro-German propaganda.[21] On the

---

[20]"Maramarosh-Sihotskii sbor," *Karpato-rus'kii vîstnyk*, December 23, 1918; "Protokol Maramarosh'koi Rus'koi (Ukrains'koi) Narodnoi Radŷ, December 18, 1918, reprinted in Ortoskop, *Derzhavni zmahanniia*, pp. 20-21.

[21]"Memorandum Narodnago Soveta Russkago Prikarpat'ia," Sanok, December 13, 1918, reprinted in Peška and Markov, "Příspěvek," pp. 528-531. Ukrainian

other hand, Dr. Iulii Brashchaiko and his brother Mykhailo were
pronounced Ukrainophiles who thought clearly in terms of union with
an independent Ukrainian state when they put forth their demands at the
meetings in Khust and Marmaţiei Sighetul.

Ukrainian developments proceeded beyond Subcarpathian
expectations. Ukrainophile parliamentarians from Galicia organized a
national council in late October and on November 1, 1918, met in L'viv
where they called into being an independent West Ukrainian
Republic.[22] The new republic claimed jurisdiction over "the Ukrainian
parts of Galicia, Bukovina, and Subcarpathian Rus', but its authority
was immediately challenged by Polish forces who by the end of the
month pushed the Ukrainians out of the city. Until April 1919 the
beleaguered national council of the West Ukrainian Republic met in
Stanyslaviv. The situation in former Russian Ukraine was not much
better. There, the Directorate of the Ukrainian National Republic
(originally based in Kiev), was from December 1918 fighting for
survival against the forces of the Soviet and White Russian armies. On
January 22, 1919, in the midst of a critical military situation, a
delegation from the West Ukrainian Republic went to Kiev in order "to
unify the century-long separated parts of one Ukraine . . . Galicia,
Bukovina, Uhors'ka Rus' [Subcarpathia] with Great Ukraine beyond the

writers have confused the geographical term Rus' (Ukraine) with Ukrainian
nationalism and have erroneously considered Nevyts'kyi and the Lubovňa Council
to be Ukrainophile. See Ortoskop, *Derzhavni zmahanniia*, pp. 8-17; Stefan, *From
Carpatho-Ruthenia*, pp. 19-20; Stercho, *Karpato-ukraïns'ka derzhava*, p. 117;
Vasyl' Hryvna, "Vplyv Zhovtnia ta natsional'-no-vyzvolnyi rukh ukraïntsiv
Chekhoslovachchyny," in *Zhovten' i ukraïns'ka kul'tura* (Prešov, 1968), pp.
127-130; Smiian, *Zhovtneva revoliutsiia*, pp. 30-34.

[22]Ukrainian leaders claim that at the October 19 meeting of the National Council
in L'viv a letter from Subcarpathian leaders (unnamed) was read; it concluded with
the request: "You, our brethren, must stand behind us and unite with us. Our people
demand such salvation so that finally we can be liberated from the yoke of another
people." Cited in a work by the Chairman of the L'viv National Council, Kost
Levyts'kyi, *Velykyi zryv: do istoriï ukraïns'koï derzhavnosty vid bereznia do
lystopada 1918 r. na pidstavi spomyniv ta dokumentiv* (L'viv, 1931), p. 118. See
also Mykhailo Lozyns'kyi, *Halychyna v rr. 1918-1920* (Vienna, 1922), p. 29. No
work by a Subcarpathian author, however, has mentioned the sending of a letter to
L'viv as early as October 1918.

Dnieper."[23] Actual territorial unification, however, was not to be achieved.

While there was an undeniable sense of kinship felt by Subcarpathian Rusyns for those people, in Galicia and Bukovina who spoke a similar language, it was the social issue which especially provoked interest in the lands beyond the Carpathians. Returning soldiers and other refugees, who could be considered Bolshevik "in sentiment, if not by conviction,"[24] spread tales of how the lords were driven away and the land given to the people. Thus, the Svaliava Council manifesto called for union "with the councils in Ukraine because these Councils give the peasants the gentry and state lands."[25] Likewise, "in the area around Khust ... the movement for emigration to Ukraine has been strengthened. The landless hope to get there good, fertile land."[26] A petition from one small mountain village summed up Subcarpathian national and social desires:

> We are Rusyns who live in the Carpathians near the Galician border, we want to unite with Russian Ukraine where we will use state lands and forests so that everything will be for the common citizen; here we are

---

[23]The Kiev universal is cited in Lozyns'kyi, *Halychyna*, pp. 68-69. For the complicated circumstances under which this so-called Fourth Universal was issued, see John S. Reshetar, *The Ukrainian Revolution* (Princeton, N.J., 1952), pp. 110-113.

[24]Jászi, *Revolution*, p. 37. "Young soldiers returning from Russia have in particular brought the irresistible Bolshevik propaganda. They are causing an uproar against priests." From an article entitled "Bolshevism in Máramaros," *Görög-katholikus szemle* (Uzhhorod), December 15, 1918. On the impact of soldiers returning from the Russian front, see also *Shiakhom Zhovtnia: zbirnyk dokumentiv*, Vol. I (Uzhhorod, 1957), docs. 17, 19, 20, 22, 26, 28, 29.

[25]Cited in Stefan, *From Carpatho-Ruthenia*, p. 20; Smiian, *Zhovtneva revoliutsiia*, p. 36; V.I. Netochaiev, "Vplyv Velykoï Zhovtnevoï sotsialistychnoï revoliutsiï na Zakarpattia i rozhortannia borot'by trudiashchykh za vozz'iednannia z usim ukraïns'kym narodom v 1918-1919 rr.," *Naukovi zapysky*, III (Uzhhorod, 1957), p. 53.

[26]*Görög-katholikus szemle*, November 24, 1918. For examples of village petitions that called for union with Ukraine in late 1918, see Netochaiev, "Vplyv," pp. 52-53, and *Shliakhom Zhovtnia*, Vol. I, docs. 38-41, 49-51.

very poor people because the landlords have pressured us so much that one cannot even survive.[27]

Another indication of Rusyn opposition to Hungary took place in the far eastern village of Iasynia. In the early morning of January 7, 1919, a group of demobilized Rusyn soldiers led by Dmytro and Vasyl' Klempush, Stepan Klochurak, Dmytro Nimchuk, and in cooperation with troops sent by the West Ukrainian Republic, drove out the garrison of 250 Hungarian militiamen. The new force occupied Marmaţiei Sighetul for a while, but was soon forced back home by the Romanian army. The local leaders favored unification with an independent Ukraine, but since this was not yet feasible they established instead on February 5 their own "Hutsul Republic," which came to control the territory surrounding Iasynia (representing about 20,000 inhabitants). This "miniature state," administered by a forty-two member elected council and a four-man government, existed until June 11, 1919 when Romanian troops occupied the area.[28]

Thus, by the beginning of 1919, the Subcarpathian Rusyns responded to the political crisis by creating a series of national councils which proposed four possible solutions: federation with Czechoslovakia (Prešov), autonomy within Hungary (Uzhhorod), union with Ukraine (Maramorosh), or independence (Iasynia). The first months of the new year were to witness a struggle between these four orientations, but it was not until the spring that the outcome became clear.

Events during the month of January revealed an increase in the influence of the Czechoslovak and Ukrainian orientations. On January 7, 1919, Dr. A. Beskid invited local leaders and Galician Russophiles (the Lemko Council) to Prešov, where they declared for union with Czechoslovakia.[29] A few days later Beskid conveyed this decision to

[27]Cited in Fedor Vico, "Ohlas Mad'arskej republiky rád v ukrajinských obciach Zakarpatska," Nove obzory, I (Prešov, 1959), p. 48.

[28]Despite aid from the West Ukrainian Republic, leaders like Vasyl' Klempush emphasized that the "Hutsuls [term used by the local Rusyns] themselves created the uprising and not the Galicians. Our Hutsul National Council decided to break away from Hungary and unite with the Ukraine." Shtefan, Ukraïns'ke viis'ko, pp. 11-21; Smiian, Zhovtneva revoliutsiia, pp. 55-59; "Hutsulska Republyka," Nedîlia Rusyna, I (Uzhhorod, 1923), pp. 54-55, 59-60.

[29]The protocol of the Prešov meeting is included as an annex to the

Czech politicians in Prague, who immediately sent him as the Rusyn delegate to the Peace Conference in Paris. The Czechoslovak solution was put in writing on January 31 at another meeting of the Prešov Carpatho-Russian National Council. After stating that the Rusyns are members of the Great Russian people, the manifesto regretted that unfavorable political conditions made union with a united Russia impossible; thus "we desire to live for better or worse with our Czechoslovak brethren."[30]

The situation in Uzhhorod was not yet clear, although here, too, the Czechoblovak orientation seemed to be gaining ground. While many Rusyn leaders had accepted an autonomous status for their land within Hungary, the procrastination of the Budapest government led to increased disillusionment summed up later by a leading figure in the Uzhhorod Council, A. Voloshyn: "When it became clear that Magyar autonomy for Rus'ka Kraina was not a serious thing, we met already on January 1, 1919, with Milan Hodža, chief representative of the Czechoslovak Republic in Budapest, and asked whether the Republic would occupy all of Subcarpathian Rus'."[31]

Since November 1918, Milan Hodža had been in Budapest where he was negotiating with the Károlyi government for the evacuation of Hungarian troops from Slovakia. The Czechoslovak representative was approached by several Rusyn leaders. The first of these was a delegation of twenty-two members led by Mykhailo Komarnyts'kyi of

---

Czechoslovak Delegations's *Mémoire No. 6*, reprinted in *La Paix de Versailles*, Vol. IX: *Questions territoriales*, pt. 1 (Paris, 1939), pp. 99-100, and in Stercho, *Diplomacy*, pp. 404-405.

[30]Manifesto reprinted in Peška and Markov, "Příspěvek," pp. 531-532. The anti-Ukrainianism of Beskid and his Galician allies was emphasized: "We consider the separatism of Ukrainian politicians a temporary phenomenon—anti-Slavic, anti-cultural and anti-social—a product of Austro-German imperialism." The decision of the Prešov Council was opposed by its former chairman Emiliian Nevyts'kyi, who issued proclamations the same day calling for union with Ukraine. Reprinted in Ortoskop, *Derzhavni zmahannia*, pp. 14-16. Despite Nevyts'kyi's rhetoric calling for Ukraine, his discontent was not motivated by displeasure with the Russophile attitude of the Prešov manifesto, but rather with the usurpation of the council's leadership by Beskid and his supporters.

[31]Voloshyn, *Spomynŷ*, p. 92, and his *Dvi polytychnî rozmovŷ* (Uzhhorod, 1923), pp. 6-7.

the Svaliava Council, who "demanded the separation [of Subcarpathian Rus'] from the Hungarian state and union (preferably) with Ukraine, or if that were not possible, with the Czechoslovak state.[32] The Svaliava delegation also left with Hodža a memorandum stating:

> The Rusyn people desire autonomy on the territory of the counties of Ung, Bereg, Ugocsa, and Máramaros; as an autonomous body, they request to be attached either to a Ukrainian state or, for reasons of an economic and geographic nature, preferably to the Czecho-Slovak Republic.
>
> The delegation submits at the same time a request that the High Command of the Allied armies order the occupation of Rusyn territory in Hungary by a Ukrainian or Czechoslovak army so that the population can freely decide its fate.[33]

These requests fit in well with Hodža's desire that Czech troops occupy territory at least as far east as the city of Uzhhorod.

The Czechoslovak representative was less well disposed toward Voloshyn and Petr Legeza, whom he met in Budapest on January 1, 1919. Hodža considered these Uzhhorod Council members to be "opportunists," basically satisfied with the concept of autonomy (i.e., Rus'ka Kraina) within Hungary, but afraid that the Károlyi government would renege on its promises. Although Voloshyn asked for help from the Prague government, he refused to make a written request until Czech troops would occupy Uzhhorod.[34]

Two days later, Hodza met again with Komarnyts'kyi, whose Svaliava Council he considered to be more representative of the popular will than the pro-Hungarian Uzhhorod Council. Komarnyts'kyi reiterated the request for Czech troops, and according to Hodža the

---

[32]Report of Hodža to the Ministry of Foreign Affairs in Prague, December 19, 1918, in *Slovenský rozchod s Maď'armi roku 1918: dokumentárny výklad o jednaniach dra Milana Hodžu ako čsl. plnomocníka s Károlyiho maď'arskou vládou v listopade a prosince 1918* (Bratislava, 1929), pp. 68-69.

[33]Annexe No. 1, dated December 18, 1918, attached to *Memoire No. 6*—reprinted in *La Paix de Versailles*, Vol. IX, pt. 1, pp. 98-99; and Stercho, *Diplomacy*, pp. 403-404.

[34]Report of Dr. Milan Hodža, representative of the Czechoslovak Republic in Budapest, to the Minister of Foreign Affairs in Prague, January 3, 1919, in A. Kocman et. al., eds., *Boj o směr vývoje československého státu*, Vol. I (Prague, 1965), doc. 28.

Rusyn leader "completely agreed today to the union of Uhors'ka [Hungarian] Rus' to us [Czechoslovakia]."[35] Later in Paris, the negotiations between Hodža and Komarnyts'kyi were to be used as one of the justifications for the incorporation of Subcarpathian Rus' into Czechoslovakia.

The arrival of the Czechoslovak Legionnaires in Uzhhorod on January 15 put the city definitely within the new country's sphere of influence and two weeks later came the news of the pro-Czechoslovak decision reached by Rusyn immigrants in the United States. As early as June 1918, immigrant leaders decided to concern themselves with the political fate of the homeland, and on July 23 formed an American National Council of Uhro-Rusyns. This body first demanded autonomy within Hungary, union with the Galician and Bukovinian Rusyns, or complete autonomy; it was not until September that association with the new state of Czechoslovakia was seriously considered. As a result of negotiations between President Woodrow Wilson, the Rusyn-American activist Gregory T. Zsatkovich, and the future president of Czechoslovakia, Tomáš G. Masaryk, the idea of union with Czechoslovakia was accepted. This request was incorporated into a resolution signed by Rusyn leaders in Scranton, Pennsylvania on November 12 and approved in a plebiscite held the following month among members of the two largest Rusyn-American fraternal organizations. The pro-Czechoslovak decision was acknowledged by the United States government and was to be of extreme importance in bolstering the arguments of Czech diplomats at the Paris Peace Conference.[36]

[35]*Ibid.* According to Ortoskop, *Derzhavni zmahannia,* p. 9, and Kaminskii, "Vospominaniia," no. 49, Komarnyts'kyi never signed any memorandum requesting union with Czechoslovakia. Nevertheless, the latter did sign the December 18, 1918 *procès verbale* and later, the May 8, 1919 formal declaration of union with Czechoslovakia.

[36]The activity of Rusyn-American immigrants is analyzed by Victor S. Mamatey, "The Slovaks and Carpatho-Ruthenians," in Joseph P. O'Grady, ed., *The Immigrant's Influence on Wilson's Peace Policies* (Lexington, Ky., 1967), pp. 224-249; Joseph Danko, "Plebiscite of Carpatho-Ruthenians in the United States Recommending Union of Carpatho-Ruthenia with the Czechoslovak Republic," *Annals of the Ukrainian Academy of Arts and Sciences,* XI, 1-2 (New York, 1964-68), pp. 184-207; and Walter K. Hanak, *The Subcarpathian-Ruthenian Question:*

"Only at the end of January," wrote Voloshyn, "did we find out from two Czech captains (Písecký and Vaka), sent to us in Uzhhorod by President Masaryk, that you, [our] American brothers, already decided that we be united to the Czechoslovak Republic."[37] Voloshyn and other members of the Uzhhorod Council continued to maintain relations with the Hungarian government,[38] but the presence of Czechoslovak troops in the city, together with knowledge of the Rusyn immigrant decision, helped persuade many Subcarpathian leaders that their interests could best be safeguarded by reaching an accord with Prague.

The Ukrainian orientation received its strongest and, as it turned out, last impetus during the first weeks of 1919. At the Council of the West Ukrainian Republic held on January 3 in Stanislaviv, two Subcarpathian representatives proclaimed: "Our hearts long for the Ukraine. Help us. Give us your fraternal hand. Long live one unified Ukraine."[39] The most important expression of pro-Ukrainian sentiment, however, was reserved for the General Council of Hungarian Rusyn-Ukrainians (Vsenarodni zbory uhors'kykh Rusyniv-Ukraïntsiv) which met in Khust on January 21. Arranged by Drs. Iu. and M. Brashchaiko, the dominant figures at previous meetings in Khust and Maramaţiei Sighetul, the General Council was made up of 420 delegates chosen by 175 smaller councils throughout Subcarpathian Rus'. The estimated 1200 Rusyns present made Khust the most representative of the many national councils to date.[40] Its resolution expressed a desire to belong to a United Ukraine (Soborna Ukraïna), requested that Ukrainian armed

1918-1945 (Munhall, Pa., 1962), pp. 7-13.

[37]Voloshyn, *Dvî polytychnî*, p. 7, and his "Interv'iu" in *Rusyn* (Uzhhorod), March 21-23, 1923.

[38]As late as February 9-10, 1919, the Uzhhorod Council under S. Sabov and A. Voloshyn submitted a memorandum to Rus'ka Kraina's Minister O. Szabó demanding implementation of Law 10. Kaminskii, "Vospominaniia," no. 42.

[39]Lozyns'kyi, *Halychyna*, p. 60. The letter of invitation to Brashchaiko, dated December 25, 1918, is reprinted in *Shliakhom Zhovtnia*, Vol. I, p. 496n. 34. The Subcarpathian delegates to the Stanislaviv meeting were the Hutsul leaders, S. Klochurak and D. Klempush. Shtefan, *Nashe viis'ko*, p. 9; I. Nahayewsky, *History of the Modern Ukrainian State, 1917-1923* (Munich, 1966), p. 135.

[40]Kaminskii, "Vospominaniia," no. 35. See also Rauser, "Připojení," p. 66; Stefan, *From Carpatho-Ruthenia*, p. 21; Netochaiev, "Vplyv," pp. 56-61; Smiian, *Zhovtneva revoliutsiia*, pp. 61-70.

forces (presumably from the West Ukrainian Republic) occupy their land, and, claiming to represent all Rusyns south of the Carpathians, rejected Hungarian Law No. 10 and autonomous Rus'ka Kraina.[41] Plans were also made to send a delegation to Stanyslaviv and even to Kiev, but the Polish occupation of eastern Galicia and the unstable political situation in the Dnieper Ukraine soon caused a decline in enthusiasm for the Ukrainian solution.

Meanwhile, the Károlyi regime in Budapest, concerned about the widespread pro-Ukrainian sentiment expressed at the Khust Council, made an effort to organize as soon as possible an administration for Rus'ka Kraina, then centered in Mukachevo. On February 5, 1919, temporary authority was invested in a council composed of forty-two members drawn from four Rusyn counties and presided over the Minister Oreszt Szabó and and Governor Dr. Agoston Stefan.[42] Elections to a thirty-six member Soim (Diet) were held on March 4 and a week later the first session was held, but the representatives adjourned the body until the Hungarian government defined clearly the borders of the province. In fact, the government was also under pressure from conservative factions in Budapest who felt that Károlyi "gave the Rusyns more than they desired ... and that this 'more' was detrimental to Hungary."[43] As for the issue of borders, the Minister of Interior declared that "not even a small part of the Magyar population ... can ever be left under the authority of an uncultured and economically backward Rusyn people."[44] Such opinion did not augur well for any kind of Rusyn autonomy in Hungary.

Before the Soim was to meet again, Bolshevik elements under Béla Kun replaced the Károlyi regime on March 21. A Soviet Rus'ka Kraina was proclaimed, but this had little effect on the governing personnel; the non-Communist Dr. Stefan was reappointed, this time with the title of commissar. The Kun government hoped that local national councils

---

[41]The resolution is reprinted in Stercho, *Diplomacy*, p. 401, and partially in Ortoskop, *Derzhavni zmahannia*, pp. 21-22.

[42]"Ukaz pravytel'stva Uhorskoî Narodnoî Republyky chysla 928/1919 v dîlî orhanyzatsiî Rus'koho Pravytel'stvennoho Sovîtu" (dated Budapest, February 5, 1919), *Karpato-rus'kii vîstnyk*, February 3, 1919.

[43]*Budapesti hirlap*, January 6, 1919, cited in Smiian, *Zhovtneva revoliutsiia*, p. 47.

[44]*Budapesti hirlap*, February 2, 1919, cited in *ibid.*, p. 51.

would administer the area, and elections to such bodies were held on April 6 and 7. As a result, Soviet Hungarian Rus'ka Kraina, which maintained real authority only in the county of Bereg, had two legislative bodies: the recently elected national councils and the Soim chosen under the Károlyi government. The Soim did meet on April 17, but after a brief session it again refused to conduct further business unless the Hungarian goverment, within a period of eight days, specified the boundaries of the province.[45]

During its few weeks of existence, Rus'ka Kraina was provided with a constitution "that recognized the independence of the Rusyn people" within the Hungarian Soviet Republic. With regard to the troublesome question of boundaries, the constitution avoided the issue by stating that "now the establishment of borders for Rus'ka Kraina is not necessary because the Soviet Republic does not recognize legally established state borders."[46] Cultural autonomy seemed guaranteed, Rusyn was declared the official language, a few school texts were published, and a Rusyn language department was established at the University of Budapest.[47] Under the influence of a generally far left-oriented political atmosphere, various decrees were promulgated that called for nationalization of mines, industry, and transportation, and for requisition of property from landlords and the church. A Rusyn Red Guard was also formed as part of the Hungarian Soviet Army and death penalties were imposed for "counterrevolutionaries" and speculators who with held foodstuffs.[48]

[45]Mel'nikova, "Kak byla vkliuchena," pp. 123-124; V.V. Usenko, *Vplyv Velykoï Zhovtnevoï sotsialistychnoï revoliutsiï na rozvytok revoliutsiinoho rukhu v Zakarpatti v 1917-1919 rr.* (Kiev, 1955), pp. 131-135; Kaminskii, "Vospominania," no. 33; Eva S. Balogh, "Nationality Problems of the Hungarian Soviet Republic," in Ivan Völgyes, ed., *Hungary in Revolution, 1918-19* (Lincoln, Nebraska, 1971), pp. 101-103; Mykhailo Troian, *Uhors'ka komuna 1919 r.* (L'viv, 1970), pp. 129-131; Smiian, *Zhovtneva revoliutsiia*, pp. 95-109.

[46]"Konstytutsiia Rus'koi Kraini," *Rus'ka pravda* (Mukachevo), April 12, 1919. Also reprinted in *Shliakhom Zhovtnia*, Vol. I, doc. 125.

[47]Usenko, *Vplyv*, pp. 150-151; Troian, *Uhors'ka komuna*, pp. 136-138; Balogh, "Nationality Problems," pp. 103-104; Iuliian A. Iavorskii, "Literaturnyi otgoloski 'rus'ko-krainskago' perioda v Zakarpatskoi Rusi 1919 goda," in *Karpatorusskii sbornik* (Uzhhorod, 1930), pp. 79-87.

[48]Usenko, *Vplyv*, pp. 136-154; Troian, *Uhors'ka komuna*, pp. 131-135; *Shliakhom Zhovtnia*, Vol. I, docs. 78-153.

The decrees passed in Rus'ka Kraina during the month of April had only limited effect in the region surrounding the cities of Mukachevo and Berehovo (Beregszász). Czechoslovak troops were slowly moving eastward from Uzhhorod, while the Hutsul Republic had control over most of Máramaros county. But despite its tenuous existence, the nominally autonomous province of Rus'ka Kraina was to be important in future ideological disputes. Indeed, Marxist historians have overestimated the importance of "Soviet rule" that began in late March. They see the period as an unsuccessful though important precedent for the future dictatorship of the proletariat which was not to be reestablished until 1944.[49] In 1919, however, Soviet rule never established deep roots in the area, and even some Marxists have had to admit that "many [in fact, most—PRM] of the decrees of the Soviet government were not implemented."[50] Of more immediate significance for the subsequent history of Subcarpathian Rus' was the fact that in Rus'ka Kraina Rusyns legally had their own autonomous province and Soim. During its twenty years of administration in the province, the Czechoslovak regime was to be continually reproached vith the argument: "Our land as Rus'ka Kraina already received autonomy from the Magyars at the end of 1918 .... In the framework of Rus'ka Avtonoma Kraina the leaders of our people saw a guarantee of our national liberty."[51]

Fearing the growth of Bolshevik power in east-central Europe,

---

[49]"Despite the relatively short period of existence of Soviet rule in the Mukachevo area . . . its importance was very great . . . . [Soviet rule) was an important moral and political victory for Bolshevik ideas . . . . The age-long struggle of the workers of Transcarpathia against the internal exploiters and external counterrevolutionaries came to a close in late October 1944 with the liberation of Transcarpathia from fascist occupation by the heroic Red Army and the union with Soviet Ukraine." M.V. Troian, "Borot'ba trudiashchykh Mukachivshchyny za Radians'ku vladu v 1918-1919 rr.," *Naukovi zapysky*, XXX (Uzhhorod, 1957), pp. 83-84.

[50]*Ibid.*, p. 76. There is no indication in Soviet or other sources that the decrees were greeted with favor by the local populace, and it is quite likely that the forced acquisition of foodstuffs (*Shliakhom Zhovtnia*, Vol. I, docs. 89-91, 109, 112, 128) was opposed by the peasantry.

[51]I.V. Kaminskii, quoted in "Postupova abo konservatyvna polytyka?," *Rusyn*, February 6, 1923. See also his "Nasha avtonomiia (samouprava)," *Ruskii zemledîl'skii kalendar* (Uzhhorod, 1922), pp. 69-70.

Czechoslovak Legionnaires under the French General Edmond Hennocque were given orders in mid-April to attack Soviet Hungarian troops. Moreover, Soviet rule in the area was at the same time being undermined by a series of "counterrevolutionary" uprisings that were supported by the Rus'ka Kraina commissar himself, Dr. A. Stefan. In conjunction with the Czechoslovak military action, a Romanian Army moved in from the southeast, and by the end of the month all governing remnants in Rus'ka Kraina were dissolved.[52] The Hungarian orientation in Subcarpathian Rus' was doomed.

Assured that the Soviet and non-Soviet Hungarian apparatus was driven out of the region, the remaining Rusyn leaders no longer felt threatened by the "Bolshevik menace" and prepared to implement the pro-Czechoslovak solution. Since early March, the Rusyn-American delegate, G. Zsatkovich, was negotiating in Uzhhorod with the Rusyn Club (Rus'kii Klub), a group of local leaders (many of whom only recently favored autonomy within Hungary) under the leadership of A. Voloshyn. Plans were made to call a general meeting made up of representatives from the former Prešov, Uzhhorod, and Khust Councils.[53]

On May 8, 1919, some 200 delegates from these councils gathered in Uzhhorod to form a Central Russian National Council (Tsentral'na Russka Narodna Rada). The proceedings were chaired by A. Voloshyn, and about 1200 hundred people were present. After reviewing the varied decisions of the previous national councils, the following resolution was unanimously accepted: "The Central Russian National Council publicly declares that in the name of the whole nation it completely endorses the decision of the American Uhro-Rusyn Council to unite with the Czecho-Slovak nation on the basis of full national autonomy."[54] Before adjourning, A. Beskid was elected (in absentia)

---

[52]Usenko, *Vplyv*, pp. 159-177; Balogh, "Nationality Problems," pp. 104-105.

[53]Iaroslav Kmitsikevych, "1919-i rik na Zakarpatti (spohad)," *Naukovyi zbirnyk Muzeiu ukraïns'koï kult'ury v Svydnyku*, IV, pt. 1 (Bratislava and Prešov, 1969), pp. 381-384; G.I. Žatkovič, *Otkrytie-Exposé byvšoho gubernatora Podkarpatskoj Rusi, o Podkarpatskoj Rusi* (Homestead, Pa., 1921), pp. 10-15 and idem, "Polnoe spravozdanie h'na H.Y. Zhatkovycha," *Amierykanskii russkii vîstnyk* (Homestead, Pa.), June 5, 1919; Kaminskii, "Vospominaniia," no. 64.

[54]*Protokoly obshchago sobraniia podkarpatskikh russkikh rad i ... Tsentral'noi Russkoi Narodnoi Rady*, reprinted in *Karpatorusskije novosti* (New York), May 15,

chairman, and A. Voloshyn, Miron Stripskii, and Dr. M. Brashchaiko, vice-chairmen.[55] In five subsequent sessions of the Central Russian National Council held between May 9 and 16, the Rusyn leaders worked out details regarding the future relationship between the "Russian State" (Russkii Shtat)—as Subcarpathian Rus' was called—and Czechoslovakia. The concept of statehood was undoubtedly devised by Zsatkovich, who thought the territory should be internally self-governing, i.e., analogous to the political situation in the United States. Already on the first day of debate, the Galician Russophiles (well represented on the Central Council) stressed "that our task is to free and unite all Carpatho-Rusyns, including the [Galician] Lemkos."[56] Both Voloshyn and Zsatkovich agreed in principle, but they thought it unwise to deal with matters concerning Galicia until the problem of Subcarpathian Rus' was satisfactorily solved. Nevertheless, the Galicians did manage to have a motion passed to request school textbooks from the Russophile Kachkovskii Society in L'viv. The Central Council also decided to

1944.

[55]Kmitsikevych claims that Beskid was present on May 8, but this is not borne out by the protocols or by another participant, G. Zsatkovich, who reported that Beskid remained in Prešov awaiting (in vain) to be called by the government to Prague. "Uriadovŷi report Amerykanskoi Komyssii Rusynov," *Amierykanskii russkii vîstnyk*, July 3, 1919.

[56]Protocol of May 8 in *Karpatorusskije novosti*, May 15, 1944. The pro-Czechoslovak Prešov National Council had all along demanded union with the non-Ukrainophile Galician Rusyns (or Lemkos as they were called). See the Prešov Council resolutions of January 7 and 31, 1919, and memorandum of May 1, 1919, addressed to President Wilson: reprinted in Peška and Markov, "Příspěvek," pp. 531-534. Similar demands were formulated by Dr. A. Beskid in a memorandum, dated March 12, 1919, to the Czechoslovak government (reprinted in *Boj o směr*, Vol. I, doc. 54) and one, dated April 20, 1919, to the Entente powers: Anthony Beskid and Dimitry Sobin, *The Origin of the Lems, Slavs of Danubian Provenance, Memorandum to the Peace Conference concerning their national claims* (no date or place of publication). The second document clearly defined territorial demands which did not include all of Galicia but only the lands of the non-Ukrainian "Russes des Carpathes (Lemki)"—an area north of the Carpathians stretching roughly from Nowy Sącz in the west to the source of the San River in the east. The farthest northern extent included the Galician towns of Dukla and Sanok.

recommend Gregory Zsatkovich "as minister with full power for our state."[57]

The last session made clear the Rusyn view of Subcarpathia's future political status. The Central Council decided to accept a fourteen-point plan (drawn up by Zsatkovich) as the basis for unification with Czechoslovakia. Point one stated that "the Rusyns will form an independent state in the Czecho-Slovako-Russian Republic [Chesko-slovensko-russka respublika]." Great stress was put on the fact that "in all administrative and internal matters the Ugro-Russian state will be independent" (point 4). The boundaries of this state would eventually be decided upon by a joint Ugro-Russian-Czechoslovak Commission (point 2). Until such time, the "Russian State" should include not only Rusyn territories east of the Uzh River, but also the northern portions of Szepes, Sáros, and Zemplén counties (point 13)—at that time under Slovak administration. The plan's last point reserved the right of the "Russian State" to appeal to the projected court of a League of Nations, which would decide on disputes that might arise with the Czechoslovak goverment.[58]

On May 23 a delegation of 112 members from the Central Russian National Council arrived in Prague to meet with President Masaryk and to express its desire for union. As Avhustyn Voloshyn later recalled, great faith was placed in "our Czech brothers." "Golden Prague solemnly greeted [and] sincerely cared for the Rusyns, and we returned home with hope for a better future."[59] Nevertheless, the question of internal autonomy, for the resolution of the Slovak-Subcarpathian boundary, and the cultural policy to be adopted for the province—issues already raised at several sessions of the Central Russian National Council—developed into serious problems that were to plague relations with the central government for the next two decades.

Thus by May 1919 Czechoslovak troops occupied a significant portion of Subcarpathian Rus', and local leaders had formally demanded unification with the new state. All that remained was that the

[57]Protocols of May 14 and 15, *Karpatorusskije novosti*, May 15, 1944; *Amierykanskii russkii vîstnyk*, July 3, 1919; N.A. Beskid, *Karpatskaia Rus'* (Prešov, 1920), pp. 105-106.

[58]Protocol of May 16 in *Karpatorusskije novosti*, May 15, 1944.

[59]Voloshyn, *Spomynŷ*, p. 94.

Czechoslovak solution be accepted in international diplomatic circles.[60] Although Subcarpathian Rus' had not entered the original plans for a Czechoslovak state,[61] the negotiations between Masaryk and Rusyn immigrants in the United States and the demands of the Prešov and Svaliava National Councils forced Prague officials to revise their ideas concerning the eastern boundary. By February 1919 the Czechoslovak delegation to the Paris Peace Conference formally proposed the inclusion into their state of Rusyn territory south of the Carpathians.[62] Indeed, representatives of Ukrainian, Hungarian, anti-Bolshevik Russian, Russophile Galician, and even the Romanian governments submitted counterclaims for Subcarpathian territory, but Allied statesmen considered Ukraine politically unviable, looked upon Hungary as a defeated power which should not be taken seriously, and disregarded Russia because of the continuance of Bolshevik rule and the undetermined outcome of the civil war there.[63] Furthermore, the

[60]The best account of these developments is found in D. Perman, *The Shaping of the Czechoslovak State* (Leiden, 1962), pp. 213 ff., and Stercho, *Diplomacy*, pp. 29-38.

[61]Masaryk originally expected the area would be part of a united Russia. He claimed that only in 1917, during his stay in Kiev, was the problem "discussed many times" with Ukrainian leaders. Supposedly, the latter "had no objection to the unification of Subcarpathian Rus' with us." Tomáš G. Masaryk, *Světová revoluce za války a ve válce 1914-1918* (Prague, 1938), p. 290. Curiously, none of the Ukrainian leaders (D. Doroshenko, P. Khrystiuk, A. Margolin, I. Mazepa, V. Petriv, V. Vynnychenko) mention in their memoirs any conversation with Masaryk about Subcarpathian Rus'. Nor does O.I. Bochkovs'kyi in his informative account of Masaryk in Kiev—*T.G. Masaryk: Natsional'na problema ta ukraïns'ke pytannia* (Poděbrady, 1930), pp. 135-153—say anything about discussions regarding the Subcarpathian problem. The silence is intriguing since subsequently the West Ukrainian and Ukrainian National Republics claimed sovereignty over all "Ukrainians" living south of the Carpathians.

[62]Czechoslovak Delegation, *Mémoire No. 6: The Ruthenes of Hungary* (Paris, 1919).

[63]*Mémoire sur l'indépendence de l'Ukraine présenté à la Conférence de la Paix par la délégation de la République ukrainienne* (Paris, 1919); *Aide-mémoire adressé aux puissances alliées et associées* (Vienna, 1919)—actually a declaration by Magyarone Rusyns living in Budapest, reprinted in *The Hungarian Peace Negotiations*, Vol. I (Budapest, 1921), pp. 483-489; "Memorandum of the Russian Political Conference," May 10, 1919, reprinted in John M. Thompson, *Russia, Bolshevism and the Versailles Peace* (Princeton, N.J., 1966), p. 399; Dmitrij

influential French delegation to the Peace Conference desired the creation of a large Czechoslovak state which, via Subcarpathian Rus', would have a common border with a future ally, Romania. In such a situation, the Czechoslovak delegation had little difficulty in having its demands accepted. On September 10, 1919, the Treaty of St. Germain-en-Laye recognized the incorporation of "Ruthene territory south of the Carpathians" into Czechoslovakia.

The Czechoslovak solution to the problem of Subcarpathian Rus' reflected not only the requirement of Entente diplomacy, but also the demands of local Rusyn leaders. During the critical months of late 1918 and early 1919 they formed many national councils which proposed various political alternatives for the future of their homeland. These choices, whether pro-Hungarian, pro-Russian, pro-Ukrainian, or pro-Czechoslovak, were not simply reflections of recent events, but were indicative of a Subcarpathian political and national tradition that were formulated in the late nineteenth century. The national and social factor, which fostered the desire to unite with Russia or Ukraine, was balanced by political realism and the potential of reaching an accord with the Hungarians or the Czechoslovaks. Hence, the decision of May 8, 1919, to unite with Czechoslovakia was not imposed by the "imperialistic" Entente powers, as Marxist writers suggest, or an unjust stifling of Ukrainian national desires, as Soviet and some non-Soviet Ukrainians conclude, but rather was the logical result of a coincidence between traditional Subcarpathian Rusyn interests and the particular international circumstances in post-war Europe.

Markoff, *Mémoire sur les aspirations nationales des Petits-Russiens de l'ancien empire austro-hongrois* (Paris, 1919). For Romania's claim to Subcarpathian Rus' and its rejection by the Entente, see Sherman D. Spector, *Rumania at the Peace Conference: A Study of the Diplomacy of I.C. Bratianu* (New York, 1962), pp. 127-128. The Polish government demanded only a small part of Rusyn-inhabited territory near Stará L'ubovňa: Commission polonaise des travaux préparatoires au Congrès de la paix, *Le Spisz, l'Orawa et le district de Czaca* (Warsaw, 1919) and *Territoires polonais en Hongrie septentrionale* (Paris, 1919).

CHAPTER 7

Magyars and Carpatho-Rusyns in Czechoslovakia[*]

A lmost at the moment that Czechoslovakia came into existence seventy years ago, political observers were quick to point out that the new country was, in a sense, the former multinational Austro-Hungarian Empire rewrit small. Indeed, with the exception perhaps of Yugoslavia, Czechoslovakia was the most ethnically complex country of Europe. The subject of this study is two of those peoples, the Magyars and Carpatho-Rusyns, in particular their internal development and their relationship to Czechoslovakia from its establishment in 1918 to the present.

Of Czechoslovakia's 13,600,000 inhabitants recorded in 1921, the Czechs, who numbered 6,747,000, made up barely half of the population (50.4 percent), the other half being divided into several nationalities: Germans (23.4 percent), Slovaks (15 percent), Magyars (5.6 percent), Carpatho-Rusyns (3.5 percent), and others (Jews, Poles,

[*] This study was commissioned for a conference in celebration of the seventieth anniversary of Czechoslovakia held at the University of Toronto in Ocotober 1988. An abridged version was published in H. Gordon Skilling, ed., *Czechoslovakia, 1918-88: Seventy Years from Independence* (London and Oxford: Macmillan/St. Antony's College, 1991), pp. 105-129. The full version republished here first appeared as, "Magyars and Carpatho-Rusyns: On the Seventieth Anniversary of the Founding of Czechoslovakia," in *Adelphotes: A Tribute to Omeljan Pritsak by his Students/ Harvard Ukrainian Studies*, XIV, 3/4 (Cambridge, Mass., 1990), pp. 427-460.

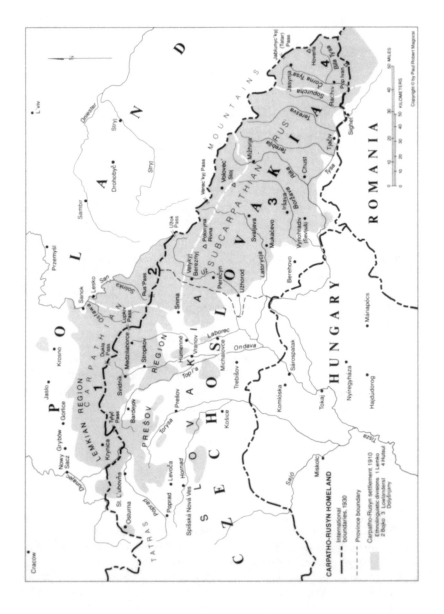

CARPATHO-RUSYN HOMELAND

International
boundaries, 1930

Province boundary

Carpatho-Rusyn settlement 1910
Ethnolinguistic divisions 1 Lemko
2 Bojko 3 Lowlanders/ 4 Hutsul
Dolyšňany

Gypsies, together 2.1 percent).[1] The Magyars and Carpatho-Rusyns were to be found almost exclusively in the eastern provinces of the republic—in Slovakia and Subcarpathian Rus'.[2]

The 1921 percentages of Magyars and Carpatho-Rusyns were obviously larger in these eastern provinces than throughout the country as a whole. In Slovakia, Magyars numbered 637,000 and Carpatho-Rusyns 86,000—respectively 21.5 percent and 2.9 percent of the population in that province. In Subcarpathian Rus', the analogous figures were 373,000 (62.1 percent) Carpatho-Rusyns and 192,000 (17 percent) Magyars.[3] Geographically, the two groups inhabited ethnically compact areas; the Magyars in the southern lowlands of Slovakia and Subcarpathian Rus', and the Carpatho-Rusyns in the foothills and mountainous terrain of Subcarpathian Rus' and far northeastern Slovakia.

At the outset of the period, these two groups numbered together nearly 1,200,000 people (in 1921), or 8.9 percent of the total population of Czechoslovakia. Since 1945, as a result of border changes and assi-

---

[1]Václav L. Beneš, "Czechoslovak Democracy and its Problems, 1918-1920," in Victor S. Mamatey and Radomir Luža, eds. *A History of the Czechoslovak Republic, 1918-1948* (Princeton, N.J., 1973), p. 40. Here and elsewhere in this text, the figures have been rounded off to the nearest thousand and nearest half percentage point.

It should be noted that Czechoslovakia's official statistics before World War II did not distinguish between Czechs and Slovaks, but provided only the rubric "Czechoslovak." The calculation for Czechs indicated here is based on the total number of "Czechoslovaks" living in Bohemia, Moravia, Silesia, and Subcarpathian Rus' (Ruthenia); the calculation for Slovaks reflects the total number of "Czechoslovaks" in Slovakia. As for Carpatho-Rusyns, the official rubrics used to describe them have varied: *podkarpatoruský* (Subcarpathian Rusyn), *ruský* (Russian/Rusyn), and since 1945 *ukrajinský* (Ukrainian), *ruský* (Russian), *rusínsky* (Rusyn). The figures appearing here and elsewhere in this study reflect all of the above terms (two or more of which are sometimes indicated separately in one statistical source), although the group will be described throughout using the name Carpatho-Rusyn, which in other sources is sometimes rendered as Ruthenian, Rusyn, Carpatho-Russian, or Carpatho-Ukrainian.

[2]As for other parts of the republic, the 1921 census recorded in Bohemia, Moravia, and Silesia only 6,100 Magyars and 3,300 Carpatho-Rusyns; the 1931 census recorded 11,600 Magyars and 11,100 Carpatho-Rusyns. Beneš, "Czechoslovak Democracy," p. 40.

[3]*Ibid.*

milatory processes, the number of Magyars and Carpatho-Rusyns has been reduced by half (in 1980—560,000 and 37,000, respectively), and together they comprise a mere 4.1 percent of the population of the country.[4] Despite their relatively small numbers, both Magyars and Carpatho-Rusyns have, because of their strategic geographic location and their relationship to peoples of neighboring states, remained an issue of serious political concern throughout most of the seven decades of Czechoslovakia's existence.

How and why did the Magyars and Carpatho-Rusyns come to be a part of the new state of Czechoslovakia? Since this is not the place to elaborate on the formation of the new Czechoslovak state, suffice it to say that its final form was justified by using historic and ethnographic arguments, despite the fact that these at times might seem contradictory. While the ethnographic argument was used to justify the inclusion of Slovak-inhabited areas with Czech lands farther west, the solid Magyar-inhabited regions of what was to become southern Slovakia were demanded neither on historic nor ethnographic grounds but for strategic purposes: the Czechoslovak delegation to the Paris Peace Conference was convinced that a "border along the Danube was of utmost importance to the Czechoslovak republic," which, "to be more precise, must be a Danubian state."[5] As for Carpatho-Rusyn territory, this unexpected "gift to Czechoslovakia" came as a result of a request by immigrants from that area living in the United States, although Czech leaders were quick to point out that what was to become the province of Subcarpathian Rus' (and was eventually to border on Romania) had strategic value as well.

The history of the Magyars and Carpatho-Rusyns within Czechoslovakia can be said to fall into three periods: 1918-1938; 1938-1944; and 1945 to the present. Given the limitations of space, it is not possible to describe except in the most general terms the evolution of these two groups and to compare and contrast their development and status during these three periods.

---

[4]Ivan Bajcura, *Cesta k internacionálnej jednote* (Bratislava, 1982), p. 27.

[5]From the memorandum to the Paris Peace Conference submitted by Czechoslovakia's minister of foreign affairs, Edvard Beneš, cited in Ferdinand Peroutka, *Budování státu*, pt. 2: *rok 1919* (Prague, 1934), pp. 1103-1105.

The interwar years (1918-1938)

During the first period, 1918-1938, there was in effect a basic difference in the legal status of the Magyars and Carpatho-Rusyns. The Magyars, for instance, were a national minority, in contrast to both the Czechs and Slovaks (more precisely "Czechoslovaks"), who were considered the state or dominant people of the country, and to the Carpatho-Rusyns who had a special status at least in the far eastern part of the republic.

The minority status of the Magyars was made even more dubious because in the early years of the new republic their status as citizens of Czechoslovakia remained uncertain.[6] Whereas the Treaty of Saint Germain (10 September 1919) granted "without the requirement of any formality" Czechoslovak citizenship to former Hungarian citizens of Slovakia and Subcarpathian Rus' who had possessed legal residence in a given commune (the so-called *Heimatsrecht*), a subsequent Czechoslovak constitutional law (9 April 1920) specified that to obtain citizenship automatically, persons had to have had legal residence before 1910. As for those who did not have legal residence before that year, the Czechoslovak government reserved for itself the right to decide whether they were worthy of receiving citizenship. The practical result of this law was to encourage between 56,000 and 106,000 Magyars (mostly former officials if the first figure is accepted, officials as well as laborers if the second is accepted) to emigrate southward to postwar Hungary. This left stateless for varying periods of time during the interwar years anywhere from 15,000 to 100,000 Magyars in the southern region of Slovakia and Subcarpathian Rus'.[7]

In sharp contrast was the situation of the Carpatho-Rusyns. While they were not a state people like the "Czechoslovaks," they held a special status, spelled out as part of the postwar international peace agreements (Treaty of Saint Germain, 10 September 1919) and then reiterated in the Czechoslovak constitution (29 February 1920): "the Ruthene territory south of the Carpathians" would become "an

---

[6]The complicated question of the status of the Magyars and the devastating effect statelessness had on individuals is discussed in C. A. Macartney, *Hungary and Her Successors: The Treaty of Trianon and Its Consequences, 1919-1937* (Oxford, 1937), pp. 160-165.

[7]*Ibid.*, pp. 158 and 164.

autonomous unit" accorded "the fullest degree of self-government compatible with the unity of the Czecho-Slovak State."[8] Among the autonomous characteristics granted the territory that came to be known as Subcarpathian Rus' (Czech: Podkarpatská Rus) were its own diet, governor, and "equitable representation" in the Czechoslovak parliament.

Whereas it is true that the specific nature of that autonomy and even the boundaries of Subcarpathian Rus' were to become issues of controversy, the fact remains that Carpatho-Rusyn territory became part of Czechoslovakia precisely because it was inhabited by a group of Slavs who, by joining voluntarily the new republic, gained a special status that at least in their own province made them more like the "Czechoslovak" state nationality than the national minorities (Magyars, Jews, Germans, Gypsies, Romanians) living in their midst.[9]

The Magyars, then, were classified as a national minority. In the Treaty of Saint Germain and again in its constitution, Czechoslovakia pledged that members of national minorities would be equal with other citizens before the law and have the right to schools in their native tongue. In actual practice, as spelled out in the constitutional language law no. 122 (29 February 1920), this meant that in judicial districts where at least 20 percent of the population comprised a linguistic minority, that minority was entitled to use its language to make submissions to the court and to receive replies. In those instances where the minority comprised at least 50 percent of the population, it was entitled to have all judicial proceedings conducted in the minority language. If a rural community had a minimum of 40 children (calculated on a three-year average) or a town 400 children, then that community or town had the right to a school in the minority language.[10]

For instance, with regard to the Magyars in Slovakia, by 1934 there were 741 Magyar rural elementary schools (1,800 classes) accommo-

---

[8]*Traité entre les Principales Puissances Alliées et Associées et la Tchécoslovaquie* (Paris, 1919), pp. 26-27; "Ústavní listina Československé republiky," in *Sbírka zákonů a nařízení státu československého*, pt. 26 (Prague, 1920), p. 256.

[9]On the particular status of Subcarpathian Rus' within Czechoslovakia, see Zdeněk Peška, "Podkarpatská Rus," in *Slovník veřejného práva československého*, Vol. III (Prague, 1934), pp. 107-115.

[10]Macartney, *Hungary and Her Successors*, pp.154-155 and 165.

dating 91,500 pupils. This meant that 86.4 percent of the Magyar children in the republic received elementary education in their own language. The status of Magyar-language schools beyond the village was not as favorable. There were only 15 Magyar elementary schools in towns, so that only 31 percent of Magyar pupils at that level received education in their own language. In addition to elementary schools, the Magyars had 5 *gymnasia*, 1 teacher's college, and parallel classes in 2 more *gymnasia* and 1 teacher's college. Therefore, 72 percent of Magyar pupils at the secondary level attended schools in their own language. In contrast, there was a pronounced shortage of technical education in Magyar (2 agricultural schools, 1 commercial academy, 1 trade school) and no Hungarian chairs at the university level.[11]

The Magyars perceived their cultural status in Czechoslovakia, based on their educational opportunities, to be even worse than the above statistics would imply. By 1934 the number of Magyar elementary schools, which before the war numbered 2,200, had been reduced by two-thirds. Not only was university education in Magyar completely abolished, but for those Czechoslovak Magyars who ventured (often with difficulty) to study in Hungary, their diplomas were not recognized when, and if, they returned home. Such perceptions of seeming cultural injustice added fuel to the Magyars' political discontent, which was often expressed in votes for parties whose representatives spoke out frequently about the shortcomings of Czechoslovakia's educational and cultural policy toward its Magyars.[12]

Regardless of the reality or the perceptions of Czechoslovak policy,

---

[11]The figures in this paragraph are drawn from *ibid.*, pp. 166-167. For greater detail, see Juraj Purgat, *Od Trianonu po Košice: k mad'arskej otázke v Československu* (Bratislava, 1970), pp. 41-48.

[12]For a recent concise, if often overstated, review of Magyar discontent during the interwar years, see chapter 2 of Charles Wojatsek, *From Trianon to the First Vienna Arbitral Award: The Hungarian Minority in the First Czechoslovak Republic, 1918-1938* (Montreal, 1981), pp. 31-44. There are, of course, a large number of contemporary anti-Czechoslovak tracts that emanated from Hungary during the interwar years, the most comprehensive of which is the Hungarian Revision League's *Memorandum Concerning the Situation of the Hungarian Minority in Czechoslovakia* (Budapest, 1934), as well as works by sympathizers abroad, like the Swiss geographer, Aldo Dami, *Les nouveaux martyrs: destin des minorités* (Paris, 1930), esp. pp. 145-208.

it must be stressed that there was a significant percentage of Magyars who simply could not conceive, being as they were geographically so close to Budapest, that they would one day be living in any country other than Hungary. Moreover, even though they were now under Czechoslovak rule, this was surely of a temporary nature until the borders were redrawn to include at the very least Magyar-inhabited villages and cities, if not all of Slovakia and Subcarpathian Rus' (the traditional Hungarian Highland—Felvidék) right up to the crest of the Carpathians. Such an attitude was summed up in a speech to the Czechoslovak parliament within a week after its Magyar members had pledged their loyalty to the Czechoslovak republic. Addressing the assembly—of course in Hungarian—the spokesman for the largest Magyar party at the time, Deputy Lajos Ékes-Körmendy of the Regional Christian Socialists, stated:

> We consider it necessary to inform world opinion that we were against our will forcibly torn away from the Hungarian body; that we were torn from the most ideal thousand-year-old Hungarian state; and that our presence here [in the Czechoslovak parliament] should not be construed as a denial of the deeds done against [four] human rights, but rather as representing a living and solemn protest against the inhuman and unjust decisions made concerning us, but without consulting us.[13]

The obvious discontent with Czechoslovakia and the anticipation of some kind of future border revisionism was typical of all Magyar political parties in Slovakia and Subcarpathian Rus' during the interwar years. The most important of these were the National Christian Socialist party (Országos keresztényszocialista párt) and the Magyar National party (Magyar nemzeti párt), which in 1936 joined together to form the United Magyar party (Egyesült magyar párt) under the leadership of Count János Esterházy (1901-1957), Andor Jaross (1896-1946), and Géza Szüllő (1873-1957). These purely oppositional Magyar parties garnered on an average nearly half the votes in each of the four parliamentary elections (1920, 1925, 1929, 1935), while the rest of the Magyar vote went to the pro-government Agrarian and Social Democratic parties or to the Communist party, which was anti-

---

[13]Cited in Purgat, *Od Trianonu po Košice*, p. 68.

government until the signing of the Soviet-Czechoslovak pact in 1935.[14] The relative strengths of these political parties provide perhaps some insight into the attitudes of the Magyar minority in interwar Czechoslovakia. Certainly the established elements of pre-World War I Hungarian society that remained in Czechoslovakia—the landowners, Catholic and Protestant clergymen (likely to be magyarized Slovaks), Magyar and magyarized Jewish lawyers, school teachers, and other petty intelligentsia and former civil servants—were to remain unreconciled to Czechoslovak rule. It was they who often formed the leadership of the Magyar parties.

The attitudes of the Magyar peasantry were more difficult to ascertain. First of all, the peasantry clearly made up the majority (65.4 percent) of the Magyar population, followed by industrial workers (16.9 percent), merchants and financiers (6.3 percent), and civil servants and professionals (3.8 percent).[15] At first glance, it would seem that a certain percentage of the peasantry was content with Czechoslovak rule. The land reform carrried out in the early 1920s helped to redistribute land more equitably (79.8 percent of the large landholdings had formerly belonged to Magyar landlords), even though the landless class did not always benefit from the reform.

Even more important was the autarchic economic policy of the Czechoslovak government, which protected grain producers from potentiafly cheaper imported foodstuffs. The result was that the wheat-producing areas along the southern frontier inhabited primarily by Magyars were materially better off than before the war, and the peasants living there were certainly more prosperous than their fellow Magyars across the frontier in Hungary. Nonetheless, as C. A. Macartney observed during a visit to several Magyar peasant households in the 1930s, the sentiment he frequently encountered was the following: "We are better off under the Czechs than we should be

---

[14]For details on Magyar political parties in interwar Czechoslovakia, see Purgat, *Od Trianonu po Košice*, pp. 60-126; E. Arató, *Political Differentiation in the Hungarian Population of Czechoslovakia in the Post-World War I Years* (Budapest, 1975); and P. Komora, *Mad'arské buržoázne strany na Slovensku (1919-1929)*, Zborník Filozofickej fakulty University Komenského: Historica (Bratislava, 1970).

[15]Purgat, *Od Trianonu po Košice*, p. 48.

in Hungary, but if a vote came, I should still choose for Hungary."[16]
Such attitudes were confirmed at the ballot box during the communal
elections in June 1938, when Esterházy's United Magyar party received
58 percent of the vote in Magyar-inhabited regions, the highest any
anti-government party had received throughout the whole interwar
period.[17]

In contrast to the Magyar minority, which actively or passively awaited
the day when it would no longer be part of Czechoslovakia, the
Carpatho-Rusyns, who also demanded changes in their status and often
voted for anti-government parties, did so not because they were bent on
disrupting Czechoslovak political life but rather because they genuinely
hoped to improve their own group's status within a Czechoslovak polity
in which they planned to remain. Among their demands were: (1) a
definition of the territorial extent of the province of Subcarpathian Rus';
and (2) implementation of the autonomy guaranteed Carpatho-Rusyns
at the Paris Peace Conference.

With regard to territory, the original agreement reached in the
United States between Tomáš Masaryk and Carpatho-Rusyn immigrants
(Scranton, Pennsylvania, 12 November 1918) and the declaration of
Carpatho-Rusyn unity with Czechoslovakia proclaimed in the homeland
(Uzhhorod, 8 May 1919) spoke of nine historic counties as comprising
an autonomous "Rusyn state," including at the very least and until the
final Slovak-Rusyn border was drawn the northern portions of
Spiš/Szepes, Šariš/Sáros, and Zemplín/Zemplén counties west of the
Uzh River. This principle was then seemingly enshrined in the Treaty
of Saint Germain and the Czechoslovak constitution, which stated that
all "Ruthene territory south of the Carpathians" would become part of
a single province that was to be granted autonomy.[18]

Certainly, at that time no one doubted that the northern portions of

---

[16]Cited in Macartney, *Hungary and Her Successors*, p. 183.

[17]See the table in Purgat, *Od Trianonu po Košice*, p. 113.

[18]For details on the Carpatho-Rusyn/Czech negotiations in the United States and
at Paris, as well as on developments in the homeland in late 1918-early 1919, see
Paul Robert Magocsi, *The Shaping of a National Identity: Subcarpathian Rus',
1848-1948* (Cambridge, Mass., 1978), pp. 76-102; and Ivan Vanat, *Narysy novitn'oï
istoriï ukraïntsiv Skhidnoï Slovachchyny*, Vol. I: *1918-1938* (Bratislava and Prešov,
1979), pp. 46-102.

Spiš, Šariš, and Zemplín counties were inhabited by Carpatho-Rusyns. However, the peacemakers in Paris decided to fix the river Uzh as the western boundary of Subcarpathian Rus', and it was subsequently to be enshrined in the Czechoslovak constitution as the provisional boundary between the two provinces. Immediate protests lodged by Carpatho-Rusyn leaders in Paris were rebuffed by the Czechoslovak foreign minister Edvard Beneš, who correctly stated that the Slovaks would never agree to changes, since they were already discontent at not having their own border moved even farther east to include the "Slovak city" of Uzhhorod. Finally, in 1928, when the republic was administratively reorganized into four provinces, the boundary between Subcarpathian Rus' and Slovakia was definitely fixed along a line slightly west of the Uzh River (more or less the present Soviet-Czechoslovak border).

In effect, this meant that throughout the interwar period, Carpatho-Rusyns were to be administratively divided into two provinces: those living in the former counties of Uzh/Ung (only that part east of the Uzh River), Bereg, Maramorosh/Máramaros, and Ugocha/Ugocsa (numbering 372,000 in 1921) were part of the theoretically autonomous Subcarpathian Rus'; those living west of the Uzh River in western Uzh, Zemplín, Šariš, Spiš, Abov, and Gemer counties (86,000 in 1921) were part of Slovakia.

Such administrative division also affected the status of these two groups. Carpatho-Rusyns in Subcarpathian Rus' were virtually the state nationality, whose language and cultural institutions were considered representative of the area. On the other hand, Carpatho-Rusyns in northeastern Slovakia were only a national minority, whose rights were guaranteed to the degree that they fulfilled the requirements of the other minorities living on "Slovak" territory.

Left with at most only three-quarters of the Carpatho-Rusyn population in Czechoslovakia, the province of Subcarpathian Rus' and its political leadership was also unsuccessful in attaining its other demand—autonomy. Again, the Treaty of Saint Germain spoke specifically of the "fullest degree of self-government compatible with the unity of the Czecho-Slovak State."[19] However, the question of the degree of that autonomy was to be decided by the central government in Prague.

Carpatho-Rusyn expectations regarding self-rule had been established

---

[19]*Traité entre les Principales Puissances*, p. 27

during the initial negotiations in the United States between Masaryk and the Rusyn-American immigrant spokesman, Gregory Zhatkovych, in late 1918 and again at the act of union carried out in Uzhhorod in May 1919. There, and subsequently in Prague, when Subcarpathian leaders met with then President Masaryk, clear reference was made to "the Rusyns who will form an independent state in the Czecho-Slovako-Rus' Republic."[20] Great stress was put on the fact that "in all administrative and internal matters the Ugro-Russian state will be independent."[21] The American citizen Zhatkovych, who formulated most of the demands, obviously assumed that Subcarpathian Rus' would be comparable to a state in the United States. Czechoslovak reality, however, was to be far from such self-governing expectations.

The Treaty of Saint Germain and the Czechoslovak constitution both called for a governor and diet for Subcarpathian Rus'. However, the diet was never convoked, and although a Carpatho-Rusyn governor held office, his authority was virtually non-existent, since a Czech-appointed vice-governor representing the Prague government was in charge of the provincial administration. As a result, the honeymoon between Carpatho-Rusyn political leaders and the new state of Czechoslovakia dissipated rather quickly. Already in March 1921, the first governor of the province, the Rusyn-American Gregory Zhatkovych, resigned in protest over the border and autonomy issues and returned to the United States.[22]

Although another governor was appointed in 1923, Prague continued its tight control over the province, which it hoped to integrate politically

---

[20]Protocol of the Central Rusyn National Council in Uzhhorod, 16 May 1919 session, cited in Magocsi, *Shaping of a National Identity*, p. 99

[21]*Ibid.*, p. 99.

[22]The governor's disillusionment with Czechoslovak rule was spelled out in Gregory I. Žatkovič, *Otkrytie-Exposé byvšeho gubernatora Podkarpatskoj Rusi, o Podkarpatskoj Rusi*, 2nd ed. (Homestead, Penn., 1921); and then later elaborated upon in several protests by Carpatho-Rusyn-American leaders, the most extensive by Michael Yuhasz, Sr., *Wilson's Principles in Czechoslovak Practice: The Situation of the Carpatho-Russian People under the Czech Yoke* (Homestead, Penn., 1929). For details on the legal relationship of Subcarpathian Rus' to the rest of Czechoslovakia during the interwar years, see Hans Ballreich, *Karpathenrussland: Ein Kapitel tschechischen Nationalitätenrechts und tschechischer Nationalitätenpolitik* (Heidelberg, 1938), esp. pp. 19-82.

even further with the rest of the country. Therefore, in 1928, when a new administrative structure was created for Czechoslovakia, Subcarpathian Rus' received instead of an autonomous diet a twenty-four-member provincial assembly (one-third of whose members were appointed), to be headed by the Czech vice-govemor, whose title was now changed to that of president of the renamed Subcarpathian Rusyn Land (Země podkarpatoruská). While there was still a Subcarpathian governor, his largely ceremonial functions were, as critics were quick to comment, appropriately carried out from an office located in the building of the city museum.

Because of the uncertain political atmosphere in Subcarpathian Rus' during the first few years of Czechoslovak rule (the unresolved provincial borders, the yet-to-be convened diet, the presence of Romanian troops occupying nearly half the province until June 1920), Carpatho-Rusyns did not participate in the parliamentary elections of 1921. When the Prague government finally thought the province was ready to participate in such elections in 1924, the result was a rude shock. Sixty percent of the votes cast were for opposition parties, the Subcarpathian Communists alone receiving 39.4 percent of the vote. The following year, in elections to the second parliament (1925), the results from the central government's perspective were not much better, with 54 percent of the vote going to opposition parties.[23]

Whereas discontent with unfulfilled autonomy and the border question were issues that motivated part of the anti-government vote, popular discontent was primarily related to economic concerns. There was no industry in Subcarpathian Rus', and as high as 74.5 percent of the Carpatho-Rusyn population (1930) was engaged in small-scale agriculture or forestry work. Even after the land reform of the 1920s, Carpatho-Rusyn peasants (of whom 75 percent had holdings of less than 5 hectares) were at best only able to eke out a subsistence-level existence on their tiny and often unproductive mountainous plots.[24] Before World War I, economic catastrophe had been avoided by the possibilities of seasonal work on the fertile Hungarian plain or permanent emigration abroad, mostly to the northeast United States. Now, in the postwar circumstances of Czechoslovakia, the new border

---

[23]Magocsi, *Shaping of a National Identity*, p. 206.
[24]Macartney, *Hungary and Her Successors*, pp. 235-236.

with Hungary cut off the option of summer work nearby, while United States restrictions on immigration (1921, 1924) effectively eliminated the American safety valve.

Such harsh economic reality boosted the popularity of the Subcarpathian Communist party, which called for a total transformation of society, and the fortunes of other opposition parties (Carpatho-Rusyn Agricultural Autonomist Union and various Magyar parties) that played on both economic and political discontent. The result was consistent electoral losses for the pro-government Czechoslovak parties. The only exception to this pattern was the parliamentary elections of 1929. The partial relief from the land reform and the enormous governmental investments in communication, transportation, economic development, and education, combined with a concerted effort during the electoral campaign, led to a slight majority of 54 percent for pro-government parties in the Subcarpathian vote. However, the effects of the world economic depression and the worsening status of the Carpatho-Rusyn peasantry in the early 1930s resulted in the most serious electoral condemnation of Czechoslovak rule. As high as 63 percent of the Subcarpathian electorate voted for opposition parties in the 1935 parliamentary elections.[25]

Another cause of discontent was in the area of local culture, in what came to be known as the nationality question. From the very outset, when Subcarpathian Rus' was still under military rule (1919-1920), the popular (*lidový*) or Carpatho-Rusyn (*rusínský*) language was designated for use in schools and, after 1926, for use as the official language (together with Czech) in the courts, the administration, and in other official activities. In this regard, the Czechoslovak authorities genuinely wished to allow Carpatho-Rusyns to develop their own language and culture.[26]

No one, however, in either the Czechoslovak governing circles or among the Subcarpathian leaders was certain just what the local language was—a dialect of Ukrainian, a dialect of Russian, or a distinct

---

[25]Magocsi, *Shaping of a National Identity*, pp. 207-209 and 224-225.

[26]Magocsi, *Shaping of a National Identity*, pp. 136-138; Peška, "Podkarpatská Rus," pp. 114-115; and George Y. Shevelov, "The Language Question in the Ukraine in the Twentieth Century (1900-1941)," *Harvard Ukrainian Studies*, XI, 1/2 (Cambridge, Mass., 1987), pp. 196-208.

Slavic language. Arguments and counterarguments for each position were put forth, so that before long the language question was transformed into a nationality question: Was the local population Ukrainian, Russian, or a distinct Carpatho-Rusyn nationality? What would each of these positions mean for the territorial integrity of Czechoslovakia? And, therefore, which orientation should the Prague government support?

The Czechoslovak government's position regarding the Subcarpathian nationality question was never really consistent. Initially, until about 1923, Prague supported the Ukrainian orientation, then (until the early 1930s) the Russian orientation, and finally (by the mid-1930s) the local Carpatho-Rusyn orientation. These changes in Czechoslovak policy were not only the result of political developments in Subcarpathian Rus'; they also reflected the increasing awareness among Czechoslovak leaders of the strategic importance of the province for the country's foreign policy. However, the government's frequent shifts in cultural policy alienated the local spokespersons for each of Subcarpathia's three national orientations.[27]

Besides the discontent caused by the Czechoslovak government's changing attitudes on the Subcarpathian language and nationality questions, another cause for increasing concern was the status of an entirely new minority that made its appearance among the Carpatho-Rusyns, namely, the Czechs. Whereas there were no Czechs in Subcarpathian Rus' before 1919, within two decades they numbered more than 35,000. The Czechs formed a virtual army of local and provincial civil servants who, together with their families, descended on the province. Not only did they take jobs away from potential Carpatho-Rusyn candidates, they also took advantage of the law on schools for national minorities (40 students in villages, 400 in towns). By 1936 the number of Czech-language schools—attended as well by many local Jews—increased from 0 to 204 (177 elementary, 23 municipal; 3 *gymnasia*, 1 teacher's college).[28]

It would be an error, however, to overstate the level of Subcarpathian

---

[27]Magocsi, *Shaping of a National Identity*, pp. 202-233 passim.

[28]For details on the relative presence of Czechs, Carpatho-Rusyns, and other minorities in the Subcarpathian administration, see Macartney, *Hungary and Her Successors*, pp. 224-228.

discontent with Czechoslovakia during the first republic. The criticism directed by Carpatho-Rusyn politicians and commentators was perhaps more a reflection of the success of the democratic process at work than it was an indication that some fundamental change, such as opting out of Czechoslovakia, was a desired alternative. In fact, subsequent events were to prove the basic loyalty of most Carpatho-Rusyns toward the Czechoslovak republic.

The Munich Crisis and the war years (1938-1944)

The international political crisis of 1938 that began with Hitler's demands for border revisions in order to rectify the problem of the *Volksdeutsche*—Germans living outside the Third Reich—culminated on 28 September 1938 with the signing by Germany, Italy, Great Britain, and France of the Munich Pact. This agreement had a profound impact not only upon Germans living within Czechoslovakia but also upon the status of Magyars and Carpatho-Rusyns. In fact, an annex to the Munich Pact, together with a declaration signed the same day, specified that the problems of the Magyar and Polish minorities were to be resolved within three months by Czechoslovakia, Hungary, and Poland; otherwise, a new conference of the four Munich signatories would be held to resolve this issue.[29]

Encouraged by the Munich declaration, the Hungarian government, whose interwar rhetoric was based continually on calls for border revisionism, now saw its chance. Backed especially by Italy, Budapest was able to force Czechoslovakia to the bargaining table, a process that lasted with interruptions throughout the month of October. For their part, United Magyar party activists in Czechoslovakia, János Esterházy and Géza Szüllő, established a Magyar National Council which openly demanded the "reunification" of a large part of Slovakia with Hungary.[30]

The Budapest government heightened political tension by partially mobilizing its army and by allowing irredentist bands to infiltrate the

---

[29]The text of the Munich Pact and its annexes is reproduced in Wojatsek, *From Trianon*, pp. 205-206.

[30]For details on the Czechoslovak-Hungarian negotiations and the activity of Czechoslovakia's Magyars, see Wojatsek, *From Trianon*, pp. 151-170; and Loránt Tilkovszky, *Južné Slovensko v rokoch 1938-1945* (Bratislava, 1972), pp. 27-40.

border into southern Slovakia and Subcarpathian Rus'. Finally, both Czechoslovakia and Hungary agreed to arbitration, which resulted in the so-called Vienna Award of 2 November 1938. Slovakia and Subcarpathian Rus' together lost to Hungary 4,500 square kilometers and 972,000 inhabitants, including the important regional centers of Košice (Hungarian: Kassa) and Uzhhorod (Hungarian: Ungvár). The vast majority of Czechoslovakia's Magyars now found themselves once again within the borders of Hungary.[31] While it is true that 66,000 Magyars were left within Slovakia (2.5 percent of the total population), for all intents and purposes the Magyar question within Czechoslovakia ceased to exist for the duration of the war.

With the transformation of Czechoslovakia into a federative republic following the Munich Pact, Subcarpathian Rus' finally was able to obtain its long promised autonomy. This was achieved through orderly negotiations between Carpatho-Rusyn parliamentary leaders and the government of the second, now federated, Czecho-Slovak republic. While it is true that the first autonomous government of Subcarpathian Rus', convened in October 1938, was initially dominated by individuals (Andrei Brodii and Stepan Fentsyk) who worked for reunion with Hungary, it was replaced on October 26 by a new government headed by the local Ukrainian-oriented activist, and Greek Catholic priest, Avhustyn Voloshyn (1874-1945).[32]

Like neighboring autonomous Slovakia, Subcarpathian Rus' faced the loss of its southern Magyar-inhabited regions (including the province's capital of Uzhhorod and its second largest city, Mukachevo), which were returned to Hungary by the Vienna Award of November 2. However, Carpatho-Rusyns now formed a larger percentage of the population (78 percent as opposed to the previous 63 percent), and the policy of the Voloshyn government reflected in large measure the basic pro-Czechoslovak orientation of the province's increased Slavic majority. Even though it had taken the international crisis at Munich to force Prague to grant autonomy to Carpatho-Rusyns, the Subcarpathian

---

[31]Tilkovszky, *Južné Slovensko*, pp. 48-81; and Theodore Prochazka,"The Second Republic, 1938-1939," in Mamatey and Luža, *History*, pp. 258-259.

[32]For details on the Subcarpathian/Carpatho-Ukrainian autonomous period, see Peter G. Stercho, *Diplomacy of Double Morality: Europe's Crossroads in Carpatho-Ukraine, 1919-1939* (New York, 1971), esp. pp. 107-144 and 226-283.

or, as it was soon renamed, Carpatho-Ukrainian autonomous government genuinely hoped to work on an equal basis with the Czechs and
Slovaks in the truncated but federated second republic, a structure
which more closely fitted earlier Carpatho-Rusyn expectations of what
the first republic was supposed to have been like when it was created
two decades before.

Whereas there may have been talk in German circles of making little
Carpatho-Ukraine a piedmont for a future anti-Soviet Ukrainian state,
and whereas local Ukrainian-oriented leaders (with help from refugees
from neighboring Polish-controlled Galicia) may have been dreaming
of their Subcarpathian homeland as part of an independent Ukrainian
state that included land beyond the Carpathians, the local Subcarpathian
population was for the most part oblivious to such schemes. It was with
this in mind that the Voloshyn government prepared for elections to the
province's first diet (*soim*) in February 1939. Despite the fact that there
was only one party on the ticket, the autonomous government argued
that the vote would be a kind of plebiscite whereby a positive result
would not only indicate support for the present Carpatho-Ukrainian
government but also support for the federative alliance with Czechs and
Slovaks. It was this pro-Czecho-Slovak frame of reference that helped
to produce an overwhelming majority (245,000 to 18,000) for the
Ukrainian ballot.[33]

However, the Czecho-Slovak federative solution was doomed because
of decisions made by Hitler in Berlin. In contrast to his treatment of the
Slovaks, who were given the choice to declare their independence or be
annexed by Hungary, Hitler gave no options to the Carpatho-Ukrainian
government. Hungary was simply given the green light to march into
Carpatho-Ukraine. Without any help from the Czechoslovak army
stationed in the province, a local militia known as the Carpathian Sich,
backed by the hasty but symbolic declaration of the independence of
Carpatho-Ukraine on 15 March 1939, fought for three days against the
invaders until they were entirely overwhelmed.[34]

For all intents and purposes, 15 March 1939 ended Subcarpathia's
relationship with Czecho-Slovakia, which itself had ceased to exist. The

[33]Stercho, *Diplomacy of Double Morality*, pp. 144-153; Magocsi, *Shaping of a
National Identity*, pp. 243-244.
[34]Stercho, *Diplomacy of Double Morality*, pp. 284-389.

Carpatho-Rusyn minority west of the Uzh River that numbered about 91,000 was to remain under the rule of what became a semi-independent Slovak state allied with Nazi Germany, although, as a result of subsequent border adjustments with Hungary (April 1939), their number was reduced to about 70,000.

In their new political circumstances within a Slovak state, the Carpatho-Rusyn minority became the object of suspicion because in the months after the Munich Pact their leaders had campaigned hard for unification with autonomous Subcarpathian Rus'. Now they were governed by a Slovak clerical-fascist version of national socialism, whose representatives strove to slovakize all aspects of their territorially reduced country. Prewar Carpatho-Rusyn political organizations and publications were banned, and, although the school system was allowed to function under the leadership of the Greek Catholic Church, Slovak administrators, especially at the local level, began to emphasize that minority rights were unnecessary because, as was said, "the so-called Rusyn people in the Carpathian Basin are by origin and character Slovak."[35]

From 1945 to the present

With the reestablishment of Czechoslovakia at the close of World War II, the legal status of the Magyar and Carpatho-Rusyn minorities within the reduced boundaries of the renewed state differed substantially. Yet today, after more than four decades since the end of the war, it is ironic to note that the situation of the minority that had the most difficulty in Slovakia—the Magyars—is in many ways substantially better than that of the Carpatho-Rusyns, who were ostensibly in a favorable position because of their loyalty to Czechoslovakia on the eve of and during World War II.

When hostilities ended on Czechoslovak soil in the spring of 1945 and the country was, with the exception of Subcarpathian Rus',

[35]From an extensive 1943 report by the wartime head of the East Slovak district, later published as Andrej Dudáš, *Rusínska otázka a jej úzadie* (Buenos Aires, 1971), p. 25. For further details, see Paul R. Magocsi, "Rusyns and the Slovak State," *Slovakia*, No. 29 (West Paterson, N.J., 1980-81), pp. 39-44—reprinted below, Chapter 10; and Vanat, *Narysy*, Vol. II: *veresen' 1938 r.-liutyi 1948 r.* (1985), pp. 17-191.

reconstituted according to its pre-Munich boundaries, the Magyars of Slovakia were viewed in much the same way as the Sudeten Germans of Bohemia and Moravia. In short, the Magyars, like the Germans, were held collectively responsible for the destruction of Czechoslovakia in 1938-1939, and it was felt that they should be expelled en masse from the country. While forced expulsion had not necessarily been the position of Czech and Slovak politicians in exile during the war, by early 1945 the Czechoslovak government-in-exile based in London, the Slovak National Council (Slovenská Narodná Rada) in the homeland, and the Moscow leadership of the increasingly influential Czechoslovak Communist party all agreed on this solution.[36]

As a result, when the new Czechoslovak government was set up in Košice, its first program, dated 5 April 1945, included the following sweeping policy. Those Germans and Magyars who had fought actively against nazism and fascism would retain full rights as Czechoslovak citizens, but the remainder described as "other"—which effectively represented the vast majority—were to be dealt with under the following provision:

> Czechoslovak citizenship of other Czechoslovak citizens of German or Magyar nationality will be cancelled. Although they may again opt for Czechoslovakia, public authorities will retain the right of individual decision in the case of each application. Those Germans and Magyars who will have been prosecuted and condemned for a crime against the Republic and the Czech and Slovak people, will be declared to have forfeited their Czechoslovak citizenship and, unless they are under sentence of death, will be expelled from the Republic forever.[37]

The expulsion of the Magyar minority as envisaged by the Košice program was reaffirmed one year later (11 April 1946) by all the political parties in Czechoslovakia's National Front, which at the same time instituted another principle: that henceforth Czechoslovakia was to

---

[36]On the complicated evolution of the policy of Czehoslovak leaders in exile toward the Magyar minority question, see Purgat, *Od Trianonu po Košice*, pp. 256-293; and Kálmán Janics, *Czechoslovak Policy and the Hungarian Minority, 1945-1948*, English-language adaptation by Stephen Borsody (New York, 1982), pp. 51-100.

[37]Cited in Ludvík Němec, "Solution of the Minorities Problem," in Mamatey and Luža, *History*, p. 417.

be a national state of Czechs and Slovaks only.

The announcement of Czechoslovak policy vis-á-vis the Magyars led in 1946 and 1947 to protracted negotiations initiated by Hungary, which attempted to block expulsion. The subject was also discussed at the Paris Peace Conference, whose treaties signed in February 1947 regulating the end of the war did not accept Czechoslovakia's desire for the expulsion of its Magyars.[38] Despite such intervention, the practical result for the Magyar minority was hardly enviable. Those Magyars, the so-called *anyás* (literally, those pampered and tied to the motherland's apron strings), who had arrived in southern Slovakia with the Hungarian occupation forces after 2 November 1938, were expelled immediately. By 1 July 1945, this category included 32,000 people. These, together with other volunteers, totaled about 92,000 Magyars who by 1947 left for the Hungarian motherland. Another 23,000 Magyars were arrested on charges of collaboration (an accusation which included persons who committed serious crimes as well as those who may have done little more than publish a Magyar-language article during the war). Added to these were 73,000 Magyars who, on the basis of a Hungarian-Czechoslovak accord, emigrated to Hungary in 1947-1948 in return for an equal number of Slovaks who immigrated to Czechoslovakia. Finally, after the Czechoslovak desire for total expulsion was rejected at the Paris Peace Conference, the Czechoslovak government, under the provisions of its "mobilization of manpower act," forced 42,000 Magyars to leave southern Slovakia between November 1947 and February 1948 to work in the depopulated Sudeten borderland regions.[39]

By 1948, therefore, as many as 206,000 Magyars had left southern Slovakia (forcibly, voluntarily, or on an exchange basis). Based on an estimated 600,000 Magyars living in Slovakia at the end of the war, there were still about 400,000 left. Although the remaining Magyars

---

[38]It was the United States delegation, later joined by Great Britain, which argued against including in the treaty any clause calling for the forcible removal of the Magyars from Czechoslovakia. The Soviet delegation supported Czechoslovakia's call for expulsion. Janics, *Czechoslovak Policy*, pp. 128-151.

[39]Němec, "Solution," pp. 422-425; Janics, *Czechoslovak Policy*, pp. 152-190; and Juraj Zvara, *Maďarská menšina na Slovensku po roku 1945* (Bratislava, 1969), pp. 56-73.

were stripped of their citizenship, Czechoslovakia was blocked by international accord from its desire to expel them.

Another solution was to slovakize or, as was said at the time, "re-slovakize" a population which ostensibly represented a considerable number of originally Slovak persons who themselves or whose parents had forcibly been magyarized during the late nineteenth century. The policy, which was initiated by the government in June 1946, was based on the following principle:

> Under the name of re-Slovakization it is necessary to understand the effort of the Slovak nation to get back that which was originally ours. . . . We are undertaking a program in which each person who feels him or herself of Slovak origin will have the possibility to choose voluntarily whether to become a Slovak with all its implications or to share the fate of a people without legal citizenship.[40]

Given the unenviable choice between becoming a Slovak and remaining stateless, it is not surprising that by December 1947 as many as 200,000 Magyars declared they were Slovak. The result was that by 1948, only 190,000 people in Slovakia claimed they were of Magyar nationality.[41]

Not only were these remaining 190,000 Magyars deprived of their citizenship, they were also deprived of cultural institutions. Angered by the decision of the Paris Peace Conference in not allowing Czecho-slovakia to expel its Magyar minority, the minister of foreign affairs, Jan Masaryk, declared toward the end of the diplomatic negotiations that "Czechoslovakia would not adopt any statute on minorities, and that children of citizens of Magyar nationality who remained in Czecho-slovakia will have to attend Slovak schools."[42] In fact, until 1948 there were no Magyar schools in Czechoslovakia, only 154 Magyar classes in Slovak schools attended by 5,400 students. Until 1948, there were also no Magyar newspapers, journals, or cultural organizations of any kind in Czechoslovakia.[43]

Following the Communist accession to power in February 1948, the situation of the Magyars gradually improved. It should be remembered

---

[40]Cited in Zvara, *Mad'arská menšina*, p. 68.

[41]Zvara, *Mad'arská menšina*, pp. 88-89.

[42]From a speech delivered in October 1946, cited in Zvara, *Mad'arská menšina*, p. 63.

[43]Zvara, *Mad'arská menšina*, p. 150.

that, until 1948, the Communists did agree with their otherwise bitter political enemies on one thing—the desirability of expelling the Magyars. However, by the time the Communists came to power, international accords had blocked the expulsion solution and the success of the re-Slovakization program (which Slovak Communist leaders had supported) had already reduced the size of the Magyar problem. Moreover, Marxist-Leninist policy frowned on national discrimination, which seemed particularly inappropriate when directed against a group that had traditionally provided a significant number of Czechoslovak Communist party leaders as well as rank-and-file members. Finally, neighboring Hungary was by then ruled by a Communist regime, and it would be inappropriate within the new postwar Soviet sphere of Eastern Europe to treat harshly a national group whose cultural homeland was now a brotherly Communist country.

All of these factors contributed to a change in Communist Czechoslovakia's policy toward its Magyars, although it is important to note that in the country's new socialist-oriented constitution of 9 May 1948 nothing was said and no provisions were made regarding national minorities. And, while the new Communist leadership condemned nationalist extremism, it did not oppose the policy of "re-Slovakization." In fact, Magyars were not mentioned as a group warranting any kind of protection until 1956, when a constitutional law indicated that the Slovak National Council had the task "to guarantee in the spirit of equality favorable conditions for the economic and cultural life of citizens of Magyar and Ukrainian nationality."[44]

In the interim, however, certain steps were taken to improve the status of the country's Magyars. In the fall of 1948, Czechoslovak citizenship was restored to the Magyars, and those who had settled in the Sudetenland were allowed to return to southern Slovakia. One year later, Magyar elementary schools were again permitted to operate, leading to a restoration of the educational system that by the 1963/1964 school year saw 611 Magyar-language schools with 3,064 classes and 88,000 students.[45] By 1965, twenty-one Magyar-language newspapers and journals were appearing in a total printing of 295,000 copies and

---

[44]From a constitutional law dated 31 July 1956, cited in Zvara, *Maďarská menšina*, p. 104.

[45]See the statistical table in Zvara, *Maďarská menšina*, p. 152.

included the weekly and then daily *Új Szó* (New Word: 1948-present), the weekly *A Hét* (The Week; 1965-present), and the important literary and cultural quarterly and then monthly, *Irodalmi Szemle* (Literary Review; 1958-present). Book production (not including school texts and translations) averaged about seven titles a year, so that between 1949 and 1965, 117 original Magyar-language works (in a total printing of 643,000) appeared in Czechoslovakia. The existence of such publications made possible the development of a regional Magyar-language literature, for which the most important representatives were Tibor Bábi (b. 1925), Oliver Rácz (b. 1918), Viktor Egri (1898-1982), Béla Szabó (1906-1980), and most especially Zoltán Fabry (1897-1970). Other cultural developments begun after 1948 included a Magyar-language radio program (1,287 hours by 1965), the establishment of amateur folk ensembles (600) and theaters (300), and a regional theater in Komárno that opened in 1952.[46]

The most important cultural organization created was Csemadok, the acronym for Csehoszlovákiai Magyar Dolgozók Kultúregyesülete (The Cultural Union of Hungarian Workers in Czechoslovakia). It began functioning in March 1949 from its headquarters in Bratislava and branches throughout Magyar-inhabited towns and villages. Its goal was to coordinate and promote all aspects of Magyar cultural development in Czechoslovakia, not only among members of the group but also, in a spirit of international and socialist brotherhood, among fellow Czech and Slovak citizens. The Csemadok Society was in particular called upon to fight against any remnants of "chauvism, revisionism, and national extremism" among Czechoslovakia's Magyars.[47] In 1951, Csemadok was reorganized so that it could become a part of the Slovak National Front.

Because of the organization's close links to the Czechoslovak government during the height of the Stalinist 1950s, many Magyars considered Csemadok members "tratiors," calling them "state" or

---

[46]These figures and further details may be found in Zvara, *Mad'arská menšina*, pp. 147-180. Cf. the more recent data in Bajcura, *Cesta*, pp. 195-199 and 209-213; and Juraj Zvara and Imre Dusek, eds., *A magyar nemzetiség Csehzlovákiában* (Bratislava, 1985), pp. 85-145.

[47]From the founding statue of Csemadok, dated 15 June 1949, cited in Zvara, *Mad'arská menšina*, p. 181.

"czechified Magyars."[48] However, by 1968, with the movement for reform that accompanied the Prague Spring in Czechoslovakia, Csemadok, still under its first chairman, Julius Lőrincz (b. 1910), stood in the forefront demanding improvements in the status of Magyars.[49] In March, even before the call of the Czechoslovak Communist party's Action Program (5 April 1968) to "strengthen the unity, integration, and national individuality of all nationalities,"[50] Csemadok issued a resolution based on the concept that Czechoslovakia's national minorities should henceforth be treated not only as individuals but as coporate entities. As such, they should be entitled to group autonomy, which in the case of Magyars should be instituted through the creation of predominantly Magyar districts (okresy), a separate Magyar representative body to speak on behalf of these districts, and a Slovak government ministry staffed by Magyar officials to deal with the Magyar minority.

In the course of 1968, Csemadok was joined by the Magyar section of the Union of Slovak writers which included further demands, such as official repudiation of the Košice government program of 1945 (stripping most Magyars of their Czechoslovak citizenship), the policy of re-slovakization, and the postwar trials of Magyars with compensation for the victims. On the cultural front, demands were made for the creation of several new Magyar institutions.

Not surprisingly, Slovak spokespersons responded with sharp criticism of Csemadok and Czechoslovakia's Magyar press for propagating what was described as its "chauvinist" and "separatist" tendencies. Tensions rose: throughout southern Slovakia anti-Magyar slogans followed by anti-Slovak responses appeared on walls, and in some instances their appearance was accompanied by minor clashes between the two groups. Yet, in the end, Slovaks had nothing to fear because, following the Warsaw Pact intervention of August 1968 and

---

[48]Zvara, Mad'arská menšina, p. 182.

[49]The following discussion of the Magyars in 1968 can be supplemented with information from Robert R. King, Minorities under Communism: Nationalities as a Source of Tension Among Balkan Communist States (Cambridge, Mass., 1973), pp. 109-123; and H. Gordon Skilling, Czechoslovakia's Interrupted Revolution (Princeton, N.J., 1976), pp. 606-610.

[50]Cited in Zvara, Mad'arská menšina, p. 99.

the subsequent period of "political consolidation" that began in 1970, there have been no specific advances in the status of the Magyar minority.[51]

While in 1969 the Magyars did get a new publishing house (Madach) and their own minister without portfolio (László Dobos) in the first government of the Slovak Socialist Republic, within two years the ministerial post was abolished and Csemadok was removed from the Slovak National Front, thereby changing its status from an organization which represented the interests of the group as a whole to a unit within the Slovak Ministry of Culture. As for the school system, the high point of 1970/1971, when 83 percent of Magyar children were attending Magyar-language schools, was followed by a gradual decline that reached 73 percent in 1977/1978. These same years also witnessed an increase from 14.8 to 26.6 percent of Magyar children attending Slovak schools.[52]

The demographic picture has, however, changed dramatically (at least in terms of statistical reporting) since 1948, when a mere 190,000 inhabitants claimed their nationality as Magyar. After their Czechoslovak citizenship was restored (1948) and the "re-slovakization" decree declared void (1954), Magyars began returning to their true nationality. Already by 1950 their numbers almost doubled to 355,000, and by 1970 the figure stood at 573,000. Whereas there has been a recent decline, the 1980 census figure of 560,000 still makes Magyars

---

[51]As part of the new constitutional law of 27 October 1968 transforming Czechoslovakia into a federal state, the Magyars, together with the Germans, Poles, and Ukrainians (Carpatho-Rusyns), were recognized as the country's four national minorities (*národnosti*), each of which comprised a corporate entity (*státotvorní činitelé*). Csemadok welcomed this new definition of minorities (as groups, not simply individuals), although it regretted that the law made no mention of their respective political, economic, and cultural equality with the Czech and Slovak nations (*národy*). The Slovak text of the 1968 federalization law is reproduced in Zvara, *Mad'arská menšina*, pp. 100-101. For its subsequent effect on the minorities, see Skilling, *Czechoslovakia's Interrupted Revolution*, pp. 875-877; and Bajcura, *Cesta*, pp. 186-193.

[52]Gyula Dénes, "The Status of the Hungarian Minority in Slovakia and its Problems: A Reply to Milan Hubl, Czech Historian," *East European Reporter*, I, 4 (London, 1988), p. 6.

by far the largest national minority in Czechoslovakia.[53]
There is another important factor that has contributed to Magyar
cultural and language retention as well as to self-pride—the proximity
of the group to Hungary. By the 1970s, nearly every household had a
television whose Magyar-language programs from Budapest could easily
be received in southern Slovakia. Moreover, in the past decade,
Hungary has itself come to attain a new level of respect, if not envy, in
the eyes of Czechoslovakia's Slavic inhabitants. This is because of the
reforms in the Hungarian economy that have provided a new prosperity
and availability of western-like consumer products, sought after and
now more easily obtained by Czechoslovak citizens of both Magyar and
non-Magyar origin who regularly flock to Budapest and other nearby
Hungarian cities on shopping sprees. Hence, the success of the
Hungarian economic experiment, coupled with the impact of a
Magyar-language mass media originating in Budapest, has contributed
at the very least to a positive self-image and the general cultural
retention of the Magyar minority in nearby Czechoslovakia.

The same four decades since the close of World War II have witnessed
a marked decline in the status of the Carpatho-Rusyns. The period
began with an immediate drop in their numbers, following Czechoslovakia's cession of Subcarpathian Rus' to the Soviet Union.[54] As a

---

[53]Cf. the tables in Dénes, "Status of the Hungarian Minority," pp. 27 and 32; and
in Vladimír Srb, "Demografický profil mad'arské menšiny v Československu,"
Český lid, No. 72 (Prague, 1985), pp. 218-222. It is interesting to note that of the
560,000 Magyars listed in Slovakia in 1980, 40,000 are Roma/Gypsies who claimed
Magyar nationality.

[54]The seeming last-minute decision of the Red Army to liberate by itself (without
the presence of the Czechoslovak Army Corps) Subcarpathian Rus' and thus prepare
the region for its "voluntary" request to be united with its "maternal homeland,"
Soviet Ukraine, has become the subject of extensive historiographical controversy.
The basic points of view are: (1) the Soviet Russian: I.F. Evseev, *Narodnye
komitety Zakarpatskoi Ukrainy—organy gosudarstvennoi vlasti (1944-1945)*
(Moscow, 1954); (2) the Soviet Ukrainian: Mykhailo V. Troian, *Toho dnia ziishlo
sontse vozz"iednannia: pershyi z"izd narodnykh komitetiv Zakarpats'koï Ukraïny*
(Uzhhorod, 1979); the non-Soviet Ukrainian: Vasyl Markus, *L'incorporation de
l'Ukraine subcarpathique à l'Ukraine soviétique* (Louvain, 1956); and the (3)
Czech: František Nemec and Vladimir Moudry, *The Soviet Seizure of Subcarpathian
Ruthenia* (Toronto, 1955); and Ivo Ducháček, "Jak Rudá armáda mapovala střední

result, four-fifths of Carpatho-Rusyns living south of the Carpathians (an estimated 500,000 in 1945) found themselves within the Transcarpathian oblast of the Ukrainian SSR. This left approximately 100,000 others within the borders of post-World War II Czechoslovakia. These were the same Carpatho-Rusyns west of the Uzh River in eastern Slovakia who, despite promises, were never united with the province of Subcarpathian Rus' after it joined Czechoslovakia in 1919 and who therefore functioned as a national minority in the province of Slovakia. The group had, during the interwar years, come to be known as the Carpatho-Rusyns of the Prešov Region (Priashivshchyna, or Priashivs'ka Rus'), because their religious and secular cultural center since the early nineteenth century had been the Slovak-inhabited city of Prešov.

In post-World War II Czechoslovakia, the Prešov Region Carpatho-Rusyns became a national minority separated from their brethren in neighboring Soviet Transcarpathia (old Subcarpathian Rus') by a state border, which before very long became a heavily guarded barbed-wire and watch-tower barrier between villages and their inhabitants that for centuries had never been divided. As a minority, Prešov Region Carpatho-Rusyns naturally fell into that category of post-World War II problems that statesmen had hoped to resolve, whether by voluntary or forcible evacuation or by population exchange. We have seen how the Czechoslovak authorities of that time urged the expulsion of Germans and Magyars from its borders. Similarly, just north of the Carpathians, in what was southeastern Poland, Carpatho-Rusyns (known locally as Lemkos) and Ukrainians were voluntarily deported eastward to Soviet Ukraine (1945-1946) and then forcibly to other parts of western and northern Poland (1947).[55]

Therefore, in an era in which the displacement of national minorities seemed to be an acceptable policy, the Carpatho-Rusyns living in northeastern Slovakia were also encouraged to move eastward to what was

Evropu: Těšínsko a Podkarpatsko," *Svědectví*, XVI [63] (Paris, New York, and Vienna, 1981), pp. 541-581.

[55]For a discussion of population movements, including those in Czechoslovakia and neighboring countries in the context of the world-wide trend at the time, see Joseph Schechtman, *Postwar Population Transfers in Europe, 1945-1955* (Philadelphia, 1962), pp. 151-179.

described as their maternal homeland in Soviet Ukraine. In 1947-1948, over 12,000 Prešov Region Carpatho-Rusyns voluntarily went eastward as part of a population exchange that saw an approximately equal number of Czechs from Volhynia in western Ukraine (where they had lived since the eighteenth century) "return" to Bohemia and Moravia. Nonetheless, the vast majority of the approximately 100,000 Prešov Region Rusyns remained within Czechoslovakia.[56]

Unlike the other national minorities in postwar Czechoslovakia, the Carpatho-Rusyns were the only group that could not be accused of working for the break-up of the first Czechoslovak republic on the eve of and just after Munich. And, even though the new Czechoslovak regime discounted as illegal all acts that occured in Czechoslovakia after 28 September 1938, it could not be forgotten that Voloshyn's Carpatho-Ukrainian government remained loyal to the idea of a federated Czecho-Slovakia until the very end.

Pro-Czechoslovak Carpatho-Rusyn loyalty became even more evident during the war years. After the Hungarian army took over what remained of Subcarpathian Rus' in March 1939, more than 20,000 Carpatho-Rusyns who opposed the occupation remained underground until the end of the year when they fled northward and eastward to what was then Soviet-occupied East Galicia. The Soviets viewed these refugees as spies and sentenced them to labor camps, but in mid-1941, when a Czechoslovak Army Corps under General Ludvík Svoboda was formed on Soviet soil, it was discovered that there were numerous Czechoslovak citizens held in Soviet detention camps. After long negotiations they were freed, so that by the end of 1943, Carpatho-Rusyns comprised 66 percent of the 3,348 troops in the Czechoslovak Army Corps.[57]

These Carpatho-Rusyn soldiers, who fought for the restoration of pre-Munich Czechoslovakia, endeared themselves to General Svoboda, and when at the end of the war it turned out that their Subcarpathian homeland was not to become part of a restored Czechoslovakia, they were singled out in the Soviet-Czechoslovak treaty of June 1945 (which confirmed the exchange of territory) as having the right to move westward within the new boundaries of Czechoslovakia. About half

[56]Vanat, *Narysy*, Vol. II, pp. 264-266.
[57]Vanat, *Narysy*, Vol. II, pp. 159-178.

chose to do so, settling for the most part in Bohemia where, because of their wartime record and participation in the liberation of the country, they were given well-placed jobs in the postwar Czechoslovak military establishment and ministry of interior.[58]

As for the Prešov Region Carpatho-Rusyns who remained at home, they founded as early as 1944 an underground partisan organization known as KRASNO (Karpatorusskii Avtonomnyi Soiuz Natsional'nogo Osvobozhdeniia—Carpatho-Russian Autonomous Union for National Liberation), which fought against the "fascist" Slovak state and joined the Czechoslovak Corps and Red Army when they arrived on Czechoslovak territory.[59] Because of their loyal record toward Czechoslovakia and their desirable leftist political orientation, these partisans, together with veterans from the Czechoslovak Army Corps who had already been members or who now joined the Communist party, were given jobs in the postwar administration of Eastern Slovakia and in the ministry of interior in Prague (especially in the Communist-controlled security organs).[60]

Although the new Czechoslovak government did not make any special provisions for the country's national minorities, the Carpatho-Rusyns were able to establish legally recognized political and cultural organizations even before the war had ended. In March 1945, a Ukrainian National Council of the Prešov Region (Ukraïns'ka Narodna Rada Priashivshchyny) was set up in Prešov, proclaiming itself the legitimate representative of the Carpatho-Rusyn population. It is interesting to note that the new council, like its predecessors going back to 1918, at first called for union with their brethen in what was about to become Soviet-ruled Transcarpathia.[61] When the Soviet authorities

---

[58]Magocsi, *Shaping of a National Identity*, pp. 252-255.

[59]Vanat, *Narysy*, Vol. II, pp. 130-159.

[60]Among the best known Carpatho-Rusyns to rise through regional and then national political ranks was Vasyl' Bilak, who until his retirement in late 1988 was the leading pro-Soviet conservative leader in Czechoslovakia. He was not, however, a partisan or member of the Czechoslovak Army Corps, since as a young boy he had emigrated in the 1930s to Bohemia, where he remained during the war years

[61]Also in 1945, as in 1918-1919, the Lemko Rusyns just across the border in Poland had requested to be united with their brethen south of the mountains. Their request was turned down by Czechoslovakia in 1919 and by the Soviet Union in 1945

proved unreceptive to their requests, the council's leaders argued—as their predecessors had done at the end of World War I—that the reconstituted Czechoslovakian republic should be comprised of three equal partners: Czechs, Slovaks, and Ukrainians. The platform of the Ukrainian National Council was made known to its constituents through a newly founded weekly newspaper *Priashivshchyna* (The Prešov Region; 1945-52).[62]

During 1945-1946, Carpatho-Rusyn leaders also set up a Ukrainian National Theater, an office for Ukrainian schools, a book publishing house (as part of the Ukrainian National Council), and a youth organization (Soiuz Molodezhi Karpat—Union of Carpathian Youth). The school system, which had functioned more or less uninterruptedly since the interwar years, was now able to expand, so that by 1950 there were 284 schools (266 elementary, 14 municipal, 3 *gymnasia*, 1 pedagogical school, and 1 commercial academy) operating in Carpatho-Rusyn communities.[63]

The existence of schools as well as newspapers and a national theater inevitably led to a discussion about the national orientation of the local Carpatho-Rusyn population and its representative institutions. During the Czechoslovak years, and for that matter during the Hungarian and Slovak domination in the course of World War II, the nationality or language question (was the local population Russian, Ukrainian, or distinctly Carpatho-Rusyn?) had never been decisively resolved. In neighboring Transcarpathia, after the war the Soviet authorities simply declared the local population was Ukrainian and the matter was closed. In part, that move was based on earlier decisions of the Ukrainian Communist party (Bolshevik) in 1926. Since many of the post-World War II Prešov Region Carpatho-Rusyn leaders were Communist party members or Communist sympathizers, the Ukrainian orientation was adopted at least for the names given to the group's new organizations, such as the Ukrainian National Theater and the Office for Ukrainian Schools.

Regardless of their names, these organizations did not use Ukrainian at all but rather Russian or the so-called Carpatho-Rusyn language

[62]For details on the Ukrainian National Council's political demands, see Vanat, *Narysy*, Vol. II, pp. 218-236 and 267-276.

[63]Bajcura, *Cesta*, p. 201; Vanat, *Narysy*, Vol. II, pp. 276-289.

(local dialect mixed with Russian and Church Slavonic). This seemingly paradoxical situation was a function of local tradition in the Prešov Region, which (in contrast to neighboring Subcarpathian Rus') never had a serious Ukrainian orientation. Thus, literary Russian was taught in the schools, which, moreover, the local population considered to be their own, since the terms *russkyi* (Russian) and *rus'kyi* (Rusyn) sounded virtually the same to the undiscriminating and barely educated local peasantry. The point is that whatever they were called, the Carpatho-Rusyns in early post-World War II Czechoslovakia had political, cultural, and educational institutions that they considered their own.

Change was on the horizon, however. Slovaks of whatever political persuasion were already displeased when in 1945 the Ukrainian National Council called for union with neighboring Transcarpathia and then for a Czechoslovak republic in which Carpatho-Rusyns would be equal to Czechs and Slovaks. Then, on the eve of the Communist ascent to power in February 1948, the Slovak National Council turned down the request of the Ukrainian National Council to become a permanent political body representing Carpatho-Rusyns/Ukrainians. The situation worsened: between 1949 and 1952, the group's recently established youth organization, publishing house, and, finally, the Ukrainian National Council itself were all liquidated on the grounds that they were all set up before the Communists came to power and were therefore probably guilty of "bourgeois nationalism."[64]

In their stead, the government supplied funds to set up in 1951 a nonpolitical and acceptably socialist organization, the Cultural Union of Ukrainian Workers in Czechoslovakia (Kul'turnyi Soiuz Ukraïns'kykh Trudiashchykh), known by its acronym KSUT. Similar to Csemadok among the Magyars, KSUT was designed to work closely "with existing state organs" in order "to educate Ukrainian workers toward national consciousness and pride, and to instill in them the consciousness of belonging to the great Soviet Ukrainian people."[65]

Despite the liquidation of several recently established political, cultural, and educational institutions, the worst was yet to come. At the

---

[64]Pavel Mačů, "National Assimilation: The Case of the Rusyn-Ukrainians of Czechoslovakia," *East Central Europe*, II, 2 (Pittsburgh, 1975), pp. 113-114.

[65]From the founding statute of KSUT, cited in Mačů, "National Assimilation," p. 114.

outset of the 1950s, during the height of the Stalinist period, the Carpatho-Rusyn population of Czechoslovakia was to lose the three elements that for all intents and purposes defined their very existence, namely, their religion, their land, and their national identity.[66]

Following the example in neighboring Soviet Transcarpathia, in April 1950 Czechoslovak authorities organized in Prešov a meeting of some Greek Catholic priests and laymen, who declared the union of their church with Rome (dating from the seventeenth century) null and void. The Greek Catholic Church ceased to exist legally. The nearly 75 percent of Carpatho-Rusyns who were of this religion were forced to become Orthodox, their bishops (Pavlo Goidych and Vasyl' Hopko) were arrested and sentenced to life imprisonment, and all Greek Catholic institutions, including the historically important theological seminary in Prešov, were closed.

As for the land, a decree abolishing private ownership struck particularly hard at the agriculturally based Carpatho-Rusyn minority. Peasants were at first encouraged voluntarily and then were forced administratively to sign over their holdings to village cooperatives. This process, known as collectivization, was particularly intense in Carpatho-Rusyn villages in 1951-1952, and by the end of the decade 63 percent of landholdings were collectivized.

Finally, in June 1952, following the complaints about the nationality question lodged by some Carpatho-Rusyn delegates to a Communist party conference held in Prešov, the authorities in Bratislava decided, again following the Soviet model in Transcarpathia, to introduce Ukrainianization by fiat. Consequently, Russian was no longer to be used in the schools, and instead Ukrainian became the language for all subjects. Furthermore, the name "Rusyn" was not to be accepted in official documents or in census declarations. Later, in 1968, when it became possible to speak openly about many matters, one Carpatho-Rusyn summed up the early 1950s in a radio interview: "Today I am like that dumb sheep; I don't have anything. I had my own God, you took him from me. I had my own nationality, but you took it away too. I had a little piece of land, even that you took. Everything that I had you

---

[66]The following discussion is based largely on Ivan Bajcura, *Ukrajinská otázka v ČSSR* (Košice, 1967), pp. 105-165.

took."[67]

In return for what it took away, the Czechoslovak Communist authorities did make a concerted effort to improve the cultural and educational levels of the Carpatho-Rusyn population. KSUT began to publish a Ukrainian-language weekly newspaper (*Nove zhyttia*, 1952-), a monthly magazine (*Druzhno vpered*, 1951-), a quarterly, later bimonthly, literary journal (*Duklia*, 1953-), and original works of literature and scholarship. Fellowships were provided for young members of the local intelligentsia to study in Soviet Ukraine. Like their predecessors, Prešov Region leaders invariably identified themselves as Russians (some even denying that a separate Ukrainian people existed), but under the new conditions they had to become Ukrainian if they wished to remain teachers, editors, or retain other posts in the cultural establishment. Hence, Russian-language authors like Fedir Lazoryk (1913-1969), Vasyl' Zozuliak (1909-1994), and Ivan Matsyns'kyi (1922-1987) were among many who changed their national orientation and began to write in Ukrainian.[68]

Several other well-funded institutions were founded in rapid succession: a Ukrainian National Museum (1950); a Ukrainian Department and Research Institute at Šafárik University in Prešov (1953); and a professional song and dance ensemble named Duklia (1955), not to mention hundreds of local folk ensembles and annual festivals of folklore and culture. It seemed no amount of money was spared to provide new institutions that would give Carpatho-Rusyns a Ukrainian cultural identity in a socialist mold.

For the most part, however, the Carpatho-Rusyn masses rejected a cultural policy that was linked to the destruction of their Greek Catholic Church, the loss of their land, and the imposition of a Ukrainian identity.[69] They expressed their response in the one area where at the time

[67]Cited in Mač^u, "National Assimilation," p. 108.

[68]Some switched nationality allegiancies for opportunistic reasons; others did so through conviction based on intellectual evolution. For a good example of the latter, see the historical introduction to Ivan Matsyns'kyi, *Rozmova storich* (Bratislava and Prešov, 1965), pp. 13-230.

[69]Bajcura, *Ukrajinská otázka*, p. 193, points out that whereas those who accepted the new orientation argued that Ukrainian was simply an older name for Carpatho-Rusyn, the "broad masses" felt that Carpatho-Rusyn and Ukrainian were two different peoples and identities.

they could make their voice heard—in the matter of the language to be taught in village schools. If we cannot have our own Carpatho-Rusyn schools, they argued, then it is better to have Slovak than Ukrainian ones. In 1961, when a resolution of the Czechoslovak Communist party declared that citizens had the right to choose which language their children were taught in schools, village after village where Carpatho-Rusyns lived voluntarily requested that Slovak replace Ukrainian in the local elementary school. Between 1961 and 1963 alone, parents in 160 Carpatho-Rusyn villages requested that Ukrainian-language schools become Slovak, and by 1966 there were only 68 Ukrainian-language schools left. This represented a decline of 74 percent from 1950, when Russian or Carpatho-Rusyn was taught in 266 elementary schools.[70]

Not surprisingly, with the change to Slovak schools and the lifting of other restrictions in the use of the name Carpatho-Rusyn, the statistical size of the group declined as well. Whereas in 1930, 91,000 Carpatho-Rusyns were recorded in northeastern Slovakia, by 1960, when only a Ukrainian identity was permitted, a mere 35,000 declared themselves as such.[71]

The Prague Spring of 1968 brought to the Carpatho-Rusyns, as to other national minorities in Czechoslovakia, the hope that their situation could be improved. The local intelligentsia realized that the Ukrainian cultural policy followed since 1952 was a failure, and in an attempt to stave off the rapid trend toward assimilation with the Slovaks, concrete plans were made to introduce publications, theatrical performances, and radio programs in the local Carpatho-Rusyn vernacular instead of in Ukrainian, which the masses said they could not understand. Meetings were also held with the aim of restoring a political organization to be called the National Council of Czechoslovak Rusyns or, simply, the Rusyn National Council.

As with the Magyars at the time, there were calls for administrative restructuring that would allow for a Carpatho-Rusyn autonomous territory. Newspapers (now partially in Carpatho-Rusyn) were also filled with letters from readers who demanded that they be "given back" their Carpatho-Rusyn schools taken from them during the Ukrainianization process. Finally, Greek Catholic adherents pressed the government for

[70]Bajcura, *Ukrajinská otázka*, p. 159; and idem, *Cesta*, p. 201.
[71]Mač11,"National Assimilation," pp. 105.

the legal restoration of their church, which actually took place in June 1968. The proponents of these various political and cultural measures hoped that they would restore pride in things Carpatho-Rusyn, and they began planning for the upcoming 1970 census, which might more accurately record the estimated 130,000 Rusyn-Ukrainians—as they were now being called—who actually lived in the Prešov Region.[72]

However, the Warsaw Pact intervention of 21 August 1968 and the subsequent "political consolidation" in Czechoslovakia put a stop to all such experiments. Before long, those who favored the restoration of a Carpatho-Rusyn national orientation were branded as part of the "anti-Socialist, right opportunist, and revisionist forces" that dominated KSUT and other Ukrainian organizations in 1968-1969.[73] The result was the removal of the most outspoken intellectual and party leaders (even those who favored a Ukrainian orientation), and the return to a policy of administrative Ukrainianization reminiscent of the 1950s.

During the two decades since 1968, the status of the Carpatho-Rusyn minority in Czechoslovakia has declined further. The demands for Slovak instead of Ukrainian schools at the village level has continued, so that by 1987 there were only 23 Ukrainian-language schools left, with a mere 1,450 pupils.[74] Cultural institutions like the Ukrainian National Theater cannot attract audiences for its performances; print runs of books (generally 600 to 800) and newspapers (2,000) are minimal because of a lack of readers; and the latest census (1980) has recorded only 37,000 Ukrainians in Eastern Slovakia.[75]

Aside from the fact that the peasant masses and the intelligentsia have traditionally identified themselves as Carpatho-Rusyns (in local terminology, Rusnaks) or as Russians, since World War II there has not been any advantage for Carpathio-Rusyns to identify themselves as Ukrainians. In a Slovak environment, identity as a Ukrainian inevitably has meant association with the Soviet Union, hardly a favorable alternative in Czechoslovak society, most especially after 1968.

---

[72]Mačku, "National Assimilation," pp. 119-124.

[73]Ivan Bajcura, "Vývoj a riešene ukrajinskej otázky v ČSSR," in Michal Čorný, ed., Socialistickou cestou k národnostej rovnoprávnosti (Bratislava, 1976), p. 29.

[74]Speech of Mykhailo Popovych, inspector for Ukrainian schools in Eastern Slovakia, in Nove zhyttia (Prešov), 11 December 1987, p. 3.

[75]See the statistical table in Bajcura, Cesta, p. 32.

Moreover, there has never been easy contact with neighboring Transcarpathia, closed off, like the rest of the Soviet Union, since 1945. There has not even been the possibility for linguistic and cultural reinforcement from Soviet Transcarpathia via radio or television since Czechoslovakia's Carpatho-Rusyns, when they finally obtained widespread access to such media during the 1970s, never tuned into Soviet programming—and if they did, that media would in any case be primarily in Russian, not Ukrainian. Even the Greek Catholic Church, the only "experiment" to survive from 1968, has become during the past decade an instrument of slovakization.[76]

Thus, while Ukrainian institutional life for the Carpatho-Rusyn minority has remained well financed by the Czechoslovak Communist government during the past four decades, the practical results of an administratively forced Ukrainian orientation combined with an unfavorable international environment and the natural assimilatory trends resulting from intermarriage with Slovaks and/or displacement to Slovak cities in search of employment are all factors that have created a situation in which the national minority, whether its members call themselves Ukrainians, Carpatho-Rusyns, Rusnaks, or Russians, is on a path of irreversible numerical decline and perhaps eventual disappearance.

Conclusion

Looking back on the seven decades of Czechoslovakia and its relationship to the Magyar and Carpatho-Rusyn inhabitants within its borders, it seems inevitable that the country's policy towards these two national minorities would from the outset be fraught with difficulties. This is because with one exception every Czechoslovak government, regardless of its political persuasion, has been committed to the concept of a unitary Czechoslovak state, which in practice has been dominated since 1918 by the Czechs and since 1945 by Czechs and Slovaks as the leading or "state peoples." The one exception to this approach was the second republic, whose federative structure was but a short-lived tenuous interlude that in any case was forced upon the country after September 1938 by the events of Munich. Even after Czechoslovakia

---

[76]Paul Robert Magocsi, "Religion and Identity in the Carpathians," *Cross Currents*, No. 7 (Ann Arbor, Mich., 1988), esp. pp. 97-101.

was "re-federalized" in 1968, the country has remained a nation-state of Czechs and Slovaks in which the minorities are subordinate, with no possibility of functioning within the system as political groups or corporate entities.

From this perspective, it becomes clear why during the interwar years the Carpatho-Rusyns were simply refused any real autonomy, even though they were guaranteed such rights through an international treaty (St. Germain) subsequently enshrined in the first Czechoslovak constitution. As for the Magyars, it is unlikely they would ever have been satisfied, whatever degree of self-rule they may have obtained, since their basic outlook was that the Czechoslovak "occupation" was at best to be tolerated as a temporary solution until the inevitable return of their territory to the Hungarian homeland.

With the end of World War II, the Carpatho-Rusyn minority was reduced in size by three-quarters while the Magyars, like the Germans, were to be expelled from Czechoslovakia en masse. If these expectations had been fulfilled, the country would finally have become a nation-state of Czechs and Slovaks. But the exclusion efforts and subsequent "re-slovakization" program toward the Magyars ultimately failed. The group was numerically restored, remaining culturally strong and ethnically aware, so that with its 580,000 (official data) to 700,000 (unofficial estimate) members it is today the largest national minority in Czechoslovakia.

Entirely different tactics were used against the Carpatho-Rusyns. As a people that did not work for the break-up of Czechoslovakia on the eve of World War II and that fought at home and abroad for the restoration of the republic, the Carpatho-Rusyns became in a sense a privileged minority after 1945. Initially, they were allowed to create their own national organizations; then after the Communists came to power in 1948, Carpatho-Rusyns were showered with funds to set up a revised cultural infrastructure that was concerned with building socialism through the medium of a new national and linguistic orientation—Ukrainian. The practical result of this change was to encourage an increasing trend toward assimilation with Slovaks and the demise of the group to a mere one-quarter its potential numerical size. The future, moreover, looks bleak, since today less than 1,500 students attend Ukrainian-language schools, a mere fraction of the group's total school population.[77]

Nonetheless, too much emphasis should not be placed on the change in nationality orientation as the only reason for the decline of Carpatho-Rusyns as a national group. As great a cause for the decline lies in the social mobility that has accompanied their improving economic status under Communist rule. The prevalence of economic backwardness in peripheral rural areas is perhaps the safest way to assure the maintenance of traditional cultures and identities. By the late 1950s, mountainous Carpatho-Rusyn villages were for the first time all connected with daily bus routes to lowland Slovak cities, making daily commuting to work, and eventually permanent settlement, possible. For instance, whereas in 1930, 89.6 percent of Carpatho-Rusyns in the Prešov Region were engaged in agriculture or forestry, by 1980 that figure was only 28.5 percent.[78] The result is that today Carpatho-Rusyn villages have become home to people who are in most cases sixty years and older. Young people have left and there is little need for schools, regardless of language of instruction. Carpatho-Rusyn villages are literally dying out demographically or in several instances are being destroyed to make way for seemingly more productive use, such as reservoirs.[79]

For those who began to work in the towns farther south and who eventually settled there, the setting is purely Slovak. The assimilatory linguistic and cultural environment has been encouraged further by the advent of Slovak-language radio and television, which is also widespread in Carpatho-Rusyn villages. Thus, Czechoslovakia's policy of industrialization in Eastern Slovakia has brought concrete improvements in the well-being of Carpatho-Rusyns, which in turn has contributed to

---

[77]Even the local Ukrainian intelligentsia sends its children to Slovak schools, an embarrassing fact brought out from time to time in the local press when it engages in a rare exercise in soul searching. Cf. "Shchob 1988 rik stav perelomnym," *Nove zhyttia*, 11 December 1987, p. 3 and "Shkodymo sami sobi," *Nove zhyttia*, 15 January 1988, p. 7.

[78]Vanat, *Narysy*, Vol. I, p. 212, Bajcura, *Cesta*, p. 177.

[79]In the early 1980s, seven Carpatho-Rusyn villages in the Upper Cirocha River valley were inundated to make way for a reservoir, and from time to time there has been talk of turning cther parts of Rusyn-inhabited lands into a state ecological reserve.

undermining the group through what has become a "natural" trend toward social mobility and slovakization.

National assimilation has, of course, been made easier by the similarity of the Slavic dialects spoken by the two peoples (East Slovak and Prešov Region Rusyn dialects), the similarity in religion (many East Slovaks are, like Rusyns, Greek Catholic), and the continuance of a traditional pattern of intermarriage, in which more often than not Slovak becomes the dominant medium in ethnically mixed households.

In contrast, it is a lack of these same factors that has worked against any significant assimilation among the Magyars. The Magyar language, with its non-Indo-European roots, is the first significant barrier against slovakization, which is being reinforced by a Magyar-language school system that in 1980 still served over 70 percent of the group's children. Intermarriage with Slovaks is not common, and in churches (whether Catholic or Protestant) Magyar is the language of the liturgy and services. Finally, in the economic sphere Magyars too have shared in the general increase in Czechoslovakia's standard of living, at least through the 1970s, but in contrast to the Carpatho-Rusyn experience, socioeconomic mobility has not contributed to national assimilation.

Whereas there has been some Magyar out-migration in search of work, that trend has been largely tempered by the presence of sixty new factories and forty other reconstructed works established in or near Magyar-inhabited lands in southern Slovakia. This has made it possible for Magyars to gain a livelihood outside the traditional agricultural sector without, nonetheless, having to leave a Magyar linguistic and cultural environment. Moreover, agriculture has remained a viable occupation in Magyar-inhabited southern Slovakia, so that 34.4 percent of Magyars are still engaged in that sector, a percentage that is the highest of any nationality in Czechoslovakia.[80]

It is also true that since the 1970s there has been a slight decline in the number of Magyars and in the percentage of their children attending Magyar-language schools. These trends have even prompted protests from newly established underground groups like the Committee for the Defense of the Rights of the Magyar Minority in Czechoslovakia, which, since its establishment in 1978, has issued appeals to civil rights

---

[80]Bajcura, *Cesta*, pp. 176-177.

groups within the country (Charter 77) and abroad.[81] Despite the recent assimilatory trends, the achievements of the 1950s and 1960s toward preserving the Magyar minority in Czechoslovakia, combined with the increased access since the 1970s to Magyar-language radio and television programs from Budapest and the traditional patterns of cultural self-maintenance (social stability, language use at home, endogamous marriages), are all factors that have worked toward sustaining group identity.

Thus, from the perspective of preserving the culture and identity of national minorities in Czechoslovakia, the Carpatho-Rusyns have had a negative experience, especially during the last three decades, despite governmental support and encouragement for what is considered their culture. On the other hand, whereas the Magyars may have suffered sometimes extreme political and administrative deprivations at the hands of Czechoslovakia after World War II, their own clear sense of self-identity, their proximity to Hungary, and the development of economic opportunities in or near their native villages are factors which have allowed them to continue functioning as a viable minority.

[81]The committee is led by a Bratislava geologist, Miklós Duray, whose essays critical of Czechoslovak policy toward its Magyars have been published abroad: *Kutyaszorító* (New York, 1983). For further details, see Stephen Borsody, ed., *The Hungarians: A Divided Nation* (New Haven, 1988), pp. 174-190.

CHAPTER 8

The Nationalist Intelligentsia and the Peasantry in Twentieth Century Subcarpathian Rus'*

This is a study of the interaction between two social groups. It is especially concerned with the manner by which the intelligentsia tries to reach the peasants in order to instill in them a national consciousness, i.e., an awareness of belonging to a larger nationality. Focus will be on the Rusyn population of Czechoslovakia, which inhabited that former country's easternmost province, Podkarpatská Rus, or Subcarpathian Rus'during the years 1918 to 1938.

The idea that one segment of a society, the intelligentsia, has to convince another, the peasantry, of an identity it supposedly was not already aware of, presupposes certain assumptions concerning the problem of nationality. First of all, there is no simple equation between language and nationality, so that ethnic groups may be closely related linguistically but still belong to different nationalities. Further, individuals are not born with a national consciousness; rather, this has to be cultivated through various forms of indoctrination or education. In the words of one writer on the subject, "nationalism ... is a sentiment which is recreated in each generation by acculturation and is

*This study was commissioned for presentation at the ninth international seminar of the Inter-University Consortium for the Study of Eastern Europe, organized by Robert H. Lord at Harvard University, May 13-16, 1975. It is published here for the first time.

transmitted from mind to mind by education."[1] Finally, the national affiliation of individuals and even ethnic groups may be altered, a process frequently defined in positive terms as an awakening and in negative terms as assimilation, but which might perhaps more objectively be called reeducation.

Nationalist movements, most especially among ethnic groups that did not have direct control over their own political futures, i.e., "stateless" peoples, have been fashioned by a modern secular elite, the intelligentsia. In the simplest terms, the intelligentsia is a group that is distinguished (and frequently alienated) from its own society by the level of its education.[2] The other crucial element involved in national movements is the people—the *volk* among Germanic peoples, or the *narod* among the Slavs. Although it was not always the case, after the writings of the German philosopher Herder became known, the *volk/narod* came more and more to be associated with the nation. In fact, the *narod* soon was considered to be the embodiment of the nation.[3] Thus, the nationalist intelligentsia could justify its own existence to the degree that it interacted successfully with the *narod*.

Until well into the nineteenth and twentieth centuries, the majority of the population throughout Europe belonged to agriculturally-based peasant societies. This was particularly the case in Subcarpathian Rus', where in 1910, 89.6 percent of the region's Rusyn inhabitants were peasants. While the percentage of the population engaged in agricultural pursuits decreased in subsequent years, it was still as high as 83.1 percent in 1930 and even 70 percent in 1956.[4]

---

[1]Louis Snyder, *The Meaning of Nationalism* (New Brunswick, N.J., 1954), p. 90. On the sometimes tenuous equation between linguistic and national identity, see Joshua A. Fishman, *Language and Nationalism* (Rowley, Mass., 1972), esp. pp. 44-55.

[2]Anthony D. Smith, *Theories of Nationalism* (New York, 1972), pp. 83-150.

[3]Hans Kohn, *The Idea of Nationalism* (New York, 1958), pp. 427ff.; Elie Kedourie, *Nationalism* (London, 1961), pp. 54ff.

[4]These figures also include very small percentages of the populace engaged as shepherds and woodcutters. The figures for 1910 and 1930 refer to the Rusyn population in both Subcarpathian Rus' and northeastern Slovakia; those for 1956 apply to the entire population of the Soviet Ukraine's Transcarpathian oblast. See *Magyar statisztikai közlemények*, Vol. LVI (Budapest, 1915), pp. 330-433; *Československá statistika*, Vol. CXVI (Prague, 1935), pt.1, p. 17; pt.2, pp. 33-35,

In such circumstances, the nationalist intelligentsia in Subcarpathian Rus' had to concern itself primarily with the peasantry, and it is of interest here to see what communicational transmission belts the intelligentsia used to reach its constituency. In essence, the national message was carried through cultural organizations, including reading rooms, libraries, and theaters, and most importantly through the educational system. Before reviewing in some detail the specific developments in each of these areas, it may be useful to review briefly the particular national situation existing at the time in Subcarpathian Rus'.

The years 1919-1938 marked the most intense period in the embryonic stage of national development among Subcarpathian Rusyns, i.e., a time when the local intelligentsia tried to work out a nationalist ideology that would be acceptable and attractive to the populace. This does not mean that efforts in this direction were not made previously; they were, in particular during a few decades after 1848, but this development soon atrophied as a result of a policy of magyarization during the last years of the Hungarian Kingdom, which for the most part encouraged the assimilation of the local intelligentsia.[5] In contrast, under Czechoslovak rule the Subcarpathian intelligentsia functioned in a relatively uninhibited atmosphere in which external pressures were at a minimum.

Subcarpathia's intelligentsia was not, however, united behind one national ideology. Rather, there existed three factions: (1) the Russophiles, who argued that the population was a part of one Russian nationality from the Carpathians to Vladivostok, or in the alliterative phrase, from the "Poprad to the Pacific"; (2) the Ukrainophiles, who stressed the existence of an independent Ukrainian nationality stretching from both sides of the Carpathians to the Caucasus; and (3) the Rusynophiles, who felt that Subcarpathian Rusyns made up a separate Slavic nationality. Subcarpathian Rus' became a kind of market place where the leaders of these various factions were promoting their ideological wares in the hope that the peasant masses might purchase

---

51-53; *Narodne hospodarstvo Zakarpatskoï oblasti: statistychnyi zbirnyk* (Uzhhorod, 1957), p. 122.

[5]On early Rusyn national developments, see Ivan Žeguc, *Die nationalpolitischen Bestrebungen der Karpato-Ruthenen, 1848-1914* (Wiesbaden, 1965).

one product instead of another.

Considering these factors, the present discussion must inevitably be two-fold: an analysis of how the nationalist intelligentsia tried to reach the peasantry, and also an attempt to explain why one orientation proved to be more successful than the others. For all practical purposes, the Rusynophile faction did not operate on an organized level, so that emphasis here will be on the Russophiles and Ukrainophiles.

Cultural organizations

In the spring of 1920, the first attempts were made to establish a cultural organization for Subcarpathian Rus'. On April 29, a general council of local leaders met in Uzhhorod under the leadership of Iulii Brashchaiko. The Czechoslovak administration supported these cultural endeavors, and among the official guests were Jan Brejcha, the Provincial Administrator, and Josef Pešek, Superintendent of the School Administration. Nothing positive, however, came as a result of this first meeting, because those leaders present fought among themselves regarding the national and linguistic orientation of the proposed organization. The Russophile leaders Andrei Gagatko, Ilarion Tsurkanovich, and Antonii Beskid vigorously opposed the proposals of the populist-Ukrainophile organizers, Iulii Brashchaiko and Avhustyn Voloshyn. The result was a complete disruption of the proceedings—a symbolic indication of the deep rift between Subcarpathian leaders that was to be a standard feature of political and cultural life in the province for the next two decades.

Subsequently, on May 9, 1920, Iulii Brashchaiko called together only populist Ukrainian- oriented leaders and this led to the establishment of the Tovarystvo Prosvîta Pôdkarpatskoî Rusy (hereafter Prosvita Society).[6] The aim of the Prosvita Society was "to uplift, both culturally and economically the Rusyn people (*rus'kyi narod*) living within the borders of the Czechoslovak Republic."[7] This task was to be

---

[6]Pavlo Iatsko, "Spomyny pro pershi zbory 'Prosvity'," in *Z nahody desiat'litn'oho iuvileiu istnovannia tovarystva 'Prosvita' na Pidkarpats'kii Rusy: 29.IV. 1920-29.VI.1930*, Vyd. Tovarystva 'Prosvita', No. 152 (Uzhhorod, 1930), pp. 3-8; Avhustyn Voloshyn, "Zasnovannia i rozvytok t-va 'Prosvita'," in *Kalendar 'Prosvita'* (Uzhhorod, 1938), pp. 70-72.

[7]*Statut Tovarystva 'Prosvîta' v Uzhhorodî* (Uzhhorod, 1924), p. 3. The original

carried out by the publication of all kinds of popular and scholarly books "written in the national tongue and accessible to every Subcarpathian Rusyn."[8] In addition, the original constitution intended to set up agricultural cooperatives, to help farmers obtain tools and machines, to organize musical, gymnastic, theatrical, and educational circles, and to establish libraries, national homes, and a "Central National Museum for all Subcarpathian Rus'."[9]

The Prosvita Society was divided into publishing, literary-scientific, organizational, library, theatrical, museum, and economic sections and the example to be followed was cultural activity in neighboring Galicia. The name Prosvita, which means enlightenment, was copied from the Prosvita Society established in Galicia's provincial capital of L'viv as early as 1868. Moreover, many Galician Ukrainians like Ivan Pan'kevych, Volodymyr Birchak, and Vasyl' Pachovs'kyi, who emigrated to Subcarpathian Rus' during the early 1920s, brought with them the valuable experience they gained in working to improve the national and educational conditions of the Rusyns in Galicia. Welcomed by the Czechoslovak government, the Galician Ukrainians received positions in many governmental, educational, and cultural institutions, and it is not an exaggeration to say that "of all the Ukrainian lands where ... Ukrainian emigrants worked, their efforts had the greatest importance in Transcarpathia."[10]

The Galician experience, which transformed Rusyns into nationally conscious Ukrainians must, according to these leaders, be repeated in Subcarpathian Rus'. In the words of Vasyl' Pachovs'kyi, "'Prosvita' set for itself one task: in Galicia there should not be one illiterate Rusyn. ... And should not Subcarpathian Rusyns take up the example of their brothers? Subcarpathian Rusyns must also uplift the education of the people and make each Rusyn aware of his rights and obligations towards his people."[11]

constitution (1920) referred only to the Rusyns of Subcarpathian Rus'.

[8]*Statut tovarystva 'Prosvîta' Pôdkarpatskoî Rusy* (Uzhhorod, 1920), p. 6.

[9]*Ibid.*, pp. 6-7.

[10]Symon Narizhnyi, *Ukraïns'ka emigratsiia: kul'turna pratsia ukraïns'koï emigratsiï mizh dvoma svitovymy viinamy,* Studiï Muzeiu vvzvol'noï borot'by Ukraïny, Vol. I (Prague, 1942), p. 321.

[11]Vasyl' Pachovs'kii, *Chto Prosvîta?*, Vŷd. Tovarystva 'Prosvîta', No. I (Uzhhorod, 1920), pp. 8-9. It should be emphasized that when Galician-Ukrainian

The catalyst for this national transformation was to be the village reading room, where Subcarpathian peasants could obtain newspapers and books and hear lectures. A minimum of ten members was required to set up a local affiliate of Prosvita, and the aim of these grass-root cultural organizations was clear: "In the reading-rooms our peasants must first of all be taught that they are Rusyns.... The reading room must teach our peasant to love his mother tongue; in short, everything that is Rusyn."[12]

Many of the reading rooms contained libraries, and the Prosvita Society set up a broad publishing program to make available material for all segments of the population. Initially, most of the publications were written in a dialectally based language in the traditional orthography, but by 1930 the gradual approach toward literary Ukrainian was augmented and the modern orthography employed. Of importance was the publication of a popular-oriented series of books, including about sixty different titles which were primarily agricultural, literary, and historical in content; a children's journal, *Pchôlka* (1922-32); eighteen short monographs dealing with the language, literature, and history of the province; and the erudite fourteen-volume *Naukovŷi zbornyk Tovarystva 'Prosvîta'* (1922-38), edited by the Galician emigrés, I. Pan'kevych and V. Birchak, and the local Ukrainophiles, V. Hadzhega and A. Voloshyn. As part of creating a focal point for the Prosvita reading room network, plans were made to construct a Narodnyi Dom (National Center), which came to fruition in October 1928, when the Society celebrated the opening of a modern center in Uzhhorod that included a museum, library, reading room, and movie theater.[13] Although the impact of the world economic depression and the cutback in government support during the 1930s resulted in a decrease in Prosvita's publishing and theatrical program, the society nevertheless continued to be an important feature in the cultural life of the province.

emigrés and Subcarpathian Ukrainophiles used the term *Rusyn* they did not think in terms of a separate nationality, but used the name as a synonym for Ukrainian and considered that their task was to make Subcarpathians aware of belonging to a larger Ukrainian nationality beyond the Carpathians.

[12]"Iak zakladaty y vesty chyt. 'Prosvîta'?'" (undated pamphlet), p. 2.

[13]"K slavnostnímu otevření 'Národního domu v Užhorodě'," *Lidové listy* (Prague), October 20, 1928.

The Russophile faction of the local intelligentsia which boycotted the Prosvita Society met in Uzhhorod on March 23, 1923 to set up a rival organization, the Russkoe Kul'turno-Prosvietitel'noe Obshchestvo imeni Aleksandra Dukhnovicha (hereafter, the Dukhnovych Society).[14] Evmenii Sabov, a long time defender of the so-called "Carpatho-Rusyn tradition," was chosen chairman, although the organizing and guiding spirit was the younger political activist, Dr. Stepan Fentsik. The Dukhnovych Society attracted those elements within the Subcarpathian intelligentsia who for various reasons were dissatisfied with the Ukrainian-oriented Prosvita Society. The aim of the new organization was to foster the "cultural development of the Russian (*russkii*) people living within Czechoslovakia, and most importantly to educate them in a moral, patriotic and Russian spirit, exclusive of all political activity."[15] In subsequent years, the Russian character and anti-Ukrainian attitude of the organization were to be continually emphasized. A resolution from 1930 declared: "in the course of its one thousand year history, our people always called themselves Russian. They always considered their language, their lineage, their customs, their church and other institutions as Russian."[16]

Even flags, the symbolic trapping of national sovereignty, were employed. While the Prosvita Society displayed the blue and yellow flag that was used by the independent Ukrainian Republic in Kiev and by the Western Ukrainian Republic in L'viv (1918-1919), the Dukhnovych Society chose the "Russian (*obshcherusskii*), tricolored, national flag [as] ... a symbol, an external mark that we are Russian and ... a part of the great Russian nation (*velikaia russkaia natsiia*)."[17]

---

[14]The society was named after Aleksander Dukhnovych (1803-1865), the "national awakener of the Subcarpathian Rusyns." "Protokol sostavlennyi 27.XII.1923 . . . na pervom ocherednom sobranii Obshchestva im. A. Dukhnovicha," *Karpatskii krai*, I, 3-4 (Mukachevo, 1923-24), pp. 35-39.

[15]*Ustav Russkago kul'turno-prosvietitel'nago obshchestva imeni Aleksandra Dukhnovicha* (Uzhhorod, 1923), p. 3.

[16]"Rezoliutslia 8-ogo obshchago sobraniia Obshchestva im. A. Dukhnovicha, I.VI.1930," *Karpatskii sviet*, 111, 5-6 (Uzhhorod, 1930), p. 1003. Of the many anti-Ukrainian statements made by the Dukhnovych Society, see especially the "Protokol 9-ago godichnago obshchago sobraniia Obshchestva im. A. Dukhnovicha, 7.VI.1931," *ibid.*, V, 6 (1932), pp. 1315-1347.

[17]S. Fentsik, *Nash natsional'nyi gimn*, Izdanie Obshchestva im. A. Dukhnovicha,

Similarly, the local Prosvita Society maintained close relations with the Ukrainian Shevchenko and Prosvita Societies in L'viv, while the Dukhnovych Society stressed its affinity with the Russophile Kachkov-skii Society in Galicia and Russian emigré organizations in Prague, Sofia, Belgrad, Paris, and the United States.[18] Nevertheless, despite these external signs of allegiance to a nationality beyond the borders of Subcarpathian Rus', the Prosvita and the Dukhnovych societies always stressed their loyalty to the Czechoslovak Republic.[19]

The Dukhnovych Society was divided into twelve sections, organizational and educational, scientific-literary, publications, theatrical, musical, choral, sports, Russian Scouts, National Center, National Archive, Russian Women, and sanitary-hygienic. Among the society's activities were the erection of monuments to Subcarpathian national leaders[20] and the celebration of an annual Russian Day (Russkii Den'), which in effect was a folk festival where speeches, parades, folk dancing, and singing were the order of the day. Another important achievement was the opening of the Russkii Narodnyi Dom (Russian National Center) in Uzhhorod in December 1932. Finally, the Russophile orientation propagated its ideology among youth through the Dukhnovych Boy Scouts. Like the schools, the scouting organizations had a great impact on determining the national orientation of young people.[21] By 1929, the Dukhnovych Society claimed to have 29

No. 26 (Uzhhorod, 1926), pp. 4-5.

[18]Besides the émigré representatives at the Dukhnovych Society's Russian Day celebrations, local leaders also travelled abroad. See Stepan A. Fentsik, "Moia poiezdka v Bolgariiu na V. S'iezd Russkikh Uchenykh, 14-28. IX.1930," *Karpatskii sviet*, III, 7-8 (Uzhhorod, 1930), pp. 1036-1051, and idem, *Uzhgorod—Amerika: putevyia zametki, 1934-1935* (Uzhhorod, 1935).

[19]"Above all I want to stress that in cultural-national matters our attitude towards the Czechoslovak government must remain loyal." Speech by Fentsik at the Eighth Congress (I.VI.1930) of the Dukhnovych Society, in "Dieiatel'nost' Obshchestva im. A. Dukhnovicha v 1929/30 godu," *Karpatskii sviet*, III, 5-6 (Uzhhorod, 1930), p. 1001.

[20]Statues were erected to A. Dukhnovych in Sevliush (1925), Uzhhorod (1929), Khust (1931), and Prešov (1933); to Evgenii Fentsik in Uzhhorod (1926); to Aleksander Mitrak in Mukachevo (1931); and to Aleksander Pushkin in Chynadiiovo (1937).

[21]Stepan A. Fentsik, "Russkoe kul'turno-prosvietitel'noe Obshchestva im. A. Dukhnovicha v Uzhgorodie na Podkarpatskoi Rusi," in A. Popov, ed.,

scouting affiliates with 500 members.

The publication section of the Dukhnovych Society sponsored the journals *Karpatskii krai* (1923-24) and later *Karpatskii sviet* (1928-33), which contained articles of a literary, scholarly, and polemical nature whose purpose was "to strive for an awakening of Carpathian Rus', which could then feel more deeply its profound intimate relationship to Russian culture and Russian literature."[22] The Dukhnovych Society also published 115 pamphlets (*Izdanie*, 1924-37), many of which were reprints of articles from *Karpatskii sviet*, while some others included original plays and collections of poetry. In contrast to the Prosvita Society, which published many pamphlets of practical use for the Rusyn peasants written in a dialectally based language, the material of the Dukhnovych Society was usually limited to the relatively esoteric realms of literature and cultural history. Moreover, since the Russian literary language was employed, the Subcarpathian reader could understand the texts only with great difficulty.

The Dukhnovych Society was most proud of its work in the establishment of reading rooms throughout the province. Like Prosvita affiliates, a minimum of ten members was required to set up a village reading room which then served as a local center for educational, theatrical, musical, and scouting activities.[23] The number of reading rooms was the criterion used by Dukhnovych Society in its claims to superiority over its rival Prosvita; a greater number supposedly represented superior cultural activity and thus justified a claim to more government funds. Unfortunately, we could find no two sources which agreed as to the relative number of reading rooms existing in any given year.[24] Such discrepancies may be explained by the existence of

Karpatorusskaia dostizheniia (Mukachevo, 1930), pp. 90-116; "My preodolieli krizis," *Karpatskii sviet*, VI, 1-2 (Uzhhorod, 1933), p. 1353.

[22]"Nasha programma i nasha tsiel'," *Karpatskii krai*, I, 1 (Mukachevo, 1923), p. 3.

[23]Stepan A. Fentsik, "Rukovodstvo k organizatsii Russkikh Narodnykh chitalen im. A.V. Dukhnovicha . . .," *Karpatskii sviet*, II, 10 (Uhhorod, 1929), pp. 743-753.

[24]For 1931, two Russophile sources—*Podkarpatskaia Rus' za gody 1919-1936* (Uzhhorod, 1936), p. 115, and Georgij Gerovskij, "Jazyk Podkarpatské Rusi," in *Československá vlastivěda*, Vol. III (Prague, 1934), p. 514—listed Dukhnovych affiliates at 274 and Prosvita at 111; while a third source—"Deklaratsiia kul'turnykh i natsional'nykh prav karpatorusskago naroda," *Karpatskii sviet*, IV, 5-6-7

fabricated statistics, but also because of the fluctuating relationship between a local reading room and its professed national orientation. Most often the affiliation of the reading room was dependent on the attitude of the local teacher, and the arrival of a new teacher might have prompted a change in affiliation. Furthermore, the Czechoslovak Ministry of Education and Culture supplied funds for the establishment of state reading rooms and libraries which were not dependent on either the Dukhnovych or Prosvita Societies, although the latter frequently claimed them in the statistics.

At best we can offer in Table 1 a representative sample of the number of reading rooms based on a modified version of statistics compiled in 1929 by the Russophile Podkarpatorusskii Narodoprosvietitel'nyi Soiuz (Subcarpathian-Russian Popular Education Association). These were the only detailed statistics available, and according to this source, the Dukhnovych Society had 202 reading rooms while Prosvita only 83. Most interesting was their geographical layout. The Dukhnovych Society was unquestionably strongest in central Bereg county, particularly in the areas around Mukachevo, Svaliava, and Nyzhni Verets'ky. In western Ung county, the proportion was roughly two to one in favor of Dukhnovych, while in eastern Máramaros, a stronghold of Ukrainianism, the proportion was reversed in favor of Prosvita.[25] The last available statistics showed that the Prosvita Society increased its total number to 253 (1937), although the 297 (1936) affiliates of the Dukhnovych Society revealed the continued leadership

(Uzhhorod, 1931), p. 1208—listed respectively only 230 and 70 affiliates.

[25]The geographical layout suggested by Table 1 is confirmed by an analysis of the membership (1934) in the Ukrainophile teachers organization, Uchytel's'ka Hromada. While only 355 (49 percent) of teachers in Bereg county belonged to the Ukrainophile Hromada, 186 (60 percent) were members in Ung county, and 486 (75 percent) in Máramaros county. *Uchytel's'kyi holos*, V, 6 (Mukachevo, 1934), p. 109.

Table 1: DUKHNOVYCH AND PROSVITA SOCIETY READING ROOMS IN SUBCARPATHIAN RUS, 1929

	UNG COUNTY			BEREG COUNTY			UGOCSA COUNTY			MÁRAMAROS COUNTY		
	School District	D	P	School District	D	P	School District	D	P	School District	D	P
	Užhhorod	24	7	Berehovo	1	2	Sevlush	20	5	Khust	6	6
	Velykyi Bereznyi	14	13	Irshava	26	5				Rakhiv	7	18
				Mukachevo	17	2				Tiachiv	3	8
				Orysvyhiv	27	0				Volovoie	6	14
				Svaliava	51	3						
Totals		38	20		122	15		20	5		22	46

Source: "Statistika o dieiatel'nosti kul'turnykh i prosvietitel'nykh organizatsii na Podkarpatskoi Rusi," *Karpatskii sviet,* III, 5-6 (Uzhhorod, 1930) pp. 995-999.

of the Russophile organization in reading room activity.[26] As for membership, the Dukhnovych Society claimed 21,000 members, Prosvita, 15,000.[27]

Notwithstanding these figures, it must be stated that the Dukhnovych Society was the less dynamic of the two cultural organizations during the 1930s. For example, its publication program was severely curtailed. This was in part the result of a decrease in governmental support, but this also struck the Prosvita Society. More significant were the attitudes of leaders in each institution. Whereas Prosvita was headed by individuals like A. Voloshyn, V. Birchak and I. Pan'kevych—teachers and scholars continually in close contact with Subcarpathian cultural life—the Dukhnovych Society was under the influence of Stepan Fentsik and Iosif Kaminskii, individuals more interested in local politics and personal advancement than in serious, sustained cultural work among the masses.

In 1934, the nominal head of the Dukhnovych Society and the highly respected priest and national leader, Ievmenii Sabov, died. It was not long before the Dukhnovych Society became little more than a platform for the propagation of Stepan Fentsik's political views. An attempt to depoliticize the organization came with the election of Edmund Bachinskii as chairman in June 1936, but he resigned three months later in protest against the secretary Fentsik's continued use of the organization for political purposes.[28] By 1937, Fentsik's relations with the revisionist movement in Poland and Hungary became common knowledge and the Dukhnovych Society was discredited in the eyes of many inhabitants throughout the province.[29]

---

[26]*Karpats'ka molod'*, I, 6-7 (Velyka Kopania, 1937), p. 15. In eastern Slovakia, the Dukhnovych Society, with 37 reading rooms, was by far the superior organization. Cf. Ivan I. Zhidovskii, "Priashevskaia Rus' v bor'bie za svoi prava," in *Podkarpatskaia Rus' za gody 1919-1936*, pp. 89-91.

[27]Evgenij Nedzielskij, "Spolek Alexandra V. Duchnoviča" and Ivan Pan'kevič, "Spolek 'Prosvita' v Užhorodě," in Jaroslav Zatloukal, ed., *Podkarpatská Rus* (Bratislava, 1936), pp. 298-299.

[28]*Nedîlia* (Uzhhorod), June 14 and September 27, 1936.

[29]A letter by one villager (from Rostoky) to the editor of an anti-Fentsik Russophile newpaper concluded: "And since Fentsik carried on his politics even in the Dukhnovych reading room, we decided to establish a Prosvita instead of a Dukhnovych reading room." "Komu éto nuzhno?," *Russkii viestnik* (Uzhhorod),

An indication of the ever-growing popularity of the Ukrainian orientation and the simultaneous decrease of the Russian orientation can be observed in the degree of success registered by the Prosvita and Dukhnovych Societies in organizing public manifestations during the late 1930s. Prosvita convoked a series of congresses which met in Svaliava, Rakhiv, Perechyn, and other villages throughout Subcarpathian Rus'. Although aimed at stimulating Ukrainian national pride, these gatherings frequently turned out to be political and especially anti-government in nature. Prosvita's dominance in garnering popular support was indisputable after the General Prosvita Congress, which took place in Uzhhorod on October 17, 1937. Upwards of 30,000 persons gathered in one of the largest manifestations ever organized in the city. The Ukrainian and anti-governmental character of the general congress was made explicit by a wide range of speakers, among whom were Social-Democratic as well as Communist and extreme nationalist delegates.[30]

The Dukhnovych Society could hardly match the massive support behind its Ukrainian rival. Fentsik's last attempt was to announce the celebration of another annual Russian Culture Day on September 12, 1938 in Mukachevo, the center of Russophile strength. Nevertheless, despite the call to members of the Duchnovych Society, to its scouts, and to local students, only 190 people participated.[31] The poor showing was not only a reaction to Fentsik's foreign political ventures. It also revealed that in the struggle between the two cultural societies for the allegiance of the local population, by the late 1930s Prosvita had proved to be the most successful.

The constitutions of both the Prosvita and Dukhnovych Societies expressed an intent to organize theatrical circles throughout Subcarpathian Rus'. It was early recognized that theatrical performances would be an important stimulus to national allegiance and pride among the Subcarpathian population. The psychological effect of seeing heroic and patriotic deeds performed on stage and in the national language was a force that could not be underestimated. Undoubtedly, the type of reper-

January 26, 1936.

[30]Petro Stercho, *Karpato-ukraïns'ka derzhava* (Toronto, 1965) pp. 40-42.

[31]*Nova svoboda* (Uzhhorod), September 15, 1938.

toire and choice of language to be used were crucial questions which had to be faced by both amateur and professional theaters.

The first theatrical organization was an amateur circle set up by the Prosvita Society which from July to September 1920 gave seven performances of the patriotic Ukrainian play, "Natalka Poltavka." Public interest was so great that it was decided to establish a permanent theater, made easier by the presence of many professional Ukrainian actors in Czechoslovakia. On January 1, 1921 of the Rus'kii Teatr Tovarystva 'Prosvita' (Rus' Theater of the Prosvita Society) was established. The following summer Uzhhorod's Rus' Theater received a subsidy of 250,000 crowns from Czechoslovakia's President Masaryk and was reorganized by the renowned Ukrainian director, Mykola Sadovs'kyi.

Despite subsequent financial difficulties, the Rus' Theater played ten seasons (1921-29) and averaged 133 performances a year. Most popular were the Ukrainian patriotic operas and dramas: "Zaporozhets' za Dunaiem," "Taras Bul'ba," "Bohdan Khmel'nyts'kyi," "Natal'ka Poltavka," and "Oi, ne khody, Hrytsiu." All performances were given in the Ukrainian language, and the theater's frequent tours throughout Subcarpathian Rus' helped to create a lively interest and feeling of allegiance towards Ukraine.[32]

Unlike Prosvita, the Dukhnovych Society never had a professional theater. In fact, the only productions in the Russian language by a professional group were the few performances given in Uzhhorod by the Moskovskii Khudozhestvennyi Teatr (Moscow Art Theater) of Prague. The existence of local theatrical circles, however, was of great importance, and in this realm the Dukhnovych Society was most active. In 1936, the Dukhnovych reading rooms had 214 theatrical circles, 144 of which had their own stages, while Prosvita had 143 circles with 64 stages. The total number of performances in 1931 was listed as 574, while in 1936 there were 1000.[33] The Czechoslovak government, in turn, was generous in its support of local theatrical activity, contributing thirty to ninety thousand crowns annually. In the words of one historian: "Even with the lack of leadership, theatrical activity grew,

---

[32]Iurii Sherehii, "P'iadesiatyrichchia ukraïns'koho teatru na Zakarpatti," *Nove zhyttia* (Prešov), January 16, 29 and February 5, 1971.

[33]Evgenii Nedziel'skii, *Ugro-russkii teatr* (Uzhhorod, 1941), p. 7.

and for this small land and people took on fantastic proportions! With regard to the number of performances, the village began to overtake the city."[34]

In the individual reading room and theatrical circle the local teacher played a crucial role. It was he who urged the peasant villagers to participate as actors or spectators, he who chose the repertoire, he who stimulated an appreciation for the theater among the Rusyn masses. In response to necessity, these amateur productions were performed in the local dialect. As for material, Subcarpathian authors like Dimitrii Antalovskii, Antonii Bobul'skii, Vasyl' Grendzha-Dons'kyi, Iryna Nevyts'ka, Sion Sil'vai, and Pavel Fedor wrote a series of simple plays that could easily be adapted for amateur productions.

Despite Prosvita's dissociation from the Rus' Theater in late 1929 and the virtual end to government funding, the company still played for a few more seasons. Under the direction of another Ukrainian immigrant, Mykola Arkas, the Rus' Theater gave 230 performances during the 1931-32 season, but without further subsidies it was impossible to continue, and by the 1935-36 season only one drama was performed.[35]

The widespread interest in the theater expressed by the population in Subcarpathian Rus' prompted a the provincial government of Subcarpathian Rus' to decide in September 1931 to organize and subsidize a professional company. These plans, however, were not realized until the summers of 1934 and 1935 when courses were organized to develop talent. Both Russian and Ukrainian immigrants were employed as instructors. Finally, in April 1936, the Zemskii Podkarpatorus'kii Narodnyi Teatr (hereafter: Subcarpathian Rusyn National Theater) was established. Although the ruling board included the region's Rusynophile governor, Konstantin Hrabar, the Ukrainophile A. Voloshyn, and the Russophile I. Kaminskii, policy was actually determined by the Czech Superintendent of Schools, Viktor Klima and his successor František Hlavatý. In theory, the Subcarpathian National Theater was to perform all plays in the Rusyn dialect and to draw especially on the repertoire of local dramatists. In practice, Russian works were translated into Rusyn while Ukrainian plays were performed in the original.

[34]*Ibid.*, p. 54.
[35]Sherehii, "P'iatdesiatyrichchia," February 12, 1971.

If in Prague and other Czech cities the Subcarpathian Rusyn National Theater was lauded with praise, at home it was harshly criticized by both Russophile and Ukrainophile leaders for its use of an "artificial" Rusyn language. The steady barrage of criticism contributed to a leadership crisis during the 1937-38 season, and despite a large government subsidy of 450,000 crowns annually, in that season the theater gave only seventy-two performances.[36]

One reason for the crisis was the appearance of a new Ukrainian theater in Khust, the Nova Stsena (New Stage). Founded by the brothers Iurii and Ievhen Sherehii in February 1934, New Stage became in 1936 an affiliate of the Prosvita Society in Khust, and two years later a self-supporting corporation under the direction of Ivan Hryts Duda. In the tradition of the Rus' Theater, the New Stage performed a repertoire of classical Ukrainian plays and operettas. After unsuccessful plans in 1938 to unite the Subcarpathian Rusyn National Theater with the New Stage, many members of the former company resigned and went to Khust. Despite only a minimum subsidy from the state (10,000 crowns in 1938), the New Stage nonetheless managed to give 236 performances.[37]

If plays in Rusyn dialect written by Subcarpathian authors dominated the repertoire of local amateur theatrical circles, at the professional level the Ukrainian orientation was by far the superior. In the 1920s, the presence of Ukrainian immigrants in Czechoslovakia provided a strong cadre of professional performers who had a decisive influence in the formation of younger talent that was to come to the fore during the following decade.[38] Another explanation for the success of the Ukrainian orientation in the theatrical world may be found in the repertoire itself. While Russian dramatic and operatic literature was characterized by the grand and heroic, the Ukrainian tradition found its strength in rural themes and folk motifs. The enormous popularity

---

[36]Nedziel'skii, *Ugro-russkii teatr*, pp. 63-74; Sherehii, "P'iatdesiatyrichchia," February 19, 1971; František Gabriel, "Otázka zemského divadla podkarpatoruského," *Podkarpatoruská revue*, I, 2 (Bratislava, 1936), pp. 6-8.

[37]Sherehii, "P'iatdesiatyrichchia," February 19, 1971

[38]Writing about the theater during the 1920s, one author rightly concluded that "these theatrical undertakings existed exclusively thanks to the forces of the Ukrainian and Russian immigrants." Stepan S. Fedor, "Teatral'noe dielo na Podk. Rusi," in *Podkarpatskaia Rus' za gody 1919-1936*, p. 142.

throughout the province of works like "Zaporozhets' za Dunaiem" or "Oi, ne khody, Hrytsiu" could not be matched by any Russian works.[39] Thus, while the amateur theaters propagated themes drawn from life in Subcarpathian Rus', the professional Ukrainian-language theaters, centered in the larger cities, fostered among the intelligentsia and especially students a sympathy and love for the culture and traditions of Ukraine.

Besides the Prosvita and Dukhnovych Societies there were many other social and cultural organizations in Subcarpathian Rus', such as the Rusyn National Museum, the *Shkol'naia Pomoshch* (Educational Benevolent Association), which from 1920 operated a library and four student dormitories, various choral groups, and a short-lived opera group headed by Z.G. Ashkinazi and under the patronage of Russophile leaders in Mukachevo.[40]

Also of great importance for crystallizing a feeling of national consciousness in the local youth was the Ukrainophile Plast scouting organization. Like the Dukhnovych scouts, Plast played a decisive role in forming a national consciousness in young boys. The nationalist aspect was stressed by long-time scout master, the Ukrainian émigré from Galicia, Leonyd Bachyns'kyi: "To love the fatherland, its customs, traditions and language, to learn how to help and show the way to his nation so that it can become great and powerful, to defend the nation with tenacity and character from any harm, to raise the culture of the homeland—these are the primary and basic tasks of the Plast scout."[41]

---

[39]The author is thankful here for the opinions expressed in interviews (June 1971) with Ivan Hryts'-Duda, the founder of the Nova Stsena (New Stage).

[40]*Školství na Podkarpatské Rusi v přítomnosti* (Prague, 1933), p. 48. Iurii Borzhava [Sevestiian Sabol], *Vid Uhors'koï Rusy do Karpats'koï Ukraïny* (Philadelphia, 1956), pp. 31-35; "Osnovania Rus'koho Natsional'noho Muzeia v Uzhhorodî," *Podkarpatska Rus'*, VII, 6 (Uzhhorod, 1930), pp. 123-124; Petr Sova, "Spolek 'Školnaja Pomošč' v Užhorode," in Zatloukal, *Podkarpatská Rus*, p. 300; *'Kolomŷika': zbôrnyk prysviachenyi I. zîzdu Rus'kykh Natsional'nykh Khorov Podkarpatskoî Rusy* (Uzhhorod, 1926).

[41]L. Bachyns'kyi, "Plast y relygiia," *Podkarpatska Rus'*, V, 3 (Uzhhorod, 1928), p. 34. See also Mykola Vaida, "Pered vidznachenniam 50-richchia Plastu na Zakarpatti (1921-1951)," *Vistnyk Karpats'koho soiuzu*, II, 2-3 (New York, 1971), pp. 10-11.

To foster its goals, Plast published the monthly journal *Plastun* (1923-35) and a series of pamphlets (adventure stories, playlets, and moral tracts) in which Ukrainian themes and a gradual trend from Rusyn dialect to literary Ukrainian was characteristic. By the 1930s, Plast was fully associated with the Ukrainian movement and its more than 3,000 scouts (1935) formed an important component in pro-Ukrainian manifestations throughout the province.

Educational developments

The most important mechanism for implanting a national consciousness within a given population is the educational system. From the beginning Subcarpathian leaders were keenly aware of this fact: "The future of our land and our people lies in the state of our culture, which in turn is dependent upon our schools. . . Our future is in our schools."[42] Thanks to the enormous investments of the Czechoslovak government, elementary schools were established in almost every Rusyn village, so that between 1920 and 1938 the number of Rusyn elementary schools increased from 321 to 463. As Table 2 reveals, there were similar increases in the number of Rusyn municipal schools, *gymnasia*, teacher's colleges, and technical schools.[43]

[42]Aleksander Markush, *Shkolný voprosý* (Uzhhorod, 1922), p. 42.

[43]Between 1919 and 1929, Prague invested more than 41 million crowns which provided for repairs, extensions, and 52 new schools in Subcarpathian Rus'. Pavel St. Fedor, "Krátký nástin školství na Podkarpatské Rusi," in *Publikace pro zem Podkarpatská Rus, 1919-1932* (Uzhhorod, 1932), pp. 65-69; *Školství na Podkarpatské Rusi*, pp. 25-26.

Both pro- and anti-Czechoslovak writers recognize these achievements. For the Russophile view, see A.V. Popov, "Shkol'noe dielo na Podk. Rusi v 1919-1929 godakh," in *Karpatorusskiia dostizheniia*, pp. 41-53; for the Ukrainophile, A. Stefan, "Education and Schools—Transcarpathia, 1919-29," in *Ukraine: A Concise Encyclopedia*, Vol. II (Toronto, 1971), pp. 381-383; for the Marxist, A.M. Ihnat, "Stan osvity na Zakarpatti v 20-30kh rr. XX st.," in *Velykyi Zhovten' i rozkvit vozz'iednanoho Zakarpattia* (Uzhhorod, 1970), pp. 212-221.

TABLE 2: SCHOOLS IN SUBCARPATHIAN RUS', 1920-1938

Language of instruction	Elementary			Municipal			Gymnasia			Teacher's Colleges			Professional and Technical		
	1920	1931	1938	1920	1931	1938	1920	1931	1938	1920	1931	1938	1920	1931	1938
RUSYN[1]	321	425	463	7[a]	16[b]	21	3	4[d]	5[e]	3	3	4	3	5[f]	5[f]
CZECH	22	158	188	1	2	23			1		1	1			
HUNGARIAN	83	101	117	2		1									
OTHER	49	43	35					1	2						
Totals	**475**	**727**	**803**	**10**	**18**	**44[c]**	**4**	**5**	**8**	**3**	**4**	**3**	**6**	**5**	**5**

Source: *Školství na Podkarpatské Rusi v přítomnosti* (Prague, 1932); František Stojan, ed., *Representační sborník veškerého školství na Podkarpatské Rusi při příležitosti 20 leteho trvání ČSR* (Uzhhorod, 1938).

Explanations:

[1] Rusyn is used here as a translation for the official Czech term "podkarpatorуský," which referred to a school whose language of instruction might have been Russian, Ukrainian, or Rusyn.

[a] 5 schools with Hungarian classes

[b] 12 schools with Czechoslovak classes, 4 with Hungarian classes

[c] This number represents schools that also contain 30 Hungarian classes, 6 German classes

[d] 3 *gymnasia* with Czechoslovak sections, 1 with Hungarian

[e] 2 *gymnasia* with Czechoslovak sections, 1 with Hungarian

[f] 1 school a with Czechoslovak section, 1 with Hungarian

Of course, the existence of a physical plant does not automatically guarantee the presence of students, and one enormous difficulty encountered by the Czechoslovak regime was the resistance of the local population to education. Typical of peasant societies, the population in Subcarpathian Rus' was tradition bound and apt to be wary of any kind of change. If peasants were urged to send even one of their children to school, the response was given: "He's not going to be a notary or a priest, so why should he know how to read and write?" Furthermore, "Grandfather could not read nor write and he still went on living." The stubbornness of Rusyn parents, particularly in the rural areas, was not easily surmounted, yet in the course of a few years the School Administration could claim a great psychological victory. While in 1919-1920 only twenty-five to thirty percent of children in Subcarpathian Rus' attended school, by 1933 the percentage reached as high as ninety.[44]

The School Administration was also concerned with the uneducated adult segment of the population, and special courses for illiterates were established. Between 1919 and 1930, 1,473 courses were organized which included 64,700 participants.[45] Like the Prosvita and Dukhnovych Societies the state set up village reading rooms and libraries which by 1930 numbered 19 and 291 respectively.[46] The School Administration also sponsored a series of publications including a children's magazine, *Vînochok* (1919-1924), and pedagogical and official journals for teachers, *Uchytel'* (1920-36) and *Uriadovŷi vîstnyk* (1921-38). Associated with the School Administration was the Pedagogychne Tovarystvo (Pedagogical Society), which published the children's journal *Nash rodnŷi krai* (1923-38) and the more scholarly *Podkarpatska Rus'* (1923-36), which strove to provide information dealing with all aspects of the homeland, in short, "to serve primarily

---

[44]Josef Pešek, "Školství v Podkarpatské Rusi," in Josef Chmelář et al., eds., *Podkarpatská Rus* (Prague, 1923), p. 169; René Martel, *La Ruthénie subcarpathique* (Paris, 1935), p. 106.

[45]*Školství na Podkarpatské Rusi*, p. 48; Cyril Kochannyj, *O Podkarpatské Rusi*, Občanská knihovna, No. 83 (Prague, 1929), p. 33.

[46]"Statistika o dieiatel'nosti kul'turnykh i prosvietitel'nykh organizatsii," *Karpatskii sviet*, III, 5-6 (Uzhhorod, 1930), p. 999. Again, there is no agreement among the sources, Kochannyj, *O Podkarpatske Rusi*, p. 33, claiming that by 1927, 140 state reading rooms and 179 libraries were in operation.

instructors as an aid to teaching."[47] The Pedagogychne Tovarystvo also published a series of forty-five text books for Subcarpathian schools, that were, in the words of A. Voloshyn, "written in the simple, national, literary language," which for him meant a dialectal variation of Ukrainian in the traditional orthography.[48]

It is also important to note that at the lower educational levels two distinct trends were in evidence: a steady decrease in the number of church-run schools and a rapid increase in Czech-language schools. In 1920, there were 249 elementary schools, but by 1938 only 84 were left. This meant that the formerly predominant role of religion in the formation of young minds could give way to civic and especially national concerns. On the other hand, the number of Czech schools increased from 22 to 188 during this same period.[49] This was a direct challenge to the local nationalist intelligentsia and only further complicated their task by adding a potentially new national option to the many that already existed in the region. In short, a solid network of educational establishments was set up, but with regard to nationality policy the Czechoslovak School Administration was never able to adopt one ideology that could be implemented throughout all phases of the educational process.

One reason for this was the way in which the government obtained its teaching and administrative personnel. Many teachers who had staffed Subcarpathian schools during the Hungarian administration were opposed to the Czechoslovak regime, and in 1919 almost half the teaching force, a total of 428, were released.[50] Where were replacements to be

[47]This journal also published the series, Byblioteka novynky 'Nash rodnŷi krai', 17 vols., which included translations and original literary works by local authors.

[48]"Besîda predsydatelia Pedegogychnoho T-stva na II. zahal'nom z'îzdî, 8.V.1926," *Podkarpatska Rus'*, III, 6 (Uzhhorod, 1926), p. 132. After 1935, literary Ukrainian with modern orthography was employed.

[49]The decrease in Greek Catholic church schools was especially marked—from 164 in 1920 to 19 in 1938. The decline in the number of Roman Catholic (20 to 17) and Evangelical (44 to 31) administered schools during these years was less marked. František Stojan, ed., *Representační sborník veškerého školství na Podkarpatské Rusi* (Uzhhorod, 1938); Josef Pešina, "Národní školství na Podkarpatské Rusi," in Zatloukal, *Podkapatská Rus*, pp. 259-262.

[50]The situation was particularly critical in secondary schools: "Of the 80 professors teaching during the 1916-1919 school year, only 6 were willing to serve

found? The lack of trained local cadres compelled the School Administration to call on external aid.

Coincidentally, the social and political upheavals that accompanied the postwar period throughout Europe provided a fund of educated elements among Russian and Ukrainian émigrés and Czech Legionnaires. Within ten years the number of teachers in Subcarpathian Rus' more than doubled from about 1,000 in 1920 to 2,362 in 1931. Many of these new teachers were either Russians and some Ukrainians from the former Russian Empire, or Russophile and especially Ukrainophile immigrants from neighboring Galicia. The Subcarpathian classroom became a platform from which these émigrés could propagate national and social ideas that they were unable to do in their own land.[51] Moreover, the local Subcarpathian intelligentsia welcomed the fact that schools could be used for the spread of national ideals. In the words of one commentator:

> One of the most important tasks of education in elementary schools is the development of the national spirit.... The school must give to the children and future citizens the feeling of nationality so that they know what they are and who they are. The future of our people depends on our national, that is on our educational upbringing.[52]

---

the Czechoslovak regime after the revolution." *Školství na Podkarpatské Rusi*, p. 32.

[51]Unfortunately, statistics on the precise number of Russian and Ukrainian emigré teachers are not available, although one source for 1922 recorded 106 immigrant teachers in Subcarpathian Rus', 79 of Ukrainian nationality, and only 27 of Russian. Archiv Národního Musea (Prague), Fond Dr. Starý, karton 1, folder 2.

The Czech Legion, formed in Russia (1917) by Czech and Slovak prisoners of war, was intended to serve with the tsarist armies in the struggle against the Central Powers. The Russian revolutions of 1917, however, precluded the realization of such plans, and the Legion returned to Europe via Siberia and Japan. In the new Czechoslovak Republic, the Legionnaires were lauded as national heros and given many of the highest positions in the country's economic and military life. Some lower echelon individuals who may have had some knowledge of Russian from their military days were given positions as teachers in Subcarpathian Rus'. In "Rusyn" elementary schools there were 37 teachers of Czechoslovak nationality (probably Legionnaires) in 1920 and 49 in 1931. *Školství na Podkarpatské Rusi*, pp. 14-15.

[52]V. Hasynets, "O rozvyvaniu narodnoho dukha," *Uchytel'*, XII, 1-2 (Uzhhorod, 1931), p. 14.

The role of the local teacher, then, was to be crucial. If he was a Russophile, then the students would study literary Russian and learn to idealize Pushkin, Turgenev and Tolstoy. If a Ukrainophile, then Taras Shevchenko, the "melodious" Ukrainian language, and tales of Bohdan Khmel'nyts'kyi and the Zaporozhian Cossacks would be propagated. If a Rusynophile, as were many who were educated and who taught in Hungarian schools before World War I, then Hungarian cultural and political heroes would be replaced by local Rusyn historical figures and instruction given in a personal variant of what was claimed to be the "Carpatho-Rusyn language." Finally, for those Rusyn children who might have been enrolled in one of the many Czech-language schools, national identity would be emphasized in terms of Czechoslovak citizenship and in some cases a Czech national consciousness might result.

The influence of the teacher was, of course, largely dependent on how he (and increasingly she) was viewed in the village. In fact, respect for teachers was very great among the peasantry. Of all the so-called influential village *panove* (priests, notaries, shopkeepers), the teacher was the one most trusted by the people. "During the revolution [1918-1919] the teacher was the only *pan* in the village who did not have to flee, who was not maltreated, driven away, or beaten by the people, because the simple people considered him their own."[53] Herein lies the reason for the domination of the village teacher's influence not only in the schools, but also in the reading rooms, theatrical circles, and other rural sociocultural activities.

The type of village teacher (i.e. his national orientation) was in large part dependent upon the Superintendent of Schools in Uzhhorod (all of whom were of Czech nationality) and his subordinates, the fourteen district school inspectors. The first superintendent, Josef Pešek (1919-1924), favored Galician émigrés of the Ukrainian orientation, whereas his successor, Josef Šimek (1924-1929), was inclined to hire former Czech legionnaires. Add to these categories Russian emigrés and local Rusyn instructors and the reader may get some idea of the variety of influences to which children in Subcarpathian Rus' were exposed. Unfortunately, this combination was often pedagogically unsound, as it was not uncommon for students to receive instruction in Russian, in

---

[53]Markush, *Shkolnŷ voprosŷ*, p. 23.

some Carpatho-Rusyn dialect, or in Ukrainian. At the secondary level, students might be obliged to respond in Russian to one teacher, in Ukrainian to a second, and in some Rusyn dialect to a third. Because of the lack of personnel, the Czech school superintendents had no choice but to rely largely on émigrés to fill teaching posts during the 1920s. This situation changed somewhat during the 1930s, when graduates of Subcarpathia's three teacher's colleges began to fill positions throughout the province. The national orientation of this new generation of teachers was determined by which institute they attended. If an alumnus of the Greek Catholic male and female institutes in Uzhhorod (headed by A. Voloshyn, Viktor Zheltvai, and Vasyl' Lar) then they were likely to be Ukrainian; if they attended the state institute in Mukachevo, then they were usually partisans of the Russian orientation. Based on the number of students in these institutes 346 in Uzhhorod and 151 in Mukachevo (1931/32) one would assume that in the future the Ukrainian orientation was likely to be the dominant one among teachers (and hence students) in Subcarpathian Rus'.[54] An analysis of the various teacher and student organizations tends to support such a premise.

The first organization which temporarily united the teaching force was the Uchytel'ske Tovaryshchestvo Podkarpatskoî Rusy (Teacher's Society of Subcarpathian Rus'), established in 1920. Although the Society planned to provide a broad program of cultural and social aid to students and to its own members, in practice it "spent much time and money on conferences, at which much was said but little done."[55] Debate at these conferences centered on the question of language, and the lack of any clear orientation was indicative of the broad range of opinion that existed among Subcarpathian teachers. In later years, however, the society and its journal, *Narodna shkola* (1921-38), became a platform for the Russophile orientation.[56]

Adherents of the populist-Ukrainian orientation were first concentrated

---

[54]*Školství na Podkarpatské Rusi*, p. 36; Mykola Shtets', *Literaturna mova ukraïntsiv Zakarpattia i Skhidnoï Slovachchyny pislia 1918*, Pedahohichnyi zbirnyk, No. I (Bratislava, 1967), p. 23.

[55]Pešek, "Školství," p. 167. See also the Statut 'Uchytel'skago Tovarystva Podkarpatskoî Rusy" (Uzhhorod, 1920).

[56]Shtets', *Literaturna mova*, pp. 37 and 98-99.

in the Pedagogychne Tovarystvo (Pedagogical Society), founded by a group of 100 delegates in 1924.[57] As an affiliate of the Uzhhorod School Administration, the Pedagogychne Tovarystvo tried to avoid active participation in the language and national controversies. "To care for our youth, to care about its education, this is the most important aim of our society."[58] Nonetheless, the society did take a stand on the national issue, and at its 1928 Congress "accepted the scientific principle that Subcarpathian Rusyns are a Little Russian [Ukrainian] people."[59] A critical turning point in the fortune of the populist-Ukrainian movement was the 1929 Congress of the Uchytel'ske Tovaryshchestvo. Having failed to reach agreement on the language question, a few Ukrainian teachers founded a new organization, the Narodovets'ke Uchytel's'ke Tovarystvo (Populist Teacher's Society). Led by Avhustyn Shtefan and Aleksander Polians'kyi, the new association was uncompromising on the language and national issues. "The people themselves speak their own language, Ukrainian, and so the language question is solved."[60] The new Society was especially opposed to the use of any textbooks other than Ukrainian in Subcarpathian schools "because our people are Ukrainian, and their children Ukrainian."[61]

The rapid increase in membership of the Narodovets'ke Uchytel'ske Tovarystvo, later renamed the Uchytel's'ka Hromada, was indicative of the Ukrainian movement's growing strength during the 1930s. While only a few years previous the Uchytel'ske Tovarychchestvo contained the majority of teachers, by 1934 the Uchytel's'ka Hromada claimed 1,211 of the 1,874 "Rusyn" teachers throughout Subcarpathian Rus'.[62]

---

[57]"Spravozdania o diial'nosti Pedagogychnoho T-va Podk. Rusy do kontsia ianuara 1926," *Podkarpatska Rus'*, III, 2 (Uzhhorod, 1926), p. 39.

[58]Iu. Revai and A. Voloshyn, "Vpysuitesia v chlenŷ Pedagogychnoho Tovarystva," *ibid.*, II, 1 (1925), p. 16.

[59]"Rezolutsiî predlozhenî na zahal'nôm z'îzdî Pedagogychnoho Tov. dnia 6 okt. 1928," *ibid.*, V, 8-9 (1928), p. 176.

[60]*Uchtel's'kyi holos*, III, 1 (Mukachevo, 1932), p. 2.

[61]*Ibid.*, III, 2 (1932), p. 1. See also "Iz zvychainykh zahal'nykh zboriv Kruzhka Narodovets'koho Uchytel's'koho T-va v Uzhhorodi," *Ukraïns'ke slovo* (Uzhhorod), May 1, 1932.

[62]*Uchytel's'kyi holos*, V, 6 (Mukachevo, 1934), p. 109. In 1935, to the Hromada was attributed 1,650 members—Vasyl' Markush, "Zakarpattia," in *Entsyklopediia*

Moreover, the Hromada professed a clear-cut program of Ukrainianization, while its rival Uchytel'ske Tovaryshchestvo continued to call for the use of an undefined language and national affiliation "which conforms to our tradition and our past."[63] The Ukrainian-Russian dichotomy was also evident in student life. Students at the university level were the first to organize, and in 1920 the Vozrozhdenie (Renaissance) association was founded in Prague. Only temporarily, however, could the Vozrozhdenie unite all students from Subcarpathia Rus', and in 1922 a populist-Ukrainophile group set up the rival Kruzhok Sotsiial'noï Pomoshchy Pidkarpatskykh Studentiv, later the Soiuz Pidkarpatskykh Rus'kykh Studentiv (Union of Subcarpathian Rusyn Students).[64]

The Vozrozhdenie founded a chorus, a balalaika orchestra, and later published a monthly (*Molodaia Rus'* [Prague, 1930-31]) and two literary anthologies (*Almanakh Vozrozhdenie* [Prague, 1933 and 1936]) which clearly defined the association's Russian orientation.[65] In 1927, an attempt was made to unite both groups in a Tsentral'nyi Soiuz Karpatorusskykh Studentiv (Central Union of Carpatho-Russian Students), but disputes over the national issue caused the secession of the Ukrainophile Soiuz. Other associations of Subcarpathian students which were set up in Mukachevo (1929), Chynadiiovo (1930), Prague (1931), Bratislava, Khust, Svaliava, and Prešov (1933) also failed to unite the opposing factions and were strictly either Russian or Ukrainian in orientation.[66]

ukraïnoznavstva: slovnykova chastyna, Vol. II (Paris and New York, 1955-57), p. 721. Two years later the Hromada contained 1,555 of the 2,222 teachers in Subcarpethian Rus'—St. Merekht, "Uchytel's'ka Hromada—nasha hordist'," *Nash prapor* (L'viv), October 15, 1937.

[63]Shtets', *Literaturna mova*, pp. 65-72.

[64]Š. Antalovskij, "Karpatoruské studentstvo," in Zatloukal, *Podkarpatská Rus*, pp. 102-104.

[65]See especially the anti-Ukrainian articles by Aleksei A. Farinich: "Kto vrag narodnoi kul'tury," *Molodaia Rus'*, 3-4 (Prague, 1930), pp. 24-25, "Iz sviataia sviatykh ukrainskoi kul'tury," and "Ukrainskii vopros," in *Al'manakh Vozrozhdentsev* (Prague, 1933), pp. 86-88 and 98.

[66]Ivan S. Shlepetskii, "Vozrozhdenie karpatorusskago studenchestva," in *ibid.* (1936), pp. 71-75; L.K. Gumetskii, "Kratkaia istoriia o-va karpatorusskikh studentov 'Vozrozhdenie' i ego dieiatel'nost' v nastoiashchee vremia," in *Karpatorusskiia*

By the 1930s some basic differences in attitudes between the Russian and Ukrainian oriented student factions were obvious. In general, Russophile students were primarily occupied with cultural and other pedagogical activities not directly related to contemporary problems. Typical was the Samoobrazovatel'nyi Kruzhok (Self-education Circle), formed at the Mukachevo *gymnasium* in 1932 which was dedicated to the propagation of classical and Soviet Russian literature.[67]

On the other hand, Ukrainian oriented students, imbued with national conviction, became what in modern terminology are known as social and political activists. Simultaneous with the founding in 1929 of the Narodovets'ke Uchytel's'ke Tovarystvo, there was organized in Uzhhorod the first Z'ïzd Narodovets'koï Molodi (Congress of Populist Youth) which identified itself and the people of Subcarpathian Rus' as Ukrainian. At the Second Congress (1934), held in Mukachevo in honor of the Subcarpathian medieval hero, Fedir Koriatovych, more than 9,650 students from 84 villages participated. By the late 1930s, then, the Ukrainian student movement could be considered the more active and certainly the more vociferous of the two factions.[68]

The success of the Ukrainian movement was due in large part to the energetic leadership of confident and uncompromising leaders like Stepan Rosokha, a university student in Prague and co-editor of the journal, *Proboiem* (Prague, 1933-44). The radically nationalist and in some cases demagogic nature of the Ukrainian student movement was indicated by the tenor of many articles that appeared during the late 1930s. Opposed to the government's indecisive nationality policy in the province, Rosokha declared that "the nationality and language of Subcarpathia is Ukrainian. ... Likewise we are, were, and will remain

dostizheniia, pp. 145-158; P.F. Komanitskii, "OKS 'Vozrozhdenie' i studencheskie organizatsii," in Ivan S. Shlepetskii, ed., *Priashevshchina* (Prague, 1948), pp. 301-307.

[67]Oleg Grabar, *Poeziia Zakarpattia, 1939-1944* (Bratislava, 1957), p. 23.

[68]Stercho, *Karpato-ukraïns'ka derzhava*, pp. 40-41. "This nationally conscious Ukrainian youth formed later the most important cadres in the formation of the Carpathian Sich [military force] and similar societies during the period of the recent national upheaval. This youth displayed sacrifice and dignity during the revolutionary events of 1938 and 1939." Narizhnyi, *Ukraïns'ka emigratsiia*, p. 329.

Ukrainian."[69] Another young nationalist expressed his frustration with
the attitude that "the struggle between the nationalities can be solved
'reasonably, democratically, [and] justly'."[70] This same author concluded that soon the Ukrainian orientation would dominate, even if
force had to be used. In fact, suggestions of this sort reflected the
atmosphere of increased national tension that caused not only ideological but also physical clashes between the opposing factions.[71]

As a result of Czechoslovakia's democratic tolerance toward the
strivings of the various national factions of the Subcarpathian intelligentsia, and the lack of a single nationality policy on the part of the
state's School Administration, a situation developed whereby it was not
uncommon to find many peasant families that included a "Russian" son,
a "Ukrainian" son, and compromising "Rusyn" parents. Indeed, youth
was a reflection of its elders, students of their professors. Thus, the
national antagonisms of the nationalist intelligentsia were being propagated by young people, and in the absence of political change it is
likely that these controversies would have continued for generations to
come.

In a study such as this, it is relatively easy to describe the transmission
belts along which the intelligentsia attempted to reach the peasantry. In
the case of Subcarpathian Rus', I have placed emphasis on cultural organizations and especially the educational system. The process was complicated somewhat by the fact that there were several national orientations in conflict with each other for the allegience of the peasantry.
In this struggle, the main contenders proved to be the Ukrainophile and
Russophile orientations.

Although the latter-day observer may weigh the relative strengths and
weaknesses of these factions and speculate with some assurance on the
reasons why one was more successful than the other, it is exceedingly

[69]S. Rosokha, "'Protypravne' chy polityka?," *Proboiem*, III, 3 (Prague, 1936), pp,.
39-40.
[70]V.H., "Baika pro lis, toporyshche ta klyn (abo chomu biemo peredovsim
ukraïntsiv)," *ibid.*, p. 35.
[71]In 1929, a Ukrainophile student from the Uzhhorod Teacher's College attempted
to assassinate the head of the Dukhnovych Society, Evmenii Sabov. *Dielo o
pokushenii na E.I. Sabova*, lzdanie Obshchestva im. A. Dukhnovicha, No. 99
(Uzhhorod, 1930).

more difficult to determine to what degree the ideals of the nationalist intelligentsia entered the psyche of the peasantry. We may follow the fate of the peasant's children and assume that their own national orientation reflected that of their teachers, but even this was not always the case, since as pointed out in the introduction, national affiliation was always subject to change.

How then, can we know if the peasant masses were influenced by the nationalist intelligentsia? There were, of course, frequent elections at the local, provincial, and national levels, in which the majority of the population participated, but the inordinately large number of political parties and splinter groups, many of which changed their own positions on the nationality issue, does not reflect in any real way the attitude of the peasantry.[72] Unfortunately, there were no Gallup polls or other surveys conducted, for instance, as those in Austria during the past twenty years which are designed to gauge whether Austrians recognize themselves as Germans or as an independent nationality.[73]

Hence, the researcher is forced to rely on indirect evidence, and interestingly this does not confirm what we have observed in our present analysis, i.e., that the Ukrainophile orientation seemed to be the more dynamic both in cultural activity and in the educational system. In 1937, a kind of poll, billed as a language plebiscite, was taken among parents of Subcarpathian elementary school children in order to

[72]The pro-Communist Agrarian party and oppositional Communist party were the strongest in the region. The Agrarian party at first was neutral concerning the Rusyn nationality issue; then in 1927 it adopted a Russophile orientation, but after 1934 also included a Ukrainophile branch. The Communists (dominated by Magyars and Jews) first followed a Rusynophile orientation, but after 1926 came out in favor of Ukrainianism.

Ukrainophile writers in the West (Stercho, Stefan, Sabol) frequently point to the elections of February 1939 conducted by the autonomous Carpatho-Ukrainian government in Khust as an indication of the widespread acceptance of the Ukrainian orientation among the populace. The fact that the authorities allowed only one party in the elections, the Ukrainian National Union, and that a yes vote was billed as an indication of support for (1) the present government—dominated by the Ukrainophiles A. Voloshyn and Iuliian Revai and (2) the federative alliance with the Czechs and Slovaks, is hardly a sign of Ukrainian strength at the grassroots level.

[73]William T. Bluhm, *Building an Austrian Nation* (New Haven, Conn., 1973), pp. 220-241.

determine which type of grammar, a Russian or Ukrainian one, should be used in schools. The Ukrainian one was billed as *malorus'kyi* (*ukraïns'kyi*), the Russian one as *russkii*. The result was 313 schools for the Russian and only 114 for the Ukrainian. Since the parent might confuse *russkii* (Russian) with *rus'kyi* (Rusyn), it is difficult to determine with absolute certainty the relative strengths of these two orientations, but clearly the Ukrainian alternative was in the minority.[74]

Another piece of indirect evidence comes during the first census held under the Soviet regime in the summer of 1945. A student census taker who was accompanied by a Soviet official later informed me that, when asked, most peasants responded to the question of nationality: *Ia rus'kyi*; to which the official responded with the question, "Where were you born?" The answer, of course, was: "I was born here"; to which the official instructed the census taker: *Napishi ukrainskii*—write down Ukrainian.

Such incidents suggest that despite the efforts made by the Subcarpathian intelligentsia during twenty years of relatively favorable Czechoslovak rule, the peasantry seemed to maintain the same national identity they always had, i.e., Rusyn or Carpatho-Rusyn, and not one that their leaders wished them to have, Russian or Ukrainian. One may conclude from this study that what is needed in order for a national ideology to be accepted among a given population is a strong government with a clear policy that can consistently and over a long period of time be taught in the school system, be applied at all levels of civil administration (birth records, identity cards, passports, etc.), be written about in newspapers, magazines and other publications, and be propagated via such modern means of communication as radio,

---

[74]Probably the vote favored the *russkii* grammar because the Subcarpathian populace thought it was voting for a text in its own *rus'kyi*, i.e., the Rusyn language. In local terminology, Russian in the sense of Great Russian is rendered as *rossiis'kyi* or *moskovs'kyi* (Muscovite), but never *russkii*.

The grammars in question were those of the Galician Ukrainian Ivan Pan'kevych and the local Russophile Evmenii Sabov. The plebiscite was called for by the Czechoslovak Ministry of Culture in response to President Beneš's earlier suggestion that "on the language and school questions the Rusyns must theoretically and practically in a democratic manner come to agreement themselves." Cited in A. Raušer, "President dr. Eduard Beneš a Podkarpatská Rus," *Podkarpatoruská revue*, I, 1 (Bratislava, 1936), p. 7.

television, and motion pictures. Neither the Czechoslovak regime during the years 1919 to 1938, nor the Hungarian government, which ruled the region during World War II, was ever willing or able to do this. Thus, the widespread indecisiveness about national identity in Subcarpathian Rus' could only be resolved after 1945 under the all-encompassing rule of a Soviet regime.

CHAPTER 9

The Nationality Problem in Subcarpathian Rus', 1938–1939: A Reappraisal[*]

The literature dealing specifically with the nationality question during the brief period of autonomy in Subcarpathian Rus' is not extensive and is limited basically to two sources, Marxist historians within the Soviet Union and Czechoslovakia, and Ukrainophile émigrés from the territory who reside in the West. To the first group belong authors like Iurii Slivka, Borys Spivak, Andrii Kovach, and Štefan Pažur,[1] who accept the Ukrainian nature of the population but characterize the Voloshyn autonomous government as a "bourgeois-nationalist regime" that was little more than a puppet of imperialist Hitlerian Germany. On the question of national identity, they dismiss the Russian

---

[*] This is a revised text of a paper delivered at the Seventh Annual Congress of the Czechoslovak Society of Arts and Sciences, held at New York University on November 17, 1974. It is published here for the first time.

[1] Borys I. Spivak, *Narysy istoriï revoliutsiinoï borot'by trudiashchykh Zakarpattia v 1930-1945 rokakh* (L'viv, 1963), especially, pp. 255-284; Iurii Iu. Slyvka, *Pidstupy mizhnarodnoï reaktsiï na Zakarpatti v 1938-1939 rr.* (L'viv, 1966); Andrii Kovach, "Stanovyschche zakarpats'kykh ukraïntsiv (rusyniv) i zanepad ChSR," *Naukovyi zbirnyk Muzeiu ukraïns'koï kul'tury v Svydnyku*, VI, pt. 1 (Bratislava and Prešov, 1972), pp. 7-33; Štefan Pažur, "O vývoji národnostných pomerov na východnom Slovensku v jesenných mesiacoch roku 1938," *Nové obzory*, no. 10 (Prešov, 1968), pp. 13-25.

and Rusyn orientations as reactionary or antiquated ideologies that were harmful to the "Ukrainian" people of Subcarpathian Rus'.

On this latter point, the émigré writers like Peter Stercho, Vikentii Shandor, Stepan Rosokha, Avhustyn Shtefan and Sebastiian Sabol are in full accord.[2] Unlike their Marxist counterparts, however, the émigrés emphasize the successes of the short-lived Voloshyn regime and view its destruction as a result of German indifference and Czech and Hungarian treachery. On the nationality issue, they view the autonomous period as the culmination of a process that resulted in the full acceptance of Ukrainianism by the local populace.

Unfortunately, the apriori positions of both the Marxist and nationalist writers have precluded an unbiased analysis of the nationality issue in Subcarpathian Rus' during the ciritical months of late 1938 and early 1939. On the basis of evidence drawn from unpublished archival sources and the contemporary press, the following conclusions seem more appropriate: (1) that the Russian or Rusyn national orientations did not disappear during the autonomous period; and (2) that the tenuous political successes of the Voloshyn government do not necessarily mean that the local population had accepted wholeheartedly the Ukrainian national orientation.

During the previous two decades of Czechoslovak rule, Subcarpathian Rus' was still experiencing what be called an embryonic stage of national development, i.e., a time when the local intelligentsia was formulating an ideology that would reflect the ideals of a particular ethnic group and provide a national identity that would be accepted by all members of the given group. Peoples like the Czechs, Slovaks, Slovenes, and Serbo-Croatians had gone through an anlogous development in the first half of the nineteenth century. Such a process

---

[2]Peter G. Stercho, *Karpato-ukraïns'ka derzhava: do istoriï vyzvol'noï borot'by karpats'kykh ukraïntsiv v 1919-1939 rokakh* (Toronto, 1965) and *Diplomacy of Double Morality: Europe's Crossroads in Carpatho-Ukraine, 1919-1939* (New York, 1971); Vikentii Shandor, "Karpats'ka Ukraïna—zfederovana derzhava," *Zapysky Naukovoho tovarystva im. Shevchenka*, CLXXVII (New York, 1968), pp. 319-339; Stepan Rosokha, *Soim Karpats'koï Ukraïny* (Winnipeg, 1949); Augustin Stefan, *From Carpatho-Ruthenia to Carpatho-Ukraine* (New York, 1954); Iurii Borzhava [Sebastian Sabol], *Vid Uhors'koï Rusy do Karpats'koï Ukraïny* (Philadelphia, 1956). An early exposition of the Ukrainophile position is found in *Karpats'ka Ukraïna v borot'bi* (Vienna, 1939).

did not effectively begin among the Subcarpathian Rusyns until 1918, and during the following two decades an internal struggle broke out between separate factions of the local intelligentsia which adhered to a Russian, Ukrainian, or Rusyn national viewpoint.

Briefly, the Russophiles argued that the inhabitants of Subcarpathian Rus' were part of one Russian people that stretched from the Poprad River (in present-day eastern Slòvakia) to the Pacific Ocean, and that this people was culturally united by an Eastern-rite Christian religion and by the so-called common Russian, or *obshcherusskii*, language. Local Ukrainophiles retorted that Subcarpathian Rus' was actually the farthest western territory inhabited by members of a distinct Ukrainian people whose cultural and linguistic heritage stemmed from the medieval days of Kievan Rus'. Supporters of the Rusyn orientation at times suggested that the Subcarpathian Rusyns were a separate Slavic nationality; usually, however, their ideology did not get much past the stage of negation, i.e., rejecting the Russian and Ukrainian viewpoints for an undefinable something else.[3]

These nationalist ideologies, especially the Russian and Ukrainian, were propagated by cultural organizations (the Duknovych Society for the Russophiles and the Prosvita Society for Ukrainophiles), by political parties, and by numerous publications. Most important, supporters of all three orientations staffed the school system where they most efectively fostered their respective ideologies among the youth.[4] After almost two decades of relatively unhampered cultural and national development within the Czechoslovak Republic, it could be argued that the Ukrainian

---

[3]The three national orientations were frequently expressed in contemporary belles lettres. The Russophile position was best revealed in the works of Andrei Karabelesh (1905-1964) and Mikhail Popovich (1908-1955), and in the journals *Karpatskii krai* (1924-25), *Karpatskii sviet* (1928-38), and the newspaper *Russkii narodnyi golos* (1934-38). The Ukrainophiles were represented by Vasyl' Grendzha-Dons'kyi (1897-1974), Iulii Borshosh-Kumiats'kyi (1905-1978), Oleksandr Markush (1891-1971), and by the journals *Uchytel's'kyi holos* (1930-38) and *Ukraïns'ke slovo* (1923-38). The Rusyn viewpoint was most prevalent in the weekly newspaper, *Nedîlia* (1935-38), edited by the Greek Catholic priest, Emyliian Bokshai (1889-1976).

[4]Paul R. Magocsi, "The Role of Education in the Development of a National Consciousness," *East European Quarterly*, VII, 2 (Boulder, Colo., 1973), pp. 159-165.

orientation was the most dynamic.[5] Nonetheless, the Russian and to a lesser degree Rusyn orientations were still very much alive. In essence, by 1938, when the Czechoslovak Republic was subjected to a series of international and internal political crises, the nationality issue in its far eastern province was far from resolved.

The political developments in Subcarpathian Rus' during the last months of 1938 and early 1939 are rather well known and will only be given in barest outline here.[6] In the spring of 1938, Russophile and Ukrainophile politicians led by parliamentarians Andrei Brodii (1895-1945), Stefan Fentsik (1892-1945), Edmund Bachinskii (1880-1947) and Iuliian Revai (1899-1978), put aside their national and political antagonisms and united in an attempt to achieve the two outstanding demands of all Subcarpathian politicans: (1) "to introduce in the shortest possible time elections to a Subcarpathian autonomous soim [diet]; and (2) to unite with Subcarpathian Rus' that territory in eastern Slovakia inhabited by Rusyn-Ukrainians."[7] During the summer months, these leaders were not successful in negotiations with the Czechoslovak government, but in the weeks of political crisis following the signing of the Munich Pact on September 30, 1938, both Slovakia and Subcarpathian Rus' received their long-awaited autonomous status.

The cabinet of the first Subcarpathian government, appointed on October 11, 1938, was dominated by the Russophile faction under

---

[5]This was particularly the case regarding literature and language as seen in the analyses by the impartial Czech observers: Antonín Hartl, *Literární obrození Podkarpatských Rusínů v letech 1920-1930* (Prague, 1930), p. 24 and František Tichý, *Vývoj současného spisovného jazyka na Podkarpatské Rusi*, Knihovna Sboru pro výzkum Slovenska a Podkarptské Rusi, Vol. XI (Prague, 1938), pp. 125 and 134. Even the Russophile émigré literary scholar, Evmenii Nedziel'skii, acknowledged the superiority of the Ukrainian orientation in belles lettres: *Podkarpatskaia Rus' za gody 1919-1936* (Uzhhorod, 1936), p. 133

[6]The international aspect of the problem has bean stressed in the latest work by Stercho, *Diplomacy*. The Marxist interpretation has been supplemented by Ivan Pop, "Zakarpats'ka Ukraïna v ievropeis'kii kryzi 1938-1939 rr," *Duklia*, XV, 1 (Prešov, 1967), pp. 62-66 and Ladislav Suško,"Nemecká politika voči Slovensku a Zakarpatskej Ukrajine v období od septembrovoj krízy 1935 do rozbitia Československa v marci 1939," *Československý časopis historický*, XXI, 2 (Prague, 1973), pp. 161-196.

[7]From the resolution of the First Russian-Ukrainian Central National Council formed on May 29, 1938. Cited in *Nova svoboda* (Uzhhorod), June 15, 1938.

Prime Minister Andrei Brodii. Brodii's government lasted only fifteen days, during which time the former Czechoslovak regime was attacked for its pro-Ukrainian and thus "anti-Russian educational and cultural policy."[8] The process of closing Czech-language schools in Subcarpathian Rus' was begun and active propaganda efforts were made in eastern Slovakia "to unite all the Russian (*russkaia*) territories in the Carpathians (from the Poprad tò the Tisa Rivers) into one unitary, free state."[9] Ministers Stepan Fentsik and Ivan P'eshchak were immediately sent to eastern Slovakia to organize demonstrations, and Slovak police files during the month of October were filled with reports of meetings, intercepted telegrams sent to Ministers Fentsik and Bachinskii, and leaflets, all of which revealed the desire of local Rusyns to unite with their brethren in Subcarpathian Rus'. Teachers and Greek Catholic priests were especially active in these activities.[10] But the primary goal of the Brodii administration was to introduce a plebiscite in order to decide the political future of the province. Since the mid-1930s Brodii was being subsidized by the Hungarian government and a plebiscite was viewed as a trouble-free way to achieve Budapest's revisionist aims. It was the public revelation of these intrigues which led to the demission of the first autonomous cabinet and the arrest of Brodii.[11] On October 26, a new government headed by Prime Minister Avhustyn Voloshyn (1874-1945) was appointed, and this began the domination of the Ukrainian orientation in the political life of the province.

After less than a week in office, the Voloshyn regime faced its first crisis. As a result of the Vienna Award of November 2, 1938, the southern Magyar-inhabited fringe of Subcarpathian Rus' (including the cities of Uzhhorod, Mukachevo and Berehovo) was incorporated into

---

[8]*Russkii viestnik* (Uzhhorod), October 16, 1938. See also *Priashevskaia Rus'* (Prešov), October 29, 1938 and the pointed article, "Likvidatsiia ches'kykh shkil' tam, de nemaie dostatochnoho chysla ditei ches'koï narodnosti," *Nova svoboda*, October 21, 1938.

[9]Cited from an October 12 speech by Brodii, *Russkii viestnik*, October 16, 1938.

[10]Štátny slovenský ústredný archív (Bratislava), Fond Prezídium Krajinského úradu, karton 237, folder 62212/33 and Fond Ministerstva vnútra, kartón 3, folder 4/38.

[11]Brodii's closest collaborator, Fentsik, escaped to the Polish Embassy in whose service he was since the mid-1930s. Brodii was released from prison and both men eventually made their way to Budapest and then Hungarian-occupied Uzhhorod.

Hungary. Direct rail communication with the rest of Czechoslovakia was broken and the autonomous government was forced to move hastily eastward to the town of Khust. The Russophile leaders, Brodii and Fentsik, found their way to Uzhhorod where they embarked on a propaganda campaign to gain the rest of Subcarpathian Rus' for Hungary, while Bishop Aleksander Stoika (1890-1943), as well as other dignitaries of the Greek Catholic Church (Aleksander Il'nyts'kyi, Irynei Kontratovych) also stayed in Uzhhorod where they soon came out in support of Hungary.[12] Since ranking members of the Greek Catholic clergy were the strongest supporters of the separate Rusyn national viewpoint, that orientation was effectively left without leadership within the reduced territory of Subcarpathian Rus'.

Meanwhile, to protect the province against future incursions by Hungarian terrorists, the recently established Ukrainian National Defense was transformed into a military force, the Carpathian Sich. Recognized by the Czechoslovak government in mid-November, the Sich was led by local Ukrainophiles although its ranks were soon filled with avid Ukrainian nationalists from Galicia. To facilitate relations with the central government, a Subcarpathian Bureau, led by Ukrainophiles, was set up in Prague,[13] while on November 22 a bill was passed in Parliament which gave legal recognition to the authonomous province. Interestingly, in its final form this bill accepted Podkarpatská Rus as the official name, and only on November 30 did Prague consent to recognize as an alternative form, Carpatho-Ukraine (Karpats'ka Ukraïna), the name being used in all official communiques of the

---

[12]The pro-Hungarian Russophile leaders who remained in Uzhhorod (Iosif Kaminskii, Viktor Gomichkov, Mikhail Demko, Petr Gaevich) formed a Russian National Council (Russkii Natsional'nyi Soviet) and "saluted the one and undivided Carpathian Rus' from the Poprad to the Tysa River, autonomous within the borders of the Hungarian Kingdom." Cited from the masthead of Fentsik's *Karpatorusskii golos* (Uzhhorod), November 27 and December 15, 1938.

[13]Presided ever by Vikentii Shandor, the Subcarpathian Bureau included seven members. A Central State Economic Council was also set up in Prague which included five representatives from Subcarpathian Rus'. Shandor, "Karpats'ka Ukraïna," pp. 9-10. In January 1939, a weekly Czech-language newspaper *Karpato-ukrajinská svoboda*, began publication in an attempt to inform the Czech public about Subcarpathian Rus' and general Ukrainian affairs.

Voloshyn regime.[14] Most important, the bill included a provision which called for elections to a diet (*soim*) within five months. The diet was to decide on the question of the official name and language of the province.

While the future diet was to be given final say regarding the controversial issue of the language to be taught in schools, it was soon clear that in educational and cultural matters the Voloshyn administration had already adopted distinctly Ukrainian characteristics. Premier Voloshyn was responsible for education and culture, although he delegated these affairs to Avhustyn Shtefan (1893-1986), an ardent Ukrainophile and head of the Economic Academy in Mukachevo. The various *gymnasia*, professional schools, and teachers' colleges located in Hungarian-controlled areas were transferred to small towns in the north and east of the province. Ukrainophiles dominated school administrations and, according to a decree passed on November 25, all teachers, directors and inspectors were required to use the Ukrainian language. The closing of most Czech schools begun during the Brodii administration was completed, and plans were made to transfer the Ukrainian Free University from Prague to Khust.[15]

As for publications, most of the periodicals that had existed up until 1938 were discontinued, while the editorial boards of the remaining and new journals were staffed by Ukrainophile personnel. The first two numbers of the autonomous government's official journal, *Uriadovyi vistnyk*, appeared with Russian and Ukrainian texts, but subsequent issues only used Ukrainian. Other publications included *Nova svoboda*, *Karpats'ka Ukraïna*, *Nastup*, *Hoverlia*, and *Nova stsena*. Despite their short-lived existence, all were written in literary Ukrainian and each

---

[14]The autonomy proposal was first introduced in the Czechoslovak Parliament on November 17 by the Ukrainophile deputy and minister in Voloshyn's cabinet, Iuliian Revai. It was identical with the Slovak autonomous bill, except that Revai proposed the terminology "Carpatho-Ukraine," "Carpatho-Ukrainian government," and "Ukrainian language." "Návrh poslance Juliana Révaye na vydáni ústavního zákona a autonomii Karpatské Ukrajiny," *Poslanecká sněmovna N.S.R.C. 1938*, IV volební období, item 1433. The bill finally recommended is found in *ibid.*, item 1434.

[15]"Zakryite ches'ki shkoly po selakh," *Nova svoboda*, November 25, 1938; Volodymyr Birchak, *Karpats'ka Ukraïna: spomyny i perezhyvannia* (Prague, 1940), pp. 26-27; Borzhava, *Vid Uhors'koï Rusy*, pp. 42-43.

emphasized the Ukrainian character of the new autonomous state.[16] The young Ukrainophile intelligentsia came out in full force behind the Khust government. Overjoyed at spending his first Christmas in an autonomous Carpatho-Ukraine, Mykola Rishko wrote:

> For centuries we awaited this festive day ...
> While suffering under enemies in our own homes.
> Rejoice my great, invincible people
> Join in shining ranks
> To greet a holy Christmas in unity
> from the Tysa to the Don, and beyond to the Caucasus.[17]

But despite the domination of the Ukrainian orientation, the Russophiles did not remain inactive. To be sure, the traitorous pro-Hungarian activities of Fentsik and Brodii discredited the Russian national orientation, yet most Russophile leaders remained loyal subjects and supported the concept of a federated Czecho-Slovak state. To replace the influential Agrarian party and the autonomist parties of Fentsik and Brodii, some Russophiles established the Russian Populist National party (russkaia vsenarodnaia natsional'naia partiia).[18] In Khust, a group of twenty-five Russophiles met on November 14 to establish a Central Russian National Council. Their aim was to defend Russian interests in the autonomist province, and they sent a memorandum to the Czechoslovak government in Prague, which demanded that the Voloshyn government be replaced by a cabinet headed by Minister Edmund Bachinskii and including parliamentary deputy Pavel Kossei and the former governor of Rus'ka Kraina, Agoston Stefan (1877-194?).[19]

---

[16]Arkadii Zhyvotko, *Presa Karpats'koï Ukraïny* (Prague, 1940), pp. 19-20.

[17]Cited in Stercho, *Karpato-ukraïns'ka derzhava*, p. 91.

[18]Ivan S. Shleptskii, "Rus' ne pogibnet," *Dnevnik* (Prague), November 30, 1938. While no Russian-language newspaper was published in Subcarpathian Rus' during the Voloshyn regime, *Dnevnik*—"an organ of Carpatho-Russian youth"—continued to appear in Prague and was one of the few sources of information on the Russophile movement.

[19]Police telegram-report sent to the Ministry of Defense in Prague, dated Bratislava, November 15, 1938 (Štátny slovenský ústredný archív, Fond Prezídium Krajinskáho úradu, karton 298, folder 2695/39); also *Dnevnik*, November 30, 1938. Rus'ka Kraina was the Hungarian-supported autonomous regime which functioned for a few months in early 1919. Dr. Agoston Stefan later returned to his homeland, repented his pro-Hungarian attitudes, and in 1925 was elected an Agrarian party

The Central Russian National Council was led by Vasilii Karaman, Petr P. Sova (1894-1984), and Pavel S. Fedor (1884-1952), all of whom served in the local School Administration of pre-Munich Czechoslovakia. They protested the dismissal of Russophiles from the School Administration, the general "Ukrainian terror," and the excesses of the Carpathian Sich which maintained "concentration camps exclusively for *katsapy* [pejorative term for local Russophiles] and Moskaly."[20] Unquestionably, one such detention camp was set up as early as November 20, 1938 on orders from Voloshyn at Dumen near the town of Rakhiv, and there were rumors that two others existed as well. Operated by the Carpathian Sich, Dumen included refugees from Galicia, and also local Russophile activists who refused to accept the Ukrainian orientation of Voloshyn's regime.[21] Another source of discontent was the Orthodox population. Traditionally, Orthodox adherents in Subcarpathian Rus' represented a stronghold of Russophile sentiment, but pro-Ukrainian authors have subsequently pointed out that certain Orthodox hierarchs allegedly supported the Voloshyn government.[22] Contemporaries reported, however, that the majority of the Orthodox population, organized in 140 parishes, was indoctrinated by their love of all things Russian and rejected the Ukrainian ideology of the Khust regime.[23]

---

deputy to the Prague Parliament. He should not be confused with the active Ukrainophile, Avhustyn Shtefan.

[20]*Dnevnik*, December 15, 1938.

[21]The existence of the Dumen camp was confirmed by the Ukrainophile leader, Iuliian Revai, in an interview with the author (January 1971). See also Michael Winch, *Republic for a Day: An Eye-Witness Account of the Carpatho-Ukraine Incident* (London, 1939), pp. 95-96; and the report by V. Karaman, Prezídium policajného riaditel'stva v Prešova, December 31, 1938 (Štátny slovenský ústredný archív, Fond Prezídium Krajinského úradu, kartón 297, folder 310/1939).

[22]Stercho, *Karpato-ukraïns'ka derzhava*, p. 86.

[23]The confusion about attitudes to Voloshyn's Ukrainophile government may, in part, be related to the divisions within the Orthodox community. Although the established Orthodox Eparchy of Mukachevo-Prešov was within the jurisdiction of the Serbian Orthodox Church, there were also some parishes that were loyal to Archbishop Savatii of Prague under the jurisdiction of the Ecumenical Patriarch of Constantinople. Stercho, *ibid.*, speaks of an Orthodox Metropolitan Josyf (without specifying which jurisdiction) as having "consistently expressed loyalty to the government of Carpatho-Ukraine." On the widespread opposition of the Orthodox Church, see Winch, *Republic for a Day*, pp. 114-117, as well as the frequent

There was also discontent from outside the province. In Prague, Sub-carpathian university students of Russophile orientation opposed the use of the name Carpatho-Ukraine, while Minister Bachinskii and Deputy Kossei complained to the Prague government about the forced Ukrain-ianization being perpetrated by the Khust regime.[24] Finally, Rusyn immigrants in the United States—the vast majority of whom were either Russophiles or Magyarones—sent "protests against the establishment of Ukraine on an immemorial Russian land as ordered by Premier Voloshyn."[25]

Meanwhile, the Voloshyn cabinet was plagued by increased difficulties with the central government in Prague. The two issues of conflict concerned the appointment on January 16, 1939 of the Czech general, Lev Prchala, as a minister in the Khust government, and the fate of many "former Czechoslovak" officials who were released from their jobs, in particular the 820 school teachers from the liquidated Czech-language schools. At the same time, Voloshyn had difficulties with Slovakia's new autonomous government, since pro-Ukrainian elements, like their predecessors in the Brodii cabinet, continued to demand the union of Rusyns in eastern Slovakia with Subcarpathian Rus'. In Khust, the agressive nationalists were fond of proclaiming "that

articles in the official newspaper of Voloshyn's government which carried warnings addressed to Russophile recalcitrants: "'Russkii' tabor, chy madiarons'kyi smitnyk?" and "Rosiis'ki emigranty provokuiut'," *Nova svoboda*, November 27, 1938.

[24]"Protest Tsentral'nago Soiuza Podkarpatorusskikh Studentov," *Dnevnik*, November 30, 1938. See also Jan Brandejs, "Unpublished memoirs" (Archiv Národního Musea, Prague; Fond Brandejs, karton 2), p. 843

[25]"Kabelagrammy pereslannyia Karpatorusskim Soiuzam, November 6, 1938," reprinted in *Dnevnik*, December 15, 1938. In the 1930s, an important Rusyn-American organization was the American Carpatho-Russian Union headed by Aleksei Gerovskii (1883-1972), a staunch Russophile who in the spring of 1938 went back to the Subcarpathian homeland where he was instrumental in uniting local Russophile and Ukrainophile politicians. Stercho, *Diplomacy*, pp. 257-261, 281-283, also speaks of the role of the United States-based Committee for the Defense of Carpatho-Ukraine. Actually, this organization was not composed of immigrants from Subcarpathian Rus' but primarily of Ukrainians from Galicia. The position of the Committee and its displeasure with the non-Ukrainophile majority among Rusyns in the United States is expressed in Ivan Karpatskij, *Piznajte pravdu* (New York, 1939).

the Ukrainian flag will fly over the Tatras."[26] Slovakia's autonomous administration was angered by these demands, although on the ground itself in strongly Russophile eastern Slovakia, the previously widespread desire to unite with Subcarpathian Rus' virtually disappeared when it became clear that the Voloshyn government was Ukrainian in orientation.[27]

Notwithstanding these enormous difficulties, the pro-Ukrainian administration in Khust undertook preparations for elections to an autonomous diet. On January 12, 1939, Voloshyn decreed that elections would be held exactly one month later. In an attempt to clarify the internal political situation in the weeks since the establishment of autonomy, all political parties were declared invalid[28] and new parties were called on to submit candidates by January 22. A new party, the Ukrainian National Union (Ukraïns'ke Natsional'ne Ob'iednannia), presented a list of 32 candidates, many of whom were prominent local members in various interwar political parties, but who were now united

[26]*Nastup* (Khust), January 17, 1939.

[27]Recent studies—Pažur, "O vývoji," pp. 13-25 and Kovach, "Stanovyshche," pp. 25-26—have tried to prove that the desire of Rusyns in eastern Slovakia to unite with Subcarpathian Rus', which was openly expressed during the summer of 1938, was still evident after October. But there is overwhelming evidence in Slovak police reports (otherwise exceptionally sensitive to the slightest indication of Russophilism or Ukrainianism) that for Rusyns in eastern Slovakia "the Ukrainian orientation is alien and in the end they reject any kind of revision of borders in favor of Carpatho-Ukraine." See Prezídium Policajného riaditel'stva v Prešove, January 11, 1939, in Štátny slovenský ústredný archív, Fond Prezídium Krajinského úradu, kartón 297, folder 310/1938, and also kartón 298, folder 62212/38. Despite protests regarding election procedures to the Slovak autonomous parliament, the Russian National Council (Russkii Narodnyi Soviet) in Prešov came out in favor of Slovakia's autonomous government.

[28]Actually, Communist party activity was declared illegal as early as October 20, 1938 in a decree passed by the Czechoslovak government and enforced by the Uzhhorod police authorities. "Donesennia Uzhhorods'koï politseis'koï dyrektsiï . . . pro zaboronu diial'nosti komunistychnoï partiï, November 2, 1938," in *Shliakhom Zhovtnia: zbirnyk dokumentiv*, Vol. IV (Uzhhorod, 1964), doc. 216. According to Iuliian Revai (interview with the author, October 1970), the Voloshyn regime promised to leave the Communist organization alone if it agreed not to organize strikes or other protests against the Khust regime. Both sides concurred, and there was in fact a remarkable lack of Communist public activity after November 1938.

under one dominant force—"the idea of Ukrainian nationalism."[29] Others, including the former Czechoslovak senator and Subcarpathian cabinet minister, Edmund Bachinskii, the so-called "Group of Subcarpathian Rusyns" (Hrupa podkarpats'kykh rusynov) headed by a local teacher, Mikhail Vasilenko, and Orthodox candidates from the village of Iza were not accepted by the electoral commission. The reason given was that there were some kind of administrative difficulties which Voloshyn's government could not solve.[30] Thus, the populace was presented with only the list of the Ukrainian National Union.

In response to Fentsik and Brodii, whose newspapers in Hungarian-occupied Uzhhorod were calling for the union of Subcarpathian Rus' with Hungary, the Voloshyn government argued that the upcoming elections to an autonomous Soim would be a kind of plebiscite that would reveal the attitude of the people regarding the present political situation. The party organ, *Nova svoboda*, stated clearly that by voting for the Ukrainian list one favored the present government of Carpatho-Ukraine as well as the federative alliance with Czechs and Slovaks.[31] In this context, the results of the February 12, 1939 election turned out overwhelmingly positive. A substantial majority of 244,922 persons accepted the Ukrainian list, while only 17,752 were opposed.[32] It has

[29]Stepan Rosokha, *Soim Karpats'koï Ukraïny* (Winnipeg, 1949), p. 29; Stercho, *Diplomacy*, pp. 147-150. The breakdown included 10 previous members from Voloshyn's Christian National party, 10 Social Democrats, 7 Agrarians, 2 representatives of Ukrainian Nationalist Youth, and 1 member of the party representing Subcarpathia's German minority.

[30]The list of the Subcarpathian Rusyn group was rejected on grounds that it did not represent a political party and did not supply the necessary funds for printing a list of candidates—both provisions stipulated in the Czechoslovak law regulating electoral practices. N. Lemko, "Cherovyi uspikh," *Karpato-ukrajinská svoboda* (Prague), February 3, 1939; Stercho, *Diplomacy*, pp. 150-151. According to Winch, pp. 156-153, Russophile leaders headed by Deputy Pavel Kossei and Dr. Agoston Stefan were put into jail until after the January 22 deadline for submitting the lists.

[31]"Narode, nekhai bude volia Tvoia," *Nova svoboda*, February 5, 1939. Cited in Stercho, *Diplomacy*, pp. 151-152, note 36

[32]Of the 376 villages participating in the elections, only 19 returned clear majorities against the Ukrainian ticket. In Khust, the capital and largest settlement in the province, 8330 votes were cast—6208 for the Ukrainophiles, 2122 apposed. Cf. the list of election returns in Stercho, *Karpato-ukraïns'ka derzhava*, pp. 242-252.

generally been accepted that "the elections ware held in calmness and respectfully, without terror, without corruption,"[33] although one English observer remarked that obvious pressure was placed on voters by the presence of armed Carpathian Sich propagandists in most vlllages.[34]

Notwithstanding the electoral success registered by the Khust government, it was to be allotted little more than four weeks more existence. By February 1939, it had become evident to many political observers in western Europe that Hitler was only waiting for the right moment to dismantle the remainder of Czechoslovakia and to give Hungary the signal to occupy the rest of Subcarpathian Rus'. Along the Hungarian and Polish borders terrorists renewed their attacks, while internally the remaining weeks of the Voloshyn administration were marked by increased friction with the Prague government. Furthermore, reports from various sources continued to accuse the Ukrainian regime of terrorism against the local Russophiles, perpetrated especially by extremists in the Sich military organization. One reporter claimed to have witnessed several such conversations. Sich guard to peasant:

> "You are a Ukrainian."
> "No, I am a Rusyn."
> "What, you are a Ukrainian, yes?"
> "I am a Rusyn."
> "Come along; you—are—a—Ukrainian."
> "All right, I am a Ukrainian."[35]

On March 6, 1939, Prague reorganized the autonomous Khust government, reappointing Voloshyn. Nevertheless, tension between Czech and local Ukrainophile leaders increased to such a degree that an March 14 a pitched battle broke out between the Carpathian Sich and

---

[33]Brandejs, "Unpublished memoirs," p. 849. See also Shandor, "Karpats'ka Ukraïna," p. 14; and Rosokha, *Soim*, pp. 32-51.

[34]Winch, *Republic for a Day*, pp. 151-155. Even one Ukrainophile journalist admitted that the pre-election campaign had taken on a "fanatical character." Cited in Rosokha, *Soim*, p. 52. Moreover, voting was obligatory in Czechoslovakia and boycotters could be fined.

[35]Winch, *Republic for a Day*, p. 131. There were also reports of beatings perpetrated by Sich guards against Russophile teachers who, like the above peasant, refused to comply. *Dnevnik*, December 15, 1938.

Czechoslovak soldiers stationed in Khust.[36] That same day, at Hitler's suggestion, Slovakia's Premier Tiso proclaimed his country's independence, while farther east the Hungarian Army began to march on Subcarpathian Rus'. As fighting was taking place between Carpathian Sich units and Hungerian troops, Voloshyn convened the diet, and on the afternoon of March 15, 1939, the 22 elected representatives who were present accepted a symbolic act which called into being the Republic of Carpatho-Ukraine.[37] A few hours later the members of the Carpatho-Ukraine's new government were forced to leave the country. On orders from Prague, Czechoslovak Army units did not put up any resistance and the defending Carpathian Sich was overwhelmed by the advancing Hungarians. By March 16, the Hungarian Army had control of Khust and in the next few days occupied all of Subcarpathian Rus'.[38] Such was the end of the "republic for a day."

The events which took place in Europe during 1938-1939 had a direct effect on the political and national status of Czechoslovakia's eastern territories. After the Munich crisis, the province of Subcarpathion Rus' was to enjoy almost six months of autonomy within a federated Czechoslovakia. The year 1938 also witnessed a temporary alliance of local Russophile and Ukrainophile leaders, although after November the Ukrainian national orientation had come to dominate internal affairs in the autonomous province.

This does not mean, however, as many pro-Ukrainian writers assert, that the population of Subcarpathian Rus' rejected the Russian or Rusyn national orientations. While it is true that some leading Russophile and Rusynophile leaders were compromised because they supported Hungary, at the same time most others remained loyal to Czechoslovakia and even tried, if unsuccessfully, to reorganize themselves during the

[36]The military clash occurred when the Sich refused Prchala's orders to disarm. Stercho, *Diplomacy*, pp. 131-137.

[37]Voloshyn was chosen president and Iuliian Revai (in absentia) prime minister and minister for foreign affairs. The protocols of the five consecutive sessions of the Soim are reprinted in Rosokha, *Soim*, pp. 60-88. See also Stercho, *Diplomacy*, pp. 153-159.

[38]Details on Carpatho-Ukraine's demise are found in Avhustyn Shtefan, *Ukraïns'ke viis'ko v Zakarpatti* (Toronto and New York, 1969), p. 27, and in *Karpats'ka Ukraïna v borot'bi*.

Voloshyn period. Moreover, the outcome of the February 1939 elections to an autonomous Soim was as much a vote of confidence in the continued existence of a federated Czechoslovakia as an indication of Ukrainian national consciousness. In essence, the rejection of Hungarian revisionist propaganda was not necessarily an indication of conscious Ukrainianism on the part of the local population.[39] The majority of Russophile leaders remained anti-Hungarian, and the fact that they were excluded from participation in the Voloshyn government did not mean that the Russian or even Rusyn national orientations were dead.[40]

Nevertheless, it must be admitted that the Ukrainian orientation did increase its influence and prestige among large segments af the local population during the stormy months of autonomy. At a time when Russophiles like Andrei Brodii and Stepan Fentsik and Rusynophile Greek Catholic Church leaders like Bishop Aleksander Stoika opted for Hungary, the Ukrainophiles basically remained loyal subjects of Czechoslovakia and opposed all Hungarian and Polish intrigues against the homeland. Because of its pronounced anti-Hungarian stance, there was an infectious spread of Ukrainian national ideology, especially among the younger generation. Yet, as this study has shown, the embryonic stage of national development did not come to a close with the general acceptance of Ukrainianism during the autonomous period of 1938-1939. Five years of Hungarian occupation and another "liberation," this time a Soviet one, had to be experienced before the identity question would be resolved.

---

[39]Not only the masses, but also a large segment of the intelligentsia was far from having a Ukrainian national consciousness. After twenty years of educational work in Subcarpathian Rus', the Galician-Ukrainian émigré, Volodymyr Birchak, wrote that "after 1919, the intelligentsia began to call itself Rusyn (*rus'ka* and *rusyns'ka*), Russian, and Carpatho-Rusyn, but was still not [in 1939] nationally [i.e., Ukrainian] conscious." Birchak, *Karpats'ka Ukraïna*, p. 5.

[40]Hence, it was clearly premature for Premier Voloshyn to have declared: "Thank God, Russophilism is completely liquidated." *Karpato-ukrajinská svoboda*, January 20, 1939.

CHAPTER 10

Rusyns and the Slovak State[*]

T he status of Rusyns living within the boundaries of the Slovak State between the years 1939 and 1944 was greatly influenced by developments during the interwar period and most especially during the period of the Second Czechoslovak Republic in late 1938 early 1939.

The Rusyns, or as they are known today, Ukrainians, who inhabit the so-called Prešov Region[1] of present-day northeastern Slovakia had lived for centuries in harmony with neighboring Slovaks. Both groups were ruled by Hungary and both groups were characterized by general economic and social backwardness. This situation changed after 1918 when Rusyns and Slovaks found themselves within the new Czechoslovak Republic. Both groups now had the opportunity to function as a political as well as cultural force whose demands had to be taken into

---

[*] This essay was originally prepared for a panel, "14 March 1939 and the Slovak State," at the XIth National Convention of the American Association for the Advancement of Slavic Studies, held at Yale University, New Haven, Connecticut, October 10-13, 1979. It was first published in *Slovakia*, XXIX (West Paterson, N.J., 1980-81), pp. 39-44.

[1] The Prešov Region takes its name from the city of Prešov, the traditional religious and cultural center for Rusyns in Slovakia, which is, however, located outside of Rusyn ethnographic territory.

consideration by the Czechoslovak state.[2] This, however, led to friction between these otherwise friendly Slavic groups.

Already toward the end of World War I Rusyn immigrants in the United States began to talk about autonomy, or even statehood, which they hoped to obtain for their Carpatho-Rusyn homeland at the close of the war. These leaders spoke of uniting all Rusyn inhabited areas, including the northern portions of the old Hungarian counties of Spiš, Šariš, and Zemplín. This demand was opposed, however, by Slovak leaders who felt that all three of these counties should belong to Slovakia.[3]

When the Rusyn province of Subcarpathian Rus' (Czech: Podkarpatská Rus) was established in 1919, its western border with Slovakia (along the Už River) was initially only a provisional one, and Rusyn politicians both in Subcarpathian Rus' as well as in the Prešov Region called upon the Prague administration to unite all Rusyn-inhabited areas into one autonomous province. But Slovaks adamantly opposed any proposed cession of Spiš, Šariš and Zemplín counties. Finally in 1929, the boundary of Subcarpathian Rus' was moved slightly westward, still

[2]For a survey of socioeconomic and cultural developments in the nineteenth century among Rusyns, see I. G. Kolomiets, *Sotsial'no-ėkonomicheskie otnosheniia i obshchestvennoe dvizhenie v Zakarpat'e vo vtoroi polovine XIX v.*, 2 vols. (Tomsk, 1961-62); and Ivan Žeguc, *Die nationalpolitischen Bestrebungen der Karpato-Ruthenen 1848-1914* (Wiesbaden, 1965). On the Slovaks,, see R. W. Seton-Watson, *Racial Problems in Hungary* (London, 1908); and František Bokeš, *Dejiny Slovákov a Slovenska od najstarších čias až po oslobodenie: Slovenská vlastiveda*, Vol. IV (Bratislava, 1946), esp. pp. 130-339.

On Slovak-Rusyn relations before 1918, see Mykhailo Mol'nar, *Slovaky i ukraïntsi* (Bratislava and Prešov 1965); and Helena Rudlovčaková, "K otázkam vzájomných kultúrnych stykov Slovákov a zakarpatských Ukrajincov v polovici minulého storočia," *Sborník Ševčenkovský Filozofická fakúlta Univ. P.J. Šafárika*, V (Bratislava, 1965), pp. 149-165.

[3]For further details on the immediate post-World War I developments, see Paul Robert Magocsi, *The Shaping of a National Identity, Subcarpathian Rus', 1848-1948* (Cambridge, Mass., 1978), pp. 76-102; and Marián Mark Stolárik, "The Role of American Slovaks in the Creation of Czecho-Slovakia, 1914-1918," *Slovakia*, VIII (Cleveland and Rome, 1968), pp. 7-82.

leaving more than 90,000 Rusyns as a minority within the province of Slovakia.[4]

Rusyn leaders in Subcarpathian Rus' continued to lay claim to what became their Prešov Region irredenta, but it was not until late 1938 that a new drive toward Rusyn unification was undertaken in earnest. After the Munich Crisis and the establishment of a federalized Czechoslovakia in October 1938, Prešov Region Rusyn parliamentary deputies Ivan P'eshchak and Petro Zhydovs'kyi supported the demands of the Rusyn National Committee in Prešov (est. 1937), which called for unification with the autonomous Subcarpathian Rus'. These efforts lasted barely a month, however, because in November, after a Ukrainophile government led by Avhustyn Voloshyn came to power in Subcarpathian Rus', Prešov Region Rusyns, who were traditionally Russophile in national orientation, wanted nothing to do with the Carpatho-Ukrainian government farther east. Instead, in December 1938, the Rusyn National Committee in Prešov supported elections to the Slovak Provincial Diet to which two Rusyns were chosen—Anton Symko and Adal'bert Horniak.[5]

---

[4]For details on the problem of the Slovak-Rusyn border during the interwar period, see the comprehensive recent monograph by Ivan Vanat, *Narysy novitn'oï istoriï ukraïntsiv Skhidnoï Slovachchyny*, Vol. I: *1918-1938* (Bratislava and Prešov, 1979), pp. 103-135 and 272-287.

[5]There is controversy over the extent to which Rusyn leaders in the Prešov Region supported the call for unification with autonomous Subcarpathian Rus'. Pro-Ukrainian writers in Slovakia, in an attempt to show that Rusyns in 1938 were in opposition to Slovak political activity and that they were anxious to express solidarity with their "Carpatho-Ukrainian" brethren just to the east, argue that contemporary Slovak police reports revealed widespread support for unity with Subcarpathian Rus'.   Cf. Stefan Pažur, "O vývoji narodnostných pomerov na východnom Slovensku v jesenných mesiacoch roku 1938," *Nové obzory*, X (Prešov, 1968), pp. 13-25. While this is true for the month of October and very early November, those same police reports (located in the Štátny slovenský ustredný archív—ŠSÚA in Bratislava), indicate that by November a clear change had taken place in Prešov Region public opinion. Rusyns were now against the idea of unity, because the "Ukrainian orientation is alien and in the end they [Prešov Region Rusyns] reject any kind of revision of borders in favor of Carpatho-Ukraine." Prezídium Policajného riaditel'stva v Prešove, January 11, 1939, in ŠSÚA, Fond Prezídium Krajinského úradu, kartón 297, folder 310/1938. See also kartón 298, folder 62212/38.

Within a few months the question of unity with Subcarpathian Rus' became a moot issue. This is because on March 15, 1939, Hitler decided to liquidate what remained of Czechoslovakia. The provinces of Bohemia and Moravia were incorporated into the Third Reich; Slovakia (without its southern region annexed by Hungary in November, 1938) was allowed to become a German-oriented state; and Subcarpathian Rus' was taken by Hungary. In late March, the anxious Hungarians sliced off a piece of land in eastern Slovakia, placing 36 Rusyn villages (20,000 people from the Prešov Region) under Hungary for the duration of the war. As a result of these political changes, most Prešov Region Rusyns were now under the control of a state governed by Slovaks in Bratislava.

The Slovaks had struggled for more than two decades to gain greater autonomy from the Czech-dominated centralized Prague government. Now they finally had their own state, even if its existence depended on the good will of Hitler's Germany. The new government in Bratislava was dominated by patriots whose goal was to slovakize all aspects of the country. The Rusyns of the Prešov Region were especially a target for discrimination, because just after the Munich Crisis they had expressed a desire to unite with Subcarpathian Rus'. Consequently, the Greek Catholic Church and especially its bishop, Pavel Goidych, was accused of disloyalty and pro-Hungarian feelings. For instance, in 1939, the President of Slovakia, Msgr. Jozef Tiso, and in 1940 Minister of Propaganda, Šaňo Mach, visited Prešov. On two occasions during these visits it is alleged that both Slovak leaders slighted the bishop in public and questioned his loyalty.[6] Also in 1940, Andrej Dudáš was appointed to head the administrative district (Šariš-Zemplín župa) for all of eastern Slovakia, a post he was to hold for the remainder of the war. Dudáš was convinced that the idea of a Rusyn nationality was created by the Hungarians, and in 1943 he wrote a book on the subject, concluding

---

[6]These incidents are based on an unnamed eyewitness report and are given in Atanasii V. Pekar *Narysy istoriï tserkvy Zakarpattia*, Analecta OSBM, Series II, Sectio I (Rome, 1967), pp. 144-146; and Julius Kubinyi, *The History of Prjašiv Eparchy*, Editiones Universitatis Catholicae Ucrainorum S. Clementis Papae, Vol. XXXII (Rome, 1970), pp. 161-163.

that the "so-called Rusyn people (*rusínsky l'ud*) in the Carpathian Basin are by origin and character Slovak.[7]

It was in such an atmosphere that Prešov Region Rusyns now found themselves. In early 1939, the Rusyn National Committee and Carpatho-Rusyn National Council were banned, the newspaper *Priashevskaia Rus'* (Prešov, 1938-39) was closed, and the activity of the local Rusyn cultural Dukhnovych Society was restricted. Rusyns were allowed one more deputy, Mykhailo Bon'ko, who was appointed to the Slovak Diet in 1941, but like his elected predecessors (Symko and Horniak), he was expected to support the government's policy.[8] Only the Greek Catholic Church led by Bishop Goidych could effectively defend Rusyn national interests.

As a result of Goidych's efforts, the Slovak government passed a decree in 1940 making all elementary schools the responsibility of the Greek Catholic Church. This allowed for the maintenance of Rusyn teaching, and for that purpose four new textbooks were published. Other

[7]Andrej Dudáš, *Rusínska otázka a jej úzadie* (Buenos Aires, 1971), p. 25. The Slovak denial of the existence of Rusyns in the Prešov Region was widespread already during the interwar period: "These people [in northern Šariš and Zemplín counties] are our Slovaks, who only because of the Greek Catholic faith inadvertently call themselves Rusnaks or of the Rusnak faith. But teachers infect them by saying that they are also of Rusyn nationality. This is ridiculous, but it is happening . . . There are no Rusyns up there, nor Rusnaks, only Slovaks of the Greek Catholic faith." *Slovenská politika* (Bratislava), September 2, 1928—cited in Ivan Bajcura, *Ukrajinská otázka v ČSSR* (Košice, 1967), p. 44. The politically and emotionally charged question of whether all Greek Catholics in eastern Slovakia are Rusyns or whether all, or most, are Slovaks has acquired an extensive polemical and scholarly literature. Among the better works which present opposing views are: Volodymyr Hnatiuk, "Rusyny Priashivs'koï eparkhiï i ïkh hovory," *Zapysky Naukovoho Tovarystva im. Shevchenka*, XXXV (L'viv, 1900), pp. 1-25; and Ondrej R. Halaga, *Slovanské osídlenie Potisia a východoslovenskí gréckokatolíci* (Košice, 1947).

[8]For details on the policy of the Slovak autonomous government and later the Slovak state toward the Prešov Region Rusyns, see Andrii Kovach, "Stanovyshche zakarpats'kykh ukraïntsiv (rusyniv) i zanepad pershoi ChSR," *Naukovyi zbirnyk Muzeiu ukraïns'koï kul'tury*, VI, pt. 1 (Svidník, Bratislava, and Prešov, 1972), esp. pp. 23-30; and his "Natsional'na polityka Slovats'koï Respubliky po vidnoshenniu do rusyniv-ukraïntsiv (1939-1945 r.r.)," in *Zhovten' i ukraïns'ka kul'tura* (Prešov 1968), pp. 132-143.

cultural activity was limited, however. The Slovaks wanted to remove Prešov as the cultural center for Rusyns, and in that regard tried, though unsuccessfully, to have Bishop Goidych's residence transferred from Prešov northward to Medzilaborce. One newspaper was permitted, *Novoe vremia* (Medzilaborce, 1940-44), which like the Greek Catholic school system used the so-called "traditional Carpatho-Rusyn language" (i.e., Russian with local dialectisms) and propagated a Russophile national orientation.[9] Prešov Region authors were generally isolated from each other during the war years, although some cultural activity took place among Rusyn university students in Bratislava through their student club, the Dobrians'kyi Society (Obshchestvo Dobrianskogo) and publications: *Studencheskii zhurnal* (Bratislava, 1940-41) and *Iar'* (Bratislava, 1942-43).[10]

The economic situation of the mass of Rusyn peasantry did not change from what it was during the interwar years, even though a few thousand went to Germany to work, while some who remained home were able to take advantage of the arianization laws (September, 1941) and receive proprietorship over former Jewish land and shops. Moreover, Slovakia did not suffer any destruction until the last months of the war, and some improvements, especially in roads and communications, took place.

It is beyond the scope of this short study to discuss the partisan movements in any detail. Suffice it to say that the first partisan unit in the Prešov Region was organized already in 1943, and an underground movement, the Carpatho-Russian Autonomous Union for National Liberation (Karpatorusskii Avtonomnyi Soiuz Natsional'nogo Osvobozhdeniia—KRASNO), was formed in 1944. The latter maintained contacts both with the Slovak underground movement and

---

[9]Beginning in the second half of the nineteenth century and continuing down to as recently as the early 1950s, most members of the Prešov Region Rusyn intelligentsia considered themselves part of one Russian nationality which lived from the Carpathian Mountains to the Pacific Ocean.

[10]On cultural developments during the war years, see Andrii Kovach, "Ukraïntsi Priashivshchyny i deiaki pytannia kul'turnoï polityky Slovats'koï Respubliky," *Naukovyi zbirnyk*, IV, pt. I (Svidník, Prešov and Bratislava, 1969), pp. 401-412; and his "Ukraïntsi Skhidnoï Slovachchyny naperedodni slovats'koho narodnoho povstannia," *Z mynuloho i suchasnoho ukraïntsiv Chekhoslovachchyny*, Pedahohichnyi zbirnyk, No. 3 (Bratislava, 1973), pp. 196-215.

with the Czechoslovak Army Corps in the Soviet Union. KRASNO was dedicated to the principle of a liberated Czechoslovakia, and it welcomed the October 1944 declaration of the underground Slovak National Council that the "new republic must be . . . a fraternal republic of three equal nations—Czechs, Slovaks, and Carpatho-Rusyns."[11]

In summary, the close and often supportive relations that existed for centuries between Slovaks and Prešov Region Rusyns were replaced in the twentieth century by friction often caused by the opposed political and cultural goals of the two groups. Neither the first or second Czechoslovak Republics, nor the Slovak state contributed in any way to a lessening of political friction between Slovaks and Prešov Region Rusyns, a situation which only seemed to get even worse after World War II.[12]

[11]Cited in Edo Friš, *Myšlienka a čin: úvahy o Československu 1938-1948* (Bratislava, 1968), p. 104. For details on the Rusyn underground and partisan movement, see the studies by Stepan Pazhur, Vasyl' Horkovych, Andrii Kovach, as well as several eyewitness recollections from the period contained in *Shliakh do voli*, in *Naukovyi zbirnyk Muzeiu ukraïns'koï kul'tury*, II (Svidník, Prešov and Bratislava, 1966).

[12]For a discussion of Slovak-Rusyn relations between 1945 and the mid-1960s, see Bajcura, *Ukrajinská otázka v ČSSR*. On the worsening of those relations after the Dubček era in 1968-69, see Pavel Mačů, "National Assimilation: The Case of the Rusyn-Ukrainians of Czechoslovakia," *East Central Europe*, II, 2 (Pittsburgh, 1975), pp. 101-132.

CHAPTER 11

National Assimilation: The Case of the Rusyn-Ukrainians of Czechoslovakia[*]

During the past century and a half various ethnic groups in eastern Europe have been consolidated into clearly defined nationalities. The intelligentsia has played a crucial role in this process. An ethnic group represents a population which usually possesses a distinct territory, related dialects, and common ethnographic, historical, literary, and religious traditions. However, members of ethnic groups are not necessarily aware of these interrelations and it is the task of the intelligentsia to foster in them a sense of national consciousness. Possession of such

[*]First published under the pseudonym Pavel Maču in *East Central Europe*, II, 2 (Pittsburgh, Penn., 1975), pp. 101-132. This study was subsequently translated into Vojvodinian Rusyn by Diura Latiak and published under the title, "Natsionalni i kulturno-sotsiialni rozvoi Rusinokh-Ukraïnstsokh Chekhoslovatskei," *Shvetlosts*, XXVIII, 1 and 2 (Novi Sad, Yugoslavia, 1990), pp. 77-96 and 213-235.

A short version was published under the title, "The Present State of National Consciousness among the Rusyns of Czechoslovakia," *Europa Ethnica*, XXI, 4 (Vienna, 1974), pp. 98-110; and also under the pseudonym Pavel Maču with the title, "The Rusyns of Czechoslovakia," *The Cornish Banner*, I, 2 (Trelispan, U.K., 1975), pp. 4-6.

a state of mind among a significant portion of a given population allows for the transition from the status of an ethnic group to a nationality.[1]

In the initial stages of this consolidation process, there were frequently several choices open to the intelligentsias of eastern Europe. For instance, in the multinational Austro-Hungarian, German, and Russian Empires, a member of a national minority could have identified with the ruling nationality or with the ethnic group into which he was born. Hence, Czechs or Poles might have become germanized; Ukrainians or Belorusans russified; Slovaks, Jews, or Croats magyarized. For those who did not join the ruling group, there were sometimes other choices: an ethnic Ukrainian in the Austrian province of Galicia could identify himself as a Pole, a Russian, or a Ukrainian, while an ethnic Slovak in northern Hungary might become a Magyar, a Czech, or remain a Slovak. The respective intelligentsias did not operate in an ideological vacuum; their decisions were influenced by the limitations and requirements of contemporary political reality. It was the degree of skill in balancing intellectual ideals with political exigencies which determined the success or failure of national movements.

By the early twentieth century, and especially after the political changes brought about by World War I, many of the former ethnic minorities had developed into full-fledged nationalities. Some even had their own states, and most enjoyed the fruits of universal education in their own language. A few groups, however, did not yet achieve national consolidation. Among these might be mentioned the inhabitants of Macedonia, where Serbian, Bulgarian, Greek, and Macedonian ideologists competed for the allegiance of the people. It was not until 1945 that within Yugoslavia a clear-cut Macedonian orientation was implemented. Indeed, the process of national consolidation has still not been achieved in every part of eastern Europe. One such territory is the

---

[1]The view that one is not born with a national identity and that the acquisition of such an identity is the result of a process of ideological and social indoctrination is an assumption that has been accepted implicitly or explicitly by most modern theorists. See Hans Kohn, *The Idea of Nationalism* (New York, 1958), p. 6ff; Carlton J.H. Hayes, *Nationalism: A Religion* (New York 1960), pp. 9-10; Karl W. Deutsch, *National and Social Communication* (Cambridge, Mass., 1966), passim; Elie Kedourie, *Nationalism* (London, 1971), pp. 81-85; Boyd C. Shafer, *Faces of Nationalism: New Realities and Old Myths* (New York, 1972), p. 13.

Prešov Region of northeastern Czechoslovakia,[2] inhabited by a people known officially as Rusyn-Ukrainians.[3]

Before World War I, Rusyns had the choice of identifying themselves with the Russian, Magyar or Slovak nationalities. After 1918, the Magyar option became less feasible, though new choices—Carpatho-Rusyn, Ukrainian and "Czechoslovak"—were added to the list. Since 1945, the competition has been limited basically to three orientations: the Russian, Ukrainian, and Slovak. This study will attempt to explain why the Slovak orientation has proved to be the most successful.

A borderland people

Rusyns who live south of the Carpathian Mountains (both in Czechoslovakia and the Soviet Union) have traditionally inhabited a border region and as a result they share ethnic characteristics with peoples in the surrounding territories. Most important among these are the Galician Ukrainians north of the Carpathians, the Slovaks to the west and southwest, and the Magyars on the lowland plains to the south. Although there is evidence of earlier settlement, most Rusyn villages were founded by colonists who came from north of the Carpathians in several successive waves of immigration between the thirteenth and

---

[2]The Prešov Region (Priashevshchyna) is a term designating the geographical region where Rusyns live. This name has never been an official one, though it appears often in local publications and speech. Other terms used are Priashevskaia Rus' (Prešov Rus'), Skhidna Slovachchyna (eastern Slovakia), and recently Piddukliańs'kyi krai (The land below the Dukla Pass). Ivan Vanat, "Do pytannia vzhyvannia terminiv 'Zakarpattia' ta 'Priashivshchyna'," in *Zhovten' i ukraïns'ka kul'tura* (Prešov, 1968), pp. 602-603. In this study, the term Eastern Slovakia will be used only to designate the present-day administrative unit, Východné Slovensko.

[3]Historically, Rusyns living south of the Carpathian Mountains were known in western literature as Ruthenians, Subcarpathian Ruthenians, Rusins, Carpatho-Ukrainians, or Carpatho-Russians. Traditionally, Czechs referred to these people as *rusíny* or *podkarpatští rusíny*; Slovaks called them *rusňáci* or *rusíny*. Hungarians used the terms *magyarorosz, ruszin, rutén*, now *ukrán*; Ukrainians called them *karpato-rusyny*, and recently *zakarpatoukraïntsi*. In Czechoslovakia, the people invariably still refer to themselves as *rusnatsi* (Rusnaks) or *rusyny* (Rusyns), terms used also by the most famous national writers (Aleksander Dukhnovych, Aleksander Pavlovych, Iulii Stavrovs'kyi-Popradov).

fifteenth centuries.[4] These newcomers brought with them a language closely related to the Ukrainian then spoken in Galicia, as well as an Orthodox culture which had predominated among the East Slavs. In their new homeland, however, the Rusyns were geographically and politically separated from Galicia. Physical movement was restricted by the high crests of the Carpathians, which coincided with the northern boundary of the Hungarian Kingdom. Within Hungary, the Rusyns, like the Slovaks, never had any separate political status; rather, they were spread among several counties in the northeastern part of the country. In terms of social status, they were almost exclusively peasants, and hence without any effective political or social influence.[5]

Their primary cultural institution, the Orthodox Church, also underwent transformation in the Hungarian environment. In 1646, the Union of Uzhhorod was signed which established the Uniate or Greek Catholic Church to accommodate adherents of Orthodoxy. Initially, most of the eastern rite traditions were maintained, but the new church was placed within the jurisdiction of Rome and came under the direct influence of the Hungarian Roman Catholic hierarchy. Despite the increasing Hungarian influence, especially during the nineteenth century, the Greek Catholic Church held within its ranks the only educated segment among Rusyns, and for a long time this institution set off the population as distinct from the neighboring Roman Catholic or Protestant Slovaks and Magyars. As with many ethnic groups before the period of their national revivals, religion became the carrier of the national idea.

As for other characteristics, Rusyn habitation, dress, customs, folklore, occupations, and general life-style came to be hardly

---

[4]The best historical surveys on the Prešov Region Rusyns are by L'udovít Haraksim, *K sociálnym a kultúrnym dejinám Ukrajincov na Slovensku do roku 1867* (Bratislava, 1961) and Georgii Gerovskii, "Istoricheskoe proshloe Priashevshchiny," in Ivan S. Shlepetskii, ed., *Priashevshchina: istoriko-literaturnyi sbornik* (Prague, 1948), pp. 57-93. A more general work intended for popular consumption is by Iurii Bacha, Andrii Kovach, and Mykola Shtets', *Chomu, koly i iak: vidpovidi na osnovni pytannia z zhyttia ukraïntsiv Chekhoslovachchyny* (Prešov, 1967).

[5]In 1910, 89.6 percent and in 1930, 83.1 percent of the Rusyn population was engaged in agriculture. *Magyar statisztikai közlemények*, Vol. LVI (Budapest, 1915), pp. 330-433; *Československá statistika*, Vol. CXVI (Prague, 1935), pt. 2, pp. 33-35 and 51-53.

distinguishable from those of their immediate Slovak and Magyar neighbors. Their historical experience was determined by the same geopolitical unit that linked all the peoples of the Danubian Basin. Those few Rusyns who went to secondary schools received their training in a Hungarian educational system and even the language spoken at the village level was heavily laden with Slovak and Magyar vocabulary. Moreover, the potential maintenance of cultural relations with Ukrainians north of the mountains was after the eighteenth century actively opposed by the Hungarian government. Finally, even the Greek Catholic religion was no longer the unique preserve of Rusyns, since both Slovaks and Magyars (in some, but not all cases slovakized or magyarized Rusyns) were members of this church. Hence, as a result of geographical and political conditions, the Rusyns who lived for several centuries south of the Carpathians developed a culture which was clearly distinct from the one that existed in the lands from which their ancestors came.[6]

This was the status of the ethnic "raw material" during the second half of the nineteenth century, when the first indications of a national revival began.[7] As a result of the revolutionary and counterrevolutionary events of 1848-1849, a few Rusyn leaders, led by the politician Adol'f Dobrians'kyi (1817-1901) and the writer Aleksander Dukhnovych (1803-1865), tried to instill in their people the sense of a larger national unity. But what was that unity to be? These leaders as well as

[6]On ethnographic, cultural and linguistic interrelations, see Jan Húsek, *Národopisná hranice mezi Slováky a Karpatorusy*, Knižnica 'Prúdov', no. 2 (Bratislava, 1925), pp. 220-342; Tivadar Bacsinszky, "A ruszin nemzeti öntudat útjai," *Zoria-Hajnal*, III (Uzhhorod, 1943), pp. 194-198; Ivan Pan'kevych, *Ukraïns'ki hovory Pidkarpats'koï Rusy i sumezhnykh oblastei*, Knihovnu sboru pro výzkum Slovenska a Podkarpatské Rusi, no. 9 (Prague, 1938), pp. 14-31; Michal Blicha, "Slovenské prvky v ukrajinskom nárečí na severovýchodnom Slovensku," *Zborník Pedagogickej fakulty v Prešove*, VII, 2: *Spoločenské vedy* (Prešov, 1968), pp. 31-58; and P.M. Lizanec, *Magyar-ukrán nyelvi kapcsolatok: a kárpátontúli ukrán nyelvjárások anyaga alapján* (Uzhhorod, 1970).

[7]It is interesting to note that during the nineteenth century, the most important leaders among Subcarpathian Rusyns were natives of the Prešov Region. Among them are: Andrei Bachyn'skyi, Petro Lodii, Mykhailo Baludians'kyi, Ioann Churhovych, Aleksander Dukhnovych, Adol'f Dobrians'kyi, Aleksander Pavlovych, Anatolii Kralyts'kyi, and Iulii Stavrovs'kyi-Popradov.

their successors proclaimed that the Rusyns are part of one Russian people which stretched from the Carpathians to the Pacific Ocean. They adopted Russian as the medium for writing and often thought that national liberation would be brought about someday by the tsar in St. Petersburg.

Despite the efforts of a few individuals, the national movement did not really get off the ground; Rusyn newspapers and cultural organizations were short-lived and ineffective, and what is worse, they were competing with a government in Budapest which by the 1870s embarked on a concerted policy to assimilate the non-Magyar minorities. The result was that in the decades before World War I, the national movement among Rusyns was in abeyance, while most educated individuals adopted either a Magyar or Slovak identity.

After 1918, the Rusyns of Hungary were incorporated into the Czechoslovak Republic—372,000 into the province of Subcarpathian Rus' (after 1945 the Transcarpathian oblast' of the Soviet Ukraine) and about 100,000 into northeastern Slovakia.[8] The new state proclaimed that it would rectify the national, cultural and socioeconomic injustices that had existed under the Hungarian regime, and, indeed, the Rusyn population was in several instances better off in Czechoslovakia than in pre-war Hungary. Yet, in the case of Rusyns in the Prešov Region, by 1970, a little over half a century later, their number has decreased statistically by two-thirds, and, on the basis of several indicators, one can conclude that today the active level of national consciousness among the inhabitants is on a steady decline. Why are so many Rusyns unwilling to identify themselves as such and why is the trend toward assimilation with Slovaks so pronounced?

One indicator of the decline can be obtained by surveying briefly the official statistics.[9] According to the first Czechoslovak census of 1921,

[8]It was Rusyn intelligentsia (led by the Beskid family) centered in Prešov which became the most active group calling for union of all Subcarpathian Rusyns with Czechoslovakia. See Paul R. Magocsi, "The Ruthenian Decision to Unite with Czechoslovakia," *Slavic Review*, XXXIV, 1 (Seattle, Wash., 1975), pp. 360-381.

[9]In the 1921 and 1930 censuses for Slovakia, the nomenclature *ruská* (actually meaning Russian in both Slovak and Czech) was used to describe the Rusyn population. If a person declared him or herself Rusnak, Rusyn, or Karpato-Rus', these would be placed under the *ruská* rubric. In the censuses after 1950, the terms *ukrajinská* (Ukrainian) and *ruská* were listed under one rubric. More crucial,

there were 85,628 Rusyns living in Slovakia. Ten years later that number had risen to 91,079. Because of border changes on the eve of World War II, it was not until 1950 that a comparable census was taken,[10] but then only 48,231 Rusyns were recorded. By 1961, that figure had reached an all-time low of 35,435. On the eve of the 1970 census, a substantial effort was made to stimulate the populace to identify itself as Rusyn or Ukrainian, but the final result recorded only 42,146 persons who were willing to do so! These great statistical fluctuations are not the result of natural demographic changes but reflect the changing national and political climate in the Prešov Region as well as an absolute decline in national consciousness among Rusyns.

A critical problem is that of self-identification. Traditionally a local inhabitant referred to him or herself variously as a Rusnak, Rusyn, Uhro-Rusyn, Carpatho-Rusyn, Greek Catholic, Šarišan, Zemplínčan, or simply as a person from this or that village or river valley. This lack of certainty regarding a national nomenclature was the result of a pattern set by the local intelligentsia which itself was never of one opinion. Until well into the twentieth century, the Rusyn intelligentsia was composed mainly of Greek Catholic clergymen. Before 1918, many of these priests, especially among the upper echelons of the hierarchy, succumbed to the official policy of magyarization.

Following the incorporation into Czechoslovakia, the Magyar trend was generally discounted, and the national leaders, who now included teachers and lawyers as well as priests, identified themselves and their people as members of the Russian or of an independent Carpatho-Rusyn nationality. This development was somewhat analogous to the situation

---

however, was the police registration for identification cards where Ukrainian or Slovak were the only acceptable names for the local Rusyn population. Whichever name was chosen for personal identification, this was the one most frequently used in the next census reports. *Štatistický lexikon obcí na Slovensku* (Prague, 1927), p. 159; *Štatistický lexikon obcí v republike československej*, Vol. III: *Krajina Slovenská* (Prague, 1936), xviii; *Československá statistika*, Nová Řada, A, sv. 35, part 1 (Prague, 1965), p. 4; *Nove zhyttia* (Prešov), January 7, 1972.

[10]Despite the generally unfavorable conditions for Rusyns under the Slovak Republic, as many as 69,116 were recorded in the census of December 1940, although this figure did not include the approximately 20,000 more in 36 villages annexed to Hungary the previous August. Andrii Kovach, "Ishly v bii," *Duklia*, XVII, 4 (Prešov, 1969), pp. 45-47.

in eastern Galicia during the nineteenth century and in neighboring Sub-carpathian Rus' during the first half of the twentieth century. In those two areas, the Ukrainian national orientation came to be most important, but in the Prešov Region it was virtually absent and the Russian and Carpatho-Rusyn ideologies predominated. After World War II, however, some leaders felt obliged to follow the official policy of the Czechoslovak government and to adopt Ukrainian as a national designation, although many individuals continued to identify themselves as Russian or Carpatho-Rusyn, while others began to accept Slovak nationality. From this brief survey, it is evident that the local intelligentsia has never been of one mind with regard to national identification, nor as will be shown below, are they any closer to being so today.

The impact of Communist rule

Lacking clear-sighted and effective leaders, the largely uneducated Rusyn masses were vulnerable to the assimilation process. As indicated by the statistics quoted above, this trend has been especially pronounced since World War II. In the period after 1948, the year in which the Czechoslovak government came under Communist control, three deve-lopments occurred which proved to have an overwhelmingly negative effect on Rusyn national self-consciousness. These developments were collectivization, de-Catholicization, and Ukrainianization.

Despite general satisfaction with the present-day economic situation, there is no denying that Rusyn agriculturalists avidly opposed the forced end to private land ownership which began in earnest during the years 1951-1952. Collectivization was particularly odious to the basically rural Rusyn populace, whose land holdings were incorporated into the new cooperatives. Within a decade, the government succeeded in collectivizing an average of sixty-three percent of the farmland located in Rusyn-inhabited areas.[11]

At the same time, the state decided to dismantle the most important Rusyn cultural and social institution, the Greek Catholic Church. Taking its cue from the Soviet regime in neighboring Subcarpathian Rus' (Transcarpathia), Czechoslovak authorities arranged a conference in Prešov on April 28, 1950 which negated the seventeenth-century Union

---

[11]Ivan Bajcura, *Ukrajinská otázka v ČSSR* (Košice, 1967), p. 141.

of Uzhhorod and recognized Orthodoxy as the only valid eastern Christian religion for the local population. The popular Bishop Pavel Goidych was arrested and sentenced to life imprisonment, and numerous priests were interned.[12] The liquidation of the Greek Catholic Church had a crucial impact on the nationality question. As one Marxist writer observed:

> The Greek Catholic religion . . . was in many cases a factor which united the people at least as much as national feeling. This is shown by the fact that that part of the [Rusyn] Ukrainian population which did not accept Orthodoxy did not accept Ukrainian nationality either and today declare themselves to be of Slovak nationality.[13]

Almost simultaneous with collectivization and de-Catholicization came Ukrainianization. Rusyns in the Prešov Region, unlike their brethren in Subcarpathian Rus' were traditionally not receptive to the Ukrainian movement. In the interwar period, for instance, there were 10 newspapers which appeared in Russian or in local dialect and 37 local cultural centers affiliated with the Russophile Dukhnovych Society, while at the same time there was only one short-lived Ukrainian newspaper and but one reading room supported by the Ukrainophile Prosvita Society.[14] In elementary schools, local dialect and literary Russian were the media of instruction, and in 1936 a Russian *gymnasium* was established in Prešov.[15] The dominant attitude

---

[12]Michael Lacko, "The Forced Liquidation of the Union of Užhorod," *Slovak Studies*, I: *Historica*, I (Rome, 1961), pp. 158-185; Ministerstvo spravodlivosti, *Proces proti vlastizradným biskupom Jánovi Vojtassákovi, Michalovi Buzalkovi, Pavlovi Gojdičovi* (Bratislava, 1951), pp. 7-24 and 115-223.

[13]Bajcura, *Ukrajinská otázka*, p. 132.

[14]Ivan P'ieshchak, "Priashevskaia Rus'," in *Podkarpatskaia Rus' za gody 1919-1936* (Uzhhorod, 1936), pp. 87-91; Mykola Shtets', *Literaturna mova ukraïntsiv Zakarpattia i Skhidnoï Slovachchyny pislia 1918*, Pedagogichnyi zbirnyk, No. 1 (Bratislava, 1969), pp. 101-129. See also Ivan Vanat, "Do kul'turno-natsional'-nykh problem ukraïntsiv Priashivshchyny v period domiunkhens'koï respubliky," *Druzhno vpered*, XVII, 6 (Prešov, 1967), pp. 18-19; and Olena Rudlovchak, "Literaturni stremlinnia ukraïntsiv Skhidnoï Slovachchyny u 20-30-kh rokakh nashoho stolittia," in *Zhovten' i ukraïns'ka kul'tura*, pp. 146-154.

[15]Feodor Roikovich, "Radostnaia viest," *Russkoe slovo* (Prešov), May 12, 1936; Andrii Dutsar, "30 rokiv vid zasnuvannia rosiis'koï gimnaziï v Priashevi," *Narodnyi kalendar 1966* (Bratislava and Prešov, 1965), pp. 88-89.

concerning nationality orientation was expressed in an editorial in *Russkoe slovo*, a newspaper published in local dialect by the Greek Catholic Eparchy of Prešov:

> If Germans, Czechs and Slovaks can study the Great Russian language, so the Subcarpathian Rusyn (*podkarpats'kyi rusyn*) with a secondary education (*gymnasium*) must more than anyone know the common Russian (*obshcherusskii*) language; but the first duty of Ivan and his wife under the Carpathians is to love and support our local Subcarpathian Rusyn language ... our national local culture, schools, and literature must follow the way of our ancestors—i.e., *po nashemu*![16]

It was not really until after World War II that the process of Ukrainianization began, but even then only slowly. In 1945-1946, the Ukrainian National Council of the Prešov Region (Ukraïns'ka Narodna Rada Priashevshchyny), a Ukrainian National Theater, and an office for Ukrainian schools (Referat ukraïns'kykh shkil) were set up, but despite the names of these organizations, the language used in all publications and in most theatrical performances was Russian.[17] Going one step further than during the interwar period, the local dialect was no longer employed and literary Russian was used exclusively for all subjects in elementary schools and *gymnasia* where young students were weaned on Pushkin, Tolstoy and Dostoevsky. Even the annual celebration of "Russian Days," begun in 1933, was maintained in many villages.[18] Thus, in the first few years after 1945, the Russian and to a lesser degree Rusyn cultural orientations predominated. At a regional conference of the Slovak Communist party held in Prešov in 1950, the Rusyn delegates who were present lamented: "Five years after the war

---

[16]*Russkoe slovo* (Prešov), August 30, 1924.

[17]The Ukrainian National Council published the weekly newspaper, *Priashevshchina* (1945-52), *Karpats'ka zvezda* (1946-48) and the children's journal *Kolokol'chik*, with a Ukrainian section *Dzvinochok* (1946-49). The "Ukraino-Russian section" of the Democratic party also published its organ, *Demokraticheskii golos* (1946-48), in Russian. Ivan Matsyns'kyi, "20 lit ukraïns'koï vydavnychoï spravy na skhodi respubliky," *Duklia*, XVII, 3 (Prešov, 1969), pp. 1-5. On the predominance of Russian language in the theater, see *25 rokiv UNT* (Bratislava and Prešov, 1971), p. 30.

[18]Shtets', *Literaturna mova*, pp. 130-134; Shlepetskii, *Priashevshchina*, pp. 46-51 and 297-301.

and we don't know who we are: Russians, Ukrainians, or Rusyns. This is shameful."[19]

The government attempted to rectify this situation by adopting the Ukrainian national orientation for the Rusyn population. The ideological justification for such an act could be traced back to a decision made in December 1925 at the Ninth Congress of the Communist party (Bolshevik) of Ukraine: all individuals within Ukrainian ethnographic boundaries—and this included the Rusyns of Subcarpathian Rus' and the Prešov Region—were to be henceforth considered of Ukrainian nationality. Any other names (Rusyn, Rusnak, Uhro-Rus', Russian) or national ideologies were proclaimed to be "anti-progressive."[20] The Czechoslovak Communist party followed the Soviet example with regard to this question and, disregarding local conditions, decided to introduce Ukrainianization by administrative fiat. This process began in June 1952, when the Slovak Communist party in Bratislava decreed that the Ukrainian language should be introduced into all Russian schools in the Prešov Region. Actually, since 1949 Ukrainian was taught two hours per week, but in 1953 it abruptly became the language of instruction for all subjects.[21]

It was in the school system that the most tragic consequences of the rapid transformation to the Ukrainian national orientation occurred. For young students the linguistic change was pedagogically devastating. Not even basic preparations were made. Texts were hastily imported from the Soviet Ukraine, and Russian language teachers were expected to teach in the new medium. Many refused and were expelled from their jobs. Of those that remained, an average of sixty percent were unqualified to teach.[22] The parents, too, were incensed at the introduction of the Ukrainian language, and they responded by

[19]Cited in Bajcura, *Ukrajinská otázka*, p. 132.

[20]Shtets', *Literaturna mova*, pp. 55-60; Ivan Bajcura, "KSČ a ukrajinská otázka," in *Z mynuloho i suchasnoho ukraïntsiv Chekhoslovachchyny*, Pedagogichnyi zbirnyk, No. 3 (Bratislava, 1973), p. 9-12.

[21]Shtets', *Literaturna mova*, pp. 138-140; Bajcura, *Ukrajinská otázka*, p. 132, and Bajcura, "KSČ a ukrajinská otázka," pp. 26-27.

[22]The actual breakdown of unqualified teachers according to type of schools in 1953/54 was: kindergartens, 77.7 percent; elementary, 37.2 percent; junior high (*strednyi*), 80.4 percent; gymnasia, 71.7 percent. Pavel Uram, "Vývoj ukrajinského školstva v rokoch 1948-1953," in *Zhovten' i ukraïns'ka kul'tura*, p. 525.

demanding that if their own language (which they often confused with Russian) could not be used, then it would be better to teach in Slovak than in Ukrainian. Already during the 1953/54 school year, seventeen Rusyn villages requested and were allowed to use Slovak in their schools.[23]

At this point it may be useful to analyze the problem of terminology. Ukrainian authors would argue that Rusyn or Rusnak—terms widespread in the Prešov Region—were archaic forms, though fully synonymous with the more modern name Ukrainian. The term Rusyn had also been used by the East Slavic population in Ukraine's neighboring regions of Galicia and Bukovina, even if there in recent decades the name Ukrainian has almost completely replaced the older form. The point is that for Ukrainians there was no conceptual difference between being a Rusyn or Ukrainian. They failed to realize, however, that their own preconceptions could not be readily applied to the situation in Subcarpathian Rus' or in the Prešov Region. This problem was poignantly summed up by the Prešov Region political scientist, Ivan Bajcura, in his study *The Ukrainian Question in Czechoslovakia*:

Among the broad masses, a Rusyn national consciousness predominated. National consciousness consists of several factors: the realization of national identity, a definite inclination to national values and traditions., a feeling of national pride. The realization of belonging to the Ukrainian nation did not exist. The concept 'Rusyn' in scholarly literature is used as a synonym for the word 'Ukrainian', but in the mind of the masses this concept of synonyms was not there. 'Rusyn'—this was *something separate, different than Ukrainian!* [italics mine]

The realization of belonging to a definite national group is an elementary part of national self-consciousness, and thus such a problem cannot be decided by decree.... For such a profound change to occur it is necessary to proceed gradually, to create favorable conditions and sufficient leeway for the realization of a new orientation so that the masses do not feel that their nationality was being forcibly taken from them.[24]

To say the least, "favorable conditions" were not provided, and the

---

[23]Bajcura, *Ukrajinská otázka*, pp. 152-158; Shtets', *Literaturna mova*, pp. 141-144.

[24]Bajcura, *Ukrajinská otázka*, p. 133.

masses could not simply understand why "overnight" they were changed from Rusyns to Ukrainians.[25] In the words of one peasant:

> Today I'm like that dumb sheep, I don't have anything. I had my own God, you took him from me. I had my own nationality, but you took it away too; I had a little piece of land, even that you took. Everything that I had you took.[26]

In return, he received a new identity: Ukrainian. Nor was this concept a favorable one in the post-war Czechoslovak environment. Ukrainianism was popularly associated on the one hand with extreme nationalism and on the other with banditry, as symbolized by the anti-Soviet Ukrainian Insurgent Army (UPA), whose remaining forces fought against the Communist regime while retreating from southern Galicia across northeastern Czechoslovakia during the late 1940s.[27] Furthermore, all these developments were completed during a period of intense political repression in a police state that before the death of Stalin in 1953 did not tolerate even the slightest diversion from the "official" line.[28] Collectivization, de-Catholicization, Ukrainianization—these were the forces which set the stage for the denationalization of the Rusyns in the Prešov Region.

Rusyn national character and relations with Slovaks

Two other factors must be kept in mind: (1) the psychological state of

---

[25]Bajcura, "KSČ a ukrajinská otázka," p. 27.

[26]From a radio report cited in *Nove zhyttia*, March 23, 1968.

[27]Rusyn children were warned in school about the "extreme danger" of the "Banderovtsi" (Stepan Bandera was a leader of the UPA) and were asked to report to the authorities any knowledge about them. During the trial against the Greek Catholic bishop, Pavel Goidych, he was accused of espionage "for supporting the Banderovtsi." *Proces*, p. 118 ff. See also Bajcura, *Ukrajinská otázka*, pp. 99-103; and František Kaucký and Ladislav Vandůrek, *Ve znamení trojzubce* (Prague, 1965).

[28]Some voices were raised against the administrative introduction of Ukrainianization, but the critics (most of whom were Russophiles) were either silenced, released from their jobs, or imprisoned. In the jargon of the times, they were paradoxically labelled "Ukrainian bourgeois nationalists." *Nove zhyttia*, February 17, 1968. For details on those unjustly arrested, see the revealing articles by V. Kapishovs'kyi, Pavlo Uram, and Ivan Baitsura in *ibid.*, February 17; April 17 and 20; June 17, 1968.

Rusyns; and (2) the attitude of the Slovaks. If one could enumerate the chief character traits of the Subcarpathian Rusyn, a sense of inferiority would be placed high on the list. During Hungarian rule prior to 1918, the Rusyn, like his neighbor Slovak, was not considered much better than a beast of burden. If an individual wanted to be anything in life, he would have to adopt the "superior" Magyar culture and scorn the Rusyn or Slovak "dialects" and traditions of his or her youth. During the first Czechoslovak Republic, the possibility for Slovak self-respect was substantially improved, but the Rusyn almost inevitably was relegated to a lower level in the popular mind.

Without doubt, geography and economic status were influential in fostering such an inferiority complex. Rusyns inhabited the upper mountain slopes, an area devoid of mineral resources and not hospitable to large-scale farming. Despite substantial investments by the Czechoslovak government and marked economic growth since 1945, the northeastern corner of the country remained the least developed. In the Prešov, Bardejov, and Humenné *okresy* (counties)—the territory where most Rusyns live—only seventeen percent of the population was employed in industry in 1968, while the per capita annual income was almost two-fifths below the national average.[29] The eastern region also had the lowest percentage of doctors, hospitals, and other health facilities, and as late as 1957 in counties where Rusyns predominated only fifty-nine percent of the villages had electricity.[30] These statistics are visually confirmed as one descends toward Slovak and Magyar ethnographic territory in the broader valleys and plains. There the

[29]The average per capita income for Czechoslovakia in 1968 was 10,220 crowns; in Bardejov and Humenné *okresy*, the income was only 7,666 crowns and 7,909 crowns respectively. *Biuleten dlia vnutrishnykh potreb orhanizatsiï KSUT*, No. 1 (Prešov, 1969), pp. 15-17. Statistics by village breakdown indicating mode of employment are found in *Východoslovenský kraj v číslach* (Prague, 1964), pp. 266-310. See also Bajcura, *Ukrajinská otázka*, pp. 141-148; idem, "KSČ a ukrajinská otázka," pp. 20-24; and Vasyl' Kapishovs'kyi, "Ekonomichni peredumovy rozvytku ukraïns'koï kul'tury v ChSSR" in *Zhovten' i ukraïns'ka kul'tura*, pp. 484-495.

[30]The 59 percent figure is the average based on the percentage of villages with electricity in the following *okresy*: Bardejov—65.8; Medzilaborce—64; Sabinov—54; Snina—62; Stropkov—57; Svidník—52. *Štatistické zprávy slovenského štatistického úradu*, č. 2 (Bratislava, 1958), p. 20.

impression of material wealth and well-kept homesteads is in sharp contrast to the situation in Rusyn villages. In short, poverty is associated with the Rusyn, prosperity with the Slovak.

The physical location of Rusyn villages also renders communication difficult and this, in turn, has had a negative impact on national consolidation. Rusyn settlements are located in river valleys which run in a north-south direction. Usually, the only way to reach a neighboring valley is to travel first through Slovak towns farther south. Thus, contact among Rusyns is severely limited or is frequently achieved only in a Slovak environment. Finally, the trend toward urbanization has markedly increased. A high percentage of young Rusyns have flocked to Czech and Slovak towns and cities, where they have intermarried and proved remarkably susceptible to national assimilation.[31]

But what about the Slovaks and their relation to the Rusyns? Both peoples had for centuries shared the same fate within the Hungarian Kingdom, a historical experience which, in the face of increased Magyarization at the end of the nineteenth century, was marked by friendly relations between the two Slavic peoples.[32] This state of affairs began to change after the establishment of the Czechoslovak Republic. Slovak leaders claimed that Slovak territory continues as far east as the Uzh River, that is, it included areas inhabited by Rusyns. In subsequent struggles to hold their own in the republic against the Czechs, the Slovaks were not about to be outdone by Rusyns in territories that they considered to be their own.

The problem of the boundary with Subcarpathian Rus' was particularly the cause of much friction. Drawn provisionally in 1919 along the Uzh River, it separated the 100,000 Rusyns under Slovak administration from their brethren farther east. Despite protests by Rusyn politicians, the boundary with only slight changes was made

---

[31]In the decade 1962-1971, a total of 80,424 people moved from Eastern Slovakia to other parts of Czechoslovakia or abroad. More than half of these came from rural villages of less than 2000 inhabitants. *Československá statistika*, Nová Řada, sv. 34, 38, 39, 40 (Prague, 1965-68); *Statistická ročenka ČSSR* (Prague, 1966-72).

[32]See Mykhailo Mol'nar, *Slovaky i ukraïntsi* (Bratislava and Prešov, 1965), pp. 9-109, and the articles by A. Rot and F. Tichý in *Z istoriï chekhoslovats'ko-ukraïns'kykh zv'iazkiv* (Bratislava, 1959), pp. 307-344 and 588-593.

permanent in 1928. Moreover, Slovak promises made back in 1918 for "full autonomy" in ecclesiastical and educational affairs as well as a university were never fulfilled.[33] Despite the fact that by 1934 there were 110 Rusyn schools in the Prešov Region, lay and church leaders continued to demand "that Rusyn children in Rusyn villages be taught in Rusyn."[34] Tension increased during the 1930s when Slovak nationalism adopted a distinctly chauvinist character. Some Slovak circles even refused to recognize the existence of Rusyns:

These people [in northern Šaris and Zemplín counties] are our Slovaks, who only because of the Greek Catholic faith inadvertently call themselves Rusnaks or of the Rusnak faith. But teachers infect them by saying that they are also of Rusyn nationality. This is ridiculous, but it is happening.... There are no Rusyns there, nor Rusnaks, only Slovaks of the Greek Catholic faith.[35]

This is not the place to enter into the long polemic of whether all Greek Catholics are Rusyns or slovakized Rusyns, as Russian and Ukrainian writers claim, or whether the majority is of Slovak

[33]"Proclamation of the Slovak National Council," Turčiansky Sv. Martin, 30.XI.1918, reprinted in Zdeněk Peška and Josef Markov, "Příspěvek k ústavním dějinám Podkarpatské Rusi," Bratislava, V (Bratislava, 1931), pp. 527-528.

[34]"Memorandum biskupa Gojdiča prezidentovi o ruskom školstve," Prešov, 26.VI.1934, in Archív Gréckokatolíckeho biskupstva, Fond Prez. spisy, karton 12, folder 69/1934. See also "Memorandum russkaho naroda na Slovakii . . . v dělě peremény slovackoho predpodavatel'naho jazyka na russkij," Prjašev, 24.III.1937, in ibid., karton 13, folder 71/1936. Statistics are drawn from Annuaire statistique de la République tchécoslovaque (Prague, 1937), pp. 244-245.

[35]Slovenská politika (Bratislava), September 2, 1928. As early as 1921, the head (župan) of Zemplín county, M. Slavík, declared: "In Slovakia there are neither Rusyn men nor Rusyn women." Cited in Vikentii Shandor, "Rusyny-ukraïntsi i slovaky," Suchasnist', X, 3-4 (Munich, 1970), p. 118. For an example of the contemporary polemical literature, see the brochure of the Slovak League: Jan Ruman, Otázka slovensko-rusínskeho pomeru na východnom Slovensku (Košice, 1935) and the Rusyn response: Otzyvy po voprosu karpatorussko-slovatskikh otnoshenii (Prešov, 1936). The most extreme example of the Slovak nationalist point of view is a 1943 manuscript written by a local official and published recently by Slovak émigrés in Argentina: Andrej Dudáš, Rusínska otázka a jej úzadie (Buenos Aires, 1971).

nationality, as Slovak authors suggest.[36] The problem was complicated by the fact that national identification had traditionally been associated with religion—theoretically Roman Catholicism was the Slovak religion, Greek Catholicism the Rusyn religion. After the local intelligentsia replaced religion with language as the primary element in determining nationality, the uneducated masses were frequently confused, and during the late nineteenth century there were several instances in which whole villages would claim themselves Slovak in one census and Rusyn in the next.[37] Disputes over this issue produced charges and countercharges of rusynization or slovakization which tended to worsen relations between the two peoples.

This does not mean that the majority of responsible Slovaks in the administrative center, Bratislava, was either then or now specifically anti-Rusyn in its outlook.[38] However, Eastern Slovakia does have

[36]On the basis of linguistic evidence, the Ukrainian ethnographer, Volodymyr Hnatiuk, divided Prešov Region Rusyns into (1) Rusnaks and (2) *Slovjaks*. These groups, together with a few ethnic Slovaks and Magyars, make up the Greek Catholic Church. See his "Rusyny Priashivs'koï eparkhiï i ikh hovory," *Zapysky Naukovoho tovarystva im. Shevchenka*, XXXV (L'viv, 1900), pp. 1-25. Slovak writers count the *Slovjaks* as Slovaks, who consequently form the majority of Greek Catholics. Ladislav A. Potemra, "Ruthenians in Slovakia and the Greek Catholic Diocese of Prešov," *Slovak Studies*, I: *Historica*, 1 (Rome, 1961), pp. 199-220. The term *stara vira* (the old faith) had come to be synonymous with Greek Catholicism, but one Slovak specialist has pointed out that in older documents this concept has a broader connotation and in some cases might even refer to Protestantism or Roman Catholicism. Ondrej R. Halaga, *Slovanské osídlenie Potisia a východoslovenskí grékokatolíci* (Košice, 1947), p. 11.

[37]Húsek, *Národopisná hranice*, pp. 398-460. For an analysis of the various pre-1914 censuses, see *ibid.*, pp. 461-484; Alexei L. Petrov, *Prediely ugrorusskoi riechi v 1773 r. po offitsialnym dannym* (St. Petersburg, 1911); idem, "Zamietki po etnografii i statistikie Ugorskoi Rusi," *Zhurnal Ministerstva narodnago prosvishcheniia*, II (St. Petersburg, 1892), pp. 439-458; Lubor Niederle, *Národopisná mapa uherských Slováků na základě sčítání lidů z roku 1900*, Národopisný sborník, Vol. IX (Prague, 1903); idem, "K sporu o ruskoslovenské rozhraní v Uhrách," *Slovanský přehled*, V (Prague, 1903), pp. 346-349; and Stepan Tomashivs'kyi, "Etnohrafichna karta Uhors'koï Rusy," in V.I. Lamanskii, ed., *Stat'i po slavianoviedeniiu*, Vol. III (St. Petersburg, 1910), pp. 178-269.

[38]On the other hand, publicists and scholars have done little to inform the Slovak public about the existence of Rusyns. For instance, in a chapter on national minorities in the Slovak encyclopedia published during the Slovak Republic, Rusyns

certain characteristics which tend to overemphasize national differences. The area is an ethnographic transition zone for Poles, Slovaks, Rusyns, and Magyars. There are also significant colonies of Germans and Gypsies. Recently, significant numbers from all groups have assimilated into the dominant Slovak nationality, but even the eastern Slovaks (*vychodniare*) themselves have been latecomers in this process. Before 1918, there was a movement among some who felt that they composed an independent "Slovjak," or eastern Slovak nationality (*vichodoslovenski narod*),[39] and even the influential nineteenth-century Slovak nationalist, L'udovít Štúr, subscribed to a similar theory which in turn supported his desire to have the "pure" central Slovak dialects accepted as the literary standard.[40] At the outset of the twentieth century, the Slovak linguist Samo Czambel declared: "Our language developed completely under different influences than western [Slovak]. The *Slovjak* and Slovak, no matter how close they are to each other in everyday affairs, are not one; they are two—two languages and two peoples."[41]

One might suggest that it is only in the years after World War II that

are not even mentioned: *Slovenská vlastiveda*, Vol. III (Bratislava, 1944), pp. 375-383. More recently, general histories of Slovakia do not discuss Rusyns and at best make passing reference to the activity of the Rusyn leader, A. Dobrians'kyi, during the 1848 revolution: *Dejiny Slovenska*, Vol. II (Bratislava, 1968) and the newer encyclopedia, *Slovensko*, Vol. I: *Dejiny* (Bratislava, 1971).

[39]Halaga, *Slovanské osídlenie*, pp. 53-54; Húsek, *Národopisná branice*, pp. 343-349.

[40]Accordingly, the western Slovak dialects were heavily influenced by Czech, while the eastern dialects were not really considered Slovak. Štúr and his Pan-Slavic supporters also argued that "He who is a Greek Catholic is a Rusyn." Cited in Halaga, *Slovanské osídlenie*, pp. 105-107.

[41]Cited in *Naša zastava*, XVI (Košice, 1942), p. 22. The problem of the Slovjaks and their failure to develop into a separate national group is an intriguing question which warrants further attention. Ladislav Tajták, the specialist in eastern Slovakia's history, dismisses the incipient Slovjak movement as an anti-Slovak political venture of the pre-1918 Hungarian government, but he has provided valuable data in three articles: "K otázke vydávania učebníc vo východoslovenskom nárečí," *Nové obzory*, VI (Prešov, 1964), pp. 43-57; "*Naša zastava*—nástroj politiky mad'arských vládnúcich tried," *ibid.*, VIII (1966), pp. 78-106; "Revolučné prejavy l'udu na východnom Slovensku v roku 1918 za pripojenie k ČSR," *ibid.*, X (1968), esp. pp. 96-115.

the slovakization of the eastern Slovaks has been completed. As is wont with latecomers to a movement, they tend to be the most extreme propagators of the accepted ideology. Joined by slovakized Poles and Germans, the eastern Slovaks have often acted intolerantly toward any divergence from the standard language and state categorically that the so-called Sotaks and Cotaks who live along the Slovak-Rusyn ethnographic boundary must be considered Slovak. And as for those Rusyns farther east, why cannot they speak "correct" Slovak?—as if the Šariš, Zemplín, and other dialects spoken by eastern Slovaks were anything near the literary norm.[42]

Another negative feature, though a quite natural human phenomenon, is the need to have someone inferior to look down upon, or some lesser soul next to whom you can feel superior. The Czechs struggled for a century to outdo the Germans, and finally they established an independent state. They, of course, could feel sorry for their less advanced wards, the Slovaks. As for the Slovaks, those in the western and central regions traditionally looked down upon their own brethren in the east. The popular saying still exists: "The farther east you go, the worse everything is." The eastern Slovaks, not to be outdone, denigrate the Sotaks, and both console themselves in time of anger by attacking the "šaleny Rusňák."

In the midst of Eastern Slovakia lies the city of Prešov. Though unquestionably within Slovak ethnographic territory, Prešov has also traditionally, if perhaps unfortunately, served as the cultural center for Rusyn life. Since 1818, it has been the seat of a Greek Catholic eparchy, and many of the more important national leaders like the Rusyn "national awakener," Aleksander Dukhnovych, lived and worked

---

[42]The Sotak dialects are spoken in several villages around the city of Humenné. Húsek, *Národopisná hranice*, pp. 108ff; Ján Šárga, "Zprávy o štúdiu 'sotáckeho' nárečia," *Carpatica*, XI, Řada A (Prague, 1939), pp. 204-241; and Ivan Paňkevič, "K otázce sotacismu ve vychodoslovenských nářečchí," *Universitas Carolina—Philologica*, II, 1 (Prague, 1956), pp. 67-75 consider that most Sotak dialects are of Rusyn origin. For an opposing view as well as a discussion of the whole problem of eastern Slovak dialects, see Jozef Liška, *K otázke pôvodu východoslovenských nárečí*, Spisy jazykového odboru Matice Slovenskej, Vol. IV (Turčiansky Sv. Martin, 1944), and the older though still indispensable Samo Czambel, *Slovenská reč a jej miesto v rodine slovanských jazykov* (Turčiansky Sv. Martin, 1906).

in the city. In the twentieth century, Prešov became a center for Rusyn political activity. Rusyn leaders gathered there in 1919 and declared for unity with the new Czechoslovak Republic. Indeed, their original and subsequent goal was to unite Rusyn-inhabited lands with Subcarpathian Rus', but this request was diametrically opposed to the Slovak position. Thus, as a result of latent national consolidation among the eastern Slovaks and the polarized political goals of Rusyn and Slovak leaders, the whole region has frequently been the focus of national antagonism which has worked to the disadvantage of the Rusyn minority.

The nationalist intelligentsia and Ukrainianization

How have Rusyn leaders—the nationalist intelligentsia—responded to the situation and have they been successful in preserving the identity of the populace they ostensibly serve? The leaders active since the 1950s are for the most part natives of the Prešov Region, born between the years 1910 and 1925.[43] They most likely attended the Russian-language *gymnasium* in Prešov during the 1930s and 1940s, where they developed a sense of belonging to the Russian nationality. If they went to the university, it was either in Bratislava or Prague. For those who accepted the Communist regime after 1948 (and only those who did so could hope to hold a responsible position), the change to Ukrainianization during the early 1950s was viewed by some as a legitimate intellectual resolution to a problem of self-identification and by others as a necessary step for maintaining one's own role in society. Many leaders in the educational system and theater were sent to be reeducated in Kiev, where former Russophiles were transformed into avid Ukrainophiles. In essence, the Prešov Region intelligentsia has tended to associate themselves with a larger civilization—first Russian, then Ukrainian—and to disregard for the most part the individual cultural

[43]Among the exceptions, there are several individuals from neighboring Subcarpathian Rus' who either came to Slovakia during the war years or who opted for Czechoslovak citizenship when their homeland was incorporated into the Soviet Union. In this group are both Russophiles (Andrei Karabelesh, Evgenii Nedziel'skii) and Ukrainophiles (Vasyl' Grendzha-Dons'kyi, Ivan Hryts'-Duda, Iulii Borolych, Fedir Ivanchov). There are also conscious Ukrainians from other parts of Ukraine who have settled in Czechoslovakia and who have played an active role in Prešov Region intellectual circles (Vyktor Hainyi, Mykhailo Kachaluba, Orest Zilyns'kyi).

values of their own people. This policy has unquestionably had a negative impact on Rusyn national growth.

Initially, the Rusyn leadership tried its hand in the political arena. In
March 1945, several activists established the Ukrainian National
Council of the Prešov Region, which declared itself to be the legitimate
representative of the Rusyn population and on an equal status with the
Slovak National Council in Bratislava. The Ukrainian Council had no
legal basis, however, and in May 1947, when it made a formal request
to become a recognized political organ, the Slovak National Council
refused. The Slovaks were particularly bothered by the Ukrainian
Council's claim that the reconstituted Czechoslovak Republic should be
composed of three equal partners: Czechs Slovaks, and Ukrainians.[44]

In the new Czechoslovak constitution of May 1948, no provision was
made for a separate Rusyn political body, and in an effort to centralize
authority, the government decided to do away with various organizations (frequently labelled "bourgeois") that were established before the
Communists came to power. The Ukrainian National Theater and Radio
Studio (in existence since 1934) were permitted to continue, but between 1949 and 1952 the Office for Ukrainian Education, the youth
organization Soiuz molodi Karpat (Union of Carpathian Youth), the
publishing and printing plant Slavknyha (Slavic Book), and the Ukrainian National Council were liquidated.[45] The government then supplied
funds to set up in 1951 a non-political and acceptably socialist
organization, the Kul'turnyi soiuz ukraïns'kykh trudiashchykh ChSSR
(Cultural Union of Ukrainian Workers in Czechoslovakia—hereafter
KSUT). As originally conceived, KSUT was to work "in close cooperation with the existing state organs and community organizations, to
care for in all ways the cultural uplifting of citizens of Ukrainian
nationality," and "to educate Ukrainian workers toward national consciousness and pride, instill in them consciousness of belonging to the

---

[44]Bajcura, Ukrajinská otázka, pp. 72-80, 89-99, and 109-119.

[45]According to contemporary rhetoric, "the Ukrainian National Council fell from
the true path . . . and instead became the organization of a narrow clique of
Ukrainian nationalists and Catholic clergy. . . ." Iurii Mynchych, "Nazustrich
Ustanovchii konferentsiï KSUT," Druzhno vpered, II, 10 (Prešov, 1952), p. 15. See
also Bajcura, Ukrajinská otázka, pp. 124-125 and "Nezakonno zlikvidovana," Nove
zhyttia, April 25, 1968.

great Soviet Ukrainian people."[46]

To fulfill these tasks, KSUT began to publish a weekly newspaper, *Nove zhyttia* (New Life), a monthly magazine, *Druzhno vpered* (Forward in Friendship), and various pedagogical and propagandistic pamphlets. KSUT organized lectures throughout Rusyn villages and by 1963 supported the creation of 242 local folk ensembles. It also sponsored annual drama, sporting events, and folk festivals, the largest of which is the Ukrainian Song and Dance Festival in Svidník. By 1967, KSUT, with central offices in Prešov, had 230 local chapters and 8,000 members. Government funds were also provided to establish a Ukrainian National Museum (1950) now in Svidník, and a Ukrainian Department (Katedra) and Research Institute (1953) at the P.J. Šafárik University in Prešov. That city was also the center for a Ukrainian publishing house (actually a branch of a Slovak publisher in Bratislava), for the section of Ukrainian Writers—a group of ten authors who form an integral part of the Slovak Writers' Union—and for the famed professional Dukla Ukrainian Song and Dance Ensemble, organized in 1955 as a division of the Ukrainian National Theater.[47] At their inception, all these institutions were Ukrainian in character and, perhaps with the exception of the Dukla Ensemble, they have continued to maintain a Ukrainian façade.

The language of all publications, radio broadcasts, and theatrical performances is literary Ukrainian, but this fact has caused several problems with regard to their acceptance among the local populace. As pointed out above, the change to Ukrainianization came abruptly in the early 1950s without any psychological, ideological, or pedagogical preparation. Neither the writers, teachers, or other leading cadres were prepared to use standard Ukrainian, nor was the local population—which spoke several dialects far removed from the literary norm[48]—

---

[46]Cited in Ivan Humenyk, "KSUT-u desiat rokiv," *Duklia*, X, 3 (Prešov, 1961), pp. 5-6

[47]"Ukraïnistyka v Chekhoslovachchyni," *Narodnyi kalendar 1966* (Bratislava and Prešov, 1965), pp. 108-109; Ivan Chabyniak, "Muzei ukraïns'koï kul'tury ta ioho zavdannia," *Naukovyi zbirnyk Muzeiu ukraïns'koï kul'tury*, I (Bratislava and Prešov, 1965), pp. 25-30; "Zvity pro diial'nist' ukraïns'kykh ustanov Chekhoslovachchyny," *ibid.*, III (1967), pp. 378-436.

[48]Modern Ukrainian dialectology recognizes four main Carpathian dialectal groups: Lemko, Boiko, Hutsul, and Transcarpathian. F.T. Žylko, *Narysy z*

ready to accept the new language. There resulted a kind of passive boycott of the cultural institutions and their programs. For instance, performances of the Ukrainian National Theater which are given in Rusyn villages are poorly attended. The local folk perplexingly explain: "If you spoke in our language (*po-nashemu*), we would come, but we don't understand how you speak now." The Prešov Ukrainian radio program is avoided for the same reason.[49]

It should be noted that such a viewpoint regarding the radio and especially theater is hardly encountered in KSUT publications. These are ever ready to praise in superlative terms supposed cultural successes, and Ukrainian writers, especially in the West, glibly accept such claims as an indication of an ostensibly active and vibrant Ukrainian cultural movement in the Prešov Region.[50] At the grassroots level,

---

dialektolohiï ukraïns'koï movy (Kiev, 1955), pp. 89-155. The Rusyn dialects of the Prešov Region belong primarily to the Lemko group, which also includes territory north of the Carpathians. In the Prešov Region itself, seven distinct dialects have been isolated. Despite differences, they are mutually understandable. Usually, a Prešov Region Rusyn will describe the dialect he speaks as *po-rusnats'kŷ* (in Rusňak) or *po-nashemu* (in our own way). As the farthest western Ukrainian group, the Lemko dialects are considerably different from the contemporary Ukrainian literary norm. It is interesting that in the Lemko Region north of the Carpathians, a codified Lemko language (and distinct national consciousness) was developed in the early twentieth century, although for the most part this trend remains active today only among immigrants in the United States, represented by the Lemko Soiuz in Yonkers, New York, and its weekly, *Karpatska Rus'* (Yonkers, N.Y., 1939-). A separate Lemko consciousness has never developed among Rusyns in the Prešov Region, and while linguists classify them with Lemkos, they never use the term to describe themselves. On the dialects of the Prešov Region, see the basic works of Pan'kevych, *Ukraïns'ki hovory*; Georgii Gerovskii, "Jazyk Podkarpatské Rusi," in *Československá vlastivěda*, Vol. III (Prague, 1934), pp. 460-517; idem, "Narodnaia rech' Priashevshchiny," in Shlepetskii, *Priashevshchina*, pp. 94-144; and the survey of existing scholarship by Olena Pazhur, *Bibliohrafiia pro doslidzhennia ukraïns'kykh hovoriv Skhidnoï Slovachchyny* (Prešov, 1972).

[49]"I think also that on Radio Prešov it is necessary to broadcast in the mother tongue, because many people complain that although they listen to Prešov they understand little." Letter to the editor, *Nove zhyttia*, June 1, 1968.

[50]Examples of uncritical praise for Ukrainianism can be found in Vasyl' Sofronov-Levyts'kyi, *Klanialysia vam try Ukraïny: reportazh pro turystychnyi maraton pro ukraïns'kykh poselenniakh u Iugoslaviï, Chekhoslovachchyni i Pol'shchi* (Toronto, 1970); V. Markus, "Ukrainians Abroad: in Czechoslovakia," in

this could not be farther from the truth. The situation is even worse when we turn to publications. Newspapers, magazines, and journals published by KSUT are sent to all schools and libraries, but their circulation is small among the masses. The novels, poetry, and scholarly works, of which over 225 titles have already appeared, are almost exclusively read by the small intellectual cadres in Prešov. In the words of one candid Ukrainian activist writing at the time: "Separated from the people, the writers are left without strength, like generals without an army."[51] A book club called Druzhba (Friendship) has been set up specially to stimulate the distribution and purchase of publications from Prešov, but it has not met with much success. Not only is the Rusyn peasant traditionally averse to reading, but these publications are in many cases more easily obtainable in the West than they are in Eastern Slovakia.[52] Local critics have since 1958 been complaining about the publication crisis and about the unavailability of Ukrainian books, but to no avail. Ukrainian writers in Czechoslovakia are not only alienated from their own constituencies,

---

Ukraine: A Concise Encyclopaedia, Vol. II (Toronto, 1971), pp. 1244-1248; Petro Kravchuk, *Nezabutni zustrichi: dorozhni zamitky* (Toronto, 1970), pp. 26-50; Anna Halia-Horbach, "Za tumanom nichoho ne vydno," *Suchasnist'*, VIII, 10 (Munich, 1968), pp. 111-126. Better informed are the studies by Dariia Rebet, "Priashivshchyna na perekhresnykh shliakhakh," *ibid.*, IX, 8 (1969), pp. 93-110; Mykhailo Marunchak, *Ukraïntsi v Rumuniï, Chekho-Slovachchyni, Pol'shchi, Iugoslaviï* (Winnipeg, 1969), pp. 13-32; Grey Hodnett and Peter J. Potichnyj, *The Ukraine and the Czechoslovak Crisis* (Canberra, Australia, 1970), pp. 39-44.

[51]Mykola Hyriak in "Z dyskusiï do nashoï literatury i zhurnaliv," *Druzhno vpered*, VII, 24 (Prešov, 1957), p. 20. The serious lack of a broader spectrum for criticism is discussed by Orest Zilyns'kyi in *Literatura chekhoslovats'kykh ukraïntsiv, 1945-1967: problemy i perspektyvy* (Bratislava and Prešov, 1968), pp. 93-101 and "Nasha literaturna sytuatsiia," *Duklia*, XVII, 2 (Prešov, 1969), pp. 1-7.

[52]Only two bookstores in Prešov, and one each in Medzilaborce, Svidník, and Humenné, carry local Ukrainian publications. These outlets are actually Slovak bookstores with one or two shelves of Ukrainian books that are not prominently displayed and in some cases not obtainable unless specifically asked for. Moreover, the printings are consistently small, some important scholarly publications (which sell out almost immediately) appearing in only 600 or 800 copies. Olena Pazhur, *Bibliohrafiia knyzhkovykh vydan' slovats'koho vyd. khudozhn'oï literatury v Bratislavi, ukraïns'koï redaktsiï v Priashevi (1956-1970)*, appended to *Duklia*, XIX, 6 (Prešov, 1971).

they are also cut off from an otherwise enormous market of readers in the Ukrainian SSR. The Soviet government does not allow the free circulation of Prešov Ukrainian-language publications, which are virtually non-existent in the Ukraine. Moreover, complaints are constantly lodged that in contrast to Poland and Hungary, which foster close relations with the Polish and Hungarian minorities in Czechoslovakia, the Soviet Ukraine maintains only minimal contacts with the population in the Prešov Region.[53]

The basic problem, however, is that literary Ukrainian is not easily understood by the local population. One writer quoted the plaint of a Rusyn peasant who in the course of a conversation retorted: "You have become a gentleman, live and write like a gentleman. Don't write such newspapers for us because we don't need them."[54] Parents rebelled against Ukrainianization and demanded that their children be taught in Slovak, the state language which was more easily understood. The process of adopting Slovak for instruction in Rusyn elementary schools has led to almost catastrophic results. In 1948, there were 275 elementary schools in which Russian was the language of instruction. After the change to Ukrainian, the number had declined to 245 in 1955 and to only 68 in 1966. Similarly, between 1948 and 1966 the number of middle schools has declined from 41 to 3 and the *gymnasia* from 4 to 1.[55]

---

[53]While Prešov leaders often lament the lack of contact, they also realize that the Ukrainian SSR has its own problems and "itself cannot develop satisfactorily. There the Russian language is primarily used." *Nove zhyttia*, February 24, 1968. See also Iurii Bacha, "Umovy rozvytku ukraïns'koï kul'tury v ChSSR pislia 1945 roku," *Duklia*, XVI, 2 (Prešov, 1968), pp. 118-125.

The plaints of Prešov leaders are somewhat overstated. It is true that while travel to and from Poland and Hungary is virtually unlimited, stringent visa formalities effectively limit personal contact between Czechoslovakia and the Soviet Ukraine. Nonetheless, most actors and directors from Prešov's Ukrainian National Theater and scholars from the university community are trained in Kiev. For these and other contacts, see V.U. Pavelko, *Druzhba narodiv—druzhba kul'tur: Ukraïns'ka RSR u radians'ko-chekhoslovats'komu kul'turnomu spivrobitnytstvi 1945-1970 rr.* (Kiev, 1973), pp. 43-44 and 140-144.

[54]"'Nashi cherhovi zavdannia': prysutni vyslovylys' ZA,'" *Duklia*, XII, 2 (Prešov, 1964), pp. 109-111.

[55]Uram, "Vývoj," p. 523; Kapishovs'kyi, "Ekonomichni peredumovy," p. 489; Bajcura, *Ukrajinská otázka*, p. 159.

It should be stressed that the adoption of the Slovak language has come as a result of voluntary requests from the parents. And why shouldn't they ask for Slovak? If the school were a Ukrainian one, the young student would have to learn literary Ukrainian, Slovak, and later Russian. None of these languages would be considered the native tongue,[56] and of the three, Slovak would be the most practical since it is the language used in higher education and in government administration. Economic, social, and cultural advancement can be achieved only by knowing Slovak. Moreover, the textbooks used in Ukrainian elementary schools do not reflect local needs. Until the late 1950s, most books were imported from the Soviet Ukraine, later, when the first texts were published in Czechoslovakia, they were, because of the lack of qualified "local Ukrainians," often written by Soviet Ukrainian immigrants whose choice of language and subject matter included very little from the Prešov Region.[57] These factors influenced and

---

[56]"Often in various discussions with parents we heard such questions: Why don't they teach in our schools like they used to, with texts like Dukhnovych or Pavlovych [19th century authors who published in dialect] used to write." A. Chuma and Iu. Zheleznyk, *Znachennia ridnoï movy u vykhovanni i navchanni* (Prešov, 1965), p. 15. Nor is it easy to convince the young student that Ukrainian is his native language. In the course of reading lessons in Ukrainian elementary schools, students have to make their own notebook dictionaries with lists of Ukrainian words and their equivalents *po-nashemu*, that is, in their own language. How can Ukrainian be said to be the mother tongue if, *po-nashemu*, the words are something else. Even in Subcarpathian Rus', where some of the dialects are closer to literary Ukrainian, more than eighty percent of the words used most frequently by agricultural societies are totally different from the Ukrainian norm. See Iosyf O. Dzendzelivs'kyi, *Linhvistychnyi atlas ukraïns'kykh narodnykh hovor v Zakarpats'koï oblasti URSR (Leksyka)*, 2 vols., *Naukovi zapysky Uzhhorods'koho derzhavnoho universytetu*, XXXIV and XLII (Uzhhorod, 1958-60).

[57]Pavelko, *Druzhba narodiv*, pp. 84-86. A perusal of readers shows that most excerpts are from classic Ukrainian writers Shevchenko and Franko, or from Czech and Slovak writers, and that the only local subject matter is based on the Slovak National Uprising of August, 1944. For instance, not one reader contains the famous poem of Dukhnovych, "I was, am, and will be a Rusyn." In contrast to the modern history text used in Hungarian-language schools in Slovakia, the Ukrainian-language edition includes 4 pages devoted specially to the cultural achievements of Subcarpathian Rusyns during the interwar period. *Istoriia dlia 9 klasu osnovnoï dev'iatyrichnoï shkoly*, trans. from Slovak (Bratislava, 1973), pp. 130-133.

continue to influence parents in Rusyn villages who respond by demanding Slovak schools.

By the 1960s it became clear to the well-paid Ukrainophile intelligentsia sitting in Prešov that they were rapidly losing touch with their constituencies.[58] The more permissive atmosphere in the years prior to 1968 produced long discussions in the local Ukrainian press concerning the specific problems of the Prešov Region. Again, the perennial question of language arose. Realizing that through literary Ukrainian the local population could not be reached, some writers favored the use of dialect in their works. A conference held in 1963 at the Šafárik University's Ukrainian Department decided that a more dialectal medium should be introduced in some publications and on radio.[59] In fact, writers like Mykhailo Shmaida did publish novels in which dialectisms were used freely. To be sure, the intelligentsia was not of one mind: some favored the use of dialect, others criticized such "reactionary" moves and propounded the continued use of literary Ukrainian. For instance, Shmaida was severely criticized for incorporating dialectal words into his novel, *Lemky*. In defense, he responded:

> Some of the Ukrainians who came here as emigrants or who have just come recently from the Soviet Ukraine ... often poke fun at the local language which is spoken by the Ukrainian population of Eastern Slovakia. Even though there are many Lemko dialectal words in Ukrainian dictionaries, just because they [i.e., Ukrainian emigrants] do not understand something, they consider it non-Ukrainian. They forget that the local population did not suckle the Ukrainian language together with the milk of the mother-Ukraine. They were left to themselves. The small corner of Eastern Slovakia ... is not the Ukraine where pure Ukrainian [is spoken].[60]

---

[58]Vasyl' Turok, "Rusyns'ki paradoksi," *Nove zhyttia*, January 6, 1968. Complaints were lodged that certain leaders, realizing the tenuousness of the situation, have begun to send their children to Slovak schools. *Ibid.*, February 24, 1968.

[59]Mykola Shtets', "Za chystotu movu," *Duklia*, XI, 2 (Prešov, 1963), pp. 65-67.

[60]Mykhailo Shmaida, "Povchannia zhart chy zhart z povchannia," *ibid.*, XII, 3 (Prešov, 1964), p. 87. The original attack on Shmaida was made by the Soviet-born wife of Mykhailo Mol'nar, the Ukrainian scholar in Bratislava, Larysa Mol'nar, in "Zharty z movoiu chy zharty movy?," *ibid.*, XII, 2 (1964), pp. 66-73.

The unsophisticated manner in which the local intelligentsia imposed upon itself the Ukrainian language during the 1950s was best summed up by Ivan Matsyns'kyi. "To learn the Ukrainian literary language we couldn't do any better than to stretch out our hands for books by Kharkiv, Bilhorod, and Chernivtsy [writers]. Unlike those writers, we came to our medium in another manner: not from the Ukrainian dialectal language (which our mothers and neighbors taught us) to the level of literary culture, but from the bookish language culture to the dialect."[61] He then decried the fact that local dialects were consistently avoided. "Once we knew these dialects, but then it seemed we did not need them because we wrote in Russian. With the change to Ukrainian they seemed worth nothing, foolish (*zasmicheni*), in short—not Ukrainian. ... for 'the pure Ukrainian language' we went farther eastward—to Kharkiv itself.[62] Matsyns'kyi also emphasized the need for a series of publications in dialect. Beginning in early 1967, the editors of *Nove zhyttia* responded to popular requests, especially from young readers, and included in each issue two full pages written in dialect.[63]

Another bone of contention was the Dukla Song and Dance Ensemble. Writers like Iurii Bacha and Ivan Matsyns'kyi attacked the group for not being Ukrainian enough, i.e., the repertoire did not put sufficient emphasis on "true" Ukrainian bandura music and Cossack dances. On the other hand, the ethnographer Mykola Mushynka lamented that there were not enough local songs and dances in the repertoire.[64] After 1961, a concerted effort was made to add more

---

[61]Ivan Matsyns'kyi, "Kontseptsiï, bezkontseptsiinist' i—de ty kontseptsiie nashoho kul'turnoho zhyttia," *Duklia*, XIII, 2 (Prešov, 1965), pp. 40-41. An example of the kind of Ukrainian introduced is evident in signs on store fronts in the Prešov Region. Instead of the generally used and understandable *sklep*, all village stores are called *bakaliia*. This literary "Ukrainian" term is originally a Persian word which entered the Turkish language, later Russian, and from there it was introduced into Ukrainian. It finally reached south of the Carpathians and has been proclaimed the acceptable form for the Rusyn peasant.

[62]*Ibid.*, p. 41. See also Iurii Bacha, "Za pravdyvu literaturu," *ibid.*, XI, 3 (1963), p. 58, and Ivan Shelepets', "Movni pytannia," in *Literatura chekhoslovats'kykh ukraïntsiv*, pp. 102-108.

[63]The reasons for this innovation are given by the editor Iurii Datsko in *Nove zhyttia*, January 14 and March 25, 1967.

[64]Matsyns'kyi, "Kontseptsiï," p. 41; Iurii Bacha, "Kil'ka dumok pro iuvileine

musical material based on regional motifs, but some Ukrainophiles were still not convinced that the Dukla Ensemble was sufficiently "Ukrainian."[65]

1968 and the Rusyns

The Czechoslovak liberalization process, known as the Prague Spring, began in 1968 under the leadership of Alexander Dubček also affected the status of the Rusyn population. Latent political, religious, and cultural problems were brought to the fore, and as a result of the relaxation in censorship, local publications were filled with new criticisms and suggestions on how to resolve the "Ukrainian question." It should be mentioned that the other minorities in the republic also had many justified grievances. Actually, though officially the Rusyns were the smallest minority—in 1961, the Magyars numbered 533,934, the Germans 140,402, the Poles 67,552, and the Rusyns 35,435—were in a sense the most favorably treated. While the other groups had their own elementary schools, cultural organizations, and publications, they did not, like the Rusyns, have a professional dramatic theater and folk ensemble, a fully-staffed museum, a scholarly research institute, or a department at a Czechoslovak university.

The Rusyn's favored position may be explained by the fact that during World War II, they were the only minority to support the Czechoslovak Republic. For the most part the German., Polish, and Magyar minorities supported the irredentist claims of Berlin, Warsaw, and Budapest, while the Slovaks created an independent state under

---

Sviato pisni i tantsiu," *Duklia*, VII, 3 (Prešov, 1959), pp. 110-111; Mykola Mushynka, "Vos'me sviato i mistsevyi fol'klor," *ibid.*, X, 4 (1962), pp. 52-56; and idem, "IX sviato v otsintsi presy," *ibid.*, XI, 4 (1963), pp. 81-85.

[65]For praise of the new repertoire, see Iurii Tsymbora, "Uspikhy zaokhochuiut': do 10 richchia PUNA," *Druzhno vpered*, XVI, 2 (Prešov, 1966), pp. 16-17 and Mykola Mushynka, "Desiata prem'iera PUNA," *Nove zhyttia*, May 13, 1967. Nevertheless, in 1968, Mushynka severely attacked the Ensemble for not being Ukrainian in spirit (in fact half of the members are not Rusyn and the artistic director is Slovak) and for supposedly emphasizing Slovak folklore and language. See his articles, "Komu sluzhyt' UNT?" and "Progres chy stagnatsiia," *Nove zhyttia*, March 16 and May 8, 1968, as well as the long response by the director of the theater that talent, not nationality, is the criterion for choosing personnel: Ivan Pykhanych, "Spravdi sumno na dushi," *ibid.*, June 8, 1968.

Germany's protection which lasted from 1939 to 1944. In the reconstituted, post-1945 Czechoslovak state, it was almost inevitable the status of these minorities would take a change for the worse. The Magyar and especially the German minorities were deported in large numbers, and those that remained were restricted in the propagation of their national cultures. The Slovaks also soon became disenchanted with the revival of Czech centralism, whether under the guise of a democratic or communist regime.[66]

Though the Rusyns may have fared relatively better than the other minorities, they still had many complaints which were publicly articulated in 1968. Like all segments of the country's population, Rusyn leaders were strongly critical of the past. They argued that Rusyns fought in large numbers during World War II, and that during the last months of the conflict the Slovak National Council had declared: "We are for a Czechoslovak republic as an independent and unified state of three Slavic peoples: Czechs, Slovaks, and Carpatho-Ukrainians on the basis of the principle 'equal among equals'."[67] Yet after 1948 their representative political body, youth organization, printing and publishing house, school inspectorate, and Greek Catholic Church were liquidated. "The deformations of the 1950s left the Rusyn

---

[66]The fortunes of the Hungarian minority are best analyzed in two studies: Juraj Purgat, *Od Trianonu po Košice: k mad'arskej otázke v Československu* (Bratislava, 1970); and Juraj Zvara, *Mad'arská menšina na Slovensku po roku 1945* (Bratislava, 1969). The Slovak situation has been recently outlined by Eugen Steiner, *The Slovak Dilemma* (Cambridge, U.K., 1973).

The Gypsies are perhaps the minority in the worst position. Since 1945 they have not even been recognized as a separate nationality, and it was not until 1968 that they managed to acquire their own cultural organization, Roma, in Bratislava.

[67]This principle was laid down in November 29, 1944, a time when it was expected that Czechoslovakia's far eastern province of Subcarpathian Rus' would still be part of the republic. Cited in Mykhailo Myndosh, "Paradoksy nashoho zhyttia," *Nove zhyttia*, March 23, 1968. In 1943, fully two-thirds of the Czechoslovak Army Corps in the Soviet Union was made up of Rusyns from Subcarpathian Rus' and the Prešov Region. Ivan Vanat, "Zakarpats'ki ukraïntsi v chekhoslovats'komu viis'ku v SRSR," in *Shliakh do voli: zbirnyk spohadiv i dokumentiv/Naukovyi zbirnyk Muzeiu ukraïns'koï kul'tury*, II (Bratislava and Prešov, 1966), pp. 183-201.

without 'his own faith', his 'own land,' and his 'Rusyn nationality'."[68]
To put an end to national assimilation, local leaders felt it necessary "to
reactivate as soon as possible the Ukrainian National Council."[69]
That body, criticized until 1968 for being a "bourgeois-nationalist"
organization, was now lavished with praise, and concrete plans were
laid to convoke a new council.[70] On March 19, 1968, the Plenum of
the Central Committee of KSUT resolved in a special session that a
Ukrainian National Congress (Narodnyi Z"ïzd) should be convened no
later than May 30.[71] Soon petitions and resolutions from various
localities reaffirmed the call.[72] Suggestions were also made to
designate the congress as Rusyn, not Ukrainian, because "many people
react negatively to such a name [i.e., Ukrainian]. The national council
should have a name that would unite all of us and not just the little
band of intellectuals."[73]

What was the specific nature of Rusyn political demands? Clearly
some "form of self-government" was desired. While most leaders
demanded "full political, economic, and cultural autonomy," some
proposed the establishment of a "Ukrainian or Rusyn (rusyns'ka)
autonomous region with the broadest political and economic rights for
self-government."[74] All agreed that the county (okres) pattern should
be restructured. In 1961, the Medzilaborce and Snina counties—areas
with an overwhelming Rusyn majority—had been abolished and

[68]Myndosh, "Paradoksy," pt. 2, April 6, 1968. See also the article by Vasyl'
Kapishovs'kyi and the proclamation of the Central Committee of KSUT in Nove
zhyttia, March 9 and 16, 1968.

[69]Vasyl' Kapishovs'kyi, "Iak vyrishyty nashi narodni spravy?," ibid., April 6,
1968.

[70]Among the rehabilitation articles, see Ivan Shkurlo, "Ukraïns'ka Narodna Rada
v dniakh liutoho" and "Priashivshchyna v Liutnevi dni 1948 roku," ibid., February
24, 1968.

[71]The position paper and resolution are in ibid., March 23, 1968.

[72]For the petitions and resolutions from Medzilaborce, Kalinov, Bardejov,
Humenné, and Havaj, see ibid., March 30, April 10, 13, 16 and 17, 1968.

[73]Alternatives suggested were: "National Council of Rusyns," "National Council
of Czechoslovak Rusyns," or "Rusyn (Rus'ka) National Council." Ibid., April 20,
1968.

[74]Resolution from a meeting of the staffs of Nove zhyttia, Duklia, and Prešov
Radio held on March 9, reprinted in Nove zhyttia, March 16, 1968. See also
"Rezoliutsiia OK KSUT-u v Snyni," ibid., April 6, 1968.

consolidated into the larger county of Humenné. As a result, county governing organs took on a distinct Slovak hue. Rusyn leaders argued that the re-creation of the two former counties would stem the assimilation process.[75]

Initially, the National Congress was scheduled for Prešov on April 26-28, but it was postponed to May 3, then May 24, and finally to May 31.[76] Several delegates were chosen and they arrived in Prešov "with great hopes," but suddenly on May 30, in response to orders from the Central Committee of the Czechoslovak Communist party in Prague, KSUT announced the indefinite cancellation of the Congress.[77] This postponement "provoked protests and lack of faith in its organizers," so that the "Prešov intelligentsia" began to lose the popular support which had only just arisen among large segments of the Rusyn population.[78]

The initiative for a National Congress passed to the town of Medzilaborce, where a "Preparatory Committee for a National Congress" was formed in early July under the direction of the *gymnasium* professor, Stepan Bunganych. Afraid of losing influence to the Medzilaborce Committee—which already had "massive strength among the peasantry,

---

[75]For various petitions and demands, see *ibid.*, March 23, April 6, 13 and 27, 1968. As late as March, 1969, KSUT still demanded the creation of two counties, but this was never realized. *Biuleten dlia vnutrishnikh potreb orhanizatsiï KSUT*, Vol. I (Prešov, 1969), pp. 13-14.

[76]The first postponement was because of a simultaneous meeting of the Regional Committee of the Communist Party in Košice, the second because of a visit of President L. Svoboda to Eastern Slovakia. *Nove zhyttia*, April 13 and May 22, 1968.

[77]Later, various explanations were given: (1) the simultaneous meeting of the Communist party Central Committee in Prague created "a complicated internal political situation in the country."—*ibid.*, June 8, 1968; and (2) an insufficient number of delegates and the fear that a Rusyn Congress would "set a precedent" for other minorities—*ibid.*, July 20, 1968. It became known that the cancellation was ordered on May 29 by Vasil' Bil'ak, who informed the Košice Regional Party Committee that if the Congress were held, it would be considered "a secret, illegal act, and the Communists who led the Congress would be subjected to disciplinary action." Only nine of the seventeen members of the KSUT Presidium met and decided to carry out the order. Iurii Bacha, "Ne khrestyny, a pokhoron," *ibid.*, June 22, 1968.

[78]Quotation from a speech at the special session of the KSUT Plenum, held on July 9, 1968, cited in *ibid.*, July 20, 1968. See also the protests in *ibid.*, June 8 and July 13, 1968.

workers, and intelligentsia of that region"—KSUT leaders agreed on July 9 to join the renewed drive for a National Congress.[79] Various proposals for the Rusyn region were drawn up, including Bunganych's call for territorial autonomy, and several Slovak officials declared themselves unopposed in theory to a Congress.[80] The new date set was August 23, but the military intervention of the Warsaw Pact forestalled the Congress once again.[81] Plans were made for a meeting in late November, but nothing resulted, and the project was dropped.

In addition to interest shown in a National Congress, individual Rusyns were at the same time participating in the commission that was preparing a new federal structure for Czechoslovakia and in the sub-committee on nationality problems. Czechs and Slovaks were to have two separate republics, while the Rusyns, in cooperation with the Magyars, sought broader rights for the national minorities.[82] The final constitutional amendment passed on November 4, 1968 made no pro-visions for territorial or cultural autonomy, though it legalized the name Rusyn alongside Ukrainian and "in the spirit of social democracy and internationalism" guaranteed national minorities "the possibility and means for full development."[83]

The attempts to organize Rusyn youth were not successful. Demands

[79]The KSUT Plenum sharply criticized the decision to cancel the Congress made on May 29 by a minority of the Presidium. *Ibid*, July 20, 1968. In early June, members from the last Plenum of the Ukrainian National Council (November 1, 1948) met in Prešov and stressed the absolute need to reactivate the Council under a new name: The Council of Czechoslovak Rusyns. "Pravda pro Ukraïns'ku narodnu radu Priashivshchyny," *ibid.*, June 17, 1968.

[80]Bunganych's proposal was similar to one he made to the Slovak National Council back in January 1949 (Bajcura, *Ukrajinská otázka*, pp. 113-117), which was opposed by Slovak leaders, especially by then Deputy Premier, Gustáv Husák. Both the head of the Slovak National Council and its representative for national minorities, however, were not opposed to a Rusyn Congress. *Nove zhyttia*, August 3 and November 9, 1968.

[81]The August 24 issue of *Nove zhyttia* announced the convocation of a National Congress and the creation of a monetary fund for its support.

[82]*Ibid.*, June 22 and 29, 1968. On cooperation with the Magyar and other minorities, see Vladimir V. Kusin, *Political Grouping in the Czechoslovak Reform Movement* (London, 1972), pp. 153-155.

[83]*Sbírka zákonů Československé socialistické republiky*, č. 144 (Prague, 1968), pp. 402-403.

were made in April to revive the Union of Carpathian Youth (disbanded in 1949), and a preparatory committee was finally set up in Prešov on September 12. By November, however, it became clear that the best that could be achieved was a Ukrainian section in the Union of Czechoslovak Youth.[84] Rusyn failure in the political realm was complimented by partial success in religious affairs. In June 1968, the Greek Catholic Church was legalized again, but this institution was no longer able to resume its historic role as a unifying force for Rusyn nationalism. It became embroiled in disputes with the Orthodox Church over property jurisdictions and with the Slovak Greek Catholic clergy over the question of what vernacular should be used for the liturgy—and more importantly—from what national group should the new bishop come.[85]

The years 1968-1969 saw an intensification of the debate over the question of national orientation. In a sense, two factions existed: (1) the Ukrainophile—headed by former Russophiles who accepted Ukrainianism during their re-education in Kiev in the 1950s and who dominated the cultural apparatus in Prešov; and (2) the anti-Ukrainians—a heterogeneous group of individuals who hoped to end the existing alienation between the intelligentsia and the masses. The attitude of the second faction, which included Russophiles and supporters of an independent Rusyn national idea, was best revealed in the many letters to *Nove zhyttia* which criticized "our intelligentsia in Prešov who still today do not know their nationality ... [and] do not know what to fight for."[86] One villager pleaded: "Help the people have some nationality

---

[84]*Nove zhyttia*, April 20, September 28 and November 30, 1968.

[85]The Greek Catholic Church did succeed in securing control of the cathedral church in Prešov (from 1950 to 1968 controlled by the Orthodox Church). In many Rusyn villages, severe conflicts broke out between Greek Catholic and Orthodox adherents, and it was reported that at least two priests were killed. The best survey on the religious problem is by Athanasius B. Pekar, "Restoration of the Greek Catholic Church in Czechoslovakia," *The Ukrainian Quarterly*, XXIX, 3 (New York, 1973), pp. 282-296. On slovakization, see Iurii Bacha, "Reabilitatsiia chy spekuliatsiia?," *Nove zhyttia*, July 27, 1968 and *The Tragedy of the Greek Catholic Church in Czechoslovakia* (New York, 1971). For the protests lodged by the Orthodox hierarchy, see the organ of the Orthodox Church, *Zapovit sv. Kyryla i Mefodiia*, XI, 5, 6, 7 (Prešov, 1968).

[86]Ivan Siika, "Hyne nasha kul'tura?," *Nove zhyttia*, April 27, 1968.

for which they would be proud. ... Give us our own schools which our people would like and which our children would want to go to. ... If in our republic there can be Czech, Slovak, Hungarian, Ukrainian, and German schools, why can't there be Rusyn schools?"[87] Perhaps the best example of the Rusynophile attitude was revealed in a letter published at the end of March 1968. Describing the situation after World War II, the author wrote:

> Everywhere there was joy because of the liberation, but here in Prešov they established a Ukrainian National Council. Do you remember what came out of such a name? The people did not want it because they didn't like Ukrainians and didn't want to be called Ukrainians. We had, of course, our own name. Why did we begin to be ashamed of what we hadn't been ashamed of for years? Perhaps you say it was for scholarly reasons that it was necessary to call our people by a new, scientific name.
>
> That was the beginning of all our misfortune. ...
>
> Why was it necessary to change our Rusyn (rus'ki) schools to Ukrainian? Of course, there were no teachers. For centuries the people spoke in Rusyn (let it be po-rusyns'kŷ), then suddenly we were told: this is not your language, you must only be called Ukrainian and even speak in Ukrainian! ...
>
> And when we glance at the identity cards of our people, what nationality is entered? You, perhaps, will say that this was also a mistake of the past, that the security organs gave incorrect information. Nothing of the kind. Our people said directly to the police that they were Slovak, because they were afraid they would be sent to Ukraine and also because they thought their children would be educated in Ukrainian. The result is that in our villages there are Slovak schools, and so [our people] live peacefully as Slovaks. And we complain that it is the fault of the state organs, the schools, the teachers, the parents, the children. Only we are without fault. This, however, is not the case. ...
>
> It is difficult, but it will be necessary to return to a situation where once again our speech will resound in our schools, where our cultural centers will have our own gymnasia, and where we won't be ashamed of the word 'Rusyn'.[88]

[87]Ibid.

These and similar letters provoked stiff rebuttals, but even the staunch Ukrainophile, Iurii Bacha, was forced finally to admit that more than 100,000 of "our people" accepted slovakization "in protest against the forced methods of Ukrainianization." As Bacha pointed out further, the people do not understand the Ukrainian literary language; thus, in the schools, press, radio and theater the local language must be used. "Let our people (if somehow they did not accept the Ukrainian orientation) grow proud again of their own speech, their own culture, their own traditions and their own schools. Let the people again proudly and freely repeat the words of our Dukhnovych: 'I was, am and will be a Rusyn'!"[89]

In fact, the words of Dukhnovych did appear frequently in the press along with other articles and laudatory praise for the local language and traditions. The Svidník Folk Festival in June became a focal point for Rusyn self-expression. Rusyn historical motifs formed the unifying theme for the two-day program, and most of the 30,000 spectators joined at the conclusion to sing in public (for the first time in more than twenty years) the popular anthem based on Dukhnovych's poem, "I was, am, and will remain a Rusyn." Indeed, the freedom of expression permitted during the few months of 1968 stimulated a rebirth of Rusyn self-identity.[90]

The recent return of about 8,000 Rusyns from the Soviet Union further contributed to the growing anti-Ukrainian attitude. The strange fate of these people began in 1946-1947, when Rusyns living in the

---

[88]Letter of Andrii Birosh, *ibid.*, March 23, 1968. For similar statements about the Rusyn, though "non-Ukrainian" nature of the population, see Iurii Bacha., "Protses demokratyzatsiï," *ibid.*, May 22, 1968; letters to the editor, *ibid.*, July 6, 1968; and interviews from the Stará L'ubovňa region, "Ia Rusyn buv, iesm i budu," *Druzhno vpered*, XIX. 6 (Prešov, 1969), pp. 4-6.

[89]Iurii Bacha, "Treba reabilituvaty rusyniv," *Nove zhyttia*, May 8, 1968.

[90]The special program, "From the National Well-Spring," was written by Mykola Mushynka, who put special emphasis on poetry of the Rusyns. *Ibid.*, June 22 and 29, 1968, and the touching letter of A. Franko, "Ia znovu 'narodyvsia'," in *ibid.*, July 27, 1968.

Prešov Region were given the opportunity to migrate to the Soviet Union. On the basis of an agreement between Stalin and Czechoslovak President Beneš, Rusyns were to be exchanged for Czechs who had lived in Volhynia since the late nineteenth century.[91] The "Volhynian" Czechs arrived in Bohemia and Moravia, and about 12,000 Rusyns, lured by expectations of rich and fertile land (and in some cases by the chance to live in the land of "Stalin the liberator"), went to the Soviet Ukraine. The Rusyns moved into the places of the Volhynian Czechs who, like German settlers (*Volksdeutsche*) in eastern Europe, often had the better homesteads. Local Ukrainians resented the new intruders, and the Rusyns in turn felt estranged from their immediate neighbors and soon became hostile to the economic and social system around them. Many wanted to return to Czechoslovakia, but they were not permitted to do so. Information about their plight did reach the Prešov Region and Rusyns there soon became skeptical to the idea of a supposed "Ukrainian paradise." Finally, in 1966, an agreement was reached between Prague and Moscow to allow Rusyns living in the Soviet Ukraine to return home. Interestingly, these Rusyns justified their demand to return on the ground that they were "Czechoslovaks" or "Slovaks"; moreover, since they spoke a distinct dialect, they came to be considered Slovaks by the indigenous Ukrainians. About 8,000 Rusyns eventually returned to Czechoslovakia, but they went back as self-proclaimed Slovaks who were filled with unfavorable tales about their experiences in Ukraine.[92]

The established pro-Soviet Ukrainophile intelligentsia felt threatened and opposed the spread of Rusynism, especially any ideas proposing that the local population was not a part of the Ukrainian nationality. "Our citizens have a right, if they do not consider themselves of Ukrainian nationality, to declare themselves of Rusyn nationality. . . . But this does not mean a separate national minority. There is not in the

---

[91]Jan Auerhan, *Osady českých emigrantů v Prusku, Polsku a Rusku* (Prague, 1920), and idem, *Československé jazykové menšiny v evropském zahraniči*, Národnostní otázky, sv. 5 (Prague, 1935).

[92]Those Rusyns who returned home demanded in 1968 that they receive once again Czechoslovak citizenship. See the resolution of the returnees and former members of the Communist party and non-party people in *Nove zhyttia*, March 30, 1968.

world a Rusyn nation."[93] Several articles appeared which praised the achievements of Soviet Ukrainian society and criticized the adoption in the local press of the "archaic" term Rusyn. Ukrainophiles also protested the demand to revive the Russian *gymnasia* in Humenné, Prešov, and Svidník.[94] Moreover, in the optimistic months before August 1968, some thought that the Prešov Region would become an international meeting place for Ukrainians and that the local publications would serve as an outlet for Ukrainian writings not permitted in the Soviet Union.[95] The anti-Ukrainian trend was not limited simply to emotional attacks against the Ukrainophile intelligentsia. At first, many expected that the proposed National Congress would do away with the Ukrainian cultural orientation. When, in late 1968, it was clear that the Congress would not be held, interest was focused on cultural matters and in particular on the language question. In December, a seminar met in Prešov to discuss "the language problem in Czechoslovak Ukrainian publications, radio, and theater." The participants concluded that the creation of a separate Rusyn language would not be feasible, though they did suggest the

---

[93]P.A. Uram, "Hovorymo pro konstytutsiinyi zakon," *ibid.*, November 23, 1968. See also Iurii Bacha, "Vidpovid' A. Birosha," *ibid.*, March, 30 1968; Ivan Bosnovych, "Khto matir zabuvaie...," *ibid.*, June 8, 1968.

[94]*Ibid.*, May 8, 1968. Favorable articles on the Ukrainian SSR were especially prevalent between May 29 and July 10 when an exhibition, "Days of Ukrainian Culture," was on display throughout Czechoslovakia.

[95]The director of the Transcarpathian National Ensemble in Uzhhorod and the editor of the Rusyn newspaper in the Bačka (Vojvodina) region in Yugoslavia were among those who suggested that Svidník become a world center for Ukrainians. *Ibid.*, July 6 and 13, 1968. In 1968-1969, *Nove zhyttia* ran many articles on international contacts between Ukrainians from different countries, and *Duklia* several studies on contemporary Soviet Ukrainian authors as well as those liquidated during the 1930s. Also, on June 21-22, an international seminar on "the Development of Ukrainian Studies in Socialist Countries" was held in Prešov. "Mizhnarodna asotsiatsiia ukraïnistiv," *Druzhno vpered*, XVIII, 8 (Prešov, 1968), pp. 6-7. The International Congress of Slavists that took place in Prague in July and August allowed further contacts (especially with Ukrainians from the West) for Prešov Region scholars and activists. Indeed, the Soviet government was wary of these developments, especially since through Prešov many illegal Soviet writings reached the West.

incorporation of more dialectisms.[96] In May 1969, however, Ivan Matsyns'kyi was elected First Secretary of KSUT and almost immediately he published a long article proposing profound changes in nationality and language policy. He suggested that school texts, popular pamphlets, and the weekly, *Nove zhyttia*, be published in dialect, while *Druzhno vpered* and *Duklia* should remain in literary Ukrainian.[97]

The Ukrainophiles were shocked that such proposals were made by the head of their own cultural organization and they reacted bitterly. They considered the "return" to a popular language a step backward and impossible to achieve because many dialects were spoken in the Prešov Region.[98] No one, of course, stopped to think that all languages are composed of many dialects and that one of the primary functions of the intelligentsia during the embryonic stage of national development is to transform one or several of these dialects into a literary language. For instance, during the early nineteenth century, a few individuals were instrumental in codifying the literary languages of their respective peoples. Josef Dobrovský did this for the Czechs, L'udovít Štúr for the Slovaks, Ludovit Gaj for the Croats, and Vuk Karadžić for the Serbs. Similarly, the intelligentsia of the miniscule group of Rusyns (originally from the Prešov Region) living in the Bačka or Vojvodina region in Yugoslavia succeeded during the 1950s in creating a literary language, complete with modern and technical terminology, based on local dialects.[99] But the intellectual cadre in the Prešov Region never took up this linguistic challenge, and like their predecessors in interwar Sub-carpathian Rus' they found it easier to rely upon an already developed language, whether it be Russian, Ukrainian, Slovak, or Hungarian.

Matsyns'kyi prepared a separate report (never published) on language which included a thirty page dialectal codification to be used for the

---

[96]"Iazyk nashoï presy," *Nove zhyttia*, December 21, 1968.

[97]"Osnovy kontseptsiï rozhornutoï diial'nosti TsK KSUT," *Nove zhyttia*, May 23, 1969.

[98]*Ibid.*, August 8, 1969. See also the criticisms of Ivan Hryts'-Duda, Iosyf Shelepets', and Mykhailo Shtefaniuk in *ibid.*, August 22 and 29, 1969.

[99]On the phenomenal development of a literary language for only 25,000 Bačka Rusyns, see Aleksander D. Dulichenko, "Stanovlenie i razvitie rusinskago literaturnogo iazyka v Iugoslavii," *Sovetskoe slavianovedenie*, No. 3 (Moscow, 1972), pp. 38-50, and idem., "Z istorii formuvania ruskoho literaturnoho iazyka," *Nova dumka*, II, 4 (Vukovar, Yugoslavia, 1973), pp. 46-47.

local press. And in response to those who complained that present-day readers of Ukrainian periodicals would be sacrificed if dialect were used, he pointed out that *Nove zhyttia* and *Druzhno vpered* had a meager 2,670 and 1,700 subscribers—and most of these were institutions, not individuals.[100]

Ukrainophile critics, however, used other arguments. Realizing that after the Soviet invasion a return to the pre-1968 political status quo was inevitable, they equated Rusynism with anti-Sovietism. The Medzilaborce Preparatory Committee for a National Congress was attacked for wanting to introduce dialect into the local press and schools. "What is behind all of this? The formula—we don't want to have anything to do with the East [Soviet Union]. That is the true goal of political Rusynism. So it was during the [first Czechoslovak] bourgeois republic, so it is today."[101] Similarly, the director of the Prešov Ukrainian radio studio, Vasyl' Varkhol, claimed that the proposal to publish a newspaper in dialect "is water for the mill of those chauvinist and anti-Soviet forces which have wanted and still want to tear away our people from its own roots—the Ukrainian people."[102] Thus, by joining the political conservatives in late 1969-1970, the Ukrainophiles guaranteed the predominance of their orientation in an increasingly repressive Czechoslovakia.

Slovak-Rusyn tensions

How did the Slovaks respond to the political and cultural demands of their eastern brethern? In the tension-filled atmosphere created by the Prague Spring, government functionaries appointed in Slovakia before 1968 were under severe criticism and, significantly, it was pointed out that Rusyns were disproportionately represented in the Communist bureaucracy. For example, in the Prešov Region Communist Central Committee, thirty-seven percent of the members in 1951 and again in 1958 were of Rusyn origin.[103] Even more disconcerting to Slovaks

---

[100]Ivan Matsyns'kyi, "Odnache problemu nashoï presy treba rozv'iazaty, bo vona davnia i nabolila," 3 pts., *Nove zhyttia*, November 7, 14 and 21, 1968.

[101]From a statement issued by the Prešov okres section of KSUT, *ibid.*, September 18, 1969.

[102]Vasyl' Varkhol, "Vyrishal'ne zmist hazety," *ibid.*, October 31, 1969.

[103]Bajcura, *Ukrajinská otázka*, p. 106.

was the fact that the Ministry of Interior, especially the secret police in Eastern Slovakia and even in Bratislava and Prague, was largely staffed by Rusyns. This phenomenon stemmed from political patronage for Rusyns who made up almost half the Czechoslovak Army Corps of General Svoboda which arrived with the Soviet Army in 1945. Moreover, in the postwar years, the Communist party did not have difficulty attracting into its ranks uneducated young Rusyns whose opportunities for employment in the war-torn Prešov Region were otherwise severely limited. It must be admitted, however, that these party functionaries became a-national types who did little to foster or protect the national interests of their people. The most outstanding individuals of this type were Vasil' Bil'ak, the pro-Soviet First Secretary of the Slovak Communist Party in 1968, and Ivan Rohal'-Il'kiv, the former General Secretary of the Ukrainian National Council (1949-1951).[104] Nonetheless, in Slovak eyes, Rusyns were seen as an anti-democratic force whose political demands were considered an interference if not a direct threat to the achievement of Slovak autonomy.

The Slovak response took the form not only of polemical articles in the press, but also physical attacks and threats against the Rusyn population. While Slovaks were pressing for equality with the Czechs, they opposed political organization and especially any kind of territorial autonomy for the Rusyn minority.[105] They argued that especially in

---

[104]It was during Bil'ak's tenure as Commissioner for Education and Culture in Slovakia (1958-63) that the largest number of Ukrainian schools adopted the Slovak language. As for Rohal'-Il'kiv, he opposed the legalization of the Ukrainian National Council and officially requested its dissolution. Since then he was not active in Rusyn affairs, but he has risen in the ruling hierarchy and has served as Czechoslovakia's ambassador to the United States during the Soviet intervention of 1968 and subsequently as Vice-Minister of Foreign Affairs.

[105]Most of the anti-Rusyn articles appeared in *Východoslovenské noviny*, the organ of the Communist party Regional Committee in Košice. Ukrainian publicists responded with protests against: (1) the Slovak term for Rusyns, "poddukelský národ" (the people under the Dukla Pass); (2) an exhibition held in Bratislava of "Slovak icons" from Eastern Slovakia; and (3) the editorial policy of *Východoslovenské noviny*. They further stressed that Prešov is also a "Ukrainian town" and that, in contrast to Slovakia, "our people" in the United States speak their own language and "no one calls them *šalené Rusnaky* [dumb Rusnaks]." *Nove zhyttia*, April 17, 25, 27; May 15; June 1, 17; August 24, 1968.

the eastern part of the country the Slovaks themselves were since the 1950s "in an inferior position with regard to the other nationalities" and "that this fifteen year anti-Slovak movement in Eastern Slovakia ... must be liquidated."[106] Furthermore, both before and after August 21, a time when the Soviet Union (and this includes Ukraine) was not popular, Rusyns were suspected of disloyalty to Czechoslovakia: if they wanted to be Ukrainian, then "we [Slovaks] will bring a bus and carry them off to the Ukraine."[107] Many Slovaks also disliked the fact that Rusyn political activity was centered in Prešov where frequently such warnings were found on the wall of buildings: "Prešov was and will be only—and only—a Slovak city" and "Ukrainians get out of Prešov."[108]

The increased friction between Slovaks and Rusyns in 1968 and 1969 was graphically revealed in regional administrative centers like Stará L'ubovňa, Humenné, Snina, and Stropkov. Several times Ukrainian posters were ripped down, windows broken in the homes of Ukrainian teachers, and walls defaced with insulting anti-Ukrainian signs.[109] Slovak-Rusyn relations reached a dangerous extreme in the town of Stropkov. A branch of the Slovak cultural society, Matica Slovenská, was reactivated there on May 26, and from the outset this organization claimed that "in Slovakia things should be only in Slovak" while in the schools there should be only Slovak teachers."[110] In July 1968, the

[106]Cited from *Kultúrny život* (Bratislava), April 19, 1968 and *Východ* (Košice), November 29, 1968.

[107]These words were attributed to the pre-World War II Slovak nationalist leader, the Roman Catholic priest, Andrej Hlinka. See the articles critical of the 1968 "democratic process" by Ivan Shlepets'kyi and Iurii Polians'ka in *Nove zhyttia*, April 25 and May 22, 1968. As early as March 1968, some Slovaks claimed that the Rusyns wanted to unite with "their eastern brothers," yet despite rumors in August that the Soviets might annex the Prešov Region (or even all of Slovakia), the Rusyn leadership and populace remained united behind the Dubček regime. "My za iednist' respubliky," *ibid.*, September 14, 1968. Nonetheless, as late as 1970 some extremists considered Rusyn-Ukrainians worse than Gypsies because of their supposed "pro-Soviet love." *Ibid.*, July 3, 1970.

[108]"'Rivnobarvna' demokratiia," *ibid.*, April 13, 1968; Stepan Kochuta, "Oko za oko, zub za zub!," *ibid.*, May 15, 1968.

[109]*Ibid.*, May 18, June 22, October 12, 1968; August 8, 1969.

[110]See Oto Pezlár's article, "Long live the Matica Slovenská!," reprinted from *Poddukelské noviny* (Humenné) in *Nove zhyttia*, July 6, 1968. A similar resolution

Matica Slovenská in Stropkov sent a circular to all "Rusyns, Rusnaks, Ukrainians, Rus', Russians, and newly-baked (*novopečení*) Slovaks!" The authors claimed that

> the youth which you [Rusyn] teachers educate is unquestionably Slovak. ... Only past regimes deceived them, took from them their true Slovak nationality, and called them some kind of Rusyns and Ukrainians. ... They [the Rusyn teachers and the pre-1968 regime] wanted to make from this population a bridge that would link our republic to Khrushchev's Russia. Thus, the primary task of the Matica Slovenská is to clean from our schools teachers of non-Slovak nationality and to put in their place upright Slovaks, i.e., Slovaks by origin. Thus, we sincerely recommend that you immediately secure a place in your Ukrainian schools—where you belong—and from September make available your present position. ... This is our sincere advice to you. If you don't take heed of it, we will have to resort to other means, and this we will do—count on it![111]

In keeping with the theory that latecomers to an ideology are usually its most extreme propagators, it is interesting to note that the authors of the circular as well as many members of the Stropkov's Matica Slovenská were themselves Poles by national origin who settled in the area after World War II and who since then became fanatic Slovaks.[112]

As early as September 1968, Prešov's Ukrainian newspapers seemed to express a sense of relief that the Warsaw Pact intervention slowed down the "Czechoslovak liberalization," a process which had included "strong forces that spread an evil and enemy campaign against Rusyn-Ukrainians."[113] To be sure, the Slovak fear of Ukrainianization in the school system was totally unfounded. In fact, as a result of further voluntary requests from parents, the number of Ukrainian-language

---

was adopted by the main Matica Slovenská Congress held near Bratislava. Bajcura, "KSČ a ukrajinská otázka," p. 31.

[111]Circular published in the Slovak original in *Nove zhyttia*, July 20, 1968.

[112]On the other hand, for an example of a Rusyn who at all costs wants to prove his Slovak identity, see the interview with Mikhal Kovach, head of the Matica Slovenská in the Rusyn village, Radvaň nad Laborcom, "Ako to vlastne s nami je?," *ibid.*, March 21, 1969.

[113]Mykhailo Myndosh, "My za iednist' narodiv i natsional'nostei Chekhoslovachchyny," *ibid.*, October 5, 1968. See also A. Kalyna, "Stalosia—a dali iak?," *ibid.*, September 28, 1968.

elementary schools decreased in 1970 to only thirty.[114] Ukrainophiles complained of the "democratic" principle which allowed "the street to dictate its will in the schools," but the head of the Ukrainian school system more rightly concluded: "We wouldn't have come to such a situation if we ourselves were clear about what we want and the kind of schools we wanted."[115] Five commissions—over 100 people—dealt specifically with Ukrainian educational matters. "And what do we have? almost nothing!"[116]

Thus, the liberalization of 1968-1969 brought little that was positive to the Rusyn population of eastern Czechoslovakia. Attempts to organize politically and to introduce local dialect into cultural life failed. The number of Ukrainian schools continued to decline and, worst of all, relations with Slovaks became so tense that many Rusyns were afraid they may be removed physically from their homes.

It was in such an atmosphere that preparations were made for the 1970 census. Beginning in 1968, many articles appeared which stressed

---

[114]Actually, there was only one school left in which all subjects were taught in Ukrainian. In the others, subjects in the humanities were generally in Ukrainian, the remainder in Slovak. Strangely enough, however, arithmetic was taught in Ukrainian, geography in Slovak. See *Biuleten*, pp. 28-31; *Navchal'ni prohramy dlia pershoho-p'iatoho klasiv osnovnoï dev'iatyrichnoï shkoly* (Bratislava, 1961).

[115]Andrii Dutsar, "Zdrastvui, shkola!," *Nove zhyttia*, August 28, 1970. The voluntary choice of schools was outlined in a Communist party document: "if the parents decide to have a Ukrainian language school, the state language should also be taught, but if the parents want a Slovak language school, the mother tongue should be taught." Cited in *ibid.*, February 18, 1967. In elementary schools, where Slovak language replaced Ukrainian, teachers were requested "to foster love for the homeland and respect for the mother tongue and cultural richness of the Ukrainian people, especially that part . . . living in Czechoslovakia." Cited in Pedagogický ústav v Prešove, "Metodické pokyny pre vyučovanie vlastivedy a hudobnej výchovy v ZDŠ, kde nastala zmena vyučovacieho jazyka ukrajinského na slovenský" (typescript "only for internal use in schools in Eastern Slovakia"). Since the above principles are not specifically employed in any of the published school texts, their implementation is dependent on the individual discretion of the teacher.

[116]Andrii Chuma, "Zberim syly," *ibid.*, April 17, 1970. The commissions included: (1) the KSUT school commission; (2) the Ukrainian school commission in the Council of Nationalities; 3) the advisory committee in the Ministry of Education—section for Ukrainian language schools; (4) Council of the Teacher's Club; and (5) the pedagogical section of KSUT's Naukove Tovarystvo.

the need to increase the number of Rusyns so that official statistics might better approximate the actual ethnographic situation in Eastern Slovakia. Though at first the Ukrainianization process of the 1950s was blamed for the low number of Rusyns, it was later argued that the people have to be informed that the names Rusyn and Ukrainian are synonymous and that they should not fear deportation to the Soviet Union if they declared themselves one or the other.[117]

During the optimistic months in early 1968, some leaders declared that there were as many as 200,000 "Ukrainians" in Slovakia, although more realistic estimates placed the figure around 134,000.[118] Most important, the census takers would once again recognize the names Rusyn, Rusnak, or Carpatho-Russian as terms of national self-identification. In the 1961 census, for instance, Rusyn and Rusnak were unacceptable, and rather than enter Ukrainian, the local villager preferred to be considered Slovak.[119] Perhaps in the new census, the nomenclature problem would no longer be a negative factor.

But it was too late. The increased friction with Slovaks, the Warsaw Pact invasion of August 1968, and the generally tense atmosphere in Eastern Slovakia made it more convenient—and psychologically safer—to enter Slovak as nationality, notwithstanding one's language or former national identity. In 1970, only 42,146 persons were willing to identify themselves as Rusyn or Ukrainian. This was far below the 91,079 figure recorded in 1930 and hardly reflective of the approximately 130,000 to 150,000 ethnic Rusyns who live in the region.[120]

[117]"Rusyns'kyi chy rus'kyi," *Druzhno vpered*, XVIII, 12 (Prešov, 1968), p. 3; Ivan Baitsura, "Pro perepys naselennia," *ibid.*, XIX, 9 (1969), pp. 12-13; Andrii Kovach, "Perepys liudei domiv i kvartyr," *Narodnyi kalendar 1970* (Prešov, 1969), pp. 57-59; and various propaganda articles in *Nove zhyttia*, June 19, 1968; October 31, 1969; January 16 and 23, February 27, November 27, 1970.

[118]*Ibid.*, March 30, April 17, May 8, 1968.

[119]"I remember the population censuses when the people did not understand why they should be 'Ukrainians' and not 'Rusyns'. Uninformed state employees could only respond: 'Rusyns don't exist, there are only Slovaks or Ukrainians!' 'Then better put me down as a Slovak!'" Radio commentary (March 17, 1968) by Ivan Matsyns'kyi, reviewed in *ibid.*, March 23, 1968.

[120]On the basis ethnic criteria (especially language), it is extremely difficult to determine the exact number of Rusyns, because after 1950 the statistics for

Conclusion

It must be admitted that despite the substantial funds provided by the Czechoslovak government to foster Ukrainian cultural and national activity, the trend to assimilate with the Slovaks has increased precipitously. In the first years after the 1948 Communist coup, the processes of collectivization, de-Catholicization, and decreed Ukrainianization caused economic, social, and psychological dislocations which stimulated the initial trend toward assimilation. In the decades which followed, the intelligentsia did have time to rectify those unfortunate initial developments, but for the most part, this group remained in Prešov (geographically separated from the lands where Rusyns live) and set up Ukrainian institutions and publications which for all practical purposes have remained alien to the bulk of the population. They failed to make Ukrainianism an attractive force or to create in the younger or older generation of Rusyns the will to be Ukrainian.

During the 1968-1969 liberalization period, the intelligentsia made demands for political representation, but it repeatedly surrendered the initiative when the time came for actual organization. Moreover, local leaders could not provide a clear cultural policy because they were helplessly divided between Rusynophiles, who in response to popular demand called for a Rusyn cultural orientation, and Ukrainophiles, who

individual Rusyn villages (which linguistically can be isolated) are not available. Considering that Eastern Slovakia is basically similar to Central and Western Slovakia—and statistics on birth, death, immigration, and emigration rates confirm this—a simple algebraic equation based on the statistics of 1930 (despite shortcomings the most reliable on record) and 1970 can provide an estimate of the increase in the number of Rusyns in proportion to a similar increase in the number of Slovaks during this forty year period. While the Slovak population rose from 2,346,000 (1930) to 3,884,000 (1970), the Rusyn population should similarly have risen from 91,000 (1930) to 150,500 (1970). Indeed, this number might be reduced by 10,000 to 20,000 since within Eastern Slovakia the Prešov Region has experienced an absolute decrease in population due to emigration to other parts of the country.

This whole question requires a more sophisticated analysis, assuming statistics become available. In 1968, such a study was undertaken, and 133,000-134,000 Rusyns were recorded, i.e., 3 percent of the total population in Slovakia, a percentage which coincided with those of 1921 (3 percent Rusyns) and 1930 (2.9 percent Rusyns). See P. Kovtan, "Ukraïntsi v ChSSR," *Nove zhyttia*, May 8, 1968.

in the face of widespread criticism strove to maintain their own lucrative positions. Since 1970, the "consolidation process," or politically conservative atmosphere prevalent throughout Czechoslovakia, has prompted a return to administrative Ukrainianization so reminiscent of the 1950s.[121] The local press discontinued the pages written in dialect and it no longer contains heated discussions about the "Ukrainian question." Rather, it is filled with articles of self-praise for KSUT leaders and phrases about the unprecedented opportunities "given by the Communist party of Czechoslovakia for the all-embracing development of the Ukrainian national minority."[122] But such commentary can do little to disguise the fact that there are fewer schools, fewer readers of the Ukrainian press, and fewer persons willing to identify themselves as Rusyn or Ukrainian.

The Rusyn-Ukrainians of Czechoslovakia represent one of those ethnic groups which is still in the formative stage of national consolidation. The population has a sufficient number of distinct characteristics which might have allowed it to develop into a separate nationality, or be assimilated into the Ukrainian, Russian, Slovak, or even Magyar nationalities. In the past century, the leaders have at some time favored each one of these alternatives, but due to their own indecisiveness as well as the demands of the political environment, they have never really adopted a clearly defined program for any significant length of time. Whereas massive national assimilation may have been avoided in the past, at a time when the poverty-stricken Rusyn population was left largely to itself in relatively remote mountainous areas, this situation has changed radically since World War II, when increased educational opportunities and industrial development have allowed for greater physical, social, and economic mobility. The result has been a natural tendency to assimilate with the ruling (Slovak) nationality—a trend rendered especially easy in a world of radio,

---

[121]At a meeting of the Plenum of KSUT's Central Committee, held on November 12, 1970, Ivan Matsyns'kyi was removed as first secretary and Iurii Bacha, Vasyl' Datsei, Iosyf Shelepets', Vasyl' Varkhola, Iurii Datsko, and Iaroslav Sysak were released from either the Plenum, or Presidium, or both. *Ibid.*, November 20, 1970.

[122]"Rik bohatoï i plidnoï pratsi KSUT," *ibid.*, January 5, 1973. The page written in dialect was discontinued in June 1970, but the danger of the "old and worn-out assertion about the particular national identity of the Ukrainians of Czechoslovakia" seemed no longer serious. Hence, the dialect page was renewed beginning in 1973.

television, and other modern communicative facilities. Considering these factors, one must conclude that among the Rusyn-Ukrainians of Czechoslovakia the sharp trend toward national assimilation will continue in the future.

CHAPTER 12

The Hungarians in·Transcarpathia (Subcarpathian Rus')*

As in other countries of the Danubian Basin, the Hungarians/Magyars of historic Subcarpathian Rus' (Hungarian: *Kárpátalja*), present-day Transcarpathia, did not become a national minority until 1919. Before then they were simply Hungarians—and part of the dominant state nationality—living in the northeastern corner of the Hungarian Kingdom. With the border changes that occurred in 1919-1920, the Hungarians of Transcarpathia/Subcarpathian Rus' found themselves within the borders of the new state of Czechoslovakia. Since then borders and countries have changed several times, so that Transcarpathia's Hungarians have found themselves in Czechoslovakia (1919-1938), again in Hungary (1938-1944), in the Soviet Union (1945-1991), and in an independent Ukraine (1991-present). Regardless of what state may have ruled Subcarpathian Rus'/Transcarpathia, the region has remained a distinct administrative entity—at times with a degree of autonomy—throughout most of the twentieth century.[1]

---

*This study was commissioned for a collection of essays on Hungarians living outside Hungary, edited by Andrew Ludanyi, and published in *Nationalities Papers*, XXIV, 3 (Oxfordshire, England, 1996), pp. 525-534. It was also published in the journal of Uzhhorod State University's Institute of Hungarian Studies: *A Kárpátaljiai Magyar Tudományos Társaság Közlémenyei*, II (Uzhhorod, 1995), pp. 40-51.

[1]The various changes in the region's political status have included: (1) an autonomous region, Rus'ka Kraina, during the period of the short-lived Hungarian republic (December 1918—April 1919); (2) a semi-autonomous province of Subcar-

MAP 12   291

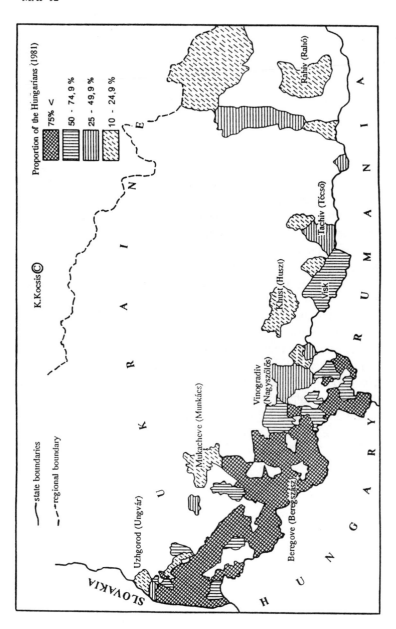

Proportion of the Hungarians (1981)

- 75% <
- 50 - 74,9 %
- 25 - 49,9 %
- 10 - 24,9 %

K.Kocsis©

—— state boundaries
–·– regional boundary

Uzhgorod (Ungvár)

Mukacheve (Munkács)

Vinogradiv (Nagyszőlős)

Beregove (Beregszász)

Khust (Huszt)

Vinogradiv (Nagyszőlős)

Visk

Techiv (Técső)

Rahiv (Rahó)

SLOVAKIA

U K R A I N E

R U M A N I A

H U N G A R Y

Hungarian Areas of Settlement in Subcarpathian Rus'

The sociodemographic setting

The settlement pattern of the Hungarian minority has been stable. The majority of Hungarians reside in agricultural-based villages on the lowland plain adjacent to the border with Hungary. Nearly two-thirds live in the district (*raion*) of Berehovo/Beregszász with most of the remainder in the immediately adjacent areas of the Uzhhorod, Mukachevo, and Vynohradiv districts. Sixty-two, percent of the population is rural, although there are also sizeable numbers of Hungarians in the region's administrative center of Uzhhorod/Ungvár (16.6 percent) as well as in the district centers of Mukachevo/Munkács (20.2 percent) and Vynohradiv/Nagyszőllős (29 percent). The largest "Hungarian" city in Transcarpathia is Berehovo/Beregszász, the center of the district of the same name where the 24,700 Hungarians living there represent as high as 85 percent of the population.[2]

According to official census reports, the number of Hungarians in Transcarpathia has in the course of the past seventy years gradually increased, although their proportion to the rest of the region's population has declined. Official data should, nevertheless, be used with caution. Since the last census, data taken annually by regional authorities has revised the number of Hungarians upward to 167,000 (1992), while unofficial estimates place their number at about 200,000.[3]

The Hungarians of Transcarpathia are a minority among minorities. Of the 1.3 million inhabitants in the province (1989), 78 percent were Rusyns and Ukrainians, 12.5 percent Hungarians, 3.4 percent Russians, 2 percent Romanian, 0.9 percent Gypsies, 0.5 Slovaks, and 1.6 percent Germans Jews, and Belarusans.[4] The minority status of Hungarians is

---

pathian Rus' in the first Czechoslovak republic (May 1919—September 1938); (3) an autonomous province of Carpatho-Ukraine in a federated Czecho-Slovak state (October 1938—March 1939); (4) the territory of Subcarpathia (*Kárpátalja vajdaság*) in an expanded wartime Hungary (March 1939—September 1944); and (5) the Transcarpathian oblast of the Ukrainian Soviet Socialist Republic (January 1946—August 1991) and an independent Ukraine (September 1991—present).

[2]The statistics on urban areas are from 1981 and are found in Károly Kocsis, "Kárpátalja," *Élet és tudomány*, XIV (Budapest, 1989), p. 436.

[3]Alfred A. Reisch, "Transcarpathia's Hungarian Minority and the Autonomy Issue," *RFE/RL Research Report*, February 7, 1992, p. 18.

[4]*Naselennia Ukraïns'koï RSR za dannymy vsesoiuznoho perepysu naselennia 1989 r.* (Kiev, 1990), pp. 153-161. The name *Rusyn* is not recognized in official

HUNGARIANS IN SUBCARPATHIAN RUS'/TRANSCARPATHIA[5]

Census	Number	Percentage
1921	104,000	17.3
1930	110,000	15.4
1959	141,000	15.9
1970	151,000	14.3
1979	164,000	13.7
1989	156,000	12.5

also evident in religious affiliation. Whereas the Rusyn and Ukrainian majority are either Greek Catholic or Orthodox, the smaller Roman Catholic and Reformed Calvinist churches are almost exclusively comprised of Hungarians.[6]

Developments before the Gorbachev era

The Hungarians of Transcarpathia began their history as a minority in 1919 under Czechoslovak rule. For nearly twenty years that experience had both positive and negative features. On the one hand, the Hungarians enjoyed the liberties provided by a democratic state governed by the rule of law. On the other hand, the former privileged position of Hungarian-speaking officials and a Hungarian-dominated milieu in

documents and is classified as Ukrainian; therefore, it is impossible to know how many Rusyns there are. Of the 977,000 Ukrainians recorded in the 1989 census, the number of Rusyns (according to Rusyn and Hungarian sources) is estimated between 600,000 and 800,000. A survey conducted in late 1991-1992 by the Institute of Sociology of the Ukrainian Academy of Sciences reported that from a sample of 1,300 Transcarpathian residents, 28 percent (by statistical projection circa 350,000) considered Rusyns to be a distinct nationality. Petro Tokar, "Tko mŷ es'me?," *Podkarpats'ka Rus'* (Uzhhorod), September 10, 1992.

[5]*Statistický lexikon obcí v Podkarpatské Rusi* [1921] (Prague, 1928), p. 45; *Statistický lexikon obcí v zemĕ podkarpatoruské* [1930] (Prague, 1937), p. xv; V. P. Kopchak and S. I. Kopchak, *Naselenie Zakarpat'ia za 100 let* (L'viv, 1977), pp. 66-71; Stephen Rapawy, *Ukraine and the Border Issues* (Washington, D. C., 1993), p. 39.

[6]According to the 1930 Czechoslovak census there was an equal number of Roman Catholics and Reformed Calvinist adherents. Since World War II, there are 84 Reformed Calvinist churches and 53 Roman Catholic parishes and affiliates. József Botlik and György Dupka, *Ez hát a hon . . . : tények, adatok, dokumentumok a kárpátaljai magyarszág életéből 1918-1991* (Budapest and Szeged, 1991), pp. 255-260.

schools, churches, and cultural life that was characteristic of the pre-World War I era came to an end. Such blows to the status of Hungarians and their culture led, in part, to the creation of several Hungarian political parties that were critical of Czechoslovak rule and that throughout the interwar years worked closely with other parties in opposition to the government.[7]

It was therefore not surprising that during the last few months of the existence of the first Czechoslovak republic that followed the signing of the Munich Pact in September 1938, local Hungarian parties campaigned for the return of the province to Hungary. This eventually took place in two stages: the southern, mostly Hungarian-inhabited regions including the main cities of Uzhhorod, Mukachevo, and Berehovo were annexed November 2, 1938; the remainder of the province was annexed in mid-March 1939. The Carpatho-Ukrainian autonomous government that came into existence in October 1938 actually resisted with armed force Hungary's final annexation, so that it could be said that World War II actually broke out in Transcarpathia (Carpatho-Ukraine) nearly half a year before Hitler's invasion of Poland. The result of this albeit limited conflict and the occupation that followed during World War II was alienation between large segments of the Transcarpathian population (most especially the Ukrainians) and the restored Hungarian government. Another factor to note was the position of the strongest political force in the region during the interwar years, the Communists. That party remained adamantly opposed to what it considered the "brutal annexation" of the region by "fascist Hungary."[8]

Such local conditions together with Hungary's subsequent defeat were to have dire consequences for Transcarpathia's Hungarian minority when, after World War II, it found itself within the borders of the Soviet Union. Already in 1945, as part of its policy against alleged wartime "collaborationist" populations within its borders, the Soviet authorities deported all Hungarian males between the ages of 18 and 50 to work camps in the remote eastern regions of the Soviet Union.

---

[7]For further details on the interwar period, see Paul Robert Magocsi, "Magyars and Carpatho-Rusyns," *Harvard Ukrainian Studies*, XIV, 3-4 (Cambridge, Mass., 1990), pp. 429-438—reprinted above, Chapter 7.

[8]On the wartime years, see Paul Robert Magocsi, *The Shaping of a National Identity: Subcarpathian Rus', 1849-1948* (Cambridge, Mass., 1978), pp. 234-249.

Estimates place the number at 45,000 who were forcibly deported. Some were held for nearly a decade, and many never returned from the vast Soviet gulag. Aside from the deportations, all existing Hungarian organizations were banned and the activity of the Roman Catholic and Reformed Calvinist churches were severely curtailed.[9] The Soviet Union was intent on creating among Transcarpathia's inhabitants a new kind of patriotism that was based on the heroic deeds of the Red Army and the remembrance of the suffering inflicted by external invaders during World War II. In that context, historic Hungary and the culture it represented was equated with oppression against the Transcarpathia's working class. These workers invariably were for the most part downtrodden Slavs whose desires for liberation were only fulfilled with the arrival of the Red Army in late 1944 and the "reannexation" less than one year later of Transcarpathia to the Soviet Ukraine. It seemed to make little difference that neighboring Hungary was also by then a Communist-ruled worker's state. In other words, Hungarian culture and therefore Hungarians themselves were scorned in immediate postwar Transcarpathia. Their only hope was to become divorced from their traditional Hungarian heritage and instead to become reeducated as socially enlightened class-conscious Soviet men and women.

In order to create "Soviet Hungarians," the regime gave support to a few writers, editors, and journalists. They were expected to publish works in Hungarian that praised the new sociopolitical order and that followed the guidelines of socialist realism, that is, were written in a manner that was both understandable and inspirational to the masses. In the administrative center of Uzhhorod, a Hungarian section of the Karpaty publishing house (Kárpáti Kiadó) was set up, and from 1951 it began to publish Hungarian translations of Soviet "classics" (Marx, Lenin, Stalin, Brezhnev) and of other Russian and Ukrainian works, a few original literary works by local Hungarian authors, and from 1957 an annual almanac (Kárpáti kalendárium). The Hungarians also got their own branch of the Soviet school book publishing house (Ragyanszka Skola Tankönyvkiadó). Several Hungarian-language newspapers were published as well, whether as organs of the regional

---

[9]For further details on the early years of Soviet rule, see Botlik and Dupka, *Ez hát a hon*, pp. 54-66 and 141-152.

(*Kárpáti igaz szó*) and district (*Vörös zászló, Kommunizmus zászlója, Kommunizmus fényei*) Communist party organizations or of the Communist Youth League (*Kárpátontuli ifjúság*). For the longest time, however, these were simply translations of Russian or Ukrainian newspapers.[10]

Of particular importance in creating new ideologically reliable citizens was the school system. Marxist-Leninist nationality policy recognized the need for schools using the languages of national minorities, and the Hungarians of Transcarpathia were no exception. To assist in these efforts, a Department of Hungarian Language was established in 1963 at Uzhhorod State University to train teachers and to carry out research, most especially on Transcarpathia's Hungarian dialects.[11] By the 1989/1990 school year there were 84 schools in which Hungarian was taught (54 elementary and 30 secondary). During the previous two decades, however, the actual composition of the school system had changed. Following a pattern common in other parts of the former Soviet Union, there was a marked trend toward replacing unilingual with bi-lingual schools. Thus, in the two decades between 1968 and 1989, the number of uni-lingual Hungarian schools decreased from 93 to 53, while the number bi-lingual Ukrainian-Hungarian and Russian-Hungarian schools increased from 6 to 31.[12] Moreover, despite their nominal Hungarian nature, for over 45 years these schools never taught students any history of Hungary, while the Hungarian literature

---

[10]For further details on the period of Soviet rule before Gorbachev, see *ibid*, pp. 67-121ff; and Steven Bela Vardy, "The Hungarians of the Carpatho-Ukraine: From Czechoslovak to Soviet Rule," in Stephen Borsody, ed., *The Hungarians: A Divided Nation* (New Haven, Conn., 1988), pp. 209-227—an expanded version of the latter work appeared as "Soviet Nationality Policy in Carpatho-Ukraine Since World War II: The Hungarians of Sub-Carpathia," *Hungarian Studies Review*, XVI, 1-2 (Toronto, 1989), pp. 67-91.

[11]Péter Lizanec, "A magyar nyelv és irodalom oktatása az uzsgorodi Állami Egyetem," in Judit Róna, ed., *Hungarológiai oktatás régen és ma* (Budapest, 1983), pp. 36-40. A comprehensive bibliography of the results of the department's scholarship appears in a recent dialectal atlas of the region by Transcarpathia's leading Hungarian linguist: P. N. Lizanec, *A kárpátaljai magyar nyelvjárások atlasza/Atlas vengerskikh govorov Zakarpat'ia*, Vol. I (Budapest, 1992) esp. pp. 59-66.

[12]Botlik and Dupka, *Ez hát a hon*, pp. 250-254.

that was allowed included only those authors from the past and the few post-1945 Soviet Hungarian writers who were deemed to be ideologically reliable.[13]

From the Gorbachev era to an independent Ukraine

All aspects of Soviet society were to be profoundly influenced following the ascendance in 1985 of the reform-minded Mikhail Gorbachev to the post of general-secretary of the Communist party of the Soviet Union. While it did take some time for his policies of restructuring (*perestroika*) and openness (*glasnost*) to reach the peripheral areas of the Soviet Union, the Gorbachev phenomenon did finally make it to Transcarpathia by the end of the decade. The Hungarian minority, moreover, was among the first groups to participate in and to profit from the new political and social environment.[14]

Neighboring Hungary was to play an important role in this process. After four decades of silence, Hungary's media began in 1987 to speak openly for the first time about the past difficulties and present situation of Transcarpathia's Hungarians. Then, during a state visit to Budapest in April 1988, the Soviet Foreign Minister Andrei Gromyko signed with the Hungarian government a joint communiqué that called for increased cultural activity (including an Institute of Hungarian Studies at Uzhhorod State University) and travel opportunities for Transcarpathia's minorities.

It was the year 1989, however, that witnessed a concerted renewal of Hungarian life in Transcarpathia. Early in the year travel restrictions were eased, which resulted in a veritable flood of Transcarpathia's Hungarians to visit relatives and friends in northeastern Hungary or simply to see for the first time what for Soviet citizens was the legendary Hungarian economic "miracle." Hungary's party and government officials

---

[13]Among the best known writers from this period were László Balla (b. 1927) and Vilmos Kovács (1927-1977). See Lajos M. Takács, comp., *Vergődő szél: a kárpátaljai magyar irodalom antológiája 1953-1988* (Budapest and Uzhhorod, 1990).

[14]The following discussion is based in large part on Reisch, "Transcarpathia's Hungarian Minority," pp. 17-23; and the chronology of events by Kálmán Móricz, "Kárpátalja (Ukrajna)," in *Magyarság és Európa: évkönyv 1992* (Budapest, [1993]), pp. 167-207.

as well as Roman Catholic and Reformed Calvinist hierarchs visited in turn and for the first time Transcarpathia.

As for the Hungarians in Transcarpathia, they set up in February 1989 their first large-scale independent civic organization, the Hungarian Cultural Association of Subcarpathia (Kárpátaljai Magyar Kulturális Szövetség—KMKS). Headed by the Uzhhorod University Hungarian-language specialist Sándor Fodó, the new organization began with 500 members and before the end of the year burgeoned into 175 chapters with 30,000 members. This meant that the KMKS had effectively become the second largest political/civic organization after the local Communist party, which at the time had about 45,000 members. During the next two years the KMKS reinvigorated the debate about culture and politics in the local Hungarian press; it pressured local authorities to reverse the bi-lingual trend in the school system and to establish for the first time Hungarian-language nursery schools (55 by 1990); and it succeeded in having Hungarian history taught in schools. Although not a political party, the KMKS did nominate candidates in the 1990 local elections. Its eleven deputies in the 124-seat Transcarpathian regional parliament (Oblastna Rada) eventually joined with other oppositional parties to form a bloc of fifty deputies.

The political situation changed dramatically in August 1991, when, following the failed anti-Gorbachev putsch, Ukraine declared its independence. This declaration was to be put to the country's citizens for confirmation in a nation-wide referendum to be held on December 1, 1991. During the intervening months until the referendum, the Hungarians reacted to the new political situation by creating the Hungarian Democratic Alliance of Ukraine. The new organization, also headed by Sándor Fodó and based in Uzhhorod, had specifically political goals. It intended to coordinate Hungarian political and cultural activities throughout Ukraine, although its emphasis was obviously on Transcarpathia where the vast majority of the country's Hungarians lived. The Democratic Alliance came out in favor of an independent Ukraine, but at the same time it condemned extreme nationalism and declared its intention to work against any possible conflict that might arise between Transcarpathia's many nationalities.

The illusion to actual or potential conflict underscored the precarious status of Transcarpathia's Hungarians as a minority among minorities. For nearly forty years, Transcarpathia's Hungarians lived in what was ostensibly a Ukrainian province, but which in fact was subject to the same policies of sovietization and russification that were typical of other parts of the Soviet Union. With the dissolution of Soviet centralized rule in the late 1980s, the Ukrainians began to reassert their linguistic, cultural, and political rights. At the very same time, one segment of the indigenous East Slavic population who identified itself by the local historic name Rusyn challenged the Ukrainians. They argued that the Rusyn national orientation was the most legitimate one to be promoted in Transcarpathia.

Consequently, two rival national orientations, which had existed before Soviet rule, arose once again. One argued that the East Slavic population was Ukrainian and that Transcarpathia should be an integral part of a unitary independent Ukrainian state. The other argued that Rusyns were a distinct nationality and that Transcarpathia should have its historic autonomous status restored in a federal Ukrainian state. The Ukrainian orientation was represented by the Transcarpathian branches of the Movement for Restructuring Ukraine, better known by its acronym RUKH, and by the Taras Shevchenko Language Society. The Rusyn orientation was represented by the Society of Carpatho-Rusyns founded in Uzhhorod in February 1990. The idea of autonomy was also supported by several members of the Transcarpathian regional parliament and other government and cultural activists.[15]

As a minority among either a Ukrainian or a Rusyn majority, the Hungarians were faced with a dilemma. Which group should they support? And after they did chose, to what degree might the other become alienated? The matter came to a head during the debates about the issue of autonomy.

Actually, the issue was first broached by the Hungarian Cultural Association of Subcarpathia already in late 1990, when it called for cultural autonomy for all Hungarians living in what should become a distinct administrative territory within Transcarpathia. That goal was then put on the agenda of the Transcarpathian parliament by its Hungarian deputies. Within a month after Ukraine was declared a sovereign state in August 1991, the Society of Carpatho-Rusyns demanded

[15]Paul Robert Magocsi, "The Birth of a New Nation, or the Return of an Old Problem? The Rusyns of East Central Europe," *Canadian Slavonic Papers*, XXXIV, 3 (Edmonton, Alta., 1992), esp. pp. 207-212—reprinted below, Chapter 15.

autonomy for all of Transcarpathia and proposed that the entire population of the province should be asked to vote on the issue in the December 1 referendum on Ukrainian independence. The Hungarians actively cooperated with the Rusyns and other minorities—Russians, Romanians, Slovaks, Germans, Gypsies, and even a small Jewish community in Mukachevo—all of whom joined together to form the Democratic League of Nationalities set up in October 1991. Not only did the Hungarian Cultural Association support the call for autonomy, but leaders in the Berehovo/Beregszász district (*raion*) called for yet another question to be placed on the December 1 referendum. If approved, Berehovo/Beregszász would be transformed into a Hungarian national autonomous district (Magyar Autonóm Körzet).

The local Ukrainians were furious at this turn of events. Ever since the Hungarian parliamentary deputies had proposed cultural autonomy, the Ukrainians opposed any kind of autonomous status for Transcarpathia, arguing that this would compromise the sovereignty of Ukraine. For them, the rights of all minorities, including the free use of their native languages in all spheres of public life and government support of minority cultures, were guaranteed by a declaration proclaimed in November 1991. In fact, Ukraine's liberal policy regarding its national minorities was noted by many international observers, including the Hungarian media which since that time has described the status of Hungarians in Transcarpathia as being better than the status of any other Hungarian minority in the Danubian Basin.

Despite strenuous protests by local Ukrainian activists during the fall of 1991 (including demonstrations and a public hunger strike), the Transcarpathian parliament reached a compromise formula with the chairman of the Supreme Soviet and presidential candidate, Leonid Kravchuk. The December 1 memorandum on Ukrainian independence was to include as well two other questions: (1) should Transcarpathia become a "self-governing administrative territory" within Ukraine; and (2) should the Berehovo/Beregszász district become an autonomous national district? This was the first time in history that the population of Transcarpathia was asked (83 percent of eligible voters participated) in an open and free election about their future political status. The results were: 93 percent in favor of Ukrainian independence; 78 percent in favor of autonomy for Transcarpathia; and 81 percent for a Hungarian autonomous national district in Berehovo/Beregszász.[16]

The euphoria and expectations surrounding the results of the December 1, 1991 referendum did not last long, however. Kravchuk, who won the presidential elections held on the same day of the referendum, had promised that autonomy could be established as early as January or February 1992. Yet to date (early 1994) neither autonomy for Transcarpathia nor a Hungarian national district has been established. Moreover, local Ukrainian activists have kept up their struggle against autonomy, characterizing any such demands as opposed to the interests of the Ukrainian state. At the same time the country has been overwhelmed by hyper-inflation and a general economic crisis, so that no decision has even been reached whether Ukraine will be a federal or unitary state. As for Transcarpathian autonomy, both the government and parliament have stalled on the issue, arguing that the region could go the way of Crimea, whose Tatar leadership in June 1991 declared their region's sovereignty.[17]

There is, indeed, some justification for such fears. Frustrated by the inaction of Ukraine's central government and Transcarpathia's parliament on the autonomy issue, the Society of Carpatho-Rusyns spearheaded a movement which, in May 1993, created a Provisional Government for Subcarpathian Rus'. At well-publicized press conferences in Budapest, Bratislava, and Vienna, the Provisional Government's spokespersons declared the 1945 treaty uniting Transcarpathia with Ukraine null and void, proclaimed that Subcarpathian Rus' is an autonomous republic, and expressed the intention to negotiate a valid treaty that would before the end of the year unite the "Republic of Subcarpathian Rus'" with Ukraine. In the interim, the region's inhabitants should "ignore the Ukrainian government's administration in Transcarpathia."[18]

The pace and direction of such developments raised concerns among the Hungarian leadership. Their support of autonomy and cooperation

---

[16]Taras Kuzio and Andrew Wilson, *Ukraine: Perestroika to Independence* (Edmonton, Alta., 1994), p. 196.

[17]The debates for and against Transcarpathian autonomy both before and after the December 1, 1991 referendum are discussed in each issue of the quarterly *Carpatho-Rusyn American*, XV-XVI (Pittsburgh, Pa., 1992-93).

[18]"Obrashchenie Vremennogo pravitel'stva Podkarpatskoi Rusi k narodam Zakarpatskoi oblasti," *Podkarpats'ka Rus'* (Uzhhorod), July 3, 1993.

with the Rusyns had clearly alienated the local Ukrainians who began to raise the spectre of "traditional" Hungarian disloyalty and anti-Ukrainianism. On the other hand, while Berehovo/Beregszász may not yet have gained the status of a national district, the Hungarian minority was enjoying the fruits of Ukraine's liberal law on national minorities. Also, Hungary and Ukraine were experiencing excellent bi-lateral relations, and both governments were pointing with pride to the favorable manner in which Hungarians were being treated in Transcarpathia.

Faced with such larger political realities, by late 1992 the Hungarian Cultural Association of Subcarpathia distanced itself from the Democratic League of Nationalities and refrained from pushing the autonomy issue. Since that time, some kind of accommodation seems to have been reached with the Ukrainian authorities. It remains to be seen what strategy the Hungarians will adopt in its relations with other nationalities in Transcarpathia, in particular toward the Rusyns and Ukrainians. In the end, the Hungarians are likely to do whatever is necessary to make the best out of their fate as a minority among minorities.

CHAPTER 13

The Lemko Rusyn Republic (1918–1920) and Political Thought in Western Rus'-Ukraine[*]

D uring the closing months of World War I in late 1918 and the break-up of the historic multinational empires that for centuries had ruled most of east-central Europe, it became common practice for the varying ethnolinguistic or national groups to form councils whose goals were to determine their group's political future. These national councils, as they came to be known, seemed to appear everywhere, but perhaps most frequently in the former Austro-Hungarian Empire. It was not only the "large" former minorities like the Czechs, Poles, Slovaks, Croats, Slovenes, Romanians, or Ukrainians who formed national councils, but many smaller groups acted in the same way. And, like the national councils of their immediate neighbors, so, too, did some of

[*] This study was originally commissioned for a session on "Ukrainian Ethnic Communities in Poland and Czechoslovakia between World War I and World War II," at the XXI Annual Convention of the American Association for the Advancement of Slavic Studies, held in Chicago, November 2-5, 1989. It was also delivered in Ukrainian at the First International Congress of Ukrainians, held in Kiev, August 27-September 3, 1990. It was first published under the title, "The Ukrainian Question Between Poland and Czechoslovakia: The Lemko Rusyn Republic (1918-1920) and Political Thought in Western Rus'-Ukraine," *Nationalities Papers*, XXI, 2 (New York, 1993), pp. 95-105. A Ukrainian translation, "Ukraïns'ke pytannia mizh Pol'shcheiu i Chekhoslovachchynoiu u mizhvoienni roky," appeared in Pavlo Robert Magochii, *Halychyna: istorychne ese* (L'viv: Toronts'kyi universytet, Katedra ukraïnoznavchykh studiï, 1994), pp. 290-303.

these smaller groups proclaim their independence. Thus, in the news-papers of the time and scholarly monographs of today one can still find references to the Baranya, East Slovak, Hutsul, or Przemyśl "republics" among others, which during the last few months of 1918 seemed to sprout up like mushrooms after a rainfall, but which for the most part ceased to exist when the borders of east-central Europe began to stabi-lize as a result of the Paris Peace Conference that opened its deliber-ations in early 1919.[1]

One of the least known, yet ironically perhaps the longest-lasting, of these postwar "republics" was the Lemko Rusyn Republic (Ruska Lem-kivska Respublyka), which existed for a full sixteen months from December 1918 to March 1920. Despite its relatively long existence in comparison with other post-World War I ephemeral "states," the Lemko Rusyn Republic has never been treated in a serious manner in scholarly literature, so that all that exists on the subject are a few small published and unpublished articles or parts of studies that deal with Lemkos in general.[2] This study will attempt to outline the basic facts concerning the existence of the Lemko Rusyn Republic and, in particular, to deter-mine how the discussions about that republic's orientation shed light on the more general problem of political thought in western Rus' (Ukrain-ian) lands during the first half of the twentieth century.

Although it was based in historic Austrian Galicia, which after the war became Polish-ruled territory, the Lemko Republic was closely linked to the fate of fellow Rusyns living south of the Carpathian mountains in the Prešov Region of what became Czechoslovakia. Using

---

[1] For information on some of these smaller and often ephemeral "republics," see C.A. Macartney, *Hungary and Her Successors: The Treaty of Trianon and Its Consequences, 1919-1937* (Oxford, 1937); and Ladislav Tajták, *Národnodemokra-tická revolúcia na východnom Slovensku v roku 1918* (Bratislava, 1972).

[2] V.R. Vavrik, "Russkaia Narodnaia Respublika 'Lemkov'" (unpublished 6-page manuscript); P. Kohutov, "Lemkivshchyna u borot'bi za vozz"iednannia" (unpublished 11-page manuscript); Andrzej Kwilecki, "Fragmenty najnowszej historii Łemków," *Rocznik Sądecki*, VIII (Nowy Sącz, 1967), esp. pp. 254-257; and Bohdan Horbal', "Lemkivska Narodna Respublyka," *Holos Vatry*, No. 5 (Bortne, 1988), pp. 5 and 12, as well as his more comprehensive "Działalność polityczna Łemkow na Łemkowszczyźnie Zachodniej i Sródkowej w latach 1918-1921" (unpublished manuscript). See also below, note 4.

more modern terminology, the political activity of Lemkos and Rusyns on both sides of the Carpathians in 1918-1920 could be considered part of the larger Ukrainian question in interwar Poland and Czechoslovakia. However, while it is true that scholarly literature, at least since World War II generally refers to the Lemkos and Rusyns as Ukrainians, most of the people that are the subject of this discussion would not in the years 1918-1920 have considered themselves part of a "Ukrainian question" for the simple reason that they did not consider themselves Ukrainians.

The explanation for this seeming paradox varies. Some commentators have argued that the Lemkos/Rusyns had not yet reached the stage of becoming nationally conscious, that is they did not identify as Ukrainians. For other commentators, however, the group was already quite conscious of belonging to an historic entity called Rus'. To avoid the potentially confusing and anachronistic use of modern terminology for earlier periods (only since World War II has the group officially been known as Ukrainians), I will use here the historic terms Rus' and Rusyn to describe respectively the territory and the East Slavic population which lived in the former Austrian province of Galicia and in the northeastern counties of Hungary, areas which after World War I became respectively parts of Poland and Czechoslovakia.

As for the term Lemko, it is a local name that had in the early twentieth century been adopted by those Rusyns who lived along the northern slopes of the Carpathians just west of the San River in historic Galicia.[3] This area was immediately adjacent to Polish ethnographic territory so that the Lemkos were geographically set off from the mass of Rusyns (Ukrainians) on the other side of the San River in eastern Galicia. The Lemko Region (Lemkovyna/Lemkivshchyna) was itself divided into a western and eastern half more or less at the point where the Dukla Pass crosses the Carpathians. The eastern Lemko Region had by the outset of the twentieth century been more influenced by the Ukrainian national revival that had gained strength beyond the San in

---

[3]On the origin of the term Lemko and its introduction as an ethnonym among the populace, see Bohdan Struminsky, "The Name of the Lemkos and Their Territory," in Jacob P. Hursky, ed., *Studies in Ukrainian Linguistics in Honor of George Y. Shevelov/Annals of the Ukrainian Academy of Arts and Sciences*, XV (New York, 1981-83), pp. 301-308.

eastern Galicia. In contrast, the western Lemko Region retained its sense of association with historic Rus'.

In the eastern Lemko Region, a meeting was called in early November 1918 by Pan'ko Shpil'ka, a Greek Catholic priest from the village of Wisłok Wielki (Rusyn: Vyslok Velykyi). Bringing together Lemkos from about 30 villages who were generally of a Ukrainian orientation, this group formed in the village of Komańcza (Rusyn: Komancha) what came to be known as the Komancha Republic.[4] The formation of the Komancha republic was only a "temporary" measure, however, undertaken until the whole Lemko Region would be united with the West Ukrainian People's Republic, founded on November 1, 1918 in L'viv, the administrative center of eastern Galicia. In fact, the Komancha Lemko Republic lasted only until January 23, 1919, when Polish troops occupied Komańcza as part of their military advance during the Polish-Ukrainian war that, by July, had driven the West Ukrainian People's Republic entirely out of Galicia.

Meanwhile, in the western Lemko Region, councils were formed in several villages. On November 27, 1918, about 200 Lemkos met in the town of Gładyszów (Rusyn: Hladyshiv; Gorlice district) to discuss their political future and, in particular, to consider the implications for them of the Wilsonian call for "the right of people to self-determination." At Gładyszów, Lemko leaders formed a Rusyn Council (Ruska Rada), which rejected the Ukrainian orientation of the Komancha Republic and called instead for union with Russia. The meeting also decided that the various smaller Lemko councils at Czarna/Charna (Grybów district), Śnietnica/Snitnytsa, later Binczarowa (Grybów district), and Krynica

---

[4]The literature on the more ephemeral Komancha Republic is slightly better than that on the Lemko Rusyn Republic. The most detailed survey is a chapter on the republic in Tadeusz Andrzej Olszański, *Bieszczady 1918-19* (Warsaw, 1984), pp. 41-52. Other descriptions of the Komancha republic, which also include brief and usually critical appraisals of the rival Lemko Rusyn Republic, are in Frants Kokovs'kyi, "Lemkivs'ki republyky v 1918-1919 rokakh," in *Istorychnyi kaliendaral'manakh Chervonoï kalyny na rik 1935* (L'viv, 1934), pp. 115-117; Iuliian Tarnovych, *Iliustrovana istoriia Lemkivshchyny* (L'viv, 1936), esp. pp. 246-258; and Ivan Hvat, "Istoriia pivnichnoï Lemkivshchyny do vyhnannia lemkiv," in Bohdan O. Strumins'kyi, ed. *Lemkivshchyna*, Vol. I, Zapysky Naukovoho tovarystva im. Shevchenka, Vol. 206 (New York, Paris, Sydney, and Toronto, 1988), esp. pp. 179-186.

(Nowy Sącz district) should with Gładyszów be consolidated at an all-Lemko national congress to be convened in the town of Florynka on December 5.

More than 500 Lemko Rusyns representing 130 villages and towns in the western Lemko Region did meet, as planned, at a national congress in Florynka (Grybów district) on December 5, 1918. Also present were representatives from among Rusyns living south of the mountains in the Prešov Region of northeastern Slovakia and from immigrants in the United States (Viktor Hladyk), as well as an official (Kazimierz Romult) from the new government in Poland at the county seat of Grybów.

At Florynka it was decided to form a self-governing entity that would include an executive council (Nachal'nyi Sovit) headed by the Reverend Mykhal Iurchakevych and a central national council (Ruska Rada) headed by the lawyer Iaroslav Kachmarchyk. This was the birth of what became known as the Lemko Rusyn Republic whose leading figure remained from beginning to end Iaroslav Karchmarchyk. Almost immediately, the new Lemko government set up a national guard and organized schools and cooperatives.[5]

Hoping that the Lemko Republic would be opposed to the West Ukrainian People's Republic and therefore of use in supporting Polish interests in the area, the Polish official present at the Florynka proceedings offered Lemko leaders the building of the former town hall in Grybów as its governmental headquarters and provided some arms for the Lemko national guard. Polish expectations of Lemko loyalty proved to be misplaced, however. Whereas the Lemko Republic was ideologically opposed to the West Ukrainian People's Republic, it did not join Poland's efforts to drive that Ukrainian government out of Galicia.[6] Whereas the Lemko Rusyns welcomed Poland's initial

---

[5]On the background to the Florynka meeting and its actions, see Ivan Krasovs'kyi, "Zakhidnio-Lemkivs'ka Respublyka," *Nashe slovo* (Warsaw), November 30, 1980, p. 4; and Horbal, "Działalność polityczna Łemków," pp. 2-7.

[6]The pro-Ukrainian Kokovs'kyi, "Lemkivs'ki republyky," p. 117, who otherwise had little sympathy for the Lemko Rusyn Republic, nonetheless concluded that "the leadership of 'this republic' conducted itself in a completely loyal manner toward the Ukrainians, and although there were efforts to divide Muscophiles [Russophile Lemkos] from Ukrainians, both sides took the position that this was only an internal matter which would be resolved among the two orientations."

support, they were primarily concerned about implementing for themselves Wilson's precept of self-determination.

For the Lemko republic's national council now based in Grybów self-determination meant union with a democratic Russian state that would "reunite" all of Galicia with the East as had only recently been the case under the leadership of the tsarist arrny during the winter of 1914-1915. Thus, one week after the Florynka meeting, the chairmen of the Lemko national and executive councils, Dr. Karchmarchyk and the Reverend Iurchakevych, joined other pro-Russian Galician leaders at Sanok, where on December 13 they signed a memorandum that rejected all foreign pretentions over their homeland, whether Hungarian, Polish, or "Habsburg-Ukrainian," proclaiming instead that, as "Russians" living in Galicia, they should be incorporated into a "single, great Russian state."[7] By 1919, however, Russia was plunged into a civil war and it seemed unlikely that any government there, whether Bolshevik or non-Bolshevik, would be able to make its influence felt in the Carpathians. In such circumstances, Lemko leaders began to look for other alternatives.

Already in January 1919, Lemko representatives met with their Rusyn brethren south of the mountains in Prešov, where under the leadership of a former member of the Hungarian parliament, Antonii Beskyd, they joined to form a united Carpatho-Rusyn National Council. This council proposed the idea that Galician Lemkos and all Rusyns south of the Carpathians formed one people who would comprise a territory called Carpathian Rus' that would seek union with the new state of Czechoslovakia.[8] The pro-Czechoslovak orientation was approved by Galician Lemko leaders at several meetings in March (at Florynka, Brunary, Krynica) and a delegation was sent to the Paris Peace Conference to support the idea of union with their Rusyn brethren south of the mountains. This proposal was formalized in a memorandum submitted on April 20 by the chairman of the Carpatho-Rusyn National Council in Prešov, Antonii Beskyd, to the Paris Peace Conference. The 23-page Paris memorandum issued in French and

---

[7]"Memorandum Narodnago Sovieta Russkago Prikarpat'ia," reprinted in Zdeněk Peška and Josef Markov, "Příspěvek k ústavním dějinán Podkarpatské Rusi," *Bratislava*, V (Bratislava, 1931), pp. 528-531.

[8]See the memorandum, dated Prešov, January 31, 1919, in *ibid.*, pp. 531-532.

English also included a fold-out map delineating the boundaries of what was called the united state of Carpathian Rus' (Karpats'ka Rus'), which included not only the Lemko Region in Galicia as far as the San River, but also the Rusyn inhabited Prešov Region in Slovakia and Subcarpathian Rus' on the southern slopes of the mountains.[9]

At the same time that the Paris memorandum was being presented to diplomatic circles at Versailles, the Lemko Republic's leader, Iaroslav Karchmarchyk, was meeting with Poland's prime minister, from whom he received assurances that the Polish government would not interfere in the affairs of the Lemko Republic until final decisions were reached at the Paris Peace Conference. Nonetheless, Polish army troops broke up manifestations in the Lemko Region and by late April 1919 arrested and put on trial the Reverend Iurchakevych for his pro-Czechoslovak activity. In the end, when diplomatic decisions finally came, they were not favorable to the Lemkos.

On May 8, 1919, Rusyns living south of the Carpathians declared at Uzhhorod their desire for union with Czechoslovakia. During the following week of talks at the Uzhhorod Central Rusyn National Council, representatives of the Lemkos asked to be included as well, but the Rusyn-American immigrant activist Gregory Zhatkovych, who later became first governor of Czechoslovakia's province of Subcarpathian Rus', opposed any union of the Lemko Region, which he considered would complicate further the yet unresolved border of Galicia.[10] Then, in June 1919, the Paris Peace Conference authorized the Polish government to occupy temporarily all of Galicia, which in theory remained under the ultimate authority of the Allied and

---

[9]*The Origin of the Lems, Slavs of Danubian Provenance: Memorandum to the Peace Conference Concerning Their National Claims* [Paris, 1919].

[10]*Protokoly obshchago sobraniia podkarpatskikh russkikh rad i pervykh 5-ti zasiedanii Tsentral'noi Russkoi Narodnoi Rady* (Uzhhorod, 1919). The question of territorial unity with the Lemko Region was discussed at Uzhhorod during the second day (May 9). It was raised by Dmytro Vislots'kyi, secretary of the Prešov National Council and native of the Lemko Region. The Rusyn-American Zhatkovych, who at the time had the greatest political influence among those assembled, expressed particular dismay over those Galician leaders (Russophiles who sometimes spoke on behalf of the Lemkos) who called for union with "Great Russia"; this, he felt, would undermine the efforts of Carpatho-Rusyns to find an advantageous political position within Czechoslovakia.

Associated Powers.

Rebuffed by fellow Rusyns south of the mountains, Karchmarchyk returned for a while to the idea of union with Russia, even if it would be under Bolshevik rule.[11] But considering the anarchic conditions in the East, union with a Russia of whatever political orientation seemed as unlikely as ever. Realizing that the international situation was working against them, on March 12, 1920 Karchmarchyk convened a second all-Lemko national congress, once again at Florynka and this time with 600 delegates. At that meeting, a government for the Lemko Rusyn Republic was formerly established, with Dr. Iaroslav Karchmarchyk as president; the Reverend Dmytro Khyliak as minister for internal affairs; the Reverend Vasyl' Kurylo as minister of foreign affairs; and Mykola Hromosiak as minister of agriculture. The Florynka congress also authorized the Lemko government to initiate once again contacts with the government of Czechoslovakia in an effort to be united with their Rusyn brethren south of the mountains.

By 1920, however, Poland and Czechoslovakia had strained relations over other areas along their long common border in Silesia (Cieszyn/ Těšín) and Slovakia (Orava-Spiš), so that neither needed the Lemko Region to be added to its problems. Thus, before the end of March, the Poles arrested Karchmarchyk and the rest of his government, effectively putting an end to the sixteen-month existence of the Lemko Rusyn Republic. More than one year later, on June 10, 1921, Karchmarchyk, Khyliak, and Hromosiak were put on trial. They were accused of trying to separate the Lemko Region from Poland and of promoting internal

---

[11]From the moment back on December 13, 1918, when at a meeting in Sanok the Lemko leaders Karchmarchyk and Iurkachevych joined Galician Russophiles in calling for union with Russia (see above, note 7), the leading prewar Galician Russophile spokesperson, former Austrian parliamentary deputy Dmitrii Markov, was empowered to speak on behalf of Lemkos. For instance, he presented the Lemko declaration made at the Florynka national congress to France's influential prime minister, Georges Clemenceau. Markov was clearly anti-Bolshevik and preferred to see some kind of democratic Russian state or even a return to tsarism. See his *Mémoire sur les aspirations nationales des Petits-Russiens de l'ancien empire austro-hongrois* [Paxis, 1919] and *Belgium of the East: An Interview with Dr. Dimitri A. Markoff* (Wilkes-Barre, Pa., 1920). According to Kohutov, "Lemkivshchyna," p. 6, the Lemko republic also dispatched two representatives to the "Soviet Union" in the spring of 1919.

conflict in the area. Although all three were acquitted of the charges, any hopes for Lemko self-government or union with Czechoslovakia definitely ended. In March 1923, the Allied and Associated Powers made a final decision regarding this part of the former Austro-Hungarian Empire. Galicia in its entirety was recognized as a part of Poland. This meant that the Lemko Region, like Ukrainian-inhabited East Galicia, became integral parts of the Polish administrative system with no provisions for any kind of territorial autonomy.

There remain several aspects of the Lemko Rusyn Republic that still need to be clarified. The basic chronology of events has not yet been established, and in existing secondary accounts they are related in a contradictory manner.[12] Furthermore, what did the texts of the Florynka national council's memoranda actually say? When and how did the change from a pro-Russian to pro-Czechoslovak political orientation actually take place? How did the Lemko government administer its territory? What territory did it actually claim and what did it effectively administer? These are only some of the basic questions that await scholarly research. Yet, as interesting as the Lemko Republic may be in and of itself, what, if anything, does it tell us about broader problems in this part of east-central Europe?

Perhaps the problem that the story of the Lemko Republic most effectively illuminates is the evolution of political thought among the East Slavic population of the former Austro-Hungarian Empire, specifically territory in eastern Galicia, northern Bukovina, and northeastern Hungary. For the sake of discussion, these three regions will be referred to as a single unit called western Rus', whose population was then known as Rusyn and today as Ukrainian.

Modern political thought in western Rus' could be said to date from 1848, when the revolution that began in that year in Austria-Hungary

---

[12]For instance, most authors mentioned above in note 2 refer to the Lemko Republic existing sixteen months and ending with the arrest of its leaders in March 1920, yet Kohutov, "Lemkivshchyna," pp. 7-8, states the arrest and end of the republic did not come until January 1921. Similarly, Kohutov states the whole movement began with the meeting at Gładyszów on October 30, 1918, while according to Horbaľ, "Lemkivs'ka respublyka," p. 5, that meeting took place on October 9. These are some examples of the many inconsistencies in the existing accounts.

opened up new possibilities for the many nationalities of the empire. The Rusyn/Ukrainians of western Rus' also took an active role in what became known throughout much of east-central Europe as the Spring of Nations. Two basic principles were initiated in 1848, and they were to remain the cornerstones of western Rus' political thought for the rest of the nineteenth and beginning of the twentieth century until the final collapse of Austria-Hungary in late 1918. These principles were: (1) that western Rus'—eastern Galicia, northern Bukovina, and northeastern Hungary—should be united, because the East Slavic inhabitants who lived there were on linguistic and cultural grounds the same people who called themselves Rusyns (*rusyny*); and (2) that since these Rusyns of Austria-Hungary were linguistically and culturally related to other East Slavs in what was at the time the Russian Empire, they should at the very least maintain cultural relations with their brethren in the East if not, as some leaders would later propose, be united with them in one state.[13]

Whereas most western Rus' spokespersons would, without exception, agree with these two basic principles, a problem arose as to the extent of the relationship to the rest of the East Slavic world. Concern with defining the specifics of the eastern relationship increased already during the last decades of the nineteenth century, but this became particularly crucial with the end of Austro-Hungarian rule in late 1918.

In short, that relationship could be visualized as consisting of three concentric circles. The first and largest circle comprised the former Austro-Hungarian or western Rus' lands together with the entire East Slavic world, referred to as Russia. This was commonly called the Russophile view. The second circle was smaller, including the western Rus' lands joined only to the southern branch of the East Slavs, namely the Ukrainians. This was called the Ukrainophile view. The third and last circle was narrower still, comprising only part of the western Rus' lands—specifically the Lemko Region (the East Slavic lands of Galicia

---

[13]For the details on western Rus' political thought in the second half of the nineteenth century, see Paul Robert Magocsi, *The Shaping of a National Identity: Subcarpathian Rus', 1848-1948* (Cambridge, Mass., 1978), pp. 42-75; Mykhailo Lozyns'kyi, "Obopil'ni stosunky mizh Velykoiu Ukraïnoiu i Halychynoiu v istoriï rozvytku ukraïns'koï politychnoï dumky XIX i XX v.," *Ukraïna*, V, 2 (Kiev, 1928), pp. 83-90; and O.A. Monchalovskii, *Sviataia Rus'* (L'viv, 1903).

west of the San River) together with the Prešov Region and Subcarpathian Rus' (the former northeastern counties of Hungary). This last approach, which retained a sense of cultural affinity with the East but which was satisfied with a reduced territorial base, was known as the Carpatho-Rusyn view.[14]

It is interesting to note that all three political orientations in western Rus' adapted to the new political reality of the immediate post-World War I era. For instance, the traditionally conservative and pro-tsarist Russophile orientation included some leaders who were willing to accept the idea of union with Russia even if under Bolshevik rule. For their part, Ukrainophiles were willing to sacrifice the idea of a united Ukrainian state (Soborna Ukraïna) if they could be assured of wide-ranging autonomy or independence for at least a western Ukrainian (East Galician) state.[15] Rusynophiles both north and south of the Carpathian mountains moved from the idea of some kind of vague unity with the East to the more realistic possibility of union with a democratic Czechoslovakia from whom they expected guarantees of autonomy. No orientation, however, ever considered association with Poland as an acceptable option.

The Lemko Region, which was examined above in some detail during the immediate postwar era, experienced all three western Rus'

---

[14]An expanded variant of the third circle existed as long as the Austro-Hungarian Empire existed. It encompassed all the western Rus' lands whose Old Ruthenian leaders, as they were known, maintained a political vision that basically was encompassed by the borders of the Habsburg Empire. The viability of such a territory, which was called Carpathian Rus', ended in 1918, after which the narrower third circle described here became a concrete and, as some thought, more feasible political goal. Cf. Paul Robert Magocsi, "Old Ruthenianism and Russophilism: A New Conceptual Framework for Analyzing National Ideologies in Late 19th-Century Eastern Galicia," in Paul Debreczyn, ed., *American Contributions to the Ninth International Congress of Slavists*, Vol. II (Columbus, Ohio, 1983), pp. 305-324.

[15]Such an orientation, which looked for a revival of the medieval Galician-Volhynian Kingdom through the establishment of an independent West Ukrainian Republic was not completely eliminated as a political option until the 1923 decision of the Allied and Associated Powers. Cf. Mykhailo Lozyns'kyi, *Za derzhavnu nezalezhnist' Halychyny: chomu ukraïns'ka Halychyna ne mozhe pryity pid Pol'shchu* (Vienna, 1921); *Nekhai zhyve Nezalezhna Halyts'ka Derzhava: zbirka statei* (Vienna, 1922); *The Case for the Independence of Galicia* (London, 1922).

political orientations. Of the two national councils and Lemko republics which evolved in late 1918, the short-lived one in the eastern Lemko village of Komańcza was clearly Ukrainian in orientation; the longer lasting republic in the western Lemko centers of Florynka/Grzybów moved between the Russian and Carpatho-Rusyn orientation.

For the rest of the interwar period, all three of the traditional political orientations remained options for the Rusyn population whether in Poland or Czechoslovakia. Russophilism was propagated by local conservatives, who together with newly-arrived Russian émigrés hoped for a phoenix-like rebirth of a democratic, even a tsarist Russia, as well as by left-wing Communist activists who hoped some day to be included in a Bolshevik Russia that at most might pay lip-service to the national distinctions among the East Slavs.[16] As for Ukrainophilism, it seemed to be the dominant force in Polish-ruled Galicia, and it was a growing movement in Czechoslovakia's Subcarpathian Rus' as well. Through both legal political movements and underground conspiratorial activity, Ukrainians awaited the day when Europe's boundaries would be revised and the western Rus' lands would finally end up in an independent, non-Bolshevik Ukrainian state.[17] Finally, the Rusynophile orientation flourished primarily south of the Carpathians, where its leaders hoped to reach a permanent settlement with Czechoslovak authorities that would grant them political and cultural autonomy as an East Slavic people somehow distinct from both Ukrainians and Russians. Such

[16]For the conservative view, see N. Pavlovich, *Russkaia kul'tura i Podkarpatskaia Rus'*, Izdanie Obshchestva im. A. Dukhnovicha, No. 23 (Uzhhorod, 1926); Antonii Lukovich, *Natsional'naia i iazykovaia prinadlezhnost' russkago naseleniia Podkarpatskoi Rusi*, Izdanie Obshchestva im. A. Dukhnovicha, No. 40 (Uzhhorod, 1929); and Ivan Teodorovich, "Lemkovskaia Rus'," *Nauchno-literaturnyi sbornik Galitsko-russkoi Matitsy*, VIII (L'viv, 1934), pp. 10-21. For the Communist view, see I.K. Vasiuta and Iu. Iu. Slyvka, "Borot'ba trudiashchykh Zakhidnoï Ukraïny, Bukovyny i Zakarpattia . . . za vozz'iednannia z Radians'koiu Ukraïnoiu," in M.M. Oleksiuk et al., eds. *Torzhestvo istorychnoï spravedlyvosti* (L'viv, 1968), pp. 434-479.

[17]Bohdan Budurowycz, "Poland and the Ukrainian Problem, 1921-1939," *Canadian Slavonic Papers*, XXV, 4 (Toronto, 1983), pp. 473-500; Alexander I. Motyl, *The Turn to the Right: The Ideological Origins and Development of Ukrainian Nationalism, 1919-1929* (Boulder, Colo. and New York, 1980), esp. pp. 129-161; Magocsi, *Shaping of a National Identity*, esp. pp. 227-233.

attitudes also remained alive among the Lemko Rusyns in Poland during the interwar years and were expressed through cultural and educational activity, including the creation in 1934 of a distinct Greek Catholic ecclesiastical jurisdiction, the Lemko Apostolic Administration.[18] It is therefore not surprising that during the wide ranging political changes that took place both on the eve of (1939) and toward the close of (1944) World War II, the Lemko Rusyns issued feelers calling for unification with their brethren south of the mountains into a single entity called Carpathian Rus'.[19]

Thus, at least in the realm of political thought, the Ukrainian question in both Poland and Czechoslovakia during the interwar years reflected patterns that had been established already during the second half of the nineteenth century. With the close of World War II and the dominant presence of Soviet power in the region, the traditional three-fold Russophile/Ukrainophile/Rusynophile political options seemed to have little validity, since most of the western Rus' lands were united with the rest of the East Slavic world, albeit within the context of a Soviet state and its politcally subordinate allies, Poland and Czechoslovakia. In such a situation, the traditional tripartite debates within western Rus' political thought were suppressed in favor of an administratively-imposed Ukrainian orientation. However, with the political changes instigated after 1985 by Mikhail Gorbachev in the Soviet Union and the Revolution of 1989 in East Central Europe, the old debates in the western Rus' world about national and therefore political identity have been revived once again. But that is a subject for another essay.[20]

[18]Jan Húsek, "Rodí se podkarpatoruský národ?," *Podkarpatoruská revue*, I, 7-8 (Bratislava, 1936), pp. 6-8; Magocsi, *Shaping of a National Identity*, esp. pp. 106-110 and 221-224; I.F. Lemkin, *Ystoryia Lemkovynŷ* (Yonkers, N.Y., 1969), pp. 154-175.
[19]Ivan Vanat, *Narysy novitn'oï istoriï ukraïnstiv Skhidnoï Slovachchyny*, Vol. II (Bratislava and Prešov, 1985), p. 220.
[20]See below Chapters 14, 15, and 16.

CHAPTER 14

Nation-Building or Nation Destroying?: Lemkos, Poles, and Ukrainians in Contemporary Poland[*]

I n 1972, the political scientist Walker Conner published in *World Politics* a provocative and still seminal essay entitled "Nation-Building or Nation-Destroying?," in which he chided scholars and political analysts concerned with state integration for having systematically avoided and effectively discounted as an "ephemeral nuisance" the existence—and persistence—of national or ethnic minorities in modern states, even those in western European countries which had ostensibly attained political integration decades if not centuries ago.[1]

Conner's essay remains a valuable corrective to the literature on nationalism and political integration, since it forces the reader to realize that the existence—some would say problem—of national or ethnic

---

[*] This study was presented as part of a panel, "Ethnocultural Survival in Borderland Regions," at the XX Annual Convention of the American Association for the Advancement of Slavic Studies, held in Honolulu, Hawaii on November 18-21, 1988, and it was delivered in Polish at a conference, "Lemkos and Their Political Orientations," at the University of Warsaw, December 2-3, 1989. It was first published under the same title in the *Polish Review*, XXXV, 3/4 (New York, 1990), pp. 197-209; and subsequently in Ukrainian translation, "Natsiotvorennia chy natsionyshchennia? Lemky, poliaky i ukraïntsi v suchasnii Pol'shchi," in Pavlo Robert Magochii, *Halychyna: istorychne ese* (L'viv: Toronts'kyi universytet, Katedra ukraïnoznavchykh studiï, 1994), pp. 304-322.

[1] Walker Conner, "Nation-Building or Nation-Destroying?," *World Politics*, XXIV, 3 (Princeton, N.J., 1972), pp. 319-355.

minorities is not the exceptional remnant of underdeveloped regions but rather the vibrantly alive and growing norm in modern states throughout the world. East-central Europe is certainly no stranger to the existence of multinational states whether in the past or present. In this regard, one of the region's typical states is Poland, which remains today, as it has throughout history, a country comprised of several national or ethnic groups.[2] Among those groups are the Lemkos.

Who are the Lemkos? What is their present status and potential future? What is their relationship to the country's dominant ethnic group, the Poles, and to the group with which they are officially associated, the Ukrainians? Or, to borrow Conner's terminology, does the existence of Lemkos represent a nation-building or nation-destroying element vis-à-vis the Poles, the Ukrainians, or both?

The Lemkos represent the westernmost element of the East Slavic world.[3] They have lived since the Middle Ages along the northern slopes and valleys of the Beskyd and Bieszczady ranges of the Carpathian Mountains. Historically, this was a border region between Catholic Poland and Orthodox Kievan Rus'. Until the fourteenth century, the area was part of Kiev's Galician Rus' kingdom; from the 1340s until 1772, it was in the Polish Kingdom; from 1772 to 1918 part of Habsburg Austria's province of Galicia; and since that time (with the exception of the German occupation during World War II) part of Poland. The historic province of Austrian Galicia was divided into western and eastern spheres separated by the San River, which also corresponded roughly to the ethnographic boundary between West Slavs

---

[2]Certainly, in territorially-reduced and ethnically "purer" post-World War II Poland, the proportion of minorities is much less than the 32 percent of the population during the interwar years. Today, less than 2 percent of Poland's population of 36.5 million people (1983) comprise national minorities. These include Ukrainians (350,000), Belorusans (165,000), Slovaks (22,000) Gypsies (15,000), Lithuanians (12,000), Russians (10,000), Greeks, Macedonians, and Czechs (5,000). S.I. Bruk, *Naselenie mira: ètnodemograficheskii spravochnik* (Moscow, 1986), p. 246.

[3]There is a significant body of literature on the Lemkos. For an introduction to their historical evolution, see Paul Robert Magocsi, "Lemko Rusyns: Their Past and Present," *Carpatho-Rusyn American*, X, I (Fairview, N.J., 1987), pp. 5-12. For futher literature on the subject, see Tadeusz Zagórzański, *Łemkowie i Łemkowszczyzna: materiały do bibliografii* (Warsaw, 1984).

(Poles) west of the river and East Slavs (Rusyns/Ukrainians) east of the river.[4] An exception were the East Slavic Lemkos, who lived west of the San River, and therefore were surrounded by lowlands to the north and west that were inhabited by Poles and to the south by the mountain crest beyond which were fellow East Slavic Rusnaks in what until 1918 had been the Hungarian Kingdom and thereafter Czechoslovakia.

As East Slavs and, therefore, as part of the world of Eastern Christianity, the Lemkos traditionally identified themselves—or more precisely distinguished themselves from neighboring peoples of different religion—by use of the names Rusnak or Rusyn, that is, the people of Rus'. The term Rus' had since the Middle Ages, become synonymous with Orthodox Eastern Christianity. During the seventeenth and eighteenth centuries, the East Slavs gradually began to differentiate themselves, and this process intensified during the nineteenth and early twentieth centuries by which time the term Rus' and its derivatives were being replaced by various ethnic names—Russian, Belorusan, and Ukrainian. The Lemkos were faced with the option to maintain their traditional name, Rusnak/Rusyn, or to adopt one of the more ethnically specific names, such as Russian, or perhaps Ukrainian, which was becoming increasingly popular among the East Slavs closest to them on the eastern side of the San River. In the end, the Lemkos chose neither option. By the outset of the twentieth century, all East Slavs in the Carpathian region and throughout the province of Austrian Galicia still called themselves Rusyns. However, one faction of the intelligentsia in East Galicia, known as the populists, argued that the term Rusyn was just an older equivalent of the modern name Ukrainian and that it would be preferable to use the new name as a means of national self-identification. With the help of the Austrian government, especially after the 1890s, the name Ukrainian gained increasing popularity among the population of eastern Galicia. But west of the San River where the Lemko Rusyns lived, the local intelligentsia actively opposed adopting the new name, Ukrainian. Moreover, in an effort to distinguish

---

[4]To be precise, the Lemkos do not even reach as far east as the upper San River, but rather only the valley between that river's tributaries, the Osława and Solinka, which is considered by many scholars as the eastern boundary of the Lemko Region. Cf. Roman Reinfuss, "Łemkowie jako grupa etnograficzna," *Prace i materiały etnograficzne*, VII (Lublin, 1948-49), pp. 84-102.

themselves from those who called themselves Ukrainian, Lemko spokespersons even went so far as to downplay the use of their own historic name Rusnak/Rusyn and thereby hope to distance themselves from the alleged Rusyn/Ukrainian nomenclature equivalency. In short, they adopted an entirely new name—Lemko.[5]

Thus, the Rusyns on both sides of the San River in old Austrian Galicia were trying to rid themselves of their historic name, Rusyn, although for different reasons. The populist-Ukrainians did so because they feared the name Rusyn was being confused with Russian; the Lemkos did so because Rusyn was being described as an older equivalent for Ukrainian, a name with which they feared being confused. In this regard, it is interesting to note that many Lemkos did not fear confusion with Russians, and some, recalling their historic name Rusyn whenever it was convenient, would openly embrace what they supposed was their association and identity as Russian. What is important to remember for future developments is that the very term Lemko began—and for some remained—a rejection of association with things Ukrainian.

But why should the question of identity with Ukrainians be a problem for Lemkos? Stated most simply, if Lemkos are East Slavs, and if the East Slavic inhabitants of the Carpathians and Galicia have come to be designated as Ukrainians, then the Lemkos are Ukrainians, too. Since modern Slavic scholarship accepts the modern term Ukrainian for the East Slavic inhabitants of the area—not to speak of the official position of the countries that rule the area (Poland, the Soviet-Union, Czechoslovakia)—then Lemkos are simply a tribe or ethnographic group of Ukrainians.

By the same taxonomic logic, the Francophone Walloons and Occitans are French; the Germanic Luxembourgers and Austrians are Germans; and if one were to accept earlier and even some present-day writings, the South Slavic Macedonians are Bulgarians, and the East Slavic Belorusans and Ukrainians are Russians. As is obvious from the few examples just mentioned, such classification—often based on

[5]Bohdan Struminsky, "The Name of the Lemkos and of Their Territory," in Jacob P. Hursky, ed., *Studies in Ukrainian Linguistics in Honor of George Y. Shevelov*, in *Annals of the Ukrainian Academy of Arts and Sciences in the United States*, XV (New York, 1985), pp. 301-307.

linguistic criteria—may be acceptable in terms of modern-day concepts of national identity for certain groups, but certainly not for others. In one sense, the problem of the Lemkos in Poland stems from the contrasting and often contradictory manner by which they are classified on the one hand by scholars and governments, and on the other by the way they perceive themselves.

The question of self-perception leads to the issue of regional identity and the related problem of what has been called the phenomenon of multiple identities. It is quite natural that individuals have several levels of identity based on family, village/town, region, ethnographic group, national group/nationality, and country, and that these identities may be complementary.[6] Thus, a person from the town of Arles mear the mouth of the Rhône River in southern France could be perfectly comfortable in choosing to identify him or herself simultaneously as an Arlésien (town), Rhodanien (region), Provençal (ethnographic group), Occitan (nationality), and French (country). Analogously, a Macedonian born in Moskohori could simultaneously identify as a Moskohorin (village), Kastorian (region), Macedonian or Slavophone (ethnographic group or nationality), and Greek (nationality or country). In the case of the Lemkos, a person born in Bartne/Bortne could simultaneously identify as a Bortnianyn (village), Gorlician (region), Lemko (ethnographic group), Ukrainian, Russian, or Carpatho-Rusyn (nationality), and Polish (country).

Such a complementary hierarchy of multiple identities would, in Conner's terminology, contribute to France's, Greece's, or Poland's nationbuilding process. However, the traditional problem in the Lemko (and for that matter in the Provençal/Occitan and Macedonian/Slavophone/Greek) hierarchy of multiple identities has been the ethnographic and nationality categories. Is Lemko only an ethnographic category? If so, then Lemkos are simply an ethnographic group belonging to the Ukrainian, Russian, or (together with their brethren just south of the mountains) Carpatho-Rusyn nationality? Or should the ethnographic and

---

[6]On the question of multiple identities, see David M. Potter, "The Historian's Use of Nationalism and Vice-Versa, " *American Historical Review*, LXVII, 4 (New York, 1962), esp. pp. 924-938; and Paul Robert Magocsi, "The Ukrainian National Revival: A New Analytical Framework," *Canadian Review of Studies in Nationalism*, XVI, 1-2 (Charlottetown, Prince Edward Island, 1989), pp. 45-62.

nationality categories be collapsed into one, with Lemko serving as a designator for a distinct nationality. The ethnographic-nationality dichotomy, or the question of whether Lemkos are a distinct nationality or part of a larger nationality, remains to this day an unresolved theoretical issue for Lemko leaders and a practical problem of self-perception for the Lemko people in general.

In one sense, it is surprising that such a problem still exists at all, since based on what is often expected as the overwhelming assimilationist tendencies of modern industrialized societies, the question of Lemko self-identity should have been decided long ago. Such assimilationist tendencies were enhanced in 1947 by the forcible removal of the Lemkos from their Carpathian homeland and their dispersal generally in small groups throughout cities and towns in western and northern Poland.[7] Driven from their homeland, resettled in a Polish environment, lacking any Lemko cultural or other organizations, having one of their churches (Greek Catholic) proscribed and the other (Orthodox) limited in its activity in a Roman Catholic environment, and finally having to send their children only to Polish schools—all these factors would certainly lead one to expect the complete assimilation of the younger generation born in the "emigration." Logic would seem to dictate that with the passing away of the older generation born and raised in the Carpathian homeland before the deportation, the Lemkos would eventually disappear and this problem would be resolved.

Yet, forty years after the dispersal of Lemkos from their homeland and after the birth and acculturation of at least one generation in the emigration, it seems that the Lemko problem has not gone away. In a

---

[7]The fate of the Lemkos was part of a larger trend in many places during the immediate post-World War II years to clean up ethnically-mixed border areas through a program of population transfers and exchanges. In Poland this affected both Ukrainians and Lemkos living along the country's southeastern borders. Of the 180,000 Lemkos in 1945, 120,000 opted or were administratively encouraged to go to the Soviet Ukraine between 1946 and 1947; of the 60,000 who remained, mostly in the westernmost Lemko Region, they were forcibly deported by the Polish government in the spring and summer of 1947 (having been accused of aiding the Ukrainian Insurgent Army—UPA) to newly acquired lands (Ziemie odzyskanie) in western and northern Poland (Silesia, Warmia, Pomerania, northern Mazuria) that had previously belonged to Germany.

real—sense as is evident from the Polish press in the 1980s—not only have the Lemkos not gone away; on the contrary, they are going through a revival, a rebirth, a rediscovery of their roots. Not surprisingly, this revival has prompted a restatement of the identity question. Who are the Lemkos—a distinct people (perhaps part of a Rusyn/Rusnak people living in the Carpathians—including, in particular, the Rusnaks in neighboring Czechoslovakia), or simply an ethnographic group that is part of a larger nationality: Ukrainian, perhaps Russian, or even Polish?

Two important factors have contributed to the recent Lemko revival. By the outset of 1980s, Poland had entered the Solidarity period of its recent history, at which time the country's inhabitants, of whatever social or national background, were swept up by a mood that called for increased criticism of present-day realities and for an inquiry into the recent past that created those realities. The 1980s also witnessed the coming of age of a new generation of Lemkos born in the emigration, who by then had reached their twenties and thirties—that classic age for self-discovery, whether as individuals or as members of a group.

During the 1980s, the Lemko revival has witnessed the following type of activity: (1) the publication of poetry in the Lemko vernacular[8]; (2) newspaper articles (mostly by non-Lemkos) on aspects of the Lemko past, especially the post-World War II deportations and the question of national identity[9]; and annual cultural festivals (Vatra), which since 1983 have each year attracted upwards of 5,000 Lemkos from all parts of Poland who in the month of July descend upon some

[8]Among the poets who have recently published Lemko, bilingual Lemko/Polish, or Lemko verse translated into Polish are: Olena Duts (*W modlitewnym bluźnierstwie*, 1985); Vladislav Hraban (*Twarz pośród cieni*, 1984); Petro Murianka (*Suchy badyl*, 1983, *Murianchŷsko*, 1984, *Jak sokół wodę z kamienia/Jak sokil vody na kameny*, 1989); Pavlo Stefanovskyi (*Lemkivs'ka ikona*, 1985); and Stefaniia Trokhanovska (*Potem, teraz, przedtem*, 1984).

[9]See the extensive list of newspaper articles in Andrzej A. Zięba, "The Lemko Question in the Polish Press, 1980-1986," *Carpatho-Rusyn American*, XI, 1 (Fairview, N.J., 1988), pp. 9-11. The recent number of books, articles, and other studies appearing within and beyond Poland about the group is no less impressive. See the 94 entries on the Lemko-Region/Lemkovshchyna/Lemkos in Paul Robert Magocsi, *Carpatho-Rusyn Studies: An Annotated Bibliography*, Vol. I: *1975-1984* (New York, 1988).

remote Carpathian village in an effort to rediscover or be exposed for the first time to the traditional Lemko heritage.

The very existence of such activity has raised administrative concerns and, by extension, the nationality question, both in terms of the problem of self-identity and the relationship of the group to the Polish state. These problems have become most evident with regard to the Vatra festival. When the organizers planned to hold their first one, in 1983, they were told by the Polish authorities that since Lemkos were Ukrainians they could only hold such affairs if they were sponsored by or under the aegis of the officially recognized cultural organization for Ukrainians in Poland, the USKT (Ukraïns'ke Sotsio-kul'turne Tovarystvo—Ukrainian Civic and Cultural Society).

Ever since 1956, when the USKT was founded, Lemkos have played an important role in that organization. However, the new generation of Lemko activists in the 1980s was displeased with how the USKT had treated the Lemkos in the past, and in any case some began to argue that Lemkos were a group distinct from Ukrainians and therefore deserving of their own cultural organization. Not surprisingly, USKT leaders (Lemko as well as non-Lemko Ukrainians) branded such demands by the Vatra organizers as "separatism." Nonetheless, the "separatists" persisted and the first Vatra took place followed by others annually that have been marked by increasing popularity and success.[10]

·What exists today in Poland is a classic example of an intelligentsia-inspired national movement. Namely, there are people who in some way identify as Lemkos and whose "interests" are represented by a small group of intellectuals—cultural activists and writers in the most generous sense of the word. Some of these leaders argue that Lemkos are Ukrainians and should function within Poland's Ukrainian society; others argue that Lemkos should not be lumped together with Ukrainians because they represent a distinct group; still others are not certain which orientation to support.[11]

---

[10]From the outset of the Vatra festivals, the organizers have been Vladislav Hraban, Petro Trokhanovskyi (pseudonym: Murianka), and Olena Duts, all three of whom are among the 10,000 or so Lemkos who have returned to live in the Carpathian homeland since the late 1950s.

[11]The independentist Lemkos include mostly members of the younger generation: Olena Duts (Duć), Vladislav Hraban, Iaroslav Horoshchak-Hunka, Andrei Kopcha (Kopcza), and Petro Trokhanovskyi (Trochanowski). The pro-Ukrainian Lemkos

Somewhat on the sideline are the Polish authorities. On the one hand, ever since World War II, Communist spokespersons in Poland have accepted the view that Lemkos are a branch of Ukrainians. After all, it was the unfounded charge of Ukrainian bourgeois nationalism and the supposed massive participation of Lemkos in support of the anti-Communist Ukrainian Insurgent Army (UPA), which was given in 1947 as the government's justification for the forcible deportation of Lemkos. On the other hand, those same authorities have permitted the unofficial Lemko "separatist" Vatra festivals to take place, although it would seem this is a result of the Polish government's inability to control many (and from its point of view much more dangerous) kinds of unofficial activity. Also, in the "Polish camp" are several Polish scholars and publicists who have written recently about the Lemko revival, describing and often siding with either the Ukrainian or Lemko orientations.[12]

The position of the Polish authorities is, not surprisingly, viewed quite differently by the participants in this process. Ukrainian and pro-Ukrainian Lemko commentators (in the Soviet Union and North America as well as in Poland) consider the "Lemko separatists"—if they mention them at all—to comprise a small group of misguided enthusiasts whose activity is "supported" by the Polish government and by "concerned" Polish writers precisely because their presence contributes to a weakening of the Ukrainian element within Poland. Polish society, it is said, has in any case been traditionally fiercely anti-Ukrainian, and the postwar Communist regime, like its interwar non-Communist predecessors, have always followed a policy of *divide et*

include the long-time cultural and political activists Mykhal Donskyi, Fedir Goch (Gocz), Mykhal Koval'skyi, Pavlo Stefanovskyi (Stefanowski), all three of whom in the 1960s spoke out forcefully that Lemkos were distinct from Ukrainians and should have their own distinct organizations. The pro-Ukrainian Lemkos have been encouraged by Volodymyr Mokryi, a professor of Ukrainian background at Cracow's Jagiellonian University and recently-elected member of the Polish parliament, and by Ivan Krasovs'kyi, a prolific author on Lemko affairs who is from L'viv in the Soviet Ukraine.

[12]Among the more well-known Polish sympathizers have been the art historian Ryszard Brykowski, the ethnographer Antoni Kroh, the historian Tadeusz Olszański, and the controversial poet Jerzy Harasymowicz, who has frequently included Lemko themes in his writings.

impera in order to weaken and eventually absorb through assimilation ethnically non-Polish groups.[13] According to this scenario, the Lemko separatists are playing into the hands of the Poles, or even worse, they are accused of being Russophiles (Muscophiles) and therefore traitors to the Ukrainian cause. Regardless of what they are accused, if such recalcitrant Lemkos do not recognize their Ukrainianness, the argument goes, they will simply become assimilated Poles.

It seems, moreover, that ideological intransigence on the question of national identity is the predominant attitude. To cite only one of many examples let us turn to an active spokesperson in the West for Polish-Ukrainian reconciliation, the American university professor, Jaroslaw Pelenski, himself of Ukrainian background. When asked by a Polish-American interviewer whether Lemkos were Ukrainians or a separate nationality, the otherwise intellectually tolerant Pelenski, who was otherwise critical of "nationalist prejudices," could himself find no room for compromise or even nuance on this issue. "If we characterize the Kashubs as Poles [which is not necessarily what all Kashubes themselves nor all scholars have done—PRM] then the Lemkos should definitely be characterized as Ukrainians. An attempt to invent a separate Lemko nationality in order to divide the Ukrainian community in Poland, for whatever purpose, reminds me of certain pre-1945 German efforts to divide the Poles. . . . It is the concensus not only of Ukrainian, but also of informed Polish scholarly opinion today, that the

---

[13]Polish-Ukrainian antipathy has a long history stretching back at least to the Cossack revolution of Bohdan Khmel'nyts'kyi in the seventeenth century, and it was fueled even more during the twentieth century by the Polish-Ukrainian war for Galicia in 1918-1919; terroristic acts by both sides during the 1920s; the Polish pacification of 1930; the mutual killing of underground military personnel, partisans, and civilians in an undeclared Polish-Ukrainian war between 1942 and 1947; the Communist Polish campaign against the Ukrainian Insurgent Army in 1946-1947; and the psychological terror against persons who identified as Ukrainian during the Stalinist era.

The past decade has seen efforts among Poles and Ukrainians both in Poland and the West to overcome their mutually destructive hate-filled sterotypes. The best reflection of this new attitude is Kazimierz Podlaski, *Białorusini—Litwini—Ukraińcy: naszi wrogowie czy bracia* (Warsaw, 1983; 2nd rev. ed.: Warsaw, 1984 and London, 1985), in Ukrainian translation as *Bilorusy—Litovtsi—Ukraïntsi: nashi vorohy—chy braty?* (Munich, 1986).

Lemkos are an integral part of the Ukrainian people exhibiting their own distinct regional and dialectal peculiarities."[14] Similarly, the very text of this essay, first delivered at the American Association for the Advancement of Slavic Studies in November 1988 and then at a conference on the Lemko question at the University of Warsaw in December 1989, was described (but never published) in the Polish press and then fiercely criticized for "separatist" or historically antiquated tendencies by Ukrainians and Ukrainian-oriented Lemkos in the Soviet Union and in the United States.[15]

In contrast, the non-Ukrainian-oriented Lemkos feel that the process of assimilation among the younger generation has occurred, in part, precisely *because* with the help of Polish government policy Lemkos have since the 1950s been identified as Ukrainians—an identity, moreover, which was hardly an easy one to have in Stalinist Poland. Older Lemkos have responded to the situation with silence or have actively tried to hide their identity; younger Lemkos have often simply rejected their East Slavic origins and identified themselves as Poles. The non-Ukrainian-oriented Lemkos also argue that it is the Ukrainians who are recognized by the Polish government as a national group, and that with the help of that government they have consistently blocked recent attempts to create distinct Lemko organizations (including the

[14]"Polish-Ukrainian Relations: An Interview with Jaroslaw Pelenski," *Studium Papers*, XII, 2 (Ann Arbor, Mich., 1988), p. 50.

[15]The Polish reports were by Andrzej A. Zięba, "O Łemkach w Honolulu," *Tygodnik Powszechny*, XLIII, 12 (Cracow, 1989), p. 5; and Andrzej Chodkiewicz, "O Łemkach," *Ład*, VIII, 6 (Warsaw, 1990). The Ukrainian commentary began with Ivan Krasovs'kyi, "Kil'ka dumok u spravi Lemkiv: z pryvodu statti A. Ziemby 'O Lemkach w Honolulu')," *Nashe slovo* (Warsaw), July 30, 1989—reprinted in *Lemkivshchyna*, XI, 3 (Clifton, N.J., 1989), pp. 14-15. It was continued by Ivan Lyko, "Lemko-rusyn—ukraïnets'-'lemko'!," *ibid.*, XI, 4 (1989), pp. 12-14; Ivan Hvozda, "Podiï, iaki khvyliuiut' lemkivs'ku spil'notu, iak i vse ukraïns'ke suspil'stvo," *Lemkivshchyna*, XII, 1 (Clifton, N.J., 1990, pp. 6-11—reprinted in *Novyi shliakh* (Toronto), May 19, 26 and June 2, 1990; Myroslav Levyts'kyi, "Politychni ta suspil'ni napriamky sered lemkiv u XX stolitti," *Nashe slovo* (Warsaw), January 21, 1990; V. Mel'nyk, "Neorusynstvo i ioho interpretatory," *Zakarpats'ka pravda* (Uzhhorod), esp. pt. 4, August 24, 1990; Diura Latiak, "Ishche raz o Lemkokh u Honolulu," *Ruske slovo* (Novi Sad, Yugoslavia), June 27, 1990; and Mar'ian Koval's'kyi, "Retsenziia na . . . ," *Duklia*, XL, 3 (Prešov, 1992), pp. 53-59.

Vatra festivals when they were first held). This seems to make present-day Ukrainians no different from their predecessors who allegedly cooperated with the Austrian authorities in the deportation of Lemkos to the Talerhof internment camp during World War I, or who cooperated with Nazi German authorities in the incarceration and eventual death of some Lemkos in concentration camps during World War II. Finally, it was the supposedly misplaced identification of Lemkos as Ukrainians that led to their forced deportation en masse during the Vistula Operation (Akcja Wisła) in 1947.[16] From such a perspective, it would certainly seem that, there is no evident advantage for Lemkos to identify as Ukrainians. The result of such attitudes, or as some would say myths reinforced as they are by historical "proofs," has been increasing recrimination between Lemkos of Ukrainian and non-Ukrainian orientation.

Unfortunately, there has been no serious effort by either Lemkos or Ukrainians to address the issue of their mutually negative stereotypes. This could be done by investigating such past events as the 1914 deportation to Talerhof (at which Ukrainians are accused of denouncing Russophile Lemkos but who, in fact, were also incarcerated themselves), or the role played by Ukrainians (frequently from eastern Galicia) in the Nazi administration of the Lemko Region, which was part of Germany's Generalgouvernement from the very outbreak of World War II. Nor, for that matter, has there yet been any serious comparative analysis of Lemko support for varying military forces in the last years of World War II (Polish partisans, Red Army, Ukrainian Insurgent Army) with a discussion of what such support says, if anything, about the group's national orientation.[17]

---

[16]The preceding interpretation of recent developments in the twentieth century is most forcibly argued by a Lemko historian in post-World War II Poland, Ioann Polianskyi, whose manuscript was published in the United States under the pseudonym I.F. Lemkyn, *Ystoryia Lemkovyny*, (Yonkers, N.Y., 1969).

[17]Peter J. Potichnyj has provided a well-documented study of Lemkos who participated in the UPA, but the figures he produces are given in isolation and tell us nothing about the perhaps greater participation of Lemkos in the Polish partisan movement or the Red Army. See his unpublished manuscript, "The Lemkos in the Ukrainian National Movement After World War II," prepared for the session on Lemkos at the American Association for the Advancement of Slavic Studies National Convention held in Honolulu (November 1988).

Instead, both non-Ukrainian and pro-Ukrainian Lemko spokespersons have reiterated their ire based on frequently unsubstantiated generalizations. In the absence of serious analysis, attention has been focussed on symbolic "black sheep." For Ukrainians, their "black sheep" is Jerzy Harasymowicz, a well-known poet of unclear Polish-Ukrainian background who has written on Lemko themes and who recently has come under attack for favoring the generally negative stereotypes of Polish society toward Ukrainians.[18] For non-Ukrainian oriented Lemkos, their "black sheep" is Pavlo Stefanovskyi, a Lemko poet and cultural activist who in the past had often called for the legalization of separate Lemko organizations and who argued that Lemkos were a people distinct from Ukrainians, but who recently (the accusation says since his return from trips among wealthy Ukrainian immigrant communities in North America in the mid-1980s) has switched to a Ukrainian orientation.[19]

Before concluding, it might be useful to return to the formulation of Walker Conner expressed at the outset of this essay. Is the recent Lemko revival, which seeks to consider the group distinct from Ukrainians and Poles, an example of nation-building (from the perspective of Poland as a country) or nation-destroying (from the perspective of Ukrainian nationhood)? At the risk of moving from a descriptive to a prescriptive mode, I might in conclusion offer a few observations that bear more on the present and future than on the past. But before doing that, there is one other matter that should be mentioned.

We in the West frequently bask in the luxury of circumstances conducive to intellectual discussion that is safely removed by thousands

[18]On Harasymowicz's current views, see "Rozmowa *Gazety Krakowskiej* z Jerzym Harasymowiczem: chwast płomienisty i złowrogi—burzan nacjonalizmu," *Gazeta Krakowska* (Cracow), No. 135, June 11, 1986, p. 3, an article which prompted a spirited response by Mykhal Koval'skii, "Iezhy Harasymovychovy, poetovy—odkrytyi lyst," *Nashe slovo* (Warsaw), No. 31, September 7, 1988 ("lemkivs'ka storynka"), pp. 5-6; and Jerzy Harasymowicz, "Łemkom pod rozwagę," *Gazeta Krakowska* No. 168, July 19, 1989, pp. 1-4—translated as "To the Lemkos for Their Consideration," *Carpatho-Rusyn American*, XIII, 3 (Fairview, N.J., 1989), pp. 10-11, and followed by a commentary by A. Dryja.

[19]For Stefanovskyi's former anti-Ukrainian views, see the text of a 1959 memorandum to the Polish government co-signed by him and reprinted in "Ukraińcy w PRL—dokumenty," *Spotkania*, No. 12-13 (Warsaw, Lublin, and Cracow, 1980), pp. 158-171.

of miles from the territory and people under analysis. It should not be forgotten that what we frequently comment upon in theoretical and often clinically antiseptic terms are issues that have often created and still create for the individuals in question profound personal and psychological problems that for us outside observers from so far a distance might seem as a rather esoteric game.[20] Hopefully, without forgetting the human dimension, we can with greater sensitivity move on to some theoretical issues.

I would think that any dispassionate observer must admit in theory, and given the right conditions in practice, that Lemkos could develop into a distinct nationality. It was such a theoretical possibility, combined with the right conditions, that allowed Slovaks, Macedonians, and Ukrainians themselves, among many others, to evolve into distinct nationalities. There is, after all, no hard and fast rule based on either historical circumstance or intrinsic characteristics that would prevent—again under the right conditions—any group of people of whatever size from evolving into a distinct nationality.[21] Having accepted this premise, then one could ask whether the Lemko revival in Poland would best advance the preservation of an East Slavic Lemko heritage by becoming a distinct nationality or by becoming a regional

[20]Both Ukrainians and non-Ukrainian Lemkos in Poland—even those seemingly at odds with each other—have suffered remarkably similar fates. For an excellent insight into the current Ukrainian psyche, see Włodzimierz Mokry, "Dzisiejsza droga Rusina do Polski," *Tygodnik Powszechny*, nos. 46 and 47 (Cracow, 1981)—republished in a shortened English translation as "A Way to Go Home: One Ruthernian's Road to Present-Day Poland," *Studium Papers*, XII, 2 (Ann Arbor, Mich., 1988), pp. 29-33 and 41. For an insight into the non-Ukrainian Lemko psyche, see Jaroslav Hunka [Horoshchak], *Łemkowie—dzisiaj* (Warsaw, 1985)—republished in a full English translation in the *Carpatho-Rusyn American*, X, 4 (Fairview, N.J., 1988), pp. 4-8; and Piotr Trochanowski, "Słowo Łemka o sebie i swoim narodzie," *Regiony*, no. 2-4 [48] (Warsaw, 1987), pp. 5-15.

[21]For an interesting survey of the current status of small, in some cases still emerging peoples (Cornish, Occitans, Frisians, Friulans, Galicians, Sards) in western Europe, see Meic Stephens, *Linguistic Minorities in Western Europe* (Llandysul, Wales, 1976). For perhaps the ultimate example of a nationality that can be made "given the right conditions," even in a territory that is less than one square mile in size, see Paul Robert Magocsi, "Monaco Becomes Monégasque: Language Revival in a Country Rediscovering Itself," *The World and I*, IV, 7 (Washington, D.C., 1989), pp. 620-631.

component of a Ukrainian nationality? Moreover, if the route of Lemko distinctiveness were chosen, just what would that mean—Polish Lemkos as a distinct nationality, or their association with other Rusyns in the Carpathians as a distinct Carpatho-Rusyn nationality?

In a sense, the very fact that the contemporary Lemko issue has become a subject of debate among the group itself suggests that an answer to the question has already been given. Namely, there does exist a group of Lemkos in Poland who have opted for an identity distinct from Ukrainians, and they have already embarked along the classic path of intelligentsia-inspired national movements with the intent to produce literary works in the Lemko vernacular for use as a full-fledged literary language, to carry out historical research on Lemko topics, and to sponsor annual festivals that encourage the masses to become aware and proud of their Lemko identity. An important step in this process was achieved in April 1989, when the first specifically Lemko organization to exist in Poland since World War II came into being. This Lemko Association (Stovaryshŷnia Lemkiv), which has 10 branches to date—3 in the Lemko Region and 7 in the western regions of Poland—and which has its own amateur theatrical group, has also begun to publish a quarterly journal, *Besida*, edited by the poet Petro Murianka-Trokhanovskyi. *Besida* is written in a language that is intended as the basis for a Lemko literary standard. To be sure, some of these activities and others were tried in the past, although their purpose was usually intended to convince Lemkos that they were either Russians, Ukrainians, or Poles. However, the present generation of often university-trained activists is different in that they are convinced that they wish to be associated with neither of the above groups when it comes to the question of their individual national identity.

Indeed, there may be Poles, both within and beyond governing circles, that see this development as a means to weaken the Ukrainian group in Poland and as a first step to assimilate the Lemkos into Poles. But, if Lemkos have survived assimilation in Poland for four decades without any national revival to sustain them, why should they now assimilate in the midst of a movement that is providing them with a concrete Lemko identity? Moreover, Ukrainian ideologists should have nothing to fear. Certainly the potential loss of the Lemko minority in Poland with, at most, approximately 100,000 members would not seriously affect the 50-million strong Ukrainian nationality. Moreover, if the "Lemko separatists" continue to base their activity on the enhancement of their local culture—and their ideology in fact forces them to do so—then Ukrainians should welcome such efforts at preserving the cultural integrity of what in any case they would call a regional variant of Ukrainian culture. While fully aware that Ukrainians at no time in the twentieth century itself have functioned in a political situation in which their culture was itself not in a precarious situation, is it asking too much for Ukrainian spokespersons to realize that if they are as evolved a nationality as their historical heritage suggests, then Ukraine must be prepared to have its Tyrols and Bavarias.

In this sense, the Lemko revival could become a nation-building phenomenon both for Poland as a state and for Ukrainians living as a minority within that state. Since the only alternative—an administratively imposed Ukrainian identity—has neither stemmed assimilation to Poles nor created in all Lemkos the desire to be Ukrainians, the present efforts to sustain a distinct Lemko identity could do no worse than previous policies. In this context, it is instructive to note that the administrative imposition in 1951-1952 of a Ukrainian identity for Rusyns living in neighboring Czechoslovakia has contributed to a devastating decline in their number (from 91,000 in 1930 to 37,000 in 1980). In stark contrast, Rusnaks/Rusyns in Yugoslavia have been recognized as a distinct nationality by that country's postwar government and they have flourished with their own schools, organizations, and standard fourth East Slavic, literary language.[22]

In the end, the success or failure of the Lemko national revival will depend less upon the policies of an increasingly decentralized Polish government or the opposition of Ukrainians and pro-Ukrainian Lemkos than upon the concentrated efforts of Lemko activists themselves. Moreover, it will do no good for Lemkos to blame the Polish government or Poland's Ukrainians for what until now has been their own tendency to waver on the question of national identity and a reluctance (or simply laziness) to undertake the difficult task of collecting, codifying, and propagating local culture. To be sure, the Lemko national revival has only begun. It will be at least a decade before we will know whether it will survive and, if so, what specific direction it will take.

---

[22]For a concise comparison of the developments in other Rusyn-inhabited lands, see Paul Robert Magocsi, *The Shaping of a National Identity: Subcarpathian Rus', 1848-1948* (Cambridge, Mass., 1978), pp. 268-271.

CHAPTER 15

The Birth of a New Nation, or the Return of an Old Problem: The Rusyns of East Central Europe[*]

A s we enter the last decade of the twentieth century, many societies throughout the world, from South Africa to Central America and from the Middle East to Europe, have already or are continuing to experience great changes in their political and socioeconomic structures. Perhaps no greater changes can be found than those that have occurred in the former Soviet Union and East Central Europe. This era of change has also reached the very heart of Europe, that is the Carpathian mountains and foothills inhabited since time immemorial by people who have traditionally called themselves Rusyns but who recently have been known as Ukrainians. One aspect of the on-going changes in the Carpathian region has to do with what has historically been called the nationality question. Today, commentators refer to this phenomenon as

[*]This study was written for and presented in Slovak at the XI International Congress of Slavists held in Bratislava, Slovakia, August 30–September 8, 1993. The text was also presented in English at the University of Toronto (February 25, 1993), at Eötvös Lóránt University in Budapest, Hungary (October 19, 1993), at the University of Pittsburgh (April 15, 1994), at the University of Aarhus, Denmark (November 6, 1997), and in Slovak at the Rusyn Renaissance Society Club in Košice, Slovakia (October 17, 1994). It was first published in *Canadian Slavonic Papers*, XXXIV, 3 (Edmonton, 1992), pp. 199-223, and republished under the same title in *Acta Etnografica Hungarica*, XLII, 1-2 (Budapest, 1997), pp. 119-138. Excerpts were published in a translation into Rusyn by Anna Plishkova in *Rusyn*, III, 4 (Prešov, 1993), pp. 1-3.

the "problem" of Rusynism (*Rusynstvo*), or Carpatho-Rusynism (*Karpatorusynstvo*).[1] Who are the Rusyns? Are they a separate people, or are they simply an ethnic group that is part of the Ukrainian people? Do they have—or can they have—a distinct Rusyn language, or is Rusyn simply a series or Ukrainian dialects? These are questions which most writers on the topic had thought were resolved long ago, and certainly by the last decade of the twentieth century. Since the revolutionary year of 1989, however, it has become obvious that not everyone living in the Carpathian region feels that these questions have been answered—or answered convincingly.

The term Rusyn refers to the indigenous East Slavs who inhabit primarily the northcentral Carpathian Mountains and who are likely to identify themselves in a variety of ways: Rusyn, Rusnak, Lemko, Ukrainian, Slovak, Czechoslovak, or Polish. The East Slavic Rusyns live within the borders of five countries, but because there is inadequate or simply no statistical data available, we can only speak in theoretical terms when discussing numbers.[2] In theory, there could be as many as one million Rusyns: 650,000 in the Transcarpathian oblast of Ukraine; 130,000 in the Prešov Region of northeastern Slovakia; 60,000 in the Lemko Region of southeastern Poland as well as other parts of that country; 20,000 in the Maramureş Region of northern Romania; and 30,000 in former Yugoslavia (Serbia's Vojvodina and Croatia's Slavonia). There is even a small but still undeterminable number of Rusyns in northeastern Hungary.[3] Looked at another way, Rusyns make

[1]The current debate could be said to have begun with a five-part article by the Uzhhorod State University professor of linguistics, Pavlo Chuchka, "Kak rusiny stali ukraintsami," *Zakarpatskaia pravda* (Uzhorod), September 12-16, 1989. The debate has since then intensified in Ukraine's Transcarpathian oblast, former Czecho-Slovakia, and Yugoslavia. Beginning in August 1990 and for nearly a year thereafter, Transcarpathia's Ukrainian- and Russian-language daily newspaper, *Zakarpats'ka pravda/Zakarpatskaia pravda*, ran a popular column entitled, "The Ukraine and Rusynism" (*Ukraïna i rusynizm*).

[2]After World War II, Rusyns were recorded in official statistics only in Yugoslavia (23,000 in 1981) and Romania (1,000 in 1977). Most recently, they have been recorded once again in Czecho-Slovak statistics (see below, note 29).

[3]The establishment of two Rusyn cultural organizations in Hungary in 1992 attests to a national revival among a segment of the population in northeastern

up 65 percent of the population of Transcarpathia, while in each of the other countries they comprise only a minuscule proportion of the total population. Not surprisingly, there are similarities in the Rusyn experience regardless where they reside, but there are also differences precisely because they have lived for most of the twentieth century in different countries. Before turning to a discussion of Rusyns in individual countries, it is necessary to address a few general issues.

Let us begin with the basic theoretical question: are Rusyns a distinct nationality? If they are not a nationality, but simply an ethnic group, or a branch of another nationality, which one? Ukrainian? Or in the case of the Prešov Region, the Slovak nationality? Or in the Lemko Region, the Polish nationality? Or are they simply a branch—as many writers used to think—of a "common" East Slavic people that had come to be called Russian (*obshcherusskii*)?

Before trying to determine the status of Rusyns, it would be useful first to define what is meant here by the concept of nationality. Stated most briefly, a nationality is a group of people who may have certain characteristics, such as a distinct territory (but not necessarily statehood), language, historical tradition, religion, and common social and ethnographic traits. In that sense, ethnic groups and branches of nationalities also may have many of these same common characteristics. What, then, distinguishes a nationality from an ethnic group? The primary distinguishing feature is not the presence or absence of one or more of the above common characteristics, but rather an awareness among members of a given group that they not only have such common characteristics but that it is these characteristics which distinguish them from neighboring nationalities. Thus, it is an awareness among a sufficient number of group members—an awareness passed on to future generations through the family and most especially schools—that ultimately defines nationalities.

Therefore, we return to our original question: are Rusyns a distinct

Hungary that was long thought to have been completely magyarized. See Philip Michaels, "Rusyns in Hungary," *Carpatho-Rusyn American*, XV, 3 (Pittsburgh, Pa., 1992), p. 2; and István Udvari, "Rusyns in Hungary and the Hungarian Kingdom," in Paul Robert Magocsi, ed., *The Persistence of Regional Cultures: Rusyns and Ukrainians in their Carpathian Homeland and Abroad* (New York, 1993), pp. 105-138.

nationality? The answer, with perhaps the exception of Rusyns in the Vojvodina, is no. Are Rusyns an ethnic group with numerous common characteristics that both define and distinguish them from their neighbors? In that case, the answer is yes. If, therefore, Rusyns are minimally an ethnic group (divided into many ethnographic sub-groups like Lemkos, Boikos, Dolyniany, Hutsuls), do they have the theoretical potential to develop into a distinct nationality or to become subsumed as part of another nationality? The answer to both parts of that question is yes. It is, in fact, the issue of whether to become a distinct nationality or to be a branch of another nationality that constitutes what has been called the "problem of Rusynism."

It seemed that this problem was finally resolved during the second half of the twentieth century. Before then the issue had been hotly debated, and of the many variant explanations three orientations became the most significant. Some Carpathian East Slavs thought they were part of the Russian nationality; others argued they were Ukrainian; still others believed they comprised a distinct nationality called Carpatho-Rusyn, or simply Rusyn.[4] At the close of World War II, however, with the establishment of Communist rule in Soviet Ukraine's Transcarpathian region, and soon after in Poland and Czechoslovakia, the issue was resolved by governmental decree. Regardless of what the East Slavic population of the Carpathians may have thought, they were obliged to accept the official view (formulated in 1924 by the Fifth Comintern and in 1925 by the Communist party Bolshevik of Ukraine) that Rusyns, whatever they may call themselves, are a branch of the Ukrainian nationality.[5] Moreover, anyone who did not accept this view was dismissed as having a low level of national consciousness, an insufficient education, or worse still, as being an anti-progressive type who might even be an "enemy of the people."

---

[4]The various orientations are discussed in detail in Paul Robert Magocsi, *The Shaping of a National Identity: Subcarpathian Rus', 1848-1948* (Cambridge, Mass., 1978).

[5]Influenced by a decision taken in December 1925 at the Ninth Congress of the Communist party (Bolshevik) of Ukraine, the Subcarpathian Communist party adopted one year later, at its own Seventh Congress, a resolution that read: "It is obvious that we are part of the Ukrainian people ... and finally we will end ... all 'language questions' [and dispense] with the names 'Rusyn', *'rus'kyi'*, or *'russkii'*." Cited in *Karpats'ka pravda* (Uzhhorod), December 5, 1926.

Indeed, at least since the early 1950s, all of the media as well as the educational system in the Soviet-dominated Carpathian homeland were in the hands of those who accepted the Ukrainian understanding of the problem. Thus, for nearly forty years, the public was continually reminded that the nationality question among Rusyns was resolved. Many, perhaps most observers, whether in east-central Europe or the West, even believed their own rhetoric. But then came the Gorbachev era and the Revolution of 1989. Suddenly, so it seemed, Rusyns came out of the woodwork. In actual fact, the nationality question had never been resolved. Like numerous other problems in the former Soviet Union and in Communist-ruled east-central Europe, the Rusyn question was repressed but not suppressed.

But to return to the question of whether a Rusyn nationality is theoretically possible. We may approach that question by examining the arguments used by those who assume that the existence of a Rusyn nationality is not possible. Here, in particular, it is the arguments of those who accept a Ukrainian understanding of the problem that warrant attention. One could also address those who, in the past and even still at present, might argue that certain Rusyn groups are really a branch of the Slovak ("Rusnaks are Greek Catholic Slovaks") or Polish (Lemkos are an ethnographic group of Poles) nationalities. To address such viewpoints seems superfluous, however, since today there is generally scholarly consensus that based on linguistic, cultural, and ethnographic criteria Rusyns are East Slavs and, therefore, cannot be classified with the West Slavic Poles or Slovaks. And as for yet another view, that Rusyns are a branch (*karpatorossy*) of a single East Slavic people called Russian, this is a theoretical construct that has had no practical significance since at least the early nineteenth century when Europe began to be divided according to nationalities. To say, therefore, as some do, that Rusyns are the same people or closely related to Russians borders on the nonsensical. Thus, it is only the Ukrainian counterargument to a distinct Rusyn nationality that deserves serious attention.

Often defenders of the Ukrainian view argue that "scholarly truth" provides unequivocal proof that Rusyns are a branch of Ukrainians,[6]

---

[6]For instance, referring to the administratively imposed Ukrainian national identity in the Prešov Region of Slovakia, one author argues that "from the standpoint of historical truth, this change was logical." Mykola Mušynka, "The

and to prove their point citations from modern encyclopedias and other "authoritative" sources are duly quoted. But what is "scholarly truth?" I would suggest that those who speak of "scholarly truths" belong to the mindset of pre-secular societies, whose beliefs were based on unquestioning religious dogmas, not on rational thought. In short, in order to understand human societies as well as the natural world, scholars cannot begin with the *a priori* belief that there is an absolute truth waiting to be discoveved, but rather that there are constantly changing realities that need to be examined or, at best, that there may be approximations to truths that if found may help us to understand a given social or physical phenomenon.

The dubiousness of "scholarly truths" may be illustrated by one specific example. According to many scholars, a Macedonian nationality for all intents and purposes did not exist before 1944-1945. All the leading Slavists of our century—Lubor Niederle, Jaroslav Bidlo, Miloš Weingart—agreed that Macedonians were a branch of Bulgarians.[7] That was the "scholarly truth" before 1945. Moreover, it remains the "truth" among Bulgarian and Greek scholars to this very day.[8] They are the

Postwar Development of the Regional Culture of the Rusyn-Ukrainians of Czechoslovakia," in Magocsi, *Persistence of Regional Cultures*, p. 60. This same book includes an essay by Oleksa V. Myšanyč, "From Subcarpathian Rusyns to Transcarpathian Ukrainians," in which the author argues that the answer to the question of nationality is "provided by the historical record" and "reliance upon historical facts," *ibid.*, p. 49.

[7]Cf. Niederle's "Ethnographic Map of the Slavic World," in Jaroslav Bidlo et al., *Slovanstvo: obraz jeho minulosti a přítomnosti* (Prague, 1912); and Miloš Weingart, ed., *Slovanské spisovné jazyky v době přítomné* (Prague, 1937). Serbian scholars at the time argued that Macedonians were a branch of the Serbs. Cf. T.R. Georgevitch, *Macedonia* (London and New York, 1918).

[8]Since World War II, Bulgarian scholarly opinion has varied depending on the country's political relationship with Yugoslavia. For the current view, applicable since 1956, which considers Macedonians and their language to be "western Bulgarian," see the study signed by the Institute of the Bulgarian Language at the Bulgarian Academy of Sciences, "Edinstvo na bŭlgarskija ezik v minaloto i dnes," *Bŭlgarski ezik*, XXVIII (Sofia, 1978), pp. 3-43. Greek writers adamantly deny that there are any Macedonians within the boundaries of present-day Greece, and they argue that the Slavs in the former Yugoslav Macedonian Federal Republic are really Bulgarians. Most recently, Greece became the only country of the European Community that refused to recognize the newly-independent state of Macedonia

exception, however, and there are few in the world who would deny that Macedonians exist as a nationality. Obviously, so-called scholarly truths can change. That being the case, it follows that some scholars might defend the proposition that Rusyns are a distinct nationality just as easily as others could argue they are a branch of Ukrainians. The point is that our understanding of social phenomena can and often does change depending on time and circumstances.

Another argument against considering Rusyns as a nationality is that they do not have their own language. One does not have to search far to realize that not all nationalities have their own languages. The Irish, the Scots, and the Brazilians are only a few of the many examples of thriving nationalities who never had or, for all intents and purposes, have lost their own languages. The issue, of course, is not spoken language but rather written literary languages. A Rusyn nationality supposedly cannot exist because Rusyns do not have their own literary language, which—the argument goes—cannot be created because Rusyns speak a wide variety of dialects. Again, it seems redundant to repeat the obvious: that all peoples speak different dialects and that all literary languages are intellectual constructs. It is precisely the task of the intelligentsia to sort out the problem of dialectal differentiation and to resolve it. In that sense, all European peoples had their language question, not simply the Rusyns. The choice of one dialect as the basis for a literary standard, or the creation of an interdialectal *koiné*, or the return to some historic literary form—these were some of the options open to intelligentsias who were faced with the reality of dialectal differentiation when trying to create a literary language. This was the *questione della lingua* of Dante as he strove to create an Italian literary language. It was the same question faced by Hus for Czech, by Luther for German, by Štúr for Slovak, by Karadžić for Serbian, by Mistral for Provençal, and by numerous other national leaders who helped to create literary languages for their own purposes.

Rusyn leaders, in particular the nineteenth-century "national awakener" Aleksander Dukhnovych, faced this question as well. While many commentators like to shower uncritical praise on Dukhnovych, he

unless it were to change its name to the Republic of Skopje or any other name that does not include the designation Macedonian. Cf. Nicholas P. Andriotis, *The Federative Republic of Skopje and Its Language*, 2nd ed. (Athens, 1966).

does not always warrant it. It is certainly true that he created the most famous texts written in Rusyn vernacular, texts which have helped perhaps more than anything else to create for Rusyns a common sense of historical memory that is so important in defining national distinctiveness. But as a language theoretician, Dukhnovych's contributions on behalf of Rusyn were basically negative. As a believer in the "high" and "low" language theory derived from the Czech Slavist Josef Dobrovský, Dukhnovych wrote for the masses in the "low" Rusyn vernacular, but for educated people in a "high" literary language that derived from Church Slavonic mixed with Russian and some local Rusyn vernacular.

Regardless of the dubious value of his "high" language, Dukhnovych's approach introduced another very unfortunate phenomenon: the belief among Rusyns that their vernacular speech lacked the prestige necessary for serious communication, and that for education and intellectual pursuit some other "higher" more "sophisticated" language had to be used. At various times that "higher" language, with the necessary *dignitas*, was either Church Slavonic, Latin, Magyar, Russian, Ukrainian, Slovak, or Polish. It seemed anything would be better than the Rusyn vernacular. Such views from Dukhnovych helped to deter the Rusyn intelligentsia from doing what many other intelligentsias did throughout Europe: create a literary language based on one or more of their people's local dialects. True, there were some experiments in the twentieth century, and vernacular-based Rusyn readers and grammars were used in the schools of Subcarpathian Rus' (Voloshyn, Pan'kevych, Haraida) or the Lemko Region (Trokhanovskii), but these were limited to elementary education. A serious sociologically complete literary standard was never created, except among the Rusyns in the Vojvodina (Kostel'nik, Kovach).[9]

Some commentators might add that efforts at creating a Rusyn literary standard were and are still unnecessary because Rusyns are too small a people. This, too, is a spurious argument. There are numerous peoples in Europe smaller in number than the Rusyns, whose intelligentsias have had the desire and courage to create literary

---

[9]For details, see Paul R. Magocsi, "The Language Question Among the Subcarpathian Rusyns," in Riccardo Picchio and Harvey Goldblatt, eds., *Aspects of the Slavic Language Question*, Vol. II (New Haven, Conn., 1984), pp. 49-64.

languages. Two examples are illustrative: one from the Slavic world, the Lusatian Sorbs of Germany; the other from the non-Slavic world, the Romansch of Switzerland. Like the Rusyns, both the Lusatian Sorbs and the Romansch have been and are likely to remain stateless peoples. As for dialectal differentiation, they have resolved this problem by creating more than one literary standard. The Sorbs, who number about 80,000 people, have two literary languages: Upper Sorbian and Lower Sorbian. The Romansch, who number only 50,000 people, have as many as five literary languages: Sursilvan, Sutsilvan, Surmiran, Vallader, and Puter—each, by the way, with its own grammars, dictionaries, newspapers or journals, and texts for use in schools. The Romansch case is of particular interest, since the five Romansch groups are divided geographically, as are Rusyns, by even higher mountains. Yet this did not deter the Romansch intelligentsia from resolving the language question in favor of the local vernacular. In any search for literary languages among Europe's smaller peoples, the Rusyns themselves, at least one branch of them, should not be overlooked. These are the Rusyns in the Vojvodina/Bačka, who today number at most 30,000 and whose intelligentsia successfully created a sociologically complete distinct Rusyn literary language. The point is that dialectal differentiation or small size are not in themselves deterrents to the creation of literary languages.[10] A literary language can be created if the local intelligentsia has the self-confidence and desire to achieve such a goal.

A third argument against the possibility of a Rusyn nationality is that Rusyns do not have their own state, and that to have their own state would require a change of international boundaries which in post-Helsinki Europe is inappropriate and even dangerous. One might agree that it is not useful to encourage changes in international boundaries, especially since a future Europe is likely to be based on regions instead of nation-states, with the result that present-day international boundaries

---

[10]This principle, albeit with the cooperation of the governmental authorities, has been confirmed in the last decade by the example of the tiny Principality of Monaco. See Paul Robert Magocsi, "Monégasque Nationalism: A Terminological Contradiction or Practical Reality?," *Canadian Review of Studies in Nationalism*, XVIII, 1-2 (Charlottetown, Prince Edward Island, 1991), pp. 83-94.

will progressively decline in significance.[11]

But boundaries are not the issue, because nationalities do not necessarily need their own states in order to survive. Many stateless nationalities in Europe are divided between one or more states, such as the Basques and Catalans in Spain and France, the Frisians in the Netherlands and Germany, or the Macedonians in former Yugoslavia, Bulgaria, and Greece. While it is certainly true that separation by international boundaries makes it more difficult for stateless nationalities to function, some nevertheless can and do exist.

Somewhat related is the issue of the use or misuse of the Rusyn idea by neighboring states for their own political interests. It is true that in the past the Hungarian government promoted the idea of what was called an Uhro-Rusyn nationality not for its own sake but as a step toward further magyarization. It is also true that some Polish officials felt that by promoting a Lemko identity they might weaken the Ukrainian movement and eventually assimilate Lemkos. Finally, it is true that Rusynism was intrinsically advantageous to interwar Czechoslovakia because that country's central government in Prague felt the Rusyn orientation would help to guarantee the loyalty of its eastern province, Subcarpathian Rus'. And it is also possible that in the last two years of their existence, Soviet state and Communist party organs were interested in promoting Rusynism because they assumed it would provide a convenient counterweight to what for them was the even greater danger of Ukrainian nationalism. But whether or not all the above may have been wholly or even partially true does not negate the value of Rusyn distinctiveness for the Rusyns themselves. All peoples have a right to their own identity, regardless whether the existence of such an identity may at certain times coincide with the interests of outside powers that have their own political agendas.

Turning to individual Rusyn communities, the largest is in Ukraine's Transcarpathian oblast (historic Subcarpathian Rus'). The reemergence of Rusynism in 1988-1990, whether in the form of an organization like the Society of Carpatho-Rusyns (Obshchestvo Karpats'kych Rusynov) or in the writings of individual activists came as somewhat of a

---

[11]Paul Robert Magocsi, "The Revolution of 1989 and the National Minorities of East Central Europe"—see below, Chapter 38.

surprise. This is because unlike other Rusyn-inhabited lands, Transcarpathia was since the onset of Soviet rule in 1945 basically closed off to the rest of the world. There was little if any access to Transcarpathia's local press, so that what was known to the outside world came from books put out by state-owned publishing houses that did little more than describe the "road to happiness" *(shliakhom do shchastia)* under Soviet rule.[12] Part of the idyllic scenario included descriptions of how the nationality question was supposedly resolved forever.

Virtually all western observers accepted Soviet rhetoric, and, therefore, the view that after World War II the only national orientation which proved to be enduring in Transcarpathia was the Ukrainian one. I, too, supported this view, as summed up in 1978 in the conclusion to a major study on the nationality question: "Although any one of the three [Russian, Ukrainian, or Rusyn national] orientations might have been implemented, because of the specific culture of the region and the demands of political reality, only the Ukrainian orientation proved to be enduring."[13] By the 1970s, it certainly seemed that Rusynism was to go the way of the dinosaur or, at best, be maintained within small or inconsequential immigrant communities like those in the Vojvodina of Yugoslavia and the United States.

But what is Rusynism in Transcarpathia? Is it a movement, or is it just the stirrings of a few individuals? We really do not know the answer to that question. We do know, however, that there has been much discussion about Rusyn distinctiveness and calls for Rusyn-language grammars, dictionaries, literary works, new histories, and encyclopedias. Some have even moved beyond cultural goals to demand changes in the political status of Transcarpathia, specifically the return of autonomy for historic Subcarpathian Rus'.[14] Not surprisingly, there

---

[12]This idyllic phrase was used as the title of the first substantial historical survey published during Soviet rule, *Shliakhom do shchastia: narysy istoriï Zakarpattia* (Uzhhorod, 1973), while a variant, "on the road to the October Revolution," was the title of a multi-volume collection of documents on the region: *Shliakhom Zhovtnia: zbirnyk dokumentiv*, 6 vols. (Uzhhorod, 1957-67).

[13]Magocsi, *Shaping of a Nationly Identity*, p. 275.

[14]On September 29, 1990, the executive committee of the Society of Carpatho-Rusyns in Uzhhorod ratified a "Declaration for the Return to the Transcarpathian Oblast the Status of an Autonomous Republic," which was published in the

was swift reaction from the local pro-Ukrainian intelligentsia. At best, they grudgingly accepted the cultural aims of Rusyn spokespersons (what Ukrainians refer to as "ethnographic or cultural Rusynism"), but they were quick to reiterate that such aims must be conceived solely as regional activity among a "branch of the Ukrainian people." As for Rusyn political aims, pro-Ukrainian observers dismiss these outright, considering them to be one or more of the following: (1) the machinations of the former KGB; (2) the efforts of pro-Hungarians or pro-Czechs to return Transcarpathia to its former "colonial status" within Hungary or Czechoslovakia; or (3) the result of interference from "wealthy capitalist" elements in the West, in particular among Rusyns in the United States and Canada. Thus, for Ukrainians, the acceptable phenomenon of "cultural Rusynism" (which they view as a regional component of Ukrainianism) is juxtaposed with "political Rusynism," a negative phenomenon that ostensibly threatens the unity (*sobornost'*) of the Ukrainian state.[15]

The Rusyn movement in Transcarpathia is spearheaded by the Society of Carpatho-Rusyns that is based in Uzhhorod and that has seven branches throughout the oblast. Since its establishment in February 1990, the Society has not yet resolved the following dilemma. Its members realize that knowledge of Rusyn history, literature, and culture—that is, pride in being a Rusyn—is lacking in broad segments of Transcarpathia's East Slavic population. They do not, however, know what to do first: to undertake popular cultural and educational work, or

society's organ, *Otchyi khram* (Uzhhorod), September-October, 1990, pp. 1-2, and sent to Soviet president Mikhail Gorbachev, to the Supreme Soviets of the USSR and the Ukrainian SSR, and to the United Nations. For the text of the "Declaration" and a discussion of its impact on current Transcarpathian political life, see the *Carpatho-Rusyn American*, XIV, 1 (Pittsburgh, Pa., 1991), pp. 4-5.

[15]The pro-Ukrainian view is stated most forcefully in Vasyl' Mel'nyk, "Neorusynstvo i ioho interpretatory," *Zakarpats'ka pravda*, August 18, 21, 22, 24, 1990; Iurii Balega, "Rusynstvo: ideolohy i pokrovyteli," *ibid.*, September 6, 7, 9, 1990; Oleksa Myshanych, "To khto zhe vony?: do ideinykh vytokiv novitn'oho 'karpatorusynstva'," *Literaturna Ukraïna* (Kiev), January 17, 1991; Iurii Balega and Iosyf Sirka, *Khto my ie i chyi my dity?: polemika z prof. P.R. Magochi* (Kiev, 1991); Mykola Mushynka, *Politychnyi rusynizm na praktytsi: z pryvodu vystupu prof. Pavla-Roberta Magochi* (Prešov, 1991); and Oleksa Myshanych, *'Karpatorusynstvo', ioho dzherela i evoliutsiia u XX st.* (Kiev, 1992).

to try to change the political system, after which governmental financial and administrative support would become available to help create in the populace a clear sense of a Rusyn national distinctiveness. A crucial aspect of cultural work, it is argued, would be the creation of a standard Rusyn literary langùage.[16]

Aside from publishing newspapers in Rusyn (*Otchyi khram* and later *Podkarpats'ka Rus'*) and the opening of a Rusyn Center at its branch in the region's second largest city, Mukachevo, the Society of Carpatho-Rusyns has been more concerned with political than with cultural activity. Its leaders participated in the Conference on Security and Cooperation in Europe meeting held in Moscow (September 1991), and they have met on numerous occasions with Czechoslovak government officials in Prague as well as with leaders of a few minor Czech political parties that have openly called for the return of Subcarpathian Rus' (Transcarpathia) to Czechoslovakia.[17] Nonetheless, whatever sympathies with its western neighbor may exist, that option was invalidated when Czechoslovakia ceased to exist on January 1, 1993. As for Transcarpathia's new neighbor, independent Slovakia, there are no Slovak political parties or activists who express any sympathy with Rusyn political goals.

The Society of Carpatho-Rusyns, in cooperation with several other organizations representing Transcarpathia's national minorities (Magyars, Germans, Romanians, Gypsies), was also the most adamant force demanding that a special question regarding Transcarpathian autonomy be placed on the referendum on Ukrainian independence that

---

[16]The cultural aims of the Rusyn movement are best elaborated in the three-part essay by Volodymyr Fedynyshynets', "Ia—Rusyn, mii syn—Rusyn. . . ," *Zakarpats'ka pravda*, August 14, 15, 16, 1990; in English translation: Volodymyr Fedynyšynec', *Our Peaceful Rusyn Way* (Prešov, 1992), pp. 92-105.

[17]The Republican party had as one of its goals—at least until the break-up of the country—the "return of Subcarpathian Rus'" to Czechoslovakia: "Zpět do Československa," *Republika* (Prague), October 18-24, 1990; "Rozhovor s předsedou SPR-RSČ, PhDr. Miroslavem Sládkem, " *ibid.*, August 1991. The National Socialist party also took the position that Czechoslovak jurisdiction still applied to Subcarpathian Rus': "NSS chtějí Podkarpatskou Rus," *Lidová demokracie* (Prague), September 3, 1991. Contacts with Czech political and other public figures have been encouraged and assisted by the Society of Friends of Subcarpathian Rus' (Společnost' Přátel Podkarpatské Rusi), established in Prague in October 1990.

was held on December 1, 1991. Despite strong protests from local pro-Ukrainian activists, a question about "self-rule" (*samosprava*) was included in the referendum. In the end, 78 percent of Transcarpathia's inhabitants opted for self-rule, while at the same time 92 percent supported an independent Ukraine. With regard to the nationality question, such results proved to be inconclusive, because it was unclear whether voters favoring self-rule were supporting Rusyn national distinctiveness or simply regional self-determination within Ukraine. The referendum results may have been more conclusive had the original proposal of the Society of Carpatho-Rusyns been adopted; namely, to provide a question with two options: (1) a distinct autonomous republic: or (2) autonomy within Ukraine. It is interesting to note that the single question on self-rule reflected a compromise suggested by the then leading and subsequently successful presidential candidate, Leonid Kravchuk, who travelled especially to Transcarpathia the week before the referendum. It was during his visit that Kravchuk stated publicly his own preference that Transcarpathia "should be given special status [in Ukraine] as a self-governing territory," as well as his belief that "there is a Rusyn nationality (natsional'nist') and a Rusyn people (*narod*)."[18]

For its part, the Society of Carpatho-Rusyns interpreted the results of the December 1 referendum as an expression of Rusyn national sentiment. The call for self-rule, however, is only the first step toward the eventual creation of an autonomous republic within Ukraine, complete independence, or perhaps re-unification with some neighboring state. To achieve these goals, the Society of Carpatho-Rusyns and the recently-founded Subcarpathian Republican party (established in early 1992) have called on Czechoslovakia to annul the June 1945 treaty with the former Soviet Union which provided for the cessation of Transcarpathia to the Ukrainian S.S.R., and they have proposed that a plebiscite under international supervision be held in Transcarpathia in order that the

---

[18]From the stenographic record of a meeting with regional parliamentary deputies in Transcarpathia, cited in *Podkarpats'ka Rus'* (Uzhhorod), June 19, 1992, p. 1.

population might for "the first time freely decide its fate."[19] In the spring of 1993, the Society's leaders created a Provisional Government of Subcarpathian Rus', which proclaimed the existence of a republic that wished to join on the basis of autonomy—and this time legally—a federal Ukrainian state. The Ukrainian government has stalled on the question of autonomy, in part, fearing another Crimean problem. It remains to be seen whether the populace of Transcarpathia will be satisfied with the status proposed by Kiev or whether they will favor one of the options proposed by the Society of Carpatho-Rusyns and the Subcarpathian Republican party.[20]

The Ukrainian government in Kiev is also faced with a dilemma. In a genuine effort to address the concerns of its multinational population, all national minorities—whether Russians, Poles, Jews, Germans, and Romanians among others—have been given legal guarantees that protect their languages and cultures. Rusyns, however, do not fall into the category of a national minority. In fact, the Ukrainian press and influential leaders within and outside the government (Dmytro Pavlychko, Ivan Drach, Mykhailo Horyn', Roman Lubkivs'kyi) have without exception criticized Rusynism as little more than an artificial construct whose propagators are considered at best "unenlightened" and at worst "treacherous" to the Ukrainian nation. The local Greek Catholic Eparchy of Mukačevo has, in particular, been accused of "separatism" and "acting against the interests of Ukraine," because it wishes to retain its historic jurisdictional status under the Vatican and not be part of the Greek Catholic Church in the rest of western Ukraine.[21]

In theory, there is no reason why Rusyns could not be accepted as a distinct national minority and yet, at the same time, remain loyal citizens of a multinational Ukrainian state. For this to happen, however, long-standing Ukrainian attitudes about the concept of Rusynism would have to change. Based on the seemingly unending polemics from sup-

---

[19]See the declaration of the scholarly seminar organized in May 1992 by the Rusyn Renaissance Society in cooperation with the Ministry of Culture of Slovakia, the Slovak Academy of Sciences, and the Matica slovenská: *Narodný novynký* (Prešov), May 20, 1992; and the "Prohrama Podkarpats'koï Respublikans'koï partiï," *Respublika* (Khust), June 10, 1992, pp. 1-2.

[20]"Zakon Ukraïny 'pro samovriadne Zakarpattia'," *Karpats'ka Ukraïna* (Uzhhorod), February 20, 1992, p. 2.

[21] *Karpats'ka Ukraïna* (Uzhhorod), July 9, 1992.

porters of both the Rusyn and Ukrainian viewpoints, there is little to suggest that such change is in the immediate offing.

In contrast to Transcarpathia, the rebirth of Rusynism in the Prešov Region of Slovakia did not come as a complete surprise. First of all, the Ukrainian orientation never enjoyed the strong roots that it did in Sub-carpathian Rus' (Transcarpathia) during the interwar years, and it was not imposed on the population of the Prešov Region until as late as 1951-1952. Moreover, during the few months of the Prague Spring in 1968, when government censorship was lifted, numerous people in the Prešov Region called for an end to the Ukrainian orientation and for the return of Rusyn schools as well as the establishment of a Rusyn National Council. While it is true that these efforts, like other attempts to establish "socialism with a human face," were brutally crushed by Soviet tanks and that Rusynism was branded as "anti-progressive," "anti-Soviet," and therefore counter-revolutionary, it seems that the Rusyn idea did not die in the Prešov Region. It simply lay dormant until the Revolution of 1989.[22]

What was perhaps surprising was the speed with which both Rusyns and Ukrainians in the Prešov Region reacted in 1989. Within one week of the November 17 revolution, a new initiative group met in Prešov to demand greater democratization for the Rusyns in Slovakia. Two months later, the Cultural Union of Ukrainian Workers (KSUT), a civic organization which had been created by Czechoslovakia's Communist government in 1952, was disbanded and replaced by the Union of Rusyn-Ukrainians of Czechoslovakia—SRUCh. But when some Rusyns felt their demands were not being met by SRUCh, in March 1990 they established their own organization in Medzilaborce, the Rusyn Renaissance Society (Rusyns'ka Obroda).

Both the pro-Ukrainian SRUCh and the pro-Rusyn Renaissance Society agreed that the greatest tragedy experienced since World War II by Rusyns in the Prešov Region was their slovakization. Both orientations also agreed that all efforts must be undertaken to reverse

---

[22]On the impact of 1968 and subsequent developments before 1989, see Pavel Mačů, "National Assimilation: The Case of the Rusyn-Ukrainians of Czechoslovakia," *East Central Europe*, II, 2 (Pittsburgh, 1975), pp. 101-132—reprinted above, Chapter 11.

slovakization and to restore an awareness among the local population that they belong to an East Slavic Rus' culture. The two orientations disagree, however, about the causes and ways to resist further national assimilation. The pro-Ukrainian SRUCh considers assimilation the result of: (1) pressure from the former Communist government in Slovakia, including veiled threats of deportation to Ukraine; (2) the unwise manner in which ukrainianization was forcibly—they say "administratively"—introduced in the early 1950s; and (3) the lack of commitment on the part of the local population toward their national identity and/or the incompetence of Ukrainian-language teachers.[23] In part, the pro-Rusyn Renaissance Society agrees with this explanation. But it then asks why the Ukrainian orientation was such a failure after thirty years of strong support from a Czechoslovak Communist government that provided generous budgets for a Ukrainian-language theater, a university department and research institute, elementary and secondary schools, radio program, museum, newspapers, journals, publishing house, and other cultural organizations?

Czechoslovak authorities and non-governmental observers also asked about the results from an investment that funded so many institutions and cultural activists. On the one hand, there have been some remarkably positive achievements, especially with regard to publications like the first-rate scholarly journal (*Naukovyi zbirnyk*) of the Museum of Ukrainian Culture. Moreover, cultural institutions like the Dukla Ukrainian Song and Dance Ensemble have given a certain renown to the group and to all of Czechoslovakia as a result of its several tours throughout Europe and North America.

But when it comes to the Rusyn population in general—as the Rusyn Renaissance Society suggests—all the arguments and justifications to the contrary cannot erase the reality of a Ukrainian orientation which, after three decades, has brought catastrophic results. For instance, during the interwar first Czechoslovak republic, there were over 91,000 inhabitants in the Prešov Region who declared themselves to be of Rusyn nationality (1930). Even under the supposedly oppressive and assimilationist Hungarian regime before World War I, more than 111,000 inhabitants in the Prešov Region declared their language to be

---

[23] Anna Kuz'miak, "Polipshyt'sia stan natsional'noho shkil'nytstva?," *Nove zhyttia* (Prešov), October 19, 1990, pp. 7-8.

Rusyn (1910). After 1952, however, when a Ukrainian orientation was introduced, the numbers steadily declined, so that by the census of 1980 there were less than 40,000 inhabitants who were willing to identify as Ukrainian. This figure represented less than one-third the estimated 130,000 persons of Rusyn background who actually inhabit the Prešov Region.[24]

The prognosis for the future is even worse, because the all-important educational system, which is a primary means of preserving national cultures, is virtually non-existent. In 1947/1948, the last school year before a Ukrainian orientation began to be introduced, there were 272 elementary schools in Rusyn villages and 5 *gymnasia* in nearby towns with a total of 22,000 students. Since that time the number of Ukrainian-language schools steadily declined, so that by 1990/1991 there remained only 15 elementary schools where some subjects were taught in Ukrainian to a total student body of only 908![25]

These developments, which have correctly been categorized as catastrophic from the standpoint of preserving an East Slavic Rusyn identity, are not the result of forced slovakization on the part of former governmental authorities (although it is likely that many Slovaks, especially in Eastern Slovakia, were not upset by the results). Nor are they result of the administrative introduction of ukrainianization, or the lack of national awareness on the part of the population. They are, instead, the result of actions by the Rusyns themselves, who under a Stalinist regime spoke out in the only way they could. They did not want to be called Ukrainians and did not want to have Ukrainian-language schools. If, they concluded, they could not have their own Rusyn identity and schools as they had had before, then they would prefer to have a Slovak identity and Slovak schools. Such action was not the mark of a lack of national consciousness. Rather, it reflected a clear awareness of what one was—and also what one did not want to be. While it may seem paradoxical, the solution proposed since 1990 by

---

[24]A discussion of Rusyn nationality estimates is found in Paul R. Magocsi, *The Rusyn-Ukrainians of Czechoslovakia: A Historical Survey* (Vienna, 1983), p. 64, n. 91.

[25]Ivan Vanat, Mykhailo Rychalka, and Andrii Chuma, *Do pytan' pisliavoiennoho rozvytku, suchasnoho stanu ta perspektyv ukraïns'koho shkil'nytsva v Slovachchyni* (Prešov, 1992), p. 13.

supporters of the pro-Ukrainian SRUCh organization has been to demand that more Ukrainian be taught in schools and to argue that the Rusyns of Slovakia should find their salvation by identifying with a newly-independent Ukrainian state in the east.[26]

The new realities set in motion in 1989 and the implementation of democratic changes in Czechoslovakia forced the Prešov Region's pro-Ukrainian leadership to alter its views on the nationality question. They began to argue that the name Rusyn is acceptable and that the literary Ukrainian langauge used in their publications should employ more words from the local dialects. This proved to be at best a semantic compromise. Hence, while the name Rusyn might be used, it should only appear in the hyphenated form, Rusyn-Ukrainian. In short, the name Rusyn must be understood as a synonym for Ukrainian.

While still in the wake of the euphoria created by the November 1989 revolution, one of the Prešov Region's most active Ukrainian spokespersons and a primary defender of the hyphenated name *Rusyn-Ukrainian* revealed quite openly the real intentions of the Ukrainian orientation by using a classic Leninist image to make his point:

> Sometimes it happens that in order to make two steps forward, it is necessary to take one step backwards. And we have taken this one step backwards. ... In the given circumstances we have moved from a purely Ukrainian position to a Rusyn-Ukrainian position. We had to do this, because if we would distance ourselves from popular (not political) Rusynism, we would simply lose what little we have. I would say that if there will be a group of Rusyns who want to be Rusyns and not Slovaks, then in ten years they, too, will sing [the Ukrainian national anthem] 'Ukraine Has Not Yet Perished': that is, they will have become convinced Ukrainians.[27]

Such statements remind Rusyn supporters of the attitude of Bulgarian

---

[26]See the 15-point declaration of the pro-Ukrainian intelligentsia in Czecho-Slovakia: "Stavlennia rus'ko-ukraïns'koï inteligentsiï Chekho-Slovachchyny do suchasnykh protsesiv nashoho kul'turno-natsional'noho zhyttia," *Nove zhyttia* (Prešov), December 21, 1990, p. 3.

[27]Interview with Mykola Mušynka, head of the Ukrainian Research Institute at Šafárik University in Prešov, following the founding Congress of the Union of Rusyn-Ukrainians in Czechoslovakia—SRUCh, cited in *Druzhno vpered*, No. 4 (Prešov, 1990), p. 2.

chauvinists who occupied Macedonia during World War II: "You Macedonians are our Bulgarian brothers, even though you might not be fully aware of the fact, but you are backward and ignorant and must obey us, your elder and wiser brothers, without hesitation or question, until you learn to behave correctly, as proper Bulgarians."[28]

In many ways, the Rusyn movement in Slovakia has been more successful than in neighboring Ukraine and Poland. First, it succeeded in getting a section of SRUCh's Ukrainian-language weekly newspaper, *Nove zhyttia*, to appear in Rusyn under the rubric, "Voice of the Rusyns" (*Holos rusyniv*). Then, in early 1991, when differences of opinion regarding the national orientation of *Nove zhyttia* could no longer be rectified, the editor-in-chief Aleksander Zozuliak and most of his staff resigned. Within a few months they joined forces with the Rusyn Renaissance Society and started to publish a new newspaper (*Narodnŷ novynkŷ*) and an illustrated magazine (*Rusyn*) entirely in Rusyn. At the same time, the Ukrainian National Theater (established in 1945) changed its name to the Aleksander Dukhnovych Theater and the language of its productions became Rusyn instead of Ukrainian. Even the newly-established Museum of Modern Art in Medzilaborce, supported by the Andy Warhol Foundation in New York City, opened its doors in the summer of 1991 with emphasis on the Rusyn roots of the famous American pop artist and media figure whose prints and paintings now adorn the walls of what might otherwise have been a largely unnoticed provincial museum. The Rusyn Renaissance Society also lobbied successfully to have the name Rusyn added and recorded as a category distinct from Ukrainian in the 1991 decennial census. This latter achievement effectively meant that Rusyns were *de facto* if not *de jure* recognized as a distinct national minority in Czechoslovakia.[29]

Perhaps the greatest symbolic achievement of the Rusyn movement in Slovakia was the decision of the Rusyn Renaissance Society to hold

---

[28]Cited in Horace G. Lunt, "Some Linguistic Aspects of Macedonian and Bulgarian," in Benjamin A. Stolz et al., *Language and Literary Theory: In Honor of Ladislav Matejka* (Ann Arbor, Mich., 1984), p. 112.

[29]The total number of East Slavs recorded in 1991 in the Prešov Region was 32,408, divided into 16,937 Rusyns; 13,847 Ukrainians; and 1,624 Russians. *Preliminary Results of the Population and Housing Census: Czech and Slovak Federal Republic, March 3, 1991* (Prague, 1991), pp. 30-31.

the First World Congress of Rusyns. It took place in March 1991 in the town of Medzilaborce in the new and grandiose cultural center which subsequently became the home of the Warhol Museum of Modern Art. Despite a history of interaction between Rusyns in the homeland and the immigrant community in the United States during the twentieth century, this was, in fact, the first time representatives from all countries where Rusyns live (Ukraine, Czechoslovakia, Poland, Yugoslavia, the United States) gathered together in one place. The congress constituted itself as a permanent umbrella organization, and its very existence had an enormous impact on instilling Rusyn national pride in the over 300 persons who attended, not to mention innumerable others who read about it through the generally widespread press coverage.[30]

At present, the Rusyn and Ukrainian movements in the Prešov Region continue their rivalry to obtain the support of their East Slavic constituency and, in particular, funding from the Slovak government. Current government policy is to provide equal support to both the Rusyn and Ukrainian orientations, and it remains to be seen which of the two will be more successful in its efforts to convince the people that they are either a distinct East Slavic nationality known as Rusyns, or a branch of the Ukrainian nationality known as Rusyn-Ukrainians.

Just north of the Prešov Region and beyond the crests of the Carpathian Mountains is the Lemko Region of Poland, where even before the Revolution of 1989 a revival on behalf of Rusyn national specificity had begun. The Lemkos were unique among Rusyns in that they were deported (voluntarily and then forcibly) from their Carpathian villages between 1945 and 1947. Two thirds went eastward to the Soviet Ukraine, the rest were resettled in the southwest (Silesia) and northwest (Pomerania) of Poland on territory that had formerly been part of Germany. Even when living in the Carpathians, the Lemkos were in the twentieth century cut off from their Rusyn brethren in Slovakia and Transcarpathia by political borders. Nonetheless, ever since the first national revival in the late nineteenth century, Lemko writers and political activists always emphasized their cultural affinity with all the East Slavs of Rus', and in particular with the Rusyns living along the

---

[30]Information on the First World Congress as well as its official declaration are found in the *Carpatho-Rusyn American*, XIV, 2 and 3 (Pittsburgh, Pa., 1991), pp. 7-9 and 8-9.

southern slopes of the Carpathians in the Prešov Region of Slovakia and Transcarpathia.[31] It is not surprising, therefore, that Lemkos welcomed the revival of a Rusyn national orientation that took place in Slovakia and Ukraine's Transcarpathia after 1989.

The Lemkos had embarked on their own path of national rediscovery already in the mid-1980s, when a group of younger writers, who had already published a few collections of poetry in Lemko-Rusyn vernacular, established an annual cultural festival called the Vatra. As in the Prešov Region and in Transcarpathia, these young activists were criticized from the beginning by Ukrainian-oriented Lemkos and by Ukrainians in Poland. They prevailed, however, and in early 1989, established a cultural organization, the Lemko Association (Stovaryshŷnia Lemkiv) as well as a Rusyn-language magazine (*Besida*).[32] The situation in Poland is somewhat similar to Slovakia in that the Rusyn orientation is headed primarily by younger people born and raised after World War II, while the Ukrainian orientation is represented by older activists born before the war and who, in 1990, founded their own Union of Lemkos (Ob"iednannia Lemkiv).

Just as the threat of national assimilation affects Rusyns in Slovakia, so, too—but in the form of polonization—does it have serious implications for Lemkos in Poland. Similarly, Ukrainians as well as Ukrainian-oriented Lemkos in Poland and Ukraine use the same arguments: support of Lemko-Rusyn distinctiveness (they call it "separatism") will ostensibly lead to further polonization.[33] Also as in Slovakia, the Ukrainian orientation in Poland has had more than thirty years to transform Lemkos into Ukrainians. Yet neither has ukrainianization occurred nor has the trend toward polonization been halted. Finally, and again like Rusyns in the Prešov Region, the Lemkos have been at work trying to standardize a literary language. This, of course,

[31]The sense of affinity was further emphasized by the name *Rusnak*, which Lemkos invariably called themselves until the introduction of the new name *Lemko* in the first decades of the twentieth century.

[32]For details on the recent Lemko-Rusyn national revival, see the series of articles in the *Carpatho-Rusyn American*, X, 1, 2, 3, 4 and XI, 1 (Pittsburgh, Pa., 1987-88).

[33]The most prolific Lemko spokesperson for the Ukrainian viewpoint is Ivan Krasovs'kyi, who emigrated to Ukraine in 1945. See his recent volume, co-authored with Dmytro Solynko, *Khto my, Lemky . . .* (L'viv, 1991).

raises a very practical side of the language question. Should each group of Rusyns create its own literary language, or should an effort be made to create a single standard for all Rusyns regardless of where they live?

Because languages have such powerful symbolic value as the embodiment of national cultures as well as the instrument by which those cultures are preserved for future generations, it is not surprising that the question of a literary standard has been raised in the publications and proclamations of virtually every new Rusyn organization founded since 1990. The only exception is the small group of Rusyns in former Yugoslavia, who already have a sociologically complete literary language that dates back to the 1920s and that since World War II has been recognized as an official medium in schools and public life.[34]

In order to resolve the thorny issue of how to create a literary standard from among several dialects spoken by Rusyns in five countries, the Rusyn Renaissance Society in Slovakia, in cooperation with the Carpatho-Rusyn Research Center in the United States, convened a working seminar, or language congress, in November 1992. Journalists, writers, amateur grammarians, and scholars from all countries where Rusyns live agreed at the language congress on the principles and mode of action in language building.[35] The participants accepted the territorial principle adopted by the Romansch of Switzerland; namely, that Rusyns in each region would: (1) create their own standard based on the region's main dialect; (2) use their new standards in publications and in schools; and (3) meet regularly to work on a single Carpatho-

---

[34]The standard Vojvodinian-Srem or Bačka Rusyn grammars are by Havriïl Kostel'nik (1923) and Mikola Kochish (1971 and 1977). This fourth East Slavic language, as Vojvodinian Rusyn is known, has in recent years been the subject of intense scrutiny among Slavists worldwide, including Sven Gustavsson (Uppsala, Sweden), Aleksander Duličenko (Tartu, Estonia), Henrik Birnbaum (Los Angeles, California), Horace G. Lunt (Cambridge, Massachusetts), and Jiří Marvan (Melbourne, Australia).

[35]The Rusyn language congress, which received wide coverage in the Slovak media, also included speakers representing the Romansch in Switzerland and the Monégasque of Monaco. For details, see the entire issue of *Rusyn*, II, 5-6 (Prešov, 1992) and Paul Robert Magocsi, "Scholarly Seminar on the Codification of the Rusyn Language," *Österreichischen Ostheften*, XXXV, 1 (Vienna, 1993), pp. 186-188.

Rusyn standard, or *koiné*, for all regions. Since the Yugoslav Rusyns already have a literary standard, three others had to be created for Transcarpathia (Ukraine), the Prešov Region (Slovakia), and the Lemko Region (Poland).[36] In fact, language practitioners in each region have already prepared preliminary versions of grammars[37] and have used the local vernacular in newspapers. To coordinate the work of the codifiers, a Rusyn Language Institute was created in Prešov, Slovakia in January 1993.

In terms of a literary language as well as an organizational infrastructure for a Rusyn national life, the Vojvodinian or Bačka-Srem Rusyns of Yugoslavia are—or were until quite recently—in the best situation. This is because the former Yugoslav government recognized them as a distinct nationality after World War II. With such favorable external support, their own intelligentsia was able to create a whole host of schools, cultural organizations, publications, and media programs— all in the Vojvodinian variant of Rusyn. The language has been particularly well developed, and besides the works of local novelists and poets, there are Vojvodinian Rusyn translations that range from the Bible, Shakespeare, and Pushkin to Marx and Engels. All of this was created for what today number less than 30,000 people. Clearly the Vojvodinian Rusyns are an outstanding, if not unique, example of what can be done if the ruling state is favorably inclined and if the local intelligentsia is willing to work effectively.[38]

Although it might seem that the nationality question has been resolved in favor of a Rusyn orientation, a closer look suggests that some spokespersons in Yugoslavia are uncomfortable with the idea that Rusyns form a nationality entirely unto themselves. These people basically consider Yugoslavia's Rusyns to be part of the Ukrainian nation-

---

[36]Rusyns from Hungary also participated in the congress, but agreed to use in their publications the same standard adopted for Slovakia's Prešov Region.

[37]These include for the Lemko Region: Myroslava Khomiak, *Grammatŷka lemkivskoho iazŷka* and *Lemkivska grammatŷka dlia dity*; for the Prešov Region: Iurii Pan'ko, *Normŷ rusyns'koho pravopysu*; and for Transcarpathia: Ihor Kercha and Vasyl' Sochka-Borzhavyn, *Rusyn'skŷi iazŷk: ocherk kompleksnoi praktychnoi gramatykŷ*.

[38]There is an extensive literature on the Vojvodinian Rusyns. Cf. Vida Zaremski et al., *Bibliografiia Rusnatsokh u Iugoslaviï* (Novi Sad, 1989).

ality, even though they are reluctant to call their people other than Rusyn (in local parlance, Rusnak/Rusnatsi) or to use a literary language other than their own standard, for fear that they would lose the support of the ordinary masses who seem quite content with being Rusyn and nothing else.

Considering the fact that Rusyns have been able to maintain their own language and identity in Yugoslavia, it may seem difficult to understand why the Ukrainian orientation has gained some adherants. In part, the attraction of the Ukrainian orientation is a reaction to the fear of national assimilation that is inevitable for a people so small in number, regardless of the support they might receive from the state. Thus, local Ukrainophiles argue that Vojvodinian Rusyns would not as-similate to Serbian or Croatian culture if they could be taught to identify as Ukrainians and associate with a culture that is larger and, therefore, ostensibly more attractive than their own.

The existence of a Ukrainian orientation among the Vojvodinian Rusyns is also, in part, a result of the peculiar legal norms adopted by the former federal Yugoslav state. Despite their small number, the Rusyns were designated in 1974 one of the five official nationalities in Serbia's autonomous province of Vojvodina. Yugoslav law required, however, that a group of people could only be considered a nationality if it had a recognized "motherland" somewhere else beyond the borders of Yugoslavia. Since at the time there was no Rusyn state or officially recognized Rusyn nationality elsewhere, the motherland (*matichna zem*) of the Vojvodinian Rusyns became, by default, Ukraine—even though in actual fact most of the ancestors of the group did not come from Ukraine (Transcarpathia) but rather from what is today southeastern Slovakia and northeastern Hungary.

In the wake of the Revolution of 1989 and the Rusyn national revival in the Carpathian homeland, the Vojvodinian Rusyns began to feel they could legitimately justify their own existence without reference to Ukraine but rather to a Rusyn nationality that was gradually coming to be recognized in Slovakia, Poland, and perhaps eventually in Ukraine as well. It was in large part these new post-1989 realities in the Carpathian homeland that encouraged the Vojvodinian Rusyns to revive an older organization, the Rusyn Matka Society (Ruska Matka), which came into existence the same year (1990) as the pro-Ukrainian Union of Rusyn-Ukrainians in Yugoslavia (Soiuz Rusinokh i Ukraintsokh

Iugoslavii).[39] The increasing differentiation between the Rusyn and Ukrainian orientations among Vojvodina's Rusyns also became evident in the Department of Rusyn Language and Literature (established in 1975) at the University of Novi Sad, which includes scholars of both persuasions. On the other hand, the two existing Rusyn secondary schools (*gymnasium* and pedagogical institute) offer instruction exclusively in the Vojvodinian variant of Rusyn, and they remain a stronghold for producing new cadres of young people who are conscious of their distinct national identity.

The internal debates among this smallest group of Rusyns have been overshadowed, however, by the more recent unfortunate turn of events in Yugoslavia. Effectively, the Rusyns in former Yugoslavia are since 1991 divided by the boundaries of two states: Serbia (which includes the Vojvodina) and Croatia (the far eastern part of which includes the second Rusyn cultural center of Vukovar, virtually levelled in 1991 during Yugoslavia's civil war). Whether the new governments of Serbia and Croatia will be as supportive of national minorities as was the old federal state of Yugoslavia remains an open question, the answer to which will clearly have a profound impact on this smallest of Rusyn minorities.

Having reviewed briefly the Rusyn movement in four countries, are there any common features that can be discerned? There are, indeed, several. We have seen that since 1989 each region has both pro-Rusyn and pro-Ukrainian orientations. But who are the individuals who have set the ideological tone for those orientations? Regardless of orientation, they comprise mostly university and *gymnasium* teachers, journalists, writers, and activists in cultural organizations, in particular the theater.

There is a difference, however, in the age and therefore attitude among the activists of each orientation. Most of the pro-Ukrainian activists are in the 55 to 65 year-old range, born before World War II.[40] As young adults, they experienced the worst years of Stalinist

---

[39]It was the head of the Rusyn Matka Society who first began to question the need for a "Ukrainian motherland." See the conceptual/ideological statement of the Rusyn Matka Society by Liubomir Medieshi," Programski osnov za diïstvovanie Ruskei Matki," *Ruske slovo* (Novi Sad), December 21-28, 1990, *dodatok*.

[40]Biographical data on pro-Ukrainian activists in Transcarpathia and the Prešov

repression as well as the forced change to a Ukrainian national identity. The authoritarian nature of the environment in which they were formed also inculcated in them the belief that decisions about social policy are best made by an educated elite who has access to "truths," historic or otherwise, that should subsequently be followed by the populace as a whole.

In contrast, the leading pro-Rusyn activists are mostly between 35 and 50 years of age, that is they were born during or after World War II and acculturated for the most part during the 1970s and 1980s.[41] That was a time when Communist rule had lost its authoritarian edge and when at least the inhabitants of Poland, Czechoslovakia, and Yugoslavia were exposed to more liberal influences from western Europe. It is also significant that almost all Rusyn activists were educated in Ukrainian schools and had accepted, passively if not actively, a Ukrainian national identity. Therefore, they had to "rediscover" their Rusyn roots. The point is that they became conscious Rusyns only after having known fully what it meant to be Ukrainian.

Partly reflective of the age differentiation is the fact that pro-Ukrainian civic and academic institutions, in particular in Transcarpathia and the Prešov Region, are still headed by individuals who held the same or similar positions during the pre-1989 Communist era. As for the pro-Rusyns, they were either too young to be part of the pre-1989 system or they held positions that were of no particular influence. Thus, in some ways, the Rusyn-Ukrainian dichotomy can be seen as a generational struggle between "fathers and sons" in which the older Ukrainian generation—and therefore orientation—is accused by its

Region are found in *Pys'mennyky Zakarpattia: biobibliohrafichnyi dovidnyk* (Uzhhorod, 1989) and "Avtory zhurnalu 'Duklia'," *Duklia*, XXVI, 1 (Prešov, 1978), pp. 57-79.

[41] Of 10 members in the executive of the Lemko Association in Poland, 9 were born after 1942; of 10 executive members in the Society of Carpatho-Rusyns in Uzhhorod, 5 were born after 1942. The founding chairmen of the five new Rusyn organizations established in 1991-1992 were all in their thirties. See the biographies in "I Kongres Stovaryshŷnia Lemkiv," *Besida*, II, 3-4 (Krynica, 1990), pp. 8-9 and "The Society of Carpatho-Rusyns," *Carpatho-Rusyn American*, XV, 1 (Pittsburgh, Pa., 1992), pp. 4-5.

rivals, sometimes with justification, of being tainted by its "Communist" past.[42]

Another characteristic related in part to age is the intellectual basis of each orientation. The Ukrainian orientation has an established body of literature explaining how Rusyns gradually developed into Ukrainians in the course of the twentieth century. Those views, moreover, generally predominate in departments that specialize in the local language and ethnography at Prešov's Šafárik University in Slovakia and at the University of Užhorod in Ukraine.[43] In contrast, the Rusyn orientation was initially comprised of youthful enthusiasts whose demands for publications about Rusyns or for the creation of a Rusyn literary language were often little more than idealistic desires well beyond the intellectual resources of the group. That situation has just gradually begun to change with the recent creation of an Institute for Carpathian Studies (Instytut Karpatyky) at the University of Uzhhorod, a Rusyn Language Institute in Prešov, and a Department of Ukrainian and Rusyn Philology in Nyíregyháza (Hungary), all of which are staffed by academics sympathetic to the Rusyn orientation.[44] Scholarship and cultural activities were also the primary themes at the Second World Congress of Rusyns that took place in May 1993 in Krynica, Poland, where specific proposals were put forward for closer coordination

[42]It is ironic that the founding chairman of the Society of Carpatho-Rusyns in Uzhhorod, Mykhailo M. Tomchanii (b. 1946), and the founding chairman of the Initiative Group for the Remoulding of Czechoslovakia's Rusyn-Ukrainians, Aleksander Zozuliak (b. 1953), are the sons of the leading post-World War II Ukrainian-language writers respectively in Transcarpathia and the Prešov Region: Mykhailo I. Tomchanii and Vasyl' Zozuliak.

[43]Among the pro-Ukrainian scholars at these institutions, all of whom have spoken out adamantly against the Rusyn orientation in newspaper articles and brochures are Iurii Bacha, Fedir Kovach, Iurii Mulychak, Mykola Mushynka, Mykola Shtets', and Ivan Vanat in Prešov, and Iurii Balega, Pavlo Chuchka, Vasyl' Hanchyn, and Mykhailo Tivodar in Uzhhorod, joined by Oleksa Myshanych from the Institute of Ukrainian Literature in Kiev.

[44]The Uzhhorod institute is headed by Dr. Ivan Pop, also editor of the prestigeous Moscow journal, *Slavianovedenie*; the Prešov institute by Dr. Iurii Pan'ko; and the Nyíregyháza department by Dr. István Udvari.

between Rusyn scholarly institutions and publications in all countries where they live.[45]

In conclusion, we may return to the question posed at the outset of this essay: are Rusyns a separate people or simply a branch of Ukrainians? At present, we still do not have an answer. All we do know is that a nationality-building process is taking place. Many of the classic building blocks needed to create a nationality—language, historical ideology, publications, cultural organizations, theaters—are being developed. But whether those building blocks will be fully constructed, and whether the countries in which Rusyns live will remain sympathetic to such efforts,[46] and, most importantly, whether the masses themselves will embrace the idea of a distinct Rusyn nationality remain open questions.

[45]"Postanova z II. Svitovoho kongresu rusyniv u Krynytsi," *Narodnŷ novynkŷ* (Prešov), June 2, 1993, p. 3.

[46]On the legal status of Rusyns in each of the countries where they live, see Paul Robert Magocsi, "Carpatho-Rusyns: Their Current Status," in Jana Plichtová, ed., *Minorities in Politics: Cultural and Languages Rights—Bratislava Symposium II* (Bratislava, 1992), pp. 212-227, also in Slovak translation with commentaries by L'udovít Haraksim, Mykola Mušynka, and Andrzej Zięba in *Slovenský národopis*, XL, 2 and 3 (Bratislava, 1992), pp. 183-204 and 317-322—reprinted below, Chapter 28.

CHAPTER 16

A New Slavic Nationality?
The Rusyns of East-Central Europe[*]

S ince the Revolutions of 1989 and the fall of the Soviet Union, it has become commonplace to read about the so-called appearance of a new Slavic nationality, the Rusyns of east-central Europe. Such a

[*]This study was written for a panel entitled "A New Slavic Nationality?: The Rusyns of East Central Europe," at the 27th National Convention of the American Association for the Advancement of Slavic Studies held in Washington, D.C., October 29, 1995. It is scheduled to appear with other panel contributions in *Harvard Ukrainian Studies* (Cambridge, Mass., forthcoming). It was presented in French at the Congress of the Maison des Pays, held in Prešov, Slovakia, August 23-24, 1996, and at the Institute of Slavic Studies of the University of Paris (Sorbonne), on May 1997, and subsequently published in its journal under the title: "Une nouvelle nationalité slave: les Ruthènes de l'Europe du centre-est," *Revue des études slaves*, LXIX, 3 (Paris, 1997), pp. 417-428.

The text in English together with a translation into Rusyn by Anna Pliškova, "Nova slavian'ska narodnost'?," appeared in the bi-lingual work: Tom Trier, ed., *Focus on the Rusyns* (Copenhagen: Danish Cultural Institute, 1999), pp. 15-29. Other translations have been published: into Rusyn (by Ivan Petrovtsi), "Novŷi slavians'kŷi narod?: Rusynŷ serydnëvostochnoi Europy," *Rusyns'ka bysida*, II, 1, 2 and 4 (Uzhhorod, 1998), pp. 3, 2, and 3; and into Slovak (by L'ubica Babotová), "Nová slovanská národnost'?: Rusíni stredovýchodnej Európy," in Marian Gajdoš and Stanislav Konečný, eds., *Etnické minority na Slovensku* (Košice: Spoločenskovedný ústav SAV, 1997), pp. 251-263. An abridged Czech translation by Bohumil Svoboda, "Nový slovanský národ: Rusíni ve východní části střední Evropy," appeared in Paul Robert Magocsi, *Rusíni a jejich vlast* (Prague: Společnost přátel Podkarpatské Rusi, 1996), pp. 51-59.

formulation raises certain theoretical problems. The term *new* implies two principles: that the nationality in question did not exist before, and that nationalities can be *created*. In this regard, I agree with those theorists of nationalism like Ernest Gellner, who argue that nationalities are "the artifacts of men's [and women's] convictions and loyalties and solidarities."[1] To paraphrase Gellner further: people are only of the same nationality if they share the same culture, which is understood to be a system of ideas and ways of behaving and communicating. Still, individuals who have a common culture can be considered to comprise a nationality "only if they recognize each other as belonging to the same nation[ality]."[2] In other words, a *common culture* and a *will* to persist as a community are the two essential ingredients of a nationality.

If nationalities evolve from cultures, the next question is: from which of the thousands of cultures that are found throughout the world are specific nationalities formed? This leads to the problem of boundaries. In other words, where does, or can, the boundary between one culture, language, and potential nationality end and where does another begin? As even a cursory glance at the last century of historical development will reveal, cultural and nationality boundaries—like political boundaries—are flexible and they do change. For instance, at the outset of the twentieth century, no Slavic scholar recognized the existence of Macedonians as a distinct nationality. Today, however, Macedonians are considered one of the twelve commonly acknowledged Slavic nationalities. Analogously, Rusyns in the past were considered by various theorists to be Russians, or Ukrainians, or a distinct Rusyn nationality. Other theorists argued that Rusyns were Slovaks or Magyars of the Greek Catholic faith. Such identities, which reflected decisions about cultural boundaries, were often imposed by political forces external to Rusyn society. Nevertheless, they were accepted to a greater or lesser degree by the Rusyns themselves.[3]

---

[1] Ernest Gellner, *Nations and Nationalism* (Ithaca, N.Y. and London, 1983), p. 7. Gellner actually uses the term *nation*; I prefer *nationality* in order to avoid confusion with a state which the English term *nation* often implies.

[2] Ibid.

[3] On the evolution of national identities among Rusyns, see Paul Robert Magocsi, *The Shaping of a National Identity: Subcarpathian Rus', 1848-1948* (Cambridge, Mass., 1978).

The recent national revival

What is new today about Rusyns is not their existence as a people or culture, since their presence in the Carpathian region of east-central Europe can be traced back at least to the ninth, if not the fifth and sixth centuries. What is new, however, is their status as a nationality. And even that is not such a new thing, since during the interwar decades, when most Rusyns lived in Czechoslovakia, many saw themselves and were recognized by state authorities as a distinct Slavic people. Therefore, when speaking of the Rusyns today, it might be preferable to speak of a "renewed" instead of a "new" Slavic nationality.

While Rusyns have never had their own state, they have had on several occasions in the twentieth century autonomous status, often with many of the political trappings of statehood (governors, prime ministers, official language, national anthem, etc.). After World War II, however, and during more than four decades of Communist rule, in every country where Rusyns lived, with the exception of Yugoslavia, their nationality was banned and they were administratively declared to be Ukrainian. As numerous officially sanctioned publications from those post-1945 decades were fond of saying, the nationality problem among the Rusyns was "resolved" because of the enlightened policies of Marxism-Leninism.[4]

It was the decline and eventual collapse of centralized Communist rule between the mid 1980s to 1991 that made possible the renewal of a Rusyn nationality. The story of that renewal has already been told several times and will only be outlined briefly here.[5] The first group

---

[4]A good example of such views are found in the many works of Ivan Bajcura, including his *Ukrajinská otázka v ČSSR* (Košice, 1967); *Cesta k internacionálnej jednote* (Bratislava, 1983); and "Vývoj a riešenie ukrajinskej otázky v ČSSR," in *Socialistickou cestou k národnostnej rovnoprávnosti* (Bratislava, 1975), pp. 11-32.

[5]Among the more analytical discussions about the recent Rusyn national revival are: Paul Robert Magocsi, "The Birth of a New Nation, or the Return of an Old Problem? The Rusyns of East Central Europe," *Canadian Slavonic Papers*, XXXIV, 3 (Edmonton, 1992), pp. 199-223—reprinted above, Chapter 16; L'udovít Haraksim, "The National Identity of the Rusyns of East Slovakia," in Jana Plichtová, ed., *Minorities in Politics: Cultural and Language Rights* (Bratislava, 1992), pp. 228-235; Ivan Hranchak, "Khto taki rusyny i choho vony khochut'," *Polityka i chas*, no. 12 (Kiev, 1993), pp. 45-54; M. P. Makara and I. I. Myhovych, "Karpats'ki rusyny v konteksti suchasnoho etnopolitychnoho zhyttia," *Ukraïns'kyi istorychnyi zhurnal*

of Rusyns to challenge the supposedly "resolved" nationality question were the Lemkos of Poland. Of all Rusyns, the Lemkos had the most difficult recent past, since between 1945 and 1947, almost the entire population (about 180,000) was resettled to the Soviet Ukraine or deported to the far western regions of Poland, in particular Silesia. During the 1960s and 1970s, about 10,000 to 15,000 managed to return from western Poland to their Carpathian villages, but it was mainly among the dispersed "immigrant" population living "abroad" (i.e., in western Poland) that in the 1980s questions began to be raised about the group's national identity and about its lost Carpathian homeland. The discussions took place through articles in the press, programs on Polish television, and at an annual cultural festival (the Vatra) that brought together from three to seven thousand people each summer to a Carpathian village for a weekend of learning and group self-discovery.

It was not until the fall of Communist regimes in 1989, however, that a full-fledged Rusyn movement began with the establishment of formal organizational structures. Again, it was in Poland where the first Rusyn organization was established, the Lemko Association in April 1989. Four other organizations followed in quick succession during 1990: the Society of Carpatho-Rusyns in Ukraine; the Rusyn Renaissance Society in Slovakia; the Society of Friends of Subcarpathian Rus' in the Czech Republic; as well as the Ruska Matka Society in Yugoslavia, the only country which never banned and actively supported a Rusyn identity and cultural life. Within two years even Rusyns in Hungary, where it was thought the group had been assimilated as long ago as before World War I, established the Organization of Rusyns in Hungary. Since their establishment, each of these new organizations has conveyed its message through the publication of Rusyn-language newspapers or magazines (*Besida, Narodnŷ novynkŷ, Rusyn, Podkarpats'ka Rus', Ruske slovo, Rusynskŷi zhyvot*), public lectures, conferences, and festivals.

Regardless of the organization or its country of location, the message of each is basically the same and consists of the following basic prin-

(Kiev, 1994), pp. 117-128; and Ivan Pop and Volodymyr Halas, "Stanú sa Zakarpatci štátotvornýn národom?," *Mezinárodné otázky*, III, 2 (Bratislava 1994), pp. 33-42.

ciples. (1) Rusyns form one people or nationality (*narod*) and, with the exception of Yugoslavia and the resettled groups in Poland, live as the indigenous population in the valleys of the Carpathians where their ancestors settled as long ago as the early middle ages. (2) Rusyns are not a branch of any other nationality, whether Ukrainian, Russian, Polish, or Slovak, but rather a distinct fourth East Slavic nationality. (3) As a distinct nationality, Rusyns need to have their own codified literary language based on spoken dialects. (4) In all countries where Rusyns live, they should enjoy rights accorded all national minorities, including use of the Rusyn language in newspapers, radio, television, and most important, for instruction in schools.

In Ukraine's Transcarpathia, where nearly three quarters of all Rusyns in Europe live, the group's expectations have gone beyond the merely cultural. First of all, Transcarpathia's Rusyns do not consider themselves a national minority, but rather the "autochtonous" majority population. Secondly, they argue that the autonomous status of the region, first as Subcarpathian Rus' within interwar Czechoslovakia and then as the Transcarpathian Ukraine during the last months of World War II (November 1944 to June 1945), was illegally abolished by the Soviet authorities.[6] Therefore, the autochtonous Rusyns feel they have a legal right to have a "republic of Subcarpathian Rus'" within an independent Ukraine. In response to that demand, a special question was placed on the referendum for Ukrainian independence in December

[6]The argument is that despite the wartime Allied decision to restore Czechoslovakia according to its pre-Munich (1938) boundaries, which would have included Subcarpathian Rus', Stalin decided to annex the region for strategic purposes—direct access for the Soviet Union to the Danubian Basin. Czechoslovakia's provisional national parliament formally agreed to give up the region in June 1945. Meanwhile, from November 1944 to June 1945, the region had governed itself and was, as an autonomous territory called Transcarpathian Ukraine, treated as a subject of international law. In January 1946, the Soviet Ukrainian government unilaterally demoted the region to an oblast without any particular autonomous rights. All these developments are considered in violation of international law by Rusyn spokespersons, the most prolific of whom is Petro Hodmash as expressed in a series of articles (1991-1995) in the Uzhhorod newspaper, *Podkarpats'ka Rus'*. An impartial discussion of these same developments is found in a recent monograph by Mykola P. Makara, *Zakarpats'ka Ukraïna: shliakh do vozz"iednannia, dosvid rozvytku, zhovten' 1944—sichen' 1946 rr.* (Uzhhorod, 1995).

1991. As high as 78 percent of Transcarpathia's inhabitants voted in favor of self-rule for their region. To date, autonomy has not been granted by Ukraine, although the struggle for its attainment continues to be carried out by several deputies in the Transcarpathian regional parliament (Oblastna Rada).

It is in Slovakia, however, where the Rusyn movement has garnered its greatest successes. In 1990, the former professional Ukrainian National Theater based in the group's cultural center of Prešov was transformed into the Aleksander Dukhovych Theater. Since then performances are given primarily in Rusyn. The use of Rusyn in publications and theatrical performances prompted increasing calls for language codification. That process began at an international conference in November 1992,[7] and culminated in January 1995 with the formal announcement of a codified Rusyn language for Slovakia that accompanied the publication of a rulebook of Rusyn grammar, an orthographic and a terminological dictionary, and school textbooks.[8] The codification process was carried out under the direction of the Institute of Rusyn Language and Culture, established in early 1993 in Prešov as the first step toward what is hoped to be a department of Rusyn language and culture at Prešov University.

The developments in Slovakia were in large part possible because in the March 1991 census of former federal Czecho-Slovakia, Rusyns were recorded as a distinct nationality (with 16,937 respondants) and Rusyn as a distinct mother tongue (49,099 respondants).[9] Since that time

---

[7]Writers, journalists, and scholars agreed to adopt the model followed by the Romansch in Switzerland, who were represented at the Rusyn language congress. This means that Rusyns in Ukraine, Slovakia, Poland, and Yugoslavia are to create standards for their own region while simultaneously working on a "fifth standard" (koiné) that in the future would be used by all. A Yugoslav Rusyn standard already exists; a Rusyn standard for Slovakia was codified in January 1995; two more standards for Ukraine and for Poland are in process. See Paul Robert Magocsi and Joshua Fishman, "Scholarly Seminar on the Codification of the Rusyn Language," *International Journal of the Sociology of Language*, No. 104 (Berlin and New York), pp. 119-125.

[8]See Paul Robert Magocsi, ed., *A New Slavic Language is Born: The Rusyn Literary Language of Slovakia* (New York, 1995).

[9]These figures are for Slovakia only. From the same indigenous population, the number who identified as Ukrainian was only 13,847 (nationality) and 9,480

Rusyns are considered a national minority eligible for funds from Slovakia's Ministry of Culture and Ministry of Education. Similarly, laws on national minorities were either passed in Hungary (July 1993) and proposed in Poland, in which Rusyns are listed as a distinct nationality. As a result, Rusyns in those two countries have been granted governmental funding for publications, for organizational and cultural activity, and, in the case of Hungary, for a university department in Nyíregyháza.[10] Despite the war in former Yugoslavia, Rusyns there are still recognized as one of the five official nationalities in the Vojvodina where they continue to receive financial support for schools, publications, the media, and other cultural activity. It is only in Ukraine that Rusyns are not recognized as a distinct nationality. This means that Rusyn organizations and publications in that country are ineligible for state support.

Thus, since the 1980s, and in particular since the Revolution of 1989, Rusyns have experienced a national revival in each country where they live. But how does this newest national revival differ from previous ones, such as the first revival which occurred during the two decades after 1848, and the second revival during the interwar years of the twentieth century? And does the most recent revival promise any more lasting success than the first two?

Characteristics of the recent national revival

One of the more striking aspects of the current national revival is its all-Rusyn or interregional context. For the first time in their history, Rusyns from every country have been meeting periodically and to a large degree coordinating their cultural activity. It is true that in the past Rusyns from one region may have cooperated with those in another region, such as the period after World War I when Rusyn-American immigrants in the United States played on active role in homeland politics, or when Lemko Rusyns from Galicia tried to unite with their

---

(mother tongue). Czech and Slovak Federal Republic, *Preliminary Results of the Population and Housing Census* (Prague, 1991), p. 38; *Narodný novynký*, August 4, 1993, p. 1.

[10]This is actually a joint Department of Ukrainian and Rusyn Philology at the Bessenyei School of Higher Education, headed by the specialist on the Rusyn language of Yugoslavia, Dr. István Udvari.

brethren south of the mountains. These and other efforts were limited, however, both in geographic scope and time (usually no more than a few months).

Recent Rusyn interregional cooperation was initiated at the First World Congress of Rusyns held in Medzilaborce, Slovakia in March 1991. Since then, meetings of the executive (Svitova Rada) of the congress have been held every six months, while the full congress itself meets every two years (1993 in Krynica, Poland; 1995 in Ruski Krstur, Yugoslavia; 1997 in Budapest, Hungary).[11] Rusyns from various countries have also participated in several scholarly conferences as well as at the "First Congress" of the Rusyn language held in November 1992, which established the theoretical and practical principles for the creation of a codified Rusyn literary language. Finally, the professional Aleksander Dukhnovych Theater from Prešov, Slovakia has become a kind of all-Rusyn "national" theater, featuring plays by Rusyn authors from Slovakia and other countries and travelling to perform for Rusyns in Poland, Ukraine, Hungary, the Czech Republic, and Yugoslavia. Aside from several concrete projects (joint work on language codification, anthologies of Rusyn poetry and prose, an encyclopedia of Rusyn history), these periodic meetings and theatrical performances have afforded writers and other cultural activists the opportunity to meet, to exchange ideas, and to realize that their own aspirations are similar to those of Rusyns in other countries from whom they can learn and work in solidarity for the achievement of both common and specific goals. In short, the present Rusyn national revival has broken out of the provincial-minded mode that had characterized previous revivals during the second half of the nineteenth century and the interwar years of the twentieth century.

Indeed, modern technology has made cooperation much easier, as texts and other communications are readily transmitted by telephone, FAX, and computer disk. Consequently, the Rusyn Renaissance Society in Prešov is able to publish the bi-monthly magazine, *Rusyn* (Prešov, 1990-present), which functions as the organ of the World Congress and which contains reports and articles in each issue on the activity of

---

[11]For the work and resolutions of the first three world congresses, see the *Carpatho-Rusyn American*, XIV, 2 and 3 (Pittsburgh, Pa., 1991), pp. 7-9 and 9; XVI, 2 and 3 (1993), pp. 11 and 10; XVIII, 2 (1995), pp. 9-10.

Rusyns in whichever country they live. The automobile has also made possible more frequent physical contact between activists from the various Rusyn regions, the farthest from each other being the Lemko Region in Poland and the Vojvodina in Yugoslavia separated by a distance of some 400 kilometers.

Aside from its technical aspect, interregional communication has also been made possible by a profound change in the political climate. For over four decades following World War II, the Communist regimes throughout east-central Europe restricted the flow of traffic across borders and actively discouraged contact between Rusyns. For instance, as late as the mid 1980s, otherwise informed leaders among the Lemko Rusyns of Poland did not even know that there were Rusyns in Yugoslavia's Vojvodina, who—in what seemed to be a miracle—had their own state-supported Rusyn schools, cultural institutions, publications, radio, and even television programs. Moreover, before the early 1990s, no Rusyns anywhere ever believed that there were still Rusyns living in northeastern Hungary as well as in that country's capital, Budapest.

This explosion of awareness in the past half decade has been significantly enhanced by the open border policies of the post-Communist regimes in Poland, Slovakia, Hungary, and Ukraine. The new democratic regimes in those countries are concerned with upholding the agreements that each has signed as members of the Conference on Security and Cooperation in Europe (CSCE). In part, the motivation driving CSCE signatories from east-central Europe is a desire to maintain a positive image among other European countries, most especially the present members of the European Community. As a result of this international political equation, Rusyns have come to enjoy the fruits of two CSCE agreements. Member states meeting in Copenhagen in June 1990 agreed that "to belong to a national minority is a matter of a person's individual choice," and that "persons belonging to national minorities can exercise and enjoy their rights individually as well as in community with other members of their group."[12] One year later in Geneva, CSCE member states agreed that individuals and organizations representing national minorities would be allowed "unimpeded contacts ... across frontiers ... with persons with whom they share a common

[12]*Document of the Copenhagen Meeting of the Conference on the Human Dimension of the CSCE* (Copenhagen, 1990), pp. 40-41.

ethnic or national origin."[13]

In a real sense, Rusyns have become the concern of many other European countries and non-governmental organizations.[14] This is because the rights of Rusyns to their own national identity and to self-expression in their own language derive from the general principles on human rights that are considered today inalienable for all Europeans. Fully aware of their status as one of Europe's many peoples, Rusyns today are in contact with several European organizations that are concerned with the fate of national minorities and of lesser-used, or threatened languages. The Rusyn Renaissance Society in Slovakia, for instance, is a founding member of the Maison des Pays minority association based in France.

There is one aspect, however, in which the present Rusyn national revival is similar to previous ones. As in the past, the present revival has what might be called "internal enemies," or antagonistic rivals. To be sure, neither in the past nor in the present did or does every individual of Rusyn heritage believe that the ethnolinguistic group to which he or she belongs should function as a distinct nationality. In the nineteenth century, the "internal enemy" consisted of magyarones, that is Rusyns who wanted at all costs to give up their Slavic heritage and become part of the Magyar state nationality. Later, during the interwar years of the twentieth century, large numbers of Rusyns believed they were—and they therefore became—Russians or Ukrainians. As a corollary, they rejected the idea of a distinct Rusyn nationality. Today, it is only the pro-Ukrainians who remain the nemesis of Rusyns.

From the very outset of the present Rusyn national revival in 1989, local Ukrainian organizations rejected what they branded as "Rusyn separatism" and "political Rusynism." Such phenomena are described

---

[13]*Report of the CSCE Meeting of Experts on National Minorities* (Geneva, 1991), p. 10.

[14]Moreover, Rusyns have become known beyond specialist literature and figure in encyclopedic works like: *An Ethnohistorical Dictionary of the Russian and Soviet Empires*, ed. James S. Olson (Westport, Conn. and London, 1994), pp. 135-140; *Encyclopedia of World Cultures*, Vol. VI: *Russia and Eurasia China*, ed. Paul Friedrich and Norma Diamond (Boston, 1994), pp. 69-71; *Minorities in Central and Eastern Europe*, Minority Rights Group International Report (London, 1993) pp. 23-26; and *The Times Guide to the Peoples of Europe*, ed. Felipe Fernández-Armesto (London 1994), pp. 267-269.

as harmful to the unity of the Ukrainian nationality and, if continued, will allegedly—at least outside Ukraine—eventually lead to the complete assimilation of Rusyns into either Slovaks, Poles, or Serbs.[15] While it is true that the protests against Rusyns on the part of Ukrainians directed especially at the governments of Poland, Slovakia, Ukraine, and Yugoslavia have at times hampered Rusyn efforts at obtaining state support, there is also a positive side to such criticism. New movements are able to focus better on specific goals when they are criticized from without. In other words, the Rusyn movement has actually been helped by pro-Ukrainians, since there is often no better way to convince an individual to define his or her frequently vague or passive sense of identity than if someone else tries to deny that identity and therefore their own existence. In that sense, the oft-repeated Ukrainian polemical phrase, "There is not and cannot be a Rusyn language and people," has helped to produce the opposite result—Rusyns who have decided to identify themselves as belonging to a distinct nationality.[16]

Finally, the gender and socioeconomic composition of participants in the present Rusyn revival is much different than those which have gone before. In earlier revivals, the leadership roles and articulate

[15]The recent anti-Rusyn polemical literature on the part of pro-Ukrainian authors is quite extensive. Among the more illustrative titles (followed by translations) include: Iurii Baleha, "Rusynstvo: ideolohy i pokrovyteli"/Rusynism: Its Ideologues and Protectors, *Dzvin*, LII, 5 (L'viv, 1991), pp. 96-109; Mikuláš Štec, *K otázke 'rusínskeho' spisovného jazyka*/On the Question of the So-Called 'Rusyn' Literary Language (Prešov, 1991); Stepan Hostyniak, *Pro 'chetvertyi' skhidnoslov"ians'kyi narod ta pro placheni vyhadky i nisenitnytsi kupky komediantiv*/About the So-called 'Fourth' East Slavic People and the Paid Fantasies and Stupidities of a Group of Comedians (Prešov, 1992); Oleksa Myshanych, *'Karpatorusynstvo', ioho dzherela i evoliutsiia u XX st.*/'Carpatho-Rusynism': Its Sources and Evolution in the 20th Century (Kiev, 1992); Oleksa Myshanych, *Karpaty nas ne rozluchat'*/The Carpathians Do Not Divide Us (Uzhhorod, 1993); Oleksa Myshanych, *Politychne rusynstvo i shcho za nym*/Political Rusynism and What's Behind It (Uzhhorod, 1993); and Ivan Vanat, *Do pytannia pro tak zvanu ukraïnizatsiiu rusyniv Priashchivshchyny*/On the Question of the So-Called Ukrainianization of the Rusyns in the Prešov Region (Prešov, 1993).

[16]A few Ukrainian writers have even recognized the counter-productive nature of their attacks. See, for instance, the insightful commentary by Andrii Kviatkovs'kyi, "Prydnistrov'ia!!! Krym!!! Zakarpattia?," *Post-postup*, No. 21 (L'viv, 1992).

spokespersons were almost exclusively male. Since 1989, however women are conspicuously present at Rusyn World Congresses, at conferences, and on the editorial staffs of newspapers. Nor are women present simply as tokens or in subordinate positions. For instance, the director of the influential Rusyn publishing house in Yugoslavia, the leading Rusyn scholar in Poland, and the editor of the only periodical about Rusyn affairs published in the Untied States are all female. Moreover, it seems that the visible presence of women in the Rusyn movement has occurred not because of any conscious effort at achieving gender balance but rather as a result of respect for individual talent and commitment to the national revival.

While it would be inappropriate to overemphasize the role of women, it is not an exaggeration to call the present Rusyn revival a movement of youth, which in many ways resembles a revolt of "sons against the fathers." In that regard, it is ironic to note that the founder of the Society of Carpatho-Rusyns in Ukraine (Mykhailo M. Tomchanyi) and the founder of the Rusyn Initiative Group just after the Velvet Revolution in Czechoslovakia (Aleksander Zozuliak—also the founding and present editor of *Narodnŷ novynkŷ* and *Rusyn*), are sons of two leading post-World War II Ukrainian writers in their respective countries (Mykhailo Tomchanyi in Ukraine and Vasyl' Zozuliak in Slovakia). Both sons were raised and educated as Ukrainians and both believed themselves to be Ukrainians until the Revolution of 1989, which served as a catalyst for self-discovery and what they came to consider their true Rusyn heritage. The emphasis on youth is evident in the founding chairpersons of the new Rusyn organizations in Poland, Ukraine, Slovakia, Hungary, and Yugoslavia. All were between 32 and 45 years of age when the present revival began in 1989-1990. Also, in contrast to leaders in previous Rusyn national revivals, who were often accused by their rivals as nationally retarded, not yet educated, and therefore not conscious of a Ukrainian identity, the present Rusyn national revival is made up of leaders and spokespersons, all of whom were educated in the Ukrainian language and who often identified as Ukrainian before, at some point, consciously rejecting that identity and "returning" to something they felt was closer to their true being.

Education is perhaps the most important of the factors that characterizes the new Rusyn movement. Until the mid-twentieth century, nearly 90 percent of Rusyns were rural dwellers engaged in small-scale agriculture and related pursuits. Illiteracy ranged from 30 to

50 percent in various regions during the 1930s, with the remainder of the population having only a few years of elementary school. The interwar Czechoslovak regime began to raise educational levels, but it was the post-World War II Communist regimes that truly brought about an educational revolution. Along with the spread of education came industrialization and the migration of thousands of rural Rusyns to work in factories in nearby towns and cities, most especially in Slovakia and to a lesser degree in Ukraine's Transcarpathia.[17]

As a result, most Rusyn national activists today have university degrees, have spent most of their lives in urban areas not villages, and are fully comfortable functioning in modern industrialized societies. Of even greater contrast with the past is the fact that the present intellectual leadership now has as much of a constituency living in towns as in villages. Regardless of where that constituency lives, nearly all its members have at least a high school (*gymnasium*) level education and are therefore more easily able to understand the value of preserving the Rusyn heritage.

The very fact that at least half the Rusyn population lives in towns has another advantage. This is related to the fact that the desire for cultural preservation often reflects a nostalgic longing on the part of urban dwellers to recapture a rural-based pristine youth surrounded by loving grandparents. While such a phenomenon is largely gone, it does remain an image that is perhaps stronger than ever in the mind. This does not mean, however, that the present-day creative Rusyn intelligentsia is satisfied simply with folk-dancing or with maintaining other forms of quaint but now antiquated rural cultural artifacts. Instead, the urban-based intelligentsia with its higher levels of education is producing forms of Rusyn culture that include experimental theater, political satire, a literature that addresses the human condition in late-twentieth century urban society, and abstract art. Again, it is an irony

---

[17]Although after 1945 the Soviets established many new industries in Transcarpathia, they frequently staffed them with managers *and* workers brought in from neighboring Galicia, far eastern Ukraine, and Russia who settled permanently in the region. Consequently, many Rusyns remained in their native villages untouched by Soviet industrialization. In order to survive many males earned extra income by doing seasonal work in other parts of Ukraine, much the same way that older generations had earned supplemental income by working in former western Czechoslovakia (Bohemia and Moravia), Hungary, or the United States.

of history that the Rusyn roots of the American Pop artist and modern cultural icon, Andy Warhol, were discovered by activists in the Rusyn national revival who managed in 1991 to create in the small town of Medzilaborce in Slovakia a large-scale Warhol Family Museum of Modern Art—complete with two kiosk-sized replicas of Campbell's Tomato Soup cans that stand at the museum's entrance in stark contrast to the lush green of the surrounding Carpathian countryside.[18]

Future prospects

But what does all of this mean for the immediate and long-term future? Does the interregional aspect of the latest national revival combined with possibilities offered by modern communicational facilities, a favorable international environment in an increasingly regionally-conscious Europe, and the existence of a gender-balanced highly educated leadership and constituency guarantee the future survival of a distinct Rusyn nationality in the Carpathian homeland? Predictions are by their very nature problematic. Therefore, it might be preferable not to make predictions but rather to point out areas of concern which, if addressed, may have a decisive impact on the present Rusyn national revival.

The rediscovery—some would say the creation—of a national heritage is one thing, its preservation for future generations is quite another. In this regard, the Rusyn movement faces the critical task of assuring the establishment of classes in the Rusyn language and programs that stress a distinct Rusyn culture and historical development in elementary and secondary schools. In order for that to happen, university departments and research centers need to be created to define and promote Rusyn disciplines as well as train teachers.

Here the role of the state and its policy toward national minorities becomes crucial. Slovakia, Poland, and Hungary seem in theory favorably inclined toward some kind of Rusyn instruction in schools where there are children of Rusyn background. Nevertheless, the governments of Slovakia, Poland, and Hungary still have to be encouraged to transform theory into practice, as is already the case among Rusyns in Yugoslavia. As for Ukraine, its public and policy makers need to be

[18]Jozef Keselica, "The Warhol Story in Czechoslovakia," *Carpatho-Rusyn American*, XIV, 4 (Pittsburgh, Pa., 1991), pp. 8-11.

persuaded that the recognition of Rusyns as a distinct nationality is not in itself a threat to Ukraine as a state. Just as Catalans can be loyal subjects of Spain while not having to identify as or speak Castilian Spanish, so too can Ukraine have within its borders a distinct Rusyn nationality and even a self-governing region in Transcarpathia, both of which could strengthen rather than weaken the Ukrainian state.

State ideology does not, of course, operate in a vacuum. It is dependent upon and is influenced by the economic health of the country. It is well known that all countries where Rusyns live, in particular Ukraine, Slovakia, and Yugoslavia, are presently experiencing difficult economic times. Nevertheless, despite such harsh realities, those states—like all European states—need to be reminded that nationalities like the Rusyns are indigenous peoples entitled to the same legal and economic rights accorded citizens of every other nationality, including the dominant or state nationality. In other words, support for minority nationalities should not be considered a kind of cultural frill removable in times of economic hardship, but rather as an economic right earned by citizens of Rusyn background who pay taxes like every other citizen. Put another way, state funding should automatically be allotted to Rusyn cultural and educational activity in proportion to the size of the Rusyn tax-paying population.

Such concerns are likely to fill the social and political agendas in each of the countries where Rusyns live. The resolution of those concerns will vary depending on the skill of Rusyn lobbyists and the changing political and ecomonic fortunes of the various states in which they live. What does seem more certain than ever before, however, is the existence of a significant percentage of highly-educated males and females who believe they are part of a distinct Rusyn nationality and who are likely to pass on that belief to future generations regardless what formal structures for cultural and identity transmission may be created by the state. The existence of such an educated population that both produces and depends upon the existence of a high culture is, to paraphrase once again the theorist Ernest Gellner, the most important guarantee for the future survival of a Rusyn nationality.

Part II

Carpatho-Rusyns in North America

MAP 13

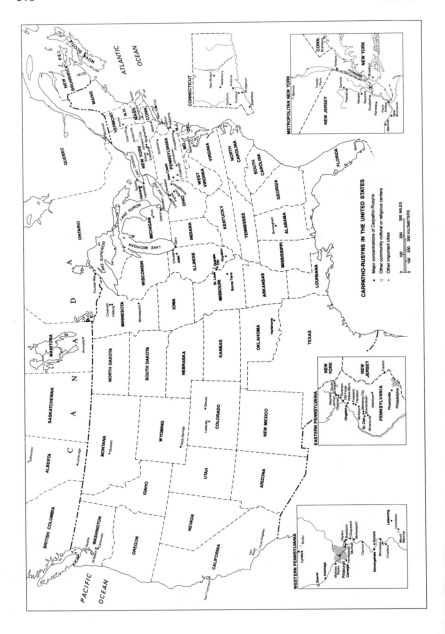

CHAPTER 17

Carpatho-Rusyns in the United States[*]

C arpatho-Rusyns began immigrating to the United States in the late 1870s and 1880s. By the outbreak of World War I in 1914, approximately 225,000 had arrived. This was to be the largest number of Carpatho-Rusyns ever to reach America. When after World War I emigration resumed, only about 20,000 came in the second wave during the interwar years. From World War II to the present, the numbers were smaller still—at the most 10,000. Upon arrival in the United States, the vast majority of Carpatho-Rusyns—also known as Carpatho-Russians, Lemkos, or Ruthenians—identified with the state that they had left. It is, therefore, impossible to know their exact number. Based on immigration statistics and membership records in religious and secular organizations, it is reasonable to assume that there are about 620,000 Americans who have at least one ancestor of Carpatho-Rusyn background.

At the time of the first and largest wave of immigration (1880s-1914), the Carpatho-Rusyn homeland was located entirely within the Austro-Hungarian Empire. The empire was itself divided into two parts: about three-quarters of Carpatho-Rusyns lived in the northeastern corner of the Hungarian Kingdom, the remainder in the Austrian province of Galicia. In both parts of Austria-Hungary, the economic situation for

---

[*] This study was commissioned as an encyclopedic entry, entitled "Carpatho-Rusyn Americans," first published in Judy Galens, Anna Sheets, and Robyn V. Young, eds., *Gale Encyclopedia of Multicultural America*, Vol. I (New York: Gale Research, 1995), pp. 252-261.

Carpatho-Rusyns was the same. Their approximately 1,200 villages were located in hilly or mountainous terrain from which the inhabitants eked out a subsistence-level existence based on small-scale agriculture, livestock grazing (especially sheep), and seasonal labor on the richer plains of lowland Hungary. Their livelihood was always precarious, however, and following a growth in the population and shortage of land many were forced to emigrate to the United States.

Most of the earliest immigrants in the 1870s and 1880s were young males who hoped to work a year or so and then return home. Some engaged in seasonal labor and, as sojourners, may have migrated back and forth several times between Europe and America in the decades before 1914. Others eventually brought their families and stayed permanently. Whereas before World War I, movement between Europe and America was relatively easy for enthusiastic young labourers, after World War II, Communist rule in the European homeland put an effective end to virtually all cross-border emigration and seasonal migration.

Since earning money was the main goal of the immigrants, they settled primarily in the northeastern and north-central states, in particular the coal mining region around Scranton and Wilkes-Barre in eastern Pennsylvania, and in the steel-producing center of Pittsburgh and its suburbs in the western part of that state. Other cities and metropolitan areas that attracted Carpatho-Rusyns were New York City-northeastern New Jersey; southern Connecticut; the Binghamton-Endicott-Johnson City triangle in southcentral New York; Cleveland and Youngstown, Ohio; Gary and Whiting, Indiana; Detroit and Flint, Michigan; and Minneapolis, Minnesota.

By 1920, nearly 80 percent of all Carpatho-Rusyns lived in only three states: Pennsylvania (54 percent), New York (13 percent), and New Jersey (12 percent). This settlement pattern was been in large part retained by the second-, third-, and fourth-generation descendants of Carpatho-Rusyns, although gradually most left the inner cities for the surrounding suburbs. Since the 1970s, there has also been migration out of the northeast, in particular to the sun-belt states of Florida, Arizona, and California.

Like other eastern and southern Europeans, Carpatho-Rusyns were not discriminated against because of their color, although they were effectively segregated from the rest of American society because of their low economic status and lack of knowledge of English. They were never singled out as a group, but rather lumped together with other Slavic and Hungarian laborers and called by the opprobrious epithet, Hunkies. This was, however, a relatively short-term phase, since the American-born sons and daughters of the original immigrants had by the late 1930s and 1940s adapted to the host society and become absorbed into the American "middle class." Effectively, today Americans of Carpatho-Rusyn descent are an invisible minority within the white middle class majority.

Acculturation and assimilation

The relationship of Carpatho-Rusyns to American society has changed several times during the more than one hundred years since they began to arrive in significant numbers in the United States. There are basically three phases or periods during which the attitudes of Carpatho-Rusyns toward American society have ranged from minimal adaptation to total assimilation and acceptance of the "American norm."

During the first period, from the 1880s to about 1925, Carpatho-Rusyns felt estranged both linguistically and culturally from the American world surrounding them. Not only did they speak a foreign language, they were also members of a distinct Eastern Christian church that initially did not exist in the United States. Upon arrival, Carpatho-Rusyns were all Byzantine, or Greek Catholics; that is, adherents of a church that followed Orthodox ritual but was jurisdictionally united with the Catholic Church under the Pope in Rome. The American Roman Catholic hierarchy, however, did not accept—and in some cases did not even recognize—Greek Catholic priests. Since religion was a very important factor in their daily lives in Europe, where Greek Catholicism had become virtually synonymous with Carpatho-Rusyn culture and identity, the immigrants, after finding a job to support themselves materially, sought ways to assure their spiritual fulfillment.

Not finding their own church and being rejected by the American Roman Catholics, Carpatho-Rusyns built their own churches, invited priests from the European homeland, and created fraternal and mutual-benefit organizations to provide insurance and worker's compensation in times of sickness or accident as well as to support the new churches. The oldest and still the largest of these fraternal societies was the Greek Catholic Union, founded in 1892 in Wilkes-Barre, Pennsylvania and then transferred to the suburbs of Pittsburgh in 1906. The churches and fraternals each had their services and publications in the Carpatho-Rusyn language as well as schools in which children were taught the language of their parents. In short, during this first period, the immigrants felt that they could not be accepted fully into American society, and so they created various kinds of religious and secular organizations that would preserve their old world culture and language.

The second period in Rusyn-American life lasted from about 1925 to 1975. For nearly a half century, the children of immigrants born in the United States increasingly rejected the old world heritage of their parents and tried to assimilate fully into American life. New youth organizations were founded that used only English, while the most popular sports clubs, even within the pre-World War I organizations, were devoted to mainstream American sports like baseball, basketball, bowling, and golf. By the 1950s, the formerly vibrant Rusyn-language press had switched almost entirely to English. Even the Byzantine Greek Catholic Church, which in the intervening years developed into a jurisdictionally distinct religious body, began to do away with traditions that were different from those in the Roman Catholic Church. In short, Carpatho-Rusyns seemed to want to do everything possible—even at the expense of forgetting their ethnic and religious heritage—to be like "other" Americans. The international situation was indirectly helpful in this regard, since throughout virtually this entire period Carpatho-Rusyn Americans were cut off from the European homeland by the economic hardships of the 1930s, World War II, and finally the imposition of Communist rule and the creation after 1945 of the Iron Curtain that restricted emigration abroad.

The third phase in Rusyn-American life began about 1975 and has lasted to the present. Like many other "assimilated" Americans, the third-generation descendants of Carpatho-Rusyn immigrants want to know what their grandparents knew so well but what their parents tried desperately to forget. The stimulus for this quest at ethnic rediscovery was the "roots fever" that surrounded the nationwide telecast of the African-American saga *Roots* and the celebrations surrounding the bicentennial of the United States in 1976.

New organizations such as the Carpatho-Rusyn Research Center and several Rusyn folk ensembles were founded in the late 1970s, and several new publications began to appear that dealt with all aspects of Carpatho-Rusyn culture. Finally, the Revolution of 1989 and the fall of Communism opened up the European homeland and provided new incentives for travel and for the firsthand re-discovery of one's roots and ancestral family ties. Thus, since the 1970s, an increasing number of Americans of Carpatho-Rusyn background have begun to learn about and maintain at the very least nostalgic ties with an ancestral culture that they otherwise never really knew. Moreover, in contrast to earlier times, American society as a whole no longer stigmatized such interest in the old world, but actually encouraged the search for one's roots.

Language

Carpatho-Rusyns are by origin Slavs. They speak a series of dialects that are classified as East Slavic and that are most closely related to Ukrainian. However, because their homeland is located within a political and linguistic borderland, Carpatho-Rusyn speech has been heavily influenced by neighboring West Slavic languages like Slovak and Polish as well as by Hungarian. Several attempts have been undertaken in the European homeland and in the United States to codify their unique speech into a distinct Carpatho-Rusyn literary language. The most successful results have been in the Vojvodina region of Yugoslavia, where a local Rusyn literary language has existed since the early 1920s, as well as in present-day Slovakia where a Rusyn literary language was formally codified in 1995.

The early immigrants to the United States used Rusyn for both spoken and written communication. As early as 1892, the *Amerykanskii russkii vîstnyk* (American Rusyn Bulletin) began to appear in Mahanoy City and eventually Homestead, Pennsylvania as the weekly and, at times, three-times-weekly newspaper of the group's largest fraternal society, the Greek Catholic Union. It was published entirely in Rusyn until 1952, after which it switched gradually and then entirely into English. That newspaper was one of fifty weekly and monthly Rusyn-language publications that have appeared in the United States, including the daily *Den'* (The Day; New York 1922-26). Traditionally, the Rusyn language uses the Cyrillic alphabet. Cyrillic was initially also used in the United States, although by the 1920s a Roman-based alphabet became more and more widespread. Today only one newspaper survives, the weekly *Karpats'ka Rus'/Carpatho-Rus'* (Yonkers, New York, 1939-), half of which is published in Rusyn using the Cyrillic alphabet, the other half in English.

First-generation immigrants, in particular, wanted to pass on the native language to their American-born offspring. Hence, church-sponsored parochial and weekend schools were set up, most especially during the period 1900 to 1930. To preserve the language, several Rusyn-American grammars, readers, catechisms, and other texts were published. The language was also used on a few radio programs in New York City, Pittsburgh, Cleveland and other cities with large Rusyn concentrations during the 1940s and 1950s. At present there are no Rusyn-language radio programs, and the language is taught formally only to students attending the Byzantine Catholic Seminary in Pittsburgh and the Carpatho-Russian Orthodox Diocesan Seminary in Johnstown, Pennsylvania.

Family and Community Dynamics

In the Carpatho-Rusyn homeland, where there was a need for agricultural laborers, families were often large, ranging in size from 6 to 10 children. Family homesteads might also house grandparents as well as a newly-wedded son or daughter and spouse waiting to earn enough to build their own home. The population of many villages comprised three or four extended families interrelated through blood or through relationship as godparents.

The immigrants who came to the United States were initially males who lived in boardinghouses. Those who remained eventually married in America or brought their families from Europe. The extended family structure typical of the European village was replaced by a nuclear family living in individual houses or apartments that included parents and on average 3 to 4 children.

Coming to the United States primarily before World War I, Carpatho-Rusyns entered a society in which there were little or no welfare programs or other forms of public assistance. The ideal was to take care of oneself, depending perhaps only on a fraternal insurance organization to which dues were paid. There was never any expectation that "the government" would assist individuals or families in what were considered their private lives. Such attitudes of self-reliance were passed on to the second and third generations, most of whom shunned public assistance even when it became available beginning in the 1930s. Only since the 1970s, with the widespread closing of steel mills and related industries in western Pennsylvania, where thousands suddenly found themselves out of work, have attitudes toward public assistance changed. This means that today third-, fourth- and fifth-generation Carpatho-Rusyns are likely to accept unemployment insurance whenever their livelihood is threatened.

The traditional old world pattern of marriages arranged by parents, sometimes with the help of a matchmaker, was with rare exceptions not followed among Carpatho-Rusyn immigrants. Instead, individuals have courted and found their own partners. At least until the 1950s, parents did not urge their daughters to continue their education after high school, but instead to get married and serve as the homemaker for a family. Boys, too, were more often than not encouraged to go to technical schools or to begin work as an apprentice in a trade. Since the 1960s, however, an increasing number of both young men and women are encouraged to attend colleges and universities, after which they work in fields such as communications, service industries, and medicine (especially nursing).

Whereas before the 1950s women were not encouraged to enter the work force, they were always welcome to take an active part in community activity. At least since the 1930s, women have served on the governing boards of Rusyn-American fraternals, have had their own sports clubs, and have been particularly effective in establishing ladies' guilds which, through social events, have been able to raise extensive funds to help local church parishes. To this day, many ladies' guilds operate catering and small food services from the basements of churches, cooking traditional Rusyn dishes like *holubtsi/holubkŷ* (stuffed cabbage) and *pirohŷ* (three-cornered cheese or potato-filled ravioli) and selling them to the community at large. The profits go to the church.

Carpatho-Rusyns had a vibrant community life during the first three decades of this century. Fraternal organizations, social clubs, political groups, and churches sponsored publications, theatrical and musical performances, public lectures, parades, and picnics, all of which were in part or wholly related to the preservation and promotion of a Carpatho-Rusyn culture and identity. Such activity virtually ceased or lost any specific Carpatho-Rusyn content in the decades immediately following World War II.

There has been a marked revival of activity, however, since the 1970s. Several new song and dance ensembles, the largest of which is Slavjane in Pittsburgh, were founded by third-, fourth-, and fifth-generation descendents of the pre-World War I immigrants. A scholarly organization, the Carpatho-Rusyn Research Center, was founded in

1978, and during its first two decades has distributed 35,000 books about Rusyn culture and history and has published a quarterly, the *Carpatho-Rusyn American* (Fairview, N. J., Pittsburgh, Pa., Fairfax, Va., 1978-97). Several other local cultural and social organizations were established or renewed in cities and towns where Rusyns have traditionally lived, such as Minneapolis (The Rusin Association), Yonkers, New York (Carpatho-Russian American Center), and Pittsburgh (Carpatho-Rusyn Society). This trend toward cultural renewal and the rediscovery of one's heritage has been enhanced by the political changes in east-central Europe after 1989. As a result, visits to families and friends that were effectively cut off by the Iron Curtain are now becoming a common occurrence in the post-Communist era.

Religion

Carpatho-Rusyns are Christians and for the most part they belong to various Eastern Christian churches. They trace their Christian origins back to the second half of the ninth century, when the Byzantine Greek monks Cyril and Methodius and their disciples brought Christianity from the East Roman or Byzantine Empire to Carpathian Rus'. After 1054, when the Christian world was divided into Roman Catholic and Eastern Orthodox spheres, the Carpatho-Rusyns remained part of the eastern tradition.

This meant that in Carpatho-Rusyn churches, Church Slavonic (written in the Cyrillic alphabet) instead of Latin was used as the liturgical language, priests could be married, and after the sixteenth century the "old calendar" was maintained, so that non-moveable feasts like Christmas were celebrated about two weeks after the western calendar. Eastern Christians also recognized as the head of their church the ecumenical patriarch in Constantinople, who resided in the capital of the former Byzantine Empire.

The question of church jurisdiction changed in the mid-seventeenth century, when some Carpatho-Rusyn bishops and priests united with the Catholic Church based in Rome. These Uniates, as they were first called, were initially allowed to keep all their eastern Orthodox traditions, although they were required to accept the authority of the Pope in Rome instead of the Orthodox ecumenical patriarch. Because the Uniates continued to use the eastern liturgy and follow eastern church practices, they were later called Greek Catholics, and eventually in the United States, Byzantine Catholics. In effect, since the seventeenth century, Carpatho-Rusyns have been divided into two branches of Eastern Christianity—Orthodoxy and Byzantine Greek Catholicism.

Regardless whether Carpatho-Rusyns were Orthodox or Byzantine Greek Catholic, the church remained a central feature of their life-cycle in the European homeland. Until well into the twentieth century, all rites of passage (birth/baptisms, weddings, funerals) and public events in Rusyn villages and towns were determined by the church calendar. In many ways, Carpatho-Rusyn culture and identity was synonymous with either the Byzantine Greek or Orthodox churches. Virtually all the early Carpatho-Rusyn cultural leaders, including the nineteenth-century "national awakener" Aleksander Dukhnovych, were priests.

Because religion was so important, it is not surprising that Carpatho-Rusyns tried to recreate aspects of their church-directed life after immigrating to the United States. From the very outset, however, the Byzantine Greek Catholics met resistance from American Catholic bishops, who before World War I were intolerant toward all traditions (especially those that used "foreign" languages and followed practices like a married priesthood) that were not in accord with American Roman Catholic norms. As a result, thousands of Byzantine Greek Catholics left the church and joined the Orthodox Church. This process of "return to the ancient faith" began as early as 1892 and was led by a priest who at the time was based in Minneapolis, Father Alexis Toth.

Aside from losing members to Orthodoxy, the Byzantine Greek Catholic Church was also having difficulty maintaining traditional practices. After 1929, the Byzantine Greek Catholics were forced by Rome to accept the practice of celibacy for priests and to turn over to their bishop all church property, which until then was generally held by councils composed of laypersons who had built and paid for the buildings. This so-called "celibacy controversy" caused great dissatisfaction, and led to the defection of thousands more Byzantine Greek Catholics who created a new American Carpatho-Russian Orthodox Church. The Byzantine Greek Catholics also gave up other traditional practices, and by the 1950s and 1960s changed to the western calendar and used primarily English in their services.

Thus, the division between Orthodoxy and Byzantine Greek Catholicism in the European homeland has continued among Carpatho-Rusyns and their descendants in the United States. Today the Byzantine

Catholic Church has four eparchies (dioceses) located in Pittsburgh, Pennsylvania; Passaic, New Jersey; Parma, Ohio; and Van Nuys, California. The American Carpatho-Russian Orthodox Church has one eparchy based in Johnstown, Pennsylvania. The Orthodox Church in America, with its seat in New York City, has twelve eparchies across the country. The approximate Carpatho-Rusyn membership in these churches is as follows:

Byzantine Catholics	195,000
Carpatho-Russian Orthodox	18,000
Orthodox Church in America	250,000

In the early years of the immigration, when Carpatho-Rusyns did not yet have their own churches, many Byzantine Greek Catholics attended and eventually joined Roman Catholic churches. Subsequently, inter-marriage increased the number of Carpatho-Rusyn Roman Catholics who today may number as high as 80,000 to 100,000. The community's internal religious controversies and the proselytizing efforts of American Protestant churches, most especially in the early decades of the twentieth century, have also resulted in the growth of several evangelical sects among Carpatho-Rusyns and conversions especially to various Baptist churches.

Employment and economic traditions

Although the vast majority of Carpatho-Rusyns who came to the United States during the major wave of immigration before World War I left small villages where they worked as small-scale subsistence-level farmers or as livestock herders, only a handful found jobs in agriculture in the United States. As one priest and community activist quipped earlier in the century: "Our people do not live in America, they live under America!"

This remark reflects the fact that many of the earliest Carpatho-Rusyn immigrants found employment in the coal-mining belt in eastern Pennsylvania. Since they lacked industrial and mining skills upon arrival, they were given the most menial tasks, such as coal splitting and carting. Carpatho-Rusyns were also attracted to the iron mines in upstate Minnesota; the lead mines of south central Missouri; the coal mines of southern Oklahoma and Washington state; the gold, silver, and lead mines of Colorado; and the marble quarries of Vermont. Even more important than mining for Carpatho-Rusyns was the growing steel industry of Pittsburgh and its neighboring towns. The steel mills and associated industries employed most Carpatho-Rusyns who lived in western Pennsylvania and neighboring Ohio.

Already during the pre-World War I decades, women were obliged to work outside the home in order to supplement the family income. With little English-language knowledge and limited work skills, at first they were only able to find work as cleaning-women in offices or as servants and nannies in well-to-do households. The second-generation American-born were more likely to find work as retail salespersons, waitresses, and workers in light industries such as shoe, soap, and cigar factories.

Like women, second-generation American-born men of Rusyn background had moved slightly up the employment ladder to work as skilled and semi-skilled workers, foremen, or clerical workers. By the third and fourth generation, there was a marked increase in managerial and semi-professional occupations. In general, however, Carpatho-Rusyns and their descendants have preferred working as employees in factories, mills, mines, and other industries rather than trying to establish their own businesses.

This dependence on the existing American industrial and corporate structure has in recent decades had a negative effect on thousands of Rusyn Arnericans who thought the jobs or industries that they and their fathers and grandfathers worked in would always be there for themselves and their children. Then came the widespread closure of coal mines in eastern Pennylvania and the collapse of America's steel industry in the 1970s, which put thousands of Rusyn Americans out of work. As a result, Carpatho-Rusyns, like other middle-class working Americans, have had in the past two decades to lower their expectations about economic advancement, and to retrain themselves and especially to encourage their children to prepare for jobs that are no longer in coal and steel, but in electronics, computers, and service-related industries.

Politics and government

At least until World War I, Carpatho-Rusyns in the European homeland did not have any experience in politics. They were used to being ruled and not to participating in the governing process. The result was scepticism and a deep-seated mistrust toward politics which was to continue after immigrating to the United States. Not surprisingly, first-generation Carpatho-Rusyns and even their American-born descendants have rarely become elected officials in the United States. It was not until the 1970s that the first individuals of Carpatho-Rusyn background were to be found in elected offices beyond the local level, such as Mark Singel, the lieutenant-governor of Pennsylvania, and Joseph M. Gaydos, Democratic Congressman from Pennsylvania. As for the majority of Carpatho-Rusyns, their relation to political life was limited to participation in strikes, especially in the coal fields and in steel and related industries during the decades of the 1890s to 1930s. While there were some Carpatho-Rusyn political clubs established during the 1930s and 1940s to support Democratic party candidates, these were generally few in number and short-lived.

On the other hand, when it comes to homeland politics, Carpatho-Rusyn Americans have in the past played an active and, at times, a decisive role. This was particularly so during the closing months of World War I, when Carpatho-Rusyn Americans, like other immigrant groups from east central and southern Europe, proposed various options for the future of their homelands following what proved to be the imminent collapse of the Russian, Austro-Hungarian, and Ottoman Empires.

In the spring and summer of 1918, both Byzantine Greek Catholic and Orthodox religious and lay leaders formed political action committees, the most important of which was the American Council of Uhro-Rusyns in Homestead, Pennsylvania. The Homestead-based council chose a young American-trained Carpatho-Rusyn lawyer, Gregory Zatkovich, to represent them. Under his leadership, the American Rusyns joined with other groups in the Mid-European Union in Philadelphia, lobbied the American government, and followed President Woodrow Wilson's suggestion that the Carpatho-Rusyn homeland might become part of the new state of Czechoslovakia. An agreement to join Czechoslovakia was reached in Philadelphia in November 1918, after which Zatkovich led a Rusyn-American delegation to convince leaders in the homeland of the desirability of joining Czechoslovakia.

The "American solution" was indeed accepted in 1919 at the Paris Peace Conference. Only the Lemko Rusyns living north of the mountains in former Austrian Galicia were left out and eventually were incorporated into the new state of Poland. In recognition of his role, Zatkovich, while still an American citizen, was appointed by the president of Czechoslovakia to be the first governor of that country's eastern province called Subcarpathian Rus'.

During the 1920s and 1930s, the Rusyn-American community followed closely political events in the homeland, and frequently sent protests to the League of Nations which called on the Czechoslovak government to implement the political autonomy that had been promised but not fully implemented in the province of Subcarpathian Rus'. The United States government was now less interested in far-away east-central Europe, so that Rusyn-American political influence on the homeland declined and eventually ended entirely, in particular after Subcarpathian Rus' was annexed to the Soviet Union in 1945 and the rest of east-central Europe came under Soviet-inspired Communist rule.

After being cut off from east-central Europe for nearly half a century, Rusyn-American contacts with the homeland were renewed following the Revolution of 1989, the fall of Conununism, and the collapse of the Soviet Union. Both secular and church bodies began once again to provide moral and financial assistance to Rusyn organizations in the homeland. Rusyn Americans also became active in the World Congress of Rusyns, established in eastern Slovakia in March 1991.

Often related to contacts with the European homeland has been the question of national identity. Throughout their entire history in the United States, politics for most Carpatho-Rusyns has meant trying to decide and reach a consensus on the question: "Who are we?" At least until about 1920, most Carpatho-Rusyns in the United States considered themselves to form a distinct Slavic nationality called Rusyn or Uhro-Rusyn (that is, Hungarian Rusyn). By the 1920s, there was a strong tendency, encouraged most especially by the Orthodox Church and Orthodox sympathizers, to consider Rusyns as little more than a branch of the Russian nationality. Hence, the term Carpatho-Russian became a popular name among group members. By the 1950s and 1960s, two more possible identities were added, Slovak and Ukrainian.

Since the 1970s, however, there has been a pronounced return to the original Rusyn identity, that is, the idea that Carpatho-Rusyns are neither Russian, or Slovak, or Ukrainian, but rather a distinct nationality. Several of the older religious and lay organizations have reasserted the Rusyn orientation, and it has been fully embraced from the outset by all the new cultural and scholarly institutions established in the United States since the 1970s. The Rusyn orientation in America has been encouraged further by the Rusyn national revival that has been occurring in all the European homeland countries (Slovakia, Ukraine, Poland, Hungary, Yugoslavia) since the Revolution of 1989.

Individual and group contributions

It is in the area of religion where Carpatho-Rusyns have made a particularly significant contribution to American life. Three individuals stand out for their work not only on behalf of Eastern Christianity, the traditional faith of Carpatho-Rusyns, but also of Roman Catholicism and American evangelical Protestantism.

The Russian Orthodox Church of America, today the Orthodox Church in America, is one of the oldest in the United States. It was founded as early as 1792, when Alaska was a colony of the Russian Empire. The real growth of that church was connected not to the Alaskan mission, however, but to its influence over thousands of immigrants from east-central Europe who settled in the northeastern United States during the decades before World War I. The expansion of Russian Orthodoxy during those years is attributable largely to Father Alexis Toth (1853-1909), a former Byzantine Greek Catholic priest who joined the Russian Orthodox Church of North America in 1891. Not only did he bring his own Minneapolis parish with him, he also set out on missionary activity in several northeastern states, converting nearly 25,000 Carpatho-Rusyns and other East Slavic immigrants to Orthodoxy. The church grew so rapidly that it moved its headquarters from San Francisco to New York City. For his services, Toth was hailed as the "father of Orthodoxy in America," and in 1994 he was made a saint of the Orthodox Church of America.

The two other influential religious activists were both born in the United States of Carpatho-Rusyn parents. Miriam Teresa Demjanovich (1901-1927) converted to Roman Catholicism as a child, became a member of the Sisters of Charity, and devoted the rest of her years to a life of pure spirituality. A year after her death, a collection of her "spiritual conferences" was published, *Greater Perfection* (1928), which became so popular that the book was translated into several languages, including Chinese. Her followers have established in New Jersey a Sister Miriam Teresa League, which is working to have her made a saint in the Roman Catholic Church.

Perhaps the best known religious activist of Carpatho-Rusyn descent in American society as a whole is Joseph W. Tkach (1927-1995), who from 1986 until his death was Pastor General of the Worldwide Church of God. Tkach served as editor of the popular religious magazine, *Plain Truth*, and he was the guiding force behind the church's syndicated news-oriented television program, "The World Tomorrow," rated in the 1980s as one of the top religious programs in the United States.

The world of entertainment and communications has also been enriched by Americans of Carpatho-Rusyn background. In the 1940s and 1950s, Lizabeth Scott (born Emma Matzo, 1922) played the role of a sultry leading lady in several Hollywood films, while Sandra Dee (born Alexandra Zuk, 1942) was cast in roles that depicted the typical American teenage girl of the 1950s and 1960s. Her very name was later used as a nostalgic symbol of that era in the film *Grease* (1978). In more recent years, other Americans of Carpatho-Rusyn descent have been active in television, including the actor Robert Urich (b. 1946) and the FOX Television newscaster, Cora-Ann Mihalik (b. 1955).

Undoubtedly, the most famous American of Carptho-Rusyn descent was Andy Warhol (born Andrew Warhola, 1928-1987), the pop artist, photographer, and experimental film maker. At the height of his career in the 1960s and 1970s, he had become as famous as the celebrities he was immortalizing. Recalling the idealized saintly images (icons) that surrounded him when he was growing up and attending the Byzantine Greek Catholic Church in Pittsburgh's Rusyn Valley (Ruska dolina) district, Warhol created on canvas and in photographs new "American icons" that epitomized the second half of the twentieth century. Since his untimely death in 1987, his older brothers (John and Paul Warhola) have become instrumental in perpetuating the Carpatho-Rusyn heritage of Andy and his family. That heritage figures prominently in the new Andy Warhol Museum in Pittsburgh. The Warhol Foundation, which funded the Pittsburgh museum, has also donated paintings and provided financial support for the Warhola Family Museum of Modern Art, founded in 1992 in Medzilaborce, Slovakia, just a few miles away from the Carpatho-Rusyn village where both of Andy Warhol's parents were born.

CHAPTER 18

The Political Activity of Rusyn-American Immigrants in 1918[*]

During the last months of World War I, many immigrant groups in the United States became actively concerned with the fate of their respective homelands. Already in early 1918 it was increasingly evident that the map of Europe would be remade after the war, and immigrant leaders hoped to influence the course of those future changes. The potential economic and political strength of the American immigration was also recognized by statesmen in eastern and southern Europe. National spokespersons like Tomáš G. Masaryk and Ignace Paderewski, for instance, spent several months in the United States where they solicited support among their overseas brethren for the idea of Czechoslovak and Polish statehood.

It was also at this time that Rusyn-American immigrants began seriously to consider organizational efforts on behalf of their native land—Subcarpathian Rus'. In comparison with other immigrant groups, Rusyns entered the political arena quite late, but in the end they were to be extremely successful in having their demands fulfilled. In a recent comparative study on President Wilson's policies, one historian concluded that: "the Ruthenian [Rusyn] immigrants in America did determine the fate of their compatriots at home—a unique case, it appears, of the

[*] First published in *East European Quarterly*, X, 3 (Boulder, Colo., 1976), pp. 347-365; reprinted in Harvard Ukrainian Research Institute Offprint Series, No. 13 (Cambridge, Mass., 1976).

influence of an immigrant group in America on the political history of Europe."[1]

Indeed, the activity of Rusyn immigrants, especially their participation in the efforts to have Subcarpathian Rus' united with Czechoslovakia, has been discussed before.[2] The older view, propounded by Czech historians, considered the Rusyn-American action a significant indication of the "voluntary" nature of Subcarpathia's incorporation into Czechoslovakia.[3] In stark contrast, interwar revisionist Hungarian writers considered the Rusyn immigrant decision unrepresentative of the population in Europe and illegal from the standpoint of international law.[4] A more recent interpretation, presented by Soviet Marxist writers, describes the same process as part of an international conspiracy to stifle the socialist revolutionary movement and to deter the unification of Ukrainian ethnographic territories.[5]

[1]Victor S. Mamatey, "The Slovaks and Carpatho-Ruthenians," in Joseph P. O'Grady, ed., *The Immigrant's Influence on Wilson's Peace Policies* (Lexington, Ky., 1967), p. 249.

[2]In western literature, the best introductory survey of this problem is by Victor S. Mamatey, *ibid.*; and Joseph Danko, "Plebiscite of Carpatho-Ruthenians in the United States Recommending Union of Carpatho-Ruthenia with the Czechoslovak Republic," *Annals of the Ukrainian Academy of Arts and Sciences*, XI, 1-2 (New York, 1964-68), pp. 184-207. See also C.A. Macartney, *Hungary and Her Successors: the Treaty of Trianon and its Consequences, 1919-1937* (London, 1937), pp. 214-221; Aldo Dami, *La Ruthénie subcarpathique* (Genéve-Annemasse, 1944), pp. 194-195; and Peter G. Stercho, *Diplomacy of Double Morality: Europe's Crossroads in Carpatho-Ukraine, 1919-1939* (New York, 1971), pp. 16-20.

[3]The Czech view is best summed up by Alois Raušer, "Připojení Podkarpatské Rusi k Československé republice," in Jaroslav Zatloukal, ed., *Podkarpatská Rus* (Bratislava, 1936), pp. 62-63; Ferdinand Peroutka, *Budování státu*, Vol. III (Prague, 1936), pp. 1599-1600; and Karel Krofta, *Byli jsme za Rakousko: úvahy historické a politické* (Prague, 1936), pp. 137-139.

[4]Gábor Dáras, *A Ruténföld elszakításának előzményei 1890-1920* (Ujpest, 1936), pp. 104-108.

[5]I.N. Mel'nikova, "Kak byla vkliuchena Zakarpatskaia Ukraina v sostav Chekhoslovakii v 1919 g.," *Uchenye zapysky Instituta slavianovedeniia*, III (Moscow, 1951), pp. 104-135 and M. Klympotiuk, *Pidstupy amerykans'kykh imperialistiv na Zakarpatti* (Uzhhorod, 1952).

Notwithstanding their polemical tendencies, these works do present the basic outline of Rusyn immigrant activity in 1918. Yet there are still several aspects of the problem which have never been elucidated. For example, when was the Czechoslovak solution first proposed and actually accepted. What were the positive and negative features of that solution? What were the programs of the various councils that were formed? And what did immigrant leaders really mean when they referred to the Ukraine? In view of the "uniqueness" of the Rusyn case, it would seem useful to clarify, on the basis of rare immigrant publications, the above-mentioned as well as related issues.

Like most immigrants from eastern and southern Europe, Rusyns came to the United States to improve their economic status. According to the Hungarian census of 1910, they numbered 447,566 and lived along the slopes and valleys of the Carpathian Mountains in the northeastern part of the Hungarian Kingdom. Toward the end of the nineteenth century, this region experienced a series of poor harvests, a demographic increase, and the general neglect of the Hungarian government—a combination of factors which made it difficult for Rusyn peasants to obtain even the basic necessities for physical survival. Although the government did attempt to improve economic conditions in Rusyn-inhabited regions,[6] these efforts were short-lived and the actual situation remained dismal. In the words of a contemporary Hungarian publicist:

> The sovereign stag should not be disturbed in its family entertainments.... What is a Ruthenian compared with it? ... Only a peasant! ... The hunting periods last two weeks. There come some of the Schwarzenbergs, the Kolowrats, the Liechtensteins,... they tell each other their hunting adventures. ... In order that they should tell each other all this ... 70,000 Ruthenians [Rusyns] must be doomed to starvation by the army of officials. ... The deer and the wild boar destroy the corn, the oats, the

[6]The so-called Highlands Action was initiated in 1890 by a Hungarian official, Edmund Egan, but his untimely death put an end to further economic or social improvements. See Egan's memoir, *Ekonomichne polozhenie rus'kykh selian v Uhorshichyni*, 2nd ed. (Prague, 1922).

potato, and the clover of the Ruthenian.... Their whole yearly work is destroyed.... The people sow, and the deer of the estate harvest.[7]

To escape their fate, many Rusyns began to emigrate, especially to the United States, where by 1914 about 60,000 had settled.[8] The former woodcutters, shepherds, and farmers were transformed into industrial workers who found employment in the mining and manufacturing centers of Pennsylvania, New York, New Jersey, and Ohio. Generally, Rusyns did not intend to remain in the New World, but only work there as long as it took to earn enough dollars so that they could return to the "old country" and pay off a mortgage or buy a new homestead and more land. But despite the "temporary" nature of their stay, they did establish several organizations, especially in the vicinity of Pittsburgh, Pennsylvania.

The largest of these was the Greek Catholic Union of Rusyn Brotherhoods (Sojedinenije Greko-Kaftoličeskich Russkich Bratstv),[9] founded in Wilkes Barre, Pennsylvania in 1892. This was basically an insurance organization concerned with the physical welfare of its members, though it also strove to preserve the integrity of the Greek Catholic Church in the United States. The Greek Catholic Union published an influential newspaper, the *Amerykanskii russkii vîstnyk* (1892-1952), and

[7] Miklós Bartha, *Kazár földön* (1901), cited in Oscar Jászi, *The Dissolution of the Habsburg Monarchy* (Chicago, 1966), p. 235.

[8] The estimates regarding Subcarpathian Rusyns range from 6,299 to 500,000. These discrepancies were caused, on the one hand, by the statistical procedures of American officials who before 1907 listed newcomers according to country of origin, not nationality, and on the other by the immigrants themselves who tended to identify themselves with the country they came from rather than by nationality. Even after the term Ruthenian (including Rusyn or Rusnak) was introduced into U.S. statistics, it was still not possible to determine how many originated from Subcarpathian Rus' and how many from Galicia or Bukovina. The 60,000 figure is based on studies by Oleksander Mytsiuk, "Z emihratsiï uhro-rusyniv pered svitovoiu viinoiu," *Naukovyi zbirnyk Tovarystva 'Prosvita'*, XIII-XIV (Uzhhorod, 1937-38), pp. 21-32, and Ladislav Tajták, "Pereselennia ukraïntsiv skhidnoï Slovachchyny do 1913 r.," *Duklia*, IX, 4 (Prešov, 1961), pp. 97-103.

[9] Proper names of Rusyn-American organizations and leaders are rendered as they appear in the Latin alphabet or "Slavish" edition of the *Amierykanskii russkii vîstnyk*. Transliterations of Rusyn dialectal works in Cyrillic alphabet follow the Library of Congress system for Ukrainian with these variations. є = ie; ы = ŷ; ѣ = î.

by 1918 counted over 90,000 members in both regular and youth lodges. A smaller group formed the United Societies of the Greek Catholic Religion (Sobranije Greko-Katholičeskich Cerkovnych Bratstv), also an insurance organization, but one administered directly by the hierarchy of the Greek Catholic Church. The United Societies published the newspaper *Prosvîta* (1917-present) and had about 9,000 members in regular, Sokol (gymnastic), and youth chapters.[10]

The ideological policies of these and other Rusyn immigrant organizations reflected traditions brought from Europe. In the late nineteenth century, Subcarpathian Rus' was still in the embryonic stage of national development and its small intelligentsia (mainly composed of Greek Catholic priests) had not yet decided upon any one national orientation. In the decades following the 1848 revolution, influential circles in Subcarpathia fostered the idea of political cooperation with both Slovaks and Galician Rusyns and adopted the Russian language and cultural ideals for local intellectual life. It should be emphasized that the Subcarpathian intelligentsia had repeatedly rejected the Ukrainian national orientation and that the Galician contacts were almost exclusively with Russophile individuals and organizations there.[11] Furthermore, since Subcarpathian Rus' was part of Hungary and subject to the assimilationist policy of magyarization, many Rusyn leaders (known as Magyarones) favored Hungarian civilization and considered themselves to be either Uhro-Rusyns (Hungarian Rusyns), or simply Hungarians of the Greek Catholic faith. Thus, a pro-Russian (and clearly anti-Ukrainian) or a pro-Hungarian cultural and political orientation, as well as a

---

[10]For the early history of Rusyn immigrant development, see Walter C. Warzeski, *Byzantine Rite Rusins in Carpatho-Ruthenia and America* (Pittsburgh, Pa., 1971), pp. 95-128; and Petr Kokhanik, *Nachalo istorii Amerikanskoi Rusi*, 2nd ed. (Trumbull, Conn., 1970), pp. 479-514.

[11]Russophile refers to those individuals in Galicia and Bukovina as well as in Subcarpathian Rus' who considered the local Slavic inhabitants to be of Russian nationality. They were opposed by the Ukrainophiles, who raised the local dialects to the level of the Ukrainian literary language used in L'viv and Kiev and who wanted to introduce this medium, not Russian, for educational and cultural affairs. Most efforts on the part of Galician Ukrainophiles to spread the Ukrainian orientation below the Carpathians were rebuffed by the Subcarpathian intelligentsia. See Evgenii Nedziel'skii, *Ocherk karpatorusskoi literatury* (Uzhhorod, 1932) pp. 256-257.

potential pro-Slovak political trend, were the predominant elements of late nineteenth-century Subcarpathian life which inevitably pervaded the intellectual framework of Rusyn immigrants in the United States.[12]

With these factors in mind, Rusyn immigrant developments can better be understood. Initially, the ecclesiastical, and to a lesser degree lay organizations, tried to include Rusyn immigrants from Galicia, Bukovina, and Subcarpathian Rus', as well as Slovaks and Magyars of the Greek Catholic rite. To avoid controversy, these organizations referred to their members with noncontroversial names such as Rusyn, or the ethnically non-specific designation, "Slavish." The Greek Catholic Union was subtitled by the catch-all phrase: "A Fraternal and Benefit Society Comprised of Catholics of Greek and Roman Rite and of Slavonic Extraction or Descent," while the Greek Catholic Church, with its Galician-Ukrainian, Slovak, Magyar, and Croatian as well as Carpatho-Rusyn adherents, tried not to favor any one ethnic group.

The tendency toward separation, however, in particular between Rusyn immigrants from Subcarpathian Rus' and those from Galicia, was already evident in 1894. In that year, a Rusyn (later renamed Ukrainian) National Union was set up to accomodate nationally conscious Ukrainian immigrants from Galicia. This new organization began to compete for members with the older Greek Catholic Union. Any attempts toward cooperation between the two groups broke down completely after 1907, when a Galician Ukrainophile priest, Soter Ortyns'kyi, was appointed bishop for Greek Catholics in the United States. Backed by the Greek Catholic Union, a group of immigrant priests from Subcarpathian Rus' opposed Ortyns'kyi, especially his "policy of making the diocese Ukrainian," and they strove "to protect the Uhro-[Subcarpathian] Rusyns and segments of the Galicians against Ukrainian propaganda."[13] The

---

[12]A useful survey of cultural and political thought in Subcarpathian Rus' before World War I is found in Ivan Žeguc, *Die nationalpolitischen Betrebungen der Karpato-Ruthenen 1848-1914* (Wiesbaden, 1965).

[13]Program of the Rusyn Civilian Church Council, May 14, 1908, cited in Warzeski, *Byzantine Rite Rusins*, p. 120. Ortyns'kyi's unpopularity also increased because he was responsible for having to administer a Papal decree, the "Ea Semper," dated July 18, 1907, which revoked several practices of the Eastern rite, among them the recognition of married priests. The more unpopular provisions of the "Ea Semper," were later revoked ("Cum Episcopo Graeco-Rutheno," 17.VIII.1914). See Stephen C. Gulovich, "The Rusin Exarchate in the United

continual disagreements between the Galician-Ukrainophile clergy on the one hand, and priests from Subcarpathian Rus' (strongly supported by the Greek Catholic Union) on the other, finally led to a papal decree of April 1916, which divided the Greek Catholic Church in the United States into a Subcarpathian and Galician branch, each to be headed by its own administrator.[14]

The Rusyn-American community was not only rent by regional Subcarpathian-Galician conflicts, but also by large scale conversions from both camps to Orthodoxy and by the attempts of the Hungarian government to gain influence over immigrant organizations. From the very beginning, Greek Catholic priests had problems with the American Catholic hierarchy concerning questions of ritual, jurisdictional authority, and the existence of married priests. In particular, the refusal of American Catholics to recognize married Greek Catholic priests resulted in the defection to Orthodoxy of more than 29,000 Rusyns between the years 1891 and 1909.[15] These Orthodox Rusyn immigrants became staunch advocates of a Russian national orientation.

The relationship to the Slovak immigrants in this early period was more positive. For instance, the Greek Catholic Union's newspaper was initially printed and to a degree influenced by Peter V. Rovnianek, the founder of the National Slovak Society. This organization, which included immigrants from "Slovakia" of all religious beliefs, as well as the Pennsylvania Slovak Roman and Greek Catholic Union, attracted many Rusyns. Cooperation between Slovak and Rusyn immigrants in political affairs was also evident, and as early as 1904 representatives of both groups addressed a petition to the Hungarian delegates of the

---

States," *The Eastern Churches Quarterly*, VI (London, 1946), pp, 477-479.

[14]Gabriel Martyak was chosen the Subcarpathian administrator; Peter Poniatyshyn, the Ukrainian. Warzeski, *Byzantine Rite Rusins*, pp. 114-124; Atanasii V. Pekar, *Narysy istoriï tserkvy Zakarpattia*, Analecta OSBM, series II, section 1 (Rome, 1967), pp. 183-187.

[15]Warzeski, *Byzantine Rite Rusins*, pp. 105-110; Keith S. Russin, "Father Alexis G. Toth and the Wilkes-Barre Litigations," *St. Vladimir's Theological Quarterly*, XVI, 3 (Crestwood, N.Y., 1972), pp. 128-149. A sociological analysis of the first community that converted and that was led by Father Alexis Toth is available in Alex Simirenko, *Pilgrims, Colonists, and Frontiersmen: An Ethnic Community in Transition* (London, 1964).

world congress of parliamentarians being held in St. Louis which protested the fate of their brethren at home.[16]

In turn, the Hungarian government tried through the Trans-Atlantic Trust Company in New York and through the Austro-Hungarian consulates in Cleveland, Pittsburgh, and Wilkes-Barre to combat the "pernicious" effect of Subcarpathian contact with Slovaks and with Galician Ukrainophiles and Russophiles and to assure a favorable attitude on the part of the Greek Catholic Union and Greek Catholic Church hierarchy. The Union successfully resisted such infiltration, but the church still remained staffed with magyarone priests who were educated and acculturized in the old world Hungarian environment.[17] Such a situation fostered frequent controversy between the Rusyn clergy and the lay leadership of the Greek Catholic Union, and this was the predominant feature of Rusyn immigrant life in the early years of the twentieth century.

Political concerns did not really take precedence among Subcarpathian immigrants until the last years of World War I and especially 1918, when Allied military victories and declarations by President Woodrow Wilson seemed to forecast imminent changes in the structure of eastern Europe. Reflecting on the fate of their homeland, Rusyn immigrant leaders considered the following alternatives: union of Subcarpathian Rus' with Russia, union with the Ukraine, full independence, autonomy within Hungary, or autonomy within Czechoslovakia.

The first public demonstration of Rusyn political attitudes came at the Russian Congress, held in New York City on July 13, 1917. Organized by the Galician Russophile, Petr P. Hatalak, this Congress was composed of Rusyn immigrants from "Carpathian Russia," i.e., Galicia,

---

[16]"Podkarpatští Rusíni v Americe před válkou a za války," *Naše revoluce*, IV (Prague, 1926-27), pp. 270-271. The St. Louis petition was signed by Michael Yuhasz, chairman of the Greek Catholic Union, and by Pavel J. Zsatkovich, editor of the *Amerykanskii russkii vîstnyk*.

[17]The first Apostolic Visitor for Greek Catholics in the United States, Andrei Hodobai (1902-06), was an important agent for the Budapest authorities. See, Mariia Maier, "Zakarpats'ki ukraïntsi na perelomi stolit," in *Zhovten' i ukraïns'ka kul'tura* (Prešov, 1968), pp. 65-70.

Bukovina, and Subcarpathian Rus'.[18] The majority of participants were delegates from Russophile organizations set up by immigrants from Galicia and Bukovina. The Subcarpathians were represented by the chairman of the Greek Catholic Union, the editor of the Union's newspaper, and by Nicholas Pačuta, chairman of a "Carpatho-Russian" political organization, the American Russian National Defense (Amerikansko-Russkaia 'Narodnaia Obrana'). Although the Orthodox hierarchy was well represented, Galician-Ukrainophile leaders and Subcarpathian clergy from the Greek Catholic Church were noticeably absent. The latter had only recently issued a resolution stating "that the most advantageous thing for those sons of our people who are citizens of Hungary would be to remain within Hungary after the war with full guarantees of autonomy."[19]

The Congress issued a memorandum which traced the unfortunate history of "Carpathian Russia" and then declared:

> The whole Carpatho-Russian people steadfastly demand the liberation of Carpathian Rus' (Prikarpatskaia Rus') from foreign domination, and with the broadest autonomy the unification of all Carpathian Rus', according to its ethnographic boundaries, with its older sister—a great, democratic Russia.[20]

This memorandum was presented to the Russian and other Allied Embassies as well as to the State Department in Washington. However, the British Ambassador's opposition to the idea of union with Russia, and especially the Bolshevik coup d'état in November 1917 ended the feasibility of the Russian solution. The chairman of the Russian Congress later recalled: "Towards the end of 1917 it was already clear

---

[18]Petr Hatalák, *Jak vznikla myšlenka přípojiti Podkarpatskou Rus k Československu* (Uzhhorod, 1935), pp. 11-21; Mamatey,"Slovaks and Carpatho-Ruthenians," pp. 240-241.

[19]Cited from a resolution signed by 32 Subcarpathian Rusyn priests who met in New York City on June 28, 1917. *Prosvita*, July 12, 1917; *Svoboda* (Jersey City, N.J.), July 17, 1917.

[20]"Memorandum Russkago Kongressa v Amerikie, sozvannago 'Soiuzom osvobozhdeniia Prikarpatskoi Rusi' posviashchaemyi svobodnomu russkomu narodu v Rossii, russkomu uchreditel'nomu sobraniiu, russkomu pravitel'stvu," cited from the Russian text reprinted in Zdeněk Peška and Josef Markov, "Příspěvek k ústavním dějinám Podkarpatské Rusi," *Bratislava*, V (Bratislava, 1931), pp. 517-518.

to all Uhro-Rusyn leaders in America that Uhro-Rus' cannot be united with Russia ... because ... in Russia the Bolsheviks already controlled the government."[21]

The proclamation of Ukrainian independence at Kiev in January 1918 and the ratification in March of the Treaty of Brest-Litovsk which recognized an independent Ukraine may have provided a stimulus for the Ukrainian orientation among a few Subcarpathians. An organization called the Ukrainian Federation of the United States claimed to represent "more than 700,000 Ruthenians and Ukrainians" and submitted a memorandum to President Wilson on June 29, 1918 asking, that he "endorse the endeavors of their mother countries for national unity and constitutional freedom" from the "unjust and incompetent rule of the Romanoff and Habsburg dynasties."[22]

But the most influential faction among Rusyn immigrants was that represented by the Greek Catholic Union. At the beginning of 1918, the Union's newspaper already called upon its readers to think in political terms and to consider four possible "alternatives" for the homeland: unity with Hungary, Czechoslovakia, Ukraine, or Russia.[23] By the end of the year, Rusyn immigrants accepted the Czechoslovak "alternative," and the reason for this can be attributed to the activity of two men: Tomáš G. Masaryk, the future founding president of Czechoslovakia, and Gregory I. Zsatkovich, the future first governor of Subcarpathian Rus'.

The change in United States policy toward the Austro-Hungarian Empire was also of crucial importance for budding immigrant politicians. Wilson's famous Fourteen Points had stated the general principle of self-determination for all nations, but it was a declaration by Secretary of State Lansing which really raised immigrant hopes.

---

[21]Hatalák, *Jak vznikla*, p. 19.

[22]Cited from United States State Department document 763.72119/1775 supplied to me by Professor Victor Mamatey. There is no indication that immigrants from Subcarpathian Rus' were members of the Ukrainian Federation. The memorandum was signed by Miroslav Sichyns'kyi, who later represented the Ukrainians at the Mid-European Union in Philadelphia, where Subcarpathian Rusyns were recognized as a separate national group.

[23]Michael J. Hanchin, "Alternatyvŷ," *Amerykanskii russkii vîstnyk*, January, 3, 1918. This, and all other references, are from the "Russian" edition of the newspaper printed in Cyrillic alphabet.

Although the United States did not specifically call for the dismemberment of Austria-Hungary, Lansing stressed on June 28 that "all branches of the Slav race should be completely freed from German and Austrian rule."[24] Statements like these provided favorable propaganda for the efforts of leaders like Masaryk who arrived in the United States on May 1 in order to gather support for Czechoslovak independence among American Czechs and Slovaks.

It was in the course of negotiations with Slovak immigrants in Pittsburgh at the end of May that Masaryk first met a Rusyn representative in the person of Nicholas Pačuta. Actually, Masaryk had not contemplated Subcarpathian Rus' in his original plan for an independent state, and only during his stay in Kiev in 1917 did he discuss the problem with Ukrainian leaders who at the time were demanding autonomy within the Russian Empire. With regard to Subarpathian Rus', Masaryk later recalled: "it was only a pious wish, but I had to consider a plan in Russia and especially in Ukraine, because Ukrainian leaders discussed with me many times the future of all Little Russian [Ukrainian] lands outside of Russia. They had no objection to the unification of Subcarpathian Rus' with us."[25]

In the United States, Masaryk found that most Slavic groups were aware of the struggle being waged on behalf of Czechoslovak independence. Following the path of Czech and Slovak immigrants, many Rusyns had already volunteered for service in a Czechoslovak regiment

----

[24]*Papers Relating to the Foreign Relations of the United States*, Supplement I: *The World War 1918*, Vol. I (Washington, D.C., 1933), p. 816.

[25]Tomáš G. Masaryk, *Světová revoluce za války a ve válce 1914-1918* (Prague, 1938), p. 290. Masaryk is the only source regarding the Ukrainian point of view. None of the Ukrainian leaders (Dmytro Doroshenko, Pavlo Khrystiuk, Arnold Margolin, Ivan Mazepa, V. Petriv, Volodymyr Vynnychenko) mentions in his memoirs any conversation with Masaryk about the Subcarpathian problem. Nor does O.I. Bonchkovs'kyi, in his informative account of Masaryk in Kiev—*T.G. Masaryk: natsiional'na problema ta ukraïns'ke pytannia* (Poděbrady, 1930), pp. 135-153—say anything about discussions regarding Subcarpathian Rus'. The silence on this matter is intriguing, since in late 1918 the West Ukrainian People's Republic and the Ukrainian National Republic both claimed sovereignty over all "Ukrainians" living south of the Carpathians. On the other hand, it is possible that Ukrainian politicians in Kiev were initially unopposed to Masaryk's designs on Subcarpathian Rus', because in the summer of 1917 they were desperately trying to obtain military support from the Czech Legion then stationed in Ukraine.

that was fighting alongside the Allies in France. The Czechoslovak orientation was in particular being fostered by Nicholas Pačuta, a recent convert to Orthodoxy who was not only chairman of the American Russian National Defense, but until early 1918 also an editor of the Greek Catholic Union's newspaper.[26] Formerly an advocate of Subcarpathia's incorporation into Russia, Pačuta now realized the futility of such a plan. He negotiated with Slovak leaders and drew up a memorandum proposing union with Czechoslovakia, he delivered to U.S. Secretary of State Lansing in April and to Masaryk on May 30.[27] Masaryk accepted the memorandum, though he rightly surmised that Pačuta was acting more or less on his own and did not represent the wishes of the larger and more influential Greek Catholic Rusyn community.[28]

By May 1918, however, Rusyn leaders had not yet formulated any political program. A few individuals in the Greek Catholic Union may have spoken about Ukraine or Czechoslovakia, but on the whole most immigrants were either disinterested in politics or satisfied to follow their priests who were convinced that "the most responsible solution for the Rusyns of Hungary is to remain further under the Hungarian crown."[29] The official organ of the Greek Catholic Church disavowed any sugggestion "that Hungarian Rusyns (*uhorski rusiny*) be united with the Galician Ukrainians,"[30] since the clergy was reluctant "to mix in the affairs of foreign countries."[31] One group of priests met in McKeesport, Pennsylvania in March 1918 and "unanimously expressed their policy, which was that we remain loyal to Hungary."[32] Differences over these "political" questions further exacerbated relations between the Greek Catholic Union and the Greek Catholic Church.

---

[26]Mikolai Pachuta, "Cheshsko-slovenska armada," *Amerykanskii russkii vîstnyk*, January 17, 1918.

[27]The text of these memoranda were not available to the author, although in his memoirs Masaryk mentioned the one given to him, *Světová revoluce*, p, 291. For a discussion of the contents of both memoranda, see Hatalák, *Jak vznikla*, pp. 20-31, and "Carpathian Russians and the Czechoslovaks," *The Bohemian Review*, II, 5 (Chicago, 1918), pp. 70-72.

[28]Masaryk, *Světová revoluce*, pp. 290-291.

[29]*Prosvîta*, March 14, 1918.

[30]*Ibid.*, January 24, 1918.

[31]*Ibid.*, January 17, 1918.

[32]Cited in "Podkarpatští Rusíni v Americe," p. 276.

These problems were finally resolved when Rusyn clerical and lay leaders joined together at the fifteenth convention of the Greek Catholic Union held in Cleveland, Ohio and Braddock, Pennsylvania from June 9 to 22, 1918. After a heated debate, Nicholas Pačuta, the former Russophile and now advocate of cooperation with the Czechs and Slovaks, was branded an Orthodox renegade and expelled from the Union. In his stead, a new chairman, Julij Gardoš, was elected. At the instigation of the clergy, the convention decided henceforth to use only the terms "Uhro-Rusyn" or "Rusyn" when referring to its members so as to distinguish them clearly from their Galician, Ukrainian, and Russian brethren. Most important, a policy of political activism was decided upon, and at the last session a nine-man commission was formed (later to be joined by nine priests) in order "to continue intensive action with the aim to liberate Uhorska [Hungarian] Rus'."[33]

To fulfill the task of "liberation," and to work out common political aims, lay and ecclesiastical leaders met at Homestead, Pennsylvania on July 23, 1918. First, the Greek Catholic Union (Sojedinenije) joined with the smaller fraternal, the United Societies (Sobranije), to form an American National Council of Uhro-Rusyns (Amerikanska Narodna Rada Uhro-Rusinov).[34] Reverend Nikolaj Chopey was elected chairman and Julij Gardoš, A. Koval, A. Koscelnik and A. Petach vice-chairmen. The National Council then proclaimed itself the sole legal representative for Uhro-Rusyn immigrants and adopted the following resolution:

[33]*Prosvîta*, June 20 and July 4, 1918; *Svoboda*, July 2, 1918; *Amerykanskii russkii vîstnyk*, July 11, 1918. The protocols of the Greek Catholic Union's Cleveland-Braddock convention appear in each issue of *ibid.* from July 4, 1918 to January 23, 1919, and the convention is summarized in "Istorija Greko-Kaft. Sojedinenija," *Zoloto-Jubilejnyj Kalendar' Greko Kaft. Sojedinenija v S.Š.A.* (Munhall, Penn., 1942), pp. 53-55.

[34]*Prosvîta*, July 25, 1918; *Amerykanskii russkii vîstnyk*, August 1, 1918. The clergy was represented by N. Chopey, J. Hanulja, G. Martyak, V. Gorzo, A. Holosnyay, J. Szabo, Th. Szabo, N. Szabados and E. Burik. The lay leaders were J. Gardoš, A. Koval, A. Koscelnik, A. Petach, G. Komloš, I. Drimak, M. Kopas, G. Kondor, M. Yuhasz, M. Hanchin, P. Mackov. G. Munčak, G. Dandar, and G. Šepeljak.

If the pre-War boundaries remain, Rusyns, as the most loyal people—*gens fidelissima*[35]—deserve that Hungary provide her with autonomy.

If new boundaries are drawn, they should be made according to nationality; thus, Uhro-Rusyns can belong nowhere else than to their nearest brothers by blood, language, and faith, to the Galician and Bukovinian Rusyns.

But if we are divided by foreign aspirations from Ukrainians and Old-Ruthenians [Galician *starorusyny*], the National Council demands in this case autonomy for Uhro-Rusyns so that they can preserve their national character.[36]

The Homestead Resolution made no mention of the Czechoslovak solution, but rather reflected the attitudes of the pro-Hunagarian clergy and pro-Galician lay leaders. From August until November 1918, Rusyn leaders continued to debate the relative advantages and disadvantages of the various alternatives, although in general the Hungarian trend lost ground and praise was only directed toward the idea of union with "our Galician and Bukovinian brothers."[37]

[35]This term was used by Hungarian writers in recognition of Rusyn loyalty to Prince Ferenc II Rákóczi during the latter's early eighteenth-century anti-Habsburg revolt.

[36]The original text of the Homestead Resolution appears under the heading "Do vsîkh Uhro-Rusynov zhiiushchykh v Soed. Derzhavakh Amerykî," in *Amerykanskii russkii vîstnyk*, August 8, 1918 and in *Prosvîta*, August 8, 1918. This text differs substantially from the one which appears in several other studies: Masaryk, *Světová revoluce*, p. 291; Dáras, *Ruténföld*, pp. 106-107; Macartney, *Hungary*, p. 214; Mel'nikova, "Kak byla vkliuchena," p. 115; Danko, "Plebiscite," p. 188; Mamatey, "Slovaks and Carpatho-Ruthenians," pp. 242-243; and Stercho, *Diplomacy*, p. 16. These authors have based their versions on the account given by G. Zsatkovich in his *Otkrytie-Exposé byvšeho gubernatora Podkarpatskoj Rusi, o Podkarpatskoj Rusi*, 2nd ed. (Homestead, Penn., 1921), p. 3. The Rusyn-American leader was not present at the Homestead deliberations and, reflecting his own political preferences, he claimed that the first demand was "complete independence" and the last simply "autonomy." Zsatkovich clearly misrepresented the Homestead Resolution by deleting the demand for autonomy specifically within Hungary. Nonetheless, his account was accepted by every writer except those by the Czech authors: Raušer, "Připojení," p. 63, and Krofta, *Byli jsme*, p. 137.

[37]*Amerykanskii russkii vîstnyk*, August 26, 1918.

As for the Czechoslovak movement, the Rusyn press presented a very unfavorable point of view. Wrath was especially directed toward Slovak immigrants, because they claimed certain Rusyn-inhabited territories as part of a future Slovakia and because they continued "to associate with our fallen down 'bolsheviki' [Pačuta] mob leaders."[38] Stiff polemics were exchanged in the Slovak and Rusyn press over the question of to whom the nationally-mixed counties of Sáros/Sharysh, Szepes/Spish, Abaúj/Abov, Borsod/Borshod, Zemplén/Zemplyn and Ung/Uzh should belong.[39] The Rusyn message was unequivocal:

> Hold your horses [Slovak] brethren, and be satisfied with your boundaries, made a year or two ago when you thought that the Uhro-Rusyns were dead. ... We want liberty and independence ... and as Rusyns we are trying to make unity with other Rusyns, left out from Russia and Ukrainia [sic] ... in Galicia and Bukovina, and to create for our fathers and brethren a free Carpathian Republic, instead of being the gain of anybody.[40]

The so-called Ukrainian solution and the desire for a free Carpathian Republic requires some explanation. As was obvious from the ecclesiastical controversies referred to above, the majority of Rusyn immigrants from Subcarpathian Rus' felt themselves to be distinct from Ukrainians. In effect, the proposed Carpathian Republic was to include three separate districts (*kantony*): (1) Uhors'ka Rus', from Hungary; and from Galicia (2) a Ukrainian district; and (3) a Carpatho-Russian Lemko district. This was to be a kind of federation "after the example of Switzerland!"[41] The proposed territorial division of Galicia was intended to respond to the needs of the two national orientations there: the Ukrainophile, which considered the population to be Ukrainian; and the Russophile, which considered it to be "Russian" or, in local terminology, " Lemko." Most often, Subcarpathian inunigrant leaders

---

[38]Editorial in English, "Answer to our 'Bolsheviki'," in *ibid*, August 22, 1918. See also *ibid.*, September 12, 1918.

[39]The Rusyn immigrants, most of whom came from these disputed areas, were incensed at those Slovaks who refused to consider Rusyns as anything else but "Slovak Greek Catholics." *Ibid.*, August 15, 1918. See also the articles in *Prosvîta*, September 19 and October 3, 1918.

[40]"Answer to our 'Bolsheviki'," *Amerykanskii russkii vîstnyk*, August 22, 1918.

[41]*Amerykanskii russkii vîstnyk*, November 21, 1918.

called for union only with the Carpatho-Russian Lemkos. Thus, it would be incorrect to assume, as many Ukrainian writers do, that Uhro-Rusyn immigrant proposals to unite with Galicia and Bukovina were an indication of a Ukrainian national consciousness.

If the publications of the Greek Catholic immigrant organizations continued to criticize the Czechoslovak alternative, how was it that this solution was finally accepted? The answer can be found by examining the activity of the young Pittsburgh lawyer, Gregory Zhatkovich. Though a native of Subcarpathian Rus', Gregory was brought to the United States at the age of four, educated in American schools, and by Rusyn immigrant standards became successful enough to maintain a law practice. His father Pavel was a co-founder of the Greek Catholic Union and an activist in the struggle to oppose Hungarian infiltration into that organization, but Gregory seems not to have been directly involved in Rusyn affairs until the late summer of 1918. As is evident from his proposals, he advocated the idea that the Subcarpathian, or Uhro-Rusyns formed a distinct nationality. Such a view, he believed, justified their demand for separate political as well as national rights.[42]

Because of his facility to operate within the American system, the National Council of Uhro-Rusyns called upon Zhatkovich in October to prepare a memorandum for President Wilson. Having drawn up such a document, he arranged (with the help of Congressman Guy E. Campbell, D.-Penn.) a meeting with the president on October 21.[43] Zhatkovich's memorandum differed considerably from the Homestead Resolution. The first demand was "that our Uhro-Rusyn people be recognized as a separate people and, if possible, as completely independent." If this were not possible, the peace conference might propose unification with full autonomy with a neighboring Slavic people. Finally, if Hungary's borders would remain intact, then full autonomy should be sought within that country. Significantly, nothing

---

[42]Zhatkovich wrote extensive editorials in late 1918 that stressed the distinct nature of Subcarpathian Rusyns. See, for example, his "Kraj Uhro-Rusinov—Uhro-Rusinija," *Prosvîta*, October 31, 1918. Unfortunately, there is no study about the life of this influential immigrant leader except perhaps for his short obituary in *The New York Times*, March 29, 1967.

[43]At the meeting with Zhatkovich were Julij Gardoš—acting head of the American Council of Uhro-Rusyns, the priests Nikolaj Chopey and Valentine Gorzo, Andrej Petach, Georgij Komloš, and Michael J. Hanchin.

specific about unification with Galicia and Bukovina was included and no mention at all was made of Czechoslovakia.[44]

Presumably, President Wilson recommended seeking autonomy within some larger state and also advised Zhatkovich and his colleagues to enter the Mid-European Democratic Union, a group of eastern European politicians representing eleven nationalities who organized a meeting on October 23-26 at Independence Hall in Philadelphia. At Zhatkovich's request, a nationally separate Uhro-Rusyn delegation was accorded membership in the Union. Also while in Philadelphia Zhatkovich met with Masaryk to discuss the possibility of Subcarpathia's unification with the new Czechoslovak state. Zhatkovich later claimed that Masaryk told him: "If the Rusyns decide to join the Czechoslovak Republic, they shall constitute a totally autonomous state."[45] However, another member of the Rusyn delegation, Reverend Valentine Gorzo, asked skeptically: "How can we agree with you, our brother Slovaks, if as your map shows you have taken half of our population and our Rusyn land. We demand a Rusyn territory from the Poprad to the Tisa Rivers."[46] On this critical question, Masaryk, Czechoslovakia's future president, was credited with saying: "The frontiers will be so determined that the Rusyns will be satisfied."[47]

Whether or not Masaryk made these verbal promises to Zhatkovich in Philadelphia, one thing is certain: no written agreement was concluded between the two men on October 25 or on the next day when they joined other eastern European leaders to sign the "Declaration of Common Aims of the Independent Mid-European Nations."[48] On the

---

[44]The memorandum appears in *Amerykanskii russkii vîstnyk*, October 24, 1918, and in *Prosvîta*, October 31, 1918.

[45]Žatkovič [Zhatkovich], *Otkrytie-Exposé*, p. 5.

[46]Cited in *Prosvîta*, February 21, 1926.

[47]Cited in Žatkovič, *Otkrytie-Exposé*, p. 5.

[48]Both Danko, "Plebiscite," p. 189, note 12, and Mamatey, "Slovaks and Carpatho-Ruthenians," p. 244, note 38, have correctly refuted the erroneous suggestion that a so-called "Philadelphia Agreement," signed by Zhatkovich and Masaryk, pledged the union of Subcarpathian Rus' to Czechoslovakia. For the origin of the "Philadelphia Agreement" theory, see Macartney, *Hungary*, p. 215, and the earlier Vojta Beneš, *Masarykovo dílo v Americe* (Prague, 1925) p. 73. A facsimile of the Declaration of Common Aims is reproduced in Walter K. Hanak, *The Subcarpathian Ruthenian Question, 1918-1945* (Munhall, Penn., 1962), p. 10, while

other hand, Masaryk was presented with a memorandum from Nicholas Pačuta of the American Russian National Defense. Like Pačuta's first memorandum delivered to the Czech statesman in May 1918, the new one in October called for "the union of all the Carpathian Russians on an autonomic [sic] basis with the Czecho-Slovak State."[49]

On October 29, Zhatkovich reported the results of his meetings with President Wilson and Tomáš Masaryk to the American National Council of Uhro-Rusyns. He still did not, however, publicly support the idea of joining Subcarpathian Rus' to Czechoslovakia.[50] The next few weeks were marked by further negotiations, during which Rusyn newspapers were filled with discussions of whether to unite with Czechoslovakia or with Ukraine.[51]

It was not until November 12, 1918, at a meeting of the National Council held in Scranton, Pennsylvania, that the Czechoslovak solution was finally adopted. Zhatkovich succeeded in having the following resolution accepted:

> That Uhro-Rusyns with the broadest autonomous rights as a state, and on a federative basis, be united with the Czechoslovak Democratic Republic, under the conditions that to our country must belong all the original Uhro-Rusyn counties: Szepes, Sáros, Zemplén, Abauj, Borsod, Ung, Ugocsa, Bereg, and Máramaros.[52]

This territorial clause was to be the cause of future difficulty, since Slovaks were already claiming as their own the first six counties.

---

a good discussion of the work of the Mid-European Union is found in Arthur J. May, "The Mid-European Union," in O'Grady, *Immigrant's Influence*, pp. 250-271.

[49]"Memorandum of the American-Russian National Defense Dedicated to Professor T.G. Masaryk, the Illustrious and Tireless Worker for the Emancipation of the Slavic Nations" (Pittsburgh, Penn., 1918)—the citation here is taken from the reprint in Peška and Markov, "Příspěvek," p. 130. This memorandum was also signed by G. Kondor, President of the Supreme Tribunal, and I. Drimak, Supreme Recorder of the Greek Catholic Union.

[50]"Protokol yz zasîdaniia Tsentral'noho Vŷbora Amerykanskoi Narodnoi Radŷ Uhro-Rusynov, Homestead, Penn., 29.X.1918," *Amerykanskii russkii vîstnyk*, November 7, 1918.

[51]*Ibid.*

[52]"Protokol yz zasîdaniia Amerykanskoi Narodnoi Radŷ Uhro-Rusynov poderzhanoho dnia 12-ho noiabria 1918, v Skrenton, Pa.," *ibid.*, November 14, 1918.

Zhatkovich also proposed at the Scranton meeting that a plebiscite be placed before all Rusyns in the United States in order to determine "where Uhro-Rusyns in the old country should belong, as an autonomous state in a Czechoslovak or in a Ukrainian federation."[53]

On November 13, Zhatkovich met with Masaryk, who "expressed great pleasure" with the Scranton resolution and stressed the need for a plebiscite so that the decision to join Czechoslovakia be viewed not "only as a decision of members of the National Council which could be objected to at the Peace Conference in Paris."[54] The next day Zhatkovich reported these recent developments in a telegram to President Wilson who responded with congratulations "on the progress made toward satisfactory relations."[55]

Finally, the organs representing Greek Catholic Rusyn organizations came out in support of the Czechoslovak alternative. Throughout the summer, the idea of union with Galicia had been proposed, and the only objection to that solution was a fear that the more "progressive" Ukrainian language and grammatical principles would replace our "dear Uhro-Rusyn language."[56] Nevertheless, it was the practical reality of an existing Czechoslovak state as opposed to a still unrecognized Ukrainian government in Galicia that forced American Rusyns to link their destiny with Prague.[57] It should be mentioned that several Greek Catholic priests met in Pittsburgh on November 19 to protest the Scranton resolution, but their discontent was to have only limited effect

[53] *Ibid.* Protocol also reprinted in *Prosvîta*, November 28, 1918.

[54] Žatkovič, *Otkrytie-Exposé*, pp. 5-6; Masaryk, *Světova revoluce*, p. 292.

[55] The correspodence between Zsatkovich and Wilson is reprinted in Danko, "Plebiscite," pp. 203-205.

[56] The grammatical feature most feared was the modern phonetic orthography adopted by Ukrainophiles in Galicia. The Uhro-Rusyn commentator felt that if the Carpathian Mountains remained as a border, they "will defend us so that the phonetic fish will not eat our more miserable yet to us dear Uhro-Rusyn language." *Amerykanskii russkii vîstnyk*, November 14, 1918.

[57] With regard to the Slovaks, the following Rusyn commentary is of interest: "As for language, speech, literature, there is no such fear with regard to Slovaks as with Ukrainians. Slovaks don't have a literature, Ukrainians have one. Thus, we would sooner lose our Uhro-Rusyn character with Ukrainians than with the Czecho-Slovaks." *Ibid.*, November 21, 1918. See also *Prosvîta*, November 21, 1918.

on the Rusyn-American public.[58]

In December 1918, the proposed plebiscite was held in the various lodges of the Greek Catholic Union (Sojedinenije), the United Societies of the Greek Catholic Religion (Sobranije), and in Uhro-Rusyn Greek Catholic parishes. According to Zhatkovich's suggestion made at Scranton, each lodge and parish was alloted one vote for every fifty members.[59] This indirect balloting was actually conducted in less than half of the existing lodges and parishes. For example, as of May 31, 1918, there were a total of 874 lodges in the Greek Catholic Union, but only 372 returned a vote in the December plebiscite. Similarly, of the 158 chapters in the United Societies, only 46 responded.

Zhatkovich did, however, obtain the result he desired: out of 1102 votes submitted, 732 (67 perecent) were for union with Czechoslovakia, and 310 (28 percent) for union with the Ukraine. Although not among the suggested choices, 27 votes were cast for total independence, 10 votes for Russia, and 9 for Hungary.[60] Zhatkovich immediately informed Czechoslovak authorities in both Prague and Paris as well as the State Department in Washington of the results. The plebiscite gave greater credence to the decision of the American National Council of Uhro-Rusyns since it seemed to be an expression of popular will and not just an espression of the desire of a few energetic leaders.

The Scranton resolution and the subsequent plebiscite brought to a close the first stage in Rusyn immigrant political activity. Under the influence of cultural and national traditions brought from the old country, Rusyn-American leaders had wavered between a Hungarian, Russian, Ukrai-

---

[58]The opposition priests were A. Holosnyay, J. Szabo and N. Szabados—all members of the clerical representation who signed the Homestead Resolution in July 1918—and S. Roškovich, V. Lipecky, A. Šuba, E. Volkay, M. Volkay and Danilovich. *Prosvîta*, November 28, 1918. See also the recollections of the Reverend N. Szabados in the leading Hungarian-American newspaper, *Amerikai magyar népszava*, November 8, 1924.

[59]This meant that if a given lodge or parish had, for instance, 50 members—26 voting for Czechoslovakia, 24 for the Ukraine or Hungary—the one alloted vote would be cast for Czechoslovakia.

[60]The results of the plebiscite appeared in *Prosvîta*, January 2, 1919 and in the *Amerykanskii russkii vîstnyk*, January 5, 1919. They have been subsequently reprinted in Danko, "Plebiscite," pp. 191-202.

nian, Czechoslovak, and independent orientation. It was not until late 1918 that the Czechoslovak alternative was finally adopted, and this was in large measure due to the activity of Gregory Zhatkovich. This young lawyer from Pittsburgh initially favored independence, or at least a substantial degree of autonomy in a larger state, but under the influence of rapidly changing political developments in late 1918, he was forced to conclude that his goals might best be guaranteed by uniting with Czechoslovakia.

Zhatkovich headed a three-man Rusyn-American delegation, which in February 1919 presented the Scranton resolution and plebiscite to the Czechoslovak Delegation at the Paris Peace Conference. Information about the Rusyn immigrant decision had already reached the homeland and local leaders admitted that the views further stimulated them to incline toward Czechoslovakia.[61] Zhatkovich himself arrived in Sub-carpathian Rus' on March 10 and began immediately to organize a national council. Finally, on May 8, 1919, the Central Russian National Council (Tsentral'na Russka Narodna Rada) met in Uzhhorod to declare that "in the name of the whole nation it completely endorses the decision of the American Uhro-Rusyn Council to unite with the Czechoslovak nation on the basis of full national autonomy."[62] Moreover, it was Zhatkovich himself who formulated the political demands of the Uzhhorod Council regarding the future relationship between the "Russian State" (Russkii Shtat)—as Subcarpathian Rus' was referred to—and Czechoslovakia.[63] Maintaining the independist or separatist position, he also succeeded in having the Uzhhorod

---

[61]Avhustyn Voloshyn, *Dvî polytychnî rozmovŷ* (Uzhhorod, 1923), p. 7. For developments in Subcarpathian Rus' at this time, see Paul R. Magocsi, "The Ruthenian Decision to Unite with Czechoslovakia," *Slavic Review*, XXXIV, 2 (Seattle, 1975), pp. 360-381—reprinted above, Chapter 6.

[62]*Protokoly obshchago sobraniia podkarpatskikh russkikh rad i pervykh 5-ti zasiedanii Tsentralnoi Russkoi Narodnoi Rady* (Uzhhorod, 1919), reprinted in *Karpatorusskije novosti* (New York), May 15, 1944.

[63]Zhatkovich considered Subcarpathia's relationship to the Czechoslovak republic as somewhat analogous to the position of a state in the United States. This federalist view conflicted with the centralist orientation of the Prague regime. The specific political demands of Zhatkovich were included in a fourteen-point plan accepted by the Uzhhorod Council on May 16. Reprinted in Peška and Markov, "Příspěvek," IV (1930), pp. 419-422.

Council reject all attempts to have Galician Rusyns united with their Subcarpathian brothers.[64]

It is clear that the action of Rusyn-American immigrants in 1918 had a direct impact on the specific political developments in Europe. Recognizing the crucial role played by Zhatkovich, Czechoslovakia's President Masaryk appointed him to serve as head of Subcarpathia's ruling Directorate in 1919 and as its first governor in 1920. However, after repeated disagreement with the Prague regime concerning the western boundary of Subcarpathian Rus' and the implementation of autonomy, Zhatkovich resigned in March 1921 and returned to the United States.[65] There he joined other Rusyn immigrants who soon regretted their decision and who began a long campaign of protest against Czechoslovakia's administration of the homeland. This activity had little effect, however, on subsequent developments in Europe and in no way could compare to the decisive role played by the Rusyn-American community in 1918.

---

[64]Zhatkovich's position on this matter alienated him from local Russophile leaders, in particular his successor to the governorship, Antonii Beskid, whose "aim was to liberate and unite all Carpatho-Rusyns, including the [Galician] Lemkos." *Protokoly.*

[65]Žatkovič, *Otkrytie-Exposé*, pp. 11-30.

CHAPTER 19

Carpatho-Rusyn Press in the United States[*]

The Carpatho-Rusyn press in the United States is the product of a group of Americans who either came themselves or are descendants of immigrants who arrived on these shores for the most part before World War I.[1] Like other ethnic groups in the United States, the Carpatho-Rusyns brought with them the religious and political differences that existed in their homeland and to which the American experience added even greater diversity. This diversity is best expressed through the Carpatho-Rusyn press, which since its beginnings in the United States has included more than fifty newspapers and journals.[2] For this discussion, these various titles may be grouped into four categories: fraternal, religious, political, and cultural.

---

[*]This study was commissioned for a volume on the ethnic press and first published in Sally M. Miller, ed., *The Ethnic Press in the United States: A Historical Analysis and Handbook* (New York; Westport, Conn.; and London: Greenwood Press, 1987), pp. 15-26.

[1]On the Carpatho-Rusyns in the United States, see Paul R. Magocsi, "Carpatho-Rusyns," in Stephan Thernstrom, ed., *Harvard Encyclopedia of American Ethnic Groups* (Cambridge, Mass. and London, U.K., 1980), pp. 200-210; and idem, *Our People: Carpatho-Rusyns and Their Descendants in North America* (Toronto, 1984).

[2]A convenient list of most of these is found in Frank Renkiewicz, *The Carpatho-Ruthenian Microfilm Project: A Guide to Newspapers and Periodicals* (St. Paul, Minn., 1979).

Fraternal press organs

During the ninety-year history of Carpatho-Rusyn newspapers and journals in the United States, it is the press of the fraternal organizations that has reached the largest numbers of people and therefore has had the greatest influence on the group's development. The oldest, largest, and longest-lasting Carpatho-Rusyn newspaper was the *Amerykanskii russkii vîstnyk*, the official organ of the Greek Catholic Union (Sojedinenije), which, in turn, was the first fraternal society set up specifically for Carpatho-Rusyns.[3] The *Amierykanskii russkii vîstnyk* began to appear in 1892 in Mahanoy City, a coal-mining town in eastern Pennsylvania. Before long it moved to nearby Scranton, then to New York City, and finally, in 1904, went westward to Pittsburgh and then the latter's suburb of Homestead, Pennsylvania, where since 1952 it has been published under the English title, *Greek Catholic Union Messenger*.

Initially begun as a weekly, the *Amerykanskii russkii vîstnyk* appeared twice and then three times a week after World War I, before reverting back to a weekly and then bi-weekly after World War II. Its language also changed through the years. Initially, it appeared in Carpatho-Rusyn using the Cyrillic alphabet, and for several years before World War I it also had a second edition written in the Latin alphabet and using an East Slovak/Rusyn transitional dialect (the so-called Sotak dialect). During the 1920s, only a Carpatho-Rusyn edition appeared, but using a Latin alphabet. Finally, in 1952, with the change in name to the *Greek Catholic Union Messenger*, the major language used was English with a steady decrease in the use of Carpatho-Rusyn, so that today only one column appears in the native language.[4]

---

[3]Carpatho-Rusyn organizations and publishers used different transliteration systems to render in the Latin alphabet names and titles in their native language. We have reproduced the original forms used by the organizations or individuals. When no such form in the Latin alphabet is available, and for publications mentioned in the notes and bibliography that only appeared in the Cyrillic alphabet, the Library of Congress transliteration system has been used (without final hard signs or diacritics) for Russian or Ukrainian. Cyrillic publications in Rusyn follow the Library of Congress system for Ukrainian with the following additions: ѣ=î and ы=ŷ.

[4]Already in the early 1980s, the Rusyn-language columns disappeared, and in 1993, the publication ceased entirely and was succeeded by a monthly called the

It was during the interwar period that the *Amerykanskii russkii vîstnyk* reached its greatest audience, being sent to the more than 90,000 members of the Greek Catholic Union. Because of its growing influence, the editors, especially Pavel Zsatkovich (served 1892-1914), Michael Hanchin (served 1914-1919), Reverend Stephan Varzaly (served 1929-1937), and Michael Roman (served 1937-1980), had a profound impact on Rusyn-American public opinion, especially as it affected relations with churches, politics in the homeland, and the problem of national identity. Basically, the *Amerykanskii russkii vîstnyk* represented the Greek Catholic Union's self-proclaimed mission to defend and preserve in America the specific religious and national traditions of the Carpatho-Rusyns. To ensure that such efforts had an impact on future generations, the Greek Catholic Union also published a newspaper for teenagers and young adults, the weekly *Sokol Soedineniia* (Homestead, Pa., 1914-36), and another for children, *Svit d'itej/Children's World* (Homestead, Pa., 1917-73).

In a real sense, the subsequent development of other Carpatho-Rusyn press organs came about as a reaction to the Greek Catholic Union and its policies as expressed in the *Amerykanskii russkii vîstnyk*. The first Carpatho-Rusyn immigrants to split off were the Lemkos, who joined other immigrants from the Austrian province of Galicia who were discontented with the Greek Catholic and supposedly "non-Russian" orientation of the *Amerykanskii russkii vîstnyk*.[5] Representing the

---

GCU Magazine (Butler, Penn., 1994-present). For a brief early history of the newspaper and an annotated bibliography of its contents before World War I, see in James M. Evans, *Guide to the Amerikansky Russky Viestnik*, Vol. I: *1894-1914* (Fairview, N.J., 1979).

[5] As in the European homeland, so in the United States, Carpatho-Rusyns were and still are divided into at least three orientations regarding their national or ethnic identity. Perhaps the majority felt and still feel that they form a distinct Slavic nationality variously called Rusyn (often spelt Rusin), Ruthenian, or in earlier years Uhro-Rusyn. Another group—the Russophiles—feel that Carpatho-Rusyns (like Ukrainians and Belarusans) form only a branch of a single Russian nationality. The third group—the Ukrainophiles—who became active in America only after World War II, believe that Carpatho-Rusyns are the westernmost branch of the Ukrainian nationality, and, moreover, that the term Rusyn is simply the historic name for all Ukrainians.

It should be mentioned that even though organizations like the Greek Catholic Union and its newspaper, the *Amerykanskii russkii vîstnyk*, translated into English

Orthodox religious and "Russian" national viewpoint was the newspaper *Svit* (Wilkes-Barre, Penn., 1894-present), published by the Russian Orthodox Catholic Mutual Aid Society and *Pravda / The Truth* (Olyphant, Pa.; Philadelphia, 1902-present), published by the Russian Brotherhood Organization. Although both newspapers still appear today, they have little to do with Carpatho-Rusyns; instead, they represent immigrants and their descendants from all parts of former eastern Galicia, who in the United States claim themselves to be Carpatho-Russians or simply Orthodox Russians.

The next two fraternal newspapers also came into existence after former members of the Greek Catholic Union broke from that organization. In 1915, the *Pravoslavnyi russkii viestnik* (Monessen, Pa., 1915-17) and later the *Russkii viestnik / Russian Messenger / UROBA Messenger* (Pittsburgh, Pa., 1917-present) were published in order to represent the views of the recent Greek Catholic converts to Orthodoxy who also established their own fraternal society, the United Russian Orthodox Brotherhood in America.[6] Then, in 1918, Greek Catholic Union members in the New York metropolitan area, dissatisfied with the proportionally larger amounts of accident benefits being paid to miners from Pennsylvania, founded their own fraternal, the Greek Catholic Carpatho-Russian Benevolent Association Liberty, with its own newspaper *Vostok / The East* (Perth Amboy, N.J., 1919-1950).[7] Initially representing Byzantine Catholics on the east coast, by the early 1940s *Vostok* broke with the Byzantine Ruthenian Catholic Church and supported instead the recently-founded American Carpatho-Russian

the words *russkii/rus'kyi /rusyn* as Russian, for the most part they did not consider themselves similar to the "Great" Russians of Moscow, Leningrad, etc. This prompted accusations by Russophiles that the Greek Catholic Union was "non-Russian.

[6]From its earliest years, the history of the Carpatho-Rusyns in the United States has been marked by defections from the Greek Catholic (Byzantine Ruthenian) church in favor of some form of Orthodoxy. This movement was particularly pronounced before 1918 and during the 1930s. With each wave of conversions there also followed new Orthodox fraternal societies and newspapers.

[7]On the history of this newspaper, see the special issue, *Vostok—The East: Twenty Fifth Anniversary, 1918-1943* (Perth Amboy, N.J., 1945).

Orthodox Greek Catholic Church.[8]

The religious press

Religious and church-related press organs began to appear because of dissatisfaction with and the need to react to criticism from the Greek Catholic Union's *Amerykanskii russkii vîstnyk*. Among the first organs to be created was the *Pravoslavnyi amerikanskii viestnik/Russian Orthodox American Messenger* (New York, 1896-1970?), which was the official organ of the Russian Orthodox Mission and later Orthodox Metropolia in America, designed especially to serve the needs of those Byzantine/Greek Catholics (mostly Carpatho-Rusyns) who converted to Orthodoxy. In later years, both the newspaper and its successor, *The Orthodox Church* (Syosset, N.Y., 1965-present), have had little, if any, content directed specifically to Carpatho-Rusyns, but instead have become simply organs of the Russian Orthodox and now "non-ethnic" Orthodox Church in America (the OCA). More attention to the specific heritage of the OCA members of Carpatho-Rusyn background (especially descendants of the Lemko Region) is found in the local monthly newspaper, *The Orthodox Herald* (San Antonio, Texas; Hunlock Creek, Pa., 1952-present).

Among Byzantine Catholics who did not convert to Orthodoxy, discontent with the *Amerykanskii russkii vîstnyk* (especially with its criticism of church policy) led to the creation of a new organ, *Rusin* (Philadelphia; Pittsburgh, 1910-16), published by the Greek Catholic Priests Mission Association under the editorship of the cultural activist, Reverend Joseph Hanulya. Not long after its establishment, *Rusin* moved to Pittsburgh and became the official organ of the fraternal organization, the United Societies (Sobranije) of Greek Catholic

---

[8]The movement to create this new church began in the early 1930s and reached fruition in 1938. It was sparked by discontent among several Greek Catholic (Byzantine Ruthenian) priests who opposed their own hierarchy's acceptance of the Vatican's determination after 1929 to enforce certain rules governing the practices of Eastern-rite Catholic churches in the New World. The most controversial of these was the necessity of celibacy for all new priests, a demand which several Byzantine Catholics felt had violated their centuries-old ecclesiastical right to a married priesthood.

Religion. The United Societies had been founded in 1903 by Greek Catholic Union members who were displeased with that fraternal's criticism of the church. Thus, both *Rusin* and its successor, *Prosvîta/The Enlightenment* (McKeesport, Penn., 1917-present), became for more than two decades the unofficial organs of the Byzantine Ruthenians of the Catholic Church which was, especially during the 1930s, under almost constant attack from the editors of the Greek Catholic Union's *Amerykanskii russkii vîstnyk*.[9]

Perhaps because it could count on the services of *Rusin* and *Prosvîta*, the Byzantine Ruthenian Catholic church for the longest time did not have its own official press organs. A monthly, *Nebesnaja Carica/Queen of Heaven* (McKeesport, Penn., 1927-55) did serve for close to three decades as the semi-official magazine of the church, and a few attempts were made to create a diocesan newspaper during the 1940s, but these were short-lived.[10] It was not until 1956 that the *Byzantine Catholic World* (Pittsburgh, 1956-present) was begun as the official press organ of the Byzantine Ruthenian Catholic Church. Although English was the predominant language, at least during the first decade many articles appeared in Carpatho-Rusyn, and throughout most of its history the *Byzantine Catholic World* has carried much information about the Carpatho-Rusyn heritage in both Europe and America. During the 1960s, when the Byzantine Ruthenian Church was raised to the status of a metropolitan province and two new eparchies (dioceses) were created, separate diocesan newspapers eventually followed as well—*Eastern Catholic Life* (Passaic, N.J., 1965-present) for the Eparchy of Passaic, and *Horizons* (Parma, Ohio, 1979-present) for the Eparchy of Parma.

The only other religious press organ of significance is the *Cerkoynyj*

---

[9]The debate between these newspapers originated in the *Amierykanskii russkii vîstnyk*'s criticism of the Byzantine Ruthenian Catholic church's first bishop (during the years before World War I) and then its opposition to the hierarchy's position favoring celibacy for new priests (during the 1930s). For a brief history of *Rusin* and *Prosvîta*, see Basil Shereghy, *The United Societies of the U.S.A.: A Historical Album* (McKeesport, Penn., 1978), pp. 69-72. On the clashes of these newspapers with the *Amerykanskii russkii vîstnyk*, see Walter C. Warzeski, *Byzantine Rite Rusins in Carpatho-Ruthenia and America* (Pittsburgh, Penn., 1971), pp. 194-244 passim.

[10]These included the bi-weekly *Eastern Observer* (Homestead; Pittsburgh, Penn., 1942-43) and the monthly *Greek Catholic Sower* (Lisle, Ill., 1949-50).

vistnik / Church Messenger (Pemberton, N.J., 1944-present). This bi-weekly newspaper is the official organ of the American Carpatho-Russian Orthodox Greek Catholic Diocese, based in Johnstown, Pennsylvania, which was founded in 1938 by priests who had broken away from the Byzantine Ruthenian Catholic Church. Because the "Johnstown Diocese" claimed to be preserving traditional Greek Catholic or Byzantine Ruthenian traditions, its publications such as the *Church Messenger* still carry at least one page written in Carpatho-Rusyn and are concerned with the specific cultural and religious features of the group. The traditionalist and heritage-oriented approach was also pronounced in three other affiliated publications, the monthly *Holos vostočnoj cerkvi/ Voice of the Eastern Church* (Perth Amboy, N.J., 1941-45), and the English-language youth journals—*Carpatho-Russian Youth* (Johnstown, Penn.; Binghamton, N.Y., 1938-41) and the *A.C.Y.R. Guardian* (New York, N.Y., Perth Amboy, N.J., 1957-62).

Political press organs

In contrast to the Carpatho-Rusyn fraternal and religious press, those organs that were not affiliated with any organization and that were concerned largely with political and social developments have, in general, had short life spans. One of the most interesting in this category—and the only daily in the history of the Carpatho-Rusyn press in America—was the newspaper *Den' / Den* (New York, 1922-26). Published and edited by former *ARV* editor Michael Hanchin, *Den'* appeared only in Carpatho-Rusyn and carried a wide body of information about the homeland as well as coverage of American and world news of most significance for immigrants.[11]

More typical of the Carpatho-Rusyn political press were organs established to fulfill a specific goal. Sometimes that goal had to do with the European homeland, such as trying to convince the immigrants during World War I to support the idea of unification with Russia,[12]

---

[11]On the history of *Den'*, see Georgij Sabov, "Jak voznikla perva karpatorusska ježednevna gazeta v Ameriki," in Michael Roman, ed., *1973 Calendar of the Greek Catholic Union of the U.S.A.* (Homestead, Penn., 1972), pp. 78-82.

[12]*Prikarpatskaia Rus'* (New York, 1920-25), published by the Carpatho-Russian National Organization in America—mostly Lemkos and other Russophiles from Galicia; and *Narodna obrana* (Homestead, Penn., 1917), published by the American

or during World War II to cooperate with the Czechoslovak government-in-exile which expected the postwar return of Subcarpathian Rus'
(then occupied by Hungary) to a restored Czechoslovakia.[13] As often,
the political goal might have been to persuade Rusyn-Americans that
they were ethnically, linguistically, and therefore nationally Russians,[14]
or Ukrainians,[15] or simply Rusyns whose best hope would be to remain united with a non-Communist Czechoslovakia.[16]

A special category of the Carpatho-Rusyn political press is that
published by the Lemkos. In contrast to other Carpatho-Rusyns, the
Lemkos came from villages north of the Carpathian Mountains, from
the former Austrian province of Galicia, and in the United States they
have maintained their own organizations and press. Although a Lemko
journal began to appear for a short while in the early 1920s,[17] it was
not until the appearance of the monthly and later weekly *Lemko*
(Philadelphia, Cleveland, New York, 1928-39) that this group's press
was firmly established. Founded and edited throughout its existence by

Russian National Defense—mostly recent Greek Catholic converts to Orthodoxy
from Subcarpathian Rus' and the Prešov Region.

[13]*The Carpathian* (Pittsburgh, Penn., 1941-43), published by the American
Carpatho-Russian Council headed by former Subcarpathian governor Gregory
Zhatkovich and other Byzantine Catholic Rusyns; *Jedinstvo / Unity* (Gary, Ind.,
1942-43), published by the Carpatho-Russian Unity, mostly Orthodox Rusyns from
the Subcarpathian region; and *Karpatorusskije novosti* (New York, 1943-45),
published by the Czechoslovak Government-in-Exile Information Service.

[14]*Karpato-russkoe slovo* (New York, 1935-38), published by the Carpatho-Russian
National Committee, later the Russian American Union, and edited by the
Russophile émigré from Galicia, Viktor Hladik; and *Svobodnoe slovo Karpatskoi
Rusi* (Newark, N.J.; Mount Vernon, N.Y., 1959-present), published by the
post-World War II Russophile from Subcarpathian Rus', Michael Turjanica.

[15]*Karpats'ka zoria* (New York, N.Y.; Jersey City, N.J., 1951-52), published by the
Carpathian Star Publishing Company; and *Vistnyk Karpats' koho soiuza* (New York,
1970-73), published by the Carpathian Alliance, both organizations comprised of
post-World War II Ukrainophile immigrants from Subcarpathian Rus'
(Transcarpathia).

[16]*Rusin / The Ruthenian* (New York, 1952-60), published by the Council of a Free
Sub-Carpatho-Ruthenia (in Exile), comprised of post-World War II Carpatho-Rusyn
immigrants associated with the Council of Free Czechoslovakia in Exile.

[17]*Lemkovshchyna* (New York, 1922-23), published by the Lemko's Committee
under the direction of Simeon Pysh.

Dmitry Vislocky, *Lemko* became after 1931 the official organ of the Lemko Association (Lemko Soiuz). It was succeeded in 1939 by *Karpatska Rus'* (Yonkers, N.Y., 1938-present), edited for its first two decades by the group's popular writer, Simeon Pysh. Until 1980, this newspaper appeared exclusively in Carpatho-Rusyn. At times the Lemko Association has tried to attract younger members into its ranks by publishing several heritage-oriented English publications, but these have all been short lived.[18] Like other Rusyn Americans, so too have the Lemkos created new press organs because of disagreement with the older *Lemko* and *Karpatska Rus'*, in particular over the latter's generally pro-Soviet stance on political issues and their Russophile national orientation regarding ethnic identity. Thus, an anti-Soviet though Russophile faction published a short-lived newspaper during the early 1970s,[19] while anti-Soviet and nationally Ukrainian-oriented Lemkos have published two newspapers, a scholarly journal, and most recently have begun a cultural quarterly, *Lemkivshchyna* (New York, 1979-present).[20]

Cultural press

The least successful type of press put out by Carpatho-Rusyns in the United States are cultural publications that are not affiliated with any churches or fraternal societies. Nonetheless, from the earliest years to more recent times, several attempts have been made to publish literary, educational, and cultural press organs.

Already during World War I, and in the wake of the great wave of

---

[18]*Lemko Youth Journal* (Yonkers, N.Y., 1960-64); *Carpatho-Russian American* (Yonkers, N.Y., 1968-69); *Karpaty* (Yonkers, N.Y., 1978-79). The author is grateful to Michael Logoyda, former editor of *Karpatska Rus'*, for information on the Lemko press.

[19]*Lemkovina* (Yonkers, N.Y., 1971-81?), published by the former editor of *Karpatska Rus'*, Stefan M. Kitchura.

[20]*Lemkivshchyna* is published by the Lemko Research Foundation in New York City, which is a kind of umbrella organization for several Ukrainophile Lemko groups, some of which had their own organs as well, such as the newspapers *Lemkivs'kyi dzvin* (New York, 1936-40) and *Lemkivs'ki visti* (Yonkers, N.Y. and Toronto, 1958-present) of the Organization for the Defense of the Lemko Land; and the scholarly journal *Annals* (Camillus, N.Y., 1974-present) of the World Lemkos Federation.

Carpatho-Rusyn immigration, a large format literary and religious monthly, *Niva* (Yonkers, N.Y., 1916), appeared. This unique experiment in publishing an organ for Rusyn-American literature ended after only eleven issues, however. Somewhat more successful was the monthly publication, in Carpatho-Rusyn and English, of the Rusin Elite Society, *Vozhd'/The Leader* (Cleveland, 1929-30). It, too, after what seemed to be a promising start, folded when its organizers became split over of the controversies then raging within the Byzantine Ruthenian Catholic Church.[21]

It seems that the most successful and longest-lasting cultural organ was the more recently founded English-language quarterly, *Carpatho-Rusyn American* (Fairview, N.J.; Madison, Ohio; Plymouth, Minn.; Pittsburgh; Fairfax, Va., 1978-97). Published by the Carpatho-Rusyn Research Center, it is unaffiliated with any church or fraternal, and strives to fulfill the heritage-seeking needs of third- and fourth-generation Carpatho-Rusyns affected by the American bicentennial celebrations and "roots fever."[22]

Thematic content and impact of the press

With the exception of the few unaffiliated political and cultural organs that tried to represent the interests of the ethnic group as a whole, most of the Carpatho-Rusyn press has contained material directed narrowly toward and often about the members of a specific fraternal organization or religious affiliation. Organizational matters, membership lists, and reports on lodges and individual members have always filled a significant portion of the pages in the large fraternal organs such as the *Amerykanskii russkii vîstnyk/GCU Messenger*, *Prosvîta*, and *Vostok*. During the height of the Carpatho-Rusyn press between 1910 and 1940, these newspapers also carried general international and American news. In particular, they were filled with reports about the homeland, and it was through the substantive reporting in these newspapers that the Carpatho-Rusyn immigrants received the information they needed to play the crucial role in the political fate of their homeland in 1918-

---

[21]See above, notes 6 and 8.

[22]Actually, after two decades the *Carpatho-Rusyn American* ceased publication in 1997. Some of its interests have been continued by *The New Rusyn Times* (Pittsburgh, 1994-present), published by the Carpatho-Rusyn Society.

1919—unification with the new state of Czechoslovakia—a role that is generally recognized by historians of the period.[23]

The other great issue that filled the pages of the fraternal organs was the so-called celibacy controversy of the 1930s, a time when the Byzantine Ruthenian Catholic Church was obliged to fulfill the Vatican precepts against ordaining any new married priests (a traditional historical rite of the Byzantine or Greek Catholics) in the United States. The *Amerykanskii russkii vîstnyk* and *Vostok* were harshly critical of church authorities, while *Prosvîta* used its pages to defend the bishop. During the past two decades, the great political and religious debates are gone from the pages of the fraternal press, each of which is almost exclusively concerned with its own organizational matters and activity.

Similarly, the religious press in earlier years was filled with defending and/or propagating the rightness—and righteousness—of its particular orientation, whether on the pages of the Russian Orthodox Metropolia's *Pravoslavnii amerikanskii viestnik*, the Carpatho-Russian Orthodox "Johnstown Diocese's" *Cerkovnyj vistnik/ Church Messenger*, or the Byzantine Ruthenian Catholic Church's *Nebesnaja Carica* and its fraternal mouthpiece, *Prosvîta*. But during at least the past two decades, the harsh intergroup religious polemics are gone from their pages as well as from the widely-circulated *Byzantine Catholic World*, *Eastern Catholic Life*, and *Orthodox World*. Instead, each of these religious newspapers is more concerned with the general problems of the larger church within which it is affiliated, whether Catholic or Orthodox.

For many years political issues had also dominated the pages of the Carpatho-Rusyn press. These took two forms, concern with the fate of the European homeland and debates about the group's national identity. As for the European homeland, criticism of the Hungarian regime before and during World War I evolved into: (1) heated debates over the homeland's future political affiliation in 1918-1919; (2) praise and then criticism of Czechoslovak rule or attacks on the Polish regime in

---

[23]See Victor S. Mamatey, "The Slovaks and Carpatho-Ruthenians," in Joseph P. O'Grady, ed., *The Immigrant's Influence on Wilson's Peace Policies* (Lewisburg, Ky., 1967), pp. 224-249; and Paul R. Magocsi, "The Political Activity of Rusyn-American Immigrants in 1918," *East European Quarterly*, X, 3 (Boulder, Colo., 1976), pp. 347-365—reprinted above, Chapter 18.

the Lemko Region during the interwar period; and (3) general criticism of communism, the Soviet Union, and its satellite states, Czechoslovakia and Poland, after World War II. The only real exception to this general political pattern is found in the "Carpatho-Russian" Lemko organs, *Lemko* and *Karpatska Rus'*, and in the "independent" Orthodox newspaper *Vistnik* (McKees Rocks, Pa., 1936-55), which for most of their existences have expressed favorable views of the Soviet Union and its post-World War II Communist allies, Poland and Czechoslovakia.

The other political topic that has filled the pages of the Carpatho-Rusyn press is the question of national identity. As a Slavic minority coming from the Hungarian Kingdom—and precisely at a time during the four decades before World War I when Hungarian authorities were trying to magyarize their national minorities—most Carpatho-Rusyn immigrants came to the United States only with the sense that they were of the Rus' faith (i.e., they were eastern Christians). Consequently, they described themselves as Rusyns or Rusnaks. But what did this mean in terms of ethnic or national identity? Were they of Rusyn nationality also, or were they Russian, or Ukrainian, or perhaps even Slovak?[24] All these orientations were debated in the press, and often new organs were founded because of the need of often over-anxious patriots to express themselves on the question of the "correct" national nomenclature for the group.

Whereas some organs have adopted the Russian (*Svit, Pravda, Karpato-russkoe slovo, Svobodnoe slovo Karpatskoi Rusi*) or the Ukrainian (*Karpats'ka zoria, Lemkivs'ki visti*) national orientations, the vast majority of the large fraternal and cultural organs (*Amierykanskii russkii vîstnyk, Rusin, Prosvîta, Den', Karpatska Rus', Vozhd/The Leader, Carpatho-Rusyn American*) have basically adopted the position that Carpatho-Rusyns (before World War I known as Uhro-Rusins) comprise a distinct Slavic nationality. This is similarly the case with the leading

---

[24]Some writers, especially Slovaks, have argued that the term *Rusnak* (used by Carpatho-Rusyn and Slovak immigrants of the Greek/Byzantine Catholic faith who came from what is today northeastern Slovakia) is simply the traditional designator for a Catholic Slovak of the eastern rite. Therefore, so the argument goes, all Rusnaks (whether ethnically Rusyn or Slovak) should be considered Slovaks. This position is generally expressed by several Slovak publications in the United States and in *Mária* (Toronto, 1961-present), the monthly of the Slovak Byzantine Rite Catholic Diocese of Canada.

religious organs—*Byzantine Catholic World, Eastern Catholic Life, Church Messenger*. Such a sense of distinctiveness is evident even in those organs which at times have used the term Carpatho-Russian instead of Rusyn or Carpatho-Rusyn to define the group. To be sure, use of the term "Carpatho-Russian" for the first time during the 1930s by leading organs like the *Amierykanskii russkii vîstnyk, Lemko*, and *Vostok* was also accompanied by suggestions that the Rusyns were part of one larger Russian nationality, but by the late 1950s-1960s, a sense of distinctiveness from Russians, as well as from Ukrainians and Slovaks, has been revived.

Besides the few literary and cultural journals (*Niva* and *Vozhd'/ The Leader*), each of the fraternal and some religious and political organs as well have opened their pages to literary works. In fact, while there have been a few separate Rusyn-American collections of poetry, plays, and one novel published, it is on the pages of the press that the vast majority of original Carpatho-Rusyn literature produced in the United States has appeared.[25]

Related to both literary production and the debate over the group's national identity is the problem of language. Until the 1940s, most of the press appeared in various Rusyn dialects. Although a few Rusyn-American grammars were published, the norms they set out were never consistently followed by editors, who basically wrote in the language they used (or remembered having heard) in oral communication. Since most of the Carpatho-Rusyn immigrants came from what after 1919 became eastern Slovakia, the language of the press was for the most part in the Prešov Region dialects of Carpatho-Rusyn.[26] There was

---

[25]See Paul R. Magocsi, "Rusyn-American Ethnic Literature," in *Ethnic Literature Since 1776: The Many Voices of America*, Vol. II (Lubbock Texas: Texas Tech University, 1978), pp. 503-520—reprinted below, Chapter 20.

[26]The language of the Rusyn-American press has attracted the attention of several scholars: Charles E. Bidwell, *The Language of Carpatho-Ruthenian Publications in America* (Pittsburgh, 1971); Michal Łesiów, "The Language of Carpatho-Ruthenian Publications," in Richard Renoff and Stephen Reynolds, eds., *Proceedings of the Conference on Carpatho-Ruthenian Immigration* (Cambridge, Mass., 1975), pp. 32-40; Paul R. Magocsi, "Carpatho-Ruthenian," in *The World's Written Languages: A Survey of the Degree and Modes of Use*, Vol. I: *The Americas* (Quebec City, 1978), pp. 553-561; and Alexandr D. Dulichenko, *Slavianskie literaturnye mikroiazyki* (Tallin, 1981), in which one of the eleven "micro-languages" analyzed

also an evolution in the use of alphabets, Cyrillic being steadily replaced by Latin (according to Czech orthography) after World War I. The 1940s and 1950s were a bilingual transitional period for most organs. Finally, since the 1960s English predominates, with some form of Carpatho-Rusyn appearing at best in the columns written by a dwindling few older correspondants. The only exceptions to this trend are found in the Lemko-Rusyn press, which has used Lemko dialects (in the Cyrillic alphabet) up to the present (*Karpatska Rus'*), and in the organs begun by post-World War II immigrants which are either in standard Russian (*Svobodnoe slovo*) or standard Ukrainian (*Vistnyk, Lemkivs'ki visti, Lemkivshchyna*).

Conclusion

In what has been almost a century since the first Carpatho-Rusyn press organ appeared in the United States in 1892, more than fifty different newspapers and journals have been published by the group. These organs have been sponsored by various fraternal societies, the various churches, political organizations, and cultural groups. Very often the publications came into existence to propagate a specific religious, political, or ethno-national orientation. The press not only became a mirror reflecting the wide ideological diversity in Rusyn-American society, in many ways it actually defined what that society was. This, of course, was because it was through the press that the ideology and justification for the various communities within the group were to be found. As both mirror and creator of Carpatho-Rusyn society in the United States, the press today—with its almost exclusive use of the English language and its concern with American problems—is still a true reflection of the concerns and interests of the group's members.

by this Soviet sociolinguist is "karpatorusinskii."

CHAPTER 20

Rusyn-American Literature[*]

A mong the territories within and immediately adjacent to the boundaries of the Ukrainian SSR, Subcarpathian Rus' (Transcarpathia) has provided proportionately the largest number of immigrants to the United States. Recently, it was estimated that in the United States there are about 1.3 million persons who either immigrated to or are descendants of immigrants from Ukrainian territories. Of these, as many as 650,000 can trace their origin to the Subcarpathian region. The Subcarpathian Rusyns, or simply Rusyns as they are known in the United

---

[*] This study was originally commissioned in 1974 by the editor of the journal, *Queens Slavic Papers*, for a special issue devoted to East Slavic literatures in the United States. The special issue never appeared, but this study was published under the title, "Rusyn-American Ethnic Literature," in Wolodymyr Zyla and Wendell M. Aycock, eds., *Ethnic Literatures Since 1976: The Many Voices of America*, Vol. II (Lubbock, Texas: Texas Tech Press, 1978), pp. 503-520. It was reprinted in the Harvard Ukrainian Research Institute Offprint Series, No. 5 (Cambridge, Mass., 1975), and translated into Vojvodinian Rusyn under the title "Literatura rusinokh z Podkarpatia u Ameriki," *Nova dumka*, XV [55 and 56] (Vukovar, Yugoslovia), 1986, pp. 34-37 and 23-27. An abridged version was translated into Vojvodinian Rusyn by Nataliia Dudash and published twice under the titles: "Podkarpatska literatura priselientsokh," *Literaturne slovo*, No. 11—*Ruske slovo* (Novi Sad), November 24, 1995, p. 18; and "Literatura kraianokh z Karpatskei Rusi," in Nataliia Dudash, ed., *Rusinski/ruski pisnï* (Novi Sad: Ruske slovo, 1997), pp. 235-241.

States,[1] underwent a specific development and have traditionally remained separate from the Ukrainian-American community. Hence, a discussion of Subcarpathian immigrant literature might best be treated outside the context of Ukrainian émigré belles lettres.

The question of sources is a serious problem. Many literary works written by Subcarpathian Rusyns appeared over several decades in immigrant newspapers, almanacs, and other periodicals. These publications are now difficult to obtain and for some titles complete sets are no longer available. The situation for the researcher is further complicated by the fact that there is no bibliography of Rusyn-American publications and that biographical information about the authors under consideration is not readily available. Finally, scholars like Antonín Hartl, Volodymyr Birchak, Evgenii Nedziel'skii, Olena Rudlovchak, and Iurii Baleha, who have written extensively on literary developments in Subcarpathian Rus' during the twentieth century, seemed totally unaware of the literary efforts undertaken by Rusyns living in the United States.[2]

Considering such factors, this introductory study must inevitably be limited in scope. The prose, poetry and drama analyzed here comprise most of the belles lettres that were published as separate volumes.[3]

[1]With the exception of a few post-World War II newcomers who identify themselves as Carpatho-Ukrainian, or simply Ukrainian, the vast majority of Americans who trace their origins to Subcarpathian Rus' use the names Rusyn, Carpatho-Russian, or the less specific term, "Slavish." In July 1918, the American Council of Uhro-Rusyns recognized Uhro-Rusyn or Rusyn as the only correct names for their people, and these forms are used by most of the authors under consideration in this study.

[2]Even the prolific Rusyn-American writer, Joseph P. Hanulya, failed to include any references to immigrant literature in his survey, *Rusin Literature* (Cleveland, 1941). The one exception is Dmitrii Vergun, who in a published lecture on Subcarpathian literature included two paragraphs on immigrant literary activity: "Karpatoruská literatura (stručný přehled)," *Osm přednášek o Podkarpatské Rusi* (Prague, 1925), p. 55.

[3]I am grateful to the many individuals who supplied important data, but especially to Monsignor Basil Shereghy and Reverend Stephen Veselenak, O.S.B. of McKeesport, Pennsylvania, who provided most of the rare materials that made this study possible. Throughout the names of authors and their works are reproduced in

Although some works were also drawn from periodical publications, the selection is at best representative and by no means complete. Because of the limited quantity of material under review and the absence of accomplished authors or differing literary styles (all works are in a descriptive style that falls somewhere between late nineteenth-century romanticism and naturalism), I have decided to adopt a thematic approach and to determine how this literature reflects the ideals and environment of the community it represents.

Subcarpathian immigrant literature is at best an amateur enterprise. A high percentage of Rusyns who came to this country were either semi-literate or illiterate, and even the educated strata, primarily clergy, were trained in a Hungarian environment and often not capable of expressing themselves freely in any standardized Slavic language. As Sigmund Brinsky unhesitatingly admitted: "I know well that I am not a writer. Not my ability, but rather love for my people urged me to do what I did."[4]

As might be expected, the immigrant experience is an important theme in Rusyn-American bellettres, and an examination of the texts can provide insights into the reasons for immigration, the problems of acculturation in America, and the relations with the old country. Traditionally, economic hardship was accepted as the primary stimulus that forced immigrants to leave Europe, but the literature reveals that unrequited love or social approbation were also important motivations for departure. The play, *Selska svadba* (The Village Wedding), by Stefan Varzaly,[5] provides one possible scenario. Fedor, the poor young

the same form as the original, which with one exception were all published in the Roman alphabet.

[4]*Stichi* (Homestead, Penn.: Vyd. Sojedinenija Gr. Kaftoličeskich Russkich Bratstv, 1922), p. 3. Very Reverend Sigmund Brinsky was born in 1881 in Mat'aška, former Sáros county in present day Slovakia. Like his father and grandfather, Sigmund was ordained a Greek Catholic priest in 1908 after completing his studies at the Theological Seminary in Prešov. He came to the United States before the World War I, served as a parish priest, and published many articles and poems in the *Amerykanskii russkii vîstnyk*.

[5]Very Reverend Stefan Varzaly (1890-1957) was born in Ful'anka, former Sáros county in present-day Slovakia. He completed the *gymnasium* and teacher's college (1911) in Prešov. Subsequently, he attended the Prešov Theological Seminary and

hero, has to have some financial security before marrying. Thus, he follows the advice of his future father-in-law to live in America "a few years, and when you earn something, come back home, . . . buy yourself land and become a farmer."[6] By contrast, two short stories by Emilij A. Kubek[7]—"Paschal'nyj dar" (The Easter Gift) and "Komu što Boh obical" (God Promised different things to different people)—reveal that two young suitors flee to America because in both instances they are embarrassed to remain at home. One of them returns from the army to find his sweetheart already married, the other decides to leave because his proposal for marriage was seemingly ignored. Thus, America becomes a refuge, an emotional safety valve, where distraught persons can expurge their guilt or shame.

The direct relationship of immigrants to American society is not a

---

was ordained a Greek Catholic priest in 1915. Reverend Varzaly was a village priest in the homeland and continued such duties in New Castle and Rankin, Pennsylvania after emigrating to the United States in 1920. As a married priest, he adamantly opposed the policies on celibacy of the Pittsburgh Greek Catholic Exarchate, and because of his views he was suspended in 1931 and five years later excommunicated. He was a founding member (1932) of the Committee for the Defense of the Eastern Rite and acted as its chief spokesperson for several years. He joined the anti-celibate, traditionalist group of excommunicated priests led by Orest Chornock, who established in 1938 the American Carpatho-Russian Orthodox Greek Catholic Church. In 1945, Varzaly split with Bishop Chornock and associated himself for a while with a group that came to be known as the Carpatho-Russian People's Church. While editor (1930-1937) of the Greek Catholic Union's *Amerykanskii russkii vîstnyk*, he published several poems and polemical articles in opposition to celibacy. Under his direction, the publications of the Greek Catholic Union adopted the view that the Rusyns were not an independent nationality, but rather "a branch of the great Russian ethnos." Varzaly was the founding editor of *Vistnik* (1936-55) and later of Bishop Chornock's diocesan publication, *Cerkovnyj vistnik* (1944).

[6]Stefan Varzaly, *Selska svaďba: veseloihra iz žizni podkkapatorusskaho naroda* (Homestead, Pa.: 'Amerikansky Russky Viestnik', n.d.), p. 6.

[7]Reverend Emilij A. Kubek (1859-1940) was born in Štefurov, Sáros county in present-day Slovakia. He completed theological studies at the Prešov Theological Seminary and was ordained a Greek Catholic priest in 1881. In 1904 he emigrated to the United States and served as a parish priest. Reverend Kubek was clearly the most prolific and talented Rusyn-American writer who published a four volume collection, *Narodny povísti i stichi* (1922), and continued to compose short stories and poems that appeared in the publications of the Greek Catholic Union.

focal point except in a few of Kubek's short stories. In his "Paschal'nyi dar," one gets a brief insight into working class living conditions, but it is in the short story, "Palko Rostoka," that the ideals of immigrant life are most clearly displayed. Palko, or Paul Smith as he has become, has worked for seventeen years in an automobile factory. He is fully trusted by the owner who appoints him foreman, as well as by the workers who elect him union vice-president. In the course of a strike, Paul defends the integrity of the boss and asks: "Where in the world have you heard that any capitalist would help striking workers."[8] The moral is clear: work hard and like Paul you might become a foreman, get your own house and car, and maybe even become a partner in the firm.

If settings that relate Rusyn immigrants directly to American society are rare, the literature does abound with episodes that delineate the internal problems of immigrant existence. The most persistently recurring theme is drunkenness. Like other immigrants, Rusyns reacted to the alienation they encountered in the New World by drowning themselves in alcohol, though they seemed to have had trouble holding it down. Valentine Gorzo[9] wrote a three act drama *Fedorišinovy* (The Fedorišins), based on an actual episode "in the life of American Rusyns." The play centers on Hryc Fedorišin, a chronic drunkard who terrorizes his wife and five children. He is forbidden by the court to live at home, defies the order, and finally, in the course of an argument, is

---

[8]*Narodny povísti i stichi*, Vol. I (Scranton, Penn.: 'Obrana', 1922), pp. 33-34.

[9]Very Reverend Valentine Gorzo (1869-1943) was born in Bilky, Bereg county, in present-day Ukraine. He completed *gymnasia* studies in Uzhhorod and Mukachevo, attended the Uzhhorod Theological Seminary, and was ordained a Greek Catholic priest in 1892. He came to the United States in 1905 and was appointed to a large parish in McKeesport, Pennsylvania, where he also served as spiritual advisor (1908-43) to the United Societies (Sobranije) fraternal organization. As legal prosecutor for the Pittsburgh Greek Catholic Exarchate, he remained a loyal defender of the bishop during the celibacy controversies of the late 1920s and 1930s. As a founding member of the American Council of Uhro-Rusyns, Gorzo participated in the delegation which met with President Wilson in October 1918. He continually maintained a concern with the homeland and was a patron of the Subcarpathian Bank in Uzhhorod. His publications included *Osnovna amerikanska istorija* (1924) and *Ťahary svjasčennika* (1925) as well as many translations of liturgical books.

shot dead by his oldest son. Throughout, the brutality and crudeness of the father is stressed and the cause of the tragedy placed on the "stinking," "accursed alcohol." [10]

Virtually all Rusyn immigrant authors deal with the problem of drunkenness. Kubek's four volumes symbolically begin with a poem, "Dobryj tato" (Good Daddy), a rather pathetic account by a child who laments the fact that his father is always in a bar. Similarly, Kubek's hero, Marko Šoltys, at the beginning of the novel is left destitute because of a drunken father and is compelled to promise his dying mother that he will never touch alcohol.[11] Even New Year's greetings in a poem by Brinsky are accompanied by a warning not to drink too much.[12] Indeed, America's prohibition experiment did not bode well for Rusyn immigrants: in this unfortunate "draj kontry" our Ivan had to turn to "munšain."[13]

Immigrant contact with the homeland is also a subject that frequently recurs. One variant, as in several poems by Brinsky, recalls letters sent from America. If the family in the old country wanted dollars, the immigrant needed in exchange information about his former society. To maintain himself in the New World, he pleaded for psychological sustenance. There seemed to be an almost desperate desire to know "što novaho doma?"—what's new at home. Is the neighbor's daughter married, is grandma all right, do the gypsies still play, does the brook still flow? "Write me about everything that happens."[14]

Certain aspects of Rusyn-American political activity were also reflected in literary works. In 1918, the immigrants played a crucial role in the process that led to the incorporation of Subcarpathian Rus' into Czechoslovakia. Subsequently, they regretted their decision and repeatedly sent protests to the League of Nations and the Czechoslovak government, but their economic contribution to the province did not decrease. For even if their countrymen had for a brief time

---

[10]Valentine Gorzo, *Fedorišinovy: drama . . . iz žit'a amerikanskich rusinov* (McKeesport, Penn.: Sobranije Greko Katholičeskich Cerkovnych Bratstv, 1925).

[11]Emilij A. Kubek, *Marko Šoltys: roman iz žit'ja Podkarpatskoj Rusi*, 3 vols. in his *Narodny povísti i stichi* (1923), Vols. II, III, IV.

[12]"Pozdrav na novyi hod" (Greetings for the New Year) in Brinsky, *Stichi*, pp. 145-151.

[13]From the Brinsky poem "Suchota" (Dryness), in *ibid.*, pp. 154-155.

[14]Brinsky, "Pis'mo do kraju" (The Letter to the Old Country), in *ibid.*, pp. 54-56.

> Received life,—
> And a golden fate,
> Holy freedom,
> they were nonetheless
> All poor over there,
> Barefoot and in rags.[15]

Thus, the immigrants in America who were "of the same blood and bones" were asked to contribute to the material uplifting of their "brother Rusyns" at home. Kubek also informs us that groups of immigrants "from the free land, the land of Washington" returned home to "see if our Rusyns are really free?!"[16] Elsewhere, the same author describes the return from America of the politically conscious Ivan, who is distraught because "his people are suffering from the Czechs and especially from the Slovaks."[17]

Yet despite their awareness of the far from ideal situation in Subcarpathian Rus', many individuals in the Rusyn immigrant community could not help but long for the supposed joys of rustic village life that they knew in their youth. In a poem published in 1958, Peter J. Maczkov[18] (perhaps unconsciously reflecting the disillusionment of environmentalists in the United States) was convinced that

> There is where you can drink clean water morning and evening,
> There is where clothes are made at home;

---

[15]Brinsky, "Brat'a Rusiny" (Brother Rusyns), in *ibid.*, pp. 22-25.

[16]"Pozdravleniie dl'a krajevoj Rusi" (Greetings for the Old Country Rus'), Kubek, *Narodny povísti*, Vol. I, pp. 112-113.

[17]"Komu što Boh obical," in *ibid.*, pp. 180-181.

[18]Peter J. Maczkov (1880-1965) was born in Livov, former Sáros county in present-day Slovakia. His formal education was limited to attendance in the elementary school of his native village. He came to the United States in 1898 and worked for many years as a laborer in Pennsylvania and Ohio; he later became a salesman and served on the clerical staff of the U.S. Steel Corporation. Maczkov educated himself and became a prolific writer and cultural worker. At the Greek Catholic Union he served as assistant editor of the *Amierykanskii russkii vîstnyk* (1914-36), editor of the *Amerikanskij russkij sokol* (1918-36), and editor of *Children's World— Svit d'itej* (1917-32). Besides the collection of poems discussed here, Maczkov wrote a reading book for parochial school children, *Novyi bukvar' dlia greko-kaftolicheskich russkikh dietei* (Homestead, Penn., 1921), and a guide for becoming a citizen, *The Citizen's Primer* (1915).

There is where there are no factories, mines, dust, smoke,
There is where every peasant is the 'lord' of his own household.[19]

This rather simplistic vision, most likely prompted by an old-age flight into sentimental melancholy, was poignantly questioned thirty-five years earlier in a poem by Kubek entitled: "Ci lem viditsja mi?" (Does it only seem so?). Here the dilemma of the first-generation immigrant who has established roots in the United States is best expressed.

Now my thoughts gaze below the Carpathians, —
My homeland I can't forget;
Although in my youth luck did not shine on me
And a struggle with want often occurred,
I was a host to misery in the homeland;
Still my homeland is dear to me even now.

The final refrain expressed the unsettling vacillation of the immigrant who does not know if he can or if he should return.

Are the evenings, the summers, the land, the resting places more beautiful there?
Or does it only seem so to me?[20]

There are several other aspects of the immigrant experience that are not dealt with by Rusyn-American writers. For instance, there is no reference, not even indirect, to the ecclesiastical struggle either with the American Roman Catholic hierarchy, with converts to Orthodoxy, with the Galician-Ukrainian faction, or with the non-celibate traditionalists. Again quite surprising is the total lack of concern with the Ukrainian and Slovak national activists. Ecclesiastical controversies and encounters with self-conscious Ukrainian and Slovak immigrants were (and in many cases still are) the dominant features of Rusyn life in the United States, yet the authors under consideration did not consider it appropriate or necessary to refer to such problems.[21]

---

[19]"Tam selo moie rodnoje" (My Native Village Over There) in Peter J. Maczkov, *Vinec nabožnych stichov* (2nd ed.; Munhall, Penn., 1958), p. 134.

[20]Kubek, *Narodny povísty*, Vol. I, pp. 189-190.

[21]Beyond the realm of bellettres, however, there existed a large polemic literature written by Subcarpathian immigrants. A few illustrative titles include: Josif P. Hanulya, *Čija pravda? Katholikov ili ne-Katholikov?!* (1922) and his *Orthodoxy, Schism and Union* (Cleveland, 1935); G. Kotubei and I.E. Bora, *Istoricheskaia kometa ili raskrytie pokhristianizirovaniia iazychestva: temnykh viekov* (Proctor,

Besides the immigrant experience, stories dealing with village life in the homeland are well represented. An analysis of the characters portrayed provides an insight into the style, ideals, and shortcomings of Rusyn culture. As in most peasant and bourgeois societies, material concerns, particularly attachment to the land, are uppermost in the minds of most individuals. For example, the hero of Kubek's novel, *Marko Šoltys*, is driven to fulfill his dying mother's last request: "Swear to me my child that you will remain honest, good and stolid your whole life ... and so that I may rest in peace, buy back the family land."[22] To be sure, great sacrifices were needed in order to achieve such goals, so that the theme of personal happiness versus material security came to pervade much of the immigrant literature.

In Varzaly's play, *Selska Svadba*, a greedy mother wants at all costs to have her daughter marry a lazy, though rich, young man. The maiden's distress is summed up in the first scene; "My mother values wealth more than the future of her daughter. So that our parcel of land can be joined to the rich man's, my mother is ready to give me to slavery, give me to that drunkard."[23] Such an attitude is again made evident in the anonymous play, *Arendarj v klopot'i*, (The Tenant in Trouble). In an extended scene, a returning immigrant named Ivan decides to propose marriage to his childhood sweetheart. Her parents are first consulted, they consent, but their concern is only on how much the wedding will cost. A detailed discussion of food and alcohol follows. Then Ivan asks the daughter for her hand, but instead of the expected blush or outburst of joy, the girl calculatingly responds: "Oh

kometa ili raskrytie pokhristianizirovaniia iazychestva: temnykh viekov (Proctor, Vermont, 192?); Michael Yuhasz, *Wilson's Principles in Czechoslovak Practice: The Situation of the Czechoslovak People Under the Czech Yoke* (Homestead, Pa., 1929); P.I. Zeedick and A.M. Smar, *Naše stanovišče* (Homestead, Pa., 1934); Peter G. Kohanik, *The Biggest Lie of the Century—'the Ukraine'* (New York, 1952) and his *Highlights of Russian History and the 'Ukrainian' Provocation* (Perth Amboy, N.J., 1955); Sevastiian Sabol, *Katolytstvo i pravoslaviie* (New York, 1955).

[22]Kubek, *Narodny povísti*, Vol. II, p. 39.

[23]Varzaly, *Selska svad'ba*, p. 4.

I am so happy! Pray to God that it [the wedding] takes place as soon as possible. Then I will be certain that our property will not fall into Jewish hands."[24]

This negative attitude toward Jews is another characteristic of Rusyn immigrant literature. As in *Arendarj*, there was always the fear that the land of the overtaxed Rusyn peasant would someday fall into the hands of the local moneylender, invariably a Jew. Alongside Jews stand lawyers, judges, and women—the pantheon of evil characters in Rusyn-American writings. Stefan F. Telep[25] composed a short satire for children, *V sudî* (In Court), in which the forces of law and order are ridiculed. Typical of the dialogue is a query by the judge directed to an oft-convicted criminal; "As I see by your record, you have been associating with bad company for a long while." To which the accused replied: "As long as I can remember I've always had business with lawyers and judges."[26]

Women are also disparagingly treated. In almost all instances describing male-female relationships, the courtship stage is marked with promises by the suitor that he will give his fiancée everything in life. After marriage, however, the standard characterization reveals a disrespectful husband who treats his passive wife as chattel and can

---

[24]*Arendarj v klopot'i: komedija iz sil'skaho žit'a* (Perth Amboy N.J.: Vostok Publishing Co., 1929), p. 26.

[25]Stefan F. Telep (1885-1965) was not from Subcarpathian Rus', but from the village of Pielgrzymka in the Rusyn-inhabited Lemko Region north of the Carpathians in the former Austrian province of Galicia, now part of Poland. He attended a parochial elementary school in his birthplace and in 1903 emigrated to the United States. He settled in Mayfield, Pennsylvania and worked for about a decade in the local coal mines. Then he bought a hand printing press, began to support himself as a printer, and published his own editorials, poems, and plays, one of which was *Boh svîdok: trahykomediia v 4 aktakh yz amerykanskoho zhyt'ia* (Mayfield, Penn., 1929). In 1928, Telep, together with his two sons initiated *The Mayfield News*, a newspaper that circulated for close to thirty-five years. He was also a founding member of the fraternal organization, Liubov, and author of a primer and grammar for elementary parochial schools: *Russkii bukvar' dlia tserkovno-prikhodskikh shkol v Sievernoi Amerikie* (Mayfield, Penn., 1937; 2nd ed., 1938); and *Praticheskii podruchnik grammatiki dlia tserkovno-prikhodskikh shkol* (Mayfield, Penn., 1940).

[26]Stefan F. Telep, *V sudî: stsenychnŷi obrazok dlia dîtei* (Mayfield, Penn., 1944), p. 10.

only address her as *stara* (the old lady) or *baba* (grandma). In a lighter vein, Dobra's *Oženilsja s ňimoju* (I Married a Dumb Woman) combines the negativism expressed toward both lawyers and females. A judge marries a speechless woman, arranges a successful operation, and then is driven wild by his chattering companion. To make his marriage tolerable, he has himself made deaf—a solution that should not seriously effect his profession because he will not have "to hear all the lies of lawyers and the deformations of the accused."[27]

The problem of national identity had always been of prominent concern to Rusyns in Europe and the United States. On this question, Rusyn-American writers adopted basically two orientations. They identified either (1) with the local Subcarpathian region of their birth, and in some cases suggested the existence of an independent Rusyn nationality; or (2) with Russia and accepted the view that their people are part of the Russian nationality. Themes of *lokalpatriotismus* prevail in the poetry of Brinsky, Kubek, and Maczkov, who offer effusive praise for the villages, rivers, and mountains "of holy Rus' ... under the Beskyds."[28] The Rusyn-inhabited Prešov Region of northeastern Slovakia is most often described and Orestes Koman has left us a kind of guided tour of this area in his short story, Vasko šustrom?" (How Vasko became a Shoemaker).[29] A rather extreme instance of local pride is

---

[27]J. Dobra, *Oženilsja s ňimoju* (Homestead, Penn.: 'Amerikansky Russky Viestnik', n.d.), p. 15. Julius Dobra was born in the former Ung county near Uzhhorod in present-day Ukraine, and after coming to this country he served as a cantor in the Greek Catholic (Byzantine Rite) Cathedral in Homestead, Pennsylvania. During the 1930s he set up a cantor's school at the cathedral.

[28]The Beskyds are a range of the Carpathians Mountains in northeastern Slovakia and in southeastern Poland, i.e. the Lemko Region. The quotation is from "Brat'a Rusiny" (Brother Rusyns) by Brinsky, *Stichi*, p. 22. See also his "Vo našem valal'i" (In Our Village), "Maleňkoje selo" (Little Village), and "Bo vir' Topl'a" (Believe me, oh Topl'a River), in *ibid.*, pp. 57-58, 73-76, and 161-164. See also Kubek's poems, "Pod obrazom Duchnoviča" (Under the Image of Dukhnovych), "Pozdravlenije dl'a krajevoj Rusi" (Greetings for the Rus' Country), in his *Narodny povísti*, Vol. I, pp. 86-90, 112-113; and Maczkov's poems, "Tam selo moje rodnoje" (My Native Village Over There) and "Moje selo L'ivov mnohi l'udi znajut" (Many People Knoy My Native Village Livov), in his *Vinec*, pp. 135-139.

[29]*Kalendar' Greko Kaftoličeskaho Sojedinenija v S.Š.A.*, Vol. LV (Munhall, Pa., 1951), pp. 25-26, 42-45. Reverend Orestes Koman (1894-1988) was born in Beloveža, former Sáros county, in present day Slovakia. He attended the Prešov and

found in Ivan Ladižinsky's book-length eulogy on immigrants from Kamionka (*kamjonskij narod*), a small village in former Szepes/Spiš county in the westernmost portion of the Prešov Region.[30] This tendency toward ethno-political fractionalization was later underscored as a danger by Maczkov, who called on former residents of Szepes, Sáros/Sharysh, Zemplén/Zemplyn, Ung/Uzh, Ugocsa/Ugocha and Máramaros/Maramorosh counties to join together as Rusyn brothers into one "great family."[31]

If Ladižinsky has shown special allegiance to a few villages south of the Carpathian, he is at the same time one of the few who unequivocally identified both himself and his "Carpatho-Russian" people (*karpatorossy*) with the Russian nationality. In a decidedly nationalistic poem, he declared:

> We will avenge our enemies.
> Arise my people,
> Let the earth tremble
> In a struggle for what is our own;
> Let the whole world know
> How we love what is ours;
> If possible—we will die
> For all that is Russian.[32]

Budapest Theological Seminaries and was ordained a Greek Catholic priest. After emigrating to the United States in 1921, he acted as Spiritual Advisor (1944-69) to the Greek Catholic Union and from 1923 until his death served as a parish priest in Elizabeth, New Jersey.

[30]Ivan A. Ladižinsky, *Karpatorossy v Evropi i Ameriki: primir Kamjonka* (Cleveland, 1940). Very Reverend Ivan Ladižinsky (1905-1976) was born in Jarabina (Orjabina), former Szepes county, in present-day Slovakia. He attended the Prešov Theological Seminary and was ordained a Greek Catholic priest. During the 1920s, he was an elementary school teacher in the Prešov Region and emigrated to the United States in 1930. Being a married priest, he was one of those who left the Pittsburgh Greek Catholic Exarchate and joined Bishop Chornock's Orthodox Church. In 1938, Ladižinsky was elected vice-president of the Cleveland-based American Russian National Brotherhood and appointed editor of its official organ, *Rodina* (Cleveland, 1927-40). Three years later he headed the Carpatho-Russian Unity, a political organization that published the monthly, *Jedinstvo* (Gary, Ind., 1942-43), which protested Hungary's occupation of Subcarpathian Rus' during the World War II. Since then he served as a parish priest in Duquesne, Pennsylvania.

[31]Peter J. Maczkov, "My—Sojedinenije!," in *Kalendar' Greko Kaftoličeskaho Sojedinenija v S.Š.A.*, Vol. LVII (Munhall, Penn., 1953), pp. 39-41.

Ladižinsky also composed several other poems that propounded the idea of unity with Russian civilization.[33] Kubek, too, could simultaneously praise the local Subcarpathian region as well as laud the virtues of "Matuška Rossija,"[34] while Koman wrote a short story, "Košikari u Carja Nikolaja" (The Basketweavers at Tsar Nicholas's Court) which was concerned with emphasizing the existence of close relations between the people "from the Carpathians, the land of Koriatovych" and the Russian tsar.[35]

Nevertheless, political commentary is in general at a minimum in the literary works under analysis. Mention was made of the brief criticism against the Czechoslovak regime offered by Kubek, and the only other instance of a clear political stance was that adopted by Koman. Writing in the 1950s, Koman characterized the Soviet leader, Nikita S. Khrushchev as "the red tyrant," and criticized "the pressure of this red regime" in the homeland "where the Communists have forbidden religious processions (otpusty) and have refused to allow the walls and windows [of the churches] to be repaired."[36] Elsewhere, he lamented the death of Tsar Nicholas II and his family, who were not, as other émigrés, "lucky enough to get out of that red paradise!"[37] Actually, Koman's anti-Communist attitude is an exception in Rusyn-American bellettres, since most works were published before World War II, a time when the Soviet regime had not yet annexed Subcarpathian Rus'.

On the other hand, spiritual concerns continued to loom large in Rusyn-American life and literature. Since many authors were priests,

---

[32]"Narode moj" (To My People) in Ladižinsky, *Karpatorossy*, p. 118.

[33]"Spasibo" (Thanks), "Molitva" (A Prayer), and "Na Novyj hod" (For the New Year), in *ibid.*, pp. 110, 116, and 126-127.

[34]"Svobodna Rossija—1917" (A Free Russia - 1917), in Kubek, *Narodny povísti*, Vol. I, pp. 168-170.

[35]*Kalendar' Greko-Kaftoličeskaho Sojedinenija v S.Š.A.*, Vol. LVI (Munhall, Penn., 1952), pp. 28-32. The allusion to Koriatovych refers to a Rus' prince from Lithuanian-ruled Podolia, who crossed the Carpathians (according to legend leading 40,000 people) in 1395 and received the fortress of Mukachevo from the King of Hungary. Koriatovych has subsequently been hailed as one of the first great heroes of the Subcarpathian Rusyns.

[36]These citations are taken from Koman's short stories, "Vaňko Onufer," in *ibid.*, Vol. LXV (1961), p. 25, and "Medzi-Peci," in *ibid.*, Vol LVIII (1954), p. 30.

[37]"Košikari u Carja Nikolaja," in *ibid.*, Vol. LVI, (1952), p. 52.

religious themes were abundant. In a sense, all the immigrant writings are didactic in character, but beyond that a large number are exclusively religious in inspiration. Koman dramatized the birth of Jesus in a three-act play, "Viflejemskaja noč" (The Night of Bethlehem),[38] while Jurion Thegze moralized on Christ's adolescence in a short story, "Vo cerkvi Jerusalimskoj" (In the Church of Jerusalem).[39] Brinsky also wrote several poems praising the Virgin Mary, Christ, and various church holidays, while the layman Maczkov's volume of poetry is dedicated exclusively to religious subject matter. Maczkov's writings are less concerned with revealing how faith may sustain the individual than with the presentation of eulogies dedicated to the various saints, religious places, and contemporary Rusyn-American hierarchs. As for the trials and tribulations of everyday life, an anonymous poem in a journal published by a Rusyn fundamentalist sect seemed to promise what many immigrants hoped for—an afterlife in heaven for the faithful:

> Everything there will be free from all sorrow
> Closed off by gates from [this earthly] life; ...
> Enmity will cease, peace will reign,
> And freedom for all will be forever.[40]

Despite the concern here with thematic content, perhaps a few words about the aesthetic value of Rusym immigrant literature are in order. One gets the overall impression that with the exception of Kubek, Rusyn authors never had a clear conception of the works they were composing. Hence, many stories get off to a good start but end with a situation that is hardly related to what preceded. For instance, Telep's short play, *V sudî*, is basically a scene in a court room that includes

---

[38]*Kalendar Sojedinenija*, Vol. XXXIX (Homestead, Penn., 1934), pp. 65-72.

[39]Jurion, *Vo Cerkvi Jerusalimskoj i Petrova Denna Platňa* (McKeesport, Penn.: 'Prosvita', 192?). Very Reverend Jurion Thegze (1883-1962) was a native of former Bereg county, in present-day Ukraine. He attended the Uzhhorod Theological Seminary and was ordained a Greek Catholic priest in 1905. In 1912, he came to the United States where he served as a parish priest, among other places, in Whiting, Indiana. His literary efforts include the short story, *Zahraj miňi Cigane* (Homestead, Penn., 1922).

[40]"Pokoi" (Peace), in *Prorocheskoe svietlo*, IV, 9 (Proctor, Vermont, 1922), p. 5. For information on this little-known Rusyn settlement, see Paul R. Magocsi, "Immigrants from Eastern Europe: The Carpatho-Rusyn Community of Proctor, Vermont," *Vermont History*, XLII, 1 (Montpelier, Vt., 1974), pp. 48-52.

satirical exchanges between the judge and the plaintiff; suddenly, it ends with an unexpected eulogy on Rus', the Rusyn language, and the Rusyn way of life. Similarly, in *Arendarj v klopot'i*, the focal point throughout the first two acts is the problem of marriage, yet the third act concludes with a slapstick and rather boring episode in which the local Jewish innkeeper hides in a barrel to protect himself from the bridegroom.

Generally, the character sketches are clearly delineated though flat, that is, they are limited in psychological depth. Kubek cannot be accused of writing aimlessly since his stories are almost always well-conceived units; moreover, he frequently depicts in a convincing way complex characters. Nonetheless, his narrative does tend to be choppy, and it often seems that individual episodes are strung together without consideration for smooth transitions. As pointed out above, however, these immigrant writings represent only an amateur effort at literature, so that aesthetic criteria should not perhaps be applied too rigorously.

There is one area, though, in which Rusyn-American literature has undeniable value. I refer to language.[41] A noted Hungarian linguist remarked that the United States is a "museum of languages," a place where immigrants from all over the world still speak and write languages as they existed during the late nineteenth century. In most cases, this stage of linguistic development is no longer evident in the country of origin. Despite the occasional use of literary Russian, the language used in Rusyn immigrant literature is lexically and morphologically based on the dialects of the Subcarpathian region. Since today the language used in the European homeland is heavily influenced by Russian, Ukrainian, or Slovak, and since in the past local authors strove to write in either literary Russian, Ukrainian, or Hun-

---

[41]One grammatical standard was composed for Rusyn-American writers by Joseph P. Hanulya, *Hrammatyka dlia amerykanskykh rusynov* (McKeesport, Penn.: 'Prosvîta vŷdav. spolechnosty', 1918). This text, printed in the Cyrillic alphabet, strove to impose Russian vocabulary and morphology on the dialects as spoken in Subcarpathian Rus'. The authors discussed in this study nevertheless disregarded the Hanulya grammar, wrote in their own Rusyn dialect, and, with the exception of Telep, published in the Roman alphabet (1892-1952).

garian, Rusyn-American literature is one of the few places where the older spoken forms have been preserved.

Thus, words or constructions like *bandurka* (potato), *dahde* (somewhere), *falatok* (piece), *id* (toward), *kaprul'a* (dirt in the eye; a dirty person), *kapura* (gate), *klikati* (to call), *kortit mene* (I am curious), *maštalňa* (cowshed), *merkuvati* (to be careful), *obist'a* (property), *valal* (village), *žadaliste* (you asked) have already or are rapidly disappearing from use in Europe. Inevitably, there are also Americanisms, like *burder* (boarder), *dviženije obrazy* (motion pictures), *kurtina* (curtain), *majna* (mine), *O boj, ja holoden* (Wow, am I hungry), *porč* (porch), *rum* (room), but these are relatively rare. On the other hand, the "American-Rusyn" language does contain many eastern Slovak dialectal words—*apo* (father, from the Hungarian *apa*), *kadi* (to where), *kel'o* (how much), *pokl'a* (until), *pozriti* (to look at), *skadi* (from where), *vecej* (more), *zat'al* (meanwhile)—which reveals (as do place names found in the texts) that most of the authors came from Slovakia's Rusyn-inhabited Prešov Region. In any case, Rusyn-American literature is a linguistic preserve waiting to be tapped by the specialist interested in dialects or the history of language.[42]

This brief survey of selected writings has revealed the thematic nature of Rusyn immigrant literature. Life in America or in the "old country," and national and religious subjects were the most common themes. Admittedly, this was a literature of amateurs, produced in most cases by well-meaning individuals who wanted to raise the cultural level of their brethren, not produce literary masterpieces. Furthermore, the published works enjoyed only restricted circulation and, because of their limited aesthetic value, had no discernable impact on literary activity in the homeland. Nonetheless, these literary efforts do bear witness to Rusyns as a viable distinct immigrant group, and they will continue to have value as socio-historical and linguistic documents.

---

[42]The language used in the influential newspaper, *Amerykanskii russkii vîstnyk*, has been analyzed by Charles E. Bidwell, *The Language of Carpatho-Ruthenian Publications in America* (Pittsburgh, 1971).

CHAPTER 21

Carpatho-Rusyns in Canada[*]

W hy, in a volume entitled *Ukrainians in Ontario* is there an essay dealing with a group that, at the very least, is different in name from Ukrainian. This is because the Carpatho-Rusyns, or Lemkos as they are also known, come from an area that is considered by Ukrainians and by traditional Slavic scholarship to be located within Ukrainian ethnolinguistic boundaries. Moreover, the Carpatho-Rusyns are not like national minorities found within Ukrainian lands, such as Poles, Jews, Germans, or Romanians.

Carpatho-Rusyns are East Slavs like the Ukrainians. Their spoken language is related to Ukrainian and they derive from the same Eastern Christian religious tradition (although with different customs and church singing). Yet however similar their roots, those who identify as Carpatho-Rusyns do not accept and, in fact, actively reject identification as Ukrainians.

As strange as it may seem, it is nonetheless possible to find people from the same region, the same village, nay the very same family, with

[*]This study was originally commissioned for a volume entitled *Ukrainians in Ontario* and published in a special volume of *Polyphony*, Vol. X, edited by Lubomyr Y. Luciuk and Iroida L. Wynnyckyj, eds. (Toronto: Multicultural History Society of Ontario, 1988), pp. 177-190. The version published here is supplemented with information taken from the chapter, "Carpatho-Rusyns in Canada" in the third revised edition of Paul Robert Magocsi, *Our People: Carpatho-Rusyns and Their Descendants in North America* (Toronto: Multicultural History Society of Ontario, 1994), pp. 104-110; and from idem, "Carpatho-Rusyns," in Paul Robert Magocsi, ed., *Encyclopedia of Canada's Peoples* (Toronto: University of Toronto Press, 1999), pp. 340-343.

some identifying themselves as Ukrainian, and others as Carpatho-Rusyn (Rusnak, Lemko). Moreover, the latter terms are not used in a regional sense, but to convey the sense of being a distinct people.

Lest the reader think that such a seeming paradox is limited to the world of Carpatho-Rusyns and Ukrainians, he or she should be reminded of Slavic immigrants and their descendants from Macedonia, some of whom—also from the same region, village, or family—feel that they are Bulgarians, even Greeks, while others argue that they represent a distinct Macedonian Slav nationality. Or, to chose an example from contemporary western Europe, one may turn to southern France. While most of whose inhabitants there consider themselves to be French, there are also many who believe that, together with all the "French of the Midi," they represent a distinct nationality known as Occitan.[1]

Carpatho-Rusyns are further differentiated from Ukrainians in Canada in that most come from territory that is not nor ever was part of Ukraine. Instead, they trace their origins to rural villages along the slopes and adjacent lowlands in the northcentral ranges (Beskydy, Bieszczady) of the Carpathian Mountains. Their homeland, known as Carpathian Rus', consists of three regions, only one of which (since 1945) is found within the boundaries of Ukraine—the Transcarpathian oblast, or historic Subcarpathian Rus'. The other two are in northeastern Slovakia (the Prešov Region/Priashevshchyna) and in southeastern Poland (the Lemko Region/Lemkovyna). To these three regions can be added a fourth, the Vojvodina (or historic Bačka) in northcentral Yugoslavia, an area far removed from the Carpathians where Rusyns began immigrating in the eighteenth century. From there a few have re-emigrated in the twentieth century to North America, including a small community of Bačka Rusyns that exists today in southern Ontario.

Initially it was not politics or ideological concerns that prompted

---

[1]For an introduction to the problem of Macedonian versus Bulgarian identity in the European homeland, see Robert R. King, *Minorities under Communism* (Cambridge, Mass., 1973), pp. 187-219; on this problem among immigrants, see the entries, "Bulgarians" and "Macedonians," in the *Harvard Encyclopedia of American Ethnic Groups*, ed. Stephen Thernstrom (Cambridge, Mass., 1980), pp. 186-189 and 690-694. For the conflicting views on the population/nationality of southern France, see any standard history of France in contrast to works such as Robert Lafont, *La revendication occitane* (Paris, 1974), and André Armengaud and Robert Lafont, eds., *Histoire d'Occitanie* (Paris, 1979).

Carpatho-Rusyns to emigrate, but rather the economic conditions of their homeland. Until well into the twentieth century, theirs was an underdeveloped homeland that had virtually no industry, that was geographically and climatically unsuited to profitable agriculture, and that in the second half of the nineteenth century under Austrian Habsburg rule experienced a steady demographic growth that could not be sustained by the only occupations open to the inhabitants: small-scale subsistence farming and a declining pasturing and sheep-raising economy.

The result was for Carpatho-Rusyns to seek to improve their economic standards by working abroad. The most common practice was to go southward to work during the harvest season on the plains of Hungary. Some went even farther afield, eastward toward the Ukrainian steppes of the Russian Empire, then in the 1870s westward, across the ocean to North America. In the New World, however, they were forced to undergo a decided change of work habits by entering the mines, mills, and factories of the industrial northeastern United States. In fact, of all the East Slavic immigrants to the United States the earliest came from the Carpathians, from where by the outbreak of World War I in 1914 an estimated 125,000 to 150,000 had emigrated.[2]

The prewar migrational pattern would have continued, but it was disrupted first by World War I, then by the political instability of the immediate postwar years, and finally by increasing American restrictions on "undesirable" immigrants, including Carpatho-Rusyns and other Slavs, which culminated in the quota restrictions set up in 1924. On the other hand, the causes behind the immigration remained, since there were very few economic opportunities in the new state of Czechoslovakia and even less in the restored state of Poland, two countries which after World War I annexed the entire Carpatho-Rusyn homeland both north and south of the Carpathian Mountains. Not only was Carpathian Rus' hit hard during World War I (especially the Lemko Region during

---

[2]On the pre-World War I immigration, see Iuliian Bachyns'kyi, *Ukraïns'ka immigratsiia v Z"iedynanykh Derzhavakh Ameryky* (L'viv, 1914); Stanisław Fischer, "Wyjazdy Łemków nadoslawskich na roboty zarobkowe do Ameryki," *Materiały Muzeum Budownictwa Ludowego w Sanoku*, No. 6 (Sanok, 1967); and Ladislav Tajtak, "Vychodoslovenské vyst'ahovalectvo do prvej svetovej vojny," *Nové obzory*, III (Prešov, 1961), pp. 221-247.

the tsarist Russian offenisive of 1914-1915 and 1916), but after the war the populace lost an important supplemental source of income when the new Polish-Czechoslovak and Czechoslovak-Hungarian borders closed off access to the agriculturally rich Hungarian plains.

Thus, for those who still wanted to improve their economic status, a new destination was sought and found—Canada.[3] Beginning in 1922, increasing in particular in 1926, and continuing until the world economic depression that began in 1929, an estimated 15,000 Carpatho-Rusyns emigrated to Canada, settling mostly in the eastern part of the country, whether in industrial centers like Hamilton, Windsor, Brantford, and Fort William in Ontario, or in Montreal in neighboring Quebec. However, by far the greatest numbers went to Toronto, where today still as many as three-quarters of Canada's Carpatho-Rusyns and their descendants live.[4]

Whereas most of Canada's Carpatho-Rusyns are from the Lemko Region in Poland, there are also a few thousand who came from south of the Carpathians, in particular from the Prešov Region of northeastern Czechoslovakia. Small in number, they were scattered across Canada, and with few exceptions they never had any organizational structures to unite them as a specific group. As in the homeland, so too in the New World, it was their Greek or Byzantine Catholic faith which brought them together. In contrast to the United States, where Carpatho-Rusyn Byzantine Catholics had their own distinct ecclesiastical jurisdiction since 1916, the smaller group in Canada remained for the longest time jurisdictionally within the Ukrainian Catholic Church.

The situation in Canada began to change in the early 1950s, when newly-arrived priests from Slovakia, led by the Reverend Michael Rusnak (b. 1921) and aided by the already well-to-do mining magnate, Stephen B. Roman (1921-1988), began to organize new Byzantine-rite

[3]Despite the rather extensive literature on Ukrainians in Canada (who claim Carpatho-Rusyns to be part of their group), information on specifically Carpatho-Rusyn and Lemko-Canadian organizations and their history is at best sparse to non-existent.

[4]Because Carpatho-Rusyns were not designated as such in Canadian immigration records, it is impossible to determine the number who actually arrived in Canada. Based on subsequent organizational patterns, it seems that the vast majority of the estimated 15,000 came from Poland's Lemko Region.

parishes in Toronto, Hamilton, Windsor, Oshawa, and Welland in Ontario and to co-opt the already existing parish in Montreal. These parishes attracted people who called themselves Rusnaks and who felt more comfortable in churches with fellow immigrants from the Prešov Region in Slovakia than with Ukrainians who were mostly from Galicia.[5] However, for the leaders of this movement like the Reverend Rusnak and the industrialist Roman, the term Rusnak was simplistically considered to be the exclusive equivalent of an Eastern Catholic Slovak,[6] so that these churches came to be called Slovak Byzantine

[5]In a desire to be "among their own," many Rusnaks also joined Slovak Roman Catholic parishes (such as St. Cyril and Methodius Church in Toronto). For details on the establishment of the new Byzantine-rite parishes, see Vincent Dančo, "Slovenskí gréckokatolíci v Kanade," in *Slovenskí jezuiti v Kanade* (Galt, Ont., 1966), pp. 56-60; and Joseph M. Kirschbaum, *Slovaks in Canada* (Toronto, 1967), pp. 249-263.

[6]The Canadian-Slovak historian and community activist Joseph Kirschbaum summed up this view in the following manner: "Slovak immigrants to Canada," called "in Slovak vernacular 'Rusnaks', . . . are historically and ethnically beyond doubt Slovaks." *Ibid.*, p. 249. This spurious premise is not at all tenable in the face of Slavic scholarship, including that written by Slovaks.

In point of fact, the area of Eastern Slovakia inhabited by people calling themselves Rusnaks is roughly divided between: (1) the northern mountainous part (popularly known as the Prešov Region and including 302 villages), whose inhabitants speak East Slavic dialects; and (2) the southern lowlands, whose inhabitants speak transitional (Sotak, Cotak) and West Slavic (Zemplín, Šariš, Spiš) dialects. Only in the twentieth century did the transitional East/West Slavic-speaking Rusnaks begin to describe themselves in ethnic terms as either Rusyns, Russians, or Ukrainians; while the West Slavic-speaking Rusnaks as either Slovjaks or Slovaks. It seems that at least half of the Rusnaks who emigrated to Canada may have been from East Slavic-speaking villages. In that regard, the Canadian leaders of the Slovak Greek Catholics are from two southern lowland Rusnak villages in Zemplín/Zemplyn county, where transitional East Slavic/West Slavic dialects are spoken—Pozdišovce (birthplace of Bishop Rusnak, actually born Rusnachok) and Vel'ký Ruskov, today Nový Ruskov (birthplace of Stephen B. Roman). In any case, to call the whole group, whether in the homeland or in the New World, ethnically Slovak is tendentious and false.

For a depiction of the East Slavic linguistic area in Eastern Slovakia, see the maps of the Carpatho-Rusyn homeland in Magocsi, *Our People*, p. 4. For the detailed relationship between East Slavic (Rusyn/Ukrainian), transitional (Sotak, Cotak), and West Slavic (Slovak) dialects in the area, see Václav Vážný, "Nářečí slovenská,"

Catholic parishes in contrast to the Ukrainian Catholic parishes with which the "Slovaks" were still jurisdictionally united. In response to the real make-up of these new parishes—which included as many if not more ethnic Carpatho-Rusyns than Slovaks—there was even an attempt to establish a distinct Rusyn Greek Catholic parish in Toronto.

These efforts began with an older calendar Easter service in 1956 that attracted nearly 150 Carpatho-Rusyns and that was conducted by the Reverend L'udovít Miňa, a post-World War II arrival and Greek Catholic Redemptorist from Subcarpathinan Rus'. About seven more services were held in 1957 under the auspices of St. Michael Society Mission, set up specifically to encourage the creation of a permanent Carpatho-Rusyn Greek Catholic parish. However, after initial encouragement, the Ukrainian Catholic hierarchy did not supply any priests or church facilities, while Slovak Byzantine Catholics like the Reverend Rusnak (also a Redemptorist) saw the Rusyn mission as a threat that drew parishioners away from the then struggling "Slovak" Byzantine-rite Toronto parish.[7]

By contrast, the organizational framework for the "Slovak" Byzantine Catholics proved remarkably successful. In 1964, the Reverend Rusnak was named auxiliary bishop for Slovaks in the Ukrainian Catholic Church. Then, in 1980, the Vatican created a distinct Slovak Byzantine Catholic Diocese headed by Bishop Rusnak. Finally, with great fanfare during a visit to Canada by Pope John Paul II in 1984, a monumental cathedral church funded by Stephen B. Roman was dedicated in Markham, Ontario, just outside Toronto.[8]

Less encouraging has been the growth of the new jurisdiction. At its height, the Slovak Byzantine Catholic Diocese—with jurisdiction for all of Canada—could count at most six parishes and two missions, all but

in Československá vlastivěda, Vol. III: Jazyk (Prague, 1934), pp. 301-310; and Jozef Štolc, ed., Atlas slovenského jazyka, Vol. I (Bratislava, 1968), esp. plate 4.

[7]This information is based on conversations with former activists in the St. Michael Society Mission.

[8]For the organizational developments culminating in the creation of the Slovak Byzantine Catholic Diocese, see the special issue of the official diocesan organ commemorating Pope John Paul II's consecration of the cathedral, September 15, 1984: Mária, XXIV, 11-12 (Unionville, Ontario, 1984).

one being in Ontario.[9] However, at the present, only three of the parishes have full-time priests (Toronto, Windsor, Montreal), with two others (Welland and Hamilton) trying to make do with visiting clergy.

The reasons for the lack of growth and actual decline in membership are several. The Slovak profile of the movement was never received with particular enthusiasm among parishioners, who among other things have continually blocked the introduction of Slovak into services in favor of retaining the traditional Church Slavonic liturgical language. Second, there has been a chronic problem with obtaining Slovak-speaking Byzantine-rite priests, since Communist Czechoslovakia does not permit their emigration and there are no training grounds for Slovak speakers in North America. Finally, neither on spiritual nor ethnic grounds have the parishes been able to retain young people, so that the few remaining churches have become the preserve of the older generation, with no seeming prospects for future development.

Along with the arrival after World War II of slovakizing Greek Catholic priests from Czechoslovakia, there came from both the Prešov Region and Subcarpathian Rus' (which after 1945 became the Soviet-ruled Transcarpathian oblast of Ukraine) a small group of immigrants who had a clear sense of a distinct Carpatho-Rusyn ethnic identity. Led by Vasilij V. Fedinec (1890-1982), a postwar immigrant from Subcarpathian Rus', in July 1951 they established in Hamilton, Ontario the Council of a Free Sub-Carpatho-Ruthenia in Exile (Rada Svobodnoj Podkarpatskoj Rusi v Exili). The council joined with other Czechoslovak political émigrés to protest the Soviet annexation of Subcarpathian Rus' (Transcarpathia); the attempts of Hungarian émigrés to claim that territory for Hungary; and, in particular, the forced

---

[9]The first was established in Montréal, Québec (est. 1948), followed in Ontario by Windsor (1950), Toronto (1951), Hamilton (1952), Oshawa (1952), Welland (1953), and missions in Sudbury (1954) and Delhi-Simcoe (1955). Slovak writers often claim as the seventh and the oldest "Slovak" Byzantine Catholic parish a church in Lethbridge, Alberta (est. 1921). Kirschbaum, *Slovaks*, pp. 250-252.

In fact, the original Lethbridge church, known as the "Ruthenian Greek-Catholic Parish," was founded by families from three villages in southern Spíš/Spish county—Slovinky, Poráč, and Závadka—whose inhabitants speak East Slavic dialects and who well into the twentieth century identified themselves ethnically as Rusyns. When given the choice in 1980 to join the new Slovak Byzantine Catholic Diocese, the Lethbridge parish declined.

liquidation of the Greek Catholic Church and what they viewed as the artificial implementation of a Ukrainian nationality upon the inhabitants in the homeland. These views were summed up in the Council's bilingual Rusyn/English journal: "Our Ruthenian council is the only group recognized by the Canadian Foreign Service, the U.S. State Department, and the Free Europe Committee, Inc. No one has challenged our work except some people who have organized enemical [sic] groups supporting the Ukrainian Empire or the idea of St. Stephen's Hungarian Empire."[10]

The Hamilton-based Council of a Free Sub-Carpatho-Ruthenia cooperated closely with the Byzantine Ruthenian Catholic Church in the United States. It also lobbied for Rusyn-language broadcasts to the homeland over Radio Free Europe (begun in 1954), and it helped Carpatho-Rusyn displaced persons (DPs) then in camps in Germany to emigrate to North America through its affiliate organizations, the Central Committee of Subcarpathian Political Emigrés (Centralnyj Komitet Podkarpatskich Političeskich Bižencev) in Ludwigsburg, Germany. The Hamilton-based council claimed at its height over 600 members in Canada and the United States. However, with the departure to the United States of the council's founder Fedinec sometime in the mid-1950s, its activity became virtually non-existent in Ontario.

The immediate post-World War II years also saw the arrival from south of the Carpathians of a group of Carpatho-Rusyns who, already in the homeland, had adopted a clear sense of Ukrainian identity. The most active among these was Stepan Rosocha (1908-1986), who in 1949 founded the Carpathian Sich Brotherhood (Bratstvo Karpats'kykh Sichovykiv), with branches in the United States as well as Canada.

From the outset, the Sich was integrated with the rest of Ontario's Ukrainian community, and in any case it included Ukrainians from Galicia as well as those from Transcarpathia who fought with the Carpathian Sich military unit in its armed conflict against the Hungarian invasion of the independent Carpatho-Ukraine, as the Subcarpathian homeland was known in March 1939. During its early years of existence, the Sich had its own Ukrainian-language bulletin, *Karpats'ka Sich* (Toronto, 1949-53), and after it folded, information about the organization's activity as well as about the Ukrainian aspects of the

---

[10]*Rusin/Ruthenian*, III, 11/12 (New York and Hamilton, Ont., 1954), p. 7.

Transcarpathian past appeared on the pages of the weekly newspaper, *Vil'ne slovo* (Toronto, 1934-87), owned and operated by Dr. Rosocha, whose recent death has basically coincided with the end of the group's activity.[11]

More numerous and vibrant both in the past as well as the present are those Carpatho-Rusyns who came from north of the mountains and who are known as Lemkos. Even before the direct immigration to Canada from Poland's Lemko Region in the second half of the 1920s, several hundred Lemko families emigrated from the northeast United States to western Canada during the first three decades of the twentieth century. These "American" Lemkos, as they were initially called, settled on farms in the prairie provinces of Saskatchewan, Manitoba, and Alberta or in those provinces' largest cities, Winnipeg and Edmonton, where they found work in factories and mills.[12] Some "American" Lemkos went to eastern Canada as well. For instance, the oldest Greek Catholic (now Ukrainian Catholic) Church in Ontario, located in Brantford, was founded in 1911 by Lemkos from the village of Odrzechowa (Rusyn: Odrekhova).[13]

The early Orthodox Carpatho-Rusyns in Canada were also for the most part from the Lemko Region. They did not, however, join Ukrainian Orthodox churches, but rather the various jurisdictions of Russian Orthodoxy, such as the Russian Orthodox Church Abroad (the Synod) and most especially, the Orthodox Church in America (formerly the Russian Orthodox Greek Catholic Church—the Metropolia). Within such an environment, these people were unable, or because of their previous Russophile tendencies unwilling, to preserve a distinct Rusyn identity. They have tended to think of themselves as simply Russians or, if they still have any awareness of their specific heritage, they may describe themselves as Carpatho-Russians.[14]

---

[11]For details on the founding and goals of the Sich, see Vasyl' Tymko, "Bratstvo Karpats'kykh Sichovykiv," *Karpats'ka Sich*, III, 1 [7] (Toronto, 1952), pp. 2-3.

[12]V. Cheliuk, "Materiial do istoriï Lemkiv za morem," *Holos Karpat*, II, 1 (Toronto, 1933), p. 3; Van'o Hunianka, "O Lemkach" (Lemkŷ v Kanadi), in *Nasha knyzhka*, ed. D.F. Vyslotskyi (Yonkers, N.Y., 1945), pp. 504-507.

[13]From information provided in an unpublished letter to the *Carpatho-Rusyn American* by the Reverend Conrad Dachuk, Welland, Ontario.

[14]It is interesting to note that the literature on Russian immigrants and their descendants in Canada makes no specific reference to the Carpatho-Rusyn/Russian

The Russian orientation of these early immigrants to western Canada was expressed in political activity at the close of World War I. Like the larger Rusyn community in the United States, Carpatho-Rusyns in Canada began to form organizations that they hoped would influence political developments in the European homeland. The Orthodox Lemkos in western Canada joined with other East Slavs from Galicia who called themselves Russians to form organizations that were concerned with the political changes then occuring in the European homeland. They referred to that homeland in English as Carpatho-Russia, and in their own publications as *Prikarpatskaia Rus'* (literally: Rus' near the Carpathian Mountains). This meant, besides the Lemko Region and Subcarpathian Rus' (then in Hungary), the rest of Austrian Galicia east of the San River as well as northern Bukovina. Their first step was to form in July 1917 in Winnipeg, Manitoba, and Mundare, Alberta, a Congress of Russian People (Kongress russkogo naroda), which called for the unification of Carpathian Rus' with Russia. By the spring of 1919, when the Habsburg Empire had ceased to exist, the group convened on April 21, 1919, Canada's first Convention of Carpatho-Russians (Siezd Karpato-rossov) in Chapman, Alberta. This group, made up primarily of Orthodox hierarchs and lay leaders led by Stefan Nai and Roman N. Samilo, requested that "the Paris Peace Conference unite Carpathian Rus' [*Prikarpatskaia Rus'*] with Russia, so that Carpathian Rus' would finally be liberated from 600 years of Polish and Austro-Hungarian oppression."[15]

The convention also dispatched the Winnipeg Lemko newspaper publisher Viktor Hladik as part of a three-person delegation from North America to the Paris Peace Conference, and it founded the League for the Liberation of Carpatho-Russia in order to collect funds for the "Carpatho-Russian Army" in Russia (made up of refugees from Galicia fighting against Bolshevism) and to condemn all forms of what was described as "Ukrainian separatism." Cut off as they were from the European homeland, the Canadian-Rusyn activists were unaware that by May and June 1919, "Carpatho-Russia" had already been divided

component among them. Cf. T.F. Jeletzky, ed. *Russian Canadians: Their Past and Present* (Ottawa, 1983).

[15]"Memorandum Pervogo Siezda Karpato-rossov," in *Russkii narod* (Winnipeg), May 1, 1919.

between Poland (Galicia), Romania (Bukovina), and Czechoslovakia (Subcarpathian Rus').

Whether or not Lemkos believed in their own ethnonational distinctiveness or whether they identified as Russians or Ukrainians, all felt the need to establish organizations in the New World that would bring together fellow immigrants from their native region. Considering the influence of the church in the European homeland, it was quite natural to expect that Lemko immigrants might attempt to establish their own parishes and even ecclesiastical jurisdictions. However, in Canada they were never large enough to influence either the Russian Orthodox or the Ukrainian Catholic Church, where they simply became individual parishioners, among the larger number of Russians and Ukrainians in those institutions.[16]

The poverty-stricken working class environment of the Lemkos in the homeland and most especially in the New World led to strong anticlerical left-wing political and social attitudes that sought to express themselves outside the traditional framework of the church. And even though there were distinct Carpatho-Rusyn, Russian, and Ukrainian fraternals and other secular organizations in both the United States and Canada, the Lemko immigrants felt the need to have their own separate Lemko structures. Thus, not finding satisfaction in the church or in the secular organizations of fellow East Slavs, the Lemkos began to organize on their own.

Despite the relatively small size of Canada's Lemko population, whose estimated 15,000 today represents about one-tenth the size of the group in the United States, it is interesting to note that the earliest Lemko associations were not founded in the United States but in Canada. Following a few hesitant starts in the United States during the early 1920s, the first permanent and still oldest organization, the Lemko Association (Lemko Soiuz) was established in 1929. Although its main

---

[16]Even in the United States, where Lemkos certainly formed a critical mass in Eastern Christian churches, ecclesiastical lines were drawn in such a way that in the Byzantine (Greek) Catholic Church Lemkos were placed within the Ukrainian (Galician) jurisdiction, while among the Orthodox the several attempts of Lemkos together with fellow Rusnak/ Rusyn immigrants from south of the Carpathians to establish separate "Carpatho-Russian" dioceses within the various Russian Orthodox churches were ultimately all unsuccessful. For further details, see Magocsi, *Our People*, pp. 32-38.

headquarters moved in the early 1930s to the United States, the Lemko Association actually began in Winnipeg, Manitoba, where in January 1929 the first branch was established under the leadership of Theodore Kochan (1888-1972).[17] The focus of the Lemko Association in Canada soon moved eastward to Toronto, where in 1931 a branch was set up at the initiative of Nestor Wolchak (Volchak, 1903-1958) and Walter Cislak (Vladimir Tsysliak, 1900-1955). This was followed by other branches in Montreal, Hamilton, Windsor, Fort William, and Edmonton. In 1935, these various branches were joined together to form the Lemko Association of Canada (Kanadskyi Tsentral'nyi Komytet Lemko-Soiuza), based in Toronto and under the leadership of Ivan Ksenych.[18] Although the Canadian Lemkos were organizationally distinct, they still shared the same newspaper and remained closely related to the parent Lemko Association in the United States.

The basic goals of the Lemko Association were: (1) to raise the educational, political, and cultural level of "Carpatho-Russian workers in the United States and Canada"; (2) to support cultural relations with the European homeland; and (3) to provide material support for fellow North American Lemkos in need.[19] In Canada, these goals were achieved by providing settings where Lemkos could meet (including heritage schools for children and cultural and social events such as weddings and dances), by cooperating with other Slavic and "progressive" worker's organizations, and by supporting with the Lemko Association in the United States joint representative organs, such as the

[17]"Korotka ystoryia Lemko-Soiuza," in *50th Anniversary Almanac of the Lemko Association of the USA and Canada/Iubyleinŷi al'manakh 50-lityia Lemko Soiuza v SShA v Kanadi* (Yonkers, N.Y., 1979), pp. 8-9.

[18]Following its first congress (*z"izd*) held in Toronto in 1935, the Lemko Association of Canada held three more congresses during the interwar years—in Montreal (1936) and Toronto (1937 and 1938). *50th Anniversary Almanac*, pp. 16-17; "30-ta hodovshchyna Lemko-Soiuza" (Kanadska storona v Lemko Soiuzi), in *Iubyleinŷi karpatorusskyi kalendar' Lemko-Soiuza na hod 1960* (Yonkers, N.Y., 1960), pp. 51-53.

[19]*50th Anniversary Almanac*, p. 10. It should be noted that from the outset the Lemko Association in Canada as well as in the United States included within its ranks not only those persons who specifically called themselves Lemkos (that is, immigrants from Poland), but also fellow Rusyns from south of the mountains in Czechoslovakia's Prešov Region and Subcarpathian Rus'.

newspapers *Lemko* (Philadelphia, Cleveland, New York, 1928-39) and *Karpatska Rus'* (New York and Yonkers, 1938-present), and annual almanacs (*kalendary*).[20]

With regard to its ideological orientation, the Lemko Association considered itself a worker's organization and wrote favorably about the Soviet Union, which was considered to be the first worker's state as well as the homeland of the "Rus'/Russian" people. From a distance, the Soviet social experiment looked particularly attractive, especially in contrast to the economic depression of the 1930s in Canada and the United States, which hit especially hard on Lemko immigrants most of whom were unskilled laborers. Therefore, the Lemko Association published in 1938 a favorable history of the Soviet Union (A.V Shestakov, *Ystoryia Sovitskoho Soiuza*) and it pressed the Soviet authorities in Moscow and Washington to support the suggestions aired in Galicia during the 1930s that the Lemkos should emigrate en masse to the Soviet Union.[21] Despite its left-wing political orientation, the Lemko Association continued to include a majority of members who were practicing Greek Catholics or Orthodox. With regard to defining the group's national or ethnic identity, the Lemko Association was only clear on one thing—it was not Ukrainian. Otherwise, publications and members wavered between being Russophile and stressing Lemko distinctiveness.

Lemko Association publications generally referred to the group it represented as Lemkos or as *karpatorossy*, the people of Carpathian Rus', which was meant to include territory inhabited not only by Lemko Rusyns north of the mountains in Poland but also by other Carpatho-Rusyns south of the mountains in what during the interwar years was Czechoslovakia—both the Prešov Region and semi-autonomous Subcarpathian Rus' (today the Transcarpathian oblast of Ukraine).[22]

---

[20]Branches of the Lemko Soiuz in Canada operated since the 1930s their own clubs in Toronto (first at 544 King Street and then the Carpathian People's Home at 280 Queen Street); in Montreal (1465 De Boullion Street); and in Hamilton, Ontario (Carpatho-Russian Community Home at 707 Barton Street East).

[21]*50th Anniversary Almanac*, pp. 14-15.

[22]Lemko political ideology dates from the end of World War I, when leaders at a national congress in the village of Florynka (in late 1918) demanded unification with fellow Rusyns in the new state of Czechoslovakia. Their demands were

Lemko national ideology, if that is what it can be called, was best summed up in the very popular Carpatho-Rusyn language primer, *Karpatorusskii bukvar'*, published in 1931 by the Lemko Association for youngsters in North America of Lemko descent as well as for use in Lemko-language schools in Poland. Its author was Dmitry Vislocky (Dmytro Vyslots'kyi, 1888-1968), who, writing under the pseudonym Van'o Hunianka, immigrated first to Canada in 1926 before going to the United States the following year. In a section on history and geography, Vislocky argued that "Our homeland is called Carpathian Rus'," that "Carpathian Rus' is part of a united Rus', and that we, *karpatorossy*, form a part of all the Russian people."[23] The "Russian people" (*russkii narod*) being referred to meant without distinction all the East Slavs—Russians, Belarusans, and Ukrainians. Moreover, "the Lemko language was the source for all of them." "This means that our Lemko language is the original language of all the Russian people."[24]

If the logic of this enthusiastically patriotic argument were to be carried out to its fullest extent (some would say to its furthest degree of ridiculousness), and if the old nineteenth-century theory of the Carpathian Mountains as the original homeland of the Slavs is recalled and accepted, then it could be said that there is only one Slavic language—

submitted to the Paris Peace Conference (Anthony Beskid and Dimitry Sobin, *The Origin of the Lems: Slavs of Danubian Provenance*, Prešov, 1919), and to the Czechoslovak government; since that time the standard map of Carpathian Rus' (Karpatska Rus'), which has appeared in Lemko publications in North America, has always included Rusyn-inhabited lands both north and south of the Carpathians. Cf. *Nasha knyzhka*, p. 491; and *Pamiatna knyzhka 10-lityia Lemko-Soiuza v Soed. Shtatakh y Kanadi* (Yonkers, N.Y. 1939), p. 16.

[23]Van'o Hunianka, *Karpatorusskii bukvar'* (Cleveland, 1931), p. 51. For the view that considers Lemkos part of a unified Rus'/East Slavic/Russian people (*russkii narod*), see Lemko ot pradida,"Lemkŷ-karpatorossŷ y ykh natsyonal'ne proyskhozhdenye," *Karpatorusskyi kalendar' Lemko-Soiuza na hod 1967* (Yonkers, N.Y., 1967), pp. 51-73; for the view that considers Lemkos a branch of Ukrainians, see Ivan Krasovs'kyi, "Do pytannia pro etnohrafichni mezhi ukraïntsiv Karpat," *Nashe slovo*: "Lemkivs'ka storinka," Nos. 5 and 6 (Warsaw, 1987). For present-day attitudes among Lemkos in Poland (including those that consider themselves part of a distinct people), see the series of articles in the *Carpatho-Rusyn American*, X (Fairview, N.J., 1987), Nos. 1, 2, 4, and XI (1988), No. 1.

[24]Hunianka, *Karpatorusskii bukvar'*, p. 56. This view was repeated in 1967 by Lemko ot pradida "Lemkŷ-karpatorossy," pp. 54-55.

Carpatho-Rusyn or Lemko—and that the other Slavic peoples simply speak dialects of that language, such as the Polish dialect of Carpatho-Rusyn, the Ukrainian dialect of Carpatho-Rusyn, the Serbian dialect of Carpatho-Rusyn, etc. From all of this it would seem that smallness and delusions of grandeur can become comfortable ideological bedfellows.

About the same time in the late 1920s that the Lemko Association was getting its start in Winnipeg, in Toronto a few Lemkos associated with the leftist Ukrainian Worker's Organization established in February 1929 the Worker's Educational Carpathian Society (Robitnycho-Osvitn'e Karpats'ke Tovarystvo).[25] This group continued to exist even after a branch of the Lemko Association was established in Toronto. The Worker's Society published a short-lived monthly newspaper in Ukrainian, *Holos Karpat* (Toronto, 1932-33), which argued that while its rival, the Lemko Association, could be considered a "progressive worker's" organization, it was ostensibly too concerned with promoting nationalism of the Russophile variety at the expense of working class concerns.[26]

With the outbreak of World War II in September 1939, and during the first two years when the Soviet Union was allied with Nazi Germany, Canada's Lemko organizations were plunged into disarray. Not only were both of them leftist, they were also known for their support of the Soviet Union which at the time was allied with an enemy of Canada and Great Britain. Therefore, the Worker's Educational Carpathian Society was banned by the government and ceased to exist, while the Lemko Association of Canada was forced to change its name. The latter's largest branch in Toronto resurfaced in 1940 and continued first as the Carpatho-Russian Society for the Struggle Against Fascism (Karpatorusske Obshchestvo Bor'bŷ s Fashyzmom) and then, after World War II, as the Carpatho-Russian Society of Canada (Karpatorusske Obshchestvo Kanady), both of which maintained close ties with the parent Lemko Association which continued to survive under that name in the United States.[27]

---

[25]Vasyl' Chelak, *Vid shchyroho sertsia: virshi i spomyny* (Denver, Colo., 1984), pp. 22-26; and Bohdan Chumak, *Spomyny Lemka* ([Toronto], 1976), pp. 1-7.

[26]Cf. the editorial, "Iak stavyt'sia ROKT-vo do Lemkivs'koho Soiuza," *Holos Karpat*, I, 3 (Toronto, 1932), p. 4.

[27]Mykhayl Lukach, "50 rokiv ymmygratsyy s Karpat v Kanadu," *50th*

Under these new names, Canada's Lemko organization entered its most successful period, one that was to last for nearly two decades. After Nazi Germany's invasion of the Soviet Union in June 1941, Canada and Great Britain, together with the United States, became allies of the Soviet Union. The Lemkos now had a new cause around which they could unite, and one, moreover, which was sanctioned and even encouraged by the Canadian government; namely, aid to its wartorn ally, the Soviet Union, the very same Soviet Union which had become the symbol of two basic Lemko loyalties—a "progressive worker's state" and Russian national unity.

With the imprimatur of Canada, Toronto's Carpatho-Russian Society contributed over $40,000 for clothing and medicine which was channeled through the Red Cross and the Russian Relief Fund to the Soviet Army. The fervor of this new campaign also attracted Lemko youth, which under the initiative of the dynamic Michael Lucas (Mykhail Lukach, b. 1926) set up in 1943 a Carpatho-Russian Youth Organization with its own monthly publication, *Club 280* (Toronto, 1943-60). The Toronto Lemkos also had their own Carpatho-Russian Choir, dance group, and dramatic circle, each of which gave frequent concerts and performances during the 1940s and 1950s, some of which were held on Toronto's leading stage, Massey Hall.[28] The postwar decades also witnessed representation by Canada's Lemkos at youth festivals in Czechoslovakia and the Soviet Union, while closer to home the increased level of activity allowed for the opening of new national homes in Toronto and Hamilton and of a food cooperative in Toronto.[29]

With the end of World War II, accompanied by the voluntary departure (1945-1946) and then forcible deportation (1947) of Lemkos from their ancestral Carpathian homeland, many of Canada's Lemkos became concerned with the fate of their brethren scattered throughout Poland.

Anniversary, 1929-1979, Society of Carpatho-Russian Canadians [Toronto, 1979], pp. 7-10.

[28]See the several articles celebrating the 40th anniversary of the Lemko Association/Society of Carpatho-Russian Canadians in *Nash holos*, No. 17 (Toronto, 1969), pp. 5-40.

[29]Michael Lucas, "Nasha orhanyzatsyia y molodezh," in *45 Anniversary, 1929-1974, Society of Carpatho-Russian Canadians* [Toronto, 1974], pp. 20-24.

A few leaders from both the United States and Canada began to travel to Poland in the late 1950s and early 1960s in an effort to rebuild decaying Lemko churches and to help financially the few thousand Lemkos who after 1956 managed to return to their native villages.[30]

When criticism of the Polish government as well as of Czechoslovakia and the Soviet Union for their policies regarding Lemkos and other Rusyns began to dominate the pages of the weekly newspaper *Karpatska Rus'*, published by the parent organization in the United States, the Carpatho-Russian Society led in Toronto by the Communist activist, Vasyl Lucas (Lukach) and his son, the youth activist Michael Lucas (b. 1926), decided in 1963 to break entirely with the Lemko Association. They renamed their own group the Society of Carpatho-Russian Canadians (Obshchestvo Karpatorusskykh Kanadtsev), which began its own publication in Lemko dialect, *Nash holos* (Toronto 1964-72), in an attempt to counter anti-Communist "propaganda" and to show how "our people in the homeland live freely" and without any "national discrimination" against them.[31]

Not surprisingly, some Lemko Canadians did not appreciate the apologetic stance of the Society of Carpatho-Russian Canadians toward Poland and Czechoslovakia, and in response they revived the old Toronto Branch of the Lemko Association. However, since the 1970s both factions of the older Toronto organizations have dwindled to a few older members who gather from time to time to hold a social function, or to collect monies for the press fund of the Lemko Association in the

---

[30]A Lemko Relief Committee was set up in 1946 under the leadership of the Lemko-American industrialist from Bridgeport, Connecticut, Peter S. Hardy, who in 1957 was allowed to visit the Lemko Region and to sign an agreement with Poland's Gomulka government to distribute funds to needy Lemkos. See Petro S. Hardŷi, *Korotka ystoryia Lemkovskoho relyfovoho komyteta v SShA: moia podorozh' na Lemkovshchynu* (Yonkers, N.Y., 1958).

[31]Mykhayl Lukach, "Razom z prohresyvnym rukhom Kanady," *Nash holos*, I [October] (Toronto, 1964), p. 7. To combat further the criticism by the Lemko Association of Polish and Czechoslovak policies toward Lemkos (Rusyns), and "to reveal the truth" about the positive nature of Communist rule in the homeland, the Society of Carpatho-Russian Canadians issued an eyewitness report: Mykhayl Lukach, Elena Lukach, Anna Baran, Mykhalyna Volchak, *Pravda o ridnim kraiu 1963: s podorozhy 2-i delegatsyy Obshchestva karpatorusskyeh kanadtsev do ChSSR, PNR y SSSR* (Toronto, 1964).

United States. By the mid-1960s, the Society of Carpatho-Russian Canadians had branches in Toronto, Fort William, and Hamilton, Ontario, and in Montreal and Winnipeg. However, the Toronto co-operative store soon closed; the Hamilton building was sold; and since about 1980, the society's chairman, Michael Lucas, has allowed the Canada-U.S.S.R. Association (of which he is president) to dominate the activity of Toronto's Carpathian People's Home, renamed Friendship House. The vast majority of participants in the new association's programs are Canadians of non-Slavic background interested in the Soviet Union.[32]

More dynamic are those Lemkos who came to Canada after World War II. In great contrast to their predecessors, many from this postwar group were educated and of a Ukrainian national orientation. While they have joined Ukrainian Catholic or Ukrainian Orthodox churches and function easily within Canada's well-organized Ukrainian community, nonetheless these Lemkos have also felt the need to establish what are in effect Ukrainian regional societies. During the post-World War II period, the most active figure was the Lemko Ukrainian writer Iuliian Tarnovych (1903-1977), who already in Poland during the interwar years established a solid reputation (writing under the pseudonym Iuliian Beskyd) as a promoter of the Ukrainian understanding of the Lemko past and culture. Tarnovych-Beskyd continued these efforts in Canada through reprintings of his prewar publications and as editor of the Ukrainian-language newspaper for Lemkos, *Lemkivshchyna-Zakerzonnia* (Toronto, 1949-53) and *Lemkivs'ki visti* (Yonkers, N.Y. and Toronto, 1958-present).[33]

As early as 1936, Lemkos in Toronto established a branch of the American-based Organization for the Defense of the Lemko Region

---

[32]Lucas blames the lack of participation by younger Lemkos not on their opposition to his leftist "progressive" political orientation but on the dominant Canadian assimilationist trend. The solution, he argues, is to establish another "friendship society," one for Canada and Czechoslovakia. Cf. Michael Lukač, "Pät'desiat rokov vyst'ahovalectva z Karpát do Kanady," in *Vyst'ahovalectvo a život krajanov vo svete: k storočici začiatkov masového vyst'ahovalectva slovenského ľudu do zámoria* (Martin, 1982), pp. 303-306.

[33]Michael M. Marunchak, *The Ukrainian Canadians: A History* (Winnipeg and Ottawa, 1970), p. 635.

(Orhanizatsiia Oborony Lemkivshchyny), but it lasted only until 1941.[34] Exactly two decades later, recently-arrived postwar Ukrainian Lemkos revived the Toronto branch of the organization, and although it remained within the larger American umbrella group, it adopted in 1974 a new name, the Canadian Lemko's Association (Ob"iednannia Lemkiv Kanady). The Canadian Association is based primarily in southern Ontario, with its largest concentration of over 100 members in two branches in Toronto, and smaller branches in Hamilton and Windsor. For the past decade, Ontario is also the site of the group's recreational park, Lemkivshchyna, located in the Durham region, about 200 miles northwest of Toronto.[35]

The main concerns of the Canadian Lemko's Association are: (1) to help financially churches in the few Lemko villages that have been revived in the homeland since the 1960s; (2) to assist recent Lemko immigrants to Canada; and most especially (3) to commemorate through lectures, concerts, and public protests (often directed against the Polish consulate in Toronto) the deportation of Lemkos from their homeland just after World War II.[36] Beginning in 1968, the Canadian Lemko's Association took over publication of the newspaper *Lemkivs'ki visti*, but since the decline of that organ it has been a co-publisher of the American-based quarterly, *Lemkivshchyny* (New York, 1978-present).

Following the recent political upheavals in Poland connected with the Solidarity Movement, a new wave of several hundred Lemkos immigrated to Canada during the 1980s. Like their predecessors, most have settled primarily in Toronto. Those who are of a Ukrainian orientation have joined the Canadian Lemko's Association, where they now form a majority and are the most active component of the

[34]"30-yi viddil Orhanizatsiï Oborony Lemkivshchyny Zakhidn'oï Ukraïny," in Chelak, *Vid shchyroho sertsia*, pp. 31-32.

[35]Stanko Kolesar, ed., "Ob"iednannia Lemkiv Kanady: istorychnyi narys," unpublished manuscript.

[36]"The Canadian Lemko's Association directs its activity toward attaining from the Polish Communist government that it recognize the inhumanity of [its policy] of collective guilt, correct the injustices perpetrated against Ukrainians, and allow Ukrainians in Poland to return to their native [Lemko] land." *Ibid.*, p. 8. On the Association's recent activity, see the reports of individual branches (exclusively the two in Toronto) that appear in the quarterly *Lemkivshchyna* (New York, 1979-present).

membership. They frequently interact with other Ukrainian-Canadian groups. Those who do not claim a Ukrainian identity—and who are often Polish speaking—meet among themselves in informal social gatherings.

Even more recently Canada has become home to a group of Vojvodinian (Bačka) Rusyns who began arriving in the late 1980s, and whose numbers have increased gradually since the break-up and war in Yugoslavia during the early 1990s. Today there are about 75 families, most of whom have settled in the Kitchener-Waterloo area of southern Ontario or in Toronto and its suburbs. Because of Yugoslavia's recognition of a distinct Rusyn nationality and its widespread support since World War II of Rusyn culture and education, these immigrants arrived in Canada with a clear sense of distinct identity. Their active community life, including an annual summer picnic and winter ball, has been spearheaded by a Kitchener businessman, Janko Sabadoš. In late 1995, the group founded the Ruske Družtvo Sivernei Ameriki (Rusyn Society of North America), which publishes the Rusyn-language newsletter *Hlasnïk* (Kitchener, 1996-).

With the decline of the cultural and social organizations that were active in the 1940s and 1950s, and with the ongoing uncertainty among the many Canadian-born about the national heritage of their ancestors, most Carpatho-Rusyns had by the 1970s lost interest in their ethnic identity and simply identified themselves as Canadians of Slavic background. Those who felt the need for a more concrete cultural identity joined the better organized Slovak, Russian, or Ukrainian communities and identified with one of those groups. Only since the late 1980s has there been a revival of interest in a distinct Rusyn heritage, sparked in particular by the recent immigration from the Vojvodina (Yugoslavia). Although the Rusyns from the Vojvodina may be able to preserve a distinct community in Canada, their numbers are likely to remain small (the entire population in the homeland is at most around 25,000), and it remains to be seen whether the first generation will be able to instill in their Canadian-born, or acculturated children a desire to retain a Rusyn identity.

There have been, however, examples of individual Carpatho-Rusyn Canadians committed to ethnic maintenance. An outstanding example was the talented painter and amateur ethnographer, linguist, and historian Julijan Kolesar, who established in Montreal the Julijan

Kolesarov Institute of America, and for nearly two decades, until his death in 1990, he published single-handedly thousands of pages of historical, ethnographic, and linguistic works about Carpatho-Rusyns, especially those from the Bačka/Vojvodina region of Yugoslavia. But Kolesar had virtually no impact on other Carpatho-Rusyns in Canada, who never knew of the existence of him or his "institute."

More recently, Toronto business executive Steven Chepa has funded publications about Carpatho-Rusyns and, in response to the recent national revival in the homeland, has established an annual monetary prize for the best original literary work in the Rusyn language. Also, because of the activity of scholars at the University of Toronto, Canada has since the 1980s acquired a reputation in the European homeland as one of the world's major sources for publication and information about the Rusyn national revival during post-Communist erà. Although such developments have not been able to restore the kind of community life that existed in the years immediately after World War II, it does allow for certain individuals and groups to maintain the existence of a Carpatho-Rusyn identity in Canada.

CHAPTER 22

Made or Re-Made in America? Nationality and Identity Formation Among Carpatho-Rusyn Immigrants and their Descendants[*]

A distinguished Hungarian linguist once remarked that "the United States is a museum of languages." What he had in mind was the

[*] This study was originally commissioned for a series of panels entitled, "Emigration from Northern, Central, and Southern Europe, 1880-1939," held in conjunction with the Tenth International Economic Congress in Leuven, Belgium, August 19-24, 1990. It was also delivered as part of another panel, "The Persistence of Regional Culture: Rusyn-Ukrainians in the Carpathians and Abroad," held at the IV Congress of Soviet and East European Studies, in Harrogate, England, July 21-26, 1990. The first published version appeared in the journal *Coexistence: A Review of East-West and Development Issues—Special Issue: The Émigré Experience*, XXVIII (Dordrecht, Netherlands, 1991), pp. 335-348. A revised version, translated into Ukrainian ("Stvoreni chy peretvoreni v Amerytsi?: narodnost' i protses samovyznachennia sered karpatorusyns'kykh imigrantiv i ïkhnikh nashchadkiv"), was included in a repeat of the Harrogate panel that was presented as a series of conferences held in Uzhhorod (Ukraine), Cracow (Poland), Prešov (Slovakia), and Novi Sad (Yugoslavia), March 18-26, 1991. The revised text, which is reproduced here, was published in both English and Ukrainian in Paul Robert Magocsi, *The Persistence of Regional Cultures: Rusyns and Ukrainians in Their Carpathian Homeland and Abroad/Tryvalist' regional'nykh kul'tur: rusyny i ukraïnstsi na ïkhnii karpats'kii batkivshchyni ta za kordonom* (New York: Columbia University Press/East European Monographs, 1993), pp. 163-175 and 166-181. The essay was also published in a Polish translation by Andrzej Zięba under the title: "Stworzeni czy przekształceni w Ameryce?: Narodowość i procesy świadomościowe wśród imigrantów karpato-rusińskich i ich potomków w USA," *Przegląd Polonijny*, XVIII, 3 (Wrocław, Warsaw, and Cracow, 1992), pp. 5-17.

preservation among people of various ethnic backgrounds of older forms of speech which were no longer being used in the homelands they had left, where their respective languages had continued to evolve. In this sense, the United States, has always been a kind of laboratory for historical linguists.

Just as linguistic forms became frozen in time among America's immigrants, so, too, have customs, attitudes, and political convictions, including views about national identity. For instance, there are ethnic groups with a vibrant community life which still exist in the United States, but which have ceased to exist, or in some cases have never existed, in the homelands from which they departed. For instance, it would not be possible to find Acadians (Cajuns) in France or Scotch-Irish (who are neither Scots or Irish) in Northern Ireland, either today or at the time the ancestors of those groups left their native lands.[1] On the other hand, the Kashubes and Windish did exist but have basically become assimilated with either Poles or Slovenes in their respective European homelands. Nevertheless, in North America there are still communities of Kashubes and Winds who believe that they form distinct groups.[2]

The United States also includes people who adamantly proclaim they have a national identity other than the one that exists today in the homeland that they or their ancestors left. Among such people are East Slavic immigrants and their descendants from Austrian East Galicia who claim they are Russian, even though today the inhabitants of that land generally consider themselves Ukrainian. Analogous are South Slavic immigrants from Yugoslav Macedonia who identify as Bulgarian,

---

[1] On the Acadians and Scotch-Irish, see the entries in the *Harvard Encyclopedia of American Ethnic Groups*, ed. Stephan Thernstrom (Cambridge, Mass. and London, 1980), pp. 103 and 895-908.

[2] The Windish, or Winds—Slovene dialect speakers living in the Prekmurje region that was part of the Hungarian Kingdom before World War I—should not be confused with the Wends, a designation used in the United States to describe Lusatian Sorbs. Cf. Paul Robert Magocsi, "Are Armenians Really Russians?—Or How the U.S. Census Bureau Classifies America's Ethnic Groups," *Government Publications Review*, XIV, 2 (New York, 1987), p. 146; Jan Drzeżdżon, "Wśród Kaszubów kanadyjskich, "*Pomerania*, XI, 2 (Gdańsk, 1974), pp. 24-32; and Izabela Jost, "Polish Kashub Pioneers in Ontario," *Polyphony*, VI, 2 (Toronto, 1984), pp. 20-24.

in contrast to people back home who consider themselves Macedonian. It is also interesting to note that America's so-called Russians from Galicia deny the very existence of Ukrainians as a nationality in much the same way that America's Bulgarians from Macedonia reject the existence of a distinct Macedonian nationality.[3] Among the ethnic groups who have been preserved in the United States are the Carpatho-Rusyns, also known as Ruthenians, Rusnaks, Carpatho-Russians, or by a regional name Lemko, or the religious name Byzantine. The vast majority of the group's ancestors left the European homeland of Carpathian Rus' for America's shores in the decades before World War I. Nearly half a century later, after the close of World War II, the inhabitants of Carpathian Rus' (present-day northeastern Czechoslovakia, south-eastern Poland, and the Transcarpathian oblast of the Soviet Ukraine) had already come to consider themselves—or more often than not were administratively declared—to be Ukrainian. As a corollary to these administrative and politically motivated decisions, it was argued that Rusyn was an older name for Ukrainian and that, henceforth, Rusyns did not exist as other than an antiquated regional designation for people who were an integral part of the Ukrainian nation.[4] Thus, the only Rusyns left were those in the immigration, whether in the United States or Yugoslavia, who—depending on one's point of view—had either: (1) not yet attained a Ukrainian national consciousness, or (2) were spared an

---

[3]Cf. the discussion of these problems in Magocsi, "Are the Armenians Really Russians?," pp. 144-146; and the entries on Bulgarians, Macedonians, Russians, and Ukrainians in the *Harvard Encyclopedia*, pp. 186-189, 690-694, 885-894, and 997-1009. The sensitivity over the Macedonians is evident in the passionate Greek and Bulgarian responses to the *Harvard Encyclopedia*'s decision to include an entry on the group: Nicolas Martis, "A Macedonian Nation Has Never Existed and Does Not Exist Today," *Hellenic Canadian Chronicle*; "It's Greek to Some," *Boston Globe*, August 9, 1986, p. 2; and Ivan Ilcheff, *The Truth About 'The Macedonians' According to the 'Harvard Encyclopedia of Ethnic Groups in America' Published in October, 1980* (Indianapolis, Ind., 1982).

[4]On the identity question in the homeland, see Paul Robert Magocsi, *The Shaping of a National Identity: Subcarpathian Rus', 1848-1948* (Cambridge, Mass. and London, 1978); and Pavel Mačů, "National Assimilation: The Case of the Rusyn-Ukrainians of Czechoslovakia," *East-Central Europe*, II, 2 (Pittsburgh, Pa., 1975), pp. 101-132—reprinted above, Chapter 11.

administratively imposed Ukrainian identity. Some skeptics have gone so far as to declare sarcastically that as a distinct nationality Rusyns never existed in Europe but were simply "made in America."[5]

Are Carpatho-Rusyns a purely American phenomenon, or do they represent an extension of the Old World experience? Are Rusyn Americans a historical anomaly, the last members of a group that has already or will eventually die out completely in the homeland and eventually in the United States as well? Or, in the more favorable political circumstances of the United States, have they been able to preserve a national identity which has also survived, albeit clandestinely, in the European homeland where it is waiting for a chance at renewal? These are the questions that will be addressed here, first by surveying briefly the evolution of the Rusyn-American community, and then by examining how political events in the European homeland since World War II have effected the group's self-image.

The story of the Carpatho-Rusyn immigration to the United States has been told before and it will not be repeated here in any detail.[6] A few points are, however, worth remembering. Rusyn Americans represent today are for the most part descendants of the so-called older immigration. This means that the vast majority of the 700,000 or so Americans who have at least one ancestor of Rusyn origin descend from parents, grandparents, or great-grandparents who had come to the United States before 1914. Subsequent immigration from Carpathian Rus' has been minuscule. Largely as a result of this time factor, most Rusyn Americans have no knowledge at all of their ancestor's East Slavic speech and little, if any, knowledge of a distinct Rusyn culture. At best their knowledge consists of awareness of certain religious practices or of recipes and eating habits handed down from parents and grandparents.

---

[5]Orest Subtelny, "East Slavs: 'Made in the U.S.A.'," *Ukrainian Weekly* (Jersey City, N.J.), July 15, 1984. This article appeared as a response to an address by Paul R. Magocsi, "East Slavs in America," *Ukrainian Weekly*, June 24, 1984. Both articles were reprinted with reactions by readers in the *Carpatho-Rusyn American*, IX, 1 and 2 (Fairview, N.J., 1986), pp. 6-8 and 4-5—reprinted below, Chapter 24.

[6]For basic background, see Paul Robert Magocsi, *Our People: Carpatho-Rusyns and Their Descendants in the United States*, 3rd rev. ed. (Toronto, 1994); and the earlier Walter C. Warzeski, *Byzantine Rite Rusins in Carpatho-Ruthenia and America* (Pittsburgh, Pa. 1971).

In terms of self-identity, there is much uncertainty or confusion. While older folk, and in the last decade many younger people, have a clear idea of belonging to a distinct Carpatho-Rusyn nationality, there are still many who consider themselves either Russian, sometimes Carpatho-Russian (especially among the Orthodox), or Slovak (especially among the Byzantine Catholics), or Polish, Ukrainian, Czech, or simply "Slavish." Thus in one sense Rusyns, like many of America's ethnic groups, have been made—or re-made—in the course of their history. More often than not the process of "remaking" has been directly linked to events in the European homeland.

When the earliest immigrants from Carpathian Rus' started arriving on American shores in the 1890s, what distinguished them from other Slavic immigrants—and, consequently, provided a sense of cohesion—was their Greek Catholic religion. Since initially religion was the primary cohesive factor, Carpatho-Rusyns interacted and formed parishes and secular organizations with fellow Greek Catholics from the historic Austrian province of Galicia north of the Carpathians. The Galician East Slavs had also called themselves Rusyns, but by the beginning of the twentieth century an increasing number began to describe themselves as Ukrainians and to identify with the Ukrainian national movement.[7] This "change of identity" among the Galicians—as Carpatho-Rusyns viewed it—was only one of the reasons that the early Greek Catholic immigrants drew apart. Other factors included: (1) differing social outlooks (the Carpatho-Rusyns were influenced by Hungarian-Danubian culture, the Galician Rusyn/Ukrainians by Polish culture); (2) regional and personal rivalries; and (3) perhaps most important, differing liturgical practices. With regard to the last factor, Carpatho-Rusyns felt most comfortable in church services filled with the responsive singing of their folksong-like *prostopinie* (plain chant), in contrast to Galician Rusyn/Ukrainian parishes, whose more formalized choral singing and mute congregation seemed to represent another religious orientation. All of these factors contributed to the division of Greek Catholic communities into separate Galician (Ukrainian) and Subcarpathian (Carpatho-Rusyn) parishes and into separate secular and fraternal organizations.

---

[7]Many Galician East Slavs, especially those who converted to Orthodoxy, adopted a Russian identity. See above, notes 3 and 5.

Carpatho-Rusyns were most adamant in rejecting the Ukrainian self-identity of the Galicians. Whenever they felt a Greek Catholic parish or hierarch was Ukrainian in orientation, they might respond by joining the Orthodox Church, where they felt—as it turned out wrongly—that their traditional local Carpatho-Rusyn identity would be preserved. In fact, those Rusyns who became Orthodox almost invariably became Russian in terms of ethnic or national identity.

Nonetheless, a significant number of Carpatho-Rusyns remained Greek Catholic, and to avoid further defections to Orthodoxy—caused in part by the Rusyn-Ukrainian identity dispute—the Vatican decided to establish separate church jurisdictions (1916), then eparchies (1924), and finally metropolitan provinces (1969) for Carpatho-Rusyn and Ukrainian Greek Catholics.[8]

During this process of separation, Carpatho-Rusyns came to control the oldest secular fraternal organization, the Greek Catholic Union (est. 1892), and its newspaper, the *Amerykanskii russkii vîstnyk*, after 1952 the *Greek Catholic Union Messenger*. The Carpatho-Rusyns also maintained their own cultural organizations (Rusin Elite Society in the 1930s; the Carpatho-Rusyn Research Center since the 1970s), schools, and publication houses. Hence, Carpatho-Rusyns developed all the infrastructures—religious, fraternal, cultural—that allowed them to survive and at times even flourish as one of America's distinct ethnic groups.

The evolution of Rusyn American attitudes toward their national identity has also been closely linked to events in the homelands from where their ancestors derive. In short, when those relations were close, the immigrants and their descendants had a clear sense of their distinct Rusyn identity. On the other hand, as political or military events separated or cut them off entirely from the homeland, a sense of Rusyn distinctiveness was lost in favor of identifying with "internationally" recognized larger peoples, whether Slovak, Russian, Hungarian, Polish,

---

[8]The dividing line for the two American Greek Catholic jurisdictions was the crest of the Carpathian Mountains that until 1918 formed the border between the Hungarian Kingdom and the Austrian province of Galicia. This meant that Rusyn immigrants from the Lemko Region fell under the Galician-Ukrainian Greek Catholic jurisdiction, although in fact perhaps as many as three-quarters of Lemko immigrants had converted to Orthodoxy before the first jurisdictional division was put into effect.

even Ukrainian.

The height of Rusyn-American political involvement in the homeland dates back to the years immediately following World War I. Like many other western and eastern European immigrant groups, Rusyn Americans formed new organizations to address specifically the changing political fortunes and to influence the fate of their homeland in the postwar world. Ironically, the Carpatho-Rusyns, who were among the smallest of these immigrant groups, had the greatest direct impact on events in Europe. One study that compared the political activity of several European groups singled out Rusyn Americans because they "did determine the fate of their compatriots at home—a unique case, it appears, of the influence of an immigrant group in America on the political history of Europe."[9] Having chosen a capable, young, and energetic American-trained lawyer named Gregory Zhatkovich to represent them, Rusyn Americans hoped to obtain independence for their homeland, which in English they called Uhro-Rusinia (Hungarian-Rusinia), then later simply Rusinia. The proposed state of Rusinia was to comprise all the counties in northeastern Hungary where Rusyns lived.[10] (See Map 14)

It was in the course of political debates about the homeland that Rusyn-Americans were forced to address the question of their national identity. If, in the real political world, they were arguing that they deserved a political state, that very demand forced them to justify both to themselves as well as to others that they were not Hungarians, or Slovaks, or Poles, or Ukrainians, neighboring peoples who at the very same time were also laying claim to all or part of the Carpathian Rus' homeland. In the end, as a result of American political pressure at the highest level (President Woodrow Wilson), Rusyn Americans under

[9]Victor S. Mamatey, "The Slovaks and Carpatho-Ruthenians," in Joseph P. O'Grady, ed., *The Immigrants' Influence of Wilson's Peace Policies* (Lexington, Ky., 1967), p 249.

[10]The well-known American cartographic company, Rand-McNally, issued a special map of "Uhro-Rusinia—the proposed third state of the Czechoslovak republic," which included 9 counties in northeastern Hungary, 5 of which in the west (Szepes/Spish, Šáros/Sharysh, Zemplén/Zemplyn, Abaúj/Abov, Borsod/Borshod) were inhabited by as many Slovaks as Carpatho-Rusyns.

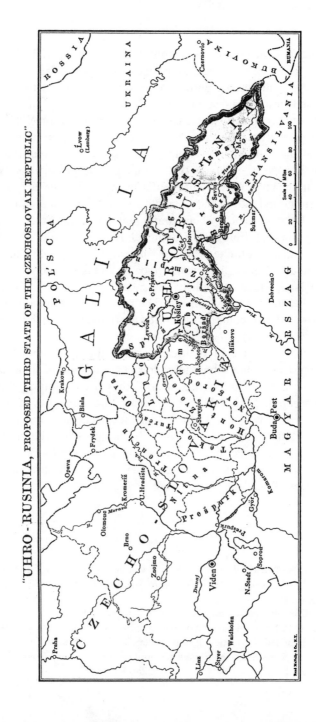

"UHRO - RUSINIA," PROPOSED THIRD STATE OF THE CZECHOSLOVAK REPUBLIC"

Zhatkovich were forced to accept the idea of unity with a larger state, specifically the new Slavic state of Czechoslovakia.[11]

While unity with Czechoslovakia might be accepted by Rusyn Americans, it could only take place on the condition that full political autonomy and self-government be implemented (similar to that enjoyed by a state in the United States, so Zhatkovich believed). These demands in themselves instilled in Rusyn Americans an awareness that, despite their union with Czechs and Slovaks, they were distinct from both those groups and, therefore, worthy of a separate political status. Carpatho-Rusyn political autonomy within Czechoslovakia was, in fact, confirmed by international treaty at the Paris Peace Conference (Treaty of St. Germain, September 1919) and by the Czechoslovak constitution (February 1920). In this way, Carpatho-Rusyns became *de facto* one of the three founding peoples of Czechoslovakia.[12] For his role and that of Rusyn Americans in this process, Gregory Zhatkovich was appointed the first governor of Czechoslovakia's far eastern province of Subcarpathian Rus' (Carpatho-Ruthenia).

Zhatkovich's tenure was short-lived, however, because the promised autonomy for Subcarpathian Rus' was never realized by the centralist Czechoslovak government. Upon his return home, Zhatkovich and other Rusyn-American leaders continued to demand that full autonomy be implemented in their homeland, and they hoped to achieve that goal by putting pressure on the Czechoslovak government through international diplomatic channels (League of Nations, Congress of European Minorities, U.S. State Department).[13] These actions,

---

[11]For details, see Paul R. Magocsi, "Political Activity of Rusyn-American Immigrants in 1918," *East European Quarterly*, X, 3 (Boulder, Colo., 1976), pp. 347-365.

[12]The Lemko Rusyns north of the Carpathians in Galicia also demanded to be united with their brethren and be part of Czechoslovakia, but Zhatkovich opposed their request. Left to their own devices, the Lemkos maintained an independent republic from December 1918 to March 1920, when their homeland was, with the rest of Galicia, incorporated into Poland. See Paul Robert Magocsi, "The Ukrainian Question Between Poland and Czechoslovakia: the Lemko Rusyn Republic (1918-1920) and Political Thought in Western Rus'-Ukraine," *Nationalities Papers*, XXI, 2 (New York, 1993), pp. 95-105—reprinted above, Chapter 13.

[13]Among the most widely-read critiques of the Czechoslovak government in Rusyn-American circles were G. Žatkovič, *Otkrytie-Exposé byvšeho gubernatora*

complemented with visits by political leaders from the homeland, further contributed to the Rusyn-American sense of worth as a distinct people who, at the very least, deserved autonomy if not full independence.

Whereas Rusyn-American awareness of and interest in the European homeland remained strong during the interwar years, the group's ability to effect politics in the homeland continually decreased. In fact, their awareness of developments in Carpathian Rus' contributed to further alienation of Rusyn Americans from the European homeland. When, following the Munich Pact of September 1938, Czechoslovakia was transformed into a federal republic and Subcarpathian Rus' finally attained its long-awaited autonomy, Rusyn Americans initially welcomed the news. But by November of that same year, when the Ukrainian-oriented government of Msgr. Avhustyn Voloshyn came to power in Subcarpathian Rus' (renaming it the Carpatho-Ukraine), Rusyn Americans became completely estranged. Discontent with the Ukrainian trend was so strong that the leading Rusyn-American organizations did not even protest against the forcible Hungarian occupation of Subcarpathian Rus' in March 1939.[14]

The Hungarian annexation of Subcarpathian Rus' and the outbreak of World War II a few months later ushered in a new phase in relations between Rusyn-Americans and the European homeland. For the next half-century, the group was to be effectively cut off from its brethren in the "old country," first because of the war and then because of the onset of Soviet Communist rule, which stringently eliminated virtually all communication with the "imperialist capitalist world" of which Rusyn Americans were seen to be an integral part. This was a particularly serious blow to an older immigration whose second- and third-

---

Podkarpatskoj Rusi, o Podkarpatskoj Rusi (Homestead, Pa., 1921), and Michael Yuhasz, Sr. *Wilson's Principles in Czechoslovak Practice: The Situation of the Carpatho-Russian People Under the Czech Yoke* (Homestead, Pa., 1929).

[14]An exception were the Lemko immigrants, who as early as 1939 protested the Hungarian occupation.They also called for the union of their Lemko homeland with Subcarpathian Rus', and they proposed the incorporation of all this territory into the Soviet Union. By 1942, the mainline Rusyn-American organizations led by Zhatkovich dropped their opposition to Czechoslovakia and worked with its exiled leaders (led by President Edward Beneš) to restore the country's boundaries as they had been before the Munich Pact. For details, see Magocsi, *Our People*, pp. 91-92.

generation descendants rapidly lost—or never had—any ability to speak Rusyn and little or no knowledge of the history of their ancestral homeland. Nor was there an infusion of new immigrants after World War II. The few that did come from Carpathian Rus' mostly identified themselves as Carpatho-Ukrainians and, not accepted by the older Rusyn Americans, they were absorbed into the Ukrainian-American community.[15] Even when travel restrictions were finally eased, in particular with Czechoslovakia during the 1970s, relatively few Rusyn Americans took advantage of what for them would have been a costly voyage to an ancestral homeland ruled by an alien political ideology whose inhabitants spoke a language that few of the English mono-lingual Rusyn Americans could speak.

Finally, there was the question of identity. Rusyn Americans, whether individually or through their religious and secular organizations, adamantly denied that they were Ukrainian, while in the homeland part of the new Communist policy was to resolve the "nationality question" by declaring simply that all Rusyns were Ukrainian. Most English-language scholarly and popular reference works also accepted this view, so that the inhabitants of Carpathian Rus' were described as Carpatho-Ukrainians or simply Ukrainians.[16]

In such circumstances, Rusyn Americans seemed to be a dying breed, the "last of the Mohicans." Whereas they might still stubbornly cling to their national identity, it was to an identity that no one anywhere seemed to recognize anymore and that, therefore, was not to be taken seriously. Cut off from the homeland and not understanding for the most part what it could mean to be part of an ethnic/national minority that never had its own state, Rusyn Americans by the 1960s lost virtually all sense of who they were. If asked, they might be able to identify themselves with the country their forebears had come

---

[15]A few Ukrainian-oriented political leaders from the homeland (Julian Revay, Augustine Stefan) did try to work with the older Rusyn immigration, but their self-identification as Ukrainians made any cooperation effectively impossible.

[16]Typical of this view were statements from a popular American reference work: "There is no ethnic or linguistic distinction between Ukrainians and Ruthenians" (from the entry "Ruthenia"); and "the majority of the population is Ukrainian" (from the entry "Zakarpatskaya Oblast/Transcarpathian Oblast," cross-referenced Carpatho-Ukraine), in the *New Columbia Encyclopedia* (New York and London, 1975), pp. 2383 and 3038.

from—Czechoslovakia, or simply Slovakia, Austria-Hungary, Poland, perhaps even the Soviet Union. More likely they would identify with the church to which they belonged—Byzantine Greek Catholic or Orthodox. The concept Byzantine was—and still is for some—even raised to the status of a kind of "Byzantine" ethnicity or nationality. The slightly more sophisticated might even describe themselves by the vague terms, "Slavish" or "Slavonic".[17]

This state of confusion among Rusyn Americans did eventually begin to change, not because of any events in the European homeland, but rather because of developments in the United States. It began with the so-called "roots fever" of the mid 1970s among America's Blacks,[18] which quickly spread to European immigrant groups and, in particular, to their third-, fourth-, and fifth-generation fully americanized descendants who were being told and encouraged by their own society to be different from the supposedly nondescript American norm.

There are, of course, varying ways to express one's individuality. Associating with a particular ethnic group is one such way. Americans of Carpatho-Rusyn background, in particular among the generation born during or just after World War II, were also struck by the "roots fever," which was enhanced further by the bicentennial celebrations of 1976. Throughout the bicentennial year, federal, state, and local officials called on the peoples of the United States to celebrate their ethnic origins and cultures which together ostensibly symbolized American civilization.

By the late 1970s, an increasing number of scholarly and popular books about Carpatho-Rusyns began to appear,[19] and in 1978 the

---

[17]With few exceptions, the group's religious and secular publications had by the 1960s dropped all references to a specific ethnic/national group, using instead euphemisms such as "our people from the old country" or perhaps our "Slavish people from Eastern Europe."

[18]This phenomenon derives its name from the novel *Roots* (1976), by the Afro-American author Alex Haley, and in particular to the six-part television series based on the book which for one week in 1975 captured the hearts and minds of millions of Americans.

[19]Carpatho-Rusyns also began to be recognized in scholarly and popular works. Aside from the major entry in the *Harvard Encyclopedia of American Ethnic Groups*, pp. 200-210, the group was treated in the newer *Dictionary of American Immigration History*, ed. Francesco Cordasco (Metuchen, N.J. and London, 1990),

Carpatho-Rusyn Research Center was founded to propagate the new "Rusyn revival" in the United States. The older fraternal organizations and churches, both Byzantine Catholic and Orthodox, were also moved by the call to respect and propagate one's ethnic roots, since in part the very existence of those churches depended on their being able to justify that they were somehow different from other Orthodox and from other Catholics, whether Roman or Byzantine-rite. Still, for skeptics, whether among Rusyn Americans or among outside observers—especially commentators in the Slovak- and Ukrainian-American communities—the Rusyn revival seemed little more than a nostalgia trip for well-meaning, if sometimes misguided, enthusiasts who were trying to sustain a national identity that no one but those American Last Mohicans seemed to have or to want.[20]

Then came the 1980s! The revival of interest in the homeland already led to the "discovery" of Rusyns living in the Vojvodina region of Yugoslavia, where since World War II they had been recognized as an official nationality with their own schools, research institutes, publications, press, radio, and even television program.[21] But as remarkable as the Yugoslav-Rusyn phenomenon may have seemed, it was applicable to less than 30,000 people—immigrants, moreover, who had begun to settle in the Vojvodina (the historic Bačka) in the eighteenth century. Back in the Carpathian homeland there were—or so it seemed —only Ukrainians, or Slovaks, or Poles. Hence, the Yugoslav Rusyns

---

pp. 105-109. It was also one of the 50 groups to whom a separate volume was devoted in the Chelsea House Peoples of North America Series: Paul Robert Magocsi, *The Carpatho-Rusyn Americans* (New York and Philadelphia, 1989).

[20]See, in particular, the polemical discussion between Vasyl' Markus', "Sproba novitn'oï istoriï Zakarpattia," *Suchasnist'*, XX, 6 (Munich, 1980), pp. 105-122 and Pavlo R. Magochii [Magocsi], "Nepravyl'ne rozuminnia istoriï: vidpovid' retsenzentovi," *ibid*, XXI, 9 (1981), pp. 65-82; with the reprints from that discussion that deal specifically with Rusyn-Americans by other commentators in the *Carpatho-Rusyn American*, IV, 3 (Fairview, N.J., 1981), pp. 4-6; V, 1, 2, 3 and 4 (1982), pp. 4-5, 4-7 and 4-5; VI, 2 (1983), pp. 6-7—see below, Chapter 26.

[21]Widespread among Rusyn-American readers was an article distributed by the Carpatho-Rusyn Research Center: Paul R. Magocsi, "The Problem of National Affiliation Among the Rusyns (Ruthenians) of Yugoslavia," *Europa Ethnica*, XXXIV, 1 (Vienna, 1977), pp. 5-8.

like the American Rusyns, seemed to be no more than a historical anomaly.

But political changes in east-central Europe soon revealed that the real situation in the Carpathian homeland was significantly different from what state-censored propagandists and historians had been writing since World War II and what, somewhat ironically, the Ukrainian-, Slovak- and Polish-American press was continually repeating in the "free world." In contrast to those views, a Rusyn identity had never died in the Carpathian homeland. It was just waiting for its moment to be publicly re-born.

The first indications of change came in Poland, where by the mid-1980 a younger generation of Rusyns—known by the local name Lemkos—began to organize annual cultural festivals (the Vatra). The goal of these festivals was, and still is, to restore a sense of pride in Lemkos and to teach them that they belong to a distinct Lemko-Rusyn nationality, which is related to Rusyns south of the mountains in Czechoslovakia and which is neither Ukrainian, nor Polish, nor Slovak. The Lemko-Rusyn phenomenon proved to be a foretaste of what was to occur in the more populous Rusyn homeland south of the Carpathians in Czechoslovakia and the Soviet Union.[22]

The Revolution of 1989 throughout east-central Europe also brought profound changes to the Carpatho-Rusyns. The first indications of what was to come occurred already two decades before. Back in 1968, during the Prague Spring, Rusyn Americans learned that, freed from political oppression, their brethren in the Prešov Region of Czechoslovakia had demanded the end to the Ukrainian cultural hegemony and the return to a Rusyn identity with Rusyn schools and institutions. But the Soviet-led Warsaw Pact intervention of August 21 brutally ended the Prague Spring, and those who supported the Rusyn orientation were branded as "anti-socialist counterrevolutionaries."[23]

[22]For details, see the series of articles on the Lemko revival in the *Carpatho-Rusyn American*, X, 1, 2, 3, 4 (Fairview, N.J., 1978) and XI, 1 and 2 (1979).

[23]See Mačů, "National Assimilation," esp. pp. 122-130, a study distributed widely by the Carpatho-Rusyn Research Center among Rusyn Americans. As a result of political changes in East Central Europe, this study has recently appeared in Vojvodinian Rusyn translation in Yugoslavia: *Švetlosc*, XXVIII, 1 and 2 (Novi Sad), 1990), pp. 77-96 and 213-235. By contrast, it was refused publication in all leading Ukrainian-American periodicals ever since 1975, when it first appeared in an

Czechoslovakia's Velvet Revolution of November 1989 has—at least for Rusyns—seemed to be a repetition of 1968. Once again there is a broad grassroots call for an end to Ukrainian cultural institutions in the Prešov Region, for giving Rusyns the status of an official national minority, for the creation of a Rusyn literary language, and for the introduction of that language in schools, the press, publications, radio, and other media. The old Communist-dominated Cultural Union of Ukrainian Workers (KSUT) was disbanded in early 1990, and the Ukrainian-oriented intelligentsia, aware of the popularity of the name Rusyn/Rusnak, has been forced to call its new cultural organization the Union of Rusyn-Ukrainians in Czechoslovakia (SRUČ). An entirely new organization has also come into being in Czechoslovakia, the Rusyn Renaissance (Rusyns'ka Obroda), whose goal is to rusynize all aspects of their people's cultural and educational life.[24]

In neighboring Soviet Transcarpathia, where it had seemed that four decades of indoctrination through schools and the closely-controlled media would have been successful in ukrainianizing the population, Rusynism has also been revived. In February 1990, the Society of Carpatho-Rusyns was founded in Uzhhorod, with branches throughout the Transcarpathian oblast. Its goals are to revive the Rusyn aspect of the region's past, to propagate a sense of Rusyn national identity in younger people, and to maintain contacts with Rusyn organizations abroad.[25]

While the European events are remarkable in themselves, they are having as well a profound effect on Rusyn Americans. These "Last Mohicans," who were criticized for nostalgic and antiquated views that had no relation to the real world, have come to have a new sense of self-confidence and pride because of the remarkable decade of the 1980s that culminated in the Revolution of 1989. No longer are Rusyn Americans cut off from a seemingly Ukrainian, Slovak, or Polish Communist homeland. Now, after nearly half a century they are restoring normalized relations with their Rusyn homeland, whether at

English-language scholarly journal—reprinted above, Chapter 11.

[24]For details on these still little-known developments, see "The Revolution of 1989," *Carpatho-Rusyn American*, XII, 4 (Fairview, N.J., 1989), pp. 5-9; and "Revolution of 1989 Update," *ibid.*, XIII, 1 and 2 (1990).

[25]*Ibid.*

the level of family or through mutual visits of religious and secular institutional representatives.[26] Admittedly, it is not yet entirely certain what precise national and cultural orientation will be adopted in the varying countries where Carpatho-Rusyns live. Nonetheless, it is already clear that the new political situation in east-central Europe, with its freedom of expression and demands for reviving some form of Rusyn identity, has reinvigorated the Carpatho-Rusyn community in the United States. The mutual interaction between Rusyns in America and in Europe seems certain to enhance a sense of Rusyn national distinctiveness for decades to come in both the Old World and the New.

[26]For the first time in half a century, two historic visits took place. A delegation of the highest ranking hierarchs of the Byzantine Ruthenian Catholic Church attended in February 1990 the consecration of the new Greek Catholic bishop of Prešov, Czechoslovakia and visited the bishops of the still illegal Greek Catholic Eparchy of Mukačevo in the Soviet Union. In April 1990, a Rusyn deputy in the Slovak parliament (Ivan Bicko) and the head of the Rusyn Renaissance in Medzilaborce (Michal Turok-Heteš) headed a delegation hosted by the Carpatho-Rusyn Research Center at its annual meeting in Pittsburgh.